A HISTORY OF
ARCTIC EXPLORATION

Venient annis saecula seris,
quibus Oceanus vincula rerum
laxet et ingens pateat tellus
Tethysque novos detegat orbes
nec sit terris ultima Thule.

(SENECA, MEDEIA 375-9)

In later years the age shall come
When the Ocean will unloose the bonds of nature
And the vast earth will stretch out,
And the sea will disclose new worlds:
Nor will the globe be utmost bound by Thule.

A HISTORY OF
ARCTIC EXPLORATION

DISCOVERY, ADVENTURE AND ENDURANCE
AT THE TOP OF THE WORLD

MATTI LAINEMA

JUHA NURMINEN

JOHN NURMINEN FOUNDATION

CONWAY

Expert Consultants
James P. Delgado, FRGS; Ulla Ehrensvärd, professor;
Alexei Postnikov, professor; Ann Savours, D. L. Hon. Litt.

Authors
Matti Lainema, Juha Nurminen

Translation
David Mitchell

Editor-in-Chief
Juha Nurminen

Picture Editors
Erik Båsk, Kaarina Pohjola

Editors
Tuula Nurmilaukas, Tuula Talasmaa-Lainema

Graphic designer and layout
Olavi Hankimo

Illustrative maps
Jari Patanen
Tiina Pystynen, captioning

Picture development
Art-Print Oy

© John Nurminen Foundation and WSOY, 2001

First published in 2001 as *Ultima Thule* by John Nurminen Foundation

This edition published in Great Britain in 2009 by Conway,
An imprint of Anova Books Company Ltd
10 Southcombe Street, London W14 0RA
www.anovabooks.com

Matti Lainema and Juha Nurminen have asserted their moral right to be
identified as the authors of this work.

British Library Cataloguing in Publication Data:
A catalogue record for this book is available from the British Library.
ISBN 978-1-84486-069-2

Distributed in the U.S. and Canada by:
Sterling Publishing Co., Inc.
387 Park Avenue South
New York, NY 10016–8810

Printed in China

ACKNOWLEDGEMENTS:

Director Kåre Berg
The Frammuseum, Oslo

Professor Victor Boyarsky
The Arctic and Antarctic
Research Institute, St. Petersburg

Librarian Tony Campbell
Assistant librarian Peter Barber
The British Library, Map Library, London

Professor Barry Cunliffe
Institute of Archaeology, Oxford

Archivist, curator Robert Keith Headland
Picture archivist Philippa Hogg
Scott Polar Research Institute, Cambridge

Curator Francis Herbert
Royal Geographical Society, London

Dr Ab Hoving
Ship-model Restoration Department
Rijksmuseum, Amsterdam

Professor Esko Häkli
Mag. phil. Leena Pärssinen
Esko Rahikainen
Helsinki University Library, Helsinki

Director Bård Kolltveit
Norsk Sjöfartsmuseum, Oslo

Commodore Evgeny N. Kortshagin
Central Naval Museum, St. Petersburg

Langfords Marine Antiques, London

The Map House, London

National Museum of Ireland, Dublin

Matti Nurmi
Expert on historical ships, Rauma

Richard Ormond, M.A. FSA
National Maritime Museum, London

Dr Monique Pelletier
Bibliotheque Nationale France

Professor Mikhail Pietrovsky
The State Hermitage Museum, St. Petersburg

Sea Captain Søren Thirslund, Humlebæk
Expert on Viking navigation

FOREWORD

LENNART MERI
President of the Republic of Estonia (1992–2001)

Discovering the world is a never-ending process. Even in this globalising world there are more than enough places where man's foot has never trod. But it is also true that as man's culture and technology grow more powerful, those horizons, discovered and yet to be found, move ever further away. We have received the news that signs of water are being sought on Mars, without much surprise. Taking it more and more for granted, we are delving deeper into the composition of water in order that we might burn the substance in place of gas, oil, coal or forests to save the earth, the air and that very same water, the basic requirements for life, from pollution. The first steps of our childhood - they too are a matter of discovering the world.

In my childhood the discovery and colonisation of Africa had not yet finished and the exploration of the polar region was given new impetus with the aid of modern technology. Throughout my boyhood years I carried with me the catch phrase 'Dr Livingstone, I presume?' and I used it in the endless deserted coasts of sub-Arctic Kamchatka when a point that appeared on the horizon turned out to be my school mate, the naturalist Erast Parmasto. I have also kept the receipt I was written in Yakutsk, the capital of the Republic of Yakut. The receipt proved that I had paid for my overnight accommodation but not for a stable, since I had not arrived by horse. I have actually travelled the routes of Bering, Nordenskiöld and Amundsen, that is to say lived simultaneously in 18th, 19th and 20th century conditions. I have been a prisoner of the snow and ice and, in the middle of the intoxicating silence, heard a Tokyo-bound aeroplane rumble above me, presumably offering steaming coffee and crisp, fresh newspapers. At such lonely and humbling moments it feels as if the globalising world does not exist and that a crackling campfire is all one needs to simplify and confirm all one's values.

What drew the sailors, traders and scientists to discover the polar lands? Furs? Walrus tusks? Shorter sea routes? All these and much more, which we can today summarise generally as man's chronic hunger for energy. The thing that has brought about the greatest change in the polar regions is the discovery of oil and natural gas in the Arctic regions of Alaska and Russia - a lucky find and quite possibly an unfortunate event, because of all nature's zones it is precisely the polar region that is the most vulnerable. Nordenskiöld describes the footprints

Fridtjof Nansen's drawing of the Aurora Borealis, on wood.
(John Nurminen säätiö)

of ancient hunters which had not been covered over in two hundred years, and the tracks of the first Fordson caterpillar tractors, tried out in 1922 on Vaigat Island, can still be seen. The polar lands have been the treasures of pure nature, and they could easily turn into man's last refuge.

This book tells the fascinating story of how the people who used the Greek or Latin alphabet discovered the polar regions. But weren't the Chinese the first to write of the polar bear? And what has happened to the Arab and Cyrillic alphabets? The polar regions have opened up to people by land and by sea. For the most part they have been populated by tribes which have known for ages of the constellations, of boat building and the necessity of vitamins while the first explorers were still dying of scurvy. It is in the ways of life and traditions of the indigenous peoples that we find the real key to discovering the polar regions. To them the polar lands were not a metro station but a world and a landscape which brought the midnight sun and the hot summer, to say nothing of Chukchi football matches which were described in astonishment by a certain Francis Bacon, Montesquieu's distant predecessor in Siberia.

Civilisation's temperate zone has been moving slowly northwards and the Hyperborean zone has withdrawn at the same rate in the opposite direction. Estonia, on the shores of the Baltic, joined the zone of civilisation 98 years after the birth of Christ in Tacitus's *Germania*, and at that time the people of Estonia were really among the first in the world to practice arable farming in the north. When, a quarter of a century ago, I was writing of the history of the discovery of the Baltic Sea, I began to think that the discoverer of my homeland, or at least of our seas, could be the Greek Pytheas of Massalia, or Marseilles, situated on the Mediterranean. Between these covers the reader will find sufficient evidence of how our distant Nordic Countries moved closer to the cradle of Europe, the Mediterranean Sea. The officials of the town of Marseilles were pleasantly surprised when I brought Pytheas, the first explorer of the polar regions, back to them from the shores of the Northern Baltic Sea to their own Mediterranean. As a gesture of gratitude I was taken to his monument. According to a widely-held concept the discoverer is considered the first person to have kept a record of his discovery. While moving about in the polar regions I have come to the opposite conclusion: the discoverer is he who does it last.

INTRODUCTION

The northern polar region long kept its secret as it was difficult to explore and map. It is almost as difficult to write an exhaustive account of the history of exploration in the north. The period of Arctic exploration covers almost 2500 years and the amount of source material, historical maps, original manuscripts, travel journals and research is enormous. Limiting such extensive and interesting subject matter has been one of our greatest challenges.

This volume, a book on voyages of exploration in the north, was inspired by a hobby shared by Matti Lainema and myself. My own expeditions, on foot and by canoe, have for years made their way to Ruija, Matti's to Alaska. We are also both collectors. My interest is directed at the history of maps and navigation, Matti collects the travel journals of northern expeditions. We are both interested in how knowledge of the Arctic area has accumulated and how man's perception of the world has changed over the centuries.

I run a small family business and Matti is a business management consultant. We have both been obliged to consider the significance and effect of synergy in our day-to-day work. We became fascinated by the idea of putting together our collective knowledge and source material. We decided to combine stories of the Arctic and ancient maps with accounts of adventure and beautiful pictures. We wrote the opening words of this book some five years ago. As dilettantes we set our aims high, copying groundbreaking, innovative companies and historical explorers in our own attempt to discover something new and unknown.

This volume is an account of the most essential and the most exciting aspects of mapping the Arctic areas from antiquity right through to the opening of the Northwest and Northeast Passages and the conquering of the North Pole. But we have also tried to consider the influences that guided researchers and explorers in their attempts to solve the mystery of Ultima Thule, the extreme north. Thousands of men, and a few women too, have for 2500 years taken part in the great adventure that has extended the boundaries of our knowledge further and further north. Hundreds of different cartographers have mapped the northern areas. So limiting and defining our task was not going to be easy.

In terms of area we concentrated on the northern part of the Arctic Circle, examining matters chronologically from Pytheas to Peary, not forgetting the indigenous peoples; the real discoverers of the Arctic. We have attempted to tell of the human victories and failures of northern expeditions both in the East and the West. We describe both the moments of joy and the tragedies of Arctic exploration, whether the expeditions were European, American or Russian. In addition, we also consider the commercial, scientific, or political considerations of the journeys, or if they were undertaken simply out of a spirit of adventure. The most difficult task was to limit the amount of visual material. We wanted to convey the beauty of the Arctic and the graphics – maps, engravings and pictures of nature – as authentically as possible. The maps show how our picture of the north has changed. The descriptions of the maps are explained by many fascinating

stories and myths. Under the supervision of the Maritime Museum of Finland, the John Nurminen Foundation had nearly twenty precise models of historic polar ships made. These are now published for the first time in this volume as well as certain unique pictures of manuscript maps. The book highlights the vessels, navigation and cartographic history of the Arctic, plus its natural history and its own special phenomena.

With the aid of these almost unbelievable, but true, stories and authentic pictures, we hope we have succeeded in conveying the adventures that people have experienced in attempting to find Ultima Thule; in attempting to open up sea routes to the Far East and in competing to reach the North Pole. The northern expeditions tell of people who made bold journeys into the unknown and penetrated areas where no man was known to have been before them.

This volume shows that those who succeeded best understood how to question old beliefs, learning both from their own mistakes and from the indigenous people of the Arctic, people who had lived and survived in the north throughout the entire period of our story. Success required both courage and wisdom. Courage meant the willingness to exert oneself to the limits of human endurance and sometimes beyond; wisdom demanded the understanding that nature cannot be beaten but that it is necessary to make it one's ally.

Matti Lainema wrote the history of exploration; I was responsible for choosing the maps and pictures and matters to be highlighted. For both of us, this process was a unique opportunity to learn and explore. I would like to thank Matti for his continued and splendid cooperation. Together we want to thank all those who made the publication of this volume possible. We thank the John Nurminen Foundation for its financial and scientific support and for editing the book and its illustrations, the WSOY Publishing House for the simultaneous publication of the work in three languages and for the tireless editing of these texts. Olavi Hankimo was responsible for the book's graphic design. We want to thank him for his creative co-operation in the editing of the illustrations. It was not an easy task to design a work of art and of science between the same covers.

The book's advisory committee, Dr. Ann Shirley from England, Prof. Ulla Ehrensvärd from Sweden, James P. Delgado, FRGS, from Canada and Prof. Alexei Postnikov from Russia did invaluable work in collecting and checking the historical material. I want to thank my friend Ulla Ehrensvärd particularly for her work in checking the cartographic material. We are also grateful to the museums, libraries and other institutions around the world for the best possible cooperation.

Finally we want to offer our special thanks to Lennart Meri, President of the Republic of Estonia. The brilliant writings of this friend, researcher and folklorist of the history of the north have provided a great deal of inspiration for our own book – *A History of Arctic Exploration*.

Helsinki, June 2001
Juha Nurminen

8

CONTENTS

PYTHEAS – PIONEER OR STORYTELLER?

HISTORY REGARDS PYTHEAS AS THE FIRST GREAT EXPLORER. IN 320 BC HE MADE A VOYAGE TO THE NORTH, TO THULE. THE LOCATION OF THULE, HOWEVER, HAS BEEN DISPUTED EVER SINCE PYTHEAS PUBLISHED HIS WORK *On the Ocean*.

HOW THE WORLD WAS SEEN IN ANCIENT TIMES

The Greeks had a pretty realistic concept of the parts beyond their world. In about 460 BC, the Greek philosopher Parmenedis divided the world into five zones. A hot zone existed at the level of the equator, either side of which ran warm zones with cold zones at the extreme poles. The Greeks believed that the hot and cold zones were unfit for human habitation.

The Greeks knew the Mediterranean well, but of the 'Hyperboreans', who lived further to the north, they had little knowledge, in spite of the fact that they conducted trade as far away as the North Sea region. According to legend, the Hyperboreans were a happy breed who lived in the forests and caves of the north because they had no houses. They were not troubled by wars or sickness, nor by ageing. When they had had their fill of the joys and pleasures of life they cast themselves from the rocks into the sea. The Hyperboreans appear for a long time on maps of the North. In the eleventh century, Adam of Bremen assumed them to be Scandinavians.

1 The Mediterranean was the cradle of European open sea sailing. Even before the beginning of our calendar sails were in use and Greek merchant vessels could travel far from their home waters even to open sea areas with no coasts. The type of vessel shown in the picture might have been used to visit ancient Thule. The John Nurminen Foundation had an exact 1/10 scale model of a Greek trading vessel made, based on the hull of the Cyrenia find.
(JOHN NURMINEN FOUNDATION)

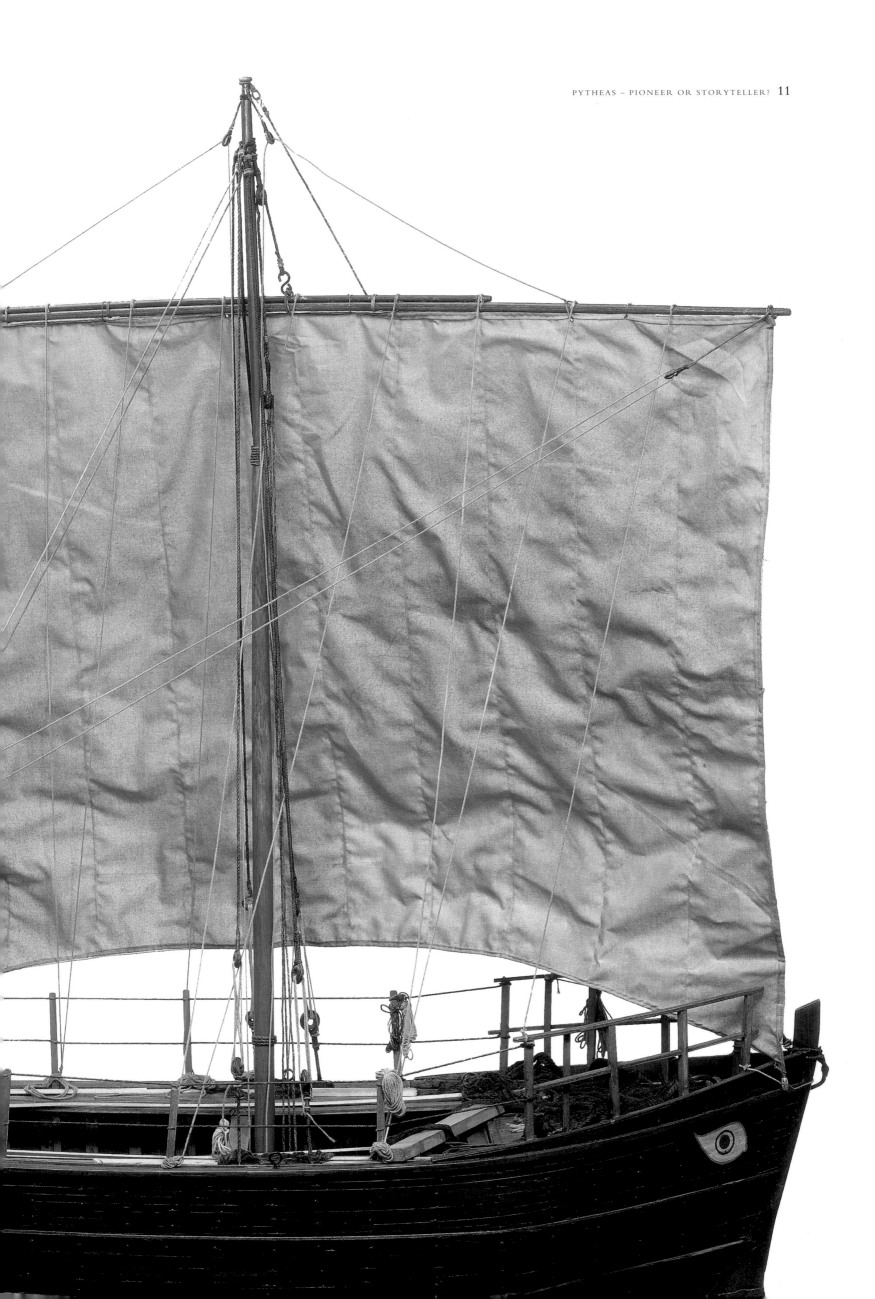

Gradually the peoples of the Mediterranean learned more about those countries from which they obtained tin and amber. Tin was to be found in France, the Iberian Peninsula and the British Isles. Amber was obtained from Jutland and the Baltic coast in particular. The northern peoples used amber as a currency with which they bought precious metals. The Romans held it in great esteem and the Phoenicians probably dealt in both tin and amber. Around 500 BC they were already sailing between the Pillars of Hercules, that is to say the Straits of Gibraltar, along the coasts, all the way to the British Isles, where even then tin had been found. The Phoenicians made no fuss about their achievements. The less known about their sea voyages, the more worthwhile their monopoly.

Of all the voyages of exploration of early history, however, the greatest was that of the Egyptian-Phoenicians around Africa when Necho II (609–594 BC) was ruler of Egypt. Herodotus tells of this voyage some 50 years later. His account was regarded with suspicion because certain details were in conflict with the prevailing conception of the world. Criticism was directed particularly at the statement according to which 'in circumnavigating Libya (Africa) they always kept the sun to the right'. To the people living north of the equator this claim seemed complete nonsense. But it put it beyond doubt that the journey did indeed take place and that the south of Africa was surrounded by sea.

PYTHEAS AND HIS CONTEMPORARIES

The only explorer of ancient times worthy of the name was the well-known astronomer and geographer Pytheas, who lived in the second half of the fourth century BC. He was the first to correct the prevailing misconceptions concerning the North Star. He concluded that the North Star was not directly over the North Pole and neither was any other star. Instead he discovered three stars whose triangular formation could be complemented in such a way as to form a quadrangle placing an imaginary star precisely over the North Pole.

In his book *Ultima Thule*, Vilhjálmur Stefánsson maintains that if Pytheas had been a typical philosopher of his time he would have been satisfied with his predecessors' definitions concerning the North Star. But he questioned these concepts and accepted only those that met scientific criteria. He was a skilful maker of instruments. With the aid of these he was the first to be able to calculate a given place's distance from the equator. He determined the location of his home town Massalia (now Marseilles) very precisely. He was also the first Greek to explain the phenomenon of the connection between the tides and the motion of the moon and to understand the rhythm of the tides. What is possibly his only work *On the Ocean* has been lost and we have only second or third-hand information as to its contents. It dealt with a voyage that Pytheas made around 320 BC.

2 Pytheas was the first to tell of Thule in his lost work On the Ocean. *"Ultima Thule" meant an area situated in the extreme north. Since Antiquity Thule was understood to be an island or land far away in the North and it was surrounded by a cold sea. There has always been an air of mystery attached to Ultima Thule. Not everybody believed in the existence of Thule, and those that did believe disagreed as to its location. The isolarios (Island Books) of the Middle Ages depicted the islands of the world's seas. On an isolario made in Italy in the 16th century there are 31 European, Asian and African islands. One of these represents the island of Thule, whose castles are depicted on the map. The island's coastline is drawn in a way typical of the isolarios as a wavy curve. The other islands depicted on the isolario are real. (THE BRITISH LIBRARY)*

Texts on and around the map:
North is on the left.
Red text: *Thule is an island with a circumference of 300 leagues situated on the far edge of the Hyperborealian Sea.*
Black text: *Servius: on the island of Thule.*
The island of Thule is located between the northern and western sea area, beyond Britain between the Hibernians and the Oxdrads, and it is the furthest island in the sea. When the sun is in the constellation of Cancer the island has no night.
Texts in the picture: farming land, fortification, town.

PYTHEAS' VOYAGE

Although the Phoenicians had successfully kept the Straits of Gibraltar closed for a long time, Pytheas sailed to the Atlantic through the Pillars of Hercules. He sailed north along the coast of Iberia and made note of the tides. He continued onwards to Celtica, from there to Cabaeum (Brittany) and to Brettanice (Britain).

According to Pytheas, Britain was a triangular island like Sicily. Its circumference, he informs us, was 23,800 stadia or a good 2100 miles. The shortest side of the triangle faced the continent. But it is unclear whether Pytheas is referring to the circumference in terms of stadia or the number of days it took to sail round the island. Nansen is convinced that the original figures were days and that the islands' measurements in stadia were made by someone else, probably Timaeus.

Pytheas made astronomical observations in different parts of the British Isles. According to his calculations, the length of the day in northern Britain in summer was 18 hours, and in the uninhabited islands to its north 19 hours. These figures correspond to the length of the days in Scotland and the Shetland Islands.

According to later accounts, Pytheas continued sailing north. After six days he arrived at Thule. On the journey he perhaps observed that the days continued to grow longer. "The barbarians showed us where the sun goes to rest." The nights were very short, two or three hours long, so that the sun rose almost immediately after it had set. When speaking of the shortness of the nights, he did not mention Thule, though this is probably what he was referring to.

Tyle ultima insula est: In hyperboreo oceano sita: q̄ mil· ccc· circuit·

Seruius de Tyles insula.
Tyle insula est oceani int̄ septentrionalem et occidentale plagam
ultra britaniam: int̄ hybernos
et Orchadas et est insula in oce-
no ultima in qua cū sol in cancro
est perpetui dies sine noc-
tibus esse dicuntur.

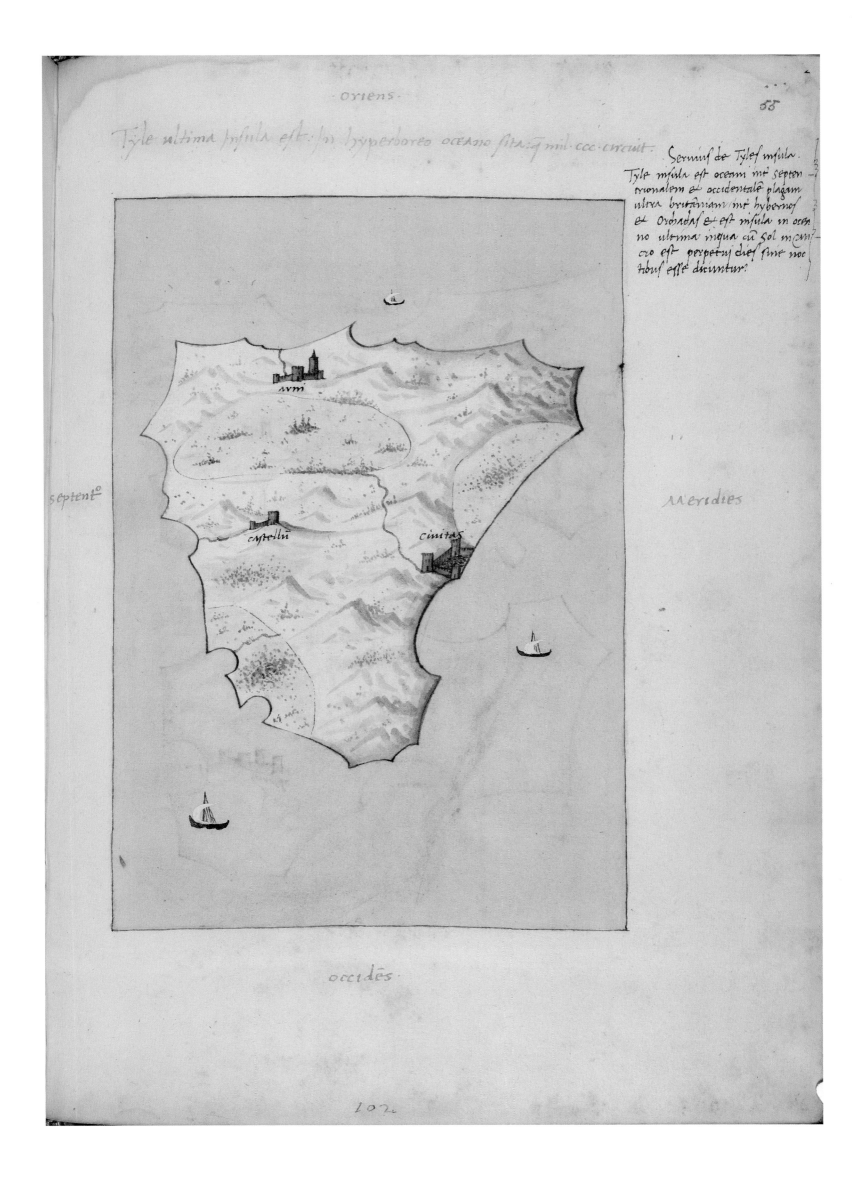

septent°

meridies

occidēs

102

3 *As far as the Mediterranean and the Indian Ocean are concerned, Ptolemy's depiction of the world is astonishingly precise. Merchants conveyed information on distant parts to the Hellenians. Even before 100 BC knowledge of the East grew by way of the Silk Road. Roman sea connections to the Red Sea and Indian Ocean were dependent on Arab sailors. The tin route to the North ran along the river valleys of France to Massalia and the amber route running further east from the Baltic Sea to the Aegean Sea. The classical Ptolemy picture draws its information from the southern Baltic Sea and the North Sea. The areas to the north of it are covered in obscurity or cloaked in the secrecy of myths. With the exception of Jutland, Ptolemy knew very little of the geography of Scandinavia. Amber merchants told of the island of Scandia which was located to the north of latitude 57°. Knowledge of the British Isles was transmitted by the tin trade and as Rome expanded. Generally Ptolemy maps end in the north at latitude 63°. The map shown is taken from the 15th century Ptolemy-Cosmography manuscript edition, in the valuable collection of Northeast Passage sailor A. E. Nordenskiöld, now kept in the Helsinki University library.*

(HELSINKI UNIVERSITY)

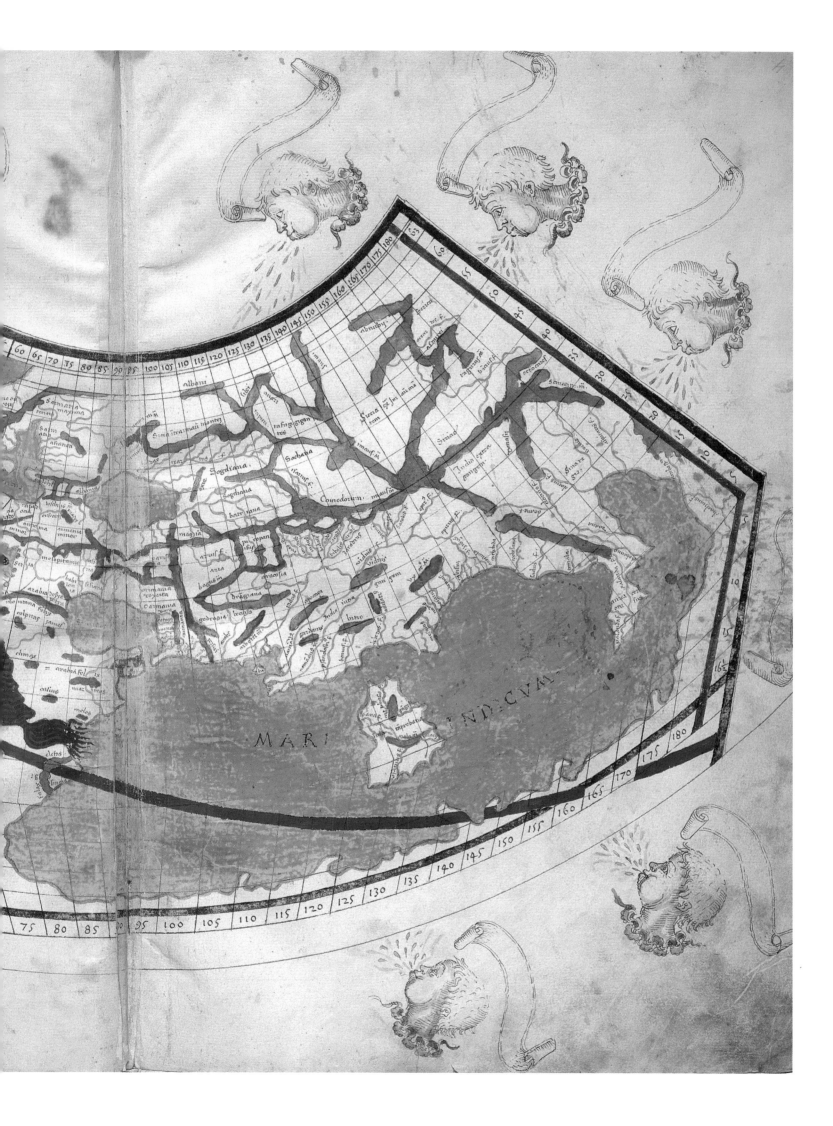

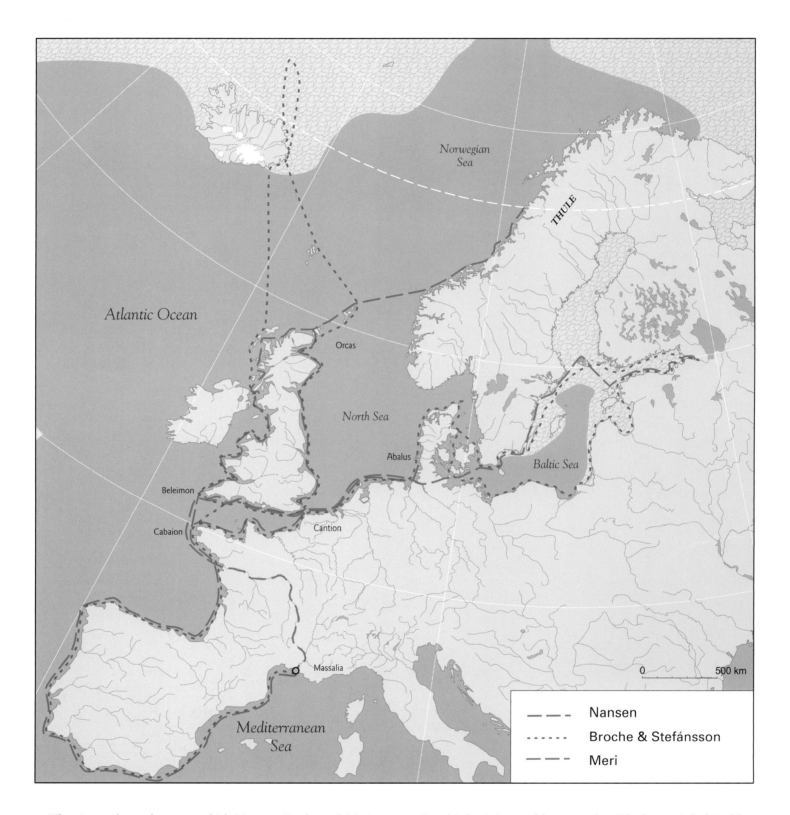

4 *The picture shows the routes which Nansen, Broche and Meri presumed Pytheas to have taken. According to Broche, Pytheas went to Iceland first and then to the edge of the pack ice area before making his way as far as the Gulf of Finland. Nansen assumed Pytheas to have sailed from the British Isles to the coast of Norway to the level of Iceland. According to Meri the island of Saarenmaa on the coast of Estonia was Thule and Pytheas went as far as the mouth of the Neva. Meri also considers the possibility that Pytheas returned home along the rivers of Russia by way of the Black Sea.* (PATANEN)

On this basis it would appear that Thule was inhabited by barbarians. Also, Pytheas must have been there himself, otherwise he would not have been able to write suchan observation. According to Pytheas the northern part of Thule stretched as far as the polar circle. He described it as the land of the midnight sun.

According to information gleaned from Pytheas' book we know the following: Thule is an island. It lies only a day's journey from the "congealed sea". According to the Greek geographer and historian Strabo, Pytheas had observed that in the north of Thule, "there was no longer any distinction of land or sea or air but a mixture of the three like a sea lung. This mixture can neither be traversed on foot nor by boat".

After Thule, Pytheas sailed along the coasts "from Gaderia to Tanais". He also provides information about Ostiae and the lands beyond the Rhine all the way to Scythia. According to Pliny, on his way to the shores beyond the Rhine, Pytheas also went to an island from which amber was obtained. He says that a Germanic people called the Gutones lived on the banks of the Metudonis Bay. From there it was a day's journey to Abalus Island where amber was washed up on the shore in spring. The amber originated in the congealed sea. Apparently different sources use different names for the same island. It is possible that Basilia Island was this same Abalus, though it was said to be a three day's sea voyage from Scythia. In those times Scythia meant that part of Europe east of the Rhine. One form of the island's name is Balcia, which may allude to the Baltic, in the same way that Ostiae, mentioned earlier, suggests Aesti, the name which Tacitus called the area now known as Estonia.

Based on the vague but unmistakable allusions mentioned above, Professor Gaston E. Broche, in his work *Pytheas le Massaliote* (1935), concludes that in visiting Thule – a question we leave open for the time being – Pytheas sailed, by way of the Kattegat, to the Baltic Sea and, following the coast, all the way to the Gulf of Riga and the remotest corners of the Bay of Finland. Nansen, however, is of the opinion that this possibly refers to a new voyage that Pytheas made after his journey to Thule.

It is difficult to arrive at a clear picture of Pytheas' voyages because many people quote from and explain his book but few have actually read it. Pytheas' most widely quoted critic Strabo, who lived in the first century AD, had not read it but quotes Polybius (200–120 BC), Eratosthenes (275–120 BC), Hipparchus (190–125 BC) and Timaeus (345–260 BC). His most important source seems to have been Polybius, who regarded Pytheas with hostility. Pliny, an important authority, gained some information directly from Pytheas but also refers to Timaeus. Many similar references to Pytheas prove nothing more than a common source, which in all probability did not quote him word for word.

It is the very fact that the information Pytheas gives us conflicts with the general views of his time which proves that he did in fact make his voyages. The biggest question in this regard is: where did he go? To Thule, there is no doubt, but from the point of view of research into exploration the most fascinating questions relate to the location of Thule. There are many alternatives.

THULE IS IN NORWAY

Nansen assumed that Pytheas had sailed along the west coast of Britain to the Scottish coast and onwards to the Shetland Islands. In his opinion the lengths of the days calculated on the basis of Pytheas' figures, provide indisputable evidence to support this. Moreover, Pytheas did not end his journey there but continued north. Thule is situated so far to the north that the day was 21–22 hours long. Observations of the sun would put it at about 64 degrees of latitude. In addition Thule stretched to the polar circle and was inhabited by barbarians. The latitude of the polar circle at that time was 66° 15'. Nansen could not believe that such a learned astronomer as Pytheas would have provided such erroneous information about the Shetlands. Neither does it become apparent anywhere that Thule was a group of islands. Pytheas had continued his journey – but where to?

In AD 825, the monk Dicuil maintained that Thule was Iceland. At that time Irish monks had already discovered the island. Nansen did not accept this assumption because in Pytheas' day, Iceland was uninhabited and had not been settled as Pytheas claimed the Thule he had discovered to be. At the time of Dicuil, in addition to the possible native Celtic population, only a few monks lived in Iceland. Secondly, how would Pytheas have known how to continue his journey into uncharted waters not knowing what he would find there? Neither, according to Nansen, could the six-day journey he mentions have taken place. And even if out of curiosity he had sailed due north, the ocean currents and prevailing winds would not have led him to Iceland anyway.

For these reasons, in Nansen's opinion, Thule could only be in Norway. The idea that someone might, in this early period, have sailed straight from Scotland to Norway, Nansen considered bold, but he believed it to be within the realms of possibility: had it, after all, been accomplished as much as 1000 years earlier than the Vikings – the pioneers of sea travel? A six-day journey would fit the Norway proposition.

According to Nansen, Eratosthenes placed Thule slightly to the north-west of Britain on the basis of the latitudes and distances given by Pytheas. The fact that Pytheas spoke of an island did not necessarily conflict with Nansen's assumption. How could Pytheas have expected that after sailing for six days from the British Isles he would have come across a continent rather than another island? In order to ascertain that Norway was part of a continent he would have had to sail to the farthest reaches of the Gulf of Bothnia. Even the boldest assumptions did not claim that Pytheas had done that.

So the Thule that Pytheas visited was situated in Norway, somewhere around Romsdal or Nordmore where the longest day of the year was 21 hours. Since there is a clear view to the north from there, it is very possible that the barbarians showed Pytheas the place where the sun went to rest. From here he would also have been able, by sailing along the coast, to continue northwards towards Bodo where it is possible to see the midnight sun. How far north he sailed also depends, of course, on what time during summer the journey was made.

The only thing that Nansen found difficult to explain was the reference to the position of the congealed sea about one day's journey from Thule and Strabo's depiction of the merging of land, sea and sky. Nansen believed that both the congealed sea and the sea lung meant a congealed or mushy mass. The phenomenon that Pytheas saw and which inspired him to employ this metaphorical expression was

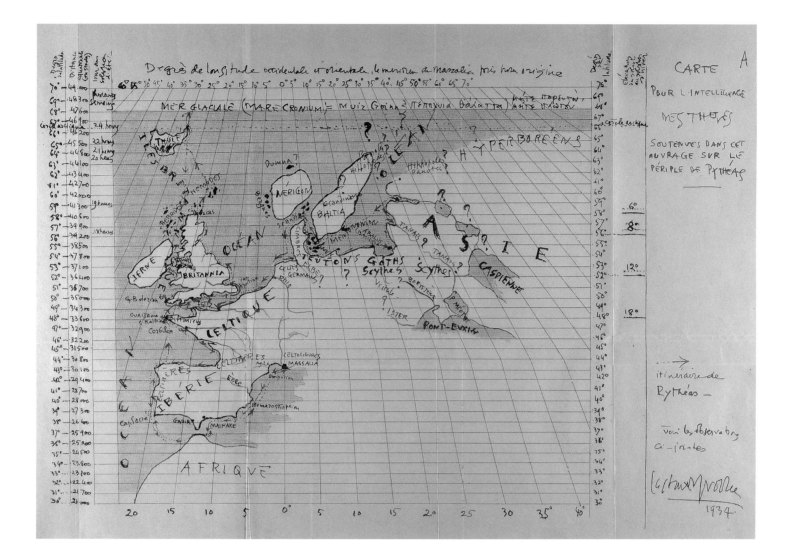

5 In his book Pythéas le Massaliote *of 1934, Professor Gaston Broche arrived at the conclusion that Thule was Iceland. If Pytheas had been to Norway instead of Iceland he would have seen the coast running from north to south. After that a geographer of Pytheas' stature would not have been able to claim that Britain was located south of Thule. Broche believes that after Thule Pytheas made his way to the Baltic Sea, that is to say to the amber coast, and went on to the furthest corner of the Gulf of Finland before turning round and returning home.*
(GASTON BROCHE, PYTHÉAS LE MASSALIOTE).

possibly the sludge which is formed in great amounts at the edge of drift-ice when the waves grind the ice into slush. Such slushy ice would fit extremely well Pytheas' description, according to which one could not walk or sail upon it. If one adds the thick fog which often hangs over areas of drift ice and which envelopes the land and sea in its shroud, the description is credible. If Pytheas stayed in Norway for the winter – and according to Nansen his journey probably lasted more than a year – he might have seen a similar, if more modest, phenomenon in the spring. There is, however, no mention in Pytheas' book that suggests he wintered there.

WOULD PYTHEAS HAVE BEEN ABLE TO SAIL TO ICELAND?

If we assume that the journey came to an end in Iceland, the maritime skill of Pytheas' contemporaries becomes decisive. The Phoenicians who sailed the waters of Western Europe five or six hundred years BC were pioneers of sea travel. But the Phoenicians always sailed close to the coast. They did not venture into the open sea nor sail in difficult conditions. How, then, would it have been possible for Pytheas to sail to the Atlantic?

Stefánsson looked to A. W. Brögger for support. Brögger believed that the open seas were sailed as early as the Bronze Age. Also, all the islands of the Atlantic and the Pacific had been discovered during the Bronze Age. According to Brögger, during the Bronze Age, in addition to those of the Mediterranean and Iberia, one of the trading areas was the North Sea and Baltic sea area. O'Neill Hencken has researched Bronze Age Cornwall and the Scilly Isles and believes that there was already a blossoming trade between the British Isles and the Mediterranean countries in 2000 BC.

The importance of sea trade later decreased with numerous river routes taking their share of the trade. Trading by sea with the Baltic Sea countries began to pick up again only around 1000 AD. On the other hand, navigational skills were already developed during the Stone Age. Stone Age Eskimos were excellent seafarers and their big umiak boats were extremely sea-worthy.

Sailing from the British Isles to Iceland was simpler than might be imagined, according to Stefánsson. The Orkneys lie in close proximity to the Scottish coast. The peripheral outermost islands of the group are only 50 nautical miles from the Shetlands. In addition, Fair Isle is midway between these two island groups. It is 160 nautical miles from the Shetlands to the Faroe Isles and from there 240 nautical miles to Iceland. For those who think the last of these distances too long, Stefánsson points out that the distance between Kingsman Reef and Hawaii is more than three times longer, and notwithstanding this the people of the South Sea probably sailed between them as early as AD 500, despite the fact that they lived in a Stone Age culture in which tools were made of stone or wood.

In Pytheas' time, *curraghs* – boats of skin with a wicker frame – were used in Scotland and Ireland. Three types of skin boats, the Eskimo kayak (which was completely covered) the Eskimo umiak (which resembled a flat-bottomed fishing boat used in the North Atlantic) and the Irish curragh (whose lines were similar to those of the canoes of the Algonquin Indians who lived in the Hudson Bay region) had sailed the open sea. All of these three boats were made of undressed skins that were stitched with waterproof seams and stretched over a wicker frame. The kayak was propelled with a paddle. The umiak used a sail, but it is not known when sails were invented. The Irish curragh, it seems, had been equipped with both oars and sails "since ancient times".

The Eskimos ventured out to sea in kayaks even in difficult conditions, and kayaks are, to all intents and purposes, unsinkable. When, in 1576, Martin Frobisher encountered the first Eskimos in the waters off Baffin Island, they easily avoided the English in their boats. And the umiak is not far behind the kayak as regards to seaworthiness. This is why American whale hunters discarded the New Bedford type of whaling boat to use umiaks for hunting the Greenland whales. The umiak can be sailed at speed onto a stony beach or onto the ice without sustaining great damage. According to Stefánsson the voyages of days gone by were not usually expeditions as such but voyages of discovery. New lands were found by chance. From the point of view of exploration the best vessels had to have two qualities, of which one is generally considered a weakness and the other an undisputed advantage. In the umiak both features are almost maximised. The umiak combines the excellent virtue of being virtually unsinkable with a tendency to be easily forced off course by the waves and the wind. Because the umiak is both light and flat-bottomed its displacement is only some ten centimetres. It is almost impossible for it to sail into the wind. A vessel like this could very easily be forced into the open sea by a change of wind. An umiak which had been blown of course could get out of trouble, however, because of its excellent seaworthiness.

Stefánsson assumed that the Stone Age Irish were just as able to build good skin boats as the Stone Age Eskimos

closer to our own time. In Irish legends there are tales of sea voyages undertaken in skin boats. In some, boats are described which could hold as many as sixty people and which could make voyages of several weeks. This was not surprising to Stefánsson. In his book he included a picture of an umiak in which there were 49 people.

A small model of a golden curragh, dating from 200 BC, has been found in Ireland. Because of its small size no details can be made out, but of its eight thwarts, oars, masts and rudder there is no doubt. The Carthaginian Hamilcar quotes a Grecian source which describes how the inhabitants of Britain used skin boats in about 500 BC. In his work *De Bello Civile* Caesar describes a river crossing in Gallia (Gaul) and says that the wooden-framed skin boats used were the same as those he had become familiar with in Britain. In his work *Historia naturalis* Pliny (the Elder) also mentions that the British used skin boats in the first century AD, to sail to the Ictis tin island. A drawing of an Irish boat dating from 1695 shows that no great changes had taken place over 1900 years. Based on this Stefánsson concluded that the boat had remained almost unchanged during previous centuries too, as advances were typically slower in early history. Dicuil, who describes the journey of the Irish to Ireland considerably later, depicts the journey as having happened in much the same way but in two-thwarted boats.

It can be assumed, then, that the Irish had boats adequate to undertake a journey to Iceland even in Pytheas' time. There is no proof, however, of such a journey having taken place before AD 800. Finally, as far as boats and their seaworthiness are concerned, it can be said that although skills at sailing the open sea were in fact on the decline in Pytheas' day, according to the respected researcher Sir Clements Markham, the vessels of Pytheas' time were bigger, and in a few respects better, than those used by Columbus when he 'discovered' America. Since Viking ships are considered to have been more seaworthy than those of Columbus, boat-building skills must have declined over the 500 years prior to Columbus' time. The prerequisites for longer sea-voyages had existed for centuries. Therefore, the question has been more one of the desire, courage and ability to navigate uncharted or little-known waters.

THULE IS IN ICELAND

Pytheas sailed from the coast of Britain and Scotland to Thule in six days in a vessel typical of the Mediterranean. He took two days to sail from the Scottish coast to the Shetland Islands. After this Pytheas had only four days left at his disposal. Was that long enough to have made the journey to Iceland?

According to Broche, Pytheas arrived in the north of Scotland in June. At that time the length of the day would have been almost exactly 19 hours, as has been possible to deduce from Pytheas' calculations. The five remaining hours are also a period of twilight, not of gloomy black night. It was here that the barbarians told Pytheas of a land where the night was

PYTHEAS BOATS – MADE OF WOOD AND LEATHER?

At the time of Pytheas' Thule voyage, the ships made in the Mediterranean area were much more advanced than vessels made elsewhere in Europe. Two seafaring nations, the Greeks and the Phoenicians, competed for supremacy in the region. In terms of size and the sophistication of their design, their vessels were in a different class altogether from the more modest vessels known then to have sailed the northern and northwestern waters of Europe. The Mediterranean ships were already fitted with sails to complement their oars. That the sail was used on the Atlantic before the beginning of our calendar lacks credible proof.

It is a common assumption that Pytheas of Massalia sailed to the Atlantic through the Pillars of Hercules, i.e. the Straits of Gibraltar, and then turned northwards. Merchant ships typical at the time on the Mediterranean remained unchanged for a relatively long period and relied mainly on the wind to propel them. Oars were only a secondary power source. Pytheas' contemporary, Aristotle, spoke of a merchant ship that sailed the wind. The "Cyrenian ship" dating from the 400s BC found in Cyprus was also this kind of a "round ship", so-called because of its shape. It is of course possible that Pytheas made his journey with a galley, which was a warship that was rowed.

It is not, however, an undisputed fact that Pytheas arrived on the Atlantic in a sailing ship. The British scholar Barry Cunliffe thinks that Pytheas went by land along the so-called tin route from Massalia (present-day Marseilles) to the Gironde at the mouth of the Garonne, and from there continued to the north using one or more local vessels.

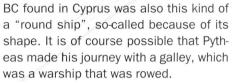

7 The Hjortspring boat is one of the oldest boat finds in the North (about 400–200 BC). A precise replica has been made to scale of the remains of this boat discovered in the Hjortspring bog in Southern Jutland. The unkeeled boat was 18 metres long and was made by sewing together aspen planks, a beam-like spine and four rib-planks. The Hjortspring boat was propelled by twenty paddlers. If Pytheas had come to land in the north and continued his journey by boat it could have been in a Hjortspring-type boat. At that time sails were unknown on the Baltic Sea. (JOHN NURMINEN FOUNDATION)

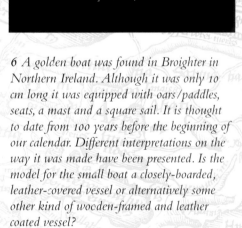

6 A golden boat was found in Broighter in Northern Ireland. Although it was only 10 cm long it was equipped with oars/paddles, seats, a mast and a square sail. It is thought to date from 100 years before the beginning of our calendar. Different interpretations on the way it was made have been presented. Is the model for the small boat a closely-boarded, leather-covered vessel or alternatively some other kind of wooden-framed and leather coated vessel?

(THE NATIONAL MUSEUM OF IRELAND)

What were the boats that perhaps transported Pytheas' escort from one place to the next? They were probably made from hide. Leather boats were common everywhere in the north - from the Eskimo kayaks and umiaks to the curraghs and coracles of Ireland. Their structure was in principle the same everywhere: skin was stretched on top of a frame made out of bones or wood. With the exception of the kayak, all the boats were open. The kayak and the curragh were used for millennia and remain in use to this day. The Eskimos used their kayaks for hunting and Irish monks used their curraghs to go from island to island on the Atlantic Coast.

Information on prehistoric skin boats is oblique. One of the oldest boat finds in Western Europe is the Danish Hjortspring boat, or Als boat from 400–200 BC. It is a reconstruction of remains discovered at the Hjortspring bog in southern Jutland at the bottom of the Als bay. The boat is built on arches and it has a bottom-board and two sideboards. It is often thought to have been inspired by the skin boat but some experts think that this find is evidence of a second, parallel evolutionary line of boats. According to this theory the dugout gradually became a boarded, keeled boat. The Hjortspring boat does not have a place for a mast and has no proper keel.

The debate on the history of wooden and leather boats and the relationship between them is further confused by the golden Broighter boat. This 20-centimetre miniature was found in a bog in Ireland. It has been thought that this boat, equipped with a mast, yard and oars, was inspired by the curragh, but the theory that a wooden boat was the source of inspiration also has some support. This find dates back to AD 100.

Whether they were wooden or made of skin, we can safely assume that Pytheas did indeed encounter boats on the Atlantic. But these boats were either rowed or paddled, they had no sails. Perhaps it was Pytheas himself who introduced the sail to the Atlantic.

8 There is no precise information on Pytheas' ship but the wreck of a trading ship found off Cyprus, the so-called Cyrenaic ship of about 400 BC, dates from the same time as Pytheas' voyages. The Cyrenaic ship was 14 metres long and 4.2 metres wide and had a displacement of 25 tons. It was almost entirely built of Aleppo pine; its frame and the wooden treenails in both the frame and keel were made of Turkish oak. The ship's hull had seen a great deal of repairs and was shored up with lead plates, among other materials. When it sank, the Cyrenaic ship had been sailing for about 80 years and by type would have been suitable for Pytheas' expeditions.

(JOHN NURMINEN FOUNDATION)

9 Pytheas is said to have found a "congealed sea" one day's journey north of Thule. According to Strabo it was here that the land, sea and air combined. This description fits the slush ice area at the edge of the pack ice well, particularly if one imagines the dense fog that usually hangs over the area. (DEREK FORDHAM)

even lighter. Pytheas was a scientist and was eager to see this unknown land. Since his ship was very seaworthy the natives agreed to go along as pilots.

On the first day, according to Broche, Pytheas passed the Orkneys; on the second the Shetlands rose into view in the east. After this he changed course towards the north-west. If the time needed to sail between the various points of the

Mediterranean is taken as a point of comparison, says Broche, Pytheas would not have found it difficult to sail at a rate of 90 nautical miles a day.

At this speed Pytheas would have passed the Faroe Isles on day four. There is no mention of an island, however. It could, of course, have been overlooked. On the fifth day Pytheas came to waters in which the period of dim light was so short that it was not necessary to slow down during the night. By changing men at the oars, the final leg of the journey could have been covered so quickly that on the sixth day, or at least in the evening of that day, he would have reached Iceland.

Stefánsson stresses that the six days mentioned by Strabo to get from Scotland to Iceland would have meant a slower speed than the three days it took to sail between Rhodes and

at the time of Pytheas' journey Iceland was still uninhabited. Apparently it was only 1000 years later that the Irish monks settled there. In Stefánsson's opinion the wording of Dicuil's writings did not suggest that Iceland was discovered in 795 but indicates that it had been known for a long time. Naturally Dicuil did not speak of Thule as if the island had just been discovered, because he believed that Pytheas had already discovered it centuries earlier.

Stefánsson still held the trump card. According to Pytheas the edge of the "congealed sea" was a day's journey from Thule. Nansen was forced to admit that this description did not fit Norway. On the other hand it suited Iceland perfectly. In his excellent work *The Arctic, A History*, Richard Vaughan wrote that 'no Norwegian would have been able to tell Pytheas of the area of pack ice which in spring is, and in all probability was in 325 BC too, about 100 nautical miles away on the northernmost coast of northern Norway. People dwelling in Iceland could have known where the edge of the pack ice lay but there were no people living in Iceland at that time, so nobody could have told about it.' In the end Vaughan does, however, state that it could not be considered completely impossible for Pytheas to have gone to the edge of the pack ice at the front off the east coast of Greenland.

Also the merging of land, sea and air, which Nansen agreed was a typical phenomenon at the edge of the pack ice, admirably suited Stefánsson's and Broche's theory. Stefánsson wrote "The Greek ships sailed from Iceland towards the Pole. After one day's sailing the scattered ice was seen which forecasted pack ice. As the journey continued the ice floes increased disturbingly rapidly. Soon the ship was only able to proceed with difficulty between ice floes in a sea on the point of freezing. Oars are of little use in this kind of slush ice, nor could it bear a man's weight. The sea rises and falls and resembles the breathing of the medusa." Stefánsson also referred to the fact that in the Mediterranean of Pytheas' time the medusa was called the sea-lung, which appears in Strabo's description of Thule. Strabo had once presented these "incredible lies" as proof that Pytheas had never been to Thule.

Stefánsson was convinced that he was right and Nansen wrong. According to Stefánsson, Nansen questioned everything which conflicted with the Norway hypothesis and believed such information to originate elsewhere than from Pytheas' original account. But Stefánsson's explanation, too, had one weakness: there was no evidence that Iceland was inhabited in Pytheas' day. Stefánsson did not, however, claim this to be the mistake of subsequent generations. Perhaps it was the Irish, who were on the journey as pilots, who told of the edge of the pack ice, and not the local inhabitants.

Alexandria. Professor William Hovgaard estimates that a Viking ship of the type of Pytheas' but with a weaker capacity would cover a maximum 170 miles per day, in other words, half as many again as Pytheas' day's journey assumed by Broche. For this reason Stefánsson did not accept the exclusion of Iceland on the basis that the journey could not have been made in six days.

On the longest days of summer one can catch a slight glimpse of the midnight sun in northern Iceland. According to Stefánsson, Iceland's latitude would then fit the picture of a place where "the barbarians showed the place where the sun went to rest". This is indeed the only direct quotation from Pytheas' book. Nansen rejected Iceland because Pytheas had said that Thule was inhabited. Nansen believed that

THULE IS IN SAARENMAA

Lennart Meri is an historian, writer and explorer and is also familiar with Russia's Arctic coast as well as the history and exploration of the Baltic Sea. In his work *Silver White* (1983)

he presents a fresh alternative regarding Pytheas' sea route. Meri interprets the same sources as his rivals. He too believes that Pytheas sailed first to Cornwall where tin mines were located. They regarded strangers with friendliness there; merchants have, of course, always been more broad-minded than others. In Britain Pytheas investigated the tides, almost completely unfamiliar to the people of the Mediterranean, and went on foot to the Bristol Channel. When travelling to Thule, according to Meri, Pytheas set out from Cornwall not from the north coast of Britain.

He made his way towards the areas where amber was produced. He was not, in fact, travelling to Thule in particular, but discovered it by accident. Meri stresses that, although Thule is in the north, it is not necessarily located at the same degree of longitude as Britain. Thule is located six sailing days away in the north, close to the frozen sea but still within the temperate zone, because they made mead from honey and threshed grain in barns.

The latter of these ideas is based on Strabo's text: "... he (Pytheas) has indeed described truthfully conditions prevailing near the cold zone: there are no cultivated plants or domesticated animals here at all or very few. For food there are roots, millet and forest corn, but where you find bread and honey there you will also find breweries. Because there are no sunny days there, corn is threshed in large dwelling places to which sheaves of corn are brought quickly to safety; because of the scarcity of sun and the plentiful rain, threshing under the open sky is not known."

Meri bases his claim on Pliny the Elder's text which itself is not based directly on Pytheas' book: "The furthestmost away of all known lands is Thule...". There are writers who mention other islands such as Scandia, Dunna, Berg and of all these the largest is Berrice, from which one usually travels to Thule.

Many Pytheas researchers have paid attention to the fact that, according to Diodorus, Pytheas measured the two sides of the triangle of Britain that extended northwards as being too long, that is to say 1665 and 2220 miles. According to this the circumference of Britain would be as much as 4717 miles or 42,500 stadia. These figures are double those of the true measurements.

Strabo regarded this mistake as proof that Pytheas was a liar. Nansen suspected that the mistake was the responsibility of some Pytheas interpreter, Timaeus for example. Since Nansen, contrary to Meri, believed that Pytheas circumnavigated Britain, the original figures, according to him, must be the number of days travelled. Meri, on the other hand, sees the distances as evidence of the fact that the eastern side of the triangle was parallel to the east coast of Scandinavia and points to the fact that Pytheas sailed north-eastward along the coast.

Pytheas arrived at the Amber coast of the Baltic Sea having crossed the Jutland Peninsula along the calm, time-honoured river route. According to Meri the Baltic Sea is Pytheas' Metuonis. After Jutland, Pytheas passed the islands named by Pliny. Scandia, according to Meri, is Skåne, he places Dumnan on the south coast of the Baltic Sea. Bergi, in his opinion, is perhaps the original form of Birkan. The largest island is Berrice, from which one generally went to Thule. Berrice is Perhedenmaa or Perheidenmaa and lies near Åland and south-western Finland. From there Pytheas turned south to Saarenmaa or Thule.

How is Meri able to prove that Thule is so far south? And why would Pytheas have gone there? What evidence is there that Saarenmaa is Thule? Meri's proof has at least literary value, as he shows both an admirable imagination and remarkable eloquence in arguing his case.

A great meteorite fell into Saarenmaa's Kaali crater lake between 700 and 400 BC. Memories of the event live still on in folk stories, to say nothing of Pytheas' day. According to Meri: "the bright flame of the explosion shook the shores of the Baltic Sea and was visible on the coast opposite... The sun had fallen from the sky and disappeared." The former is Geminos' direct quotation from Pytheas according to whom the barbarians showed the place where the sun had gone to rest. These words can also be translated as "to slumber into an eternal sleep". On the west coast of the Baltic Sea the meteorite's fall was seen as the sun setting in the east in the   middle of the day and falling into eternal sleep. This explanation is at least as good as that of the barbarians showing where the sun set for the period of the long winter night.

Pytheas calculated the latitude of Massalia extremely accurately with the aid of a gnomon, a simple stick. His measurement was based on the fact that the angle of inclination of the sun measured at the solstice shows how far north the location of any given place is compared with that of another known site. If Pytheas calculated the position of Thule just as well as he did that of Massalia, Thule cannot be located in Saarenmaa.

According to the quotation presented by Geminos, Thule's longest day lasted for 17 or 18 hours and the night for 2 or 3 hours at most. After the short night the sun rose again. If day lasted for 17 hours and the night 3, the period of twilight was 4 hours. Those who live in the north know that specifying the exact boundary between day and night in summer is rather difficult. On this basis Meri estimated Thule's latitude to be less than 60 degrees while Nansen positioned Thule between latitudes 63 and 64 and Stefánsson between 63 and 65.

Nansen assumed Thule's day to be 21–22 hours long. In his opinion many (Eratosthenes and Strabo among them) believed Pytheas to be describing Thule as the land of the midnight sun. According to Nansen a 19-hour night suggests the Shetland Islands, not Thule. Of Meri's insights the most ingenious is the specification of Thule's longitude. According to Meri the origin of the name Thule was no longer a mystery. *Tuli* is an old Finno-Ugric word and in several related languages means fire. Thule is the island of fire, the island in which the sun set into the sleep of death. It is this word and this word alone and its origin which defines Thule's longitude. So Thule is in Saarenmaa.

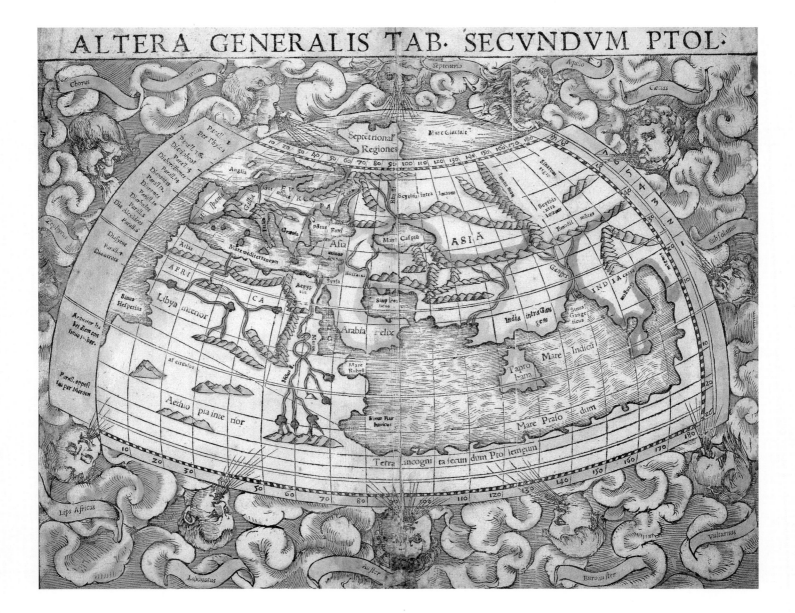

HOW THE NORTHERN COUNTRIES WERE PERCEIVED FROM PTOLEMY TO CLAVUS

Before the beginning of our calendar, western man's perception of the world was astonishingly precise. The image of the world first appeared in the Hellenistic scientific community and it encompassed continental Europe, North Africa and that part of Asia bounded by the Indian Ocean. The scientists of that time had a fairly accurate conception of the shape and size of the earth. The Greek geographer and mathematician Eratosthenes (circa 273–192 BC) understood that the earth was a sphere, and in 240 BC he calculated its circumference to be within less than 62 miles of its true dimension. The geographer and historian Strabo (circa 63–20 BC) also accepted the idea that the earth was spherical, as did many other thinkers of ancient times.

In AD 140, Ptolemy (circa AD 100–170), who lived and worked in Alexandria, drew up a map of the world based on a conical projection in which a network of meridians of longitude and parallels of latitude narrowed as they progressed northwards. A similar network, with its horizontal lati-tudes and vertical longitudes, is still the basis of modern maps. Ptolemy divided the known world into the northern and southern hemispheres and these he divided further into zones. He designated the demarcation line between the hemispheres (the equator) to be the zero degree of latitude and the geographical latitudes of the poles to be 90°. He placed the zero degree of longitude, that is to say the zero meridian, as running through the western extreme of the known world, the Canary Islands (Fortunatae Insulae).

Ptolemy also compiled a catalogue of place names and their co-ordinates; the map and the catalogue thus described the same thing in different forms. He published his data in his work *Geography*, which is considered to be the basis of modern geography. The original maps have not survived, so it is not known, for example, how he described the north, but the catalogue of names extends to the North Sea/Baltic Sea areas.

Britain is reasonably well depicted on the new Ptolemaic maps made in the 13th

10 Sebastian Münster drew up his famous COSMOGRAPHY *in 1544. An addition to the map was made above the northern world so that further information on Scandinavia would fit in. It was as though the world was distended in the north. There is a second map of the world in the* COSMOGRAPHY. *It depicts Iceland and Greenland and, as a result of the most recent expeditions, wide areas of America. The maps of the Atlas thus differ from each other.*

(JOHN NURMINEN FOUNDATION)

century. Iceland is missing, as it probably was from the original map. In place of Scandinavia there is a group of islands.

Thule, which was named by the Greek mariner Pytheas around 350 BC, is to be found on 15th century Ptolemaic maps at latitude 63°; the regions to the north were marked as "unknown land" (terra incognita). Before Ptolemy, Eratosthenes had positioned Thule at latitude 66°. Most ancient geographers and historians mentioned Thule. Pytheas' voyages were known about at the time, but they were also disputed. Pliny the Elder (AD 23–79) is the first to mention Scandinavia (AD 77). There are mentions of northern peoples and their ways in Tacitus' *Germania* of AD 98.

Ptolemy's map and catalogue disappeared from Western European consciousness in the Middle Ages. They were replaced by a diagrammatic T-map based on biblical ideas, whose central point was Jerusalem. The Europeans of the Middle Ages must have had rather a flimsy understanding of the shape of the earth. Ptolemy's legacy persisted for over a thousand years, however, in Byzantium and the Arab world, preserved and propagated by both monks and astronomers.

With the coming of the Renaissance, Europe rediscovered the geographical knowledge of Antiquity. Ptolemy's *Geography*, still with 27 maps, found its way among a group of old Grecian manuscripts from the besieged city of Constantinople to the Strozzi family in Florence. This can be considered the second coming of cartography. With the aid of the Gutenberg printing technique, the maps of Antiquity quickly spread. More than 50 new Ptolemaic atlases were published in the 15th and 16th centuries. Most contained maps printed using wood cuts.

The Finnish-born polar explorer A. E. Nordenskiöld, who was the first man to navigate the Northeast Passage, collected 49 copies of these valuable works at the end of the 19th century. His map collection, which is on UNESCO's World Heritage list, can now be found in Helsinki University Library.

During the time of the great voyages of exploration, additions were made to the Ptolemaic editions, enriching the classical perception of the world.

The Dane Claudius Clavus (born 1388) drew up a map of the north in 1427. The original was lost until 1886, when it was found in company with a Ptolemaic manuscript. It is now kept in the Nancy City Library in France. Clavus' view of the north was better than those of his predecessors in many respects. Scandinavia was no longer depicted as a group of islands but as a peninsula, and Greenland and Iceland are included. But there were also some mistakes. Clavus connected Greenland to northern Russia and, in so doing, closed off the Northeast Passage. The extension of Asia far into the northwest perhaps has its origins in the Vikings' misunderstanding of the edge of the pack ice or in their observations of Novaya Zemlya, possibly even of Spitsbergen. Norse men had in fact been sailing these waters 300 years before Clavus' time. All in all, however, Clavus' map was a valuable addition to our geographical knowledge of the north.

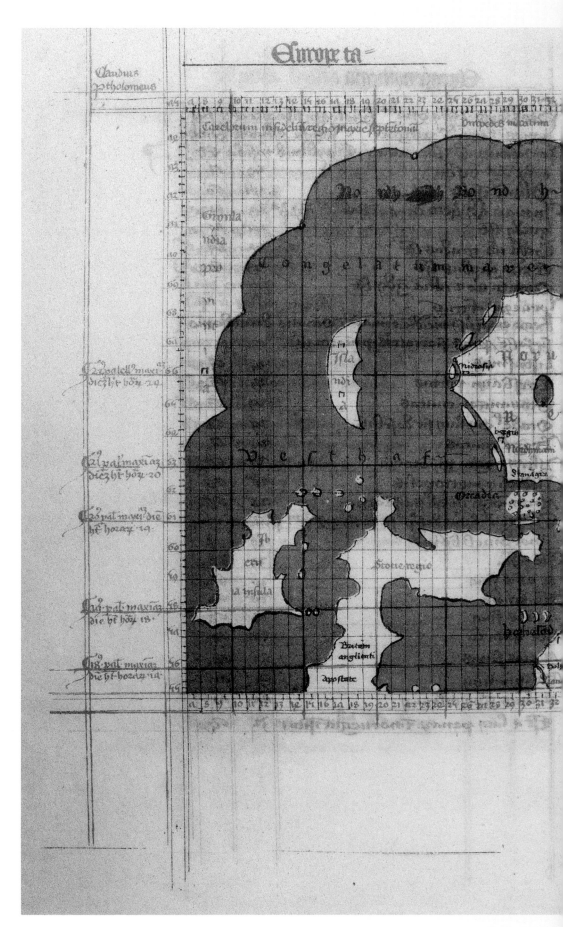

The Swede Ulla Ehrensvärd, who has made a laudable study of the history of the mapping of the north, draws our attention to an interesting point of nomenclature on Clavus' map, the background to which was only cleared up in 1904 by Carl S. Petersen. Clavus had made up place names for the coast of Greenland by putting in front of the Latin word for estuary certain words from a rhyme which begins: "Der bor en Mand i en Gronlands Aa, og Spjeldebod monne han hedde..."

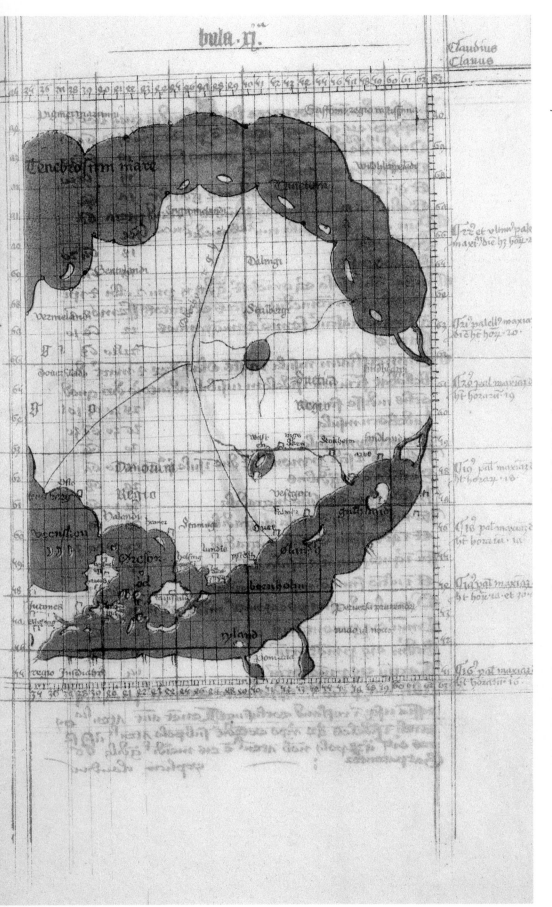

bula·II.

11 The Northern map by the Dane Clavus was found in 1886. The map was attached to a manuscript dedicated to Cardinal Filiastrus. Clavus, whose Danish name was Claudius Clausson Swart, was from the island of Fyn. He was the first to draw a map of Iceland and Greenland. The map is kept in Nancy's city library. The explorer and researcher of the history of cartography, A. E. Nordenskiöld, considered the map so important that he took a facsimile printing of it in the 19th century.

many later maps, including Zeno's first map of the North Atlantic, which contained fresh mistakes. Clavus' influence on maps of the north was considerable, however, and his insights extended not only to the versions of Ptolemy, but also, by way of later maps, to the whole of the western world.

The next modifications to maps of the north took place when the Swedish bishop, Olaus Magnus, had his own *Carta Marina* printed in Venice in 1539.

A tradition of high-quality sea charts was developed in the Italian nation states and the islands of the Mediterranean and later in Spain. Skilfully drawn on parchment, sailors' and navigators' portolan charts were very popular from the 13th to the 16th centuries. The best were made in Catalonia. During the time of the great voyages of exploration, from the 15th century onwards, information on sea areas outside the Mediterranean began to be added to the portolan charts and these were extended to include the North Sea, the Baltic Sea and the North Atlantic. The French school of Dieppe, in particular, enhanced our knowledge of northern waters with their sea charts. It is not known whether the makers of the land-drawn portolan charts and the printed geographical maps were in contact with one another; it can be presumed, however, that seafarers, at least, exchanged information on their voyages among themselves. At the end of the Middle Ages a great many seamen, explorers, fishermen and whalers from many nations travelled in northern waters. On the basis of the information they supplied, new places were put on the map.

(There dwelled a man by a Greenland river, and Spjeldebod was perchance his name...) This strange list of names is kept in Austria's National Library in Vienna.

Additions and corrections began to be made to the Ptolemaic map after 1482. Since the original system of co-ordinates extended north to latitude 65° at most, additions – the Scandinavian peninsula, for example – often had to be made outside the network of meridians and parallels. Clavus' mistakes are repeated on

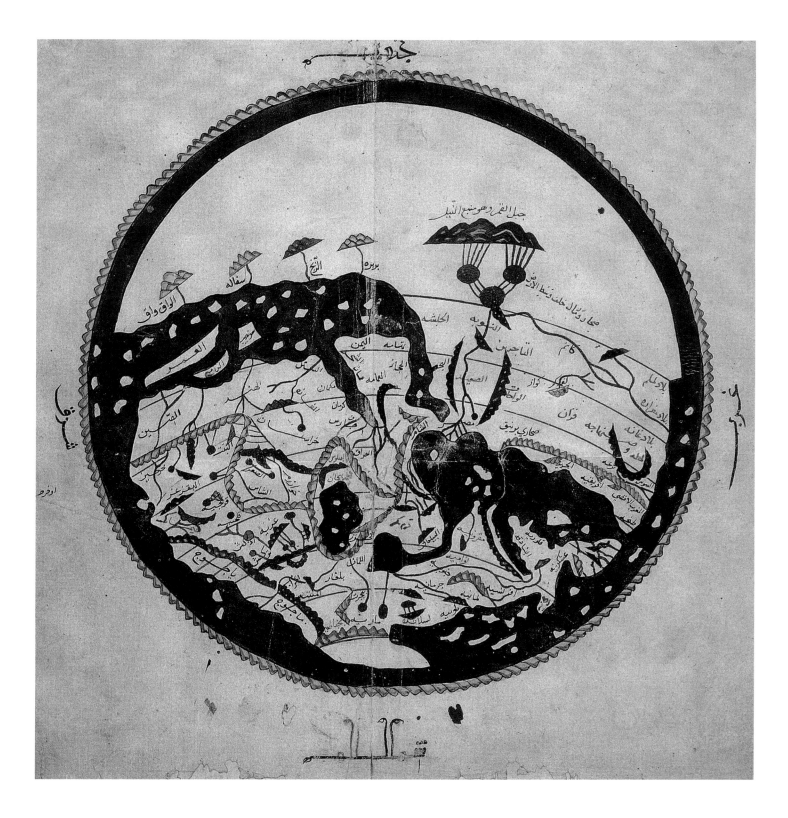

WHAT IS THE TRUTH?

So how does Meri explain Pytheas' 'sea-lung', the merging of ice and air, a day's journey away to the north? Meri is helped in solving the problem by Nansen. According to Meri, Pytheas "... had time enough to describe the freezing sea's heavy breathing in which the land, the water and the air intermingle. He calls this poetically the sea's lung. He describes for us that familiar incarceration by the ice, that thickly solidifying slush, which no longer supports a ship and not yet even a person...". The congealing created by the merging of ice and air can be found at the entrance to the Bay of Finland as the bay is freezing over.

Each contender, Fridtjof Nansen, Vilhjalmur Stefánsson and Lennart Meri not only had a command of words but was also familiar with Arctic conditions. None of them can be considered a dilettante. Nansen was a well-known scientist, an undisputed leading figure in polar exploration. Stefánsson was one of the most important 19th-20th century polar explorers, even though his reputation is more debatable. Lennart Meri is an historian who has undertaken several expeditions into the Arctic area of Russia.

All of their arguments were considered, but led to totally different conclusions. Nansen and Stefánsson maintained, at

12 Al-Idrisi visited the court of the Norman king in Palermo, Sicily, and on the basis of it drew up the famous Roger's book. The book is comprised of annotations to 70 area maps. On the basis of these Al-Idrisi drew up a world map, MAPPAE MUNDI, which differed from other Medieval world maps in two ways. It is directed towards the south and the sun, like most other Arabian maps, and it has no religious or symbolic references. Al-Idrisi's map differed from Ptolemy maps in that he did not join the southern tip of Africa to South East Asia. The Scandinavian peninsula pushes forth like a thick finger from Sythia in the north above the Ripaeus mountain range. During the Middle Ages, Arabian geographical knowledge was clearly more developed than European. The Arabs understood the validity of the ancient world view and preserved this knowledge throughout the Middle Ages. They were also familiar with the North. (BODLEIAN LIBRARY, OXFORD)

first, that the origin of the word Thule supported neither Norway or Iceland. There are many assumptions regarding the word's origin. This route did not lead to finding the location of Thule until Meri came up with his argument based on an idiosyncratic assumption.

Before arriving at his final argument, Stefánsson cited a group of his predecessors who placed Thule in Iceland. The Venerable Bede, an Anglo-Saxon monk and teacher, referred in his writings to Thule in the eighth century AD, and meant by it the Iceland of Stefánsson's interpretation. The Irish monk Dicuil most certainly meant Iceland when writing of Thule in 825. In 1075 Adam of Bremen also assumed Thule to be Iceland. According to Stefánsson, Thule meant Iceland to Columbus and Bougainville too. Prior to Stefánsson in 1935, Gaston Broche had published a work dealing with Pytheas according to which Pytheas visited both Iceland and the remotest part of the Gulf of Finland.

But Nansen was not the first researcher or writer to place Thule in Norway. The first to do this was probably Procopius in the sixth century AD who, as a Byzantine, can not however be considered a competent interpreter of conditions in north-west Europe. Nansen's prestige made Norway the unqualified favourite after the publication of *In Northern Mists* in 1911.

Meri's most important assumption is that Pytheas never circumnavigated Britain, a matter about which both Nansen and Stefánsson on the other hand were in agreement. Stefánsson certainly maintains that Polybius wrote that Pytheas claimed to have "travelled all over Britain". Both assume Pytheas to have continued his voyage, although he did go ashore in between. Nansen stresses the fact that Diodorus called the northern tip of the triangle by the name Orkas. This word perhaps stemmed from the Gaelic word *orc*. The name of the Orkney Islands perhaps originates from the same root word.

Hipparchus tells us that the length of the day in northern Britain is 18 hours and is an hour longer in the more northerly islands off the coast. According to Nansen the day in the Orkneys was 18 hours and 27 minutes at its longest. Therefore Pytheas' inability to distinguish between twilight and daytime cannot be considered as bad as Meri assumes.

One thing is certainly true, however. Regardless of whether Pytheas found Thule or not, he was the first to sail the great distance to the edge of the Arctic and knew that he was doing it. If he – as Vaughan presents as one alternative – sailed to the pack ice zone off the east coast of Greenland, he will not only go down in history as a great explorer but also as the first explorer to penetrate into the Arctic region.

Pytheas differed from the Vikings, however, who were to follow in his wake. Pytheas set out intentionally for the north to find a land of whose existence he had heard. He did not set sail in no particular direction as the Vikings did when making their great discoveries. Stefánsson asserted that as an explorer Pytheas ranks higher than Columbus. As an explorer he was more "a combination of James Cook and Galileo".

EXPLORATION OF THE ARCTIC REGION AFTER PYTHEAS

Pytheas' discoveries conflicted so deeply with the beliefs of his day that for a long time those who came after him concentrated on proving his observations and conclusions ridiculous and did not continue the work he had begun. Any evaluation of his discoveries was made more difficult by the disappearance of his writings.

Eratosthenes (275–194 BC), the founder of geography, who worked as a librarian in Alexandria, based his knowledge of the North on Pytheas. He drew the world's first atlas on which the central positions of different places were defined with the aid of longitude and latitude. He also calculated the earth's circumference and arrived at a figure of 250,000 stadia, that is to say only about 15 per cent too great. Eratosthenes placed Thule in the polar circle north of Britain. He calculated that the known world covered about a third of the earth's surface, so that the distance between the coast of Asia and Spain was about 240 degrees of longitude, which was not very far from the truth. He also claimed that "If it was not for the fact that the width of the Atlantic Ocean made it impossible we could sail from the Pyrenees to India along the same degree of latitude." He said this 1700 years before Columbus.

In the year 98 AD Tacitus wrote his work *Germania,* which increased our knowledge of the peoples of the north. According to Tacitus the north was inhabited by the Suebs, Slavs and Fenni. These were all Germanic tribes. The Aests lived on the coast of Mare Suebicum. Tacitus also tells us of a people called the Suiones whose might was built upon their men, weapons and vessels.

What Tacitus tells about the vessels is interesting in the light of Stefánsson's assumption of the advanced level of shipbuilding and seafaring in the Baltic Sea. The Suiones' vessels had a bowsprit at either end. They had no sails and their rowlocks were open so that oars could be changed from one side to the other, in contrast to the later Viking vessels in which they were closed. The description fits a ship excavated in Nydam near Flensburg well. This was a large vessel, more than 70 yards in length, and dated back to the third century AD, that is to say 600 years after Pytheas.

The Fenni lived in the north at the extreme edge of the world. They were hunters and used bows and arrows as weapons. They had no horses or other domestic animals. They lived in tents built entirely of pole-forest branches. "Among the Fenni amazing savagery and revolting poverty prevail. They have no weapons, no horses, no houses: their food is herbs, their clothing skins, their bed the ground. Their only hope is their arrows, which from lack of iron they provide with heads of bone. Hunting supports both men and women; for the women accompany the men everywhere and take their share of the spoils." From Tacitus' description it is not apparent whether the Fenni were Lapps, Kveeni or Finns.

The greatest geographer of Classical times was Claudius Ptolemy. He was probably born in Egypt and lived as an astronomer in Alexandria (126–141). Of the circumstances of his death there is no knowledge. In about AD 150 Ptolemy wrote the six-part work *Geographia*. The book provides the first definition of geography and contains systematically arranged knowledge of the geography of the time including the degrees of longitude and latitude of known places. These are estimated, not calculated, however. The essential improvement of Ptolemy's map was its new type of projection. Lines of longitude converged at the poles, a device which had already been recommended in Hipparchus' day. For a long time Ptolemy had a greater influence on Arabian science than that of the West. Ptolemy's writings found their way to the West along with Byzantine scientists when Constantinople was overthrown in 1453. Only then were his works translated into Latin. Copies of Ptolemy's maps are the only remaining remnants of the geography of Antiquity and are therefore also interesting from the point of view of the history of the Arctic regions. These copies were unsurpassable masterpieces for 1500 years, until the Middle Ages.

Ptolemy's description of the North contains nothing that is really new. As to its shape the area already resembled reality. Britain and Ireland were depicted better than on earlier maps, although the northern tip of Scotland leans strangely to the east. Ptolemy mentions the Hebrides and the Orkneys but not the Shetland Isles, unless he includes them in the Orkneys. Thule has been moved further south from the Arctic Circle to latitude 63°, that is a little to the north of the Orkneys.

The Atlantic Ocean continues into the north. The Hyperborean Sea, also called the Congealed or Dead Sea, is situated in the extreme north-west. Thule was still the most northern known place in spite of its relocation. Ptolemy had abandoned the idea that the known continents were fully surrounded by sea. The continent of Europe stretched to the

13 Hereford Cathedral's MAPPAE MUNDI *map of the world is considered the richest in information, most detailed and best preserved Medieval map of the world. This map attempted to combine the lessons of the* BIBLE *with Greek and Roman knowledge. It was also a dictionary of the world, which contained descriptions of the strange tribes and animals of the North of which the Roman historian Pliny had already written.*

At the upper edge of the map the figure of Christ depicts the East. On Medieval maps East was always upwards because the maps were directed to the East. Jerusalem was situated in the centre of the map. The Medieval MAPPAE MUNDI *maps are also called T-O maps because of their typical round shape. The Black Sea, the Red Sea and the Mediterranean together form a T shape.*

Richard of Haldingham (Richard de Bello), a Lincolnshire priest, drew up the Hereford map on parchment (1290–1300). The map has been on the wall of Hereford Cathedral since it was made. The maker based his work on late Roman sources of the Diocletian period (284–305). In the lower corner the Emperor gives an order to three surveyors: 'Go forth and measure the world and give the Senate knowledge of its parts'. The cartographer has situated the British Isles and Ireland at the top of the picture. A little higher a Norwegian skier symbolised Scandinavia.

On the left of the Northern Bear drawn on the map, below Norway, there are three islands on which are written FAREIE, YSLAND, *and* ULTIMA TILE *– The Faroe Islands, Iceland and the mysterious Ultima Thule. Haldingham has placed Ultima Thule at the very edge of the T-O map, in the extreme north.*
(THE CATHEDRAL LIBRARY, HEREFORD)

east and north-east and he made no assumption as to how it continued.

By the beginning of the Middle Ages, geography had not advanced in essence since Pytheas' day. Although the details of the area south of the Arctic Circle had increased, it can be said that knowledge of the North had decreased. New and fresh views of the northern regions were limited to the more southerly areas or, in Tacitus' terms, Hibernia (Ireland), Albion (England) and Germania as well as the areas close to it.

THE INDIGENOUS PEOPLES OF THE ARCTIC
– THE REAL CONQUERORS OF THE POLAR CIRCLE

ALTHOUGH, ON THE BASIS OF RECENT FINDS, MAN IS BELIEVED TO HAVE LIVED IN SIBERIA'S
YAKUT, FOR EXAMPLE, MORE THAN 200 000 YEARS AGO, SETTLEMENT OF THE ARCTIC REALLY
BEGAN AFTER THE LAST ICE AGE, A GOOD TEN THOUSAND YEARS AGO.

FEATURES PECULIAR TO THE ARCTIC

Formerly there was a bridge of land at the place we now call the Bering Strait over which people moved from Asia to America. Some of them roamed southwards. The Eskimos, creators of the most sophisticated culture of the polar region, migrated to the area they now inhabit only a few thousand years ago, after the Bering Strait came into being. During the last two thousand years or so, climactic conditions in the polar region have continued to change to some extent. For example, during the period of its settlement around AD 1000, Greenland's climate was considerably warmer than it was when the island's population was decimated in the 16th century. Its climate has subsequently become milder again.

The most important peculiarity of the North polar region is the amount of, and variation in, the light it receives. Though each year the Arctic receives as much sunlight as do the tropics, this is concentrated into a period of six months and the sun shines from an extremely acute angle, filtered through a thick atmospheric layer. Under such conditions the prerequisites for life are quite different from those in milder zones. Unlike in a situation governed by a 24-hour-cycle, the flora and fauna have to be able to adapt themselves to a short period of growth and a long and dark winter. Correspondingly, changes

On Stone by J. Brandard, from the original Drawing by Captain Ross

K E M I G .

in temperature are also severe. In winter the temperature often falls to 50°c below freezing, but summers, particularly in places further from the sea, are warm and hot spells are not at all uncommon. In central Alaska, for example, temperatures often rise to above 25°c, and this is not the only Arctic area to experience this kind of heat.

Although snow and ice are characteristic of the Arctic, this does not necessarily mean that there is a particularly heavy precipitation of snow. Over wide areas the snow cover is no more than twenty centimetres or so, but this can vary considerably. For the Netsilik Eskimos or Inuit living in the Boothia Peninsula in Northern Canada autumn was the most difficult time, since it meant that there was only the short period between summer and winter with enough snow to build an igloo before the onset of winter. In the polar region there is no autumn as such.

Because a great deal of heat is expended in melting the ice, in many places the waters are freed only in August. For example, Roald Amundsen, who was the first to sail the Northwest Passage, was able to leave his winter port only on 13th August, 1905, to become a prisoner of the ice again as early as 2nd September. On the other hand, the thickness of the sea ice varies greatly from year to year. At the beginning of May 1904, Amundsen and his companions measured the

14 In the warmth of the shelter the Eskimos lived half-naked during winter too. The children played in scant clothing but the adults wore light "loincloths". (JOHN NURMINEN FOUNDATION)

On Stone by J. Brandard, from the original Drawing by Captain Ross.

15 The woman's coat in the picture is typical of the Eskimo of the central Arctic area. With their tails stretching from back to front the coats resembled a tailcoat. Eskimo medicine was based on shaman spells and a few plant remedies. A wooden Eskimo leg depicted by John Ross between 1829-1833 was made by Ross's carpenter in return for Eskimo help. (JOHN NURMINEN FOUNDATION)

thickness of the sea's ice sheet as 3.8 metres, but the following year it was only 1.9 metres. Despite the severity of the Arctic winter, there are also areas which remain unfrozen throughout the winter – what the Russians call polynyas. These are found both in close proximity to land masses and in the open sea, and their position does not vary from year to year. The prevailing winds, ocean currents and tidal changes are factors that play a part in the way they are formed. Cloud cover catches the light of areas of open water and may be seen as dark patches that might be thought to be land.

Generally speaking, trees as such do not grow in the Arctic region, although spruce, pine and mountain birch thrive in some river valleys in the mountainous regions of North Alaska and Lapland. A few willow trees and dwarf birch, which grow along the ground, also flourish in the area, but they are more like shrubs than trees. Trees need warmth and nutrients as well as light. In the polar region these conditions prevail only at the earth's surface. The effect of the icy winds is so strong that 30 centimetres above ground level the air might be almost 10°c warmer than it is at a height of one and a half metres. In summer the earth's surface thaws out to a depth of between 10–20 centimetres at most. Below this the ground is frozen and roots can only grow along the surface.

The severe Arctic conditions do not mean that there is no life in northern climes. There are, however, only a few species able to survive in such extreme circumstances. Of the world's more than 4000 species of mammal, only 23 live permanently north of the tree line. These include the grizzly bear and the polar bear, as well as a few other furred animals like the wolf, fox, wolverine, ermine, weasel and mink. Rodents found above the tree line include chipmunks, lemmings and some moles. Deer and caribou, musk-ox, elk and moose are important game. Of the world's 9200 bird species only a few effectively winter in the Arctic: ravens, a few gulls, one owl and one willow grouse. On the other hand migratory birds are more numerous; as many as 70 species. Only some 600 species of insect thrive in the polar circle; some of them, like the mosquito, make an indelible impression on visitors.

Animals have to be able to adapt to the Arctic conditions. Many are able to live at times in a frozen state or can lower their metabolism when the temperature falls. Many insects spend the winter in a frozen state, coming to life when the air becomes warmer.

Bears and chipmunks go into hibernation and for a time their vital functions are slowed down. Fish and some insects make use of glucoproteins to ensure their survival in the freezing conditions. All plants and animals of the Arctic must be able to take full advantage of the short growing period. Plants need only a few days to make the change from winter to summer. Many flowers bloom in spring in places where the snow has just melted, 20 centimetres from the snow's edge. Migratory birds must reach their destination at the very outset of spring, otherwise they have insufficient time to raise their offspring to be strong enough to survive the autumn. This narrow margin increases the sensitivity of life to the changing conditions. A cold spell in June or a sudden frost in August can destroy the chances of survival of an entire generation.

Although there are only a few species, the number of individuals is enormous. Once upon a time there could have been hundreds of thousands of caribou in a single herd, spending days or even weeks making their way to summer pastures. In some areas seals may be so numerous that they provide the local inhabitants with all they need. In some rivers salmon are so abundant that in the headwaters one stumbles across the remains of spawned fish at nearly every step. Until the lamp-oil and soap industries realised their value as raw material and fashion began to favour the use of whale bone to frame

mirrors and in the making of corsets, the number of whales was sufficient for the needs of the earlier population. There are still plenty of mosquitoes, however, and swarms of them can still obscure the sun.

The Arctic landscape seems monotonous. Wide areas of Siberia and the terrain of King William Island in northern Canada are completely flat for as far as the eye can see. But such apparent monotony, emphasised in winter when clear definitions disappear under a blanket of snow, ice and fog, is deceptive. The history of Arctic exploration is full of stories of signals left behind for future visitors showing that even the most insignificant feature stands out clearly from its surroundings. The indigenous people were able to recognise changes in the winds, the forms which snow and ice took, and the rhythm and surges of nature. Anyone with a trained eye will find enough differences to use them in order to check their position or to stay on course.

Special characteristics of the terrain and climate have created phenomena which have brought hope to exhausted

16 The North Canadian Eskimos hunted deer that were migrating to the south on lakes. They made camp on the southern shores of a lake, waited until the deer crossed the narrow channels to swim and set out into the water in their kayaks. The women and children remaining on the shore waved wolf skins and frightened the deer back into the water to within range of the hunters' spears. (SCOTT POLAR RESEARCH INSTITUTE)

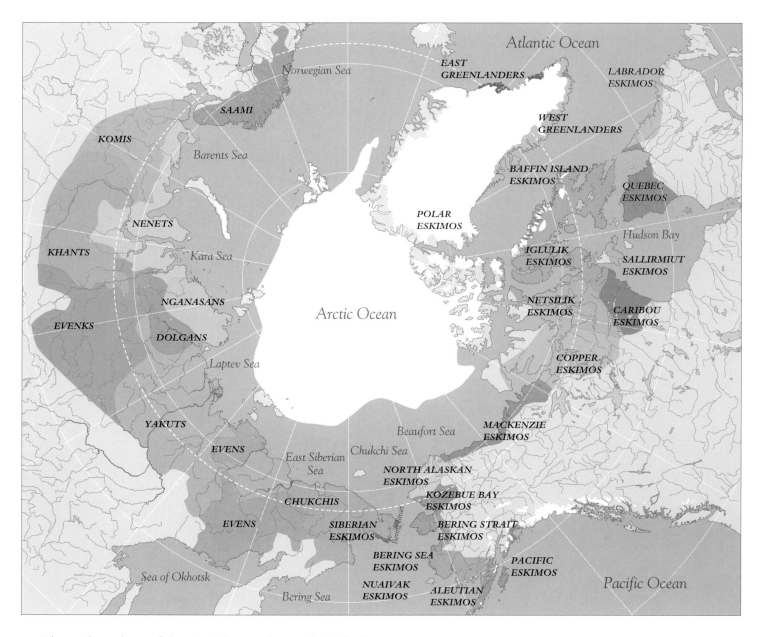

17 The northern shores of the Arctic Ocean, along with the food they provided, were within the reach of the peoples living inland. Reindeer herders moved over hundreds of miles with their reindeer and dwellings to the verdant coastal pastures in summer. There were fish, walrus and whale for the hunting and fishing tribes. Their diet varied according to regular annual cycles.
(PATANEN)

wanderers or have caused explorers to experience hallucinations. In 1818, John Ross identified the "Croker Mountains" and turned back from the Lancaster Sound at the very time when the opening to the Northwest Passage was about to be discovered. Before this he had seen the "Barnard Mountains" blocking off Jones Sound. In 1892, Robert Peary discovered the "Peary Channel" in northern Greenland. It appeared to be detaching itself from the main island of Peary Land. Three years later he visited the same district but made no further mention of his discovery. Subsequent explorers have not come across the channel. "Crocker Land" which Peary observed in north-eastern Greenland in 1906 has never been seen since, in spite of many attempts to find it.

THE PEOPLES OF THE ARCTIC

Of the present-day languages of the Arctic, the Eskimos or Inuit and the Chukchi belong to the Paleosiberian languages. The Samoyed language spoken by the Nenet or Yuraki Samoyed and the Nganasan are Ural languages. Another group of Ural languages are Finno-Ugrian languages spoken by the Sami in Fennoscandia, the Zyrian or Komi living around the Pechora River, and the Ostyak and the Vogul mostly concentrated in the regions around the Okohtsk Sea. The area inhabited by the Eskimos is extensive, stretching as it does from the Bering Strait to eastern Greenland. Although the name Eskimo suggests homogeneity, the Eskimo people are, in fact, composed of many tribes. They do, however, speak two fairly closely related languages: Yupik in the Chukchi Peninsula and western Alaska, Inuit-Inupiag in the area stretching from West Alaska to Greenland.

The Chukchi live in north-eastern Siberia on the Chukchi Peninsula, the Nganasan on the Taymyr Peninsula in northern Siberia, the Nenet to the west of them in the area between the Yenisey and Pechora rivers and the Sami on the Kola Peninsula and in the northern parts of Finland and Scandinavia.

Other smaller peoples live, or have lived, in Siberia; for example the Yakut who speak the Turkish languages, but their culture does not differ significantly from those others mentioned. The Sami people have been called by different names during the course of history.

The oldest references to them are found at the end of the first millennium. The names Finni, Fenni and Scrithfinni refer to the Sami people or Lapps. Of all the aboriginal or indigenous peoples of the Arctic area the ancient Greeks and Romans knew only of the Sami. Their culture had at no stage been very uniform. They hunted deer and domesticated them, their economy thus becoming based on reindeer husbandry. And they fished, particularly in the Arctic Ocean. The Sami people's adaptation to their surrounding environment and the development of their culture has taken place slowly over a long period of time. The special features of their culture have been preserved despite the influences which came with migration from the south. At present the Sami people live in four countries: Russia, Finland, Sweden and Norway.

The Samoyed people have moved relatively recently to the area they presently inhabit, where they possibly displaced the Sami tribes that had lived there earlier. The Yuraki Samoyed called themselves Nenet, which means 'people' or 'real people'. According to legend, the forefathers of the Nenet lived half underground in the Tundra.

The Russians first made contact with the Nenet in the 12th century, and long believed them to be cannibals. Western Europeans had their first experience of the Nenet when English and Dutch sailors were looking for a Northeast Passage in the 16th century. In spite of their connections with Russia, the Nenet led a very insular life and they did not allow the Novgorodians or Muscovites to land at their summer camp on Vaygach Island, situated in the channel between Novaya Zemlya and the mainland. Explorers were able to speak with the Nenet in Russian as they had learned the language from Russian traders. The Nenet used bows and arrows as weapons and they had tamed reindeer to pull their sledges. The Nenet were a nomadic people, living inland in winter and moving to the coastal regions and islands of the Arctic ocean in summer.

The Nganasan lived further to the north than any other of the inhabitants of Siberia and, for this reason, they long remained untouched by European civilisation. The Russian anthropologist A. Popov carried out research among them as late as the 1930s. At the turn of the 20th century there were only 900 Nganasan and they were nomads. They often lived in dwellings dug into the ground, built with stones and corked with peat. Unlike other Eurasian peoples they were not familiar with skis or snowshoes. The Nganasan hunted deer and tamed reindeer to draw sledges.

The Nganasan followed the deer, sometimes moving inland to the mountains, sometimes to the coast, hunting them in the same way as the Netsilik Eskimo, driving them with sticks into a lake. While some of the hunters frightened them deep into the lake with the aid of dogs, their companions, waiting on the opposite shore, would attack the deer from

18 The igloo was the only winter dwelling place for the Eskimos of the central Arctic area. In the Thule area of Greenland and North Alaska the Eskimos only lived in igloos while on a trek or when hunting. Building an igloo required snow of a sufficiently hard composition from which large rectangular blocks were cut. They were piled on top of each other in a spiral formation. A roof was formed by gradually decreasing the radius of the circle. When the cracks between the blocks were sealed it was possible to move into the igloo an hour after work had begun.
(JOHN NURMINEN FOUNDATION)

their punts and kill them with spears. In winter the deer were driven through fenced off areas into bottlenecks where they were slaughtered. Like other Arctic peoples, the Nganasan supplemented their diet by hunting birds and by fishing.

The meaning of the word Chukchi is 'many caribou' which is probably descriptive of this peoples' original culture. The Russians first came into contact with the Chukchi as early as the 17th century but they were described more accurately only in the 19th century. The first person to report on them between 1820–1823 was Ferdinand Wrangel, whose experience was limited to chance encounters. The crew of the English ship HMS *Plover* got to know the Chukchi in 1849, when they wintered in the Chuchki Peninsula. They were also observed by the Finnish-born Adolf Eric

19 The Eskimos encountered by John Ross on the Boothia Peninsula travelled to the coast in winter to hunt seals. The size of a village was determined by the seal population. Generally speaking some 50–100 people, one third of whom were hunters, lived in a winter camp. Usually one family lived in a single igloo. A family igloo was from less than three metres to four and a half metres in diameter and was less than two metres in height.
(JOHN NURMINEN FOUNDATION)

Nordenskiöld when his ship the *Vega* was beset in the ice during the winter of 1878–1879.

The Chuchki were divided into those tribes that lived near the coast, and those that lived inland, and their ways of life and cultures differed from each other. Coastal-dwelling Chuchki gained their livelihood from the sea and erected permanent walrus-skin tents with a whale-bone framework in the places they settled. Their most important game were seals and walrus, whose skins and tusks they traded with the nomadic Chuchki for deer meat and hide. The coastal-dwelling Chuchki made boats of walrus skin and heated their tents with blubber lamps in the manner of the Eskimo.

THE DEVELOPMENT OF INUIT CULTURE

Although the various Inuit tribes are able to understand each other's language, they have never formed a coherent unified people. Functioning communities consisted of groups of a few dozen or a few hundred people.

The forefathers of the Eskimo migrated little by little, in small groups from Asia across the Bering Strait. The oldest known Eskimo culture has been given the name "Arctic Small Tool Culture". It is thought to have come into being some 5000 years ago and to have endured for about 3000 years. This culture was extremely widely distributed. It stretched from Wrangell Island, near the south-eastern tip of Siberia, all the way to Peary Land in northern Greenland.

Finds in Peary Land were classified as belonging to the Independence culture, after Independence Fjord where they had been discovered. It is known for its tools made of flint or obsidian, typically some three-centimetres long, and less than a centimetre wide. The camping places of the small tool culture were apparently temporary and were used for only a few weeks. These Palaeo- or early Eskimos gained their livelihood by hunting. Their game was musk-ox, polar bear, fox, rabbits and birds. According to one theory the Small Tool Culture spread eastwards, pursuing their most important quarry, the musk ox.

The Palaeo-Eskimos' tools were primitive, and they lived in tents made of skin. They had discovered neither the blubber lamp nor the sledge, let alone learned how to tame dogs as draught animals. Because the coasts of bays in the Arctic region were still unfrozen a few thousand years ago, they used driftwood for fuel – the wood that was torn off and borne out to sea when the great rivers of Siberia and North America flooded. The coasts on which the early Eskimos lived have since risen by 4–10 metres above sea-level and have become covered in ice as the climate has cooled.

The Small Tool Culture was followed by other early Eskimo cultures; the Norton Culture, which appeared on the coast of Alaska, named after the Norton Sound, and the Saqqaq Culture, on the west coast of Greenland. The Small Tool Culture probably disappeared about 3500 years ago with the onset of the Little Ice Age, which lasted for more than 1200 years. As conditions became more difficult, the primitive tools of those early inhabitants were not sufficient for them to sustain life.

The Dorset Culture, which was also named after its place of discovery, the Dorset Peninsula located on Baffin Island, spread to both Canada and Greenland. Although the Dorset Eskimos are considered to be Palaeo-Eskimos their culture did not die out until 700 years ago.

Technologically the Dorset Eskimos were considerably more sophisticated than their predecessors. They invented

20 and 21 When an Eskimo makes a picture of a bear he shows his gratitude to the bear's spirit for the gift he has received but, in the background, lies the hope to possess some of the strength of his prey. The art of the Dorset Eskimo (800 BC–1300 AD) surpasses the cultural achievements of both their predecessors and their successors. These swans carved from walrus bone were worked with tools cleaved from stone. (CANADIAN MUSEUM OF CIVILISATION)

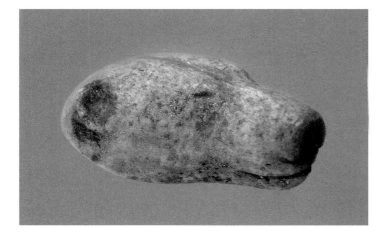

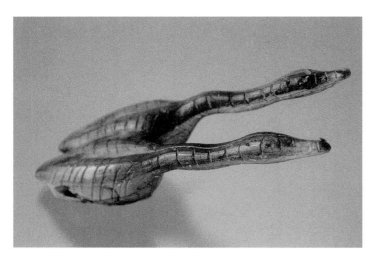

the igloo and their dwelling places were more permanent. They knew how to make kayaks and their most important source of meat was the seal.

The art of making lamps by carving out a cavity in soapstone in which to burn seal or walrus oil was discovered a little before the birth of the Dorset Culture. The Dorset Eskimos tamed dogs and built small sledges. They had better tools than their predecessors, although they too were based, for the most part, on the skilful working of the bones of the animals they hunted. On the other hand, they had no bows and arrows and did not use dogs to pull their sledges. In one respect, with their unique sculptures, the Dorset Eskimos were more advanced than the Thule culture which followed them. Art was associated with objects of use and with the beliefs of the people. With the aid of their beautiful sculptures they aimed to pacify their prey, or hoped that they would protect their bearers.

After the Little Ice Age the climate began to get warmer. The warmest period was 900–1100 AD. It was at this time that the Thule Culture superseded the Dorset Culture, during which period the people of Canada and Greenland called themselves Inuit. Although the Thule culture received its name from Northwest Greenland it originated in Alaska from which it spread to Canada and Greenland. This migration took place about 1000 AD. According to one theory, the Thule Eskimos followed the Greenland whales which moved further north when the climate became warmer. They needed big skin boats, umiaks, and considerably improved harpoons for hunting whales. The people that the early explorers encountered were Thule Eskimos. But those encountered by the Vikings in Vinland in the year 1000, which they called "skraelings", were still Dorset Eskimos.

THE INUIT AND THEIR CULTURE BEFORE WESTERN INFLUENCE

According to Kaj Birket-Smith the Eskimos can be divided into seventeen tribes from three cultural groups: the Alaskan, the Central and the Eastern Eskimos. The Eastern group comprises the Eskimos of the west and east coasts of Greenland and those polar Eskimos of the island's north-western area. The way of life of the Eastern Eskimos resembled the original Thule Culture, while the culture of the Central Eskimos had features typical of those of the interior. In the culture of the Alaskan Eskimos, too, there were features of the early Thule Culture, since this evolved in the west. There was continuous contact between the various tribes and groups of tribes and there was still migration east from the central area in the 19th century. Peter Freuchen describes how the grandfather of his Eskimo wife Navarana, Mequsaq, travelled with his tribe from Admiralty Inlet in the northern region of Baffin Island to the coast of Smith Sound in north-western Greenland.

The worsening climate, the disappearance of animals to hunt in traditional hunting grounds and the threat of starvation were the reasons for this migration. The journey, which progressed by way of Devon and Ellesmere Islands,

22 In 1884 the Danish Captain Gustav Holm received a wooden map from the Eskimo Kumiti who had carved on it the outline of the East Greenland coast north from Angmagssalik where Holm had not been earlier. According to Kumiti it was not at all uncommon for Eskimos to familiarise their friends with new districts in advance with the aid of this type of wooden map. The maps in the picture are used in conjunction. The one on the left depicts the coast with its fjords and the one on the right shows the islands off the coast. It is necessary to place the wooden maps together correctly so that they are in the correct position in relation to the coast. The maps are read from left to right. (THE GREENLAND NATIONAL MUSEUM)

took several winters. Expeditions travelling in the area at the beginning of the 1860s witnessed this minor migration.

Despite being closely related and having a common language, it was not easy for these people to settle in Greenland. Squabbles between the newcomers and the indigenous people of the area sometimes broke out into violence. The migrants already had plans to return to their home district when they finally succeeded in finding their place in the Etah region. It was easier for them to adjust to the situation for the reason that the polar Eskimos, the indigenous inhabitants of the area, had no kayaks or bows and arrows: they had forgotten how to make and use them.

Generally speaking, the Eskimo culture was based on four technologies, each of them connected to a single important raw-material: snow (and ice), skin, bone and stone.

Snow was an important prerequisite for life. In northern Canada it was used to make winter dwellings, storage space for food and privies. The sleeping space, kitchen and doors of Eskimo homes were built of snow with windows made of ice. For successful seal hunting, sea-ice had to be of a specific kind. When the ice was new and even, it was possible to find the seals' breathing holes and to catch them when they came up for air. When the winter winds had hardened the snow, it was easy to travel by dog sledge. When the

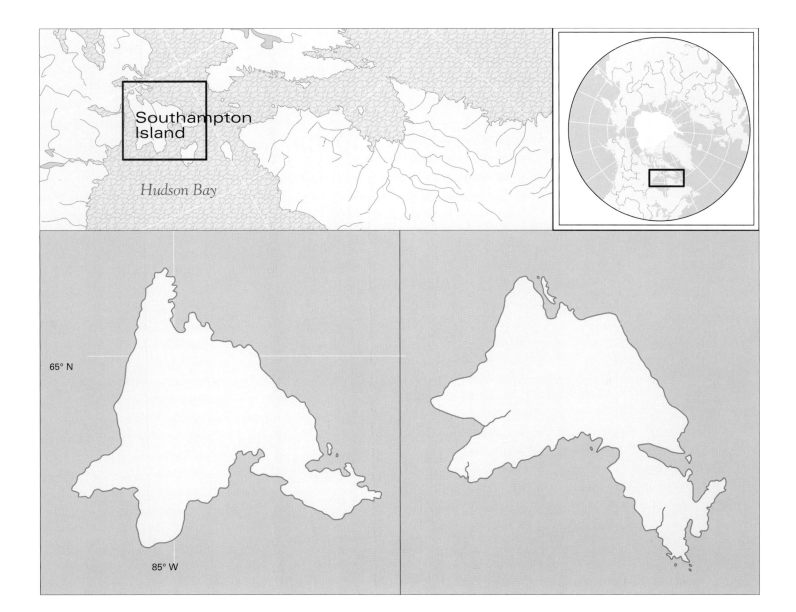

Southampton
Island

Hudson Bay

65° N

85° W

*23 Numerous explorers have attested to the accuracy of the
Eskimo map 'memory'. The American zoologist George Sutton
visited Southampton Island in the northern part of Hudson Bay
in 1929. Because he had no good map of the island he asked for
one from two Aiwilik Eskimos. Their map (on the right), which
covered the more-than-190-miles-long island, is compared in the
picture with a modern map. The accuracy of the map's proportions
covering the enormous area is astonishing. (PATANEN)*

snow melted in spring it was difficult and dangerous to
travel. Igloos were built only when there was enough snow
and it was of the right consistency. It was then possible to cut
the snow with a knife made from caribou horn. A skilled Eskimo could make a warm shelter for his family in an hour.
Drinking-water was obtained with the aid of a soapstone lamp
by melting old sea ice which had lost its salinity over the year.
The ice was broken into pieces using a chisel made of bear
bone.

If the snow technology was the field of men, the working
of leather was almost exclusively the job of women. After the
men had skinned the animals, the women would dry, spread,
cure and stretch the leather. If soft leather was required, someone would spend the night rolled up in dried leather with the
flesh side next to her naked skin. In the morning the leather
would be soft and ready for fleshing, after which it was frozen
for a few days. Tanning required strength and was man's work.
Some Eskimos used their own urine for tanning.

Leather had to be treated according to its use, so different
kinds of leather were used for different purposes. Careful use
was made of the caribou. Children's clothes were made from
the pelts of young animals. The thick pelts of the plump caribou slaughtered in late Autumn made good bed-clothes, the
pelts of animals killed in early Autumn good anoraks.
Footwear was made from the short-haired skin of the animal's
shanks, as this was the sturdiest. The white skin of the belly
was used for women's clothes. Drums and whips were made
from hide from which the hair had been removed.

Clothes were tailor-made to suit the polar conditions. For
underwear the hairy side was worn against the skin and for
outdoor-wear facing outwards, which ensured maximum
warmth. In addition the loosely-fitting clothes provided adequate ventilation. In Arctic conditions it is important to stay
dry because it is not possible to put on sweat-drenched
clothes, which become frozen stiff.

When navigating the Northwest Passage, Roald Amundsen
wore an Eskimo suit for an entire twenty month period, and

ESKIMOS – MASTERS OF SURVIVAL

The people known as the Eskimos were the only ones who were able to create a viable culture north of the tree line. Unlike all other Arctic peoples, the tundra-dwelling Eskimos do not retreat to the shelter offered by forests in even the harshest winters as most other Eskimos do. Conditions are bleakest in the area inhabited by the eastern Eskimos in eastern Arctic America and Greenland. The eastern Eskimos can with good reason be called the masters of survival.

It is not known why or when the Eskimos moved into the Arctic. On the basis of archaeological finds, the cornerstones of their technology, leather boats and sledges with runners, are dated as having been invented only about one thousand years ago during the Thule culture. But signs of an Eskimo culture dating back at least four, perhaps even six thousand years have also been found. Technology that allows mobility and habitation is an essential requirement for the birth and

survival of a culture in the Arctic. According to Kaj Birket-Smith, the skin boats, sleds and clothing called anoraks or parkas that are typical of the Eskimos are evidently a part of the ancient "ice-hunting layer" of polar culture. (Note: "Parka" and "Anorak" are both Eskimo words).

The Eskimos moved around, following animal prey. Boats and sledges were necessary to transport their equipment and personal mobility was enhanced with the snowshoe, for example. In the area that is

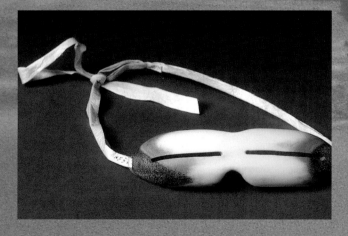

25 In spring the reflection of the sun on the snow was magnified. When stepping out from the dimness of a shelter it was absolutely blinding to the eye and without the Eskimo's wooden snow goggles the dazzle could cause painful snow blindness.
(B & C ALEXANDER)

26 The modest looking soapstone lamp burned in the snow igloo from dawn till dusk, often throughout the night too. For fuel it used seal fat and it had a wick of moss. The light from the lamp was soft and pleasant. The large size of the blocks of snow used to make this igloo speeded up building but required sufficiently dense snow.
(B & C ALEXANDER)

inhabited by the eastern Eskimos, the wind compresses the snow to such density that it is possible to build shelters, called igloos, from it. The igloo made even long stays on the treeless desert of snow feasible.

In other Eskimo areas it was not possible to build igloos but neither were they necessary. There, as in the igloo zone, the Eskimos built their permanent dwellings from stone and peat. The fuel for light and warmth was supplied by whale blubber. Fire was not needed for cooking food, for the Eskimo ate their meat and fish raw (the word Eskimo is from an American Indian language and literally means "eater of raw flesh"). Scurvy did not bother the Eskimos as the raw meat provided an adequate supply of necessary vitamins.

The material and spiritual culture of the Eskimos was based on the meagre environment surrounding them. They received only scant influence from outside their treeless domain. Driftwood on the shores was used to make spears, harpoons and boat frames. The most northerly areas had no driftwood and hence no umiaks, as the frames of boats this size could not be assembled using only animal-based materials. They used kayaks even for heavy transport; by joining several kayaks it was possible to improvise a raft that was capable of carrying both people and supplies. A flexible contraption, this makeshift raft could even endure rough seas.

The Eskimo sledge, which resembles the Finnish push sled, was either pushed or pulled. Sometimes the pulling was done by a team of dogs. The northern Eskimo were often short of suitable sledge-making materials. They always had a trick up their sleeves, however; it was possible to make a sledge from frozen fish for instance! This was also a convenient way of transporting spare food. If there were no fresh catches the party would first eat their supplies, then the dogs would be eaten, starting with the weakest, and finally the sledge itself would be digested. If the winter was a favourable one, the sledge would only be eaten in spring when the fish started to melt.

Today, there are only about a hundred thousand living Eskimos, and their distinct culture, which had remained in the Stone Age for so long, is now largely history. Their reputation, however, survives.

24 When hunting sea mammals in open water the kayak was essential for all the Eskimo peoples. It was swift, silent and light. When the paddler had tightened his waterproof anorak to the edges of the hole in the kayak and around his wrists and head, the kayak and the hunter were inseparable. Then, in spite of its lack of stability, the kayak was seaworthy even in heavy waves. A skilful paddler could turn a capsized kayak back upright using his hands without a paddle. (B & C ALEXANDER)

27 The way a dog team was used varied from area to area. The Eskimos of the central Arctic area transported their property by dog team throughout the entire winter. The dogs pulled the sledges in a row so as not to entangle their harnesses in trees. In Greenland the dogs pulled more heavily built loaded sledges over the glacier in a fanned out formation. The dogs' paws were protected with skin booties so that the jagged snow did not harm them. The sledges were mostly used for transporting hunting equipment and game. The team driver usually ran alongside the sledge guiding the dogs with orders and careful lashes of the whip. It was mostly the sound of the whip that guided the dogs, but a skilful handler could also get a stray dog back into line with a well-aimed lash.
(B & C ALEXANDER)

considered it an incomparable item of winter clothing. On the other hand, deerskin clothes were easily soaked through in summer and Amundsen would use sealskin underclothes.

The practicability of Eskimo decoration is demonstrated by the following story. When the members of the Northwest Passage expedition had acquired Eskimo clothing, all of them except Amundsen cut off the decorative tassels which they considered ridiculous on a man's attire. One fine day, however, those anoraks from which the decoration had been removed began to curl upwards. They would have soon become neck-bands if the tassels had not been sewn back on.

Sealskin was just as valuable as that of the caribou. Its most important use was for the building of kayaks, but it was often used for tents, too. The best kayaks were made with the skin of the female seal. The hairless skin of a young seal was an excellent material for coats and shirts. Summer boots were made from sealskin with soles of bearded-sealskin. Bearskin had a number of uses. It was used to trap lice, which found it irresistible. It was also used as an effective blanket. Because the furry side of bearskin was impervious to damp it was sometimes used fur-side-out as a sledge. For the same reason it was used as an aid in the freezing and polishing of sledge runners.

Since iron was unknown, most weapons and tools were made from the bones of animals. The size, hardness and pliability of the bone determined what it would be used for. The bone of the bear is hardest, while that of the musk-ox is extremely flexible. Caribou horn was a basic raw material. It is hard but resilient so that it can be bent and drilled.

Before iron was obtained from Europe, flint was used to work bone. The tips of weapons and knife blades were made of flint. Objects of religious significance, such as the miniature sculptures of the Dorset culture, were also made of bone. The subjects of Eskimo art came from their beliefs, hunting and everyday life. With their primitive power, Eskimo artists were close to the modern masters. One Eskimo artist visiting a white man's museum could understand only two western artists: Henry Moore and Marino Marini.

Soapstone was the most important mineral: it was used to make lamps and utensils. The Netsilik quarried the stone in the south-western part of Pelly Bay and in winter they transported it in great blocks by sledge. Those tribes in whose districts no soapstone could be found used goods of their own to barter for it.

The soapstone lamp resembled a shallow flat-bottomed boat. On hunting trips a small version of the large igloo oil lamp was used. A lamp for domestic use could be as long as half a metre. Cotton-grass or moss-down was used as a wick, adjustment of which could increase or decrease the size of the flame. In principle the lamp was smokeless but it needed constant adjustment. The lamp was fuelled with oil extracted from seal blubber. In winter it was successfully extracted by freezing the fat, but in summer the women and children chewed the fat and spat out the oil into some kind of vessel.

In spite of the long distances they had to travel to do so, the Eskimos traded among themselves. Eskimos of the northwest Alaskan coastal region, the Nuvugmiut, traded with the Nunamiut, the Eskimos of the interior. In winter the Nunamiut made trading trips to the Colville River. In addition to their own catches, the Nuvugmiut traded in goods they had obtained from the Russians: knives and other iron articles, copper pots and tobacco. The Nunamiut, too, bought these directly from their old enemies, the Chukchi.

As well as selling their goods at the Colville market, the Nuvugmiut traded goods they had bought from the Russians with the Mackenzie River Eskimos. For these they received narwhal, wolf and fox pelts, which they had got from the Copper Eskimos, and goods originating from the Hudson Bay Company's trading. At the end of a four-winter-long trading chain, a Russian knife might end up with the Copper Eskimos of Canada's Victoria Island.

THE BASIS OF THE ESKIMO SPIRITUAL WORLD

As nomads, the Eskimos moved from place to place in accordance with the rhythm of nature. They knew that they were dependent on nature. Their technological skills helped them take full advantage of nature's bounty. No part of the animals they hunted were wasted. There were several uses for each and every part; if an animal's blood was not drunk, for example, it would probably have been used to make glue. The Eskimos understood that in nature everything affects everything else.

It is this understanding of the relationship between the whole and its constituent parts that helped the Eskimo survive in the kind of environment which to Europeans was desolate and monotonous. As he moved from place to place, the Eskimo took note of the signs and signals he observed in nature that we never even notice. He had to be constantly aware of the direction of the winds, for example. He sensed changes immediately by watching how the wind affected the formation of snowdrifts. While paddling his kayak in thick fog he observed both the wind and the sound of the waves. In this way he could find his way to his destination even though he had not a glimpse of land nor of the stars. The Aivilik of Southampton Island had at least twelve expressions for the various winds. They described the direction, temperature, strength and effects of the winds. It was of less importance to know which way the wind was blowing than to understand how the wind affected life. When a certain northerly wind blew the ice floes away, it was a good time for hunting seals. When a southerly wind drove the floes back, it was time to begin hunting the walrus. Edmund Carpenter tells of an Eskimo who was asked to keep a diary. Almost every entry began with a comment about the wind. Like Carpenter, many observers of the Eskimo have made particular note of their phenomenal ability to observe details accurately.

One of the most impressive examples of the Eskimo's ability to see the whole and the details simultaneously is their 'mental map'. In his mind the Eskimo has a picture that is almost as precise as a modern aerial map. Even those early explorers who had the good sense to ask the Eskimos for information noticed this. Eskimos also have the ability to draw their mental map on

28 The Vikings lived alongside the Eskimos in Greenland for about 300 years after the turn of the millennium. The newcomers, originally from Scandinavia, and the indigenous people retained their harmony by living in their own cultural circles. The Norsemen line died out before the start of the new age. When Europeans met the Eskimos again in the 16th century, their confrontations were not always friendly. Whalers and explorers often considered the Eskimos an inferior breed of wild man. Frobisher brought Eskimo prisoners from Baffin Land but also lost men of his own to the indigenous people. The map above is of Cunningham's expedition of the beginning of the 17th century, which was carried out at the instigation of the Danish king. On his return Cunningham told of the conditions and Eskimos of the area. Eskimos kayaks are drawn on the banks of a Greenland fjord. The four live Eskimos brought from this journey as "souvenirs" would hardly have left of their own accord.
(The British Library)

paper. This was facilitated by an old custom. If some individual wished to visit an area with which he was not familiar, someone who knew the area drew him a map in the snow. First the relative positions of a few important features were sketched in the snow and then the details were added. It was astonishing how extensive an area a single Eskimo was able to remember. The Eskimos, it is true, did depict their own hunting ground as being larger than it actually was and, in respect to hunting, also exaggerated important bays and islands.

Carpenter makes much of the Eskimo's excellent ability to conceptualise time and space. They do not separate the two, but see them as part of the same whole. Their concept of space is always linked to direction and activity. Their way of thinking can be described with the words "let us listen to what we can see", while we, on the other hand, would say "let us look at what we can hear". The white man believes his eyes, the Eskimo his ears. When an Eskimo living in the village of Anuktuvuk in northern Alaska was asked what he did when he came to a new place he replied: "I listen". When the Eskimo Ayako returned from a journey with Knud Rasmussen during which they almost starved, he went to the bank of a fjord, bent down and filled his cupped hands with water, lifted the water up to his face and breathed its salty smell in deeply. Thus, in his mind he sensed the smell of walrus, narwhal and seal blubber, which meant food and well-being. He felt at home again.

The Eskimo's attitude to death was also different from that of a person from the West. When the old folk no longer had the strength to hunt and roam they were left behind to die.

In some areas baby girls were allowed to die because women did not hunt. Girls meant only an increase in the number of mouths to feed. In addition to all this, a family's labour force was reduced when the young women got married. According to Balicki this led to a scarcity of wives among the Netsilik, which endangered their survival in a different way.

A person who lives continuously at the mercy of nature relates to the world in a different way from us. When Knud Rasmussen asked an Eskimo of the interior what he believed in he replied: "We do not believe, we fear." Fear means recognition of the fact that life lived on nature's terms is often violent and tragic. The best things in life are simple. As another Eskimo put it: "Happiness is when you come across a fresh bear trail and you know you are ahead of the others." In one sense the history of polar exploration describes man's learning process in understanding and adapting to Arctic conditions. The skills evident in the Eskimo culture are demonstrated by the fact that it took almost 400 years for Europeans to reach the North Pole. And they only succeeded in this with the help of the Eskimos.

THE INUIT AT THE TIME WHEN THE WHITE MAN MADE HIS WAY INTO THE ARCTIC

The Eskimos had lived in the north for thousands of years before the Europeans knew anything about the area. So it is no longer possible to talk in terms of 'discovery'. Almost all regions, not including the North Pole, had been discovered and "mapped" before the first expedition set out to find out whether it was possible to reach China by way of a north-western or north-eastern sea route. In the competition between Europeans – a contest which, as time went by, the North Americans joined – it was a question of who would succeed in re-discovering the lands and islands of the North and reach the pole itself, a place that had not even occurred to the Eskimos as worth discovering.

The Eskimos lived further to the north than any other people. It is not known from where and why they moved there. Peter Freuchen is convinced that the Eskimos did not leave their forested habitat voluntarily. They had been forced to migrate to the shores of the Arctic Ocean and to develop the skills necessary to control and master the unique conditions they found there. As time went by they became completely independent of forests and trees. Their lives were always uncertain and dangerous. Freuchen wrote in his work *Book of the Eskimos*: "Any unexpected event, the least change in their routine might lead to disaster. A lack of ice at the right time meant starvation, perhaps, because fishing and hunting trips would have had to be postponed indefinitely. The Eskimos constantly set out on long and hazardous journeys, not only due to inclination or restlessness; their daily needs made it imperative for them to be at the right time just where they would find the animals necessary for their survival. They needed blubber which they could get only from certain sea animals, but at the same time they had to go far inland to get the reindeer skin and sinews they used for thread. They needed walrus skins and sealskins, but they also had to fish for salmon in the lakes. On the tiny islands out at sea they found birds and eggs. All year round the Eskimos had to be on the go. Their cooking utensils were made of stone, and to renew them the Eskimos had to travel a considerable distance before they found the right kind of soft stone. Such expeditions might take a year or two and fashioning the stone into pots and pans from lumps of stone was a strenuous job which demanded a great deal of time and patience with the primitive tools at their disposal."

The white man brought both good and bad to the peoples of the Arctic. At first their influence was in almost every respect positive. Expeditions left behind them utensils and equipment originating from a much more modern technology than that which the Eskimos had at their disposal. In the beginning, the negative aspects were almost exclusively concerned with whaling. Since the whale population was continuously decreasing, the further the 19th century progressed, the wider the areas into which whaling spread. Ever more frequently the whalers wintered in the ice. Eskimos and Indians were press-ganged into shooting musk-ox and caribou to provide the crews with nourishment. The game the Eskimos hunted also paid a heavy toll at the hands of the explorers. Along with his six compatriots, Roald Amundsen consumed one hundred caribou in a single winter. Slaughter on this scale inevitably had an effect on the Eskimo's own living conditions.

American whalers wintering in the north brought with them at least three scourges to the Eskimos: whiskey, smallpox and diphtheria. The Eskimos had no resistance to any of these. The diseases destroyed whole villages and tribes during the 19th century. In addition to whiskey, tea and tobacco caused dependence among Eskimos as time went by. Roald Amundsen tells of an Eskimo arriving at his winter camp whose first word was "tobacco".

The Hudson's Bay Company's way of establishing trading posts strengthened the co-existence of the Eskimo and the white man. The manager of a new post would bring building materials and trading goods along with him into the wilderness. He would build a house there, open a shop and begin working. In the early stages he needed the help and goodwill of the Eskimos and this imposed a limit on any superior attitude he may have had. The method made the company's employees independent. They often befriended the Eskimos and managed to combine the interests of both the company and the customers. In Freuchen's view this was why the Eskimos of Canada rarely regarded the white man with hostility. An Eskimo who had journeyed from afar to the trading post would be the guest of the company for two days, during which time news was exchanged and trading conducted.

PL.II.

ESKIMO BOATS

The Eskimo had two types of boat: the covered, one-man kayak meant primarily for hunting and the large, open umiak mainly used for transport. The kayak was paddled and the umiak rowed. George Dyson, who has studied the history of these boats on the American side of the Pacific, says that primitive boats evolved there in two ways. The flat-bottomed rowing boat and the planked boat that was developed from it was a "product of the forest" whilst the Aleutian *baidarka* (kayak) was completely a "creation of the sea".

Erik the Red was the first European to see the skin boats of the eastern Eskimo when he landed on the shores of Greenland in AD 985. It is probable that Columbus too was referring to Eskimos when he mentioned seeing "Chinamen in small boats" on the voyage that took him north of Iceland in 1477. He even considered this proof of the existence of a northwest sea passage from Europe to China. One hundred years later, Martin Frobisher took

an Eskimo in a kayak he had spotted to be one creature – just as the Indians had thought the conquistador to be organically linked to his horse. This misconception was curiously apt, in that in the eyes of a European the Eskimo and his kayak was a combination capable of astonishing feats.

Kayak

At first, the kayak started out as a streamlined hunting boat capable of carrying one person. In principle, its design was the same throughout the region inhabited by the Eskimo from the Aleutians all the way to Qaanaaq or Thule in southwest Greenland, 3100 miles away as the crow flies and 25° to the north. The kayak was usually propelled by a twin-bladed paddle, but in some areas, mainly in Alaska, Russia and the Aleutians, a single-bladed paddle was favoured.

The kayak can be roughly divided into two categories according to whether it was used to hunt caribou, or aquatic mammals

29 The smaller covered boat was called a kayak. Kayaks were built in the same way as umiaks but the kayak was completely covered with skin except for an opening for the paddler. When the paddler was getting into place in the opening he would fasten the end of his anorak around the opening which made the kayak completely watertight. Kayaks differed from each other in type from place to place as they were designed to meet the needs of the local way of hunting.
(JOHN NURMINEN FOUNDATION)

such as seals and whales. It is easier to tell the difference from the fittings, but there are also structural differences.

In principle, kayaks were made the same way everywhere. First, the frame was built from driftwood and whalebones. Sealskin was then used to cover the frame. Only the hole in which the kayak's

Tab. I.

30 Skin-covered, wooden-framed boats were used all over the Arctic area. The Eskimos had two types of boat: the smaller streamlined and covered kayak for hunting and the larger, open umiak, which was used for transport. The umiak, which was also called the woman's boat, was paddled, flat-bottomed and light and carried from 15 to 20 people. The frame was built of either driftwood or whalebone and was covered with walrus skin rubbed with oil.

(JOHN NURMINEN FOUNDATION)

occupant sat was left uncovered and this was made watertight once the hunter was on board.

The frame most commonly had three to five rigid (longitudinal) stringers: the keel and two or four gunwales. The ribs and deck-beams acted as transverse stiffeners. It may be slightly misleading to speak of stiffeners, as the hull of a kayak was 'alive'; in other words it moved with the waves. All timbers and whalebone battens were joined together using thongs or wooden nails. This made the joints strong but flexible. When the skins were stretched on the frame, they were soaking wet. This means that they contracted somewhat as they dried and so tightened the frame. When the boat was used the skin was soaked again and gradually became looser, allowing the frame to expand again. In this way the hull effectively breathed and also retained its rigidity as

conditions changed. The kayak was truly an organic artifact, which metal nails would have ruined.

There were dozens of different types of kayak hulls. They were different both in cross-section and horizontal and vertical dimensions. The entire boat was usually 5–5.5 metres in length, 40–50 centimetres in width and some 30 kilos in weight (the weight varying between 20 and 70 kilos). Lightness was desirable both for paddling properties and because it was often necessary in some parts to carry kayaks overland on long hunts.

The speed of the kayak was the subject of many a tall tale, and good paddlers were held in high esteem. The kayak did not easily exceed its hull-speed, however, and typical speeds were between 4–6 knots. *Kussarsarluni paarneq* is the Eskimo name of the technique that enables a kayak to go faster than its hull-speed. This

involves forcing the bow to go deeper than the stern of the boat. The Greenland Eskimo, Ezekias Davidsen, once paddled 17.88 miles in less than one hour; this translates to an average speed of about 15 knots. The cutter servicing the area would have completed the journey in two-and-a-half hours, but Ezekias was in a hurry to buy some tobacco from the store.

Speed was rarely important to the Eskimo, so the properties of the kayak excel in other areas instead. When the western Eskimo had chased the caribou into the water and proceeded to slaughter the animals with spears, stability and manoeuvrability were called for.

A good kayak had to be silent, too. For example, the eastern Eskimo hunted narwhal when the sea was dead calm. A group of tight-lipped hunters would first let a pod of whales swim past unharassed. A whale swimming apart from the rest, either at the back or the side, was then chosen as the quarry. The hunter closest to the unlucky whale would silently paddle after the animal. The hull of the kayak coupled with the right paddling technique hardly disturbed the water's surface and the smooth-surfaced paddle did not let a single drop fall.

31 The kayaks of the Aleutian Islands Eskimos were called baidarkkas. They were made to accommodate one, two or three persons. The sea around the Aleutians was open almost all the year round and the Aleut were very dependent on the sea as a source of food. Their kayaks were considered extremely seaworthy and they were indeed heavier than the kayaks of the Greenlanders.
(see picture 178)

On returning from the American coast to Kamchatka in 1741, Vitus Bering was the first European to visit the Aleutian Islands. Before the coming of the Europeans the Aleut mostly used kayaks with one opening. The picture is of Captain Cook's voyage of 1778.
(John Nurminen Foundation)

32 The ability of the Eskimos to make careful use of scarce raw materials can be seen from the Greenland kayak which could weigh less than 20 kilos; it was easy to carry across the ice sheets to open water. Light and functional, the East Greenland kayaks were the most slender and beautiful.
(Scott Polar Research Institute)

A kayak usually accommodates only one person. An exception was the baidarka used by the Aleutians; it could fit two, or even three individuals. Russian tax collectors demanded that they were transported on kayaks and pretty soon the Eskimo were also ferrying clergymen. The Aleutians could not understand the priests' need for rides – their finest sorcerers were able to fly from one island to the next. The Aleutians also used their baidarkas to hunt whales and walrus.

Umiak
The Eskimo also used a larger boat, which they called an umiak. The Danish colonial masters of Greenland referred to this vessel as the "women's boat" (*konebåden*). The umiak was used throughout the Eskimo-inhabited area, but not in the most northern regions where the wood necessary for making the frame was not available. The umiak was only called a women's boat in Greenland, where it was used primarily for transport. On the open shores of the Pacific the umiak – and the

Aleutian baidarka – were an important means of conveyance as well as essential equipment for hunting whales and walrus.

The make of the umiak varied somewhat between the different Eskimo tribes as they all used it for their own purposes. However, the boat was always flat-bottomed, spacious and light for its size. The length of a Greenland umiak was 32 feet, top width 5.25 feet and bottom width 3.5 feet.

Throughout the Eskimo area, the umiak was made in the same way as the kayak. It could only be used for two full days at a time, and then the soaked skin would have to be left to dry out. The skin had to be replaced every year. In summertime, the umiak could also be turned upsidedown for use as a tent. In the water, it was rowed with the rower facing back-

wards. Each rower would have his own seat and would use both hands to move the oar, which was alternately on the left side or on the right side.

For the Eskimo, forced to traverse great distances in search of prey, the umiak was an important tool. The boat could easily accommodate all that a couple of Eskimo families required: the dogs and sledges, spare kayaks, soapstone pots and seal-fat lamps, skin clothes, tents, etc.

The Greenlander painter Jakob Danielsen recollects: "My earliest childhood memory is of me sitting in a carrier on my mother's back and watching the other women, who were rowing my father's umiak. Beside them, my father was paddling his kayak. We were making our way to the salmon river, the sun was shining and I was warm".

THE VIKINGS
– PIONEERS OF EXPLORATION

Mapmakers have not always based their perceptions on voyages of exploration. In the Middle Ages the connection between maps and such voyages was broken. Pytheas' discovery of Thule was one of the events that disappeared from memory for more than a thousand years. The development of the map stopped in spite of the fact that the Irish and the Vikings made long and bold voyages into the Arctic region.

HOW THE NORTH WAS SEEN IN THE MIDDLE-AGES BEFORE THE VIKINGS

The Byzantine historian, Procopius, provides us with some interesting information on the northern lands in his work *De Bello Gothico,* written in 552. He probably got his information from the warlike Germanic tribes which he called the *Eruli.* Nansen believed the tribe to have migrated from Scandinavia, perhaps Norway from whose language the word *eruli* might stem. The Eruli were the first Vikings and they travelled through Europe all the way to the Black Sea and Spain. They are said to have conquered Lucca in Italy as early as 455 AD. In his work Procopius also describes Thule, which he places in Norway.

According to Procopius thirteen tribes, each with its own king, lived in Thule, which was a large island. All the tribes of Thule resembled one another. They worshipped several gods and their ways were cruel. A great part of the island was uninhabited. During summer the sun could be seen for forty days without a break. In winter it sank beneath the horizon for an equal number of days. When the sun returned the inhabitants of Thule held a great festival. According to Procopius they were afraid the sun would never return.

One of the tribes of Thule, the Skrithifini, lived like beasts. They wore neither clothes nor shoes. Because they did not cultivate the land they did not drink wine nor did they enjoy the other fruits of the earth. The Skrithifini hunted, along with their wives, in the forests that were their home. They clothed themselves in skins sewed together with animal gut. Their children did not drink their mother's milk but were fed on the bone marrow of the

34 A strong thread was woven from the wool from which 60-100cm wide canvas for sails was made. Sails of the sort depicted on the stone were made from one long strip. The sail was entwined over the yard in such a way that the bolt-ropes ran freely through the sides of the sails. At the bottom of the sail there were moveable ropes which were used to hoist the sails according to the wind and the course to be taken. The vessels were able to use their yard sail to sail close to the wind. (Naturhistoriska riksmuseet)

33 The church weather vane from Källunge in Gotland originally decorated the tip of a Viking ship mast. Similar gilded weather vanes, cast from bronze and decorated with beautiful ornamentation, have been found in Scandinavia. There are holes in the rim of the segment in which it is assumed were horse-tail hairs. The hairs react to the wind and indicate the wind speed. (Gotlands Fornsal)

animals they hunted. When a woman had given birth she wrapped her baby in skin, hung the bundle on a tree, left the child to suckle on marrow and went to hunt.

This description probably refers to the Finns, that is to say the Lapps, perhaps Tacitus' Fenni. The prefix of the word Skrithifini derives from a Norwegian word which means sliding or skating. This is the first reference to the skill of skiing that distinguishes the Lapps from the other tribes. The story of the children who were not fed their mother's milk might be an oblique reference to the Amazons: legend has it that they were not suckled. The marrow tale depicts the habit of the Lapps and other Arctic peoples of eating a lot of animal fat and bone marrow.

As seafarers in the north, the Irish preceded the Vikings. Irish monks sailed north in small ships to the Shetland Isles, the Faroe Islands and eventually to Iceland. The monks' voyages were not made out of curiosity, a thirst for knowledge or in a spirit of adventure. They were looking for a place to practice their religion in peace. In 825 AD the monk Dicuil wrote of the journeys to Iceland by the Irish as follows; "It is now thirty years since certain priests, who have been on the island from the 1st of February to the 1st of August, told that not only at the time of the summer solstice, but also during the days before and after, the setting sun at evening conceals itself as it were behind a little mound, so that it does not grow dark even for the shortest space of time, but whatsover work a man will do, even picking the lice out of his shirt, he may do it just as though the sun were there, and if they had been upon the high mountains of the island perhaps the sun would never be concealed by them...They lie and are in error who wrote that there was a stiffened sea around it (i.e. Thule)... but a day's sail north from it they found the frozen sea."

The Irish knew of the existence of Iceland, which they believed to be Thule, even before the journey made by the monks which had taken place thirty years earlier, that is, in 795 AD. Diciul makes no reference to the date of the discovery of Iceland; he simply states that Iceland is Thule. Although the edge of the frozen sea being a day's away is perhaps based on information supplied by Pytheas, we cannot, according to Nansen, exclude the possibility that the Irish monks also sailed there. If Pytheas was not the first to reach the edge of the sea ice, that honour goes to the Irish.

When the monks went to the Faroes there was already an indigenous Celtic population there. A number of Icelandic place-names, Papafjörður or Papey for example, tell of the monks. Celtic influences can also be seen there. In the view of some researchers these names too may stem from the Irish immigrants, but Nansen, for example, was convinced that when the monks arrived in Iceland there was already a Celtic population there. Thus the present population of Iceland would have both Celtic and Norwegian roots. The latter group soon became the majority and the native population adopted their language. Only a few place-names remain to remind us of the original people.

THE VIKINGS –
LEADERS IN THE FIELD OF NAVIGATION

The Europeans soon learned to fear the Scandinavians who sailed south in their fast boats and they gave them a common name; their Anglo-Saxon names were the *Norsemen* or the *Vikings*. In the course of time it became unclear to what extent they were Danish, Swedish or Norwegian. As the name Viking became established it meant all three peoples who, in the opinion of outsiders, were very similar and who understood each other's language.

In ancient Scandinavia *viking* meant an attack by pirates and *vikingr* a pirate or attacker. The first syllable of the word *vik* has been explained in different ways. Pirates often laid in wait at the entrance to bays (in Old Norse *vik* is bay, fjord or creek). Others explain the word's origin as stemming from the camps (*wik*) that warriors lived in. Some believed it to stem from the word *wic* (the Latin *vicus*) townsman, seafarer, trader. If the root of the word is assumed to be the Old Norse *vikja*, a Viking is swift of foot – someone who comes and goes. Although piracy was perhaps the first driving force of the Viking era, this practice was rejected over a period of centuries.

There were a number of reasons for the rise of the Vikings. They have to do with history, geography, economy and religion. During the first phase the goal was material well-being. This was attained by looting and robbery or through trading. The Vikings' significance with regard to trade at that time was considerable. They opened up trade routes to Russia along the rivers to the Black Sea and the Caspian Sea. They satisfied the needs of the Europeans and Muslims for furs and slaves, and their merchandise included wool, wood, salt, wine, horses and amber.

The further the Vikings' period of ascendancy progressed the more peaceful they became. This has happened with all military achievements. The Vikings needed to find themselves new places to settle. They were farmers and cattle breeders who practised trading and sailing as secondary occupations. There was not enough land in their home lands even for the sons of wealthier families. For those who, for one reason or another, had become undesirable or had been declared outlaws, finding a new place to live was imperative. Dissidents have never made the worst entrepreneurs.

The Vikings' success would not have been possible without sophisticated shipbuilding and seamanship. Sea travel on the Baltic had been vigorous for a considerable period before the beginning of our calendar. A ship found in Nydam dating from 300 BC is a good example of the development of Viking shipbuilding skills, although sails were never used on this craft. To sail regularly across the North Sea required sails, however. A more recent and further advanced vessel was found in Gokstad in 1880. It dates from the 6th century AD. The boat is almost eighty feet long and sixteen feet wide, but has a hull depth of only three feet. It is built of oak and the 57ft-long keel is made from a single tree. The boat's structure makes it both strong and flexible.

35 This map of 995 AD is unusual in many ways. It is drawn in rectangular form rather than circular as was usual in the Middle Ages. It also depicts the north-western part of Europe exceptionally clearly and England can be made out. The first references to the Vikings' sailing of the North Atlantic can be seen on the map. The Celts and the Anglo-Saxons also knew the islands of the Atlantic well. Iceland is apparently depicted for the first time on the COTTONIANA map. Also marked are the Faroe, Orkney and Shetland Islands, to which Irish monks sailed as well as the Vikings. Researchers assume the map was drawn by an Irish monk. Compared to this map, later Medieval maps depict the North considerably less precisely. (THE BRITISH LIBRARY)

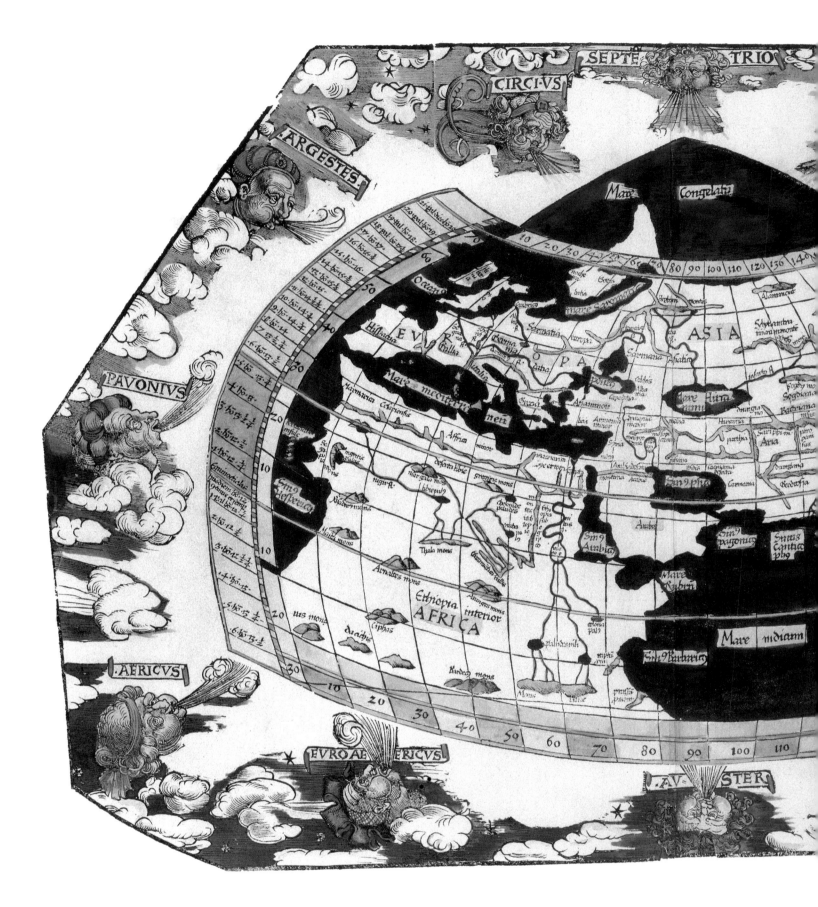

In 1893 Magnus Andersen sailed from Bergen to New-foundland in a replica of the Gokstad ship in 28 days. It was both seaworthy and efficient. Its low draught meant that it was able to navigate even the shallowest rivers. Because it had both oars and sails it was able, irrespective of the winds, to catch up with the fastest trading vessels. The Gokstad-type longboat was an excellent craft for sailing the coasts and rivers of Europe but it was not an ocean-going vessel. Stability, width, higher sides and shorter keels were essential for sailing the open seas. The long and narrow Gokstad ships were eas-ily broken under difficult sea conditions, as was the ship's Swedish replica which sank in the waters of Helgoland in 1950. The Vikings developed different kinds of ships for dif-ferent purposes. Their largest vessels were probably manned

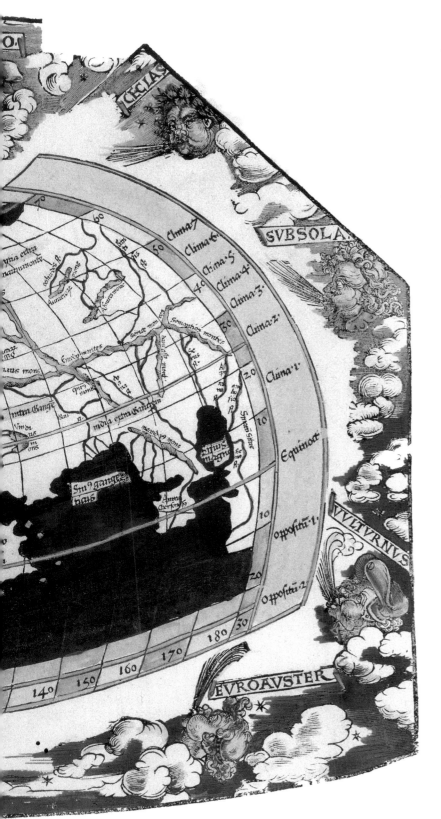

36 It was thanks to the Renaissance that ancient maps, forgotten for over 1000 years, came to the attention of Europeans once again. The maps of antiquity reached as far north as about latitude 63°. The Vikings, who were busy sailing the North Atlantic at the beginning of the second millennium, had no knowledge of these maps of antiquity. The European understanding of the world also began to take shape in the form of a relatively accurate map only in 16th century. The Vikings did not themselves draw or use maps but they sailed as far as Newfoundland nevertheless. Information from Viking discoveries did not find its way onto maps. The Ptolemy map became richer and more precise in the north only at the beginning of the 16th century, with the influence of expeditions carried out by British explorers. (Helsinki University Library)

If Pytheas' Mediterranean ship is considered even more seaworthy than those of Columbus, the same can also be said of Viking sea-going ships. As far as seaworthiness goes the Viking ship was second to none for centuries. The Vikings' navigational equipment was not so highly developed, however. They had less theoretical knowledge than Pytheas had a thousand years earlier.

How then did they manage to reach their destination in unknown waters and in difficult conditions?

The answer is that they did not always manage to do so. The Vikings preferred to sail along certain latitudes. When they wanted to reach Greenland they sailed along the coast of Norway to Stad, 30 nautical miles north of Bergen at the same degree of latitude as their destination in Greenland. If they set a strict course for the west, in a few days they passed within sight of the Shetland Islands. This meant that they passed to the south of the Faroe Islands. The same course took them onwards past the southern part of Iceland so that it became necessary to estimate the location of the country by examining the behaviour of birds or the character or appearance of the sea, particularly its tides and currents.

Basing their direction on the flight of freed birds it was possible to find out in which direction land lay. Like the Eskimos, the Vikings knew how to find their course with the aid of the wind. As long as the direction of the wind remained unchanged they steered a course based on it. But they were not always able to recognise a change in the direction of the wind.

As time went by the Vikings also learned to follow the direction and movement of whales and the appearance of ice floes and driftwood. Experienced sailors distinguished between the pure blue colour of the Gulf Stream and the green-brown shades of the North Sea. The water of the eastern Greenland drift was different from that of the Atlantic. Nansen assumed that the best sailors had learned to recognise the varying density of great red medusa in different areas of the sea and that they used this information as an aid in defining their position.

by a crew of 100. The number of pairs of oars could vary from six to thirty-four. On open-sea voyages the Vikings used the wider Knorr-type craft which had a great deal of both open and covered cargo space. This kind of vessel could carry more than 30 square metres or 20 tons of cargo. The Knorr retained all the advantages of the Viking ship; low draught, but good strength and flexibility.

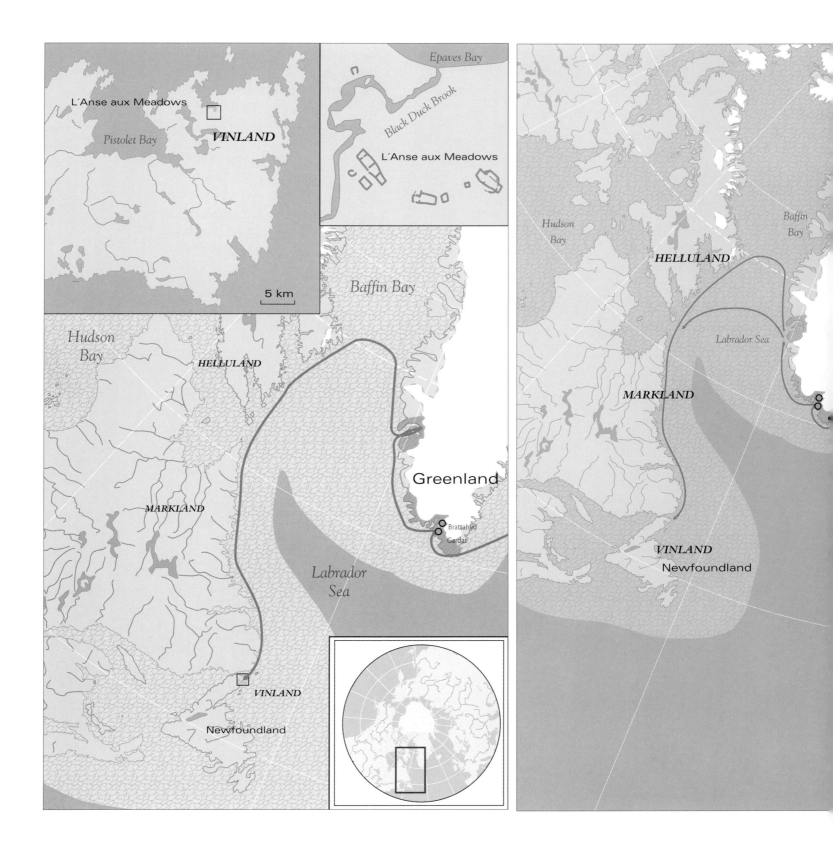

37 A map of the Vikings' route to Vinland or the northern tip of Newfoundland. First they sailed north with the ocean current until Davis Strait was at is narrowest, only about 185 miles. The sea current south along the east coast of Baffin Land helped sailing which continued along the coast of Labrador to L'Anse aux Meadows where later excavations have revealed the remains of old buildings. In all probability the Vikings sailed south and west from here, but no firm evidence of this exists. (PATANEN)

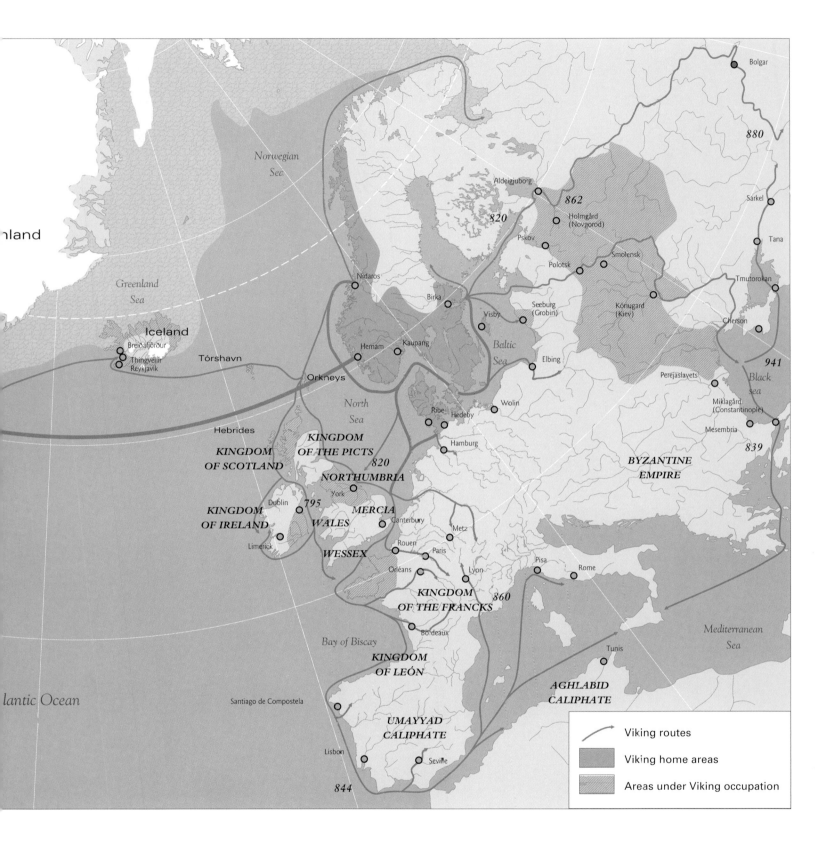

From Icelandic sagas we learn that Viking ships often drift-ed in thick fog; as clouds rolled in the sky they were tossed about by raging storms, not knowing where they were. One saga has it that the first to discover Greenland was Gunbjörn, son of Ulf Kråkason, around the year 900 AD. He drifted off course on his way to Iceland. Ulf did not even go ashore when he realised that the land rising in front of him was not Iceland. Leif Erikson lost his direction when sailing from Norway to Greenland. After drifting for a long while he came to a land of which the Vikings had no previous knowl-edge. This land he called Vinland.

VIKING EXPEDITIONS
TO THE EAST AND NORTH

The Vikings compiled new information based on their ex-periences, and also needed someone to document their knowledge of the north. In 880 AD King Alfred had made peace with the Danes and had been forced to cede the north-ern part of England to them. His most important contribu-tion to our knowledge of the northernmost area of the Arctic is the story of Ottar's journey to the north. According to Nansen, Ottar's description was a refreshing contrast to the earlier tales handed down from generation to generation which were steeped in tradition. Ottar told Alfred that he dwelt farthest north of all the Norwegians: "... the land extends very far to the north from there; but that it was quite uninhabited, except that in a few places the Finns live, hunting in the winter and fishing in the summer". Ottar wished to find out how far the land extended and whether any man lived north of the waste tracts. So he went for three days along the coast; the whole day he kept the uninhabited land to starboard. In this way he came as far north as the whalers normally sailed.

Ottar continued for a further three days until the land curved eastwards and the sea made its way inland (that is to say formed a bay). There Ottar stayed to wait for a westerly wind and with a change in the wind sailed thence eastward for five days. Then he had to wait for a due north wind because the land curved southwards. Again he sailed the following wind for five days and came to a place in which there was a great river which made its way into the land.

Ottar probably made his voyage between 870–890 AD. On the basis of the story he was the second man we know who led an expedition to the north out of a quest for knowledge. The first was Pytheas, but 1200 years had elapsed since his journey to Thule skirted the Arctic Circle. Ottar crossed the Arctic Circle and was the first person to sail to the North Cape. He continued along the coast of the Kola Peninsular to the White Sea and in all likelihood all the way to Kandalaks. Ottar was unable to demonstrate that Scandinavia was not an island.

Ottar was hardly the first Viking to sail to the White Sea; others had probably already been there on trading visits. In the White Sea he came across the Beormas, as the Russians called them. Ottar took furs as well as highly-prized walrus tusks as his spoils and took them as gifts to Alfred. Although the land of Beormas was not located near the most popular trading routes, at least three Norwegian kings went there in the 11th century. A war broke out between the Vikings and the Beormas, who managed to slay a group of Norwegians waiting on their territory.

There is no doubt at all that the Vikings went to the White Sea. But did they continue further to the east and north?

Nansen answered the question in the affirmative. The areas were good walrus-hunting grounds, as Ottar's story points out. Because of this the Vikings sailed at least as far as the west coast of Novaya Zemlya where there was an abundance of seals and walrus. According to traditional medieval Icelandic legend the coast of Siberia wound north after Beroma and formed a peninsula, the western point of which was Greenland. Since the Vikings assumed this to be the case they would certainly have come across Novaya Zemlya in the east.

It is possible that Norwegian Vikings had also discovered Spitsbergen. It is mentioned in old Icelandic writings that Svalbard was discovered in 1194. The name meant the "cold edge" so it can be assumed to be the "cold coast" here. According to the *Landnámabók,* which described the settlement of Iceland, Svalbard is a four-day journey from Iceland to the north. Certain other references to a land which is located

THE VIKING SHIP – KEY FACTOR IN EXPANDING DOMINIONS

The streamlined Viking vessels are the most beautiful ships ever built. In their time they were also the most seaworthy. Originally, the Vikings were farmers and artisans but once they took to the seas they became warriors and traders. The structure of their ships was also shaped by these uses.

The vessels built for war parties (the drake and the långskepp) were low, narrow and sometimes very long indeed. The largest warship found on the Skuldelev site in Denmark was 28–29 metres long but only 4 metres wide. It held 20–25 pairs of oars, which translates into a crew of about 40 or 50. The mast could be folded and a square sail could be raised.

Cargo vessels, called knarr, differed slightly from warships. They were high and wide. Whereas the largest warship found at the Skuldelev site had a length-to-width ratio of about 1:7, the largest cargo vessel found at the same site had a corresponding ratio of 1:4 on average (4½ metres wide and 16 metres long). The latter's sail area (a Viking vessel's sail could be reefed) was probably about 100 square metres. A crew of six was needed for sailing and the ship could carry a cargo of some 24 tonnes.

The ships were clinker-built, in Denmark mainly of oak, in Norway and Sweden pine was also used.

38 (John Nurminen Foundation)

The planks on the ship's sides were held together with metal rivets. The other joints of the ship were dovetailed or dowelled together.

The Vikings introduced the iron anchor in the 10th or 11th century. However, they were so expensive that simpler ones made of stones and stumps were a more common sight on ships.

In the Nordic countries, Viking chiefs were often buried with their ships or boats. Mead, food and weapons were provided for the final voyage to Valhalla; sometimes a horse, dog or even a servant would accompany the chief.

The Viking's ledung system was based on a territorial division of responsibilities, where a number of villages would equip and maintain a ship and a sufficient crew of armed warriors together.

The Vikings were by far the best sailors of their time; they were able to move quickly both into war and when trading. In favourable conditions, their cargo vessels could reach speeds of up to 6–8 knots and were even able to move close to the wind. This was slow, however, and had to be done from a gentle angle.

The sails were a woollen cloth woven on looms. In the 8th and 9th centuries the sails were twined between the yard and the boltrope's reefing ropes like a chip basket. Later, the strips of cloth (60–100 centimetres wide) were sewn into a single sail.

The heavy ropes in the ship were woven from walrus hide or soaked bark fibres. There was a wind vane at the top of the mast. This metal segment had horse hair attached to it that showed the navigator the wind direction.

38 The purpose of the Bayeux Tapestry was to uphold William the Conqueror's claim to England and depicts the conquest of England in 1066. The tapestry was probably made by Odo, Bishop of the town of Bayeux, and donated to a church built in the town. The church was consecrated in 1077. (Le Centre Guillaume le Conquérant)

between Iceland and the land of the Beromas made Nansen believe that Svalbard was known.

WHERE IS SVALBARD LOCATED?

In his book *In Northern Mists*, Nansen draws a map in which he shades in lands discovered by the medieval Norwegians and Icelanders. Because Spitsbergen is located at the edge of the ice in July, it is probable that the Vikings drifted there. It is also thought that Svalbard is located on the Siberian coast east of either Jan Mayen or the land of the Beormas. Jan Mayen is such a small island that it is difficult to imagine it being called a cold coast. Neither can Svalbard have been in the northern part of Greenland because this is mentioned separately in relation to Svalbard. It is possible that the Vikings drifted to Spitsbergen en route between Iceland and Norway or when seal and walrus hunting. And once the islands had been discovered, the Norsemen would certainly have taken full advantage of its excellent reserves of seals and walrus.

THE VIKINGS CONQUER ICELAND

Irish monks went to Iceland in the 700s to escape from the Vikings. They were not left in peace for long there either. Sagas tell of the discovery of Iceland and of the founding of colonies there, but the stories were only written down 300 years later. Therefore the sagas have to be regarded with some scepticism, although they do relate irrefutable historical facts.

The Irish had known about Iceland long before its colonisation; for how long we do not know, but possibly before Pytheas' day. The Vikings had learned of the island far away in the west from the Irish during the hundreds of years they had been in contact with Scotland, with the islands near to its coast and with Ireland. The most reliable early source of information is the priest Ari Thorgilsson, more commonly known as Are Frode. In the *Íslendingabók*, written 1120–1130, he tells of the 'discovery' of Iceland as follows:

"Iceland was first settled from Norway in the days of Harold Fairhair... 870 winters after the birth of Christ...The first to sail there was Ingolfur. This happened when Harold was only sixteen winters old, and for the second time a few winters later. Ingolfur settled down to live south of Reykjavík; the place is called Ingolfshövde...At that time Iceland was clothed with forest from the mountains to the strand. There were Christian men here, whom the Norsemen called 'Papar'...And then there was great resort of men hither from Norway, until King Harold forbade it, since he thought Norway would be deserted."

Other sources tell of three different men, none of whom was Ingolfur: they were the Swede Gardar Svavarsson and two Norwegians, Floki Vilgerdarson and Naddod Viking. The credit for discovering Iceland goes to both Naddod and Gardar. Each of the three gave the island a different name.

Of Naddod it is told that he was journeying to the Faroe Isles but was driven by a storm to Iceland by mistake. Naddod went ashore and climbed up a mountain to see if there were signs of human settlements but in vain. When he set out to return to the Faroes in autumn, snow was falling on the mountain and Naddod named the island the Snowland.

On the advice of his mother, a soothsayer, Gardar Svavarsson set out to look for Snowland. He arrived in Iceland, and circumnavigated the country proving that it was an island. It would be named Gardarsholm after him. Gardar built a home in the north and spent the winter there. With the onset of spring he returned to Norway.

The third voyage was undertaken by a famous Viking by the name of Floki Vilgerdarson. He set out from Rogaland in Norway to find Snowland or Gardarsholm. He took with him three ravens to guide him since there was no better navigational equipment at his disposal. He first paid a call at the Shetland Islands in the waters of which his daughter Geirhild drowned. Then he went on to the Faroe Isles where his other daughter was wed.

Floki continued his voyage. The first raven that he set free returned to the Faroe Isles. The second took flight but it returned to the ship. The third flew off in the direction of the bow where it found land. Floki followed in the direction of the raven and arrived at the east coast of Iceland. He sailed along the south coast to Breioafjörður and settled in a fjord which he had discovered.

Floki fished throughout the summer to stock up for winter. Winter arrived and the cattle he had brought with him perished. Spring was cold too and when Floki climbed to the peak of a mountain he saw that the entire fjord was covered in ice. He named the island the Island of Ice, Iceland, and this name has remained. When Floki and his companions returned to Norway in the summer he described the island as unpleasant. Herjolf told of both the good and bad points of the island, but Thorolf eulogised it, saying that each and every blade of grass oozed with butter.

The first colony to be established by the Vikings, as described by Are Frode, was the house of Ingólfur in Reykjavik around 874. The colonisation of Iceland was made more popular by Harold Fairhair, who united Norway with an iron fist. Many of the chiefs who had lost their power thought independence under bleak circumstances better than life as Harold's vassals. Colonists came not only from Norway but also from the Shetland Islands and Ireland.

THE DISCOVERY AND SETTLEMENT OF GREENLAND

After King Alfred the northern regions were described by Adam of Bremen, a learned historian who was named rector of Bremen's Cathedral School in 1067. Adam had spent some time attending the court of the King of Denmark. He heard descriptions of the north from the King and his men. On returning to Bremen he wrote a history of the archdiocese of

Tab. V.

Tegnet af H.G.F.Holm efter en Skisse af Graah.   *Stukket af Bagge.*

Bremen and Hamburg, in the third volume of which he also describes the lands and islands of the north.

Adam's work is among the most important medieval sources on the history of the northern countries. He is generally accepted as being the first to realise that Scandinavia was a peninsula and not an island. He did, however, often speak of an island when describing what was in fact part of the mainland; according to him both Courland and Estonia were islands. Adam described the Baltic Sea and its numerous islands in which there lived "savage barbarians". Because of its savage inhabitants it was necessary to be on one's guard in the Baltic Sea.

Adam also believed the Amazons to have lived on the coast of the Baltic Sea. He based this notion on an inaccurate translation of the word Kvaenland. It was assumed to refer to the old Scandinavian word *kvæn* or *kván* which meant wife. Some have assumed it to stem from the Finnish word *kainulainen*. This belief was also influenced by the idea propagated by the Greeks according to which there was an Amazon kingdom in the north.

Referring to Pytheas, among others, Adam also described Thule, which he maintained was in Iceland. He also knew that no corn grew in Iceland and that neither was there a great deal of forest there. For this reason the people lived in caves along with their animals. As well as Thule, Adam makes the first literary reference to Greenland, which was situated far

40 The ruins of some twenty churches have been found in the remains of early Norwegian settlements in Greenland; seventeen on the east coast and three on the west. The ruins of the Hvalsö/ Kakortok stone church on the east coast, shown in the picture, have been best preserved. According to the most recent assumptions the Hvälsö church was built in the 1250–1300s. The last recorded event at Hvalsö was a wedding in 1408. What happened after this is a mystery. Was the reason for abandoning the settlement a climate change, an epidemic, an attack by the indigenous people on the newcomers or perhaps the combined effect of all these?
(JOHN NURMINEN FOUNDATION)

away in an ocean "opposite Suedia and the mountains of Riphea". It took from five to seven days to sail from Nordmania (Norway) to Greenland, as it did to Iceland. Because of the sea water the people of Greenland were a bluish-green colour which is how the island got its name.

Adam wrote his history about one hundred years after the likely settlement of Greenland. Over the century the name Greenland had spread via Iceland to Norway and from there to Denmark. The oldest Icelandic reference to the discovery of Greenland is found in Are Frode's *Íslendingabók* of 1130. He says he heard of the matter from his uncle Thorkel Gellison, who had been to Greenland and spoken to a certain man who had been on the voyage of Eric the Red. Are's

41 Only when summer was well advanced did the coasts of Greenland, Baffin Land and Labrador become free of ice, allowing the Vikings to set out on expeditions to Vinland. The light nights of the Arctic helped navigation in the icy waters. (DEREK FORDHAM)

description can be considered to be relatively reliable: "Icelanders discovered and settled Greenland. Erik the Red of Breidafjord sailed there and settled down to live in the place that had begun to be called by the name Eiriksfjord. He dubbed the land Greenland because a good name would attract people to go there. He found traces of settlements, boats and stone artefacts on both the east and west coasts. On the basis of these, the people that the Vikings also saw later in Vinland and who they called by the name *skraelingar* lived there."

Since some of Are Frode's writings have been lost, we do not know whether he described the discovery of Greenland in greater detail. Several sagas mention Gunnbjorn, who had lost his way on a journey from Norway to Iceland around 900, as discovering Greenland. He drifted west and saw a great land in front of which were a number of islands which were later called the Gunnbjörn Islets. These islets were probably in the region of Cape Farewell. Gunnbjörn did not go ashore, however, realising that the land was not Iceland.

Some have claimed that the Gunnbjörn Islets are somewhere mid-way between Iceland and Greenland. But this cannot be the case. It has also been claimed that the islands were destroyed by a volcanic eruption. In descriptions of subsequent journeys no mention of the islands has been found, neither have shallows been found that would suggest their destruction.

Even if colonies had been established earlier, the settling of Greenland is strongly associated with Erik the Red, who was a war-hardened and fierce Viking and a good leader. In Nansen's words he was a born explorer who also had the ability to plan and carry out demanding enterprises. Erik was born in Norway around 950 and, having been accused of murder, moved to Iceland twenty years or so later with his father Thorvald.

Thorvald was later to die and Erik married Tjodhild, whose mother lived in Haukadal, and Erik moved south to the Haukadal region. But he quarrelled with his neighbours there and killed several of them, upon which he was banished from the district. In about 980 he moved to an island close to Hvammsfjörður, but once more became involved in controversy. Ten years after Erik's arrival in Iceland, following a new killing, Erik and Tjodhild were declared outlaws for a period of three years.

His enemies sought him out in order to slay him but he was hidden by one of his friends. Eric equipped a ship and set out to find the land discovered by Gunnbjörn. He vowed to return to his friend's if he found this land. Erik sailed along the east coast of Greenland, rounded Cape Farewell and spent his first winter in Eiriksey in the area that would become the Eastern colony. The following spring he moved to Eiriksfjord and spent the winter in Eiriksholm. For the third winter he moved once again to the neighbourhood of Eiriksey and the following spring returned to Iceland when his period as an outlaw had come to an end.

Nansen compares Erik's voyage with those made by British explorers 500 year later. When wintering the British were afflicted with scurvy, which occasionally almost wiped out entire expeditions. As becomes apparent from Floki Vilgerdarson's account, the Vikings often took cattle with them so that they could make it through the winter with the aid of milk. Thanks to his resourcefulness, Erik survived three winters in difficult conditions. It is said that not even his men complained of any problems.

On returning to Iceland Erik the Red fought his enemy Dorgest and was defeated. He later became reconciled with Dorgest and set about making arrangements for emigrating. During his three years there Erik had become so familiar with the opportunities that Greenland had to offer that he persuaded a large group to follow him. In 986, 25 ships, 14 of which would make it to their destination, set out for Greenland. If they sailed large ocean-going ships, the group in question would have been substantial. Each boat would have held 20–30 individuals with their cattle and belongings. The 14 boats that arrived would thus have transported a group of immigrants numbering some 400.

In spite of the mild climate they found when they arrived, the immigrants were confronted with numerous problems. There was little wood on the island. Although wood had been scarce in Iceland too and had to be imported, because of the long distance now involved it was considerably more difficult to obtain. Building and repairing boats required good raw materials. There was no iron to be had in Greenland either. The new settlers were obliged to refine poor bog iron ore, a process which required a great deal of energy.

The problem of obtaining wood was solved, at least in part, when the Vikings discovered the wooded Markland in Labrador. They probably discovered Labrador around 1000, approximately twenty years after their arrival in the new land.

VINLAND – LAND OF MEADOWS OR VINEYARDS

In their new homes the colonists were provided with the necessities of life but they had nothing in abundance. Hunting and fishing provided them with the essentials. Hunting trips were made into the north along Greenland's west coast. Davis Strait, which separated Greenland from Baffin Island, was no wider than 185 miles at its narrowest point. America was "within hand's reach".

The first journey to the North American continent could hardly be described as a planned expedition. The only source of information on the America–Vinland voyages were the Sagas, whose reliability is diminished by the fact that their narratives differ from one another. They do, however, provide a consistent picture of Vinland and its location and of the stages at which journeys were made there.

In the Sagas of both the Greenland and Erik the Red we learn of journeys to Vinland. According to the former, Bjarne Herjolofson sailed to Iceland with Eric the Red to follow his father and lost his way. After three days' sailing a north wind took hold of Bjarne's craft. When the storm abated he became stuck in a thick fog and for a few days Bjarne had no

idea where he was. When the sun appeared once more he took a new bearing and hoisted sail. After a day's sailing he sighted land, the hills of which were gently sloping and forested. This told him that he had not come to Greenland.

Not going ashore, Bjarne continued sailing north for two days, keeping to the coast. The terrain continued to be flat and forested. Taking advantage of a following south-westerly wind he continued to sail for three more days until a new land came into view. Its mountains were high and their slopes were covered in ice. Bjarne thought the land good for nothing and he turned about and, after sailing east for four days, he arrived in Greenland.

The Saga of Erik the Red makes no mention of Bjarne's voyage, asserting instead that Vinland was discovered by Erik the Red's eldest son, Leif Erikson. Leif and his crew were sailing to Norway from the Hebrides to which they had drifted on a voyage from Greenland. King Olav Tryggveson suggested that Leif return to take the Christian faith to Greenland. Leif agreed. On his return journey he fell into the grip of the wind for a long period and eventually came upon a new land where corn and grape trees were growing. Finally he arrived in Greenland and was given the epithet "the Fortunate".

The Greenland Saga also tells of Leif's voyage but describes it as having taken place after Bjarne's. According to this Saga it was a voyage of exploration. Leif discovered Helluland, Markland and Vinland. He built a large house on Vinland, remaining there for a year before returning to Greenland. All that the Sagas have in common is the fact that while returning from Vinland Leif rescued the crew of a shipwrecked boat.

Fridtjof Nansen considered the Erik the Red Saga the more reliable of the two because, according to him, it had been recounted earlier in the Greenland saga. He did, it is true, also defer to those opinions according to which the Sagas represented oral traditions recorded in different parts of the country. Recently a number of researchers, among them Gwyn Jones, came to the conclusion that the Greenland Saga represents the original course of events.

Helge Ingstad, who determined the location of Vinland on the basis of information gleaned from the Sagas, expresses no opinion as to their relative reliability. He used them both as his source material. The real question is; who was the first to discover North America, Bjarne or Leif? Now that it has been proved beyond doubt that the Vikings went to Vinland, they can also be considered as having discovered Baffin Island, Labrador and Newfoundland.

According to the Greenland Saga, 15 years passed after Bjarne's voyage before anybody set out to explore the land he had discovered. This is not surprising since Bjarne's journey took place only a year after the arrival of the new colonists in Greenland. Establishing the colony was such a demanding project that nobody wanted to set out on the long journey to Vinland.

After 15 years had passed, Erik the Red's eldest son Leif sailed south from his home Brattalid to Herjolfsnes to meet Bjarne, that is to say around the year 1000. He bought Bjarne's ship, persuaded a few members of his crew to go with him and set out on a voyage. He sailed Bjarne's route in the

reverse order. He gave names to important places essential to identifying the route. The first of these was Helluland, a land of flat stones, where he saw nothing but glaciers and rocks. This was the land upon the sighting of which Bjarne turned around and made his way back towards Greenland.

Leif continued sailing south from Helluland and soon dis-

covered another land which he named Markland, the land of forests. The land was flat and altogether covered with forests. The Saga also tells of wide expanses of white sand. The journey continued under a north-easterly wind and after two days' sailing Leif saw land again. First he came to an island at the northern part of the mainland. A spit extended north-

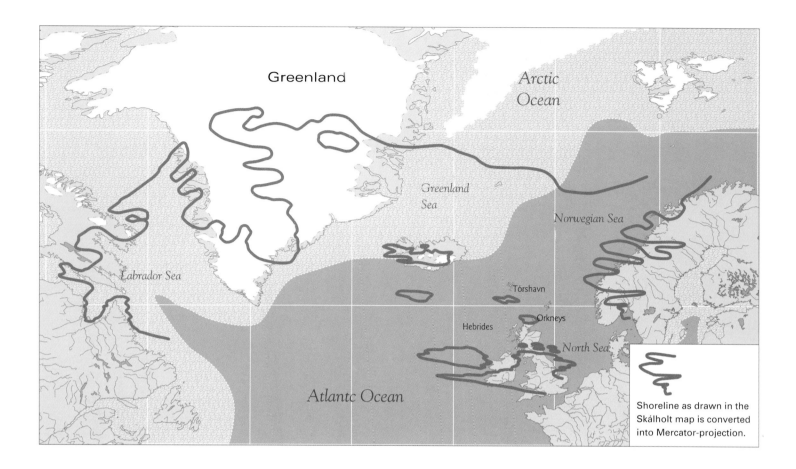

Shoreline as drawn in the Skálholt map is converted into Mercator-projection.

43 When THE SKÁLHOLT MAP *is is turned and stretched slightly in an east-west direction and this map is placed over a corresponding recent map, the result is astonishing. Regarding America with its peninsulas and bays in particular, the map fits surprisingly well. The map maker probably used information on the voyages of Cabot and his successors in addition to the Sagas. The mapmaker has visualised the geography of the area well.* (PATANEN)

42 The learned Icelander Sigurd Stefánsson probably drew the so-called SKÁLHOLT MAP. *The map gets its name from Skálholt in Iceland where the Bishop's see was located. This map is drawn on the basis of Bishop Thorláksson's original map of 1669. There are only a few Medieval influences seen on the map. The incorrect island of Frisland has its roots in the* ZENO *map. The map shows places in western Greenland named by the Vikings: Helleland, Markland and Skraelingeland as well as Winlandiae or Baffin Land, Labrador and Newfoundland.*

The Skálholt map shows influences from the Sagas and several voyages of exploration. The Sagas were kept in Skálholt. The voyages of exploration brought exciting knowledge of the New World. The Skálholt map is not based on a tradition of cartography because there was none, but depicts the Icelandic Sagas.

Later, in 1606, the Icelandic bishop Gudbrandur Thorláksson drew a second map. The map made by the Dane Poul Hans Resen in 1605 also depicts the North Atlantic. All three maps are authentic. The Skálholt map demonstrates that in the Iceland of the 16th century there was a good understanding of the geography of the North. At first sight the map, with its relationships and directions, does seem strange. It does, however, depict all the pertinent coastal areas all the way from England and Norway to Lawrence Bay. (DET KONGLIKA BIBLIOTEK)

wards from the land, at which point the ship became stuck in a shallow. Leif and his men went ashore. A river flowed from an inland lake. The boat was dragged to safety at the mouth of the river with the coming of high tide. Leif and his crew carried their leather bags onto land and decided to remain there for the winter building "great houses" near the beach. Leif named the land Vinland after its features.

The Vinland mystery has intrigued people in both Europe and America. The Sagas imbued the events with a fairytale glamour and their lack of precision allowed everyone the chance to make their own interpretation. Strange artefacts have been found on the American continent, the origins of which are shrouded in mystery. One of these is the so-called Kensington Stone which Olof Ohman, an immigrant from Sweden, found in a field in Minnesota in 1898. The runic characters scratched into the stone tell of two Swedes and 22 Norwegians who had set out on a reconnaissance trip from their camp in Vinland. Ten of their number fell in a clash with Indians and the survivors were returning to their ship, a 14-day journey away, where ten men were awaiting the arrival of the main group.

Iron objects found in Beardmore, near Ontario, are claimed to date back to the Viking era. There is doubt concerning the origin of these finds too. The Vikings were not in the habit of drawing maps. At a later time maps have been found which were compiled in the Middle Ages and which are based on Sagas and on knowledge handed down by word of mouth. The most important of these is the so-called Skálholt map drawn by the Icelander Sigurdur Stefánsson, estimated to date from 1590. Although the original has been lost, a copy of the map made by Bishop Thórdur Torláksson in 1670 has been preserved.

Some researchers doubt the scientific value of the map. Helge Ingstad is of the opinion, however, that whoever drew the map had a greater knowledge of the North American region than other map makers of the same period. The Greenland colonies have been drawn correctly. The long peninsula in the west on which Vinland is located, in Ingstad's opinion, bears a distinct resemblance to the northern part of Newfoundland. In addition, Carl Sølver re-drew the map according to the Mercator projection and claims that the distances from Norway to the colonies of Greenland and from there to the northern tip of Newfoundland correspond almost exactly to those of a modern map. There is reason to regard the maps with caution. In 1965, Yale University published a thesis on a map believed to date from 1440, that is to say before Columbus. On this map Vinland is an island close to the American continent. The Norwegian-born scholar Kirsten A. Seaver has put forward a convincing argument that this map is a fake. She has even identified the forger, and dated the forged map to have been made in the 1930s.

Although the Sagas can be considered fairly reliable, proof that the Vikings visited North America required the discovery of some conclusive evidence. In dealing with a question of a few dozen, or at most a hundred Vikings, briefly staying in an area of hundreds of miles, a solution to the mystery has seemed virtually impossible. In addition scientists have conflicting views on the location of Vinland.

The reference in the Greenland saga to Tyrker, a Turk who had accompanied them, finding wine groves and grapes, misled researchers for a long time. Because the northern limit for the dispersal of wild grapes on the west coast of North America is around latitude 42, Vinland was situated far to the south. The stories relating to the grape are a little strange. The Sagas speak of wine trees not vines. One member of the expedition collected grapes and grape wood as cargo for his boat. In the Sagas there is mention of foreigners who were able to identify grapes. The wine tree is surrounded by a kind of fairy-tale mystery.

In his own analysis, Fridtjof Nansen stressed the fact that for many countries wine trees were a symbol of wealth. He refers to a fabled island of happiness – Insulae Fortunatae – where grapevines grew. In Irish seafaring tales grapes play an important role and to eat them is intoxicating. In one of the most well-known tales, Saint Branden fills his ship with a cargo of grapes.

In addition to the wine tree, two other explanations for the word *Vinland* can be found. The first is Sven Söderberg's interpretation according to which Vinland is traced to the old word *vin* which means field or meadow. This interpretation is plausible as Icelandic sources never claim that the name Vinland refers to the grape. Based on the sagas Leif named the land according to "the opportunities it offered".

The second interpretation is that grape in fact referred to the gooseberry, which grows in the north of Newfoundland and from which wine could also be made. Even as long ago as that, wine was made from berries in Norway. According

to Finnish researcher Väinö Tanner the Nashopi Indians of northern Labrador also knew how to make intoxicating drinks from berries.

The Vinland mystery was solved once and for all by Helge Ingstad, lawyer, county governor, fur-trapper and part-time ethnologist. By solving the problem he also became an historian and part-time archaeologist who, by using simple good sense, was able to clear up a mystery which scholars had failed to solve. Ingstad's research was so convincing that all discussion about wine and meadows has been pushed aside.

THE VINLAND MYSTERY SOLVED

After his journey of exploration to Greenland in 1953 Helge Ingstad rejected the prevailing concept of the location of Vinland. Many indicators pointed to the fact that Vinland was located much further to the north. Ingstad suggested that a systematic search be made of the coast of America for signs of visitors to Vinland. Nobody came forward to take up the challenge, however.

Ingstad assumed that the Sagas provided consistent information on real matters concerning the voyages to Vinland and the circumstances relating to them. It was possible to solve the problem without taking a stand on the issue of which Saga was correct.

Ingstad was certain that the Vikings were familiar with the sea currents because recognising them helped sailing. The Vikings also made use of them when sailing to Vinland. Thanks to choosing the right route they had a favourable current for the whole of their journey. First they took a fast current which rounded Cape Farewell and continued north along the western coast of Greenland. Sailing with the current first northwards also shortened the sea-journey across the Davis Strait to the coast of Baffin Island.

In turning south from the coast of Baffin Island, the Vikings took advantage of the Labrador current coming from the north. This made their voyage easier all the way to Vinland. Because the currents carried icebergs with them, the Vikings probably waited until August before they set out. Once the Viking route had been identified, Ingstad was able to determine the lands they passed on the basis of the time they spent reaching them.

The Sagas provided information on distances in only one way: by expressing them as days travelled. Although the Sagas speak in terms of days they mean 24-hours. Because the average speed of a Viking ship was about six knots, the length of a day's journey was 150 nautical miles. Those who place Vinland in the district of the grapevine have considered the days only in a figurative sense. But they were not meant as such. Since the number of days is few, it is difficult to imagine that the true numbers changed along the years, not even when the Sagas were still based on information handed down from generation to generation.

Ingstad believed that the numbers of days journeyed given in the Sagas were correct. On the basis of them, Helluland,

44 In October 1957 an apparently revolutionary discovery was made in an American antiquarian bookshop. A map was found, estimated to be about 500 years old, that extended from Iceland and Greenland to the Vikings' legendary Vinland. Researchers at Yale University proved the map's authenticity in an extensive work published in 1965. Kirsten A. Seaver, however, has subsequently been able to show that its draughtsman was almost certainly the Jesuit Father Josef Fisher, who made the map in the 1930s. In addition, 20th century chemicals were found in the map's ink. When Skelton, an authority in the field, pronounced the map authentic the Newfoundland archaeological digs had not yet begun. In spite of the fuss, the Vinland map brought nothing new to the history of cartography.

(BEINECKE RARE BOOK AND MANUSCRIPT LIBRARY, YALE UNIVERSITY)

Markland and Vinland can be identified as Baffin Island, Labrador and northern Newfoundland. Those sailing to Vinland across the Davis Strait set out from Bjarnoey on the western coast of Greenland, a place whose location is uncertain. Those sailing from there tacked to the coast of Baffin Island. At its narrowest point the Strait was only a little more that 185 miles wide. Thus the sailing time of two days specified in the Sagas was very credible.

From Helluland the Vikings continued sailing for two days with a following wind and came to the forested land of Markland or Labrador. They passed the cape which they named Kjalarnes and long sandy beaches which they named Furdurstrandir because it took so long to pass them.

According to Ingstad the beaches of Cape Porcupine correspond fairly accurately to those described in the Sagas.

It was only two days' sailing from the sandy beaches to Vinland. This journey fits pretty precisely the northern tip of Newfoundland. According to the narrative, after two days the sailors approached land once more and saw an island in front of them which was located to the north of a greater land. They went ashore, saw the dew on the grass, collected it in their hands and lifted it to their lips. They felt they had never tasted anything so sweet.

After this they went aboard their ship and sailed through the sound which separated the island from the mainland. They continued travelling to the west of a peninsula which extended northwards. They went aground on a shallow because it was low tide. Unable to restrain themselves, they left their ship and ran to the beach at a place where a river flowed from a nearby lake.

Ingstad believed the Vikings were looking for a land that would provide them with the necessities of life. From their point of view the most important things were good grazing land for their cattle, wood to build ships or homesteads and sufficient game. Newfoundland, which they could not have sailed past unawares, met all their demands in this respect. They had certainly made journeys further to the south but it was here that Vinland was located.

Ingstad was not alone in his conclusion. There are two other writers who support his belief. W. A. Munn, himself from Newfoundland, suggested, on the basis of his knowledge of the area, the location of Vinland to be off Pistolet Bay in northern Newfoundland. The Finn Väinö Tanner came to the same conclusion. Some research was carried out in the area but without result.

In 1960 Helge Ingstad set out alone to look for traces of the Vikings. He managed to board a ship which called in at villages on the west coast of Newfoundland. Ingstad too was interested in Pistolet Bay. But he found no expansive meadows there, the likes of which he believed to have been among the most important things the Vikings would have looked for when seeking a place to settle. Later in the summer Ingstad at last came across a man who responded to the routine questions unlike the others: "Remains of buildings", he thought, scratching his head, "I think I have heard of something like that over in the L'Anse aux Meadows. But only George Decker can put you right about that, he's the boss there."

Ingstad had already sailed past the village of L'Anse aux Meadows once and had been struck by the wide fields which the name promises. The village people knew of the old ruins and told him that the first white-skinned people had settled down to live there. A river with the beautiful name "Black Duck Brook" flowed into a shallow bay. Its source was an inland lake and it wound its way through the flat terrain among moors and meadows. In this place the descriptions in the Sagas were precisely at one with reality.

Excavations carried out over the years have revealed the remains of a number of houses. The ground plan of the largest building was 16 by 20 metres. Hearths, coal-bunkers and cooking pits have been found there. Carbon dating carried out on the coal from a workshop forge has put its age at around the year 1000 just at the time when the Viking voyages took place. The latest dating places it at AD 1080.

Although many details of the finds fit the way of life and culture of the Vikings, only one Viking artefact has been

THE VIKINGS AS NAVIGATORS

The Vikings were the first Europeans to venture out on regular sailing expeditions on the dangerous waters of the North Atlantic. When navigating, they made observations of the sun and other heavenly bodies, and took note of various natural phenomena. They noted the length of the day, the height of the sun in the sky and the position of the stars – probably the elevation of the Pole Star specifically – and in doing so defined their position on a north/south course. Occasionally, however, the light summer nights made the practice of observing the stars difficult.

The Vikings did not use maps, although places they named can be found on Medieval Icelandic maps. The Norsemen did not have compasses, either, which we do not come across for the first time in Europe until the 13th century, when they were used by Mediterranean sailors, and which became more common in the 14th century. The ability of the Vikings to stay on course on long open-sea voyages has always been a source of wonder. Sailors know that, in the absence of a compass, a helmsman can make do for some time with a pennant streaming from a mast in the wind perhaps, or with the direction showed by the waves. On long voyages, however, more reliable means are needed in order to remain on course.

According to Sean McGrail, the Vikings knew how to take advantage of the prevailing North Atlantic summer winds and they steered by following their direction and strength. In addition they would note the swell of the sea, the colour of the water and the currents, and would make observations of the animals – fish, birds and insects – or even sniff the air. In volcanic areas or in the proximity of islands with bird populations, a given smell might have signalled a particular place.

Like Pytheas, the Vikings determined their latitude according to the length of the day or night. At the summer solstice the day is at its longest and at the winter sol-

stice at its shortest. At the autumnal and vernal equinoxes day and night are equally long at all latitudes. Leif Erikson, who went to America almost a thousand years ago, tells of his location in North America in sagas: "In this country night and day were of more even length than in either Greenland or Iceland. The sun passed the points of Eyktarstad and Dagmalsstad in the period of the shortest day." Leif, then, knew how to determine his position using the revolution of the sun, and realized that he had come much further south than Greenland or Iceland. Eyktarstad and Dagmalsstad mean those bearings at which Leif saw the sun rise and set. Calculations made by the Norwegian researcher, Leif K. Karlsen, show that Erikson was at latitude 49°, that is to say, at the level of central Newfoundland.

Since the Vikings had no compass, they understood what we call the points of the compass in their own way. According to Karlsen, their sense of direction was based on the west coast of Norway which, for the most part, runs north to south. They divided their horizon into eight sectors (áttir). According to some researchers, this division could be further sub-divided into 24 or 32 sectors. The sailors of ancient times also had eight "bearings". The main points of the later compass were established according to the directions of the prevailing winds at different times of the year in the Mediterranean.

The Vikings knew how to check their bearings according to the place where the sun rose and set, just as Leif Erikson

45 The woodworking skills of the Vikings can be admired not only for their ample decorations, but especially in the long, streamlined design of their ships' hulls. Their seaworthiness and speed were markedly superior to other vessels of the period.

did in America. They also observed the deviations in the sun's course at different times of the year, caused by the earth's declination. Medieval Icelandic manuscripts tell of a man called Oddi Helgason or Staroddi, who lived on the north coast of Iceland around 1050. He drew up an astonishingly accurate (+/-3°) table of the directions from which the sun rose from the winter solstice to the summer solstice. Since the compass was unknown, this could well have been an aid in determining directions.

When bearings were taken by the stars, the Pole Star (*Leidharstjarna*) was important to helmsmen, though it was difficult to see on summer nights. In storms and fogs it was, of course, no more visible than the midday sun. Clouds too, affected observations of the rising and falling of the sun. When the sun was visible it was possible to decide on a course by 'dividing up the horizon' *(deila ættir)*. If bad weather continued for a long time, one got lost, a state which was called *hafvilla*. It is possible that some islands were discovered in conditions in which the Norsemen were *hafvilla*, in other words they were somewhere they had not planned to go.

The sagas make mention of the *sólarsteinn*, the sun stone. In one tale, the Vikings tell of being able to see the sun, even through clouds, with the aid of a stone. Minerals can indeed be found in the bedrock of the north that have optical, polarising or light-enhancing properties. One example is cordierite, a silicate mineral of the gneisses, which resembles bluish quartz. It is not clear, however, how this kind of wonder stone could have been used for navigating, as some researchers have assumed.

The sea-captain Søren Thirslund has researched Viking sailing and navigation methods in both theory and practice. From sagas he has identified seven sailing directions for the open sea. These can be considered reliable, since the lives of seafarers depended on them. With their help it is still possible to find one's destination on many routes. Usually these route instructions include the places of departure and arrival and the distances between them in days travelled, for example, as well as instructions on how to stay on course.

The Vikings' longest open-sea journey began in Norway and ended on the west coast of Greenland. The sagas tell of journeys from Hernum, north of Bergen, to Hvarf at the southern tip of Greenland. In order not pass the tip of the promontory by accident, they set a course slightly fur-

46 The wooden disk in the picture was found in an archaeological dig in Greenland in 1948. From the beginning it was thought that it was used for navigation. Karl Hoberg of the Danish Police Forensic Department examined the disk using photographic techniques and it was shown to have two clearly distinctive carved grooves. One of the grooves was straight, the other curved. According to the Swedish astronomer Roslund the grooves were congruent with gnomon curves. These are drawn onto a plain by the tip of the shadow of a sundial at latitude 61 on the vernal and autumnal equinox, and the summer solstice. Hernum, on latitude 61, was the starting point for Northerners embarking on a latitudinal sail toward Hvarff, in Greenland. Gnomon curves could well have been known from sundials, used in Europe since antiquity. Perhaps the disk was used in the manner of a solar compass to guide ships on their way. The grooves have been continued on the picture to simulate the part that has been chipped off. The cardinal points have been notched around the edge of the disk, resembling the compass rose. A lot of thought has been given to the way the wooden disk was used but so far there has been no solution. Many factors, however, support the theory put forward by Roslund which Captain Thirslund has tested in practice under sea conditions. (Karl Hoberg)

ther to the north of it. They followed this route directly to the west. If they had succeeded in taking the correct bearing they passed within sight of the Faroe Islands. This method of sailing along latitudes later became the most common and the safest way to reach one's destination, and long-distance sailors were still using

it in the 18th century. It is thought the Vikings also used some kind of instruments to measure the shadow cast by the sun. In this way they would have been able to correct their course while sailing by latitude. It was possible, for example, to measure the shadow cast by the sun on the disk of a shadow instrument, floating in

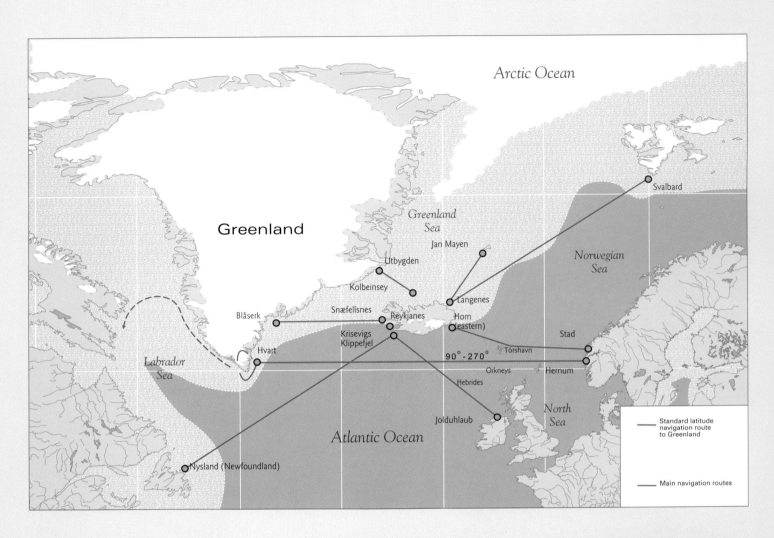

Arctic Ocean

Greenland

Greenland Sea

Jan Mayen

Svalbard

Norwegian Sea

Utbygden

Kolbeinsey

Langenes

Blåserk

Snæfellsnes

Reykjanes

Horn (eastern)

Stad

Krisevigs Klippefjel

Hvart

Tórshavn

Labrador Sea

90° - 270°

Orkneys

Hernum

Hebrides

North Sea

Jolduhlaub

Atlantic Ocean

Nysland (Newfoundland)

Standard latitude navigation route to Greenland

Main navigation routes

47 When navigating the north Atlantic the Vikings relied on traditional directions to stay on course. These usually expressed the places of departure and arrival, the direction between them and an estimated sailing time. The routes were based on experience of sailing the North Atlantic gained over many centuries. The sea captain Søren Thirslund has researched knowledge handed down from generation to generation regarding navigation recorded in 14th-century sagas. From the saga collections Landnamabok and Hauksbok he has found seven different directions in all, which were used to sail the Viking routes. These have been presented on a map and they convey a picture of the Vikings' important trade and service routes.

Route 1 is probably the most extensively travelled. According to the directions the Faroe Islands are passed to the north. Route 2 gives the shortest journey to Greenland. Route 3 includes a typical latitude navigation direction. Sticking to the latitude of the place of departure and sailing west was the surest way from Norway to Greenland. Route 5 in all probability guides the traveller to Jan Mayen Island. Route 7 leads to Nyaland, which is probably Newfoundland.

some kind of vessel. It could have been measured, in fact, simply by observing the shadow of the ship's railing on a plank. In determining the altitude of the Pole Star it would have been possible to use the vessel's mast, for example. If the shadow cast by the sun lengthened or the height of a star increased during the journey, the sailor knew that he had deviated from his latitude northwards and could make corrections to his course accordingly.

It is believed nowadays that the Vikings did not generally sail from Greenland to America by way of the open sea. A safer route would have been found by going around to the north and crossing the Davis Strait at its narrowest point. When travelling west, the sailor was also helped by the currents. Although the journey to Baffin Island (the Vikings' Helluland), Labrador (Markland) and Newfoundland (Vinland) was made longer in this way, the going was safer as the coast was within sight to starboard for most of the time. Perhaps the Norse Men learnt how to use more direct routes later. The first voyages to America were made within reach of land, however.

The Danish historian Christen Leif Vebæk made the interesting discovery of half a wooden disk in an archaeological dig carried out in Greenland in 1948. As

early as the 1950s Captain Carl Sølver had suggested the theory that the Vikings used some kind of disk as a navigational instrument. Later, the Swedish astronomer Curt Roslund examined the find again. According to him, the disk could have been used as a solar compass. There were notches showing direction along the edge and in the middle there were grooves which Roslund interpreted as gnomon lines. At latitude 61° the tip of the shadow cast by a rod placed in the centre of the disk would cast lines of this kind. The lines made by the gnomon are straight at the autumnal and vernal equinoxes and at their most curved at the summer solstice. The discovery was interesting from the point of view of the history of navigation, although it has met with somewhat conflicting interpretations. Captain Thirslund has made many tests on solar compasses resembling the disks. The instruments have proved easy to use and worked with precision at sea.

The Vikings deserve our admiration as skilful navigators. On their courageous expeditions they reached America 500 years before Columbus. At that time they settled down to live, if only for a short time, on a continent upon whose soil Columbus never really set foot.

found at the site; a Nordic spindle whorl made of soapstone. It was either brought from Greenland or was made from soapstone obtained from the Vikings. All experts, however, have been unanimous in their opinions on the origin of the find.

The Vinland mystery was solved.

THE EXPEDITIONS OF THE GREENLANDERS TO THE NORTH

The Vinland route shows that the Vikings were at home sailing in the waters of the Davis Strait and Baffin Island. How far to the north did they venture?

In the northern part of their western settlement the Vikings found excellent hunting ground stretching along the west coast from Holsteinborg to the Nugssuaq Peninsula slightly to the north of Disko Island. There they not only hunted walrus, narwhal, reindeer and polar bears but also found that important building material and fuel, driftwood. The east Greenland current still carries driftwood all the way to Disko Bay.

Nansen was of the opinion that the Greenlanders had no great need to sail further north to hunt and fish. Driftwood was to be found in greater abundance further south nor was there a greater amount of game to be found in the north. Neither were their ships suitable for sailing in icy waters. They probably also had problems regarding the condition of their ships. There was no wood for shipbuilding in Greenland, so it had to be brought all the way from Norway or Markland. The Vikings also suffered from a lack of iron nails; most of the coffins found in graves in Greenland were held together with wooden nails. In 1189 Asmund Kastanrasti arrived in Iceland from Greenland with twelve others in a ship that had been built using only wooden nails. The ship was also re-enforced with strapping; Nansen claimed that this ship was an example of Greenland's finest.

The Greenland Vikings certainly progressed much further north than Disko Bay. In 1824 an Eskimo by the name of Pelimut found a stone on Kingigtorsuak Island in the Upernavik region at latitude 72°. The runic writing on the stone told that three Greenlanders had camped there in the winter of 1333. There were also three cairns at the site, which Nansen believed the travellers had perhaps used to try to attract the attention of possible passers by.

According to old written accounts a journey still further north was made in 1267. An expedition setting out from the western settlement advanced all the way to Melville Bay at latitude 76°. This journey was one of the Vikings' rare voyages of exploration. Its purpose may have been to find out about Eskimo settlements. They did indeed find signs of Eskimo settlements but did not meet any of the people. Although there was an abundance of game in the north, particularly polar bears, there were no suitable places for new colonies there. On the return journey the expedition also saw traces of the Eskimos in the Disko Bay region.

Further to the north still, in the Smith Sound area, Viking

artefacts have been dug up from the ruins of Eskimo houses, which suggest that Greenland Vikings journeyed there or were shipwrecked there. Most of the artefacts have been dated as originating in the 13th century. They might have ended up at the places they were found as the result of trading trips. There is evidence of such trading in the form of a hinged bronze rod, a typical trading item, found in an Eskimo building on Ellesmere Island.

THE VIKING SETTLEMENTS DISAPPEAR FROM GREENLAND

There were two Viking colonies in Greenland. Both were situated in west of Cape Farewell at the western tip of Greenland, but one was called the eastern settlement and one the western. The eastern settlement was situated immediately to the west of Cape Farewell in what is now the Julianenhåb region. It was here that Erik the Red came on his first voyage and founded the House of Brattalid at the bottom end of Eiriksfjord. It was from this place that Leif Erikson and many others set out for Vinland. At its largest the eastern settlement consisted of 190 farms, 12 churches, one 'Cathedral' as well as a monastery and a nunnery. The western colony was situated in what is now the Godthåb (Nuuk) region. During its most flourishing time it consisted of 90 farms and four churches.

The combined population of the colonies grew to about 3000. Theirs was a well-organised society. Based on the Icelandic model, the settlements had their own laws and national assembly. Trading was essential to life. The Greenlanders exported furs and hides, wool, oil and walrus tusks. Greenland's hawks and polar bear skins were renowned. Important imports were grain, wood and iron, forged weapons, European clothes and various luxury goods.

There had been Eskimos in the areas of the colony before Erik the Red's arrival, and he and his men found remains of their camping places. A few colonial place names refer to the Eskimo language. There is reason to assume that there were Eskimos in the district when the colonies were established and that the new settlers made contact with them.

The Vikings arrived at an interesting time. It is believed today that the remains of dwellings and boats found by Erik the Red were those of the Palaeo- or Dorset Eskimos. Eskimos of the Thule culture migrated from Alaska to Greenland by way of northern Canada. The Dorset Eskimos were forced to move away when climate became warmer, around 1000. With the coming of the Vikings the Dorset Eskimos withdrew further to the north and left the southern regions to the newcomers.

Later references almost certainly allude to the Thule Eskimos. These came by way of Ellesmere Island to Thule and from there, further south to the west and east coasts of Greenland, from about AD 1200 onwards. There are some references according to which later relations between the new settlers and the Eskimos became tense. Haakon, Bishop of Bergen, sent the priest Ivar Bárdarsson to Greenland in 1341.

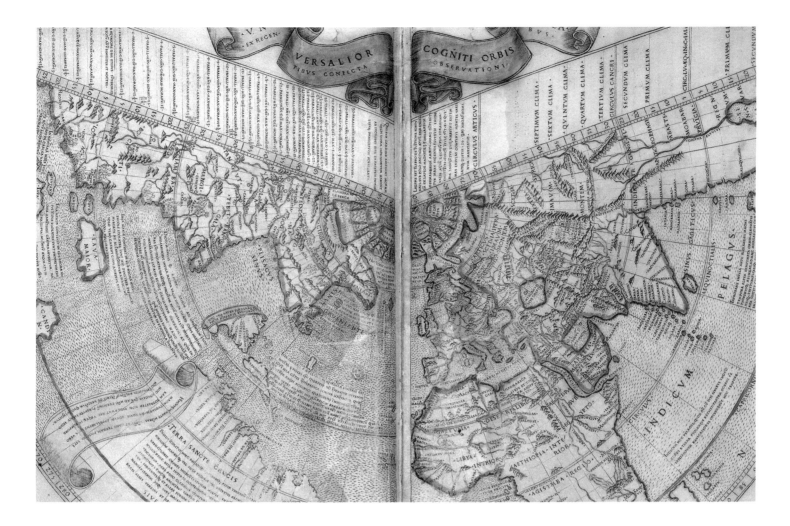

48 An Italian Renaissance monk described Johann Ruysch as an exact and conscientious geographer. Ruysch sailed west and north from England and made observations of many islands. He published his map of the world in the Ptolemy edition published in Rome in 1507. The map brought a valuable addition to what was known of America till then. Ruysch has completed the northern area with islands of which he has learnt, like Mercator later, from INVENTIO FORTUNATAE. *This legend, later to disappear, probably told of the sailing of the Norse Men, the Vikings, to Iceland, Greenland and America. It is believed that the story's teller was Thomas of Lyyn who "sailed north and who had an astrolabe". If Thomas visited the North he probably got a lift from the Vikings. In the story the islands were situated at the polar region in the same way as Ruysch had located them on his map. The hand-coloured map is in Helsinki University in the Nordenskiöld collection.* (HELSINKI UNIVERSITY LIBRARY).

Although it is not known how long he stayed in the colony his accounts, recorded by others, are available. According to Bárdarsson the entire western settlement was deserted and under the control of the Eskimos. Cattle, horses, sheep and goats ran wild in the neighbourhood of the colony. Another reference to Eskimo attacks, in which 18 men died and two boys were taken as slaves, dates back to 1379.

There is no further information on fighting between the Eskimos and the Norsemen. On the other hand, there is evidence of the good relations between the Greenlanders and the Eskimos; neither does fighting fit the picture of what is known of the Eskimo's nature. The disappearance of the colonies cannot be blamed on the Eskimos.

After 1350 the Norsemen only lived in the eastern settlement. The Ivigtut located between the two settlements disappeared after 1380. The eastern settlement survived until 1500 but then disappeared. If the explanation did not lie in the superiority of the Eskimos, what was it?

Nansen, who had lived in Arctic conditions, considered poor nourishment the reason why the colony came to an end; a deficient diet might even have led to a decrease in the birth rate. The Norwegians were used to a high carbohydrate diet. With diminishing trade, carbohydrates could only be obtained from milk and summer berries and there were no cattle to replace those slaughtered in the hunger years.

In 1294 Greenland's commerce became a royal monopoly. Only one of the royal fleet, a ship by the name of *Knarren*, plied the Greenland trade route, and when the vessel was later shipwrecked the situation became even worse. The time between voyages could stretch into as long as ten years and probably stopped completely after 1410.

Bergen, where Greenland's trade was concentrated, experienced difficult times. The Black Death raged in Norway in 1349, killing a third of its people. Forty years later an epidemic of the plague broke out again. The Hanseatic League overran Bergen in 1393 and pillaged the town. All these misfortunes had a destructive effect on Greenland's trade.

Many theories have been put forward regarding the destruction of the colonies. According to one it was physical degeneration, and to another a spiritual breakdown that led to their extinction. Skeletons found there do not support the first assumption, however. There is no evidence that the Black Death raged there either. Other theories are based on the assumption that the population migrated to Canada or Vinland. There is no evidence to support this either.

According to the latest research by Kirsten A. Seaver, the English traded with the eastern colony in the 15th century. Excavations have shown clearly that such trading took place. There is nothing to suggest that the colony had been left in a disorderly fashion or that the inhabitants had become extinct. In the churches there are is no trace of objects associated with religious services or of the remains of church bells. According to Seaver the emigrants joined Europeans on their way to the New World as they did when migrating to Greenland.

If Seaver is right, the new settlers may have been obliged to change their way of life in America and to concentrate more than before on seal hunting and on living like the Eskimos. It is believed that there is evidence to support this. In the mid-17th century somewhere around latitude 72°, the skipper of an English fishing boat tells of seeing big well-proportioned and white-skinned natives among a group of small, dark-skinned and short-legged Eskimos, whose appearance showed a marked sign of a Scandinavian blood line.

John Franklin made a similar observation almost 200 years later. In 1824, he too came across fair-skinned Eskimos and described their faces as being European in spite of their small eyes and low brows. One of the fair-skinned Eskimos had reddish skin and the longest beard Franklin had ever seen on any American native.

Thirten years later, in 1837, Peter Dease and Thomas Simpson of the Hudson's Bay Company met Eskimos in the same district as had Franklin. One of them "looked more civilised and could have been European".

Vilhjalmur Stefánsson has an explanation of his own for every mystery of the Arctic. In 1910 he saw fair Eskimos on Victoria Island. In spite of their warlike reputation they were friendly, partly perhaps because Stefánsson resembled them in appearance. The Eskimos that Stefánsson encountered claimed that fair-skinned Eskimos were not Eskimos but simply dressed and behaved like Eskimos. Three of them had beards just as long as Stefánsson's. Their skull measurements were European. Stefánsson's conclusion was clear: "If the Victorian Eskimos had European blood in their veins the only historical explanation can be that their fore-fathers were Scandinavian immigrants from Greenland."

THE VIKING HERITAGE

Although the Vikings discovered new lands, they lost most of them. Their knowledge of Spitsbergen, Baffin Island or Helluland, Labrador or Markland and of Vinland only survived in the Sagas and a few other written sources. Even the location of the eastern Greenland colony remained a secret for a long time. The Vikings' deeds did not change the world or the world view of their time. Their ability to sail in northern waters was not based on new or revolutionary navigational techniques or better mapping, but on highly developed shipbuilding and on the ability of the individual to survive in difficult conditions with the aid of simple mnemonics and their own personal experience. Such information could only be handed down from father to son, from master to apprentice.

The Vikings' success was due in part to a powerful desire to find better places to live but also to the uncertainty of their sailing methods. Motivation was the prime mover, inadequate methods took them to places other than those they wanted to reach. Individual skills helped them survive their adventures and return to tell of their discoveries to others. With the disappearance of the Greenland colonies went the information on new conquests, but through Sagas their reputation and honour survived. No one can take that away from the Vikings.

Adam of Bremen retained some of the information collected by the Vikings but not all their discoveries have come to the attention of cartographers. Certain misconceptions, on the other hand, are based on the beliefs of the Vikings. They thought Greenland was connected to the Eurasian continent. The Vikings, it seems, had progressed to Novaya Zemlya and assumed it to be an isthmus connecting Greenland with Siberia to the east of the White Sea. The discovery of Svalbard or Spitsbergen fits this way of thinking well. This belief was further strengthened by the limit of the Arctic ocean's pack ice, which ran along the southern part of Greenland to Spitsbergen and from there to Novaya Zemlya.

The best, though inadequate, presentation of the world conquered by the Vikings is to be found in an unknown writer's *The King's Mirror* of about 1240. The further to the north the writer proceeds the less his descriptions have to do with the beliefs of the Middle Ages. Although the book apparently lacks any mention of Helluland, Markland and Vinland, its depiction of Greenland is excellent. The writer gives an accurate picture of the areas settled as told of in the sagas, of the climate and of the inland ice, which he believed to have a cooling affect on Iceland's weather conditions too. *The King's Mirror* carefully depicts the shifting of the sea ice as well as the animal life in northern seas. If, of the 29 species of whale described in the book, the three that are probably species of shark are discounted, the catalogue covers all known species of whale. *The King's Mirror* also describes all species of seal living in Norwegian and Greenland waters.

Knowledge of the Vikings, particularly of Greenland and its peninsula, was handed down to later generations more accurately by the Danish cartographer Claudius Clavus-Claudius Clausson Swart, born in 1388. He made the first delineation of Scandinavia, which was to be used as an addendum to Ptolemy's maps. The earliest printing of his map is linked to a translation of Ptolemy's work which was given as a gift to Cardinal Filliastrus in 1472. Degrees of latitude and longitude were drawn on Clavus' map. Clavus' maps had a very real influence on maps of the northern regions for two centuries.

EXPLORING FOR TRADE, GOLD AND POWER

PYTHEAS WAS PROBABLY THE FIRST PROFESSIONAL EXPLORER. HIS MOST IMPORTANT MOTIVES WERE SCIENTIFIC NOT POLITICAL, ALTHOUGH IT SEEMS THAT THE SPONSORS OF HIS VOYAGES WERE MASSALIA MERCHANTS. MANY OF THOSE WHO CAME AFTER PYTHEAS MADE DISCOVERIES EVEN THOUGH THEY WERE NOT ALWAYS SEEKING THEM. THE INITIAL REASON FOR THE VIKING DISCOVERIES WAS OFTEN AN INDIVIDUAL'S ERROR OR A MISTAKEN DIRECTION CAUSED BY THE FORCES OF NATURE. THE VIKINGS QUICKLY TOOK ADVANTAGE OF THEIR DISCOVERIES TO IMPROVE THEIR LIVING CONDITIONS.

In the fifteenth century exploration became the tool of power politics. The most successful seafaring nations, Spain and Portugal, signed the Treaty of Tordesillas in 1494, in which the Pope divided the world into two. Spain was given the western half and Portugal the eastern. A demarcation line was drawn up, located in the Atlantic Ocean, 100 leagues or 1370 miles to the west of the islands of the Azores and Cape Verde. The border was later moved further to the east. At this time there was no exact understanding of the location of North America. This is why the Portuguese also took an interest in regions to the north. An attempt was made to shut two seafaring nations, the English and the Dutch, entirely out of the rich trade with China and East India, which is why these nations tried to find a new route to China. On the basis of the geographical knowledge of the time there were two possible routes. One led to China by sea across the top of America, the other north of Asia. The former was later named the Northwest Passage, the latter the Northeast Passage.

Over the centuries that followed many tried their luck at finding these seaways, and many lost their lives striving to push their way forward through freezing conditions towards China. Both routes were possible, but their financial benefit has proved to be minor in spite of modern icebreaker technology. Nobody knew this at the end of the 15th century and would not do so for almost 400 years.

Although power politics was the most important reason for journeys of exploration, there were other motives too: ambition, curiosity, the lust for gain. There was no shortage

The following is my best reading of the burnt manuscript on the left:

he nomber of those that
be in the shippe besides   136

In the Edwarde Bonaventure

Mr Lewke warde ⎰
Mr Skevington ⎰ Gentillmen
Randall Shawe ⎰
Peter Jefferye ⎰ marchauntes
Lewis a Surgeon
An appotirarye
A Jewiller
A Barbler
A Smythe
A Shewmaker
A Taylor
ij mewsitiones
ij pnrsers
iij men Mr warde
j man for the surgen
j man for the marchaunt
And all the rest to be Saylor
to the nomber of Lx

Some in all for this shipp

Lordeshippe to have
ustome and the fu
ly staye for t

mst

of men who wished to distinguish themselves. Most explorers were entrepreneurs at heart. They had chosen their occupation themselves. Perhaps the most frustrating thing for them was to convince rulers and merchants that it was worth giving them the authority to carry out the job.

49 *In 1580 the Muscovy Company sent out a two vessel expedition to seek a Northeast Passage. Arthur Pet and Charles Jackman were the ships' commanders. On the journey Hugh Smyth kept a diary, whose edges were later damaged in a fire. On the partly burnt pages a map of Vaigats Sound, in the ice of which the expedition's vessels were beset, was made during the journey. The travel report also contains a muster roll for the* GALLIONE *and the* EDUARDE BONAVENTURE, *in which there is information on the officers, the crew and their occupations.*
(THE BRITISH LIBRARY)

50 *When, on his first expedition, Frobisher met Eskimos paddling their kayaks, he thought them to be seals. The Eskimos easily paddled away from the British. They also knew how to withdraw beyond the range of the ships' guns. The picture is from Frobisher's second journey during which they sought five men captured by the Eskimos in vain. Later, based on what the Eskimos said, it was assumed that the men built a boat and sailed towards an unknown fate.* (THE BRITISH LIBRARY).

The English in Queen Elizabeth's Reign discover GRONELAND, land there & are opposed by y Natiu

EARLY SEEKERS OF THE NORTHWEST PASSAGE

Hardly anyone could have fit the description of "entrepreneur" better than John Cabot. He continued in North America where the Vikings had left off. He even had the same air of mystery as his predecessors. There is not a single picture or portrait remaining of John Cabot, not one of his letters or even his signatures has been preserved. Of Genoese birth, Cabot's original name was Giovanni Caboto. He was a contemporary of Christopher Columbus and like him moved first to Venice.

When Cabot failed to persuade the Spanish or Portuguese to finance a voyage to find a western route to China, he moved in 1498 with his wife and three sons to Bristol, England. Bristol was an important town at whose market dried cod was exchanged for Mediterranean delicacies and local woollen goods. The merchants of Bristol were interested in both a viable spice trade and the discovery of new fishing grounds.

Henry VII had rejected Columbus' suggestion for an expedition and in so doing lost the opportunity of becoming the first to reach "India". The second time round the King did not wish to fail. So it was that on 5 March 1496 Henry gave Cabot and his three sons the authority to seek, find and occupy all the new, and until that time unknown, lands to which they sailed. John Cabot was granted the right to govern these lands as a subject of the King and, since he was undertaking the journeys at his own expense, to monopolise trade conducted with these countries. One fifth of Cabot's profits was to go to the King.

In 1497 John Cabot sailed across the Atlantic in his ship named the *Matthew*. He sighted land for the first time on the 24th day of June and named the island he had discovered after St. John, the patron saint of that day; the French later called the island Belle Isle. It is interesting that the old Viking Vinland base at L'Anse aux Meadows on Newfoundland's northern peninsular is only five miles from Belle Isle. According to some sources, after declaring the land as belonging to England from that time forth, Cabot sailed northwards along the coast.

Samuel Morrison is of a different opinion, however. According to him there is so much ice to the north of Belle Isle in June that John Cabot probably sailed south along the coast of Newfoundland. Cabot returned to England having seen not a sign of a passage to India. The following year he equipped a fleet of five ships and set out on a journey from which he did not return. Only one of the ships sailed back to the home port and that was fairly soon after the expedition's departure. Nothing was ever heard of John Cabot and the rest of his fleet again.

The next to venture forth into northern waters was Gaspar Corte-Real. The inspiration for his journey was probably Cabot's first voyage. The king of Portugal, Manuel I, suspected that the land that Cabot had discovered was located east of the demarcation line agreed in Tordesilla and was thus within Portugal's sphere of power. To make sure of this he supported Corte-Real's journey, which began on 12 May 1500.

Of the first Voyage we know only that Corte-Real paid the expenses himself and that at around latitude 50° he discovered a land which was cold and on which great trees grew. He named the land, now believed to have been Newfoundland, Terra Verde.

The following spring, again at his own expense, Gaspar Corte-Real fitted out three ships and sailed west. This time he went via Greenland apparently to the entrance of Davis Strait, but continued south from there and this time found a land breached by great rivers and overgrown with pine trees. Gaspar believed he had come again to Terra Verde or Newfoundland. Two boats were loaded with 57 captured Beothic Indians. The ships returned to Lisbon but Gaspar Corte-Real apparently continued south. Nothing was heard of him after this either.

Gaspar's brother Miguel Corte-Real was given the rights to half the lands discovered by his brother. Miguel sailed to Newfoundland in spring 1502. One of his two ships returned but Miguel and his ship were lost without trace. The third of the Corte-Real brothers, Vasco, was given the rights to the lands discovered by his older brothers. The King forbade him to follow his brothers, however. The most interesting discovery made by John Cabot's expedition was Newfoundland's excellent fishing waters. The Corte-Real voyages confirmed this. On the other hand, it is possible that English fishermen had reached these waters long before John Cabot. According to Seaver they had received their information while trading with the Greenland immigrants.

The Portuguese began fishing in Newfoundland in such numbers that as early as 1506 Portugal imposed a 10 % tariff on fish caught there. Many Newfoundland place names are reminders of the Portuguese era. Legend has it that the name Labrador originated from the Portuguese Joao Ferdantes, who was a *llvorador*, a smallholder from the Azores. On one particular journey in 1501 he was the first to sight land. His companions called the land (Greenland) the Smallholder's Land (Llvorado) and that name later changed to Labrador.

THE FRENCH INTERLUDE

Giovanni da Verrazzano, like John Cabot, was of Italian origin. It seems he was of noble birth and according to the standards of the time had received a good education. Around 1506 Verrazzano moved to Dieppe and went to sea. He made many voyages east but apparently also went to Newfoundland. In 1523 the merchants of Lyon equipped Varrazzano for a voyage. He acquired a ship as a loan from the king of France. The journey west began in January 1524 and the expedition sighted land for the first time at Cape Fear in North Carolina at latitude 34°. Verrazzano sailed north along the coast of North Carolina, described New York Bay, followed the coast of Maine north and continued along the eastern coast of Newfoundland. At about latitude 50° he headed back to France.

Verrazzano appears to have been responsible for the fact that on certain maps of North America there is an isthmus

GERARDUS MERCATOR NATUS
RUPELMUNDÆ III NON.MARTII ANNO
CIƆIƆXII:VIXIT ANN.LXXXII.M.VIII.D.
XXVI:DENATUS IV NON.DECEMBRIS
ANNO CIƆIƆXCIV.

IUDOCUS HONDIUS NATUS IN
PAGO FLANDRIÆ DICTO WACKENE XVI
KALEND.NOVEMBRIS ANNO CIƆIƆLXIII:
VIXIT ANN.XLVII.M.VII.D.XXIX:DENAT:
US XIV KAL.MARTII ANNO CIƆIƆCXII.

51 The influence of Gerhardus Mercator on the field of cartography was great. As well as being a productive maker of maps and atlases he was also a skilful maker of globes. As a scientist he was interested in the question of projection, and the map he compiled in 1569 is considered revolutionary because of its cylindrical projection. Mercator was also interested in the geography of the northern area. To the right of Mercator in the picture is his son-in-law, Hondius. (HELSINKI UNIVERSITY LIBRARY)

even narrower than Panama running through the middle of the continent. The mistake seems to stem from the fact that at Cape Hatteras, Verrazzana could not make out any mainland at all beyond a narrow sandbank just off shore. He did, however, chart long stretches of the coast of the New World, and certainly knew that he had found a new continent and not Asia at all.

Jacques Cartier played an important role in the exploration of northern areas. He was born in St. Malo, a small French coastal town. Cartier made his first voyage in 1534 by order of the King and with the benefit of his appropriations. His aim was to find Terres Neuves, the new rich lands of the west. His voyage began at the end of April and land was first sighted after twenty days at Cape Bonavista in Newfoundland. Cartier, like Verrazzona, used the old Viking method of sail-

ing along a degree of latitude, since the latitudes of St. Malo and Cape Bonavista were almost precisely the same. When the wind turned westerly carrying icebergs out to sea, Cartier went north to Cape Bauld at the northern tip of the island. Thus he followed in the wake of the Vikings and Cabot. Cartier pushed further into the channel running between Labrador and Newfoundland and sailed to St Lawrence Bay, turning back between Anticosti Island and the mainland. According to Cartier Labrador was "the land that God gave to Cain".

Cartier hoped that a new route to China would be found at St Lawrence Bay. He set out once more on a voyage the following year and made his way to the St Lawrence River estuary. He dropped anchor and continued his journey by boat for 1000 miles to Hochelaga, a large Huron Indian village, nowadays Montreal. Cartier also wintered in Canada, which is an Indian name. According to Cartier the indigenous people called a village or a larger cluster of dwellings *canada*. Before long the meaning of the name spread to encompass the whole country.

Cartier explored the St Lawrence Bay area carefully. He realised what riches Canada had to offer and cemented good relations between the Huron and the French. He put into motion the development that led to the birth of the French

52 Gerhardus Mercator published his map with its epoch-making projection in 1569. Three copies of the great wall map have survived until the present day. They are kept in Paris, Basle and Rotterdam. They have 21 sheets. The purpose of Mercator's map was to help sailors and to present the countries of the world as accurately as possible. Thanks to the map's unique projection the regular routes of seafarers were represented with straight lines on the chart too. Edward Wright explained the map's projection mathematically in 1599.

Mercator used many different sources in his mapping work – both the authorities of antiquity and contemporaries such as Gasdaldi and Ortelius. The journals of explorers such as Marco Polo were also an important source.

He was in correspondence with many scientists, and with John Dee considered the possibilities of sailing to the Spice Islands by way of the northern sea. In depicting the Arctic areas he was influenced by the 14th century Oxford monk, Nicholas of Lynn. Mercator depicts Asia and America as separate continents. Thus the map inspired the sailing along a Northwest or Northeast Passage to China.

Douglas McNaughton has drawn attention to the map's astonishing accuracy in Ungava Bay (to the north of the St. Lawrence Bay). How did Mercator succeed in depicting the river mouths and coasts correctly before the first European explorer, Frobisher, had been to the area? He might have had at his disposal the secret information of Portuguese or Spanish navigators or perhaps he interviewed Basques who fished in the area. More precise charts of this American coastal area were made only much later. (MARITIME MUSEUM, ROTTERDAM)

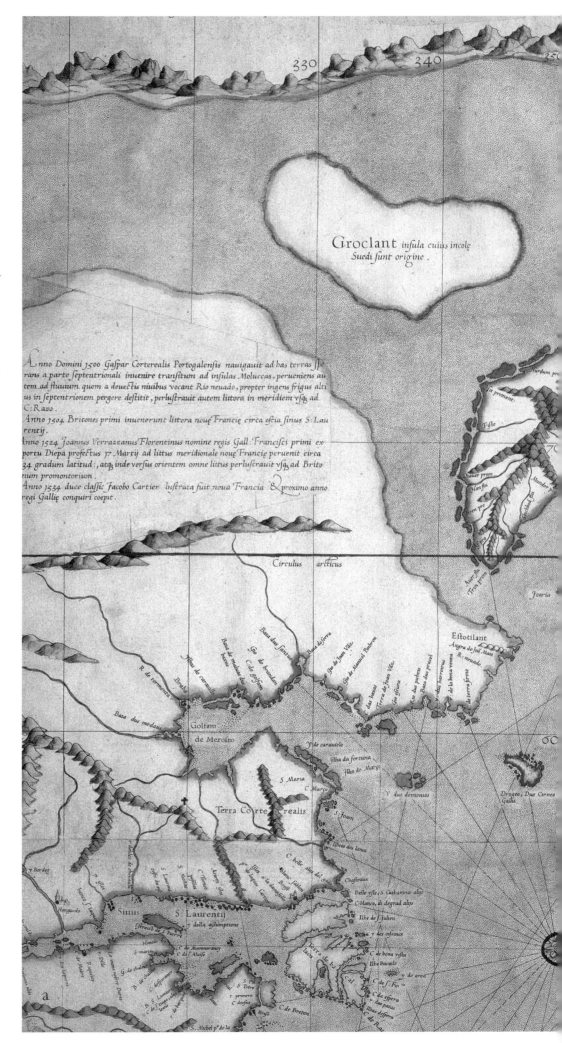

53 Jacques Cartier was a French seafarer who made three voyages to the waters of St. Lawrence Bay between 1534 and 1542 without losing a single ship or man. Cartier is considered the discoverer of Canada. He went up the St. Lawrence River to the area around what is now Montreal. On his third journey Cartier attempted to establish a colony but the venture failed. (MUSÉE JACQUES CARTIER)

colony of Quebec and the distinctive character of the province. The aim of Cartier's third voyage was to establish a colony. The journey failed, however, and the French left Canada to the Indians for a further half-century.

ENGLAND TAKES AN INTEREST IN THE NORTHEAST

Unlike his predecessor Henry VII, the English king Henry VIII was not interested in the New World. The enthusiasm of Bristol's merchants, on the other hand, never waned. One of them, Robert Thorne, had lived for a long time in Seville. From there he wrote a letter in 1527 to Henry VIII. According to Thorne the Spanish and the Poruguese had acquired a trade monopoly by sailing west, east and south. The northern countries had not yet been discovered. England should now take the initiative. Thorne claimed that "no land existed that

54 In 1578 G. Beste published the work A TRUE DISCOURSE OF THE LATE VOYAGES OF DISCOVERY, FOR THE FINDING OF A PASSAGE TO CATHAYA, BY THE NORTHWEST, UNDER THE CONDUCT OF MARTIN FROBISHER. *A simple map presented there was the first description of the opening to a Northwest Passage after Frobisher's voyage. Frobisher's voyages expanded our knowledge and the map of the North Atlantic and the west of Greenland. They also gave rise to incorrect conceptions that remained on maps for a long time. These included islands to the south of Greenland. Frobisher Strait was often incorrectly situated between these islands and Greenland.*
(PRIMARY SOURCE MEDIA AND THE BRITISH LIBRARY)

55 The Yorkshireman Luke Foxe was interested in the Northwest Passage. In 1629 he was given the use of a vessel by Charles I and set out under the patronage of some London merchants to explore the Northwest Passage and a sea route to China, Japan and the mysterious Yedso Land. Foxe sailed clockwise along the coast of Hudson Bay until he reached St. Roes in the north. On his map he marked the word Vt Ultra (forward). This was a reference to a 1625 map of his good friend Henry Briggs on which Briggs had marked Ne Ultra (no forward). When Foxe had found that the Northwest Passage did not open up from Hudson Bay, he sailed to its northernmost corner, which was named Foxe Basin after him. He returned to England without losing man nor boy, as he put it. Luke Foxe's voyage was a success. Following it the British did not conduct expeditions to the north-west for a long time.
(THE BRITISH LIBRARY)

could not be settled and no sea that could not be sailed". Therefore the English should sail north to the Pole and in so doing take a short cut to the riches of Asia. The nightless night of summer in the north would make the journey possible.

John Cabot's son Sebastian was an interesting man. He claims to have made an expedition for which no evidence remains. Sebastian failed in his attempt to get the English King to back a five-ship voyage to Newfoundland and moved to Spain. In 1584 Sebastian returned to England and succeeded in persuading a group of London merchants to finance a voyage to the east, along a new route to China which since then has been called the Northeast Passage.

As early as 880 Ottar had described the entrance to this route while sailing to the Kola Peninsular and the White Sea. Now the intention was to sail onwards from there. Sir Hugh Willoughby was put in command of a fleet of three ships. Richard Chancellor was appointed as his chief pilot. Willoughby was an accomplished soldier who knew nothing of seafaring. Chancellor and the ships' captains would be responsible for that. The ships were the *Bona Esperanza*, the *Edward Bonaventure* and the *Bona Confidentia*. The ships were equipped for wintering. Sebastian Cabot worked tirelessly to ensure the success of the expedition. He gave instructions to hold morning prayers regularly, forbade card and dice games and warned of creatures resembling naked humans in the sea, apparently mermaids!

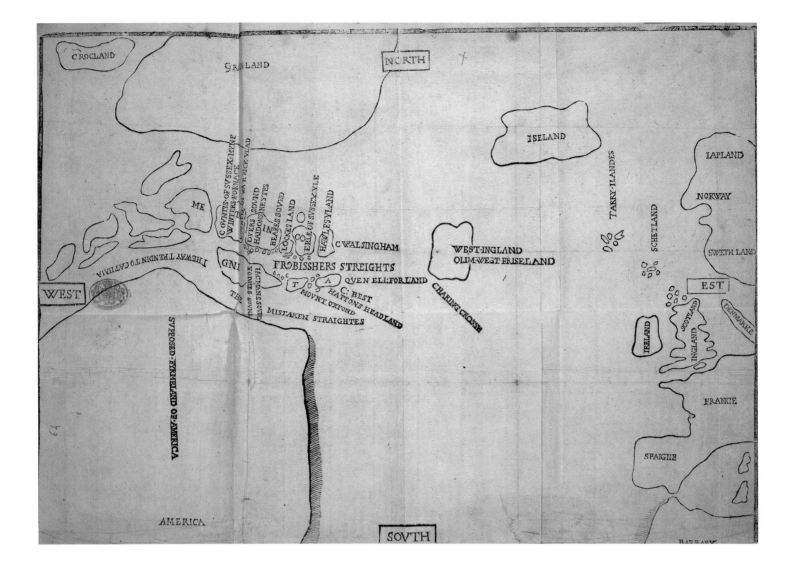

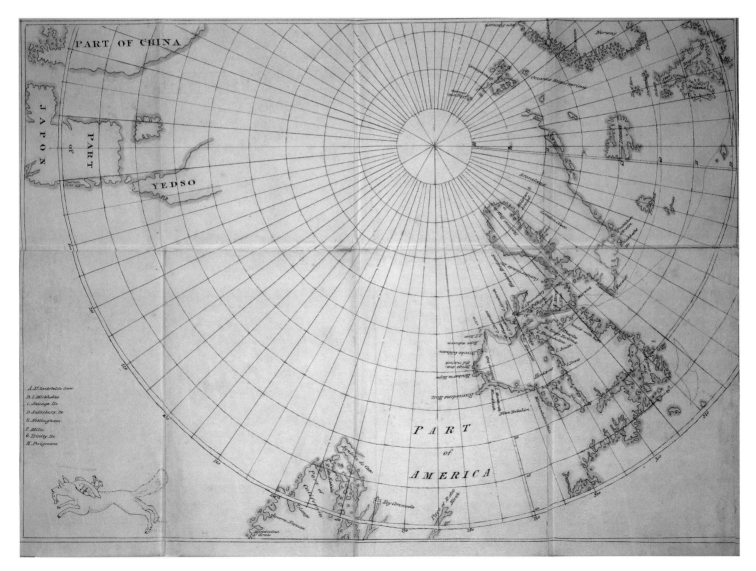

INVENTIO FORTUNATAE – A REMARKABLE PICTURE OF THE POLAR REGION

Missing links add to our interest in the history of Arctic exploration. Two important works describing the lands in the north have disappeared. One of them is Pytheas' *On the Ocean* written before the beginning of our calendar. The other, *Inventio Fortunatae*, was written by an unknown monk in the 14th century. We can examine the content of these works only from second-hand sources. Many of the philosophers, historians and scientists of antiquity make references to Pytheas' work and are sometimes critical of it. Some cartographers took *Inventio Fortunatae* as their source and for this reason it revolutionised the map of the Arctic.

The great 16th century cartographer Gerhardus Mercator, 'inventor' of modern map projection, provides us with the best clue for solving the *Inventio Fortunatae* riddle. In 1577 he sent a letter to the English geographer and polar explorer John Dee, odd fragments of which in Latin and Dutch were preserved in his estate after his death. Mercator writes:

"...The islands adjacent to the North Pole were formerly called Ciliae (perhaps Thule) and now the Septentrionales: among them is north Norway..."

"A priest who had an astrolabe told the king of Norway that in AD 1360 there had come to these Northern Islands an English Minorite from Oxford, who was a good astronomer. Leaving the rest of the party which had come with him to the Islands, he journeyed on through the whole of the north and recorded all the wonders of those islands, and gave the King of England this book, which he called in Latin *Inventio Fortunatae* ; the book began at the last zone, that is to say latitude 54° and continued to the Pole..."

"In the midst of the four countries is a Whirlpool... into which empty four Indrawing Seas which divide the north. And the water rushes round and descends into the earth just as if it were poured through a funnel. It is 4 degrees wide on every side of the Pole, that is to say eight degrees altogether. Except that right under the Pole there lies a bare rock in the midst of the sea. Its circumference is almost 33 French miles, and it is all of magnetic stone. And is as high as the clouds, so the Priest said who had received the astrolabe from this Minorite in exchange for the Testament..."

"This is word for word that which I copied from the author (Cnoyen) years ago. Farewell, most learned man, with my most affectionate esteem. 1577 Gerard Mercator."

The letter provides information on the contents of *Inventio Fortunatae*. It recounts that 'pygmies' (small people, that is to say, Eskimos) abandoned dwellings (Viking ruins) and beach driftwood (which possibly originated in the forests of Siberia) are mentioned in it. *Inventio Fortunatae* appears to tell of one or more expeditions from Norway to Greenland or even further afield. We know that there was lively sea traffic between Norway, England, Iceland and Greenland in the 14th century. We also know that King Magnus Erikson ordered a certain Paul Knudson to lead an expedition to Greenland in 1354 and that the royal knarr (a Viking trading vessel suitable for sailing the open seas) sent out from Bergen returned home in 1364. At that time, there was an established English community in the Hanseatic town of Bergen. An interesting detail can be found in a text by the 16th century historian, Richard Hakluyt, which tells that trading rights were given to the men of the *Blakeney*. The British Museum in London has an astrolabe on which is carved "Blakene 1342".

It seems probable that *Inventio Fortunatae* describes an English priest's journey to the north with some Norwegians. They probably made for Iceland, Greenland and Markland (Labrador), and perhaps

even further. In the narrative, these areas have apparently been shifted around the North Pole. When Dee inquired as to Mercator's sources he referred to the manuscript of a Franciscan monk or Minorite. Some are of the opinion that the monk in question was Nicholas of Lynn. The monk's identity has not been confirmed but he certainly measured latitude – after all, he was in possession of an expensive and rare instrument, the astrolabe.

Inventio Fortunatae tells of the geophysical conditions and inhabitants of the northern islands. The description of the whirlpool might be a reference to an ice whirl in the Davis Strait, or the Lofoten Maelstrom of which Adam of Bremen had already written as early as the 11th century: "And behold the stream of the unstable sea there ran back into one of its sources, drawing at fearful speed the unhappy seamen... into the profound chaos... in which it is said that all the back currents of the sea, which seem to abate, are sucked up and vomited forth again, which latter is usually called the flood tide."

Why did *Inventio Fortunatae* have such a great influence on the way the north was imagined? The answer is that some famous cartographers used the work as a source and situated the islands described in the narrative in the North Polar region. The Pole itself was often drawn as a rock. The islands surround an inland polar sea joined to the Arctic Ocean by streams. The first to present this view was Martin Behaim in 1492, on the oldest globe surviving to this day. It is believed that Columbus used the Behaim globe, from which America is still missing, when planning his journey.

Johann Ruysch depicts the Arctic islands on the so-called Roman Ptolemaic atlas of 1508. He had personal experience of the area as he had taken part in John Cabot's Arctic expedition of 1497–98. He tells that the polar rock was such a strong magnet that the compass did not function.

Mercator was the most important of all those who used the *Inventio*. On his wall chart of 1569, the coast of Eurasia is drawn in the Ptolemaic manner. He places the four northern islands on a separate map of the polar area. One of the islands included the southern tip of Novaya Zemlya, which was already known at that time. According to Mercator, the inhabitants of the northern islands were "pygmies". He marks the magnetic Pole oddly apart, at the entrance to the Bering Strait.

Because of its new cylindrical projection the Mercator wall chart had a revolutionary effect on geography. In addition, his interpretation of the Arctic, with its polar island and his ghost island (which had their origin in Zeno's narrative) spread all over Europe thanks to his acclaimed maps. The polar islands can also be found on Abraham Ortelius' widely distributed first commercial atlas, Theatrum

56 In 1492 the notable German scientist and cartographer Martin Behaim made the first globe depicting the world in Nuremberg. This globe depicted the whole of the known world at the time and showed the shortest sea route between Europe and Asia; it is probably no coincidence that Columbus set out on his voyage to America the year the globe was made. On Behaim's globe there are the earliest depictions of the Arctic polar islands in map form. Behaim's sources are not known but his way of depicting the islands and the positions between them suggest the Inventio Fortunatae narrative. The original globe is now housed in the Nuremberg museum.
(JOHN NURMINEN FOUNDATION)

Orbis Terrarum (1570), and on the maps of the Dutchman Petrus Plancius. The influential Plancius was one of the backers of Barents' voyages.

The Arctic was difficult to approach and explore. The first expeditions did not make their way onto the polar glacier until the 19th century. This is why the mistaken ideas about the area perpetuated by Mercator and his contemporaries remained on maps right up to the end of the 18th century. The first mistakes to disappear from "scientific" maps and the maps of northern seafarers were the northern continental islands of *Inventio Fortunatae* and the polar sea that was believed to be open. They remained on commercial maps for a long time and were still causing debate in the 19th century.

57 In 1569 Gerardus Mercator published his epoch-making world map. Mercator copied the depiction of the polar region he presented on it on his subsequently printed maps. The map in the picture is from the Mercator-Hondius atlas which was printed in 1595 in Amsterdam. Coloured by hand in beautiful baroque colours the map also depicts northern islands, shown in the corners, interwoven with the ornamentation on the sides. The four islands of the Inventio Fortunatae narrative and Zeno's phantom islands are situated on the polar map proper. An imposing mountain is situated on an island at the Pole and another rocky island near Bering Strait which shows the magnetic North Pole. This map long influenced both the concept of the Arctic area and the European perception of the Arctic. (JOHN NURMINEN FOUNDATION)

The ships set sail from London in May 1553. People had gathered on the coast to watch and courtiers followed their departure from towers and windows. The journey went reasonably well until the beginning of August, when one night the fleet was buffeted by a storm off the coast of Norway. Before the tempest a meeting place had been agreed in the eventuality that the little fleet become dispersed in a storm. Richard Chancellor waited for the others in vain for a week in Vardo in his ship the *Edward Bonaventure* before continuing his journey to the White Sea and arriving at the mouth of the Severnaya Dvina.

The other two ships stayed together after the storm and when one of them sprang a leak they went ashore at the Kola Peninsular in the vicinity of what is now Murmansk. It has been assumed that the island seen by the two ships led by Willoughby before they went ashore was Novaya Zemlya. The company wintered at the polar circle, the first western European expedition to do so. Reconnaissance parties were sent out in different directions to find signs of settlements, but with no success. All of Willoughby's 66 men perished at the beginning of 1554, apparently of scurvy, a disease which would prove to be a scourge for 300 years to come, particularly for expeditions led by English naval officers. Russian fishermen found the bodies in spring 1554, one year after the expedition had set out.

Meanwhile at the Severnaya Dvina, Chancellor met representatives of the Russian Czar, Ivan the Terrible, who invited him to Moscow. Chancellor accepted the offer and travelled the almost 1 500-mile journey by sledge. He was greatly impressed by the riches of the court. He was given a letter by the Czar to take to Edward VI. In 1555, following the journey, the Muscovy Company was established, the purpose of which was to develop trade with Russia and Persia by way of a northern route. Three decades later the town of Archangel was founded at the mouth of the Severnaya Dvina as an outpost for northern trade.

Although during the time of Chancellor's voyage no new lands or trade routes were found, the Muscovy Company which sprang from it continued exploring. The very next year Stephen Borough, captain of Chancellor's ship the *Edward Bonaventure,* sailed to Novaya Zemlya and Vaygach Island in a small craft called the *Serchthrift*. On his journey to Petsora he received the help of the Russians, who had long been sailing to both Petsora and the River Ob. In Vaygach, Borough came up against the Samoyed people and at Karanport, which led to the Kara Sea, was confronted by a belt of ice which threatened to crush his vessel. When, to cap it all, the *Serchthrift* almost collided with a whale, Borough returned to the Severnaya Dvina for the winter.

In 1580 the Muscovy Company tried once more to find a route to China. An expedition led by Arthur Pet and Charles Jackman received instructions to sail straight to China and to waste no time on trading during the journey. The ships were loaded with trading goods prized by the Chinese, from stockings to velvet shoes and glass ornaments. It was intended to trade these goods for marmalade, figs, raisins, plums, olives and other delicacies.

What was a good plan failed, however, because it was too ambitious a task. The expedition went the same way as its predecessor and was obliged to turn back from the Kara Sea after discovering Yugorskiy Shar, the strait between Ostrov Vaygac and the mainland. From there the journey to China was still 6 200 miles.

THE DUTCH ARE COMING

No sooner were the Netherlands freed from the yoke of Spanish domination than they began to make advances in seafaring and commerce. They wanted to become involved in the lucrative trade with the East and to discover the existence of a Northeast Passage. The Dutch White Sea Trading Company was established as early as 1565. It was led by Olivier Brunel, who had traded with the Russians on the Kola Peninsula. In 1584 he had failed in an attempt to sail to the East but persuaded Amsterdam and a couple of smaller towns to finance another attempt. Two expeditions were arranged in 1594 with the aim of sailing together, with William Barents and his vessel *Mercurius* at their head. Although very little is known about his background, Barents was an experienced seaman.

The expeditions parted ways at the north of the Kola Peninsula. Barents took a course towards Novaya Zemlya. Richard Hakluyt, an English historian, had sent him Pet's and Jackman's logbook in which the ice barriers at Yugorskiy Shar were described. Barents hoped to find a better route to the Kara Sea at the northern part of the island. While sailing north he charted the western coast of Novaya Zemlya. He was brought to a stop at the northern tip of the island by a wide ice floe which extended to the north and east as one solid field of ice.

Barents returned to the southern part of Novaya Zemlya and was astonished to find that the other ships of the expedition had already reached the Kara Sea, having made their way through an ice-free channel. It would be interesting to know how far the Dutch would have progressed if they had continued their journey. Encouraged by reports from Russian fishermen, according to which they regularly sailed in summer along the coast between the Kara Sea and the Yenisey estuary, they sailed back to Holland. The very next year the Dutch state sent out another expedition, this time consisting of seven ships. Barents took part once more. The ice conditions were now completely different, however. After one month they gave up and returned home. Some of the towns involved were disappointed and refused to go on. Since the government had promised a considerable reward for finding a Northeast Passage, the Amsterdam tradesmen decided to equip a further two-ship expedition. Jakob van Heemskerck, a nobleman, was chosen to lead it. He had had just as little experience of seafaring as had Willoughby before him. William Barents was responsible for navigating. The captain of the second ship was John Rijp.

The expedition decided to investigate Barents' first alternative once more and to look for a northern route to the

58 The Muscovy Company established the first trading alliance between Elizabethan England and Ivan the Terrible's Russia. There were two trade routes. The southern passage went by way of the Baltic Sea and the Neva to Russia and the northern route via the White Sea to Moscow. Thanks to the Gulf Stream the northern route remained unfrozen around the year. The Archangel harbour was established on the coast of the White Sea. From there goods were transported most often by horse team to their destination. Jenkinson, who was in the service of the company, opened up this route in conjunction with Chancellor's sailing of the Arctic Ocean. The voyage was organised by Sebastian Cabot in 1553 and its aim was to find a northern sea route to China. Chancellor perished on the voyage but the brothers Stephen and William Borrough, who had been sailing on Jenkinson's vessel, survived. Alongside Sebastian Cabot, Stephen was the mentor behind William Burrough's navigation and charting skills. Between 1556–1575 William Burrough made many voyages to both the Arctic Ocean and the Baltic Sea. He drew up a sea chart of the route between England and the Kola Peninsula whose scale was 40 miles to 1 inch.

(PRIMARY SOURCE MEDIA AND THE BRITISH LIBRARY)

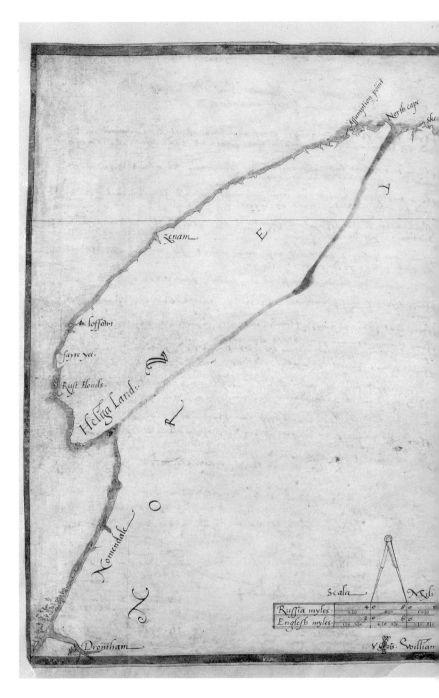

Kara Sea. It set a course north from the coast of Norway and discovered Bear Island on the 9th day of June, 1596. This small ice-covered island was named after the large polar bear that the Dutch succeeded in slaying. Its stretched fur was twelve feet long. On 19 June they sighted land to the east at latitude 80°, that is to say further north than anyone before them. A number of sharp mountain peaks rose from the island and the expedition named it Spitsbergen.

After going ashore at Fair Haven the Dutch sailed south along the west coast. Since the channels between the islands were frozen they continued south and saw Spitsbergen for the last time on 29 June. On 1 July they passed Bear Island again. After this they parted company. Rijp returned to Spitsbergen to seek a new northern route while Heemskerck and Barents set sail for the west coast of Novaya Zemlya. They arrived there on 17 July, headed north and sailed close to the coast until they came to the northern tip of the island. They headed east and made their way slowly forward.

On 24 August they became beset in the ice. Their rudder was broken into pieces, one of their boats was crushed by the ice and they feared that the same would happen to the ship. They tried to turn back but it was too late. On 26 August they drifted close to the east coast of Novaya Zemlya and found safety on a deserted beach. They gave this place the name Icy Harbour.

This was the second time that an expedition was forced to spend the winter in the polar region. The Dutchmen built themselves a shelter out of drift wood and planks removed from the ship. All 17 men crowded into this. Their furniture included wooden beds, a clock hanging from the wall and, on the recommendation of the doctor, a Turkish sauna built from wine barrels. A lamp hung from the ceiling by the light of which, on the dark winter days, the

Dutchmen read the books they had brought with them. The fuel for the lamp was oil made from bear fat.

On 4 November the men saw the sun for the last time before the onset of the long winter night. It became intensely cold. The wine and beer retrieved from the ship froze. The men heated up stones to warm their feet and they wrapped themselves in clothes made of fox furs. Collecting driftwood for fuel on the freezing beach required an almost super-human effort. They were nearly choked by the fire which they made from coal brought from the ship.

They got food and fuel for the lamp from the bears they killed. They ate the liver of a polar bear and became ill but none of them died. With the onset of the endless night the bears disappeared and the party ran out of oil for the lamp. For food the men hunted fox, whose flesh they thought the equal of rabbit. When the sun appeared above the horizon once more – thanks to the phenomenon of refraction two

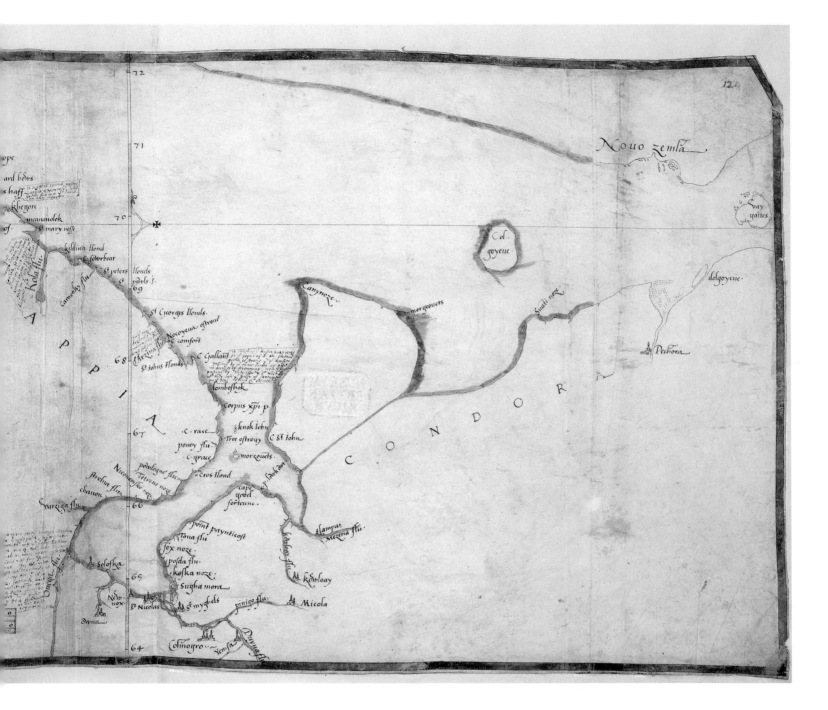

weeks earlier than William Barents had predicted – the foxes left and the bears returned.

With the new year they began to be troubled by scurvy. Although it was lighter, the frost did not let up. It snowed throughout the spring and only in June were they able to carry out repairs to the two boats. The ship was no longer fit for sailing and it is unlikely they would have been able to free it from the ice. Barents was convinced that to save themselves they would have to sail in the boats to the mainland and onwards to the Kola Peninsula, a journey of 1 550 miles. They were able to set out on 13 June. They left a message written by Barents in the shelter. Some Norwegian seal hunters found the shelter 300 years later and took with them some of the expedition's goods as proof. Others coming across the place later took the last of the 'relics'. Many of these are in the Rijksmuseum, Amsterdam.

The Dutchmen loaded their boats with the clothes, textiles and velvet intended for the Chinese. They rowed and sailed by turns or dragged their boats across the ice on the long journey south along the west coast of Novaya Zemlya.

William Barents died on 20 June. He had been the leader of one of the most successful expeditions to winter in the Arctic area. His companions arrived as planned at the mainland where they met some Russian fishermen. They continued their journey to the Kola Peninsula where they met Rijp. He had set out on a new voyage after returning from Spitsbergen. They returned with Rijp to Holland.

After the voyage led by Barents the Dutch made no more expeditions of significance to the Arctic. William of Orange had driven the last Spaniards out of Holland in 1597 while Barents' expedition was making its way towards the Kola Peninsula. The Dutch had also made inroads into the East, established factories on the Spice Islands and formed the East India Trading Company. They no longer had any need for a Northeast Passage.

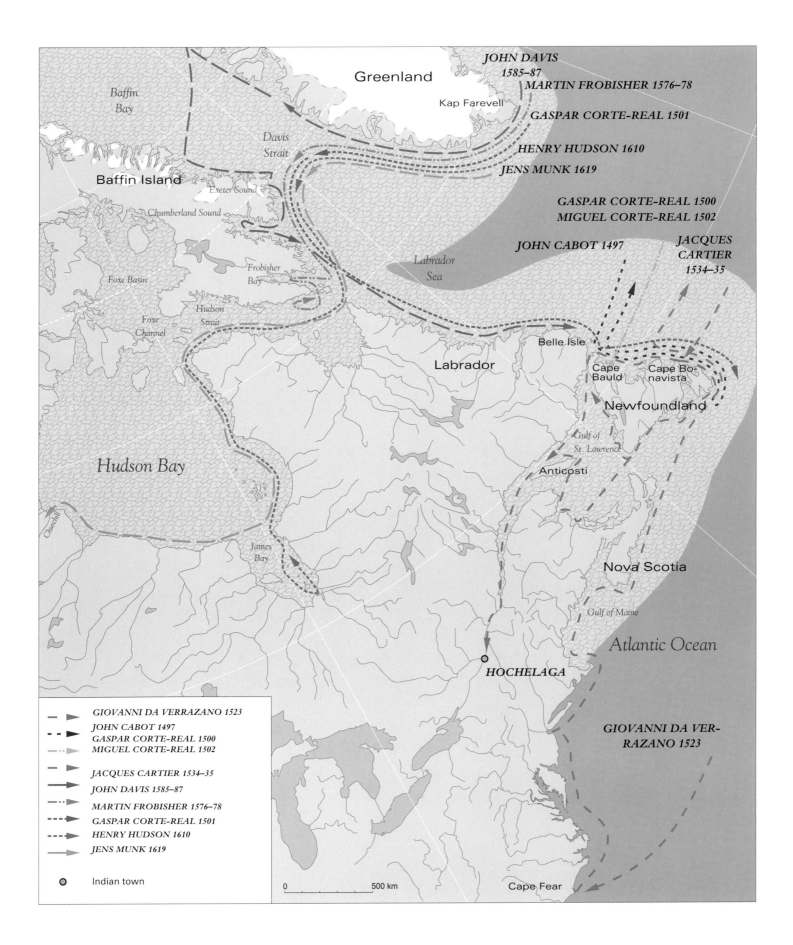

59 *The oldest voyages of exploration made their way to the coast of North America, but there is relatively little information on these for the reason that a few, such as Cabot and the Corte Reales, were lost without trace. They were followed by Verrazzano and Cartier and, at the end of the 16th century and beginning of the 17th, by Frobisher, Davis, Buffin, Hudson and Munk. The picture shows rough estimates of the routes these early sailors took.* (PATANEN)

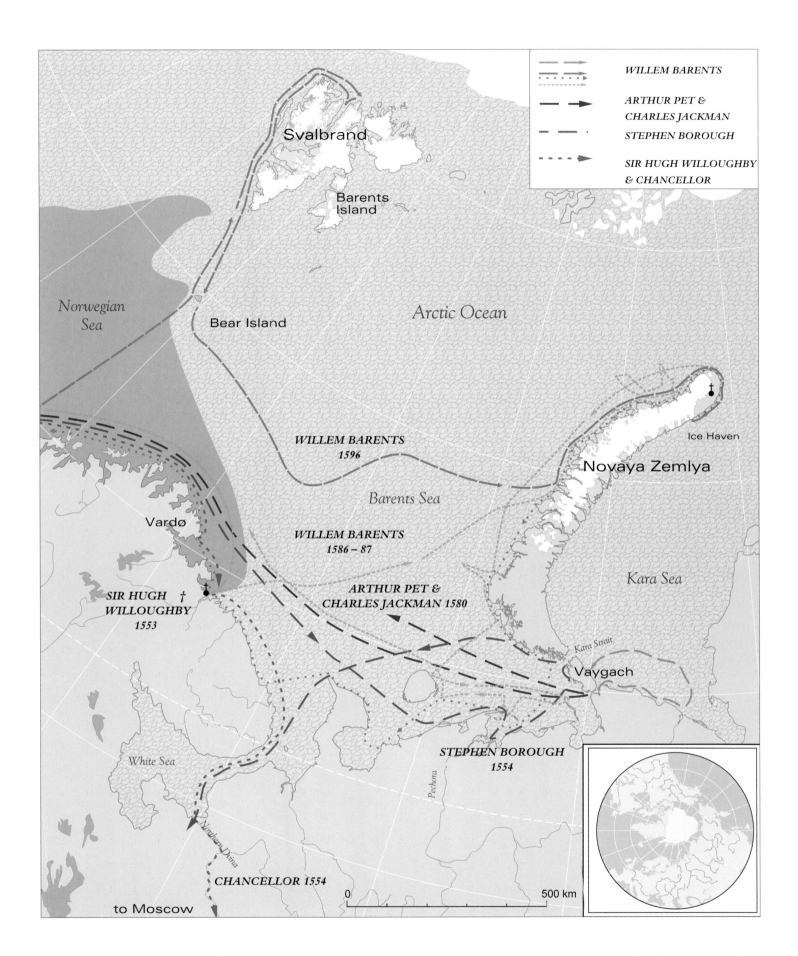

60 Those seeking the Northeast Passage came up against strong barriers in the shape of Novaya Zemlya, Vaigats Island, the straits between them and the continent, as well as the ice of the Arctic Ocean. Barents succeeded in going round the northern tip of Novaya Zemlya but was shipwrecked after this. Pet and Jackman were the first to reach the Kara Sea but were immediately forced to turn back because of the pressure of the ice. Nai and Ysbrantszoon, who were with Barents in 1594, sailed to the ice-free Kara Sea, and only turned back at the River Kara.
(Patanen)

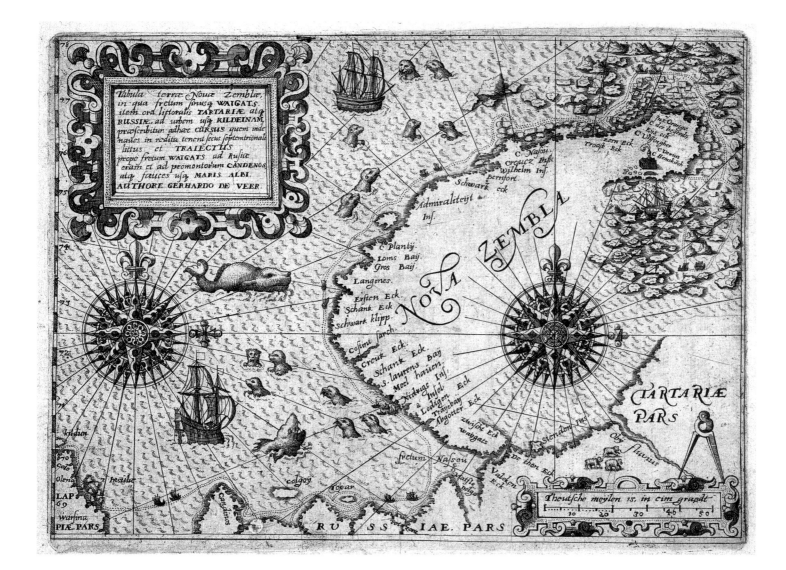

61 *De Veer's map gives a clear picture of the ice conditions in the Kara Sea that Barents and his men came up against. The Novaya Zemlya winter camp and the place where Barents' vessel was shipwrecked is marked at the north-east end of the northern island. Hunters found well-preserved remains of the camp on the coast in the 19th century. The effects, which were more than 200-years-old, were taken to St. Petersburg and Amsterdam museums. The expedition's return route to the Kola Peninsula by sailing boat is marked on the map. It was on this voyage that Barents died.* (JOHN NURMINEN FOUNDATION)

ATTENTION TURNS NORTHWEST

The Muscovy Company flourished and was no longer interested in finding a Northeast Passage. Then, in 1569, Gerhardus Mercator's new atlas of the world appeared, according to which a Northwest Passage did exist and the North Pole was surrounded by sea. As a result of an imaginary journey made by the Zeno brothers, the island of Frisland, placed in the middle of the Atlantic Ocean, was to be found on Mercator's map. The map also depicted relatively well Hudson Bay and Spitsbergen, which in 1569 had not been 'officially' discovered. The former may have been based on information received from Portuguese fishermen. Spitsbergen's name was the "Holy Russian Islands". This is an indication of the fact that the Russians – like the Vikings – had already discovered Spitsbergen before Barents.

In addition to Mercator's map, English cartographers, too, were advocating a Northwest Passage. Only by finding a Northwest Passage would the English be able to sell the fruits of eastern trade cheaper than the Portuguese or Spanish.

Eighteen enthusiastic and independent individuals joined forces under the leadership of Michael Lok and, in 1576, equipped two ships to seek a new route to China. Martin Frobisher was to lead the expedition.

Martin Frobisher was an interesting man. When he took the leadership of the expedition he was 37 years old. His widowed mother had sent Martin, one of her five children, to stay with her brother in London. His uncle found the fifteen-year-old boy a position on a ship sailing to Guinea. The journey was dangerous but Martin returned and continued his career. He advanced to the position of ship's Captain and distinguished himself "by capturing ships and cargoes that belonged or were assumed to belong to the Catholics". Queen Elizabeth I had become involved in a war with the Catholic French and gave her support to privateers acting against the French.

In 1563 Martin Frobisher and his brother were taken prisoner while they were bringing five captured ships back to London. Both were later freed. In 1565, Frobisher took both a Spanish and a Flemish vessel. He was arrested again on suspicion of piracy but was set free the very next year. It is unclear to what extent his business activities were legal and to what extent piracy. Under the patronage of the government or the ruler he was always freed eventually.

Through his uncle, Frobisher had contacts with experts on seafaring and charting, certainly with Lok, possibly also with Richard Hakluyt, Humphrey Gilbert and John Dee. And he had been interested in the Arctic region since he was young. As the planning of the expedition progressed Frobisher helped Lok, and on account of both his experience and his contribution it was a matter of course that he should become leader of the expedition.

They set off in June 1576. One of the ships turned back before they had reached Greenland and it was found that Frobisher's vessel the *Gabriel* had been lost. Meanwhile, Frobisher himself had arrived at Frisland, in fact the east coast of Greenland, north of Cape Farewell. He did not manage to go ashore and his ship ran into trouble from which, once he got free, he continued west, and on 28 July he saw in front of him a broad expanse of land which he concluded was Labrador.

62 When Barents and his men set out from Icy Harbour, Barents was so ill that he had to be transported by sledge to the boat. When he was told that one of the crew was so weak that he would not live long he replied: "I don't believe I shall live long after him." Barents asked for something to drink. Immediately after having drunk he was overcome with nausea and died. But prior to this he had ensured that his men would survive the winter and be rescued on the mainland. (NATIONAL MARITIME MUSEUM, GREENWICH)

The ice prevented him from landing, but after 16 days the sea became free of ice and the expedition continued its journey north. On 11 August they sailed into a bay which would become known as Frobisher Bay. Frobisher pushed forward 125 miles into the bay and was convinced that he had found a Northwest Passage. He presumed the land to his right to be Asia and that to his left America. A group of small objects were floating in the bay. Frobisher first thought them to be seals or strange fish. On closer inspection they were seen to be men paddling small boats made of skin; kayaks. This is the first recorded confrontation between Europeans and Eskimos. The behaviour of the Eskimos showed that they had had earlier dealings with Europeans. They realised when the ship was preparing to defend itself and immediately withdrew to beyond firing range. Having bartered with them, Frobisher sent three men to escort one of the Eskimos to the shore. Despite warnings not to do so, the men went ashore at a place close to where the other Eskimos were waiting. The Eskimos took the men away and they were never seen again. Before they left, the Englishmen managed to tempt one Eskimo in his kayak so near to the ship that he was taken prisoner. This Eskimo was taken to England, where he soon died after catching cold on the journey.

Frobisher's return increased the enthusiasm of the English to continue exploring in a westerly direction. Some of the interest was stolen by the "strange man" they had brought with them. One member of the expedition had also brought back a black stone. Although at first it seemed to be a piece of coal, when thrown into a fire it appeared to shine like nuggets of gold. Rumours of gold fired the interest of

BARENTS' YACHT

Willem Barents explored the Arctic Ocean at the end of the 16th century, financed by the merchants of Amsterdam. At that time the Dutch used such ships as the Dutch fluit and pinas. No precise information survives on the *Het Behouden Huis*, the ship he sailed to Novaya Zemlya. Detailed plans of ships were not generally introduced until the 17th century.

Pictures made of Barents' expedition afterwards generally show a three-master. It could be a pinas as it has a straight transom. It was probably not a fluit, although the ship is sometimes depicted as having a rounded transom.

A.J. Hoving gives convincing reasons for the theory that Barents' ship would have been considerably smaller than the ocean-going Dutch vessels of the time. According to him, the *Het Behouden Huis* was a yacht. It is known that these small three-masters, which were rigged in much the same way as ocean-going ships, were used in the convoys of larger vessels. Oliver van Noort, for example, had two small 25-ton yachts accompanying the two large 200–300-ton ships on his circumnavigation in 1597–1600.

The word yacht itself, now in international usage, is of Dutch derivation (*jacht* in Dutch). The word has many meanings, but always refers to a fast and easy-to-handle ship; the English adopted the word for their pleasure boats. Barents' boat would have been a far cry from the 17th-century Dutch yachts, however. These small single-masted vessels were already similar to present-day yachts, especially the fore-and-aft rig with a spritsail and a gaffsail as well as a cutwater that significantly improved the ship's sailing characteristics close to the wind. The Dutch were pioneers in Europe in developing these types of sails. In 1660 the City of Amsterdam presented a yacht rigged in this way (*statenjach* in Dutch) as a gift to King Charles II of England. The King started to enter races and so the generally known concepts yacht and yachting were born.

Barents' ship, which was square-rigged, was a yacht because at the time it would have been considered fast and agile. It had three masts made up of a lower-mast and a fixed topmast with square sails as well as a mizzenmast with a lateen sail.

If the *Het Behouden Huis* was a 30–50-ton ship, Hoving estimates that it would have been 19.25 metres long, 4.5 wide with a draught of 2 metres. Typical of such Dutch ships, it had a flat bottom, a short bottom-bilge curve and vertical sides that turned inwards at the top. It also sported a covered bow, two full-sized decks and a raised stern with a quarterdeck in front of it. The bow did not yet have a proper cabin but it did have a shelter for the gunner. Although the top hamper was light, with the two-decked design it made the ship unstable. Small two-decked ships were no longer built in the 17th century; the statenjacht, for example, was single-decked.

The *Het Behouden Huis* was crushed in the ice near Novaya Zemlya and destroyed. Disease-stricken, Barents passed away in 1597 as the crew attempted to save themselves in two boats. Of a crew of 16, twelve men made it back home to Holland.

63 William Barents made journeys to the Arctic Ocean between 1594–1596. No detailed information remains on his ship the HET BEHOUDEN HUIS. *The reconstruction of Barents' vessel is based on drawings by his contemporary Gerrit de Veer, among other sources.*

A.J. Hoving assumes that Barents' yacht had a tonnage of about 75–120t and was 19 and a quarter meters long, with a draught of 2 metres. The ship had three masts: a mizzen mast with a lateen sail and two square-rigged lower-masts that continued with fixed topmasts.

Barent's vessel was destroyed by the pressure of the ice at Novaya Zemlya. From the remains of the shipwreck the crew built a winter dwelling place in which, as far as is known, Europeans wintered for the first time in the Arctic. (JOHN NURMINEN FOUNDATION)

---

investors, and as a result Frobisher set out on a new voyage the very next spring.

The little fleet consisted of three ships, all of which stayed together this time. The primary aim of the voyage was Kodlunarn Island, where the black stone had been found. By 23 August Frobisher had collected 200 tons of black ore which the expedition's German mineralogist ascertained to be rich. No sign of the seamen captured by the Eskimos the previous year was found. All of the ships arrived safely back in England. In recognition Martin Frobisher received a one-hundred-pound reward from the Queen who christened the new land "Meta Incognita".

Frobisher's third journey can no longer be described as an expedition. The lust for gold superseded the search for the Passage. During the voyage, the fleet of 15 vessels fell into the grip of a storm close to their destination and some of them were crushed by the ice. After the storm Frobisher drifted into a new channel which he sailed for twenty days or so before turning back to attend to his main task, leading the mining venture. Thus, it seems, he fell short of discovering Hudson Bay.

When the expedition returned to England they were in for a surprise. The ore brought from the previous journey had proved to be worthless. The Cathay Company (the China Trading Company), which had been established for the purpose, went bankrupt, as did the initiator and chief financier of the voyage, Michael Lok. Martin Frobisher returned to his usual occupation. Relations between England and Spain became strained and a war broke out between the two. Queen Elizabeth set Francis Drake, John Hawkins and Martin Frobisher to defend England from the Spanish Armada of 1588. Eventually Drake and Frobisher were knighted and were promoted to the rank of Admiral.

DAVIS AND HUDSON

As the thirst for gold subsided, interest in the Northwest Passage waned. A new North-West Company was licensed by the Queen in 1584. John Davis, a quiet and unassuming man who was one of the best seafarers of his day, was chosen to lead a new expedition. Davis has also gone down in the history of seafaring for the fact that he wrote a textbook on navigation, *The Seaman's Secrets,* and developed the Davis backstaff by means of which it was easier to measure the elevation of the sun.

Davis set out on his first voyage in June 1585. The expedition comprised of two ships. Davis too came first to the south-eastern tip of Greenland. Just like Frobisher, he too failed to identify the island and called it only by the name "Land of Desolation". After rounding Cape Farewell and sailing along the west coast near to what is now Nuuk (Godthåb)

he encountered Eskimos. These Greenland Eskimos were friendly and enjoyed a performance given by four musicians that Davis had on board. Davis continued further west, landed on what was later named Baffin Island and charted Exeter and Cumberland Sounds, which he named.

Davis' next voyage was fruitless. He could no longer find Cumberland Sound, which he believed to be the entrance to the Northwest Passage. His only pleasant experience was the Eskimos who remembered with enthusiasm the performances of his musicians the previous year. Now Davis noticed a weakness in the Eskimos: they had a tendency to steal English property.

A group of London merchants sent Davis off on a voyage once again. To balance the finances of the expedition two of Davis' vessels remained further south to fish while Davis himself went north all the way to the region now known as

64 Martin Frobisher's life was full of variety and adventure. As a fourteen-year-old he went along on a sailing trip to West Africa and was one of the survivors. Ten years later he was taken hostage by the Portuguese. He later became the captain of a privateer which plundered French and Spanish trading ships; the difference between what was legal and illegal was undefined. Frobisher also spent some time in jail. His three journeys to the waters of Baffin Land between 1576–1578 made Arctic history. With England driven into war with Spain he distinguished himself, was knighted and promoted to Admiral. He died from a bullet wound in 1594.
(BODLEIAN LIBRARY)

Upernavik. On the return journey Davis followed the coast of Baffin Island and re-discovered Cumberland Sound. He passed another large sound without investigating it to any extent. This, it seems, was Hudson Strait. Davis' third voyage was not a success either. The English abandoned their exploration of the north and concentrated on repulsing the great Armada sent by Philip II of Spain.

One of the Muscovy Company's enterprises is still worth mentioning. Since China could not be reached by a Northeast or a Northwest passage, all that remained was the direct route by way of the Pole suggested by Thorne. In 1607 the merchants of London chose Henry Hudson, who was a skilful seafarer but not the greatest of leaders, to carry out this venture.

On his first voyage Hudson progressed to Spitsbergen as far as latitude 80° and explored the west coast of the islands, but the ice prevented him from going any further. Hudson saw seals, polar bears and whales and named one of the bays he discovered Whale Sound. On his second voyage in 1608 he tried once more to find a Northeast Passage to China. At Novaya Zemlya, he too ran into such impenetrable ice that he no longer believed in the existence of a Northeast Passage.

After undertaking a journey for the Dutch to what was later named New York and discovering the River Hudson he was given the task of sailing to the strait which Frobisher, Davis and Waymouth had seen but not explored. On 9 June 1602 Hudson pushed his way into the strait bearing his name and followed its south coast all the way to the entrance to Hudson Bay. From here he followed the east coast all the way to James Bay.

Hudson had run into difficulties with his men earlier and now the crew refused to go further south into the bay but Hudson, by explaining his plan, persuaded them to continue. In September his crew, led by the Mate, rose up against him again in James Bay. Hudson relieved his Mate of his duties and named Robert Bylot to take his place. During winter they suffered from scurvy and one of the crew died. Their provisions diminished threateningly and they feared these would not last for the journey home. When, in July, Hudson's vessel the *Discovery* set sail, a mutiny broke out. Hudson, his son and six other members of the crew, two of whom were sick, were forced into a boat and left to their fate without food or weapons. The ship's carpenter, still faithful to his captain, joined the company. No trace of Hudson and his men has been found since then. The crew of the *Discovery* caught birds from the islands as provisions for the journey. Four of the men were killed by Eskimos but the rest returned to England, where all of them except Bylot were accused of mutiny.

After a trial three of the mutineers were freed. According to Richard Vaughan, the fact that Bylot and one of the mutineers were able to prove that a Northwest Passage had not been found was decisive. A new expedition was fitted out immediately.

In 1612 Bylot sailed north again with Sir Thomas Button with the aim of finding a route leading from northern

America to the Pacific. After Button, the Dane Jens Munk explored Hudson Bay in 1619 and spent the winter on the River Churchill at the southern coast of Hudson Bay. Neither wine nor beer rations, nor yet the berries that were revealed under the snow in March and which Munk's crew picked as medicine, saved them from scurvy. Of the crew of 65, only Jens Munk and three others were still alive in June. Munk and his companions succeeded in sailing their small sloop the *Lamprey* back to Norway.

65 *Henry Hudson was a good seafarer but not nearly as good a leader. On his last journey in 1610 he and his men wintered in Hudson Bay. With the arrival of spring they ran out of food. The men mutinied and forced Hudson and his son, as well as all the sick men, into a boat and left them a musket, powder and a few shots. Nothing was ever heard of them again. The painting, by John Collier, depicts Hudson and his son and the faithful carpenter who volunteered to go with Hudson.* (TATE GALLERY, LONDON)

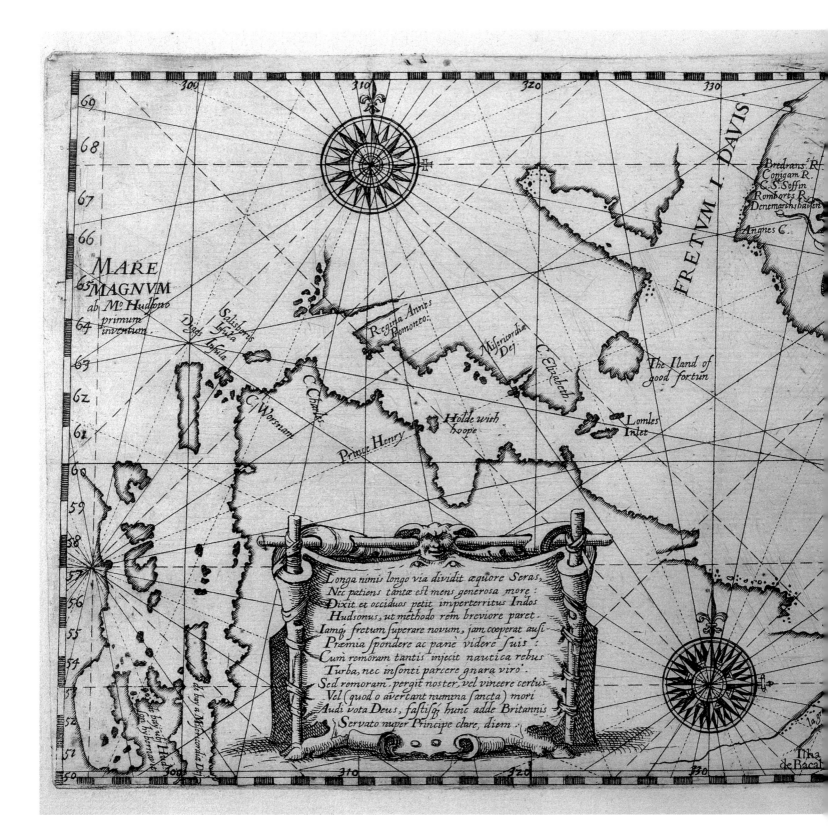

66 Robert Bylot was Henry Hudson's mate on what was to be his last expedition to Hudson Bay. Although the rebellious crew abandoned Hudson, Bylot brought the maps of the voyage with him and the Dutchman Hessel Gerritz drew a map based on them "of the great sea that Hudson had discovered". It was the first map to have Hudson Bay marked on it. Samuel Champlain immediately added the bay to his own map. Of the map's faults, the greatest is that Frobisher Bay is drawn in the wrong place. The Frisland of Zeno's narrative is also on the map, as is the phantom island, Buss.

Gerritz drew up valuable sea charts of the great oceans, particularly the North Atlantic. The greater number of his charts were drawn up on parchment in the manner of the Mediterranean portolan charts. Seafarers favoured this kind of chart, as skin was a durable material. A bronze engraving was made of the Hudson Bay chart, which is why numerous impressions of it have been preserved printed on paper.

(JOHN NURMINEN FOUNDATION)

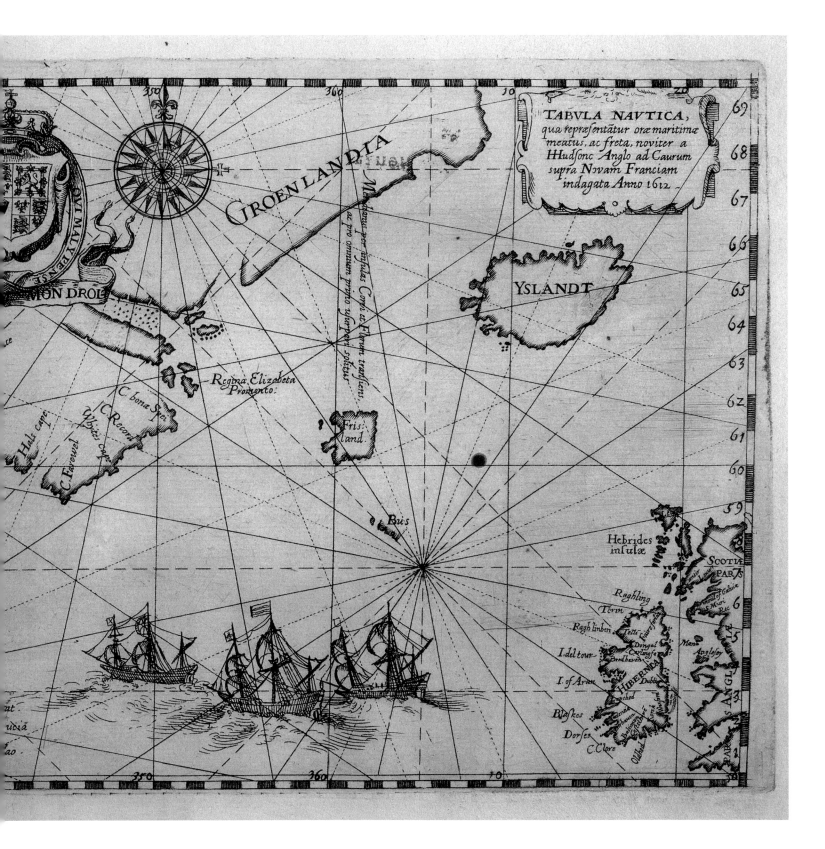

Hudson Bay was explored thoroughly at the beginning of the 17th century. Thomas James and Luke Foxe, whose names live on in the place names of Hudson Bay, continued to chart the area. Since Hudson Bay is in effect a dead end, a Northwest Passage was not found.

William Baffin and Robert Bylot also continued to explore Hudson Bay. In 1615 they sailed north through the Davis Strait. They discovered three great sounds off Baffin Bay; the Smith, Jones and Lancaster Sounds. Although they did not push on further, they discovered the key to the Northwest Passage. Yet in spite of their achievements Baffin and Bylot have remained secondary figures, because their diaries and maps were never published. The Sounds that Baffin discovered were not even marked on maps published in England at the beginning of the 19th century, on the basis of which Baffin's successors continued their exploration. Baffin himself is probably partly responsible for this. Albert Markham, an explorer and biographer of Baffin, tells of Baffin saying that neither a Northwest Passage nor "even the hope of a Northwest Passage" were found to the north of the Davis Strait.

ZENO, MERCATOR AND THE IMAGINARY ISLANDS
OF THE NORTH ATLANTIC

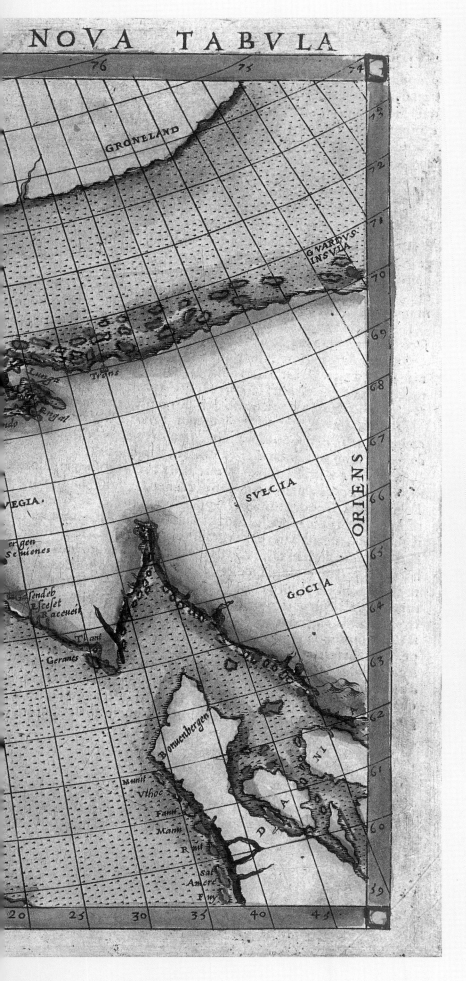

Marco Polo's famous description of his 13th century journey to Mongolia and China acted as an important spur for the great voyages of exploration. The second important publication from the point of view of the development of a cartographic picture of the world was Nicolò Zeno the Younger's account of the adventures of his forefathers in the North Atlantic, which was published in Venice in 1558. The work achieved great popularity and later appeared translated into English in Richard Hakluyt's famous series of travel accounts, *Voyages, Navigations, Traffiques and Discoveries of the English Nation*. A map of the North Atlantic published in conjunction with Zeno's account had a far-reaching effect on cartography.

Zeno the Younger based his account on an exchange of correspondence that had come into his possession via his family archives and which he destroyed after finishing his own version. In the letters his distant forefathers, the seafarer and navigator Nicolò Zeno and his brother Antonio Zeno, tell of their adventures in the North Atlantic. A fierce storm washed Nicolò onto Frisland Island, where he met the mighty ruler Zichmni. Nicolò's mission took him to many other islands and he invited his brother to join him from Venice. The brothers lived for several years on Frisland, where Nicolò was to die. After an absence of more than ten years, Antonio returned to his home town, where he had sent his brother Carlo the letters and maps that would form the subject matter for his publication.

The descriptions of the Zeno brothers' journeys contained a great deal of interesting information on the north, although Nicolò Zeno the Younger's account is largely the product of his imagination. The account does contain details which fit the picture of conditions in the north, a fact that gives credence to an actual journey having taken place. Iceland (Islanda) and Greenland (Engronelant) can be recognised from it. In addition, it mentions other islands; Drogeo, Estotiland, Icaria, Estland, Neome, Podanda and the largest and best-known Frisland. On Nicolò's map these islands are situated in the Atlantic, between Scotland and Greenland. On the first version of the map, Greenland extends all the way to Eurasia in the north, blocking off the Northeast Passage. According to Ulla Ehrensvärd, Zeno used Clavus' depiction of the north as the basis for his map. Many of Clavus' ideas and mistakes are repeated on his map.

67 *The imaginary islands of the Zeno brothers' voyages were depicted for the first time on a wood engraving by Nicoló Zeno the younger in 1558. Greenland was still a peninsula of the continent of Europe. The imaginary islands Estland, Frisland, Icaria and Estotiland could be seen to the west of Norway. Europe's leading cartographers drew the islands on their maps for more than a hundred years and seafarers sought them in vain in the North Atlantic.* (JOHN NUMISEN SÄÄTIÖ)

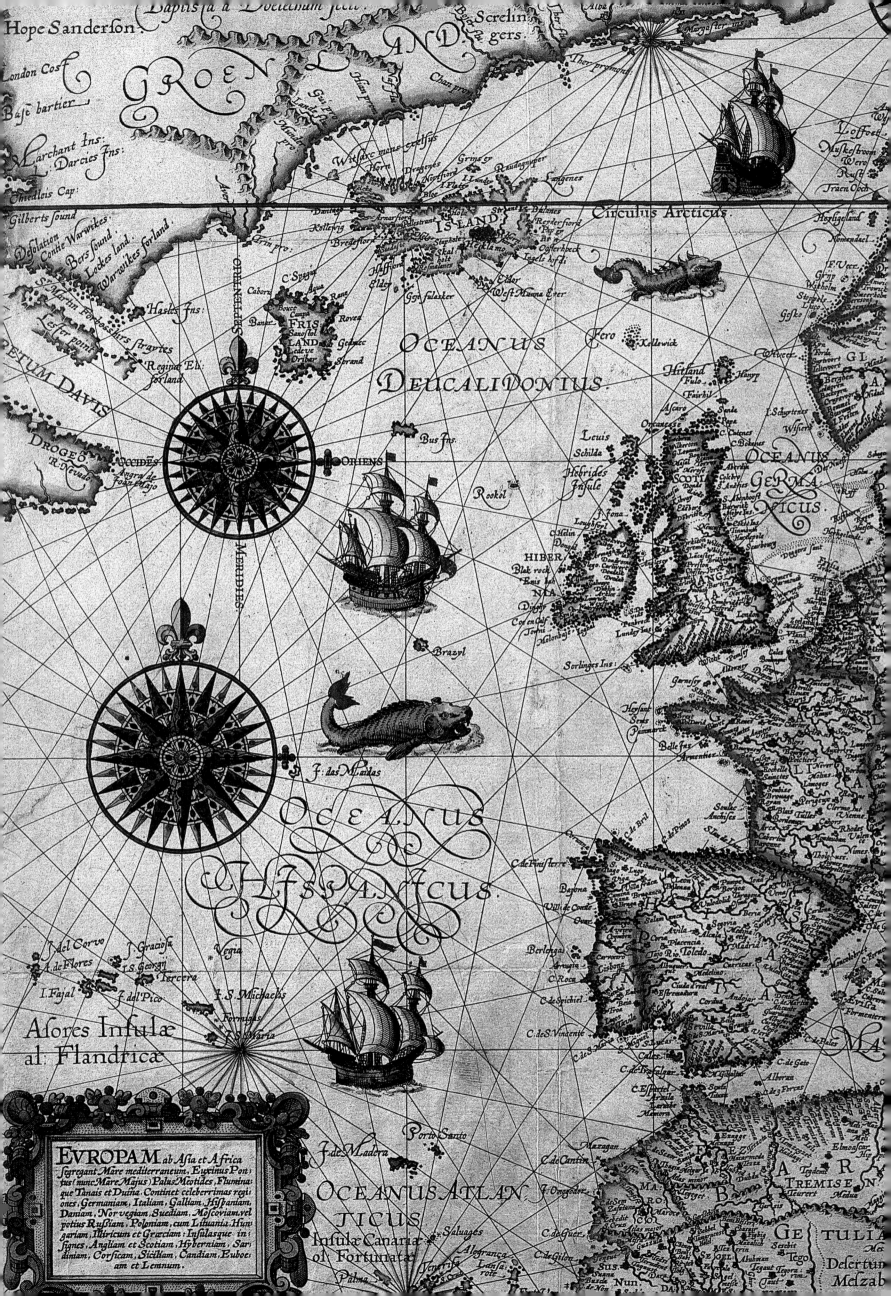

Most of the historians and cartographers of Zeno's time accepted these accounts with some reservations, and some parts of them were still believed in the 19th century. Mercator considered most of the description to be correct, as did Ortelius in his commercial atlas, and the cartographer, scientist and advocate of polar expeditions, Petrus Plancius. Mercator, in particular, had great influence on the spread of Zeno's maps.

The first of Zeno's mistakes to be corrected was the idea that Greenland was connected to the Eurasian continent. Frisland and the other imaginary islands of the North Atlantic haunted maps for much longer. Frisland was printed on most 17th century maps of the world. A map of Frisland made by an unknown 16th century Italian cartographer is kept in the Newberry library in Chicago. Even details of the island's towns and ports are drawn on it. These have their roots in Nicolò's description.

The Zeno material has been thoroughly researched and its mistakes finally came to light in the 19th century. The places in the north in the account were apparently the Orkneys, Shetlands and Faroe Islands to the north of Britain, possibly also Iceland and Greenland. In the 14th century, the Irish, Scottish and, above all, the Vikings travelled in the area. Nicolò Zeno the Younger obtained the subjects for his accounts from these seafarers. According to Nordenskiöld, it is the history of the Vikings that forms the basis for

68 Petrus Plancius (1552–1622) was a Dutch theologian and cartographer who made maps for the Dutch East India Company. He used his influence to support several northern voyages. He was also a teacher of seafaring skills and geography as well as an instructor of competent pilots. Plancius had a positive influence on Barent's voyages too. His maps were made with exceptional skill and are often recognised for the distinct handiwork of the engraver extraordinaire van Doetichum, like this map from 1594. It shows Zeno's Friesland and the mythical island Buss in the middle of the North Atlantic. (John Nurminen Foundation)

69 Gerard De Jode's knowledge of the northern parts of the globe is in keeping with the perceptions of his time. His depiction contains Anian Strait, the northern polar islands and Zeno's phantom islands. The map in the picture is a section of a larger map by De Jode that depicts both hemispheres. It was published in Antwerp in 1593. (John Nurminen Foundation)

these accounts. Many of the place names are of Scandinavian origin or suggest the history of the island's settlement. In 1200 a large cathedral was built in Greenland's Gardar, to which some of the details in the account perhaps refer.

The ideas presented on the Zeno map are not unique. The same names and locations already appear on the Zamoiski map of 1467, which is kept in Warsaw's National Library. Fikslanda, which resembles Zeno's Frisland, is mentioned on Mateo Prunes' map of 1553. When Fikslanda is compared with the shape of Iceland and the small islands surrounding it are re-examined, it becomes apparent that Iceland was the basis for both Fikslanda and Frisland. A kind of duplication has happened on the Zeno map, and information which Zeno the Younger's forefathers possibly drew from the stories of sailors has been 'superimposed' on the new island. Explanations for Zeno's other ghost islands can also be found, based on the Atlantic journeys of men from the north. There might even have been Venetian sailors on board during these voyages.

On Mercator's, Ortelius' and Plancius' maps the island of Buss, smaller than Zeno's imaginary islands, can be seen in the North Atlantic. This ghost island has a direct association with the search for the Northwest Passage undertaken by the English and particularly with Sir Martin Frobisher's third and last Arctic expedition in 1578. On the expedition's return journey, passengers on Frobisher's ship the *Emmanuel* were the first to observe the island of Buss. Frobisher had with him a Mercator map of 1569, which he had bought for more than a pound in London and on which Zeno's islands were marked. The map was based on the excellent new projection, but some of its locational data were incorrect. When he was sailing along the coast of Greenland, Frobisher thought Greenland was Frisland, because he was at latitude 60° where Mercator had placed the island. Donald S. Johnson has shown that Frobisher was probably driven by ocean currents close to the tip of Greenland and that the island of Buss seen "in the middle of the open sea" was in fact part of the Greenland coast. In this way an observation of the coast based on an incorrect location became a new island.

As far as is known, the island of Buss appears for the first time on Plancius' world map of 1594. Plancius was a friend of Henry Hudson. Hudson did not return from the journey he made in 1610–1611

to the bay bearing his name, but news of the new discoveries came to Hessel Gerritsz by way of the mutinous crew. In 1612 he published a map based on these discoveries, on which the facts about Greenland and Baffin Island became a little confused. The island of Buss was located somewhere between Greenland and Iceland, to the south of what proved to be the non-existent Frisland (See p. 96).

Buss remained on the map and in the imagination of seafarers for more than 200 years. John Seller even drew up a map of the island itself, showing its special features. On the well-known sea charts produced by the Van Keulen family enterprise, the island of Buss had shrunk to a shoal less than one third of a mile long by the middle of the 18th century. Once the North Atlantic had been sailed sufficiently, the island faded into history and, in the 19th century, disappeared from maps for ever.

Researchers have found many more imaginary islands on old maps of the Atlantic. These include Antillia, often depicted to the west of the Azores, Hy-Brazil to the west of Ireland and St. Brendan, which was located in several places between Europe and America. The Isle of the Devil was to be found off the east coast of North America. There is a history behind the birth of all these islands. The roots of Antillia lie in Antique mythology, Hy-Brazil is probably the result of mirages typical of the area, and behind St. Brendan are the sea-voyages of a priest of the same name, who was later declared a saint, and the myths attached to them.

The story of the Isle of the Devil is a curious one. After Cartier, the French made many journeys to Saint Lawrence Bay. On one of the voyages a maiden of noble birth was guilty of the sin of falling in love with a member of the crew. As punishment, the couple were left on a deserted island. The maiden was later rescued and told of the demoniacal experiences she had had. Devil's Island is usually situated off Newfoundland and Labrador, close to L'Anse aux Meadows, the place in America where archaeological digs first uncovered what proved to be a Viking settlement.

HEMISPHERIV AB ÆQVINOCTIALI LINEA, AD CIRCVLV POLI A: TARCTICI.

THE RUSSIANS ARE COMING

When visiting the White Sea, the Viking Ottar met only Permians. The Novgorod Chronicles of 1096, however, relate that fur traders from that part of the world traded with the 'Jugrians', that is to say the Ugrians. The Ugrians lived in an area which extended from the southern part of Novaya Zemlya, from the mouth of the Pechora River, which flowed into the Barents Sea, to the Urals.

In the 12th century the Novgorodians were familiar with the coast of the Arctic Ocean as far as the Urals and perhaps even as far as the Ob estuary. They sent troops to subjugate the Jurgi. The Russians were also taking an interest in the westerly direction. A Russian expedition is known to have set out from the Severnaya Dvina and to have sailed to Norway in 1320.

Kholmogory, established in 1353, was one of the first Russian bases in the White Sea area. Monasteries were also built in the White Sea area and these strengthened Russia's hold on the coasts of the Arctic. When the Muscovites overthrew Novgorod in 1478, Ivan III took matters into his own hands. The Tartars closed the road to the east. Ivan sent several civilian and military expeditions to the Urals and the River Ob. Russia increased her knowledge of both the Tartars and the Samoyeds of the Ob district. The town of Archangel was founded at the Severnaya Dvina estuary in 1584 to take care of trade to both the west and to the east of the great rivers of Siberia.

CONQUERING THE COASTS OF SIBERIA

The next step towards gaining ascendancy in the Arctic area was the decision of Czar Boris Godunov to establish the inland town of Mangazeya on the River Taz which flowed into a fork of the Gulf of Ob. The fortifications built to secure the town were probably completed in 1601. The purpose of the fortifications was to ensure the safety of Russian fur trappers as they hunted the prized Siberian sable, whose fur tithes were an important source of income to Moscow.

By way of Mangazeya it was easy to move along the rivers and isthmuses that connected them to the Yenisey, central Siberia's important waterway, and from there even further. Although the town flourished at the beginning of the 17th century, its inhabitants were evacuated to Turukhansk on the banks of the Yenisey in 1672. The town was abandoned because the sable stock plummeted and the focus of interest for the conquest of Siberia shifted eastwards.

The most important expedition was a military venture led by the Cossack Yermak Timofeyevich, through which the Russians began the complete their occupation of Siberia. The expedition was apparently organised by a merchant by the name of Stroganov who had been given the licence to trade in the areas east of the Urals by Ivan IV. Yermak was a Cossack, one of those free Russians who did not wish to tie himself to the land – to be a serf. In 1581 Yermak assembled his troops, according to one source consisting of 340 Cossacks, and advanced from the Volga to Perm and onwards to the Urals along old waterways, crossing the Urals along a 500-metre-high pass. He spent the following winter at a camp in the mountains. In the spring Yermak and his horde pushed into the area controlled by the Tartars near what are now the towns of Tobolsk and Omsk on the banks of the Ob and its tributary the Irtysh. He overpowered the Tartars but later ran into trouble that not even the reinforcements sent from Moscow could save him from. One night in 1585 the Tartars surprised Yermak and his forces and killed them as they slept.

A new division of soldiers under the leadership of Ivan Mansurov stabilised the Russians position, however. Yermak's expedition had opened up Siberia to the Russians once and for all and they were now able to make their way towards the east along the coast too.

They made their way there only in small steps. The most important navigable routes were not to be found on the northern coast but along the rivers of Siberia. In summer, however, it was easy to move from one river to another by way of the coast. Their vessels were usually of the wooden koch type, which had one mast and which could take 30

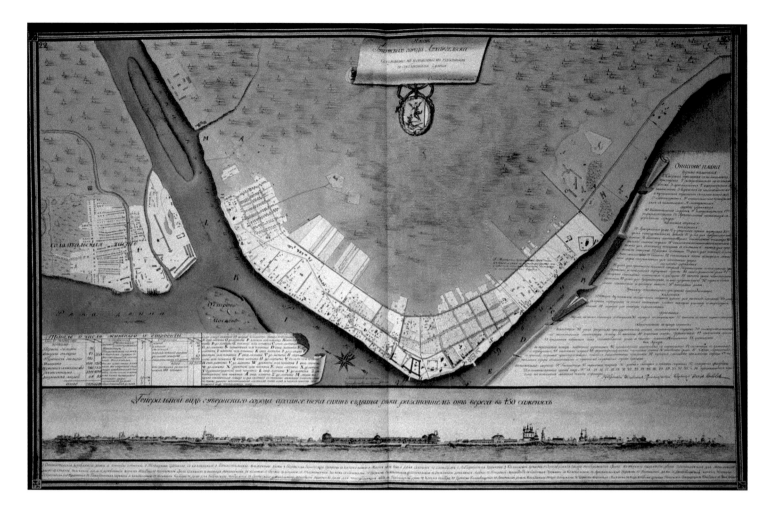

70 A land reform was implemented in Russia in 1775. Its purpose was to strengthen feudal power at the local level, in the Gubernias. The reform required more precise and serviceable maps of important areas. The map with white Archangel glistening on the coast is drawn particularly skilfully. The town silhouette depicted on the water's edge increases the beauty of the hand-made map. It is also of help to sailors. (RUSSIAN STATE ARCHIVES)

passengers and a cargo of 30 tons. Often when the Cossacks had crossed an isthmus and arrived at a new river they felled trees and built a ship. The primary aim of these men was often not to find and map new regions but to seek better hunting or fishing grounds.

In 1610 Kondratiy Kurochkin sailed east along the coast from the Yenisey estuary to the next river, the Pyasina, located west of the Taymyr Peninsula. Four years later a fort was built there as a base for fur trading. A few years later Czar Mikhail Fedorovich forbade foreigners to navigate any waters east of the White Sea; western merchants were allowed to sail to Archangel but no further. The decision was possibly a precautionary measure aimed at the Dutch and the English whom the Tsar knew to be seeking a sea-route to China. During subsequent decades the ban was forgotten.

The next step east was the exploration of the River Lena. The first expedition made its way there as early as the 1620s along the Lower Tunguska, a tributary of the Yenisey. The upper reaches of this river extended very close to the Lena. The Russians gradually tightened their hold on the middle reaches of the Lena in the Yakuts region where the first fortifications were built in 1632.

The following year, under the leadership of the officer Ilya Perfiryev and the Cossack Ivan Rebrov, the Russians were already advancing to the sea at the Lena Delta. While Perfiryev was making his way east to the River Yana, Rebrov sailed west to the River Olenek. Fortifications were built to safeguard trade with the Yakuts in the middle reaches of the Yana at Verkhoyansk which was known for its coldness. Rebrov went from the River Olenek to the Yana and continued his explorations. In 1638 he discovered the previously unknown River Indigirka estuary. The Russian expeditions did not reach the Taimyr Peninsula. Most years the ice conditions of the Taimyr were very difficult, so that the Russians made their way east along the rivers and sailed from the interior to the river estuaries. The Taimyr Peninsula between the rivers Pyasina and Olenek therefore remained unexplored.

The conquerors advanced further towards the east. Mikhail Stadukhin landed at the River Indigirka estuary, continued east and, in 1643, was the first man to discover the River Kolyma. Stadukhin claimed to have seen land to the north but nobody has seen this land since. After building a base at Kolyma and collecting furs for two years, Stadukhin and his companions built a ship and sailed with their valuable cargo back to the Lena. This voyage opened up lively traffic between these two rivers.

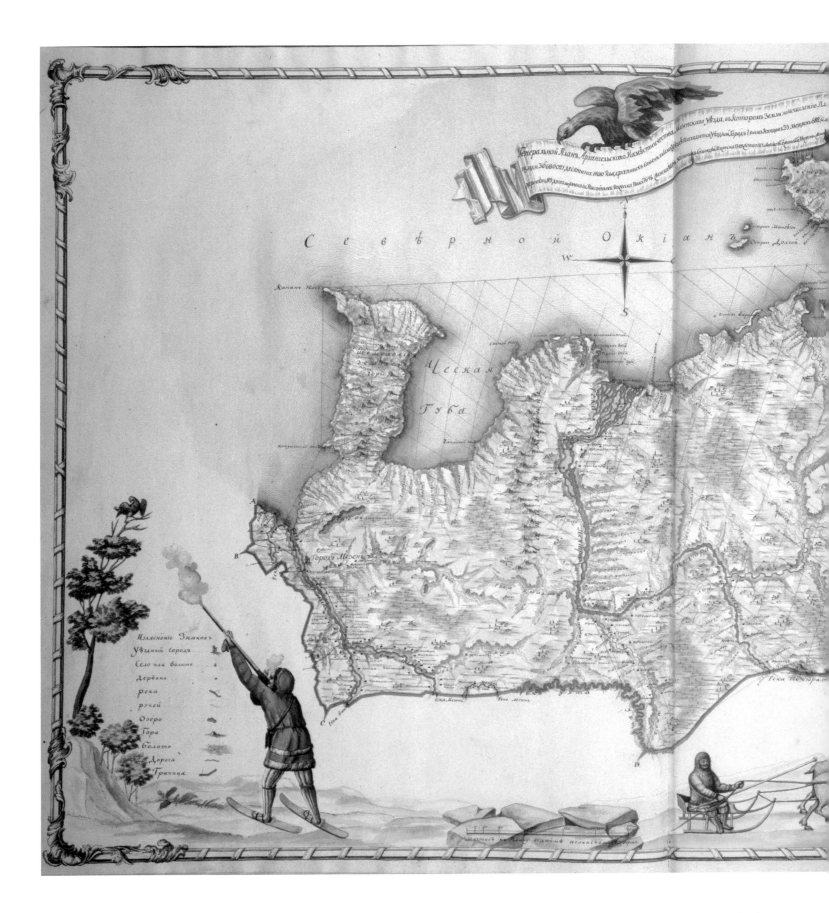

TOWARDS THE STRAIT BETWEEN
ASIA AND AMERICA

It is surprising that the greatest Russian expedition sank into oblivion for close on a century. Information about the voyage of Semen Dezhnev and his companions spread only 90 years later when the German Gerhard Friedrich Müller found Dezhnev's report in the Yakutsk archives in 1736.

Dezhnev had joined the Cossacks in his youth and worked in the area of the Lena, Yana and Indigirka rivers collecting the Crown's tithes. In the 1640s he worked with Mikhail Stadukhin in the Kolyma region. Fur trappers had heard of the Anadyr River and of the riches to its east. Fedor Alekseyev wanted to be the first to reap the benefit of these hunting grounds, and on his request Semen Dezhnev was ordered along as representative of the Government. His first attempt in

71 *Russian expansion to the east had begun by the 16th century. Yermak made expeditions of conquest into the interior. The Russians had already reached the coast of the Arctic Ocean during the Novgorod era. They conducted foreign trade via the White Sea and their interests extended to the north-east, into the areas where the Samoyed and Nenet lived. A map made in the 18th century depicts the stretches of coast from the Mezen River to the Vaigats Strait. Novaya Zemlya , which is located at the north of the Vaigats Strait does not fit on the map. In the middle of the map the Pechora River, an important trade route, flows into the Arctic Ocean. The hand-made map depicts the indigenous people near their homes as well as deer, which the Samoyed domesticated. The hunter on the left tells of Russian interest in fur hunting in the area. Fur-bearing animals, particularly the sable, tempted the Russians ever further east.* (RUSSIAN STATE ARCHIVES)

on the basis of the values of the day, corresponded to 27 red fox, 20 ermine or 180 squirrel skins. The third group included trappers led by the Cossack Gerasim Ankudinov.

The expedition set out on 20 June 1648 and of the journey itself precious little is known. We do know that the journey was stormy because four of the vessels were shipwrecked not long after the expedition set out. On 20 September, what remained of Dezhnev's, Alekseyev's and Ankudinov's fleet had already progressed beyond a strait at the easternmost tip of the Chukchi Peninsula which Cook would later name the Bering Strait and which Dezhnev and his companions found in 1681. There they became involved in a battle with the Chukchi. Alekseyev's ship became separated from the rest in storms in October and nothing has been heard of it since. Ankudinov's ship was probably lost too because there are no longer any signs of it either. Finally the ship led by Dezhnev was shipwrecked at the southern part of the Anadyr.

Dezhnev led his 25-man expedition – some of whom were probably survivors from the other ships – to the lower reaches of the River Anadyr ten weeks after the expedition had set out. Here they built the first Russian colony. Dezhnev remained in the area for 12 years.

After two years, reinforcements led by Stadukhin arrived at the Anadyr having made their way by the shortest overland route. Stadukhin had in fact tried to sail in Dezhnev's wake the following summer but the ice had prevented him.

A good 200 years later, in 1878, A. E. Nordenskiöld would sail past Kolyma and spend the winter on the Chukchi Peninsula only a few hundred miles from the Bering Strait. He christened Asia's easternmost peninsular Cape Dezhnev in Dezhnev's honour. Its official Russian name is now Mys Dezhneva. The Russians took the name into use in 1898 on the 250th anniversary of Dezhnev's journey.

Müller's finds did not convince all researchers that Semen Dezhnev had rounded the Chukchi Peninsula and sailed through the Bering Strait. The arguments continued almost up to the 300 anniversary of Dezhnev's journey. The decisive proof was the rocky peninsula, described by Dezhnev,

1647 failed because of the ice barriers. The expedition had seven vessels in all and the party consisted of three very different groups. Fedor Alekseyev led the 30-strong group of fur hunters and tradesmen, and Dezhnev the group of people in government service into which some twenty hunters had been recruited. Dezhnev's task was to protect Alekseyev's group and to collect the fur taxes due to the state. He was to collect 280 sable skins from the River Anadyr, each of which,

extending far into the sea, whose direction was, roughly speaking, east-west. In front of the peninsula were two islands inhabited by the Chukchi. In addition the tip of the peninsula pointed south to the River Anadyr. Its distance from the river was a three-day and three-night journey.

Cook visited the peninsula, which he named East Cape, in 1776. He knew of the extra peninsula appearing on Müller's map and was convinced that East Cape was Dezhnev's rocky peninsula. Some researchers suspected the Dezhnev Peninsula to be Mys Shelagski (Cape Shelagski) situated in the northwest. Dezhnev was assumed to have crossed the Chukchi by land. Later researchers, however, believe the peninsula that

72 Perhaps the most important achievement of Bering's second expedition was the charting of the Arctic Ocean coast. The whole of the coast stretching from Archangel to the Bering Strait was divided into four parts, to each of which was assigned a mapper. The names of those responsible and the date of charting are marked on the map. The ice made exploration difficult and the coast of Taimyr in particular was charted during the winter, which understandably meant that accuracy suffered. (Patanen)

was discovered by Semen Dezhnev to be East Cape.

Thanks to Dezhnev, the Siberian Russians were aware that there was a strait between Asia and America as early as the 1670s. In addition to Dezhnev, fur trappers were in continuous contact with the Chukchi and the Eskimos, and this fact became established knowledge. But the Russians only learnt of Kamchatka, a peninsula separating the Okhotsk and Bering Seas, while establishing their position in Anadyr, in around 1690. The first expedition south took place as early as 1696, but it was only the following year that the Cossack officer Vladimir Atlasov was given the task by the government of conquering the peninsula.

Atlasov set off from Yakutsk, made his way to the Kolyma and from there to the Anadyr. The expedition burned and destroyed a large native village at the mouth of the River Kamchatka, killing as many natives as they were able.

As a reward for his journey to Kamchatka, Moscow gave Atlasov the rank of Commandant, a position that he lost when pillaging a Russian caravan carrying valuable Chinese articles. Atlasov was imprisoned but was freed later to calm down the infuriated Cossacks and to quell the resistance

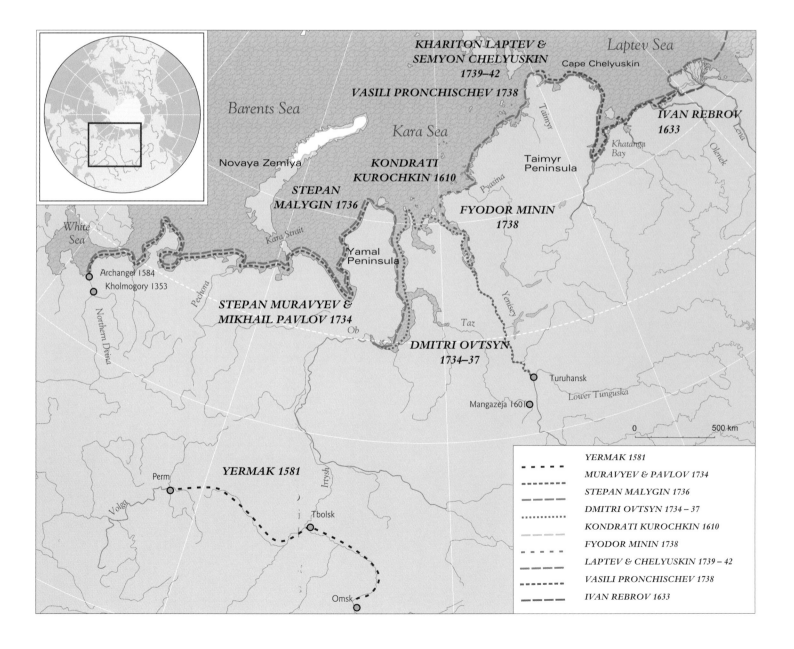

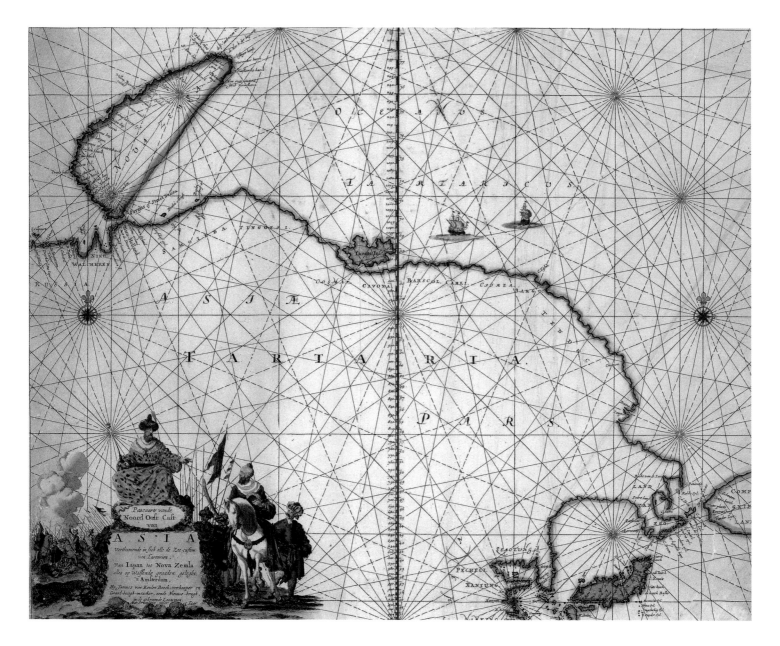

which had risen among the indigenous people. He recognised only one way of calming people down: killing them. Eventually Atlasov was killed by his own troops in 1711. Gradually the situation stabilised and the Russian position was strengthened.

PETER THE GREAT
AND BERING'S FIRST EXPEDITION

Peter the Great, who succeeded to the Russian throne in 1689, wanted Russia to be more than just a mill for the production of furs, and which exported hemp, tar and timber from its almost limitless forests. Peter founded a modern steel and armaments industry in Russia. He needed arms to consolidate Russia's position in the Baltic Sea area and to ensure access to the sea from elsewhere than Archangel. Peter was also interested in science. He established a Science Academy and recruited western scientists as its members.

It was Atlasov's discoveries that finally awakened Peter's interest in the border regions of Asia and the eastern limits of his kingdom. Atlasov had reported that a long and difficult-

73 The Van Keulen family of Amsterdam produced sea charts for several generations. It is apparent from the map of North Siberia and particularly its coast how inadequate geographical knowledge of the area still was in the 18th century. The map estimates the distance from Franz Josef Land to Bering Strait as being too short and describes the coast of the Arctic Ocean as easy to navigate. The Russians had not yet begun the mapping of North Siberia. The big river bays and deltas and the entire broad Taimyr Peninsula area stretching into the north are missing from the map. Neither does Van Keulen's map tell anything of the Chukchi Peninsula. Seafarers valued Van Keulen's maps and bought them from his shop in Amsterdam before sailing on long voyages.
(JOHN NURMINEN FOUNDATION)

to-reach peninsula, stretching far into the sea, existed between the rivers Kolyma and Anadyr. On the northern coast of this peninsula the sea was icy in summer, and in winter was completely frozen over.

In 1717 Peter went to France and held discussions with members of the French Academy. They suggested to him the despatching of an expedition to explore the border between

74 The expedition made to the North Pacific by Lieutenant Ivan Stindt in 1799 produced a lot of incorrect information on the maps of the time. The information made its way to a certain extent onto the maps of Müller and Stählin. The coast of America was depicted as a group of large islands. Cook had the maps in question with him and he found them to be inaccurate. In 1778 the engineer Captain Ivan Kurbakov drew up a map of the Russian Empire based partly on the same sources. Its purpose was to tell of both the conquests of and expeditions to Siberia. A large imaginary island is situated in the Bering Strait and the Aleuts are depicted as a wide cluster of islands. The large island appears on many western maps of the time under the name Unalaska.
(RUSSIAN STATE ARCHIVES)

Asia and America. Asia interested the French, since it had interests of its own to Canada. Peter sent an expedition himself, however, under the leadership of the Danish-born Vitus Bering. He signed the order for it to be carried out on 3 December 1742, only one month before his death.

No good map existed yet of the eastern areas of Siberia. As leader of an expanding country with growing trade and industry, Peter was interested in the development of cartography. His interest was not completely academic, however. There has been heated scientific debate over what Peter's aims were in deciding on Bering's task. In addition to the Russians, the debate was joined by American professor Raymond Fisher who, with his associates, has claimed that Peter did not

76 Peter the Great was a guest at the French Science Academy in 1717. Its members asked for permission to organise an expedition to find out if there was a physical link between Asia and America. Peter rejected the proposal but promised to consider sending a Russian expedition. He gave his orders to Bering a few weeks before his death. The orders make no mention of a possible strait but urge Bering to sail to America or a land in its immediate vicinity and acquire information on its settlement. Bering never accomplished this. (CENTRAL MARITIME MUSEUM, ST. PETERSBURG)

75 The Dane Vitus Bering had served in the Russian navy since 1703 and had advanced to the rank of Captain First Class. Peter the Great proposed that he should explore the strait that was presumed to have existed between Asia and America. Bering skilfully organised the transportation of equipment and men to the Kamchatka coast. The results of the sea journey of the First Expedition were modest, however. Bering died and was buried on the Komendorsky Islands (now the Bering Islands) in December 1741, his vessel having run aground on the coast. On the basis of finds at the grave a Danish-Russian research group reconstructed Bering's facial features in clay. An earlier, generally accepted picture, was in fact presented by Bering's uncle. (HORSENS MUSEUM)

send Bering to clarify whether or not a strait separated the Asian and American continents, but to determine to what extent the Empire was able to expand to the east. When interpreting Bering's sailing instructions there is reason to examine Homann's map of Kamchatka of 1725. It was published at Peter's request and was known by him when drawing up his orders for Vitus Bering.

On the basis of the map, Peter's instructions can be interpreted to mean that Bering's task was to sail east of Kamchatka and to follow the southern coast of the unknown Juan de Gama marked on the map. After this he was to turn north and to find out where this land joined the American continent. In addition Bering was to call at the nearest "European" town and gather all information on the area. Bering was perhaps given this map with his instructions when leaving St Petersburg. The preparations for both of Bering's expeditions, which involved transporting essential requisites through Siberia along rivers, and across the watershed regions which connected the rivers and which were completely without roads, form a unique part of the history of Arctic expeditions. It was not the least of Bering's achievements.

In January, 1724 Bering set out from the city of St. Petersburg along with his two closest officers, the Dane Martin Spangberg, who understood and spoke Russian badly, and a promising young Lieutenant by the name of Aleksey Chirikov. Their convoy consisted of 25 wagons and 26 men. Taking with them equipment for ship building and necessities for the journey, they arrived at the River Ob in Tobolsk, western Siberia.

When spring came they loaded their equipment onto barges and continued their journey along the Irtysh and Ket,

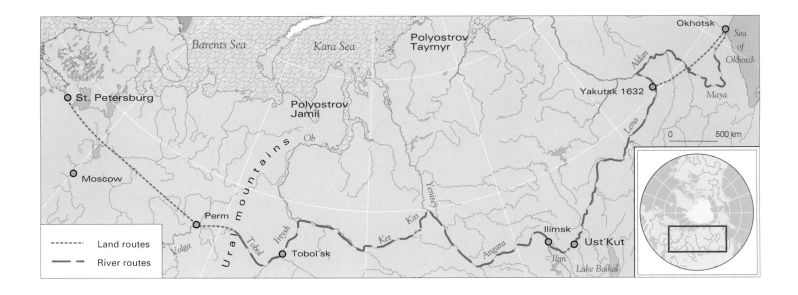

77 Probably Bering's most significant achievement was organising the transport of his men and equipment along rivers and over isthmuses across Siberia. The journey from St Petersburg to the Pacific coast is over 7 000 kilometres long. According to Bering's and Chirigov's calculations in 1733, 555 people, 300 horses and 200 ships took part in transporting 2 108 tonnes from the then Russian capital to Okhotsk. Cannons, anchors and other iron articles accounted for 708 tonnes. To provide for the expedition, 2 410 tonnes of foodstuffs was sent from St Petersburg in 1735. Difficult conditions led to some of the provisions being lost along the way. (PATANEN)

across the isthmus to the Yenisey, and made their way along the Yenisey, Tunguska and Ili rivers to Ili, where the convoy arrived in September 1724. Most of them spent the winter here, but some continued to Ust-Kut, where they built barges and ships to sail down the River Lena. Once the equipment had been transported to the Lena and loaded onto the barges, the convoy sailed down the river and, after many difficulties, arrived at Yakutsk in the middle reaches of the river. There they procured more equipment and men and the convoy was divided up into three groups. The journey continued towards Okhotsk, which is situated on the coast of the Sea of Okhotsk. Spangberg made his way, with his heavy load, along the rivers Aldan and Maya, but the others made the remaining approximate 125-mile journey as the crow flies by land. Bering headed off in August 1726, Chirikov was to follow him the following spring.

Bering arrived at the 'town' of Okhotsk in October. There were eleven buildings in the town and there was not even enough shelter for his advance guard and horses. In the vicinity of the town there were no trees with which to build a sufficiently large ship. Bering set his men to making small craft called 'shitiks'. The shitik is built by 'sewing' planks onto a keel with the aid of willow twigs and leather thongs. The shitiks were to transport Bering and his equipment across the Sea of Okhotsk to the Kamchatka Peninsula, from whose forests material for building such craft as would stand the storms of the North Pacific could be found.

Spangberg, slowed up by the freezing river, arrived in Okhotsk in January 1727 having lost a dozen men. He still needed three months to transport the equipment left behind to its destination. The *Fortuna*, a newly built shitik, made two journeys in summer 1727, transporting the expedition to Bolsheretsk on the west coast of Kamchatka. Bering did not begin to build a vessel here but only on reaching Nizhnekamchatsk on the east coast. The equipment was transported there during winter by sledge along the Kamchatka River valley and across two mountain ranges. The conditions were even more difficult than those between Yakut and Okhotsk.

On 3 April 1728, three years after the expedition had left St Petersburg, they began to build a ship. The *Svjatoi Gavriil* or *St Gabriel* was completed on 10 July. Tar was made on the spot. Salt was produced from sea-water, "butter" from fish oil, and they caught fish for the journey in place of meat. Spirit was distilled from grass in accordance with the local method. The ship had sufficient supplies to last 40 men one year. Three days after the ship was finished they began sailing north.

During a period of one month Bering discovered, named and passed St Lawrence Island about 100 nautical miles from Cape Chukotskiy. In front of him was the Bering Strait. When, on 13 August, the vessel had crossed latitude 65° and the land began to veer to the west, Bering held counsel with the ship's officers. He presented two alternatives: either they would look for new land and a place to spend the winter or they would turn back to their home port.

Spangberg suggested that they continue for three days and turn back only then. Chirikov was of the opinion that they should sail in one stretch to the River Kolyma estuary and spend the winter there. In this way they could make sure Asia and America were not connected further to the north. Bering, however, agreed with Spangberg's proposal. They continued sailing north to latitude 67°. A thick fog in the east prevented them from seeing the American continent; they did not wait for the fog to clear. The expedition returned and Bering travelled to St. Petersburg to report on the journey.

It is a pity that so mild a man as Bering has given his name to one of the most pitiless waters of the Arctic area. It is easy to agree with the words of the historian Richard Vaughan:

"Bering had shown himself to be an able administrator and navigator, but a third-rate explorer, cautious and irresolute and so lacking in courage and determination as to be almost incapable of carrying out his instructions. What explorer worth his salt would not have sailed on until ice barred his way? Nor, surely, would a real explorer have returned the way he had come. The First Kamchatka Expedition could and would have discovered and mapped the strait separating Asia and America, but did not do so. No wonder Bering's reception on his return to St. Petersburg was unenthusiastic."

THE SECOND KAMCHATKA EXPEDITION

Interest in Russian expansion to the east disappeared along with Czar Peter. Bering was not immediately awarded the usual one thousand rouble reward, neither was his salary paid for two years. Bering's advisors urged him to suggest a new broader-based expedition.

Anna Ivanova succeeded Peter, his widow Catherine I and his grandson Peter II. The decision on a new expedition was made by Anna's advisors, however, who had already been in power during the time of Peter the Great. When Bering suggested charting the coast from the Ob to the Lena, they expanded the task to cover the whole of the coast from the White Sea to the Bering Strait. When Bering suggested one vessel, they wanted two. In addition, the land to the east and south-east of Kamchatka and the Kuril Islands were to be explored. Appended to the plans was a wide inquiry embracing the history, natural science, folklore and languages of Siberia. Bering was also expected to persuade the indigenous population to accept Russia's supremacy and its right to levy taxes.

In 1731 the Admiralty asked the Academy to prepare a new map of the northern Pacific Ocean and the lands in or around it. Assigned to the project was the cartographer Joseph Delisle who the following year also wrote a memorandum: Bering took both the map and the memorandum along with him.

The land of Juan de Gama which had already appeared on Homann's map still remained, but its position had changed. The land had been moved to the south-east of the River Kamchatka, instead of being to the east of it as it had been previously.

A VAST MAPPING MISSION

First of all they began to map the Arctic coast. The coast was divided into four sections. The first stretched from Archangel to the Ob estuary, the second from the Ob to the Yenisey, the third from the Yenisey to the Lena and the fourth from the Lena all the way to the River Kamchatka. Nobody had yet been able to sail around the Taymyr Peninsular on the third stage from the Yenisey to the Lena.

Lieutenants of the Fleet Stepan Murayev and Mikhail Pavlov set out on the first stage in 1734. Since the Kara Sea

78 Homann was a significant German mapmaker. He published a map of the Chukchi Peninsula and Kamchatka together with a chart of the Caspian Sea. The anvil-shaped area represents the Chukchi Peninsula. To the west of this is a carrot-shaped island and below it a larger mainland area. The latter probably depicts the American continent. A piece of Japan can be seen at the lower edge of the map. (John Nurminen Foundation)

estuary between Archangel to the Ob was not frozen in summer, they reached the tip of the Yamal Peninsula, the northernmost point of their stretch, before autumn. From there they were forced by the ice to return to their winter camp in the River Pechora area and were only able to continue mapping the following year.

The ice conditions in the Kara Sea were more difficult than before and they were forced to return before they had even reached the place at which they had finished mapping the previous year. Murayev and Pavlov blamed each other for their failure and the Admiralty reduced them to the rank of seamen and sent Stepan Malygin to replace them in spring 1736. During the first summer Malygin progressed to the Yamal Peninsular. The second summer, too, the ice conditions were good and Malygin concluded his task. His expedition was the first to use the name the Kara Sea on its map, although the name itself is probably older in origin.

A young naval officer by the name of Dmitry Ovtsyn was given the job of mapping the second section. He, too, began in summer 1743 making his way from the Ob estuary towards the Yenisey. He set himself the goal of accomplishing his task in a single summer, but the ice conditions in the Kara Sea forced him to return fairly quickly. He spent the winter at the Ob, intending to set out again the following spring. His crew were hit by scurvy and four of them died. He was slowed down by one setback after another and was forced once again to return to the Ob. Only in 1737, in a new vessel the *Postman of Ob*, did he succeed in sailing to the Yenisey and onwards to Turukhansk. When Ovtsyn made his report in St Petersburg the following spring he heard that his patron had lost his power and that he himself had been demoted to the rank of seaman.

The third stage in the mapping of the coast was the most difficult, since it meant sailing round the still unassailable Taymyr Peninsula. The Admiralty ordered two groups to carry out the task. Fedor Minin was given the *Postman of Ob* and the task of starting to map from the west towards the Lena. Vasiliy Pronchishchev, with his wife Mariya, set out west from the Lena towards the Yenisey. Minin and his assistant Dmitri Sterlegov had been Ovtsyn's pilot and mate. Their experience was no match for nature, however. In summer 1738 the ice prevented them from reaching the Kara Sea. After the ice they were stopped in their tracks by a thick fog. Winter eventually forced the groups back before they had even reached the Taymyr Peninsula.

In winter 1739 Minin mapped the Yenisey Gulf and the following winter Sterlegov explored the east coast of the Gulf. In the summer they only succeeded in progressing a couple of hundred miles further than they had the first summer, that is to say to the River Pyasina estuary. In autumn 1740 the Admiralty relieved Minin of his duty.

Vasiliy Pronchishchev, along with his wife Mariya and Semen Chelyuskin, succeeded in reaching the River Olenk during their first summer. They also spent the winter there, their ship the *Yakutsk* having sprung a leak. During the winter some of the crew came down with scurvy, but otherwise the winter went well. The first thing they did in spring was to investigate the River Anabar copper deposits, and in August they continued north towards the Taymyr Peninsula. In August they crossed latitude 77° and, forced by the ice, they turned back just before reaching the northernmost tip of Asia.

Because they could find no suitable place to spend the winter further north they returned once again to the River Olensk. Just before their arrival at their winter camp, Vasili Pronchishchev died and two weeks later so did his wife.

Semen Chelyuskin returned to Yakutsk in the winter to report on the expedition's progress.

Hariton Laptev was ordered to continue the mission. He was a resourceful and independent man but he could do nothing against the forces of nature either. In spring 1739 he sailed west from the Lena estuary in the same vessel as Pronchishchev, the *Yakutsk*. Laptev left some of his supplies at the Gulf of Khatanga, a cove on the Taymyr Peninsula. He mapped the coast almost as far to the north as had Pronchishchev, but had to turn back with the coming of winter. He found a place to spend the winter at the mouth of a small river which flowed into the Gulf of Khatanga. When the necessary requirements for spending the winter had been completed Laptev set about planning how to continue mapping during the winter. In October he sent Zakhar Medvedev to the River Pyasina on the west coat of the peninsular to begin mapping to the east of it. Heavy frosts and biting winds forced Medvedev to make a hasty return to Pyasina and later in the spring back to the winter camp.

Laptev had also sent a patrol to the Taymyr estuary at the tip of the peninsula to begin mapping westwards towards Pyasina. This patrol experienced difficulties regarding their provisions and reindeer fodder, but succeeded in mapping 62 miles of coast before turning back and arriving at their base in May.

In July the *Yakutsk* set sail once more for the north. Even before reaching the point where they had turned back the previous year, the ship became jammed in the ice and began to leak. They were forced to evacuate both men and equipment and to go ashore. In September they marched back to their winter camp. On the journey twelve of Laptev's men were lost. They had little food left. A soldier sent by Laptev arrived in November, bringing with him provisions from the River Anadyr. Later in the winter more food was brought from the reserves left at the Ob, and the expedition survived the winter.

Laptev did not wait around passively at winter camp. When he realised that mapping would not succeed by sailing around the Taymyr Peninsular he decided to map the coast from the land. To do this he divided his men into three groups to be led by himself, Chelyuskin and N. Shekin, each aided by a team of dogs.

In spring Chelyuskin set out for the Pyasina River where he intended to map the peninsula towards the east. Shekin was given the job of starting at the northern tip of the peninsular and mapping the coast west of the Taymyr, while Laptev, with one soldier and a Yakut guide, made his way to the River Taymyr and mapped the coast to the west and in the direction of Chelyuskin's group. Both Laptev and Chelyuskin succeeded in their missions and met each other at the beginning of June. They made their way to the Pyasina and onwards to the Yenisey. Chekin failed and left his section uncompleted, which meant that the north-eastern corner of the Taymyr Peninsular still remained unmapped.

In February 1742 Laptev sent Chelyushkin to map the remaining area and to bring the mission to a conclusion. Chelyuskin himself began to map the east coast of the Taymar Peninsula while some of the group went to the River

THE KOTCH – A PIONEERING POLAR VESSEL

The underestimated kotch was long considered to be a primitive vessel used only in the northern seas of Russia. Modern research has changed this view: it seems likely that the Cossack Semyon Dezhnyov navigated the Bering sound in this type of ship, one that according to researcher Raymond H. Fisher deserves a significant place in the history of polar seafaring. The kotch was the first type of ship specifically designed to traverse the icy seas of the north. It had double hulls, for example, long before any other type of ship.

The kotch was developed as early as the 11th century on the White Sea coast. The ship's name is derived from the Russian "kotsa", which in the Novgorod region means the protective layer on the sides of boats or the runners of sledges.

Another feature characteristic of the kotch, in addition to the double layer of planking, was its hull, which in cross-section resembled half an oval. It is due to this feature that 18th century Dutch cartographer and expert on Russia, Nicolaas C. Witsen, called it the "round ship". Due to its shape, the kotch would "plop" upwards when squeezed by the ice and thus escape damage. Nansen's *Fram* was of a similar shape.

A kotch could move forward even in a narrow channel in the ice. It was also possible to push or drag it on the ice, because it was made of pine and larch and thus light in weight. A hardwood, such as oak, would have weighed too much.

The kotch had a single sail, probably a square sail. Due to its rigging, it was difficult to beat to windward with it; in other words it required a wind from behind or from the side. In northeast Siberia, where this vessel was developed the furthest, a 60-foot-long kotch that was 20 feet wide would have had a single pole-mast and a sail area of some 100 square metres. It is generally agreed among researchers that a kotch could also be rowed. Its full-length deck would also have had at least one smaller rowboat for reconnaissance, sounding or even for towing the mother ship.

A kotch is known to have reached a speed of 6.5 knots for five hours. On long journeys it was capable of sustaining average speeds of up to 3 or 4 knots at best.

79 The kotch was a clinker-built vessel. Its structural specialities included "sewn" planking and the excellent shape of the hull, particularly effective in ice.

80 Bellin was a respected French maker of sea charts. His chart of 1758 well depicts European geographical knowledge of the time of the area between Asia and America. Russia, including the Chukch and Kamchatka Peninsulas, is clearly recognisable. The northern and western parts of America are as yet uncharted. At the Bering Strait there are suggestions of Alaska. Because a reliable method of measuring longitudes was not yet in use, the longitudes of the area are imprecise. Note the location of the Date Line and the island in the Arctic Ocean, which the Line intersects. Wrangler Island was discovered in the area. According to the map the polar circle and the Date Line, which lies near meridian 180°, intersect on the Chukchi Peninsula. On Bellin's map there is no imaginary information on America or a Northwest Passage running through it or north of it. (JOHN NURMINEN FOUNDATION)

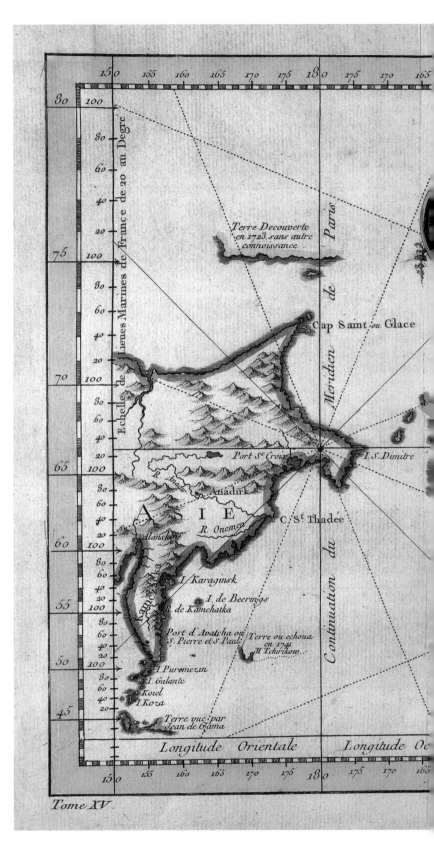

Taymyr to explore the coast towards the east. Chelyuskin advanced to the northernmost tip, which Alexander Middendorff later named Cape Chelyuskin out of admiration for the man's achievements, continuing west to meet up with the second patrol. The mission was finally accomplished seven years after Pronchishchev had undertaken the contract. And Laptev did not go unrecognised either. Nowadays the icy sea east of the Taymyr Peninsula is called the Laptev Sea.

CHARTING THE COAST COMPLETED

One section was still unexplored. The task was begun at the same time as that of the Taymar section. Planning to make his way east of the Lena, Pjotr Lasinius together with Pronchishchev sailed in his ship the *Irkutsk* to the Lena estuary in spring 1735. After this Lasinius headed east, ran into ice and was forced to make camp after hardly having begun his mission. Scurvy broke out in the camp and the first victim was Lasinius himself. By the spring 37 of the 48 men wintering in the camp had died and Dmitri Laptev, Khariton Laptev's cousin, was ordered to take command of the *Irkutsk* and continue the work.

Laptev and his crew arrived in Irkutsk by ship the following spring, but making the vessel seaworthy took so much time that they were only able to continue their journey on 11 August. Soon they became stuck in the ice and after three days decided to return to the Lena. Laptev left his men at their winter camp and reported on the progress of the journey to Bering in Yakutsk. He continued to St Petersburg where he announced that in his opinion the mission was impossible because of the ice. The Admiralty, however, ordered him to continue with the mission either by land or by sea.

The negotiations meant that explorations were put on hold between 1737 and 1738. It was only in the spring of 1738 that Laptev set out once again and by autumn had succeeded in making his way as far as the River Indigirka. In autumn he continued mapping the river delta and coast eastwards to the Alazeya River. During the early part of winter, explorations

progressed to Kolyma by land before the *Irkutsk* was freed from the ice. Laptev is possibly the first Arctic explorer to cut a passage through the ice to free a ship. In the course of the summer the *Irkutsk* reached Kolyma and a little beyond the river, but winter camp was set up at Kolyma.

The following summer was difficult. When, at the beginning of August, Laptev had failed to reach the point where the previous year's work had stopped, he returned to Kolyma. Under new instructions, Laptev collected a great deal of information on the Chukchi. He sent his men back to St

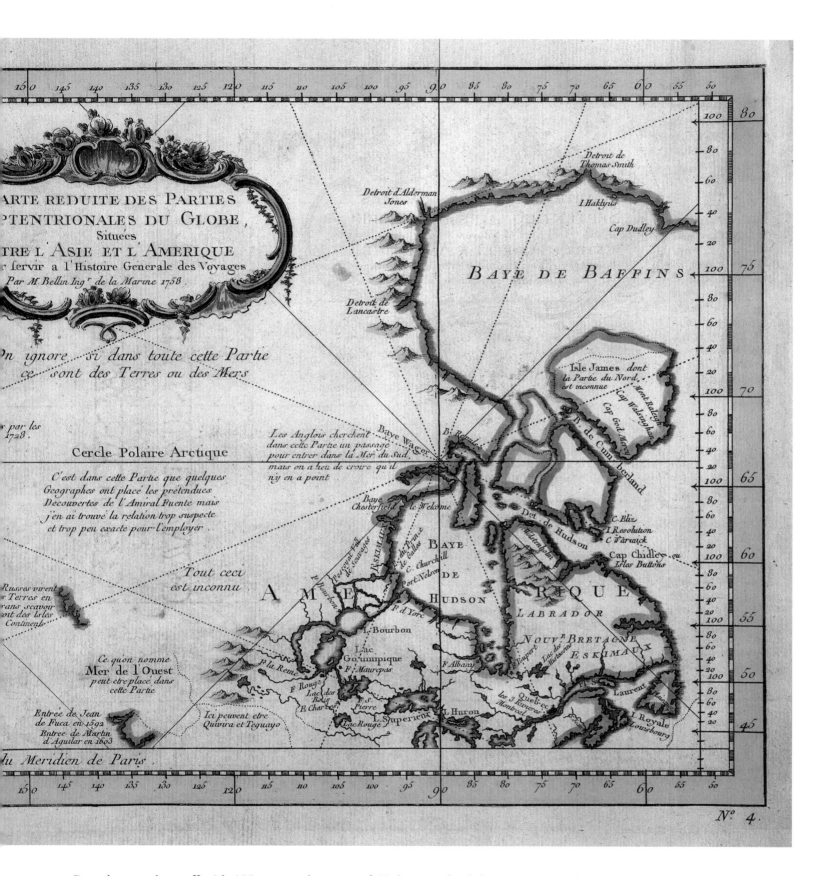

Petersburg and set off with 100 men and a team of 45 dogs straight to Anadyr, which had been his aim. From there he continued working in summer 1741 but failed to map the Chukchi Peninsula. This would be accomplished only at the beginning of the 19th century by Ferdinand Wrangel and his men, and then only by land.

Although mapping the coast of Siberia is not seen as a great feat of exploration, it was one of the most demanding projects in the history of the Arctic. Those who carried it out were afforded only scant respect. Indeed. the most common reward

for defying nature was demotion. Yet in spite of the conditions the men assigned to this arduous task did their work well. In sailing the Northeast Passage, Nordenskiöld was able to state that, considering the methods in use at the time, Cheluyskin's and Laptev's locations were accurate. Moreover, their mapping had left other signs to defy the winds of the Tundra. When, in 1911, the first steamship arrived in Kolyma from Vladivostok – exactly 170 years after Dmitri Laptev – a signal tower, just under ten metres high, that had been built by Laptev on the east bank of the river could be seen from the bridge.

81 The people of Kamchatka moved around in winter by dog sledge. They usually had four dogs pulling a sledge. The high and narrow sledges were built of birch. In place of a whip they used a curved stick at one end of which were attached small bells. These encouraged the dogs to run faster. The Kamchatka women sat sideways on in the sledge while the men stood on the runners.
(JOHN NURMINEN FOUNDATION)

Of the six island groups off the coast of Eurasia, fishermen had discovered three; Spitsbergen, Novaya Zemlya and the New Siberian Islands.

The first Russians had already arrived at Spitsbergen in 1557. In 1743, four hunters were shipwrecked on the island and survived three winters there before being rescued. The men hunted reindeer with bows and arrows, trapped foxes and killed polar bears with the spears they had fashioned. They ate frozen raw flesh, drank warm reindeer blood, chewed on herbs to ward off scurvy and kept themselves in good condition. The Russians had an admirable store of knowledge concerning the avoidance of scurvy. Dmitri Laptev ordered his men to eat raw fish and fresh reindeer meat and to drink barley water.

In 1760 Savva Loshkin – from Lake Ladoga in Karelia – was the first to circumnavigate Novaya Zemlya anticlockwise. Yakov Chirakin sailed through the Matochkin Shar, the Strait separating the two islands of Novaya Zemlya six years later.

Ivan Lyakhov, a hunter, was the first who is known to have visited the New Siberian Islands. He got the idea to look for the islands after seeing a large herd of reindeer making its way from the north across the ice-field. Lyakhov discovered the islands in 1770, but Merkuriy Vagin had probably already done

so half a century earlier. One of the most interesting things about the New Siberian Islands was the great mammoth-bone finds there. The mammoth is assumed to have been cut off on the island after the isthmus joining the islands to the continent disappeared 10 000 years earlier.

THE DISCOVERY OF ALASKA

The task of the second Kamchatka Expedition was the scientific exploration of Siberia. Four men, of whom only the youngest was a Russian, Stepan Krashennikov, shared most of the responsibility for the expedition. The project's leader was Gerhard Friedrich Müller whose responsibility it was to investigate the customs and languages of the indigenous population living between the Urals and Kamchatka as well as the history of Russian conquests. Johann Georg Gmelin's area of responsibility was the fauna and flora of the area. The task of the third foreign member, Louis Delisle de Croyère, was to determine Siberia's most important degrees of latitude and longitude. He was the half-brother of J. N. Delisle, who had made a new map for the expedition.

Müller discovered the reports on Dezhnev's journeys in the Yakutsk archives. When we compare Dezhnev's achievements with those of Lasinius and Laptev the result is astonishing. Dezhnev must have had much more favourable ice conditions. Little wonder if his accomplishment was doubted.

The exploration and mapping of Kamchatka was left to Krahennikov. He described the Kamchadals and regarded their lives with a little bewilderment but, as a real scientist, he even experimented with the effect of their diet on his own bodily functions. He found a great deal to be recommended in the way of life of the savages. They were not troubled by greed, ambition or pride. All their efforts were directed towards a happy existence.

The most interesting of his men was Georg Steller, who only joined the group in autumn 1738. Steller was a gifted but stubborn individual. He won Bering's trust, however, and became a member of his team. De la Croyère was made aide to Chirikov, who commanded the second ship.

The first members of Bering's expedition set out from St Petersburg in early 1733. Bering followed them in spring. He stopped for a lengthy period at Yakutsk since the transportation of several hundred men and their equipment to Okhotsk brought difficulties. Bering himself arrived at Okhotsk in spring 1737 and the rest of his equipment followed only in autumn 1740. Now two ships were built, the *Svjatoi Pjotr* and the *Svjatoi Pavel,* and they were ready to sail in autumn 1740. Bering took them to Bolsheretsk on the west coast of Kamchatka. A new port was built on the east coast which was given the name Petropavlovsk.

Bering's *Svjatoi Pjotr* and the *Svjatoi Pavel,* commanded by Chirikov, put to sea on 4th June 1741. Both had crews of 76 men. The expedition's officers and experts had held a meeting a month before departure. Delisle had drawn a map which included Juan de Gama Island and suggested that they try to find it first. No nation owned it because nobody had ever been there before. To avoid conflict with Delisle, Chirikov withdrew his proposal according to which they would have sailed north to the Chukchi Peninsula and from there west to the coast of America. Bering's opinion is not known.

After one week's sailing the ships became separated in a storm. Neither discovered Juan de Gama, for the reason that it did not exist. Chirikov was the first to arrive at the American coast, reaching Chichagof Island on 17 July. He sent 15 men ashore, who disappeared along with their boats – they were either drowned or killed by Indians. Since Chirikov had lost his boats he turned about and set sail for the voyage home. On his journey he saw the Kenai Peninsula and three of the Aleutian Islands; Adak, Agattu and Attu. He reached his destination, Petropavlovsk, on 10 October. One third of his crew died on the journey, among them de la Croyère.

Bering reached Kayak Island off the coast of Alaska on 20 July. Steller made his way onto land with a group sent to fetch water and he collected samples of the flora and fauna. No attempt was made to reach the mainland. Perhaps Bering was afraid of the natives, signs of whom were found on the island. After a day of indecision Bering did as before and terminated the exploration almost as soon as it had begun.

On the return journey the difficulties piled up. Bering and most of the crew came down with scurvy. On the Shumagin Islands they came up against the indigenous population. The stormy journey concluded when land hove into view, which a few hopefuls took to be Kamchatka and which, in fact, turned out to be one of the Commander Islands, later dubbed Bering Island.

Bering died on the island where the expedition was spending the winter. A boat made of planks from the shipwrecked vessel was built in the spring in spite of the fact that the adviser Ovtsyn – the same man that had been demoted for failing to map the Taymyr Peninsula – opposed the damaging of state property. In this boat the 45 survivors of the expedition made their way, under the leadership of Sven Waxell, to Petropavlosk, their port of departure, in August of the following year.

STELLER – THE EXPEDITION'S ONLY EXPLORER OF CONSEQUENCE

Bering's second voyage was not much better than his first. During this voyage America was probably discovered for the first time from the direction of Asia. The expedition's greatest achievements were, however, due to Georg Steller.

Steller managed to go to Kayak Island by forcing Bering to grant him permission to explore the island while the men were filling the water tanks. For a few hours Steller identified and collected a number of plants distinctive to the American continent, such as the Alaskan salmon-berry. Steller saw a

82 The Steller sea cow was a mammal of the siren species which grew to 7–8 metres long and weighed as much as three tons. The sea cow lived only in the waters of Bering Island and it was hunted to extinction by 1768. George Steller was the only natural scientist to have lived to see a live sea cow. A sailor assisting Steller drew precise drawings of the animal but they have been lost. A skeleton of the sea cow is in the collection of the Helsinki Natural Science Museum. It was donated by the Finnish-born Hampus Furuhjelm, who was Governor of Alaska.

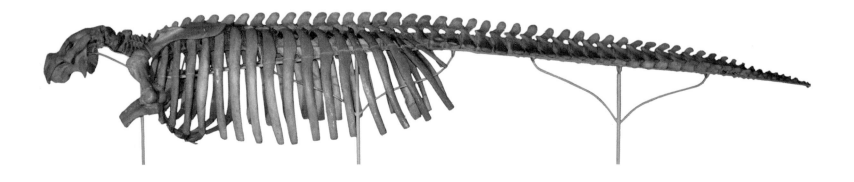

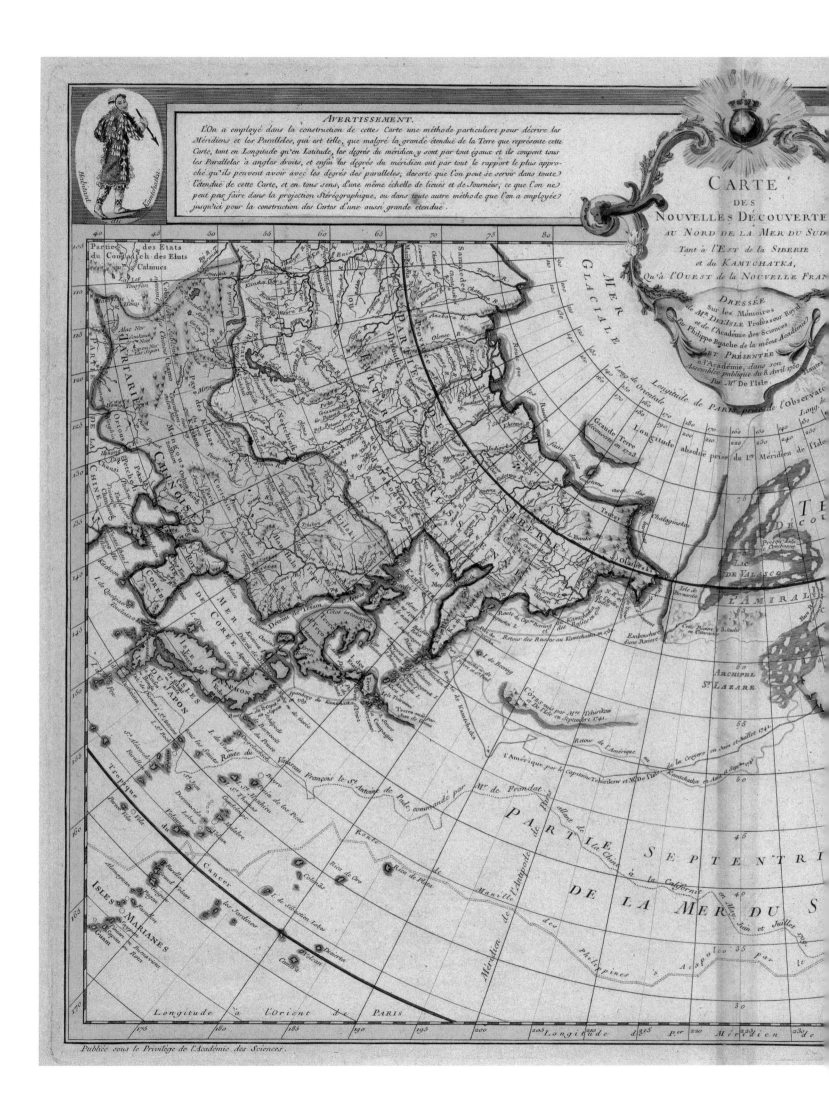

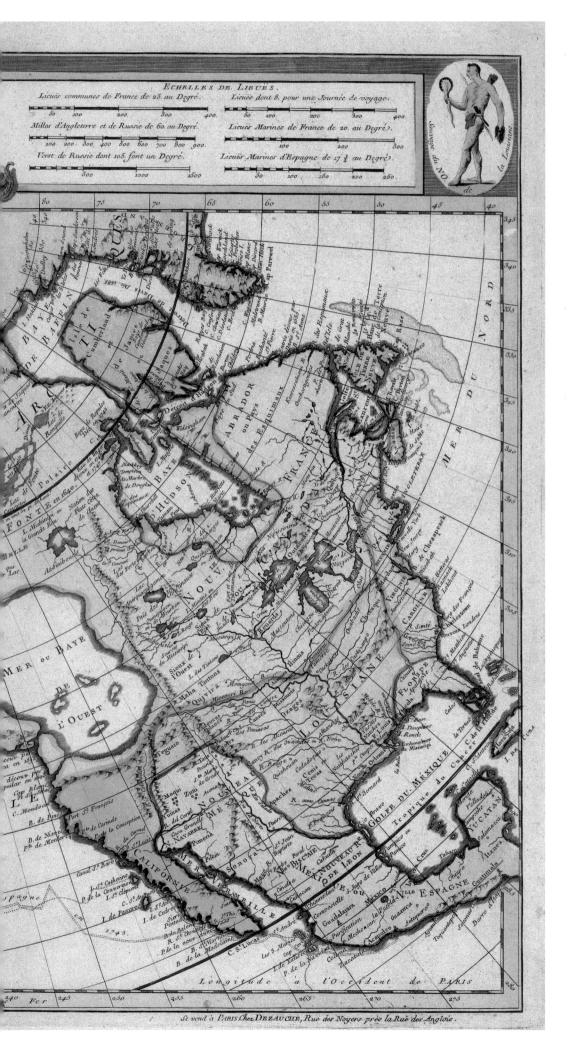

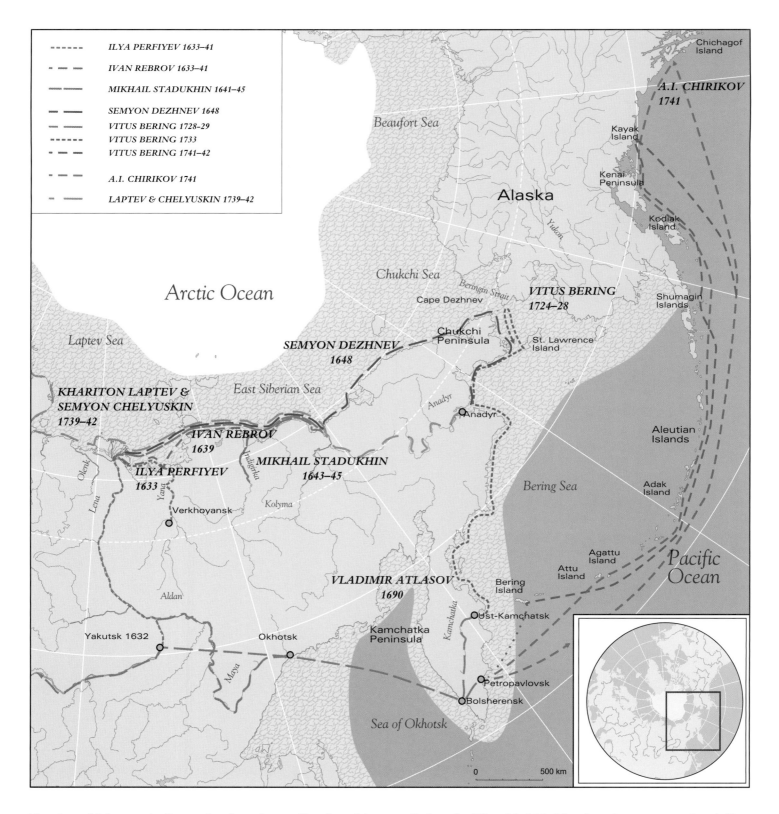

blue jay which was similar to the American roller, found in the western part of the continent. The bird was indeed related to it and was later given the name *cyanocitta stelleri* or the Steller jay. From this Steller came to the conclusion that the mainland beyond the island was America.

Steller did his most important work on Bering Island. In spring, brown eiders swarmed the coasts of the island. But Steller did not manage to catch a single specimen. But he described the bird, which was later named the Steller eider. He was also the first to identify the white-tailed eagle, which had a white patch on its head and, as it name indicates, white tail-feathers. Nowadays the bird is known as the Steller white-

tailed eagle. The third bird he found was a sensational discovery; the spectacled cormorant. The bird was just as unable to fly as the penguin and became extinct during the subsequent century. Steller succeeded in capturing this bird and his specimen is one of the six remaining.

When writing *De Bestiis Marinis,* Steller described the sea creatures of Bering Island. Of particular merit is his description of the seals, which could not be faulted later. The sea cow or dugong was an important animal for hunting but it was also one of Steller's most interesting discoveries. The Steller sea cow was only found in areas near to Bering Island. A mammal related to the *siren,* it is believed to have descend-

84 Although Semen Dezhnev was the first to sail around the Chukchi Peninsula to Bering Strait as early as 1648, the ice conditions brought difficulties to the charting of the easternmost stretches of the coast of Siberia. Both of Vitus Bering's expeditions are marked on the map. Bering's first voyage closely followed the east coast of Asia; the American coast was not spotted at all. Bering's and Chirikov's routes to the Alaskan coast closely follow the line of the Aleut islands.
(PATANEN)

85 Naval officer Semen Cheluchkin was one of the most competent men on the Great Northern expedition. He distinguished himself by mapping the Lena delta and Taimyr Peninsula with the assistance first of Vasiliy Pronchishchev and later of Khariton Laptev. In 1742 Cheluchkin advanced to the northern tip of the Taimyr Peninsula by dog-pulled sledge and erected a cairn there as proof of his achievement. The peninsula is known today as Mys Cheluchkin.

ed from the ancestors of the elephant. According to Steller it resembled a land animal as far as its umbilicus but from its umbilicus to its tail it was a fish. It is only from the description in the *De Bestiis Marinis* that science knows this animal, which became extinct a few decades after the discovery of the island. The last living sea cow was seen in 1768, only 27 years after its discovery. Steller was not able to take a specimen with him but one of the sailors made six precise drawings of the animal which were appended to the manuscript when it was sent to St. Petersburg. According to Corey Ford, who wrote a book on Steller, these drawings have never been found.

If it had not been for Steller's explorations Bering's second voyage would not be worth a longer description. Steller was the kind of person who does things according to an unswerving conviction, looks at his surroundings with eyes open and describes reality with precision. Thanks to him we have an understanding of what the fauna of Bering Island was like before the area was picked clean by plunderers.

The plundering was started by Bering's men who, upon recovering, began furiously to hunt sea otters. Alongside the sable, the sea otter was the most valuable furred animal in the region. Russian trappers hunted it just as fervently has they had the sable earlier. Hunting the sea otter was the most important motive for expeditions after Bering.

THE RUSSIANS COME TO ALASKA

Although the members of Bering's expedition were forced to give up a great number of the sea otter skins they had hunted on the island, the discovery of a new and rich hunting ground was great news to Kamchatka hunters. As a result, innumerable hunters made their way to the virgin islands of the east.

The government ordered the results of Bering's expedition to remain secret and information regarding it was not even shared with the St. Petersburg Science Academy. On a map published by the Academy in 1758, both eastern Siberia and Alaska are depicted in a way that Bering's expedition had shown to be wrong. In addition, islands that did not exist were drawn in the Pacific.

The fur hunters sailed first to Bering Island, then to the Aleutians, the Shumagin Islands and to Kodiak Island. The voyagers pooled their knowledge and used local place names as distinct to those of Bering who gave the places he saw names of his own invention. The fur trappers often travelled in the kayaks of the local inhabitants. Petr Shiskin was the first to compile a map using the new information. He sailed to the islands in 1762. In addition to Kamchatka, the Commander Island and Diomed, many of the Aleutian Islands such as Umnak and Unalaska as well as 'Kadiak' are already marked on his map.

Catherine the Great and the Admiralty were delighted with the claims the fur hunters had made. Catherine sent an expedition to make sure that Russia's supremacy would be permanent and to ensure the taxation of the fur hunters. Captains Petr Krenitsyn and Mikhail Levashev were given the task of undertaking the expedition. Their departure was

BERING'S PACKETS

The Russian Tsarina, Anna, had two fast ships built for Vitus Bering's second expedition. These vessels, which were of the type known in seafaring nations as 'packets' or 'packet boats', were brand new at the beginning of the expedition. They were built in Okhotsk on the coast of the Sea of Okhotsk and were launched seven years later. The tools and workers needed for the job were brought from the west, largely by river. The wood was brought from the east, across the Sea of Okhotsk, from the Kamchatka Peninsula.

The vessels were sister ships and were named the *Svjatoi Pjotr* (Saint Peter) and the *Svjatoi Pavel* (Saint Paul). The well-known master shipbuilder Vasili Soloyev was in 1732 given the job of designing a packet that would be quick to build, and he was asked to give a cost estimate for building two identical vessels. He drew up a precise list of the necessary materials and an estimate of the amount of skilled and unskilled labour required. According to this estimate the job required 60 carpenters or joiners, 40 assistants, from six to nine blacksmiths, five sail-makers, a few other craftsmen and a foreman.

The man chosen to supervise the work was Andrei Kusmin, who had attended a school of mathematics and navigation and had studied shipbuilding in Britain and other places. In 1733, having received the designs, he set out for Siberia

with Commander Martin Spangberg.

Oshotsk was a cluster of a dozen small and run-down dwellings on a narrow isthmus between the River Okhotsk and the Sea of Okhotsk. At Spangberg's orders a barracks and a dock were built there. The keels of the ships, which were built side by side, were laid on November 12, 1737. Three more years were to pass, however, before the vessels were completely ready. Work was slowed down by the long cold winters. Now and again there was a shortage of food supplies, which had to be brought in from very far away, and there were also long delays in getting the wood for the ships from Kamchatka. The ships' woodwork was completed in two years, that is to say by November 1739. The sail-cloth arrived the following summer. The *Svjatoi Pjotr* was launched on June 29 and the *Svjatoi Pavel* on July 2. On August 8, 1740 they had already set out on their way to Kamchatka.

Despite the difficulties experienced in building the vessels, they proved to be of excellent quality in both design and construction. In the severe conditions of the Arctic they were, of course, subject to normal damage to their rigging, and particularly to tearing of the sails. The carvel-built hulls, however, withstood the pounding of the northern seas. The *Svjatoi Pjotr* was destroyed later when she ran aground on the coastal shallows off the "island of

foxes" (known today as Bering Island) when the crew, weakened by scurvy, no longer had the strength to save her. Bering, who had been ill for a long time, died on this island. The *Svjatoi Pjotr* and the *Svjatoi Pavel* were rigged as brigs, that is to say they had two masts each equipped with three square sails. The mizzen mast also had a gaffsail and the bowsprit stays supported two headsails. The ships were coloured in a combination of white, green, red and light blue. They were 80 feet in length, and 22.5 feet in the beam with an average depth in the hold of 12 feet, but we know nothing about their draught. They carried about 1,500 kilos of flint and pig iron as ballast.

postponed and the expedition proper began only in 1768.

Before then Lieutenant Ivan Sindt had made an expedition to the Bering Sea. He rediscovered St. Lawrence Island. In other respects the expedition was a failure. On the face of it so was Krenitsyn's and Levashev's expedition. The Lieutenants' ships became separated, with one spending the winter in Unimak and the other on Unalaska Island. Both of their crews suffered from scurvy and half of Krenitsyn's men died during the winter. Before they returned Krenitsyn was drowned in an accident. The expedition's greatest contribution was Levashev's description of the way of life of the inhabitants of Unalaska.

Russian researchers consider the contribution of the fur hunters in mapping the coasts of both islands the most significant achievement of the expedition. The Admiralty continued to conceal their information and did not publish the results of the voyages. More extensive exploration of the north Pacific took place only when James Cook arrived in Alaskan waters on his third voyage.

The seizure of the Aleutian Islands was violent. Although the original names of the islands were preserved the indigenous population was subdued and coerced into the service of the Russians. When, in 1762, the Aleuts attacked a Russian camp, a war broke out. Although officials were aware of the hunters' coercive means, it was not possible for them to intervene. A hunter by the name of Soloyev led the restoration of order. The Russians, with their firearms, attacked the villages of the Aleut, killing an estimated 3 000 Indians who defended themselves with bows and arrows.

After the war the native Aleuts bowed to the power of the fur hunters and were forced to pay taxes in the form of furs and labour.

86 *Vitus Bering's vessels were so-called packets that were rigged as brigs, with two masts rigged with three square sails. The mizzen mast also had a gaff sail and two jibs were attached to the stays of the fore-bottom. The* SVJATOI PJOTR *and the* SVJATOI PAVEL *were built side by side in Okhotsk. With the exception of the ship's wooden parts all the equipment and materials, from nails to guns (including 28 cannons) were brought through road-less Mother Russia from St. Petersburg to Okhotsk. This took several years. The trees necessary for the ships' hulls and rigging were felled in the forests of Kamchatka and were floated across the Sea of Okhotsk to the docks.* (JOHN NURMINEN FOUNDATION)

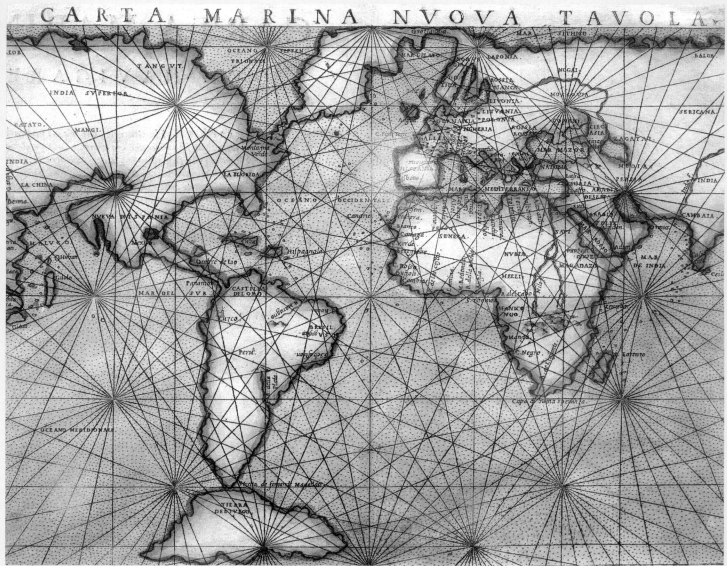

THE MAP OF THE NORTH DEVELOPS
– ASIA'S BORDER IS DEFINED

The primitive peoples of the north did not make maps, but it is said of the Eskimos that they were able to draw the most important features of wide areas of terrain in the sand or snow. The Vikings did not make maps either, although they had a precise understanding of directions and distances. After them, the northern polar regions were opened up to Europeans only with the coming of the great journeys of exploration. In 1497 John Cabot became the first European after the Vikings to go to North America. After this, numerous expeditions made their way to the north, north-west and north-east, always by sea. The first maps of the Arctic are the work of European mariners. A few unique portolan charts drawn on parchment dating from the beginning of the 16th century have been preserved in museums. Maps of the Arctic came into wider use when they began to be reproduced as wood and copper engravings in the 16th century. The art of printing speeded up the dissemination of a new perception of the world.

After the journeys of Columbus, parts of the east coast of America appeared on maps of the world; Asia and America were still thought to be a single continent. At the beginning of the 16th century, Martin Waldseemüller presented a bold hypothesis claiming that America was a separate continent divided from Asia by a strait. Gradually this idea gained more and more support. Not only did Waldseemüller correct the Ptolemaic view of the world, but he also gave the new continent a name - not, it is true, after its discoverer. It was because of the influence of Waldseemüller's maps that the name of the Italian sailor Amerigo Vespucci became associated with the new continent.

As late as 1548, Giacomo Gastaldi still depicted the New and Old World as one on his sea chart published in Venice. Europe was connected to North America by a land bridge running through Greenland. In 1550, the eminent cartographer Sebastian Münster published a map in Basle which achieved wide distribution. On it Greenland was a long peninsula pushing out from Europe far into the west, and the

87 The Italian Ruscelli's map was published in Venice in 1561 as a part of Gastaldi's Ptolemy miniature atlas. It is one of the first sea charts to depict the whole world. The map lacked a system of co-ordinates and is built on a loxodrome grid typical of portolan charts. On the Carta Marina Asia and America are still the same continent. The strangest detail of the north, however, is the land connection between Europe and America. According to the map it was possible to get to Greenland by land from America and from there to northern Norway and never get your feet wet. Greenland's land connection to North Europe originates from Clavus' geographical concept. On the other hand it is more difficult to find an explanation for the isthmus shutting off the way to a Northwest Passage.
(JOHN NURMINEN FOUNDATION)

Chuchki Peninsula stretched far to the north of America and was almost attached to Greenland. In 1566, the Bolognese cartographer Zaltieri named the waters between Asia and America the Anian Strait. Attached to Mercator's revolutionary map of 1569 there was a separate map, the basis for many other map-makers, depicting the Northern Calotte or Arctic area. On his 1592 map of the polar region, the skilful cartographer de Jode depicted the outline of Alaska and Siberia as well as the Anian or Bering Strait, though more precise information on the area was available only after Semoyen Dechnoyov sailed through the strait in 1684. De Jode's knowledge of the polar region, with its four islands, was based on Mercator's map.

The further north, north-west and northeast the Europeans pushed, the more accurate the maps of the polar region gradually became. Expeditions always sought the latest maps when planning their voyages. When Frobisher set out for the north, he had with him Mercator's map of 1569. Mercator repeated some of the mistakes of the Zeno map, but showed the existence of a navigable Northwest Passage, a fact which spurred Frobisher on. The navigator Davis had access to the information that Frobisher had found. He corrected some

mistakes and added to the information by conducting his own measurements.

Because the ice prevented sailing vessels from reaching far into the north, polar expeditions made little progress in the 17th century. More thorough geographical knowledge was compiled on the interiors of Eurasia and North America.

For a good 100 years the Russians conquered and inhabited their northern areas at record speed, and they had already reached the Pacific Ocean by the beginning of the 17th century. They made great advances in their knowledge of the north. The Cossacks generally travelled along the major rivers, and learnt about the river banks, estuaries and coasts of Siberia. The last area to be explored was the northeast corner of Asia, the Chuchki Peninsula, since the indigenous people of the area, the Chuchki, resisted Russian domination long into the 18th century.

In the west, Europeans were pushing into northwestern America with merchants and fur-trappers at the forefront. They travelled across large lakes and along the rivers flowing into the Arctic Ocean. Progress was slower than in Asia, however. The entire coastline of Siberia was mapped a lot earlier than the American Arctic, which is dotted with islands. But

88 Abraham Ortelius drew up one of Europe's first depictions of Russia. His map includes the north-eastern part of Asia and the north-western part of America, areas that were not known in Europe at the time. The vague information on Japan was based on Portuguese voyages of exploration. Ortelius situated Japan more or less in the right place on the map. At that time there was no knowledge of the Bering Strait. Ortelius, like many other map makers, supposed America and Asia to be different continents. They are divided by a strait called the Anian Strait. The portrayal of Russia's coastline is unusual: an imaginary peninsula pushes from Siberia almost to the North Pole.

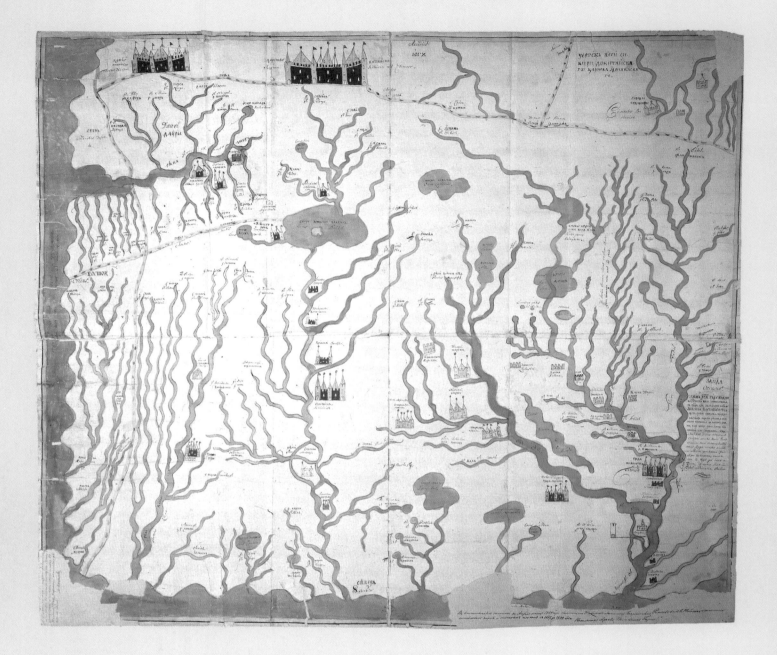

89 At first glance this early map depicting Siberia seems slightly naive. The map has no co-ordinates and it concentrates on the south. Made by an unknown cartographer, the map does however contain a great deal of information on the great rivers of Siberia, which are depicted as flowing to the lower edge. The map was made in 1673 and the information on it is congruent with that of the map made by Gudunov in Tobolsk in 1673, to which is attached an enormous amount of geographical explanations. According to this hand-made, water-coloured map the local Russians, at least, knew of the waterways which went through the eastern part of their continent and along which Semen Deshnev travelled around the Chukchi Peninsula in 1648. The map tells of later voyages by walrus hunters from the Kolyma River in the North Atlantic to the Anadyr River on the Pacific Ocean. The Chukchi told of a large continent situated on the other side of the sound. The map clearly indicates the lower left edge of the American continent.
(RUSSIAN STATE ARCHIVES)

information flowed faster in America. New discoveries were speedily communicated to map-makers, who also disseminated this new information effectively throughout Europe.

In Asia cartographic information travelled slowly. Often it came to a halt at the local level, at Yakut or Tobolsk, for example, and Moscow did not always know what had been discovered in the east. The Russians wanted to keep their findings within a small circle, which meant that maps were not usually printed. Until the 19th century, it was common practice in Russia to keep maps secret. They were considered strategic information, which the Russians had no wish to entrust to outsiders. In spite of the secrecy, Western Europe found out about the Russian discoveries, and the Dutch and later the French published them on their maps. Occasionally Russian maps were more up to date in Paris than in Moscow.

Among the Russian rulers, Peter the Great in particular understood the importance of mapping. He was the first ruler to take an interest in the outer limits of his realm and he organised great expeditions to the north which had the effect of both increasing the Russian peoples' knowledge of their own country and of advancing cartography.

In the 20th century Leo Bagrov, A. V. Yefimof and Alexei Postnikov conducted valuable research into the history of Russian cartography. Many influential people surfaced in their publications, including Remizov, Witsen and Strahlenberg.

Semoyen Ulyanovic Remizov (1663–1731) can be considered Siberia's most important cartographer. He gathered together local knowledge in the administrative centre of the area, Tobolsk, and translated it into a series of maps.

Nicholas C. Witsen, long-time mayor of Amsterdam, became interested in Russia whilst on a trip there in 1665. He found numerous sources of information, from Peter the Great onwards, and he published much better maps of Russia than had been achieved earlier.

The Swede, Philip Johann Strahlenberg, was taken prisoner at the battle of Pultava. During his long incarceration he collected extensive cartographic material on Siberia. Eventually this was published as the most progressive and accurate map of its time. Several other European cartographers, such as the Frenchman Delisle, the German Homnan and the Englishman Thornton, also increased our knowledge of northern Asia.

Russian maps were different from those of the West, which, from the beginning of the 16th century, were based on geographical and astronomical measurements. As early as the 17th century, western maps were usually drawn up on the basis of the network of latitude and longitude. Russian map makers – merchants, fur-hunters and soldiers – had no measuring instruments. Maps based on their information were therefore inaccurate as far as locations and directions were concerned. They lacked co-ordinates, their scales were uncertain and the way they presented information was naive and rather formalised. Northeastern Siberia from the Lena estuary to the Sea of Okhotsk was usually presented in a diagrammatically angular way. South was almost always up, so that the northwest corner of Siberia was always at the lower left-hand edge of the map.

Russian maps, however, did contain very pertinent information from the traveller's point of view. For example, they accurately depicted the waterways of Siberia and important places along their banks, but were found wanting in their depiction of the coast of the Arctic Ocean. They gave conflicting information about the Bering Strait, the shape of the Chuchki Peninsula and its possible connection to America was unclear, and the Kamchatka Peninsula was missing altogether. Professor Postnikov, who has researched the history of contacts between Russia and America, thinks, however, that the Russians' understanding of geography was much better than their maps would lead us to believe.

90 Information on the Far East was transmitted slowly and was often inaccurate. This influenced the understanding and geography of Europeans, and this understanding was all the more lacking the further away from Europe the area in question was. Mapping became more reliable only when seafarers received the use of more precise astronomical equipment for the taking of measurements. The picture is of Billings' sea voyage from Okhotsk at the end of the 18th century On the voyage the hydrographist Sarytchev carried out invaluable research.
(JOHN NURMINEN FOUNDATION)

WHALING IN THE SERVICE OF ARCTIC SCIENCE

MANY TOOK ADVANTAGE OF THE RICHES OF THE ARCTIC AREA BEFORE THE COMING OF THE
VOYAGES OF EXPLORATION. SEAL AND WALRUS HUNTERS HAD PROBABLY DISCOVERED THE FUR-
THEST CORNERS OF THE WHITE SEA BEFORE OTTAR. COD FISHERMEN KNEW ABOUT MANY AREAS
BEFORE CARTIER, FROBISHER, DAVIS OR BAFFIN CHARTED THEM.

THE WHALING MARKETS

Advances made during the time of the Thule culture im-
proved the Eskimos' chances of catching whales. Whaling
meant an enormous reserve of food and materials for them.
They made use of the whole whale, from its bones to its skin.
Most importantly, the Eskimos used their reserves sparingly.
Hunting did not threaten the existence of the whale.

For the European or American whale hunter the most important product obtained from the whale was the oil refined
from its blubber. The oil was used as a raw material by the
soap industry, as an additive in the leather and textile industry and as fuel for oil lamps.

Uses were also found for whalebone. It is a flexible material which can be easily shaped and polished. It was used for
making frames for photographs and mirrors, handles and
corsets. As early as the later part of the 17th century whalebone accounted for one fifth of all the revenue from whale
hunting, and at the end of the 19th century it was the single
most important commodity. In 1902 blubber accounted for

91 An 18th-century French portrayal of the Greenland whale.
(John Nurminen Foundation)

only one eighth of overall production, which is why American whalers often only kept the whalebone and left 50 tons of blubber and flesh floating in the sea.

THE WHALES OF THE ARCTIC REGION

Whales can be divided into two groups; the chenille or baleen whale and the toothed whale. Of the former there are only 11 different species, of the latter 66. The Greenland whale was the most interesting of the baleen species since it was the one most accessible to the techniques and skills of the earlier whale hunters. It was very large – up to twenty metres long – and could weigh almost 100 tons. It gained its nutrition by swimming slowly forwards, filtering nourishment from plankton through its baleen plates.

Plankton contains a great deal of the Greenland whale's most important food, krill, which is found where the warm sea currents arriving from the south meet the cold currents coming from the north; at the area where they collide the sea water is

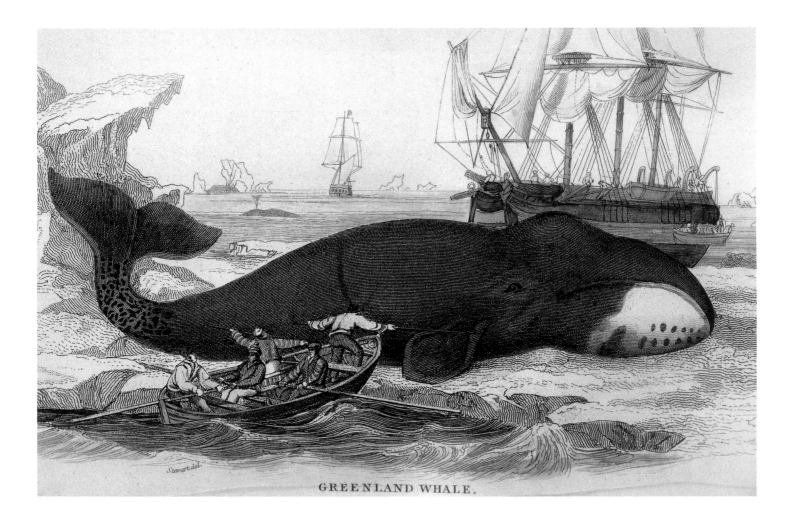

GREENLAND WHALE.

92 The Greenland whale – also called the "right whale" – is a gigantic, slow and peaceable animal which, because of the northerly climes in which it lives, has a thicker layer of blubber than any other whale. It filters plankton through its baleen for nourishment. It also yields more whalebone than other whales. Since it has no natural enemies it has never learned to fear the whalers. The Greenland whale almost became extinct before it became a protected species. (B. & C. ALEXANDER)

their way through the ice of Lancaster Sound and the waters nearby from which they move on to their wintering ground.

Many things made the Greenland whale the best ("right") whale for hunting. Because it is large, it provides a great deal of oil, bone, and baleen. In addition, its layer of blubber is thicker than that of any other whale. The Greenland whale was easy to find in its customary areas, it swims relatively slowly and it is trustful by nature. The speed of the whale is only seven knots, which is why it was possible to hunt it from boats with six oarsmen. At one time boats would set out on a hunt from coastal bases, later they were launched from whaling ships.

coloured absolutely green by plankton. The 19th century whaling captain and author, Captain William Scoresby Jr. described the Arctic seas as ultramarine, but at those places where the whales thrived the colour changed to olive-green. The colour was a sign to hunters of good whaling waters.

The Greenland whale lives in the Arctic area all year round but it needs open water in order to breathe. When necessary it can rise to the surface and break through an ice layer half a metre thick. The whales winter north-east of the Labrador Peninsula. In April they move north along the west coast of Greenland. In summer the whales go after food at the edge of the pack ice or the coastal waters freed of ice. They also mate in summer and their young are born a year later. Later in the summer they make their way further west, eventually seeking

THE HARSH WORLD OF WHALING

There was a kind of rare attraction associated with whale catching, even though the work was exhausting and was often carried out under inhuman conditions. Ice, frost, snow, thick fog, raging winds, falling icebergs and ice-floes crushing everything in their grip like a vice, put even the strongest and bravest to the test. It was big-game hunting where the quarry was the world's largest mammal and the stake was the life of the hunter – sometimes of the whole crew. Nature was as beautiful as it was merciless. In the Arctic man is surrounded by the Northern Lights, magnetic disturbances, mirages, the formation and melting of glaciers, the flowers of the Arctic, the life-giving sea currents and the nightless night.

For sailing ships the ice was a dangerous and unpredictable adversary. William Scoresby Jr. once told of counting 500 icebergs from the top of a mast, each of which was the size of a ship. But in summer the whales followed the ice. The whale hunter had to take risks and sail amongst it.

The ice did not only bring difficulties; it also had advantages. Fresh, salt-free water could be obtained from the melted ice. The sea ice provided a place of calm in a storm for ships, which might seek its shelter even under the threat that at any moment they might be crushed between the floes. Ships often found protection from the pack ice in the lee of an iceberg.

Pack ice is made up of innumerable small and large ice floes which drift with the currents and winds. In winter, too, most of the ice in the Davis strait and the Baffin bay is pack ice. In summer the belt of pack ice drifts south, following the Labrador Current all the way to the coast of Newfoundland. The whale hunters had to be able to force their way through this area of pack ice to reach the spring hunting waters. There is pack ice between Greenland and Baffin Island throughout the summer, and it is not easy to estimate its quantity or the rate and direction with which it will move.

Whale hunters made their way through the pack ice, looking for leads and for more open areas in the pack-ice zone. Since sea ice drifts constantly, danger was always lurking.

Now and again the ships were imprisoned by the ice, often for a week or two, sometimes for months. Occasionally the wooden ships sprang leaks. In 1821, eleven whalers were shipwrecked in the pack ice in the Davis Strait. In 1830, of the 91

93 Because the Greenland whale is slow, a six-man boat can keep up with it. Since the whales occasionally dived underwater for as long as twenty minutes, returning to the surface to breathe, hunters had to estimate the place where they would surface. Sometimes it was only after hours of rowing that the harpoon thrower standing in the bow of the boat succeeded in throwing a harpoon into the whale's back. Because a harpoon could not seriously wound the whale a battle began that was joined by several boats. At its longest the struggle could last for more than 24 hours.
(B. & C. ALEXANDER)

vessels sailing the Davis Strait area, 19 were lost. 1835 was a bad year for pack ice; six vessels were lost and only a few were freed from the grip of the ice late in the winter.

The solid ice of the Arctic seas is found close to the shore. In spring, in April or May, when whale hunting got under way, the amount of solid ice was at its greatest. During the summer it melted like the pack ice. In the best years the hunting waters became ice-free in August and vessels could move freely. Soon the ice began to make sailing more difficult. Those who had had no luck with hunting took greater and greater risks by remaining in the hunting waters. Delaying the journey home often led to their staying throughout the winter. In the latter years of whaling ships wintered in order to extend the season.

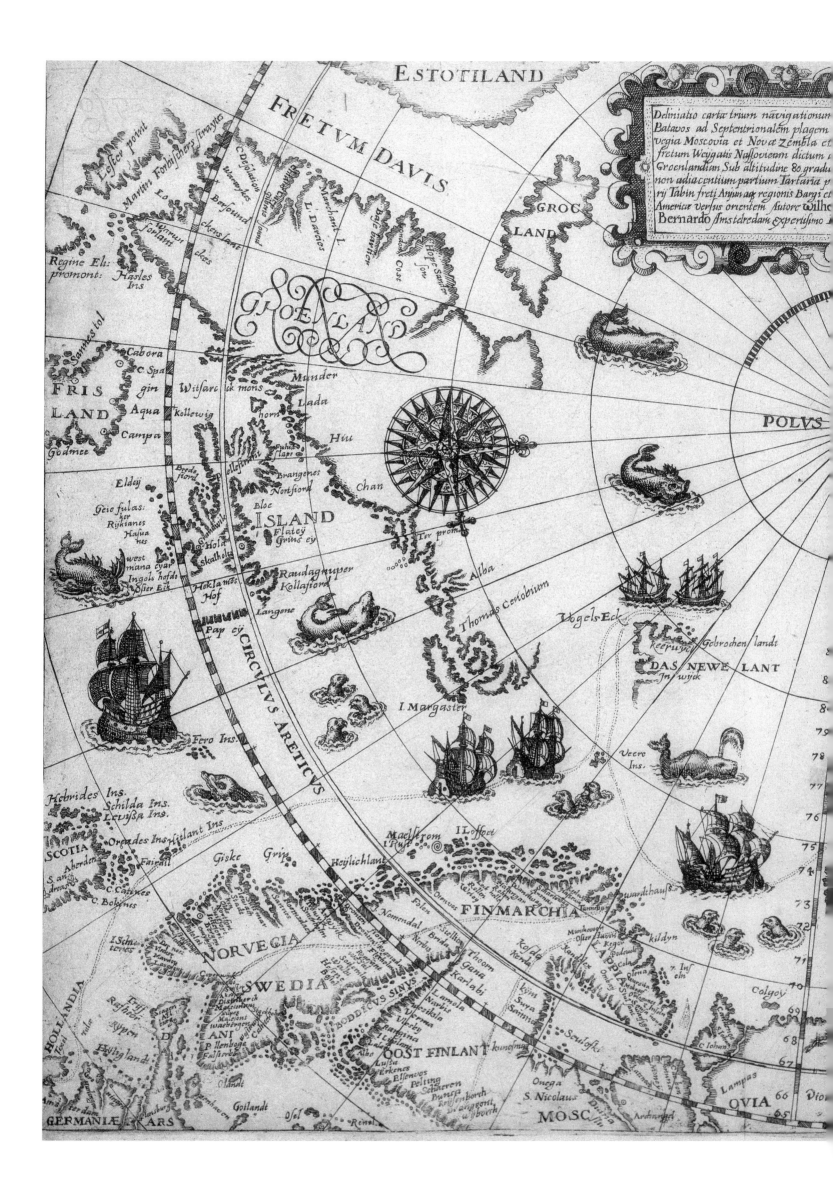

ESTOTILAND

FRETVM DAVIS

GROC
LAND

Delineatio cartæ trium nauigationum
Batauos ad Septentrionalem plagem
uegia Moscouia et Nouæ Zembla et
fretum Weygatis Naßouienm dictum
Groenlandiam Sub altitudine 80.gradu
non adiacentium partium Tartaria
rij Tabin freti Anian aꝗ regionis Bargi et
Americæ versus orientem autore Wilhe
Bernardo Amstelredam experißimo

POLVS

Lester point
Martin Forbisshers strayte
C.Desolation
Warwickes
Berfound
ckenslant
ckes
L.Davies
Marchant I.
Gilberts found
Hope Sanler
Cost
Iones

Regine Eli:
promont: Hasles
Ins.

Sannes tol

FRIS
LAND
Godmee

Cabora
C.Spa
gin
Aqua
Campa

Witsarck mons
Kollewig

GROENLANT

Munder
horn Lada
Fuha slapt
Hiu
Chan

Eldeij
Geie fulas:
her
Rijkianes
Haßua
nes
west
mana eya:
Ingols hofdt
Oster Eik

Brede
fiord
Spithvik
Hola
skatholt

Brangenes
Nortsiord
Bloe
ISLAND
Flatey
Grims ey

Hekla mos
Hof

Raudagnyper
Kollasiord

Tr. prom

Alba

Langone

Thomas Cenobium

Pap eij

Vogels Eck

Keeruyt Gebrochen landt

DAS NEWE LANT
In wyck

CIRCVLVS ARETICVS

Fero Ins.

I.Margaster

Hebrides Ins.
Schilda Ins.
Leuißa Ins.

Veere
Ins.

SCOTIA
S.and
Aberdeen
Adreos
C.Cattnes
C.Bokenis

Orcades Insul Hilant Ins

Fairhil

Giske Grip

Heijlichlant

Maelstrom
I.Tuß
I.Loffoet

75

78

77

76

75

74

73

Nomendal
Stelling
Brida
Nivus

72

FINMARCHIA

Wardhauß

Tarnihes

NORVEGIA

Folen
Thoorn
Gana
Karlabi

LAPPIA
kildyn

71

SWEDIA

HOLLAND

BODDICVS SINVS

Kosala
Kola

7. Ins.
eln

70

Colgoy

ANI
P.Ilenboge
Falstret

OOST FINLANT
Alusa
Erkenes
Elsenova
Pelting
Scharen
Panca

Lamgin
Nurbie
Uoriklo
Lecheby
I.Lesten

kym
Suya
Semina

kunchna

Sculofki

C.Iohan

69

68

67

Onega
S.Nicolaus

66

65

OVIA
Vion
Lampas

GERMANIÆ PARS

Goilandt

Osel
Renal

MOSC

Archangel

The map itself contains the following labels:

BERGI REGIO

ESTRECHO DE ANIAN

ARCTICVS

Polus Magnetis

VNG

TARCAS

CAPO DE TABIN BARGVS

MONGAL

TAIN GIN

CAROCO RAM

Die Inseln von orage
den Eck der Begerte
T. vlissinger hoof
Deus derunter Eck

CAVO NA

COLMAC

NOVA EM A

I Tasala

BAI DA

MOLGOMZAIA

TARTA RIA PA RS

OBDORA

R. Obij. Cosin

NOIEDA

DORA Obij

IVGORA Costam

SOMER MEER

Miliaria Germanica. quorum 15 um gradum respon
101 201 301 401 501 601 701 801 901 1001

94 *Theodor de Bry's map is based on the geographical findings of Barents' third voyage. It is one of the classic polar maps. The map was published in Amsterdam in 1599 in a work by Gerrit de Veer, which told of Barents' third voyage to the North. It contains the era's best knowledge of the North. Thanks to Barents' discoveries, Bear Island, Spitsbergen and Novaya Zemlya are in their right place. The incorrect islands of Zeno's narrative are depicted on the map, however, as are Mercator's magnetic North Pole in the north of the Anian Strait (Bering Strait). On the other hand the map does not have the mysterious Polar islands. In this respect it is clearly a step forward. Barents' voyage increased knowledge of the plentiful sea mammal stocks in the waters of the north. This brought numerous whalers and walrus hunters to the area. Whaling and hunting scenes have often been depicted in northern waters.*

(JOHN NURMINEN FOUNDATION)

95 *In the beginning the whalers set out around March–April and sailed to the ice belt, which at that time of the year was around latitude 70–72. The faster they got through the ice to Spitsbergen's best hunting waters, the better the hunters' haul. The captain of a whaler had to be able to sail among the icebergs and coolly weigh the risks and the potential rewards. Skilful captains could recognise the amount of plankton from the colour of the water and they quickly learned the whales' regular movements.*
(JOHN NURMINEN FOUNDATION)

96 *In the 17th century Spitsbergen was the main stage for whaling. Bases and boileries were built on land. When the whales had been caught they were towed onto land to be cut up and boiled. Only later, with the whale stock decreasing, did they give up their bases and move out to sea. When a whale was caught it was towed to the side of the ship. There both the whalebone and the blubber were removed. The blubber was cut into small pieces and stored in barrels in the ship's hold.* (JOHN NURMINEN FOUNDATION)

THE SPITSBERGEN AND WEST GREENLAND PERIOD

The Muscovy Company, founded in 1555, concentrated on hunting whales in the waters of Iceland. The journeys of Jonas Pool to Bear Island between 1604–1608 were among the first attempts to hunt in these waters. The walrus, whose stock was diminishing rapidly, was the main attraction. The situation changed when Henry Hudson set out to look for a Northeast Passage in 1607. Although he failed in his mission he returned with the news that the waters of Spitsbergen were alive with whales. Most whales were to be found in Kongfjord.

Gradually other nations, as well as the English, turned to hunting at Spitsbergen, as the whale stock had begun to decline elsewhere. Whalers from the Basque Provinces, France and Holland sailed to Spitsbergen. In 1613 there were already 26 whaling ships in the Spitsbergen area, of which the Muscovy Company, jealous of its rights, had sent seven. The English naval flag-ship, the twenty-one gun *Tiger*, seized vessels while other English ships hunted. The cargoes of some were

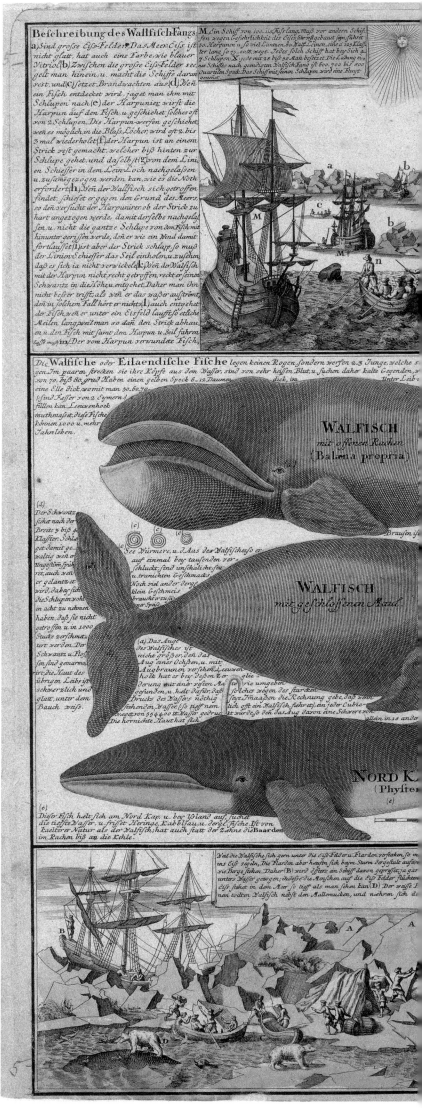

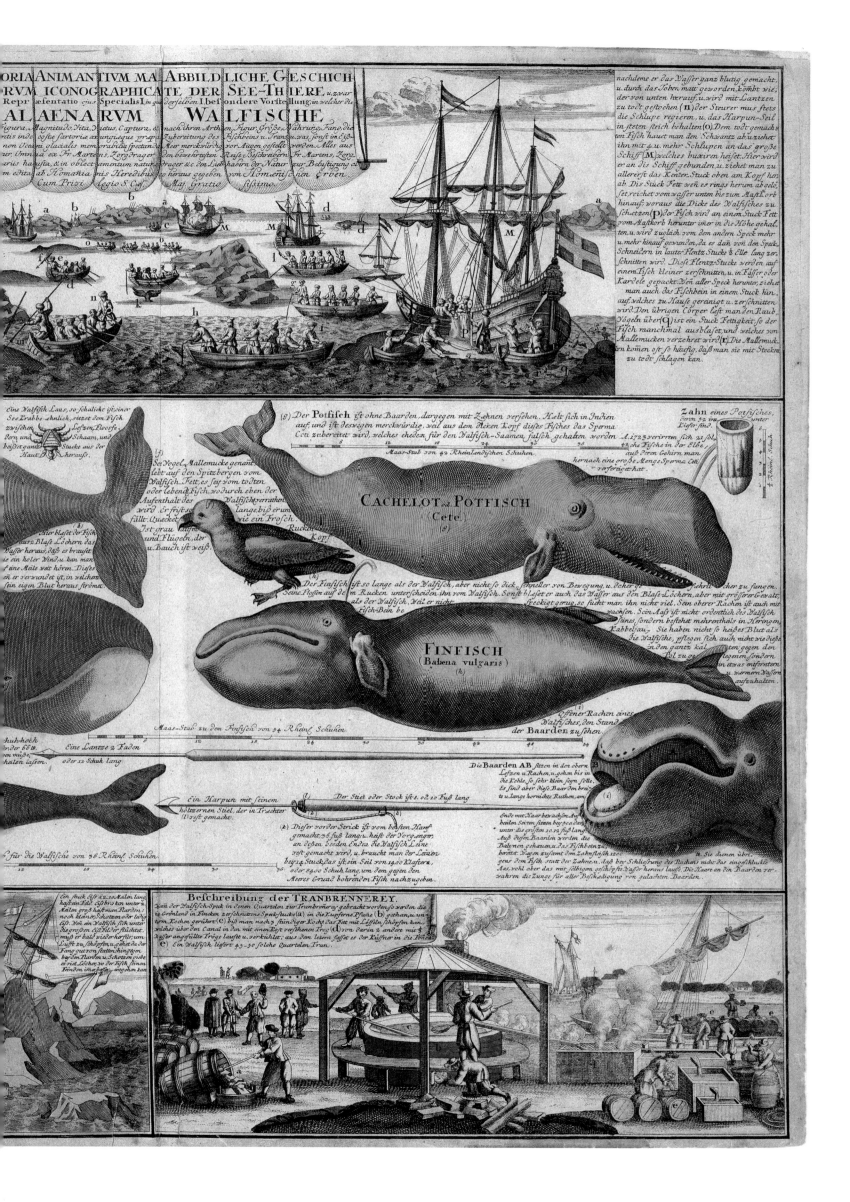

97 Cornelli's round map from 1697/1705, part of which is shown, is designed to cover the Arctic area of the globe. Coronelli's maps were known for their skilful graphics. Scenes of narwhal, walrus and polar bear hunting have been shown to illustrate the North. Because of its twisted tusk the narwhal was a highly valued catch and brought high prices in Europe.

The map's Italian text states, among other things, that certain Dutch sailors tell that on 23 June they saw the sea covered in a thick layer of ice, and some tell of the voyage being interrupted on July 24th at latitude 76 by a continuous, impenetrable and vast ice cover. Further on it mentions that Willoughby finally reached 73° latitude North and 62° longitude West but that he fell into the clutches of the ice and perished. In the same way in 1672 Friedrich Martens travelled through the ice and extreme cold without reaching his destination. Dutchmen – under the leadership of William Barents – however, were the first to discover Novaya Zemlya as early as 1594–1596. At that time it was not known if a new continent had been found. Some claimed its northern half to be the Tabin ridge and defended themselves later upon learning their mistake. (JOHN NURMINEN FOUNDATION)

confiscated and they were forced to return without their catch. The Basques were allowed to continue their hunting if they agreed to give part of their catch as a tax to the trading company. In spite of everything, the Muscovy Company had an unprofitable year.

The English were not able to take control of Spitsbergen, however. Indeed, no European state managed to do that. Before long tough but open competition held sway in the whale-hunting waters.

When the whales became fewer in the fjords of Spitsbergen, the hunters were obliged to seek their whales in the open sea or at the edge of the pack-ice belt. The whale-hunting area expanded continuously. When, in 1614, Jan Jakobsz May became the fourth man, after Henry Hudson, Thomas Marmaduke and Jean Vrolicqin, to discover Jan Mayen Island and its whaling grounds, the Dutch switched some of their operations there. In 1684 there were 246 Dutch whalers operating in the waters between Greenland and Spitsbergen. The whaling grounds were expanding continuously both to the west and to the north. The English disappeared from the picture almost completely in the mid 17th century. The Muscovy Company had given up. Holland was the leading whale hunting nation and under its leadership attention shifted to a new whale-hunting area, Davis Strait.

THE DAVIS STRAIT FLOURISHES

After having sailed as mate on the warship *Tiger*, sent by the English to Spitsbergen in 1613, William Baffin sailed to Baffin Bay three years later and praised the area as having excellent possibilities for whale hunting. In 1625 Dirck Leversteyn sent a ship from Delft to the Davis Strait. A couple of other Dutchmen hunted in the Davis Strait area that year and the following year too. This was followed by a break of a few decades.

In 1710 some ships out of Bergen came across Dutch whale hunters again in the Davis Strait. But it was not until 1719 that the number of whale hunters increased there, possibly because the number of whales in the waters of East Greenland had decreased. As many as 29 Dutch vessels sailed to the Davis Strait that year. The following year the number was up to 64 and in 1721 as many as 107.

Whaling had always involved great dangers. Between 1661 and 1718 an average of 149 Dutch vessels set out to hunt whales every year. Every year an average of six were shipwrecked – one in twenty-five. When moving to the west of Greenland the dangers increased. One in seventeen whaling voyages ended in a shipwreck and the loss of a vessel.

earlier. If a vessel became beset on its way home, the journey could last right up until the end of the year or even longer.

American whalers also joined the hunt in the waters of Davis Strait. Whaling had long been practised along the west coast of America, off New England, Long Island and Nantucket. When the whales decreased in number there at the beginning of the 18th century, ships set off from these regions, too, to hunt in the open sea. The first Americans sailed the waters of Davis Strait as early as 1732. They accounted for only six per cent of whaling trips to Davis Strait. But in one respect the Americans were pioneers. They accounted for half of all trips lasting throughout the winter.

Melville Bay on the north-west coast of Greenland was particularly dangerous. Whale hunters often reached it by going through the pack ice lying between the west coast and Baffin Bay. In a westerly wind the pack ice shut off the route and took the vessels into its pincer-like grip. The only way to survive was to cut a square dock or 'basin' for the vessel into the solid ice with a primitive ice saw.

In new hunting waters the time when hunting could begin also varied. Coastal hunting could be started as early as March; by then the winter frosts were tolerable. Because the whales moved north for the summer, hunting off the coast came to an end of April. Fishing in and along the edge of the northern pack-ice area could continue late into Autumn. Hunting trips to the east of Greenland, including the time spent travelling, took five months. The whalers set out around March–April and returned only when winter forced them to.

It was necessary to leave for the Davis Strait as early as February and to sail through the stormy and foggy frozen waters of the Atlantic to within reach of Labrador. Here they waited for the breaks to appear in the ice through which the whales set out on their journey towards their breeding grounds in Baffin Bay or still further away. Hunting was made easier by the fact that the whales congregated around latitudes 66°–69° and again at latitude 71° to wait for the ice to break up.

When setting out for the north the whales dispersed and the whale hunters had their next chance only when they returned for the south. In the eastern waters of Greenland a hunting trip could easily stretch into a month or two longer than it had

WINTERING IN THE ARCTIC AREA

Wintering was the final frontier for traditional whaling. Whales were initially hunted off the coasts, then further out at sea, but the animals were brought ashore for processing. Eventually hunters set out for the open sea and it was no longer possible to take advantage of bases on the coasts. As the whales became fewer and it was no longer possible to get a full catch during a single hunting season it was necessary to resort to wintering.

The first attempt to spend the winter in the Arctic, 1553–54, was unsuccessful. The crew of Sir Hugh Willoughby's two ships died of starvation, cold and scurvy on the Kola Peninsula. Later, Barents' expedition fared better under even more severe conditions.

The first attempt by whale hunters to winter in the area was born of necessity. In the 1620s nine men spent the winter on Spitsbergen where they starved. Their Captain left a group of men behind him for a second time in 1630. Edward Pellham and his seven companions were ordered on shore to hunt. Their ship the *Salutation* sailed home at the end of August leaving them behind. Pellham's group had no extra rations or equipment for wintering, but they survived the winter.

Pellham described the winter in his book. The fact that they survived was largely due to Pellham's leadership skills and his decisiveness. The men did pray regularly, but they did not chance their survival to that alone. They built themselves

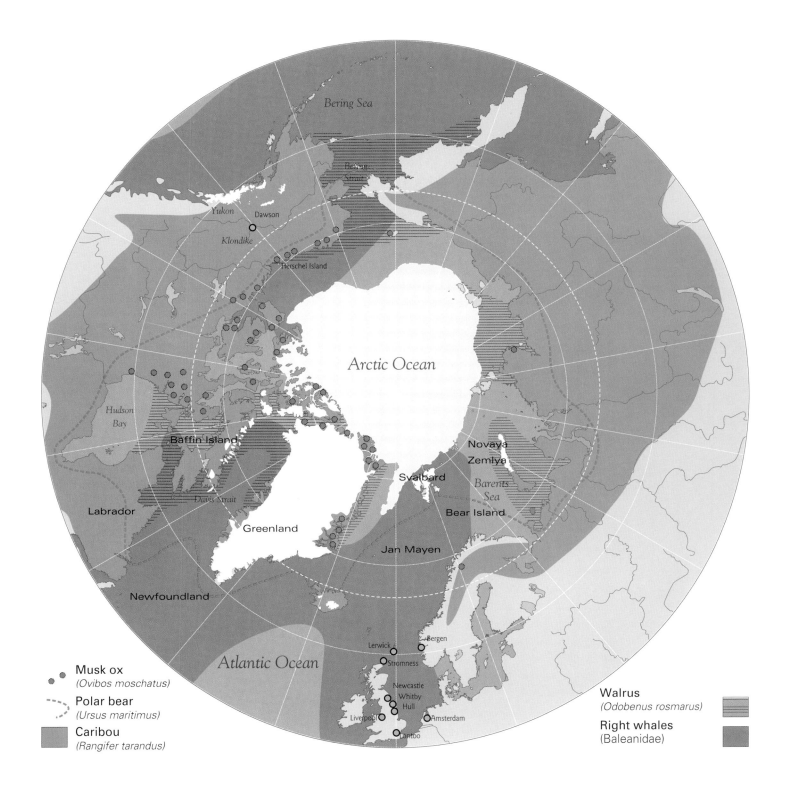

98 The most important game of the Arctic are the Greenland whale, the walrus, the musk-ox, the polar bear and the caribou, whose areas of distribution are marked on the map. (PATANEN)

sleeping places at the whaling station, insulated them as well as possible and slept covered by deerskins. They lived by eating the meat of the caribou they had been sent to hunt, complemented their diet with walrus meat and killed a polar bear with a spear. They considered its meat better than that of the reindeer. Later in the spring they bagged several bears. They also learned to trap foxes and to eat them roasted. Their most important source of nourishment, however, was the mouldy waste left after boiling blubber.

The survival of the Englishmen encouraged the Dutch to experiment with wintering. Noordsche Compagnie had earlier dismissed the idea, even though some Dutchmen had offered themselves as volunteers. In 1633 two well-equipped seven-man groups spent the winter at Smeerenburg and on Jan Mayen Island. The men managed almost as well here as had the English led by Pellham. Compared with Pellham's group though, their store of food was positively luxurious.

Wintering on Jan Mayen Island proved to be a catastrophe. In spring the group were all found dead, one in a coffin, the others lying on their beds. There was a lot of food left. The group had probably come down with scurvy, but the cause of death was trichina from poorly cooked bear meat. When even the next experiment came to a similarly fatal end, the Dutch gave up their attempts to winter.

Wintering became a routine when the move to Baffin Bay took place. Vessels stuck in the ice were forced against their will to remain where they were in winter, and members of several early crews died either of starvation or of scurvy. Gradually, however, the whalers learned to equip themselves properly to survive the winter. Wintering in the Davis Strait area and in the Bering Sea became essential in order to extend the hunting period.

WHALING IN THE BERING SEA COMES TO AN END

In 1848 the American Thomas Wellcome Roys became the first man to sail through the Bering Strait to the Arctic Ocean to hunt whales. He was long considered the first whaler to penetrate into the Bering Sea, but the earliest such attempt was probably made as early as 1819. Armed with a map made by F. W. Beechey and published in London in 1831, as well as sea charts given to him by the Russians, Roys sailed to the coastal waters of both America and Asia where his catch was good.

While whaling was getting under way in the Bering Strait, the Greenland whale was beginning to decrease in numbers in the waters of Greenland, and groups of whalers were becoming scarcer there. After 1859 steam-driven whaling vessels came into use. The steam engine improved the efficiency of whaling and helped ships cope with the pack ice.

American whalers often wintered in the harbour of Herschel Island. Wintering on Herschel Island also saw the introduction of the taxation of the North Alaska caribou stock. The Eskimos hunted the caribou and exchanged them with the whalers for food, weapons and other useful items. Such co-operation became established practice. Sometimes the Eskimos followed the ships in spring to get the provisions promised them by the whalers from the nearest port.

According to Richard Vaughan, the Dutch alone killed at least 65 000 whales in the waters of Greenland from 1661 to 1800. To this number must be added the figure of approximately 30 000 whales that were caught in the Davis Strait and Baffin Bay area. These figures do not include those caught by the English and Americans in other areas. In addition, the figure tells only of those whales that were caught. During the hunting season a great many whales were injured, escaping from the boats only to die later. During one season, the American whale hunter John Cook lost three-quarters of the whales he had harpooned. On the other hand, he claimed that the number of wounded to have got away during this one trip was more than all those of other trips put together.

The Greenland whale did not become extinct, despite the fact that in the 1980s Canadian researchers estimated the entire stock to comprise a few hundred individuals. To the east of Greenland their number was apparently even fewer. The critical point seems now to have passed, however, and the number of whales is slowly increasing.

99 *The large barrel attached to the mast of a whaler, invented by William Scoresby Sr., was called a 'crow's nest'. It was there that a lookout kept watch and shouted when he saw a whale or its spout. On hearing the shout the captain would climb the mast with a telescope. Having sent out three or four boats to pursue the whales the captain gave signals from the mast to the hunters, who could not always see the whale's movements.*

(JOHN NURMINEN FOUNDATION)

WHALERS – EXPLORERS OF THE ARCTIC

Exploration of the Arctic area was interrupted at the beginning of the 17th century after the voyages of Davis, Hudson and Baffin. No expeditions were sent out for a hundred years until that made by Vitus Bering. With the exception of whalers, traders and Samuel Hearne, who explored the northern reaches of the American continent, the absence of the English continued right up until the 1770s.

Whalers sailed to the polar region regularly every year. They learned to observe changes in the ice conditions and were able to advance far into the north if they wanted to. In 1806 Scoresby Sr. sailed all the way to around latitude 82°. In 1816 Captain Munroe sailed along the coast of Spitsbergen as far as latitude 82° 15'. He would have been able to continue even further north but since there were no whales there he turned back.

Not all whalers kept records of their affairs, much less published their records. Thanks to William Scoresby Jr., there was

THE FLUTE

This is one of the earliest Dutch ship-types with a known history. The type is first mentioned in 1595 with the name *hoorensche gaings* or *fluyt* and its characteristics are praised: the well-proportioned hull (1:4), excellent sailing qualities and ability to navigate shallow waters.

Pieter Janz Liorne is mentioned as the 'father' of the flute. This trader and seafarer was the adviser to the admiral of the Flemish coastal fleet and was sufficiently experienced and knowledgeable to develop a new breed of ship.

The original length-to-width proportions of the hull were probably inspired by Noah's Ark. As a deeply religious man and a pacifist Liorne also refused to arm his vessels. The weight of cannon on the upper deck would also have had a negative effect on the ship's stability and draught.

This type of ship was an owner's dream: inexpensive to build and operate. Its large tonnage and good sailing characteristics combined with its low taxable value, as measured by Öresund customs, made the vessel very important for the Dutch, who were participating in the lively commerce around the Baltic Sea. The narrow deck had an area of only one third of other ship types of similar size.

Different variations of the flute were developed to suit different purposes, though it has to be said that the variants designed for service in the north outlasted the ones meant for the south. The oak boards were bent to a considerable degree and did not cope well with the scorching southern sunshine, and the seams above the waterline would start to leak. In cooler waters the hulls fared much better.

The bow was reinforced with a double layer of planking to protect it against the wear and tear of the ice. In addition, the flutes called *noortsvaerder*, which were designed with whaling on the Arctic Ocean

in mind, were recognisable from the lifting booms crossing their aft decks. The rigging of the northern version of the flute differed from other versions mainly in that it had stronger lower masts.

The *houthaelder*, a type of flute common on the Baltic, was used for shipping sawn timber, which was loaded onto the ship through openings in the ship's sides or stern. Some models of this variant had no deck at all. At times there were not enough vessels for the far northern seas, and then some decked timber-carrying flutes would be equipped for whaling. The effective whaling season was 2–4 months, and the ship's owner had to find other ways to gainfully employ his vessel for the rest of the year.

The flute also gained popularity outside Holland, and these were built in France, Sweden and Germany. The Dutch began arming their flutes from the 1620s onwards, after the end of the 12-year truce. The Dutch Navy developed its own version of the flute, which was considerably larger than its civilian cousins. Some have explained the economic success of Holland's "Golden Age" by sawmills operating with industrial efficiency and the massively popular flute.

A change in the customs procedures at Öresund in 1669 had a crucial impact on the future of the flute. The type lost popularity and was eventually replaced by other models after having reigned supreme on many European shipping routes for over 70 years.

100 *The most usual trading vessel type of its time was the 17th century flute. The Dutch merchant Pieter Janszen Liorne wanted to develop the perfect trading vessel. The flute combines a number of advantages: it was cheap to build, easy to sail; its taxable value was low and its dead-weight capacity was high. Typical of the flute was its pear-shaped form, wide hold and narrow deck. Its form is explained in part by the fact that tax was paid according to the width of the upper deck. The flute's popularity is also based on its adaptability; different flute types were developed for transporting different products. Adapted for whaling, the flute had a reinforced bow, strengthened masts and davits along the afterdeck from which the whaling boats were hung on tackle.*
(HISTORISCH MUSEUM ROTTERDAM)

a substantial increase in knowledge of the Arctic. He accompanied his father on a whaling voyage for the first time when he was only 10 years old and after that almost every year until he stopped in 1823. He had also studied for longer than most of his colleagues. During his years of study Scoresby learned to take lecture notes, and this became such an ingrained habit that he even kept a diary on his honeymoon voyage. He collected an enormous amount of information on the Arctic and published it in two books, the first of which, *An Account of the Arctic Regions* he wrote at the age of 30. He had made his first voyage as captain of a whaling vessel at the age of 21.

Before Scoresby, and to a certain extent after him too, it was believed that the North Pole region was free of ice and was surrounded by open sea. On the basis of his own experience Scoresby had decided that this theory was not true. After writing an article on the polar ice he was urged to enter the scientific profession. During the lax whaling year of 1817 he also published an account of the exploration of Jan Mayen Island and conditions there. In the same year he stated that the polar ice had clearly melted, a fact which increased the chances of a successful naval exploration.

Scoresby was also prepared to lead such an expedition, but the Second Secretary of the Admiralty, John Barrow, did not want a civilian to interfere in a naval project. The Admiralty had suffered earlier for letting a civilian command a naval

102 John Phipps' map of Spitsbergen's Fair Haven of 1773. In the lower left-hand corner of the map is Amsterdam Island, at the north-east corner of which the whaling town of Smeerenburg is located. The Dutch founded it around 1619 and boiled whale blubber there right up until the 1660s. At its best the harbour was a base for twenty or so whalers, and some 200 men slept on its coast. According to some sources the men spent a wild time in Smeerenburg in summer, but later excavations show it to have been more a place of heavy work than summer joys. When Phipps sailed to the bay there were still abandoned old buildings there, and four Dutch whalers used the harbour as a base.
(PRIVATE COLLECTION)

101 When the whalers arrived at the hunting waters, boats were hung over both sides of the ship using tackle. From there they were lowered into the water when whales were spotted. There were six men to a boat, one of whom was the harpoon thrower. When the first boat had succeeded in harpooning a whale the other boats came to its assistance to secure the whale. Copper engraving of a whaler in icy waters, by Georg Balthasar Probst (1673–1748).
(JOHN NURMINEN FOUNDATION)

Seylen in 't Ys, en soeken na de Walvis
la Navigation dans la glace, et chercher du Baleine.

il Veleggiare nel ghiaccio, e cercare del Baleno.
Das Seeglen ins Eiß, und suchen des Wallfisches.

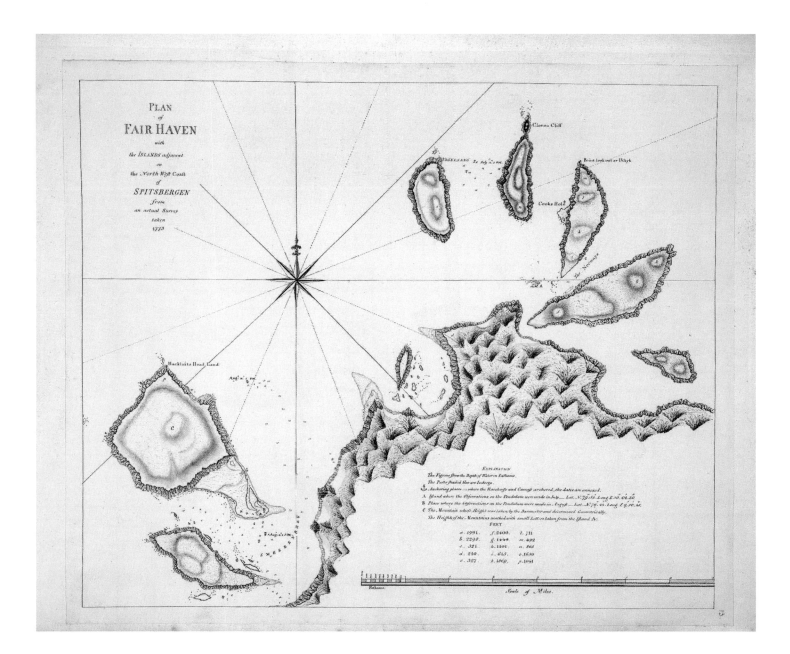

voyage. Also the Arctic was considered a training ground, in the absence of wars after 1815. It took years of experience for officers to obtain the skills that Scoresby and other leading whalers had. Some – to their misfortune and that of their men – never reached that level. The younger Scoresby was a very unusual whaler. In 1822 he charted new whaling grounds while exploring the stretch of the east coast of Greenland that would go down in history as Scoresby Sound. It tells a great deal about the relations between the Navy and the whalers that the naval officer, Captain Douglas Clavering, who was charting these regions a year later, nowhere refers to Scoresby's work, although in private correspondence he admits to having read his papers. In 1847 Scoresby was warmed by the fact that on an atlas of the world found in his American hotel, his work in mapping Greenland appeared under the heading "Scoresby Land".

Scoresby stopped whaling at a time when signs of the end were already in the air. For the rest of his life he worked as both a scientist and a clergyman; he published his theological dissertation at the age of 49. Scoresby did not, however, at any stage abandon his traditional field of investigation, but worked almost until his death to develop a better ship's compass, among other things.

Many expeditions took advantage of the help of the whalers as 'ice pilots'. In 1855 the American whaler George Henry came across an unknown ship near Cumberland Sound, Baffin Island. Volunteers sent to the vessel boarded her and said she was the British warship the *Resolute*, which Captain Henry Kellett R. N. had abandoned at the order of the expedition's commander, Sir Edward Belcher. The volunteers partook of the wine from the same carafe and from the same glasses with which Captain Kellett and his officers had raised a toast to the ship before abandoning it. As a good will gesture the United States government presented the ship as a gift to Queen Victoria.

THE WHALERS AND THE INDIGENOUS PEOPLES

When, in the 1720s, the whalers moved on to the coasts of the Davis Strait and Baffin Island and, after 1848, to the northern waters of the Bering Strait, trading, for example, brought them into continuous contact with the Eskimos and Indians.

103 Hondius was a representative of the heyday of Flemish cartography. Locations that had not been confirmed by geographical measurements are not depicted on his map published in 1630. The map has no imaginary islands, continents or waterways. The edges of the map are decorated with Dutch whale hunting and processing techniques. In the early days blubber was usually boiled on land.
(JOHN NUMINEN FOUNDATION)

The hunters bought fresh meat, furs, pelts, whalebone and livestock from the Eskimos to sell when they got home; less lucrative than before, whaling was supplemented with other products. In exchange the Eskimos received weapons, ammunition, practical goods, tools and the white man's food and stimulants. Tobacco and whiskey were in great demand.

This kind of co-operation provided the Eskimos with the chance to adapt to coexistence with the kind of culture able to produce whale meat easily and in great quantities and whose numerous tools were useful in Arctic conditions. The whalers followed with curiosity a people who in their opinion lived primitively. In some matters both parties had a similar view of each other. The Eskimos wondered at how ill-equipped the hunters were for a cold climate. The winter dress of the Eskimos, which was incomparable in the cold, did indeed became an item of trade. For their part, the Eskimos could get hold of comfortable European clothes for the summer.

The whalers collected souvenirs from the Eskimos. They also enjoyed sexual relations with Eskimo women. Since wife swapping was part of the Eskimo culture the women exchanged their favours for the things most valued by their men, like tobacco. The Eskimos wondered why the whalers left on winter hunting trips without their women. The whalers also brought with them diseases against which the Eskimos had no resistance: venereal diseases, measles, influenza and diphtheria. Epidemics could wipe out entire villages.

The wintering whalers did not eat whale meat nor generally even save it. The American whaler John Cook told of an occasion when a whale carcass was given to the Eskimos once all the bones and fat had been removed. Such co-operation was typical when the whalers were near a village. According to Albert Markham, the Captain of the *Arctia* ordered whale skin to be stored in barrels. He gave the skin to the Eskimos, who valued it as food.

Whale meat was an excellent preventative against scurvy. The whalers, however, preferred fresh game. The musk-ox was slaughtered almost to the point of extinction and the caribou stock decreased considerably as the result of hunting. When the whalers left in the early 20th century, the Eskimo found themselves without the essentials for their traditional forms of livelihood.

The Eskimos also took part in whaling. Thanks to wintering it was possible to begin whaling as early as May, when other vessels were still waiting for pack ice to disperse off the coast of Greenland. Since they could swim beneath the ice,

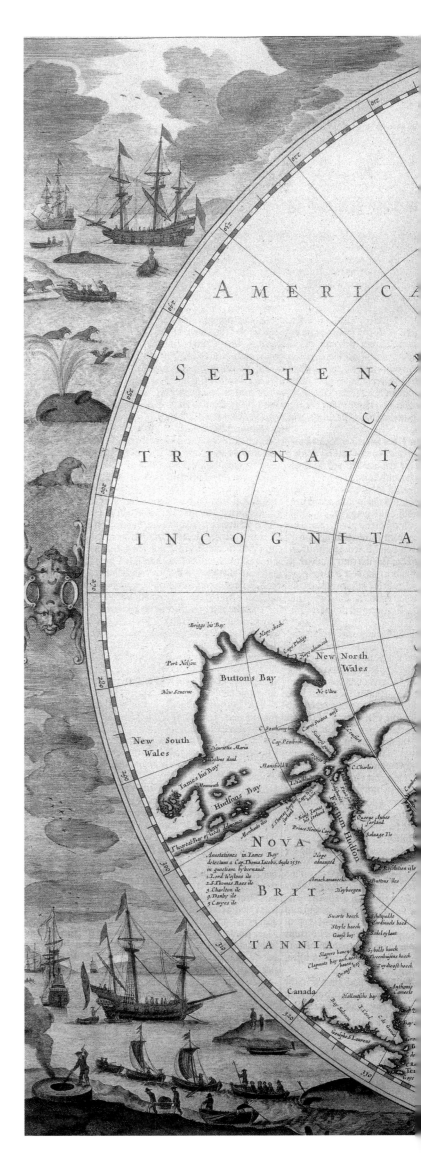

rising to the surface to breathe where the ice cover was thin, the whales made their way through the pack ice only to fall prey to the hunters who had wintered in the region. With the aid of Eskimo dog teams the whaling boats were towed to the ice's edge. The men kept guard and the Eskimos pulled the whales that had been caught to harbour with their dogs. In return the Eskimos received those parts of the whale that the hunters did not want and which they themselves prized.

104 Happel specialised in depicting ocean currents and peculiarities of the world's seas. He placed what he called the Moscol Current vortex in northern Norway. The phenomenon of eddying water, caused by tidal changes, near the Lofoten Islands was known as early the 16th century. Sailors feared it and avoided the area because they were afraid the whirlpool would swallow their vessels. In Happel's illustration the force of the eddying current has comically exaggerated the forms the waves take.
(JOHN NURMINEN FOUNDATION)

105 William Scoresby Sr. took his son William with him on a whale hunting trip when the boy was only ten years old. Seven years later, in 1806, young Scoresby became first mate of the RESOLUTION and in 1810 her captain. Scoresby was a born diarist: he kept a diary on his honeymoon. He collected his Arctic experiences in book form in 1820. Scoresby was the first to recognise that the Arctic was getting warmer, and became interested in investigating this phenomenon. In 1822 he mapped the east coast of Greenland while he was whaling there. A year later he gave up whaling, continued his studies, entered the clergy and wrote his dissertation. He investigated magnetism and until his death worked on developing the compass.
(HELSINKI UNIVERSITY LIBRARY)

106 William Scoresby Sr. was a renowned English whaler at the turn of the 18th and 19th centuries. The best whalers, like him, collected information on the Arctic, although this information was often not written down. In 1806 Scoresby achieved a new northerly record for ships by reaching 81° 30' in his vessel the RESOLUTION, an achievement which Nordenskiöld narrowly beat only in 1861.
(HELSINKI UNIVERSITY LIBRARY)

Relations between the hunters and the Eskimos varied according to which region was in question. The Danes had control of the south of Greenland. The Danes aimed, among other things, to regulate intercourse between outsiders and the Eskimos. There were no Danes in the northern part of Melville Bay, so whalers traded with the Eskimos there. The area was less attractive, however, since the conditions were worse and the whales were fewer in number.

In the areas of Baffin Island, Davis Strait and Baffin Bay the Eskimos had their first encounter with Europeans when the whalers arrived. They were keen to get hold of European weapons, tools, liquor and tobacco. The help of the Eskimos was needed and they were eager to work as boatmen, to pull teams of dogs or as hunters, jobs at which they were incomparably better than the whalers. By the time whaling had come to an end early in the 1900s the life of the Eskimos had changed considerably. This can be seen from their tools, cooking utensils, hunting equipment and dress, particularly in summer. During the whaling period and after, growing numbers of Eskimos began to practise fur trapping.

107 At the beginning of the 17th century Hessel Gerritsz was the head cartographer for both Holland's West Indian and East Indian Trading companies. His maps were printed rarely, but his finest achievements have been preserved for subsequent generations as unique hand-made parchment maps. The map of the North Atlantic drawn up in 1628 was made on more than a metre of parchment hide. It gives the latest information on expeditions. When drawing the map of the west of Greenland Gerritsz knew the results of Frobisher's, Davis', Waymouth's, Hudson's, Button's, Baffin's and Hawgeridge's voyages. The bay found near Baffin Island to the north of Hudson Bay, which the English Queen later named "Meta Incognita", is marked in the wrong place on Gerritsz's sea chart. On his voyage Frobisher had Mercator's map with him, whose longitudes were incorrect. The bay found by Frobisher was for this reason from the outset located incorrectly off Greenland instead of America. This 'Frobisher Sound' separates a large island from Greenland proper in many subsequent maps. The western and northern parts of Hudson Bay are not shown on the map because they were still unknown. Gerritsz's maps are decorated with beautiful illustrations of fishing and whaling. (Bibliothèque Nationale de France)

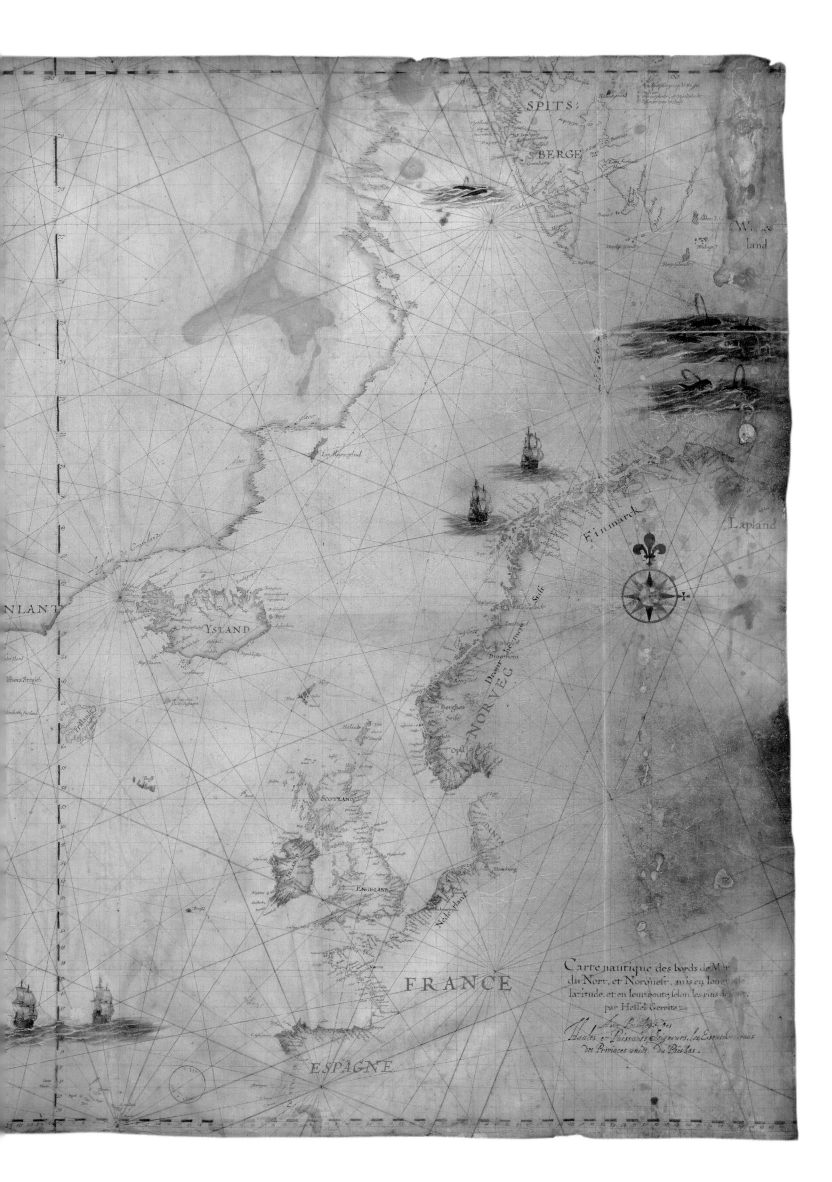

SPITS:

SBERGE

W...
land

Lapland

Finmarck

NLANT

YSLAND

NORVEG

Bergher
Stift

Opslo

SCOTLAND

IRLAND

ENGELAND

Neder-Lanc

FRANCE

ESPAGNE

Carte nautique des bords de Mer
du Nort, et Noroüest, mis en longitude
latitude, et en leur route selon les rins de vent,
par Hessel Gerritz...

Aux Puissans Des
Hautes et Puissants Seigneurs, les Estats Generaux
des Provinces unies du Pais bas.

HALOS, MIRAGES AND OTHER ARCTIC ILLUSIONS

All over the world various kinds of halo phenomena can be seen around the sun and the moon, but they are especially impressive in the proximity of the poles. When light hits ice crystals in the atmosphere, arcs and tangential arcs adjacent to them are formed around the sun or the moon. At the point where the arcs intersect, balls of light which Arctic explorers call 'sundogs' or 'mock suns' (parhelia) appear. Often, a horizontal streak of light crossing the sun can also be seen.

Descriptions of halos already appear in the reports of early polar expeditions. In de Bry's travel journal written at the end of the 16th century, a sun with a human face, complete with halo and mock suns, has been drawn behind Barents' ships. Johann Gmelin, a scientist who took part in Bering's second expedition to the north, made a study of halos and published illustrations of them in his work *Reise durch Sibirien von den Jahr 1733 bis 1743*, and subsequently many other explorers have drawn or painted them. It is difficult to photograph a halo because of the great contrasts in the firmament.

Mirages are also a common phenomenon in the Arctic, where the differences in temperature between overlapping atmospheric strata are often great. At the meeting point of these strata the light is refracted and forms mirror-like surfaces near the horizon. These are reflected in the eyes of the observer as mirages. At sea or on glaciers, these mirages appear above the horizon, often elongated or otherwise distorted. Images of islands or ships a long way

beneath the horizon can rise up to float in the air. The impression of a ship that seems to have been turned upside down by the inversion surface and appears to sail mast-downwards is particularly confusing.

The earth is slightly flattened at the poles, which is why it is possible to see farther than normal in polar regions. At latitude 60° (in Helsinki, for example), the horizon seen from a height of 5 feet is 3 miles away, but the corresponding distance at the North Pole is 7 miles. A mirage can bring points even further away into view. It can appear to bring distant ice formations into close-up as sizeable mountain ranges. Surrounded by a mirage, one feels the horizon has risen up and that one is in a gigantic ice crater.

Mirages have deceived many an Arctic traveller. It is even argued that it was this that drew Erik the Red from Iceland to Greenland. John Ross's attempt to sail the Northwest Passage in 1818 was cut off in Lancaster Sound by the "Croker Mountains". This was later understood to have been an illusion, a mirage. Eighty years later Robert Peary saw "Crocker Land" in northern Greenland, and this even appeared on maps for some time. Eight years after Peary, Macmillan could see no sign of it, however, but he did see powerful mirages. Drawings of mirages appeared in publications as early as 1820, when William Scoresby's *An Account of the Arctic Regions* was published, depicting many Arctic phenomena for the first time.

In Arctic conditions fog and clouds can

also bring about mirages. Dark areas reflected onto clouds can inform the observer of land beneath them. In winter such reflections are caused by areas of unfrozen water, polynyas. Off the coast of Siberia, such reflections have sometimes been interpreted as brought about by islands.

Sometimes the Arctic deceives the traveller because there are no points of comparison there. When one has seen nothing but expanses of snow and ice day after day, the eyes begin to deceive. When, in addition, the horizon is concealed by fog and there is no sense of perspective, estimating distances and proportions is made still more difficult. Even small blocks of nearby ice might suddenly appear to be large mountains. Sverdrup's expedition at the beginning of the 20th century came across a herd of large animals in the Cardigan Strait in North Canada. The men thought the animals were deer until Sverdrup realised he was looking at a group of some hundred rabbits. This was the effect of distorted distance.

Illusions of light and colour have also been seen in the Arctic snow and ice. At such times the explanation is often biological. John Ross tells of seeing wide areas of red snow in Greenland. The colour was due to microscopic algae which glow crimson at certain temperatures. Nordenskiöld tells of how the footprints of his companions glowed strangely in the dark on Spitsbergen. This was caused by amphipods living in the snow which began to glow when disturbed.

109 In the Arctic, explorers were faced with colour or light phenomena never seen before. In favourable conditions certain crustaceans glowed or coloured the snow. On his voyages, James Ross came across a colour phenomenon of which he made a picture in his travel report. The wide snow ridges were coloured crimson. (JOHN NURMINEN FOUNDATION)

110 Halos can surround the moon just as well as the sun. The formation of a nocturnal halo is a familiar sight for visitors to the North. (JOHN NURMINEN FOUNDATION)

XL.
PHOENOMENON IN COELO.
VRSVS IMMANIS CAPTVS. 5.

111 The halo was probably described for the first time in de Bry's publication telling of Barents' voyage to the North. In the picture the laughing suns with their halos watch Barents' crew as they struggle against a polar bear. Barents' vessels can be seen either side of the sun halo. The drawing is based on an oral description, which is why it was not possible to depict the halo properly.

(JOHN NURMINEN FOUNDATION)

112 In 1822 William Scoresby Jr. described the mirage phenomena that appeared on the horizon in his book A VOYAGE TO WHALE FISHERY. Strong differences in temperature near the surface of the sea cause boundary surfaces which function like an optical mirror. Ships rise into the sky on or beyond the horizon, often upside down and recurring. According to Scoresby the mirages usually occurred in the evening after a clear day and they almost always presaged an east wind. At the mouth of the Yenisei in Siberia an island rising on the horizon was considered a sign of a storm.
(JOHN NURMINEN FOUNDATION)

108 Backdrop courtesy of:
(SCOTT POLAR RESEARCH INSTITUTE)

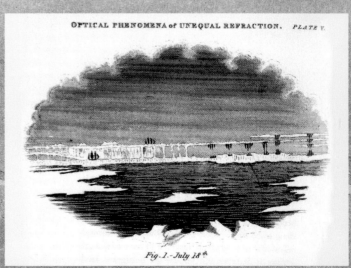

OPTICAL PHENOMENA of UNEQUAL REFRACTION. PLATE V.

Fig. 1.—July 18.ᵗʰ

TRADING POSTS AND EXPEDITIONS INTO THE INTERIOR

The first expeditions seeking to find the Northwest Passage were undertaken by sea. As the settlement of North America expanded and
the fur trade developed, expeditions were made by land ever further
to the west and north. The great rivers flowing into the Arctic Sea
opened up the way to the Arctic coast.

SAMUEL CHAMPLAIN

The French king Henry IV (1553-1610) was interested in conquering the New World. The state agreed to grant a fur-trading monopoly to private traders but only in the event that the holder of the monopoly committed himself to founding a colony. It was necessary therefore to find a man capable of doing this. Henry chose Samuel Champlain for the task, a man who had earlier been in the service of Spain, had plundered an English warship and written a book on life in the Spanish colonies. Champlain also recommended the building of the Panama Canal 300 years before the project was accomplished.

Champlain was among the first, if not the first, of a new generation of explorers. On arriving at the St Lawrence River in 1603 he allied himself with the Huron Indians, learned their language, made journeys in Indian canoes – perhaps the first white man to do so – and extended the French area of influence to the west and to the north. He forced the Iroquois to ally themselves with the English. He believed that a route to China led from the Great Lakes of Canada. In 1609 he

founded the town of Quebec which became the French Canadian centre.

Three years after the death of Champlain, Louis XIV succeeded to the throne. He applied himself with more enthusiasm than his predecessor to the affairs of the New World. Thanks to him the French colony grew stronger. Under the leadership of Pierre Radisson, the French advanced as far as Hudson Bay, but as time progressed they lost their position to the British. The Hudson's Bay Company, established in 1670, ensured British supremacy.

THE HUDSON'S BAY COMPANY

In 1668, under the patronage of Prince Rupert, 18 London merchants equipped two ships and despatched them to Hudson Bay to trade in. At the mouth of the Rupert River they built Fort Charles, a stronghold that would later be re-named Rupert House. Medard Chouart Groseilliers and Pierre Espirit Radisson spent the following winter there and managed

113 George Back's depiction of Franklin's camp at the River Coppermine estuary. Franklin notes that his measurement of the degree of latitude differed substantially from that in Hearne's report. Franklin was convinced that Hearne's description of the Coppermine estuary meant that he must have been to the coast before turning back. He in fact gave the mightiest peninsula on this coast the name Cape Hearne. The sun set behind the sea as late as eleven thirty that night. (JOHN NURMINEN FOUNDATION)

to get fur-trading underway. Their vessel the *Nonsuch* returned to England in spring 1669.

At the request of the merchants, Charles II granted exclusive trading rights to a company whose name became *The Governor and Company of Adventurers of England trading into Hudson's Bay*. Prince Rupert was made the first Governor of this venture and the company was given exclusive rights to trade in the

wilderness surrounding Hudson Bay. The Hudson's Bay Company controlled the area for the next 200 years, with powers of war and peace over 1 500 000 square miles of territory.

Little by little more trading posts were established. The first were built at the estuaries of the rivers flowing into Hudson Bay: Moose Factory on the River Moose, Fort Albany on the Albany in 1679, York Factory established on the Hayes and

concluded in 1686 and under the treaty the French were allowed to keep the areas they had conquered. Fights for possession of the Hudson Bay area, however, continued until 1713, when the conclusion of the Treaty of Utrecht confirmed the rights of the Hudson's Bay Company.

From 1714 onwards, at least one of the Hudson's Bay Company's vessels made a journey to the trading posts of Hudson Bay every spring bringing provisions and trading goods and taking the winter furs to England. They usually managed to make the return journey during the same season but occasionally they were forced to winter in the waters of Hudson Bay. Such regular voyages continued until the 20th century.

Initially the trading company did not take a positive attitude towards individual voyages of exploration. Trading posts were established ever deeper into the wilderness, however. The growth of the Hudson's Bay Company not only increased geographical knowledge of the region but also expanded the British Empire. In 1731 the new Prince of Wales Fort was built of stone at the mouth of the River Churchill to replace the earlier Churchill post.

A long break followed. French-Canadian fur traders began to advance into the west again, first to Lake Superior, then to Lake Winnipeg, from there to the Saskatchewan River and, at the end of the 1770s, to Lakes Beaver and Peter Pond. These posts attracted the Indians who had earlier taken their furs to Hudson Bay to take their wares to posts situated closer to their homes. Tighter competition forced the heads of the trading companies to look to the wilderness to the west. And in 1774 Samuel Hearne was given the task of founding Cumberland House on Lake Cumberland in Saskatchewan.

THE JOURNEYS OF SAMUEL HEARNE

Individual journeys by Hudson's Bay Company employees were already being undertaken at the beginning of the 18th century. It was not possible for the Chipewyan Indians living in the north to trade at the Hudson's Bay Company posts situated in the Cree Indians' areas since these tribes were at war with one another. William Stewart was the first European to make his way across the more than 620 miles from Churchill to Great Slave Lake to try to make peace with the Indians, an

Churchill Fort on the Severn. The Frenchmen Pierre Radisson and Groseilliers were among the founders of the Hudson's Bay Company but in 1682 they broke away and founded a competing French trading company. This was the beginning of the conflicts between the French and the English. The trading companies changed their owners and names many times at the end of the 17th century. Peace was

115 The French mapmaker Louis Renard drew up this depiction of North America, which was published in the ATLAS DE LA NAVIGATION *in 1715. Hopeful assumptions of a Northwest Passage leading from Hudson Bay have been discarded in this map. There are, on the other hand, a number of suggestions of openings to the west from Baffin Bay. The bay is located too far to the west, almost to the wrong side of Baffin Land. In addition, Baffin Bay and Hudson Bay are connected to each other on Renard's map. Two fjords penetrate the southern tip of Greenland. Renard's map follows the portolan principle. Projection is missing from this kind of sailor's chart. It is as if the map is squeezed onto its plane from the curved surface of the globe.*
(JOHN NURMINEN FOUNDATION)

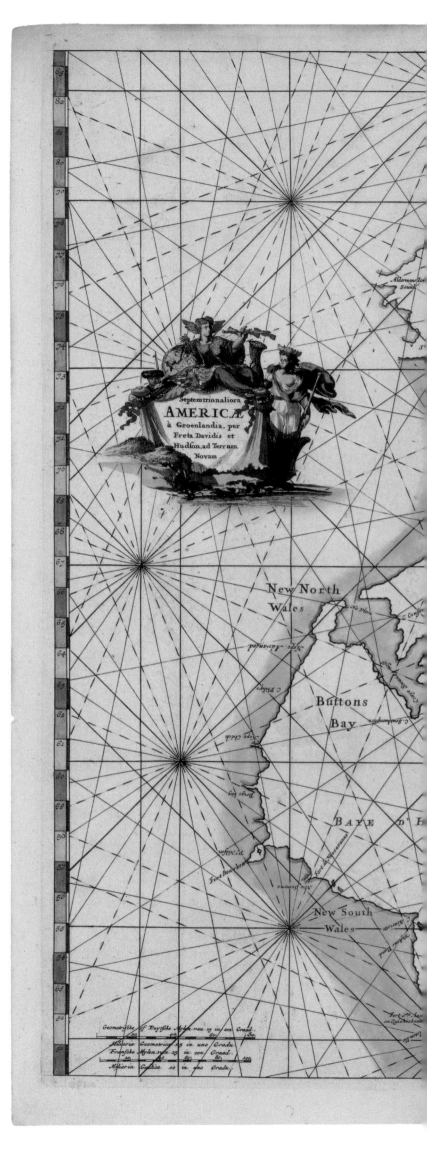

endeavour in which he was successful. James Knight, the company's overseas governor at York Factory, became interested in the riches of the northern region. To facilitate trade, Knight re-built the Churchill River trading post, which was closest to the Chipewyan hunting grounds.

James Knight was also interested in the wealth of gold and copper thought to exist north of Hudson Bay. In 1719, at the age of 70, he organised and led a two-ship expedition. The fate of the expedition became clear only 50 years later. In 1767, while on a trading and hunting trip, the Hudson's Bay Company ship, the *Success*, visited Marble Island in Hudson Bay. On the island the remains of a ship and signs of wintering were found. There was also a pile of coal under which a group of graves was discovered. The man who found them was Samuel Hearne, mate of the *Churchill*. The grave and the buildings were later found to be the remnants of Knight's expedition. Hearne returned to the island and questioned the Eskimos to try to ascertain the fate of the expedition. According to the Eskimos a great many men had been lost during the first winter and after the second only five of the group remained and they too soon perished.

In order to expand to the west the Hudson's Bay Company needed better information on the wilderness. Samuel Hearne was chosen to undertake an expedition. Moses Norton, who was the local commander at the time, was interested in the fabled Indian copper mine in the north, thought to be close to the sea. Armed with samples he had received, he succeeded in persuading the London committee to approve sending a white man to find the mine.

Moses Norton had planned everything in advance. A Cree Indian by the name of Chawchinahaw was chosen as guide. Since the Indian had never been to the copper mine, his task was to lead Hearne to the whereabouts of a better guide, Matonabbee. The journey failed because the guide lost all interest once he had been paid. Chawchinahaw left Hearne and his men, tired and hungry, in the wilderness. Hearne covered the more than 135-mile journey east to Churchill after his five-week journey, arriving at the beginning of December 1769.

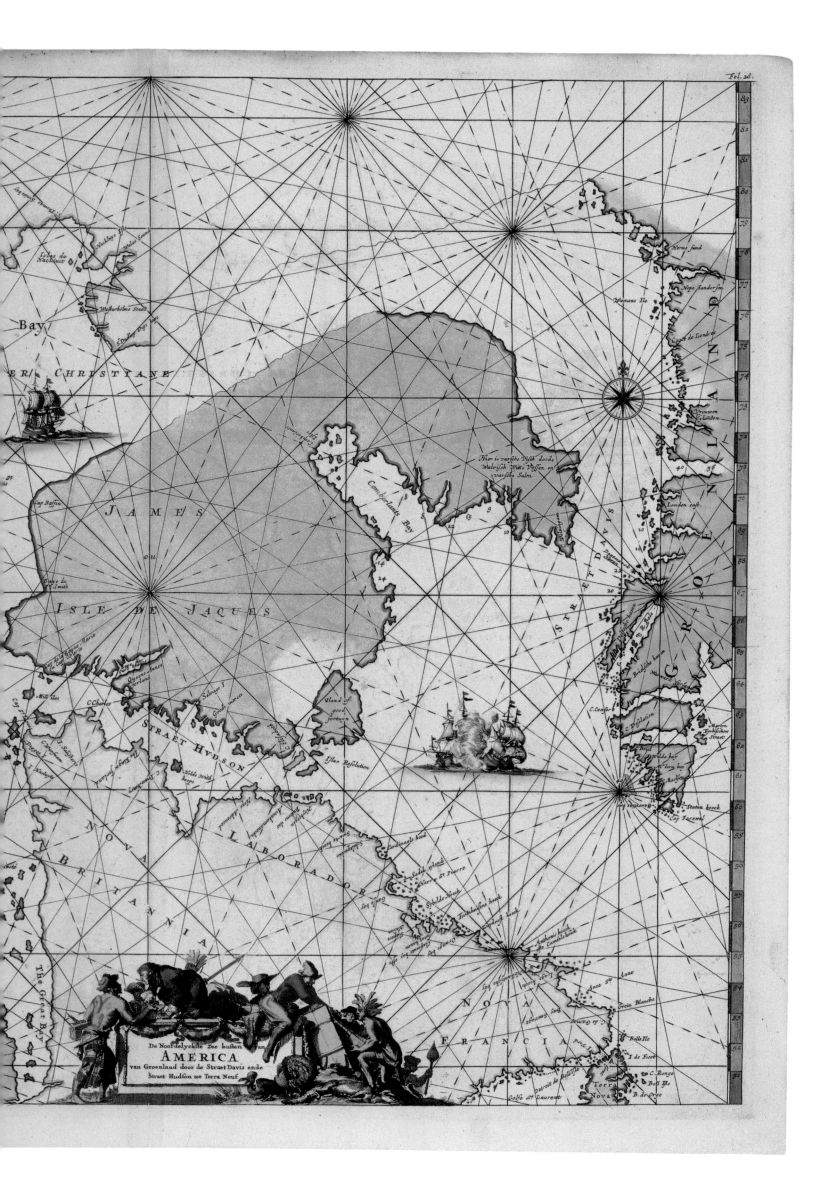

Bay

ER CHRISTIANE

Islas de Nachuit

Hackluys Illd Wales Sound

Westerholme Sound

Horns sond

Nype Sanderson

Womens Ilo

Couck de Londra

London cust

GROENLAND

STRAET DAVIS

Drouwen Eylanden

Hier is varsche Disch doode
Walvisch Witte Vossen en
varsche Salm

40 36

Cap Baffin

JAMES

ou

Drive du
C. Smith

ISLE DE JAQUES

Cumberlants Bay

12

10

14

24

20

22

Disco

GROOT

C. Lonsort

C. Desolation

Martin
Forbischers
Straet

R. Bilia

Bridsche hoeu

Cap de la Reyne Marie
Cap. S. Maria

Port Nelson
Queene Anne
fortland

Mill Illes

C. Charles

Selway I.

Goods morass

Haring I.

Iland of
good fortuun

De Brul
Mille bar
S. Terry bay
Raesfords

Cap S. Louis

C. Salisbury

Diggs Island

S. Salisbury

Cap S. Charles

Hopsby

NOVA

Noble Wield
hoeck

Langenes I.

STRAET HUDSON

Prins Hendrick

Ilas Resolution

Cap Warwiohs

Staten hoeck

Cap Farewel

Cap Queene

BRITANNIA

LABORADOR

Salisburys hoeck

Cardinaels hoed

Sadel island

Varne S. Pierre

Sybelde hoeck

Turshuysons hoeck

Anthoni hoeck
als Carnolts hoeck

The Great Bay

Ance S.te Anne

Grein Blanche

Anse S. Laurens

I. de Grange

Belle Ilo

I. de Fiset

NOVA

C. Ronge

Bell Ilo

B. de Grae

FRANCIA

Golfe S. Laurent

Detroit de Belle Isle

Terra
Nova

De Noordelyckste Zee kusten van
AMERICA
van Groenland door de Straet Davis ende
Straet Hudson tot Terra Neuf

Hearne learned a great deal on the journey. He understood that the Indians could not be managed using western methods and that the journey would be demanding. Those who were to go along had to be selected accordingly. For the second journey Moses Norten chose a Chipewyan Indian by the name of Conne-e-quese as guide, and sent the expedition off into the wilderness once more in February 1770. This journey was also unsuccessful.

The new guide had not been to the Coppermine River upon the banks of which the mines were supposed to be located either. Before long the expedition was lost. When Hearne, in addition, broke his quadrant, an instrument that was essential to calculate the degree of latitude, in other words the north-south direction, he had no chance of defining the location of the river or its estuary in the region of the supposed copper mines; in November 1770 he was forced to return to Churchill. On this occasion too Hearne was robbed of everything he possessed on the journey home.

Hearne had met Matonabbee on his journey back to the trading station and believed that the latter could guide him to the river and the copper mine. He persuaded him to become his guide. Matonabbee told Hearne that, as well as choosing the poor man Hearne had made a second mistake: he had not taken the men's wives along. Matonabbee's view of the importance of squaws was an essential part of Hearne's account of the journey. According to Matonabbee the men could not travel far and hunt if they had heavy things to carry. And if their hunting turned out to be successful who would carry the catch? Women were created to work, and one woman was able to carry or pull as much as two men. Women also put up the tents, made and repaired clothes as well as keeping the men warm at night. In order to be able to carry more or to lighten the load of the women, Matonabbee had six squaws. For this reason he was a good guide and travelling companion for Hearne.

Hearne decided to take along only Chipewyan Indians and no Cree at all. All the Cree that Norton had chosen had made poor travelling companions. Hearne's decision did not please Norton, who was part Cree himself. Although the local commander possessed all the equipment Hearne needed, he gave Hearne the station's worst quadrant.

On 7 December, two weeks after returning, Hearne set out on his third journey. During the spring they made slow progress. Occasionally either one of Matonabbee's squaws fell sick or even the guide himself, sometimes they went hungry and occasionally hunting went well. On the journey Matonabbee bought a seventh squaw. In spring they built birch bark canoes in which they crossed rivers and hunted caribou.

In May 1771 Matonabbee left most of his squaws to wait at the camp, choosing the two youngest to go with him, and set

116 The most important Hudson's Bay Company trading posts and their dates of establishment are marked on the map. Although the first expedition into the interior (with the exception of Hearne's journey to the mouth of the Coppermine) were carried out at the instigation of the Royal Navy, the Company men Simpson, Dease, Rae and later Mackenzie and Pond, mapped the wilderness and coasts of Canada. (PATANEN)

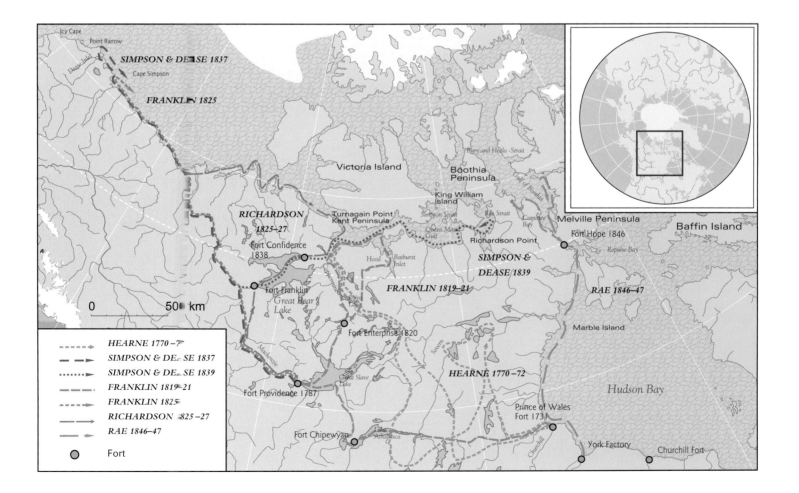

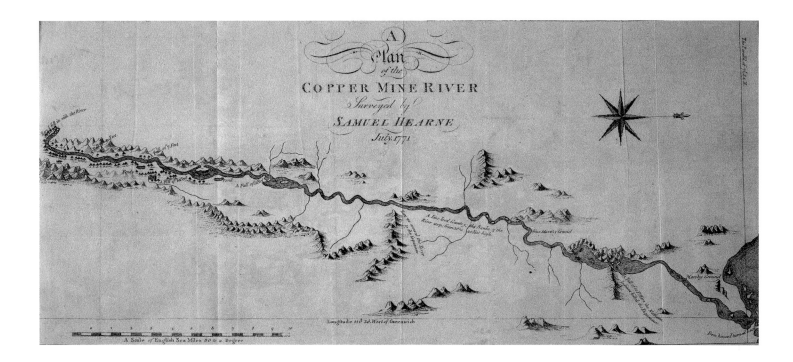

117 On Hearne's map of the mouth of the Coppermine River north is on the right. On the right-hand edge there is also a strip of the Arctic Ocean on which is written "From here I returned". Hearne has been criticised because of his incorrect locations. On 17 July 1771 he estimated his position at the mouth of the river as 71° 55' latitude North and 120° 30' longitude West. He estimates his margin of error to be 20 miles at most. In actual fact the position he gave was 275 miles too far north and 130 miles too far west. According to Hearne it was difficult to use the quadrant because of bad weather. It is strange that he was so sloppy when estimating his latitude. The mistake in longitude, on the other hand, is understandable since he could not have had the kind of clock with him that would have guaranteed a precise measurement. Hearne is described as a resolute explorer, but his skill at measuring was that of an ordinary mate. If the estimated position had been based on distance covered, the mistake could have been even greater. The mass murder of Eskimos by the Indians at the mouth of the river certainly must have shocked Hearne. The place of the tragedy is marked a little way upstream from the river estuary where the Indians were camped by a waterfall. (JOHN NURMINEN FOUNDATION)

out for the north with Hearne and a small group. On the journey Hearne learned that some of the Indians had come along with the purpose of killing the Eskimos living near the mouth of the river. Later, around June–July, they left the rest of the squaws behind and continued on a quick march. As well as caribou they hunted musk ox. Eventually, on 13 July, the group arrived at the Coppermine River. Further down the river on the western bank below some falls, there were five Eskimo tents. The Indians painted their faces black and red, tied back their hair to prevent it falling over their eyes, lightened their loads and stripped half naked. Then they attacked the Eskimos. According to Hearne only a few of the Eskimos escaped, the rest were killed early in the morning of 17 July.

After the battle the Indians came back to where Hearne had been waiting and the group advanced to the mouth of the river. Hearne put up a sign there, taking the coast into the Hudson's Bay Company's possession, and carried out the necessary observations. They immediately set out on the return journey without exploring the estuary and the sea more thoroughly. When they had made their way 25 miles to the south-east they reached the copper mine. The Indians had said that the mine was so rich that it yielded pure copper. Hearne and his companions found a copper lump weighing about three kilos, which it has been possible to admire in the British Museum since 1818. After a year the expedition returned to the Prince of Wales fort at Churchill. The entire journey had lasted almost 19 months.

Hearne was later found to have made inaccurate geographical measurements. He determined the estuary of the Coppermine River to be 185 miles too far to the north. Hearne's quadrant was lost when it fell into Point Lake on his return journey. He probably made his geographical determinations partly on the basis of distance travelled, and his estimated distances later proved to be too long. In any event Hearne made a 1 250-mile journey to the Coppermine and back, showed the river to flow into the polar sea, found the copper mine and proved that a Northwest Passage further south did exist after all. Although he had been completely dependent on the Indians he proved he was well able to adjust to northern conditions.

Doubt has been cast on the accuracy of Hearne's account of his journey, published more than twenty years after his expedition, because it was seen to differ in places from his diary. In the book he also provides information on Knight's expedition that he had not reported earlier. But there is no doubt about the fact of Hearne's journey; he had been where he claimed to have been.

In 1783–1784 some Montreal fur traders founded the North West Company. The company had a painful birth, with a number of fur traders joining forces. In spite of this it

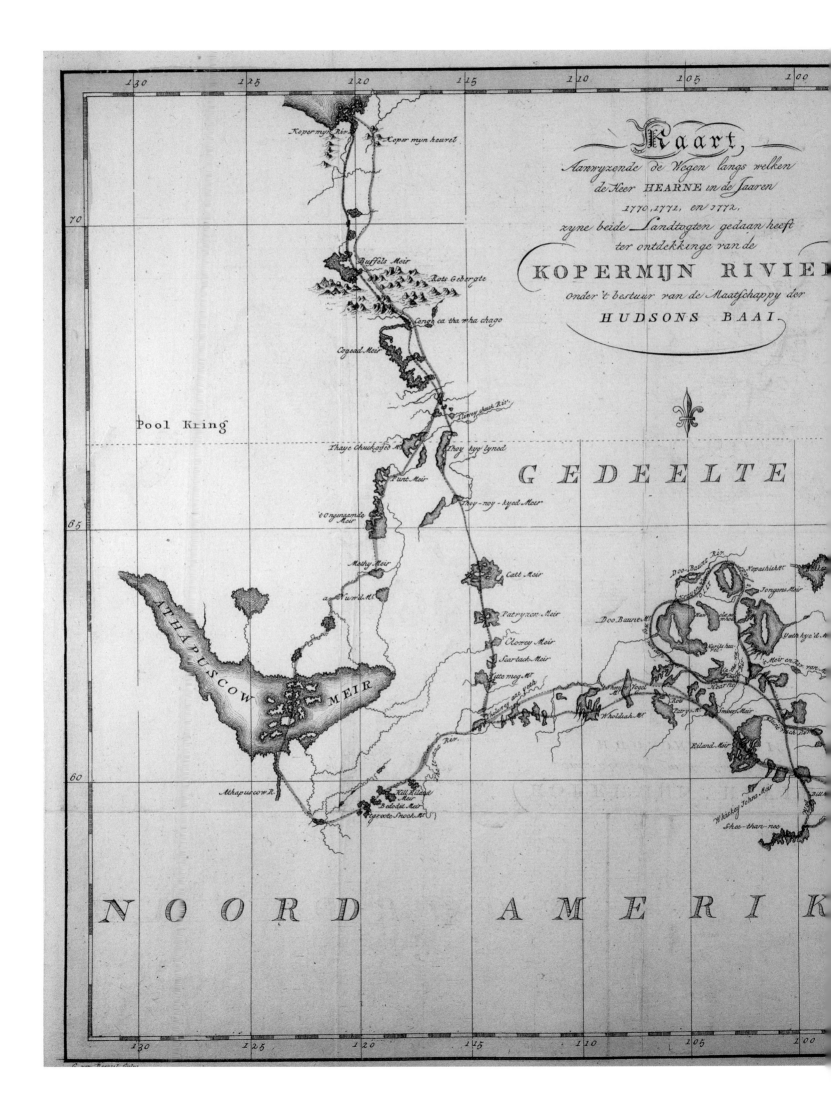

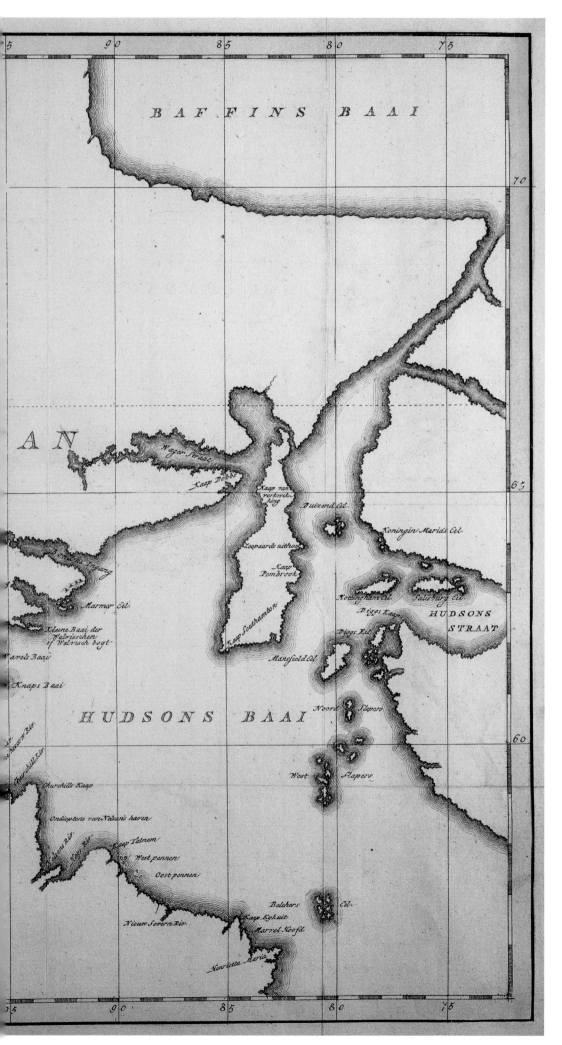

119 *Samuel Hearne (1745–1792) went to school only until the age of 11, when he decided to join the Royal Navy. Having served his time as a sailor he joined the Hudson's Bay Company.*
(CANADIAN MUSEUM OF CIVILIZATION)

118 *Hearne's map, which he published in his travel account* JOURNEY FROM PRINCE OF WALES' FORT IN HUDSON BAY TO THE NORTHERN OCEAN, *increased the world's knowledge of the geography of North America. The maps of the Arctic were above all founded on the location of the polar sea, which was demonstrated by Hearne. The mouth of the Coppermine remained for a long time the only point of reference on the Arctic coast, and it was surrounded by enormous blank areas. Hearne was a single-minded explorer and tireless trekker. In 19 months he covered 1600 miles of unknown territory. He made the journey across Hudson Bay to the Arctic Ocean accompanied by Indians. Hearne was the first white man to see the coast of Arctic America. On many contemporary maps the words "The Sea, According to Hearne" are written on the Coppermine delta.*
(JOHN NURMINEN FOUNDATION)

120 Back's evocative picture of a camp setting in a dense spruce forest where snow-covered branches give an enchanted atmosphere. A real fire provides welcome and essential warmth on a cold night. The picture is probably of Back's winter journey while he was fetching more provisions from Fort Chipewyan.
(JOHN NURMINEN FOUNDATION)

was more dynamic than the Hudson Bay's Company. One of the North West Company's leading figures was Peter Pond who, in the summer of 1737, travelled west to Lake Athabasca and the Great Slave Lake. He discovered that the source of the Mackenzie River was on the western side of the lake. Peter Pond told Alexander Mackenzie of the river and perhaps even suggested an expedition.

Mackenzie set out on the journey from Fort Chipewyan to the North West Company's trading station on Lake Athabasca in 1789. He hoped to find a passage to the Pacific Ocean, into which he assumed the river flowed. He went down the river in a bark canoe with five *voyageurs*, or French-Canadian boatmen, and a Chipewyan guide by the name of English Chief. Unlike Hearne's former guide Matonabbee, English Chief had only two wives with him.

While travelling down the river, Mackenzie came in contact with the Indians of various tribes, who told him of the extraordinary length of the river. He reached its estuary in two weeks, however, and made camp on Whale Island, which he named. It was only on the following day that he discovered that

he had arrived at what was later called the Beaufort Sea and not the Pacific Ocean. He named the river the *River of Disappointment*. Questioning the Indians he learnt of another great river, apparently the Yukon, further to the west. Mackenzie returned to Great Slave Lake at the end of August, having covered the 3 000-mile journey in 102 days. He did not give up hope of reaching the Pacific, and found his way there over the Rocky Mountains more than four years later in 1793.

THE TROUBLED BIRTH OF A LEGEND

In 1800 John Franklin, who was to become one of the most well-known Arctic explorers, joined the Royal Navy at the age of fourteen. His naval career was both active and varied; he was involved in exploring the coast of Australia in 1801, participated as a midshipman in the sea battles of Copenhagen and Trafalgar and in 1818 served as a Lieutenant on the naval expedition to the Arctic Ocean commanded by Captain David Buchan. Franklin captained one of the two vessels assigned to the expedition, HMS *Trent*. When the Admiralty ordered him to lead a new expedition, Lieutenant Franklin had experience of both exploration and of conditions in the Arctic. His mission was to explore the north coast of America east of the estuary of the River Coppermine to Hudson Bay. The expedition was linked with Edward Parry's simultaneous attempt to find a Northwest Passage.

121 Franklin's first overland expedition crossing Lake Prosperous on 8 August 1820 on his journey to Fort Enterprise, where he built his winter camp. Indians with canoes helped transport the equipment. Franklin also used a canoe on his first expedition, as had Hearne and Champlain before him.
(JOHN NURMINEN FOUNDATION)

122 An Indian family was also living at Franklin's winter camp. The family's attractive 16-year-old daughter was called Green Stockings. Both midshipmen, Robert Hood and George Back, were infatuated with the beautiful girl. To avoid a conflict Back was sent to stock up on provisions for the expedition and Hood painted more pictures of Green Stockings and her parents. As a result of their relationship a daughter was born. (JOHN NURMINEN FOUNDATION)

The expedition arrived at York Factory trading post on Hudson Bay in 1820 after an exciting sea voyage. They continued their journey by boat and, with the coming of winter, went on with a team of dogs and snow shoes until they reached Fort Providence on Great Slave Lake in summer 1820. Franklin's party replenished their supplies and built their own winter quarters, Fort Enterprise, in a forested area at the north of the lake, close to the headwaters of the Coppermine River. They ran into difficulties in acquiring more supplies because the competition between the Hudson's Bay Company and the North West Company was raging fiercely. The local governor of the Hudson Bay's Company considered the expedition unnecessary and unprofessional and suspected they would perish in the Tundra.

In addition to Franklin, the official participants in this naval expedition were midshipmen George Back and Robert

123 John Franklin was an interesting figure. He was a naval officer who had limited Arctic experience when he began his overland expedition as a 33-year-old Lieutenant. But he learnt from his mistakes, although he was never able to break free from the Navy's rigid way of thinking. Interest in him is in no way diminished by his second wife Lady Franklin, who by her persistence earned herself a place in the history of Arctic exploration.

(National Portrait Gallery)

124 After Franklin's second overland expedition of 1825–1827 there were still great gaps in knowledge of the North American continent and the islands off the Arctic Ocean. Beechey had progressed east from Icy Cape – Cook's turning point – to Point Barrow. There were still 185 miles of unexplored coast between Beechey and Franklin. Richardson had mapped the stretch between the MacKenzie and the Coppermine. Franklin's first expedition reached the Kent Peninsula. The area between it and Hecla and Fury Strait, found by Parry, was also unknown. Parry had mapped Melville Sound and discovered Prince Regent Inlet, but the Boothia Peninsula and Bay were still uncharted. Jones and Smith Sounds had not been discovered yet either. This beautiful map was published as an addendum to Franklin's travel journal.

(John Nurminen Foundation)

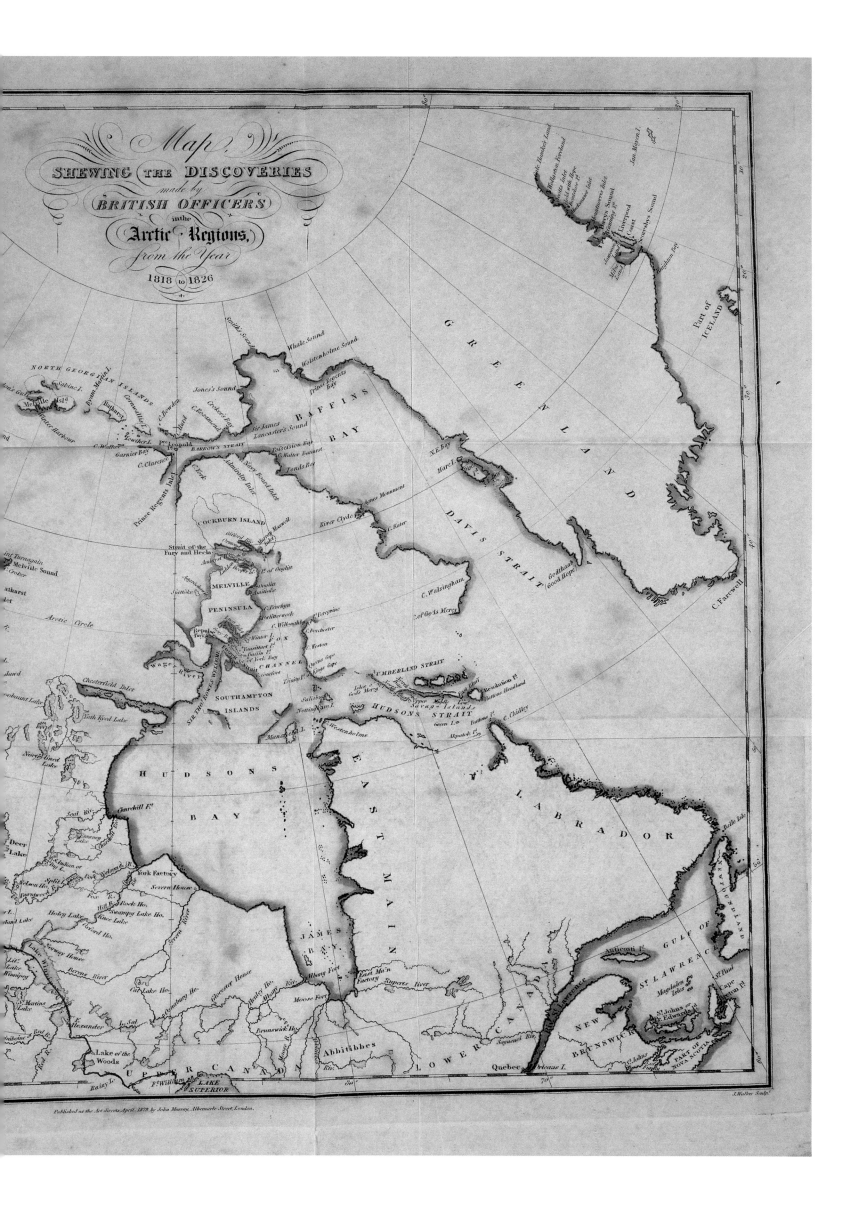

Map
SHEWING THE DISCOVERIES
made by
BRITISH OFFICERS
in the
Arctic Regions,
from the Year
1818 to 1826

Published as the Act directs, April. 1829, by John Murray, Albemarle Street, London.

J. Walker Sculp.

Hood, Doctor John Richardson and John Hepburn, who was a naval seaman. Back had served under Franklin on the *Trent*. Some *voyageurs* and two Eskimo guides also took part in the journey. For their supplies they were very dependent on the Indians who had promised to hunt caribou for them. During the winter a family of Indians whose wife made clothes, lived at Fort Enterprise. The midshipmen were said to have competed for the affections of the family's most beautiful daughter, Green Stockings, a contest of love that Hood won. Franklin had to send the losing contender back on a supplies journey during which he showed that he was able to cover a respectable distance in the wintry wilderness.

The main journey began in June 1821 and reached the estuary of the Coppermine on 20 July. Hearne's geographical positions were seen to be too far to the north, but in his honour one of the peninsulas was named Cape Hearne. Franklin named several new places after his friends or influential persons at the Admiralty. The name Porden Island was a hint as to what would come, since after the journey Franklin married Miss Eleanor Anne Porden.

The expedition covered almost 620 miles in canoes unsuited to sea conditions, mapping that part of the coast between the Coppermine and Bathurst Inlet which was navigable. Franklin took considerable risks in crossing the open sea by canoe and in setting out on the return journey along the Hood River, which flowed from Bathurst Inlet, as late as 25 August. The delay worried the *voyageurs* who were doubtful of the chances of the expedition getting back alive. If they had been aware of the return route to be taken they would perhaps have set out earlier and left the leaders of the expedition behind. The British were weakened by cold and hunger as much as their men were. Before long all that remained to eat was lichen and the bone marrow of the caribou carcasses left behind by wolves.

On 4 October, George Back led an advance group with the stronger Canadians to find Indians and get help. The weaker among them died – one of the *voyageurs*, the Iroquois Michel, killed two of the expedition's Canadians in a fight over food and later murdered Hood, who had fallen sick, too. Richardson shot Michel before he managed to kill him and Hepburn. Franklin in particular, but Richardson and Hepburn too were

125 Having reached the estuary of the Coppermine River in July 1821, Franklin continued east by canoe along the frozen coast. He named the predominantly sheer faced peninsula Cape Barrow after the Admiralty's Second Secretary. Thunder and lightning, heavy winds, fog and ice made the going difficult but Franklin travelled over 600 miles along the coast in his two birch bark canoes before setting out on the return journey up the River Hood.

(JOHN NURMINEN FOUNDATION)

on the point of dying when the Indians sent by Back brought them food on 7th November.

In England Franklin was hailed as a hero. He was promoted to the rank of Captain and Back was made Lieutenant. Franklin was also made a member of the Royal Society for his geographical achievements. Thanks to his journey there was considerably more information on a Northwest Passage.

Franklin, Richardson and Back returned to North America once more. In 1821 the Hudson's Bay Company and the North West Company merged and the new company wanted to expand and acquire more information. Franklin's new expedition was decided upon jointly by the Hudson's Bay Company and the Admiralty. The expedition began in 1824 with a boat journey down to the estuary of the River Mackenzie, where Franklin and Back parted company with Richardson. They went west towards Captain Cook's Icy Cape, to which Captain Beechey had sailed in his ship the *Blossom*. Beechey sent one of his boats east to meet Franklin but Franklin was forced to turn back 155 miles before the peninsula he named Cape Beechey.

Richardson mapped the coast from the Mackenzie River to the mouth of the River Coppermine, where he arrived on 8 August. Franklin's second expedition brought excellent results. A party led by Franklin mapped almost 375 miles of the Arctic coast and Richardson's mapped 870 miles. The expedition also made a great many scientific observations. Both parties returned without trouble to their base Fort Franklin on Great Bear Lake, Richardson by way of the Coppermine and Franklin up the Mackenzie.

Franklin and the Admiralty had learnt from the experiences of his first journey. His boats of mahogany were suitable for the Mackenzie and the sea. He received the assistance of the Hudson's Bay Company's Peter Warren Dease in matters of provisioning. For his crew he chose seamen instead of voyageurs. This time Franklin turned back in time and did not risk the lives of his crew, even though it meant that he did not reach his target. Franklin had had to leave on his journey from his wife's sickbed. On hearing of her death later he may have begun to plan his second marriage by naming Point Griffin after his wife to be, Jane Griffin, later Lady Franklin.

Back was soon given a new chance to distinguish himself. When, in 1832, Captain John Ross R.N. had been on his Arctic expedition for three years, the Admiralty sent a privately funded rescue party on the premise that Ross had made his way to the continent. Back volunteered and was made leader of the expedition. A young doctor by the name of Richard King was ordered to assist him. On his previous journey Back had heard the Indians speak of a river named the Great Fish River, which the Hudson's Bay Company's men did not believe existed.

Along with his guide Back later discovered the Great Fish River, later named Back River, canoed down it with 19 companions and arrived at a sea covered with ice. Back had been given instructions to map the coast to the west but the ice prevented him from pushing forward. There was no use waiting. King suggested mapping the east coast, but Back did not agree to that even though the sea was free of ice. This was a mistake, as Back might have succeeded in showing that 'King William Land' was an island. This fact could have been important from the point of view of Franklin's last expedition.

Richard King was even more critical in his evaluation of Back's leadership than Back himself had been in his judgement of Franklin. King was probably right. Although Back could be pleasant when he needed a favour and always gave his men a drink after a difficult stretch of rapids, he was not a good leader. Back did not take the trouble to plan and oversee the preparation of the boats, which became so heavy that it was very difficult to drag them onto land to pass the rapids. Neither did Back make a contingency plan for the eventuality that the route west might be blocked by ice.

In spite of his experience and the leadership training he had received, Back did not meet King's criteria. Back was tough and courageous, it was true, but he did not want or was not able to embrace those skills demanded of an Arctic explorer. The Navy was not able to train explorers to have the skills comparable to those of the indigenous people. The best explorers were found elsewhere.

SIMPSON AND DEASE

Franklin's second expedition and those of Back would not have succeeded without the help of the Hudson's Bay Company. Peter Warren Dease had been responsible for maintenance but did not take part in the actual exploration. Similarly, Alexander McLeod changed his plans on receiving Back's plea for help, which he got from the Governor of the Hudson's Bay Company, George Simpson, and rushed with his wife, three children and servants to his aid. He too did not take part in the expedition itself but in Back's words waited 'with four men and two Indians' for him to return from the source of Great Fish River.

One can imagine the strong and ambitious George Simpson asking why the Company should organise expeditions without gaining any credit for the results. The Company's men possessed almost all the skills required on an expedition. And the little they lacked was easier to teach them than it was to instil new ways of thinking in the Navy's men. It was also easier to conduct expeditions organised under the Company's own steam; they were faster, involved less risk and were less expensive than those organised by the Admiralty.

George Simpson gave the next mapping project to two men. The leader was Peter Dease, who was a Company man of long standing. The other was George Simpson's cousin Thomas. On George's recommendation he had entered the Hudson's Bay Company's service, initially as George's secretary. By following the governor on his travels he became a skilful explorer, a match for any *voyageur* or Indian.

Based partly on Thomas Simpson's plan, George ordered Thomas and Dease to complete the mapping started by Parry, Franklin, Ross and Back. Their main objective was to continue mapping the coast from the point where Franklin had left off. If they could not progress by water, the expedition was to continue its mission on foot. First the coast west of the Mackenzie River was to be mapped and then they were to return to Turnagain Point to the east of the Mackenzie estuary and chart the stretch left by Franklin and Back. Their instructions required them to make a particular effort to find out whether the land discovered by John Ross and named Boothia Felix was an island or a peninsula. On receiving his instructions, Thomas Simpson returned to his place of work again to improve his mathematics and to practice using astronomical instruments.

In spring 1837 a twelve-man expedition went down the Mackenzie River and on 9 July discovered the eastern branch of the river which Franklin had earlier sought in vain. At the end of July the party continued mapping beyond Franklin's Return Reef. Now the names of the heads of the Hudson's Bay Company went down in history and George Simpson had a peninsula named after him. It was not possible to go on from this peninsula by boat. Simpson offered his services and received permission from Dease to continue on foot with three men and with the aid of a small portable canoe.

Close to his destination, Point Barrow, Simpson's way was cut off by a deep bay, Dease Inlet. While his men were hunting, the resourceful Simpson borrowed an umiak from some Eskimos camping on the shore of the bay to reach Point Barrow, which according to a map drawn by one of the Eskimos was some distance away on the other side of the bay. Simpson raised the flag on Point Barrow and gave back the uimiak to its owners, who had accompanied him, and on 6 August returned to join up with Dease's group.

Having spent the winter on Great Bear Lake, the following spring Simpson and Dease went down the Coppermine to the Arctic coast. The summer of 1838 was cold. The expedition had to wait two weeks at the estuary for the ice to leave and even then progress was hopeless. Bathurst Inlet was frozen when they got there. Once again Simpson continued on foot to get even as far as Point Turnagain, which Franklin had reached by canoe in 1821. For a while he mapped the north coast of the Kent Peninsula and discovered a coast to the north which he named Victoria Land (nowadays Victoria Island). The expedition returned once more to winter quarters at Fort Confidence on Great Bear Lake.

Spring came earlier in 1839 than it had the previous year. Although the first patches of open water were seen at the mouth of the Coppermine as early as 3 July, Simpson and Dease only advanced 19 miles during the first week. After this they picked up speed and on 20 July, that is a month earlier than the previous year, they reached the hitherto uncharted coast of Kent Peninsular. They continued their journey along the south coast of what was later named Queen Maud Gulf, sheltered in part by the islands. The coast turned northwards to King William Island. The expedition had already prepared to round the northern tip of King William Island by way of Cape Felix, but on 10 August a narrow strait, later named Simpson Strait, opened up to the east.

At its mid point the strait narrowed to three miles. A deep channel ran through the middle, however, making the strait navigable. After the strait they continued south-east and passed two capes, Point Richardson and Point Ogle which George Back had already named. A raging storm pushed the expedition south and on Montreal Island they found a store left behind by Back's expedition in which there were a few packages of pemmican (a food consisting of dried minced meat and fat) rotten chocolate and goods which the expedition collected as souvenirs of the journey made by their predecessors five years earlier. The blank area left between Franklin's and Back's expeditions had now been explored. Simpson and Dease continued their journey east for another 35 miles or so, to the Castor and Pollux River, which was named after the expedition's boats. They decided to leave the charting of the coast in front of them to a new expedition. Simpson and Dease made their way back by following the south coast of Victoria Island.

Although the expedition's achievements were great – they had probably made the longest boat journey in the Arctic seas – they finished mapping too soon. They failed to correct two mistakes. Simpson presumed Boothia to be an island at the south of which a strait led to Boothia Bay. He also made a still more serious mistake and concluded that there was no strait between 'King William Land' and Boothia, but that they were connected by an isthmus. Simpson and Dease did not discover the most important section of the Northwest Passage, Rae Strait. Thomas Simpson was of the opinion that it was time for him to lead an expedition of his own. Dease was no longer interested in carrying on. Thomas suggested that the unfinished work should be continued, but George Simpson did not warm to the idea. Thomas sent his suggestion straight to London, to the Council of the Hudson's Bay Company, which approved the offer, but Thomas Simpson did not hear of the decision before setting out for England. He never got there.

The reason was that on his journey Simpson had shot two of his travelling companions and then was supposed to have turned the gun on himself in the region of Lake Winnipeg. The event was only investigated superficially. Thomas Simpson's brother Alexander and one of the late Thomas's modern colleagues, Vilhjálmur Stefánsson, believed that Simpson had been murdered. The real murderers were presumed to have been his half-breed companions who thought they had found the secret of a Northwest Passage among Thomas's papers or had killed him for some other reason – to settle old scores, for example. Simpson's work remained unfinished. When he died in 1840 he was only 32 year's old. Thomas's journal, published later, showed that he was also a gifted writer.

PORTRAIT OF A MODERN POLAR EXPLORER

George Simpson had no intention of putting an end to explorations even though he had turned down Thomas's suggestion. But he had nobody to replace his cousin. It was only in 1844 that John Rae was found, one of many explorers from within the Company's own circles who had had an education in medicine. Like Thomas and George Simpson he too was a Scot.

126 Franklin's second overland expedition of 1825–1827 charted the coast of the Arctic Ocean to both the west and east of the Mackenzie River. Doctor John Richardson led the eastern party, which spent the night on the coast of Atkinson Island in an Eskimo village in which there were 17 winter huts. The frames for these – like the hut in the picture – were made of driftwood with roofs of turf. In the foreground is the frame of an umiak. Franklin's boats were made of mahogany and ash. Because it had started to rain, the boats were covered. In the picture they are anchored near the beach, sheltered from the wind.

Immediately upon graduating at the age of 20 John Rae signed up with the Hudson's Bay Company as ship's officer on the *Prince of Wales*. The ship was forced to spend the winter in Hudson Bay. Before the arrival of spring, the head of Moose Factory had hired Rae. Besides his work as a doctor, Rae hunted and roamed the wilderness. He was later considered one of the country's most proficient snow-shoe walkers.

Rae developed the Indian canoe to make it possible to use oars instead of paddles. In spring 1844 Simpson summoned the 31-year-old Rae and offered him a new mission. The aim was to travel in two boats from Churchill to Boothia Bay and map the still unexplored area. The task was a challenge to Rae since he had not yet travelled in the northern, treeless district. Before the journey he, like Thomas Simpson, had to learn how to use astronomical instruments to find his position.

The expedition set out from York Factory on the coast of Hudson Bay on 13 June 1846. Rae had with him two boats and ten men, four of whom were from his home, the Orkney Islands, one from the Shetland Isles, one Scot and one French-Canadian. One of the men had been on Simpson and Dease's journey. At Churchill they took along an Eskimo and his sons as interpreters. After three days sailing they arrived at Repulse Bay, discovered by Christopher Middleton in 1742. They heard from the Eskimos that it was only a 35-mile journey by land to the north coast and that part of it could be covered along a lake. Rae changed his plans and travelled straight to Boothia Bay instead of from the north by way of Fury and Hecla Strait. The local Eskimos at Boothia Bay informed them that there were only two ways out of the bay, east from Fury and Hecla Strait and north from Prince Regent Inlet.

Some of the men set off to return to Repulse Bay. Rae mapped the bay he had discovered and continued north to Committee Bay along the coast of the Melville Peninsula. On 8 August his progress was stopped by the ice. Rae returned with three men to Repulse Bay to check on the condition of his party. He decided to set up winter camp there. Rae sent all but one of his men to help those returning from Committee Bay cross the isthmus and set about looking for a suitable camping place. A stone building was erected for their living quarters. The roof of the building was made from the oars and masts of the boats and was roofed with deer skin and oilcloth. The windows were made from the double glazing they had brought with them. Fort Hope was completed on 2 September and when the snow came four igloos were made which were connected by passages under the snow. With the building completed they set about hunting, fishing and collecting firewood. Rae bought six sledge dogs from the Eskimos for winter expeditions and arranged for a supply of seal oil. In autumn they practised making snow shelters under the instruction of the Eskimo guide.

The winter went well in spite of the fact that they had little fuel. On 5 April, Rae set out with three Hudson's Bay Company men and two Eskimos. The expedition travelled on foot carrying their equipment on two dog sledges. They spent the nights in snow shelters. Because the warmth of the sun made the snow slushy they started travelling at two thirty at night. They made camp after midday. Half the group – including both Eskimos – remained at Pelly Bay and Rae proceeded north from the west coast of the bay to Lord Mayor's Bay which John Ross had discovered in 1830. A small peninsula connected the Boothia Peninsula to the mainland in the west. On the return journey Rae mapped the Simpson Peninsula, which pushed north between Committee Bay and Pelly Bay. In a period of thirty days he travelled almost 620 miles.

After a week's rest Rae set out on a journey again. He took five men with him. Now they only travelled by night. After a few days the Eskimo guide, Culigbuck, could no longer stay with them and Rae left him to the care of the back-up party coming on behind. The journey north towards Fury and Hecla Strait was the most gruelling of Rae's expeditions. The group suffered from a lack of both food and fuel. After less than two weeks Rae left behind two of his men again. In spite of this he did not reach his target but, with his food coming to an end, was forced to turn back 10 miles from Fury and Hecla Strait. At the end of August 1847 the expedition returned to Churchill.

Rae's journey was an epoch-making event in the history of Arctic exploration. For the first time an expedition supplied itself with rations by hunting and fishing and by trading with the Eskimos. The group was the first to spend the winter on the treeless Arctic coast without the security of ships. When the journey ended the men were in excellent condition. In spite of the difficult conditions they were bothered by as few symptoms of scurvy as were the Eskimos or Indians.

If Rae's organisational model could be described in one word, that word would be flexibility. He prepared for surprises in many ways. The way his party acquired their food and the manner in which they wintered were adapted to the environment they found themselves in. The back-up party took care of those for whom the rate of progress or the demands of the terrain were too much. Parties were manned according to the dictates of the conditions. Rae's knowledge of the conditions and his personal qualities helped the expedition members adapt themselves to the environment in which they operated or to the individual requirements of the members of the group. He made no compromise regarding his aims, however, unless achieving them endangered the survival of the expedition.

The expedition also made considerable geographical advances. Rae cleared up once and for all – if there was any doubt after Edward Parry's second expedition – that there was no passage to the west, with the exception of Fury and Hecla Strait, leading from Hudson Bay. He proved Boothia to be a peninsula. In addition, Rae mapped over 620 miles of coast.

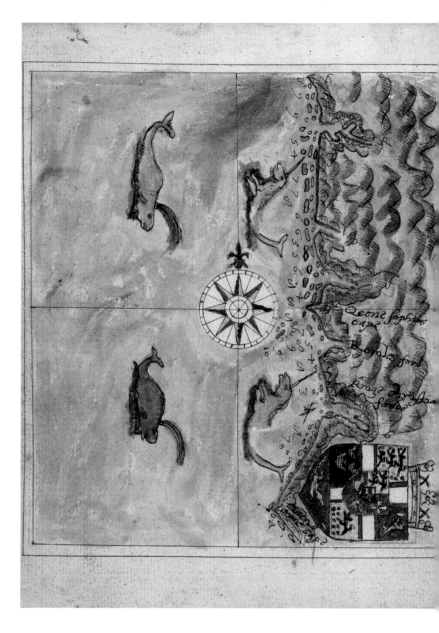

GREENLAND RE-CONQUERED

When, during the course of the 15th century, the Viking settlements were abandoned, possibly because the climate grew colder, Greenland was left in peace for 150 years. John Davis encountered the Greenland Eskimos on his first journey in 1585.

When whaling spread to the Davis Strait in the 17th century contact between the whalers and the Eskimos increased. Some whalers also dabbled in trade. Dutch and Danish merchants expanded their assortment of goods to include fabrics, clothing, tools, iron and wood. The Dutch were in control of trade and almost considered the land their own.

During the time of the old settlements, Greenland had ties with both Iceland and Norway which were parts of the Danish kingdom. The Icelander, Arngrimur Jónsson Vidalin, suggested the establishment of a colony and that trade should be commenced with the people of Greenland. Thanks to him interest in Greenland increased even though many measures were not put into practice because the Danish king was not interested in the rights to possess Greenland. A young clergyman by the name of Hans Egede became acquainted with

The coast of gromeland
with the latitudes of the
havens and harbors as
if founde them

A . Qveene arms Cape in the latitude of. 66 Seg
B . king christianvs forde in 66 deg 25 minit
C . henririk Romles ford in 66 begres 35 min
D . Qveene Sophias Cape in 67 seg 45 min
e . kinghts flandes in 67 seg 5 d minits
f . Cvninghams ford in 67 segr. 15 minnts
g . prince christianvs forde in 67 seg 30 mm
h . arnolds fovnd in 67 Seqres 45 immits
ff . Bavhovse fovnd 67 begres 56 minits
k . Brade kanfons ford in 68 segres
L . chriftin friefles cape in 68 Seg 35

127 *In 1605 Kristian IV sent an expedition led by John Cunningham to strengthen Denmark's hold on Greenland. The settlements of the Norsemen had already disappeared by then. John Cunningham was head of the expedition and under him were three vessels, the* TROST, *the* RÖDE LÖVEN *and the* KATTEN. *The expedition sailed north up the Davis Strait and charted the coast north of Itivdleq Fjord. The pilot, James Hall, dedicated the map he made to the King and named Itivdleq King Kristian Fjord. The entire stretch of coast charted north of Itivdleq was about 62 miles long. Cunningham's maps depict the fjords, Eskimos and sea mammals of the area. Cunningham brought furs, mineral samples and four Eskimos to Copenhagen.*
(THE BRITISH LIBRARY)

The number of Danish expeditions to Greenland gradually increased. Hans Egede looked for old Viking settlements. The first attempt to cross the continental glacier covering Greenland was made in 1729. In 1732 Mathis Jochimsen suggested searching for the ancient eastern colony by skiing across the ice sheet. In 1751 Lars Dalager, head of the Frederikshåb trading station, made his way with his companions onto the ice sheet. They climbed the nearby Nunatek, a peak from which a new mountain range could be seen in the north-east. They assumed these mountains to be on the east coast; in actual fact the peaks in question were 45 miles from the west coast.

At the end of the century the aims of Danish expeditions were mostly scientific. They looked into the possibilities for local farming and stock raising, looked for minerals, investigated the bedrock, plant and animal life and made improvements in mapping the coast. Interest in conquering the unknown areas of Greenland only began to grow at the end of the 1850s, when reaching the north pole became the most important challenge.

The east coast of Greenland, surrounded by pack ice, had long been impregnable. As early as 1786–1788 a Danish expedition had tried to reach Greenland's east coast to explore the ancient eastern colony, but in vain. The expedition showed that the eastern colony could not have been on the east coast but, despite its name, was located on the south-western coast, to the west of Cape Farewell.

William Scoresby Jr. charted the west coast of Greenland from latitudes 69° to 72° while on a whaling voyage in 1822, and Wilhelm August Graah continued the charting of the south-eastern coastal area. One of the most interesting projects was that carried out by the Dane Hinrich Rink in 1848–1851. As a result of it, precise maps of the Disco district were made and the first account of the birth of the Greenland continental ice sheet and glacial flows was propounded. In the mid 19th century, Greenland's Royal Trading Company had built a network of trading posts covering the whole country with the exception of the far north and eastern coast. Unlike the Hudson's Bay Company, the Greenland Trading Company established its stations in areas already inhabited by the indigenous population. More Eskimos also moved close to the trading settlements. The Royal Trading Company did not only specialise in furs but dealt in all kinds of trading goods.

Vidalin's plans, which he obtained through his wife's family, and he began to promote the proposition enthusiastically. He persuaded the merchants of Bergen to establish a trading company and the company to support his proposal to convert the population of Greenland to Christianity.

In 1721 three Det Bergenske Compagni ships set sail to establish a new colony and the company's first trading post. One of the ships was forced to turn back, but Hans Egede, his wife, four children and eight other migrants settled down to live in what was now Godthåbsfjord, later renamed Nuuk.

Without Egede the Danes would have taken an unfavourable attitude towards Greenland in the early days of colonisation because Dutch whale hunters had already established their position there. Whalers took advantage of the Eskimos whenever they could. Prices were set according to the audacity of the seller and the ignorance of the purchaser. The Danes, on the other hand, wanted fixed prices and secure growth for the indigenous population. A system of fixed purchase and sales prices was implemented in 1782. The Dutch resisted Danish advances in the north with all their might and twice burnt down trading company buildings built by the Danes in Nepisat when they were temporarily left empty.

128 In 1721 the Norwegian pr≥≤·, Hans Egede, inspired the merchants of Bergen to establisl. t.ie Greenland Trading Company and to send him to the island ≥ e missionary. Egede ensured Danish dominance in Greenlr d He was a priest, businessman and explorer. In vain he sought tl e Viking settlements which were in fact located on the west coast. Egede returned to Denmark in 1736. His book of 1741 is one cf he most important sources of Greenland's history. (JOHN NURM-IS∎N SÄÄTIÖ)

129

Hans Egede's work on Greenl≥r d, written in 1741, gives a detailed picture of life in Gree≥l≥nd at that time. The book gained considerable attention and was t≥anslated into several languages. The accompanying picture for∎ the work depicts seal hunting. Particular attention was arous≥d by the devices which the hunter stalking the seal had to ease l∙is long wait. (JOHN NURMISEN SÄÄTIÖ)

Denmark pushed aside the Dutch by shutting them off from the waters close to the co≥s⁻ but they did permit whaling in the open sea. The Royal Tr≥ding Company did not seek to make a profit but was expected to pay its own expenses as well as those of the missionary work they carried out.

At the end of the 19th century the head of the Royal Trading Company still ruled Greenland. His subordinates also took care of civil affairs. Hi∩rich Rink, one of the company's heads, claimed that the tr≥∩ing company protected the Eskimos from the kind of exploitation that would have been the inevitable consequence ∍f competition. The Eskimos were paid 20–25% of the mark≥t value of their products in Europe. Correspondingly they we⁻e sold products at a price which made a 20% coverage.

The Dane, Peter Freuch≥n, moved to Greenland and with Knud Rasmussen founded a private trading post in the north, in Thule, before the are≥ ∼as annexed to Denmark in 1921. In conjunction with annexation the trading station was taken under state control. Until World War II Greenland was closed to the Danish too ≥nd they were not allowed to come there without special permission. At first the trading company supported the practice of traditional occupations. This led to conflicts between the company and the missionaries, since the latter wished to co∩centrate the indigenous people into easily manageable village⁺. This in turn restricted the practice of hunting. Norwegiar ≥nd Danish workers were imported to do the kind of work tl·at was not traditional. The races became mixed and gave bir∩h in Freuchen's words to 'a stronger and more intelligent r≥ce'.

Monopolies function only for as long as conditions remain stable. Thus it was in Greenland too. When people learnt to know the currents of t∩e Arctic Ocean and the breeding grounds of the seal, commercial seal-hunting increased off the east coast of Greenland. This had a powerful affect on the livelihood of the inh≥bitants of the south coast. Their seal

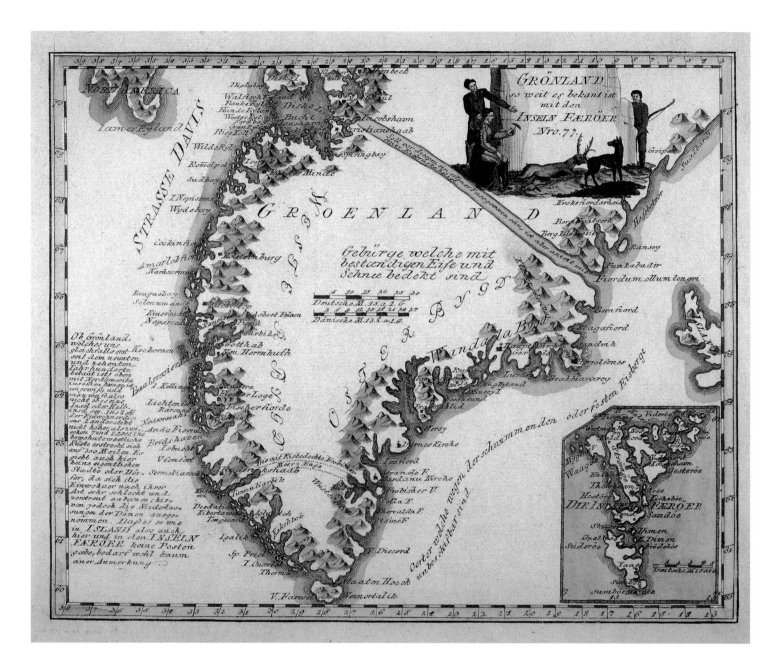

catches decreased and their welfare declined. The warming up of Arctic waters also moved the migratory routes of the seals further north and the situation deteriorated still further.

Just when the trouble was at its worst, help was found. A new fish, the Atlantic cod, moved to the waters of southern Greenland. From the point of view of society the change was a painful one. The most highly-valued occupation of this society, seal hunting, was disappearing. The trading company slowed down the change in occupations by offering only traditional trading goods. Although cod swarmed the fjords of Greenland the Eskimos, according to Freuchen, were not interested in fishing it because the money it brought in was almost worthless after their basic needs had been satisfied. Their livelihood suffered.

World War II separated Greenland from Denmark which had been occupied by the Germans. The Americans arrived on the island and after the war the monopoly was broken. The Royal Trading Company still conducts trade – among other things ice cap rocks or cubes that have been chipped from the millions-of-years-old, unpolluted, compressed ice, which melt slowly in drinks.

130 Hans Egede substantially increased the fund of knowledge on Greenland. In his work Nachrichten von Grönland mit einer nach neuesten und in diesem Werke angegebenen Entdeckung genau eingerichteten Landcharten, *Johann Andersen (1664–1743), mayor of Hamburg, drew Egede's house and told of the northern routes to which Egede had referred. Andersen also claimed that Frobisher Sound, marked on previous maps, was covered in ice and because of this could no longer be found. A waterway running through central Greenland had also been placed on the map. The mapmaker covered Frobisher Sound, mistakenly situated on earlier maps, in snow and ice. The description is in Reilly's hand, the vignette depicts the Faroe Isles.*
(John Nurminen Foundation)

DETERMINING YOUR POSITION

Very early in his history, man began to form a map of his dwelling place and the world that surrounded him. He measured distances and used landmarks and the stars to help him to take his bearings.

Of the early seafarers, it is known that the Phoenicians, at least, observed the movements of the sun and the position of the stars to determine their position. More than 3000 years ago astronomers in Mesopotamia were able to measure the elevation of the stars fairly accurately. The scientists of ancient times understood that our planet was spherical and that our position on a north/south axis could be determined with the aid of the stars. They knew that the elevation of the stars with fixed positions at certain times of the day and year showed the latitude –

that is to say, how far north the point of observation was.

In 240 BC, Eratosthenes of Alexandria had already calculated the earth's circumference with remarkable accuracy. His calculation was based on a perceptive understanding of trigonometry and an ingenious method by which he observed the shadows cast by the light of the sun at its zenith. His points of reference were a well, in what is now Aswan, where the light shone straight down to the bottom on a certain day of the year, and a square in Alexandria further to the north, in which the shadow of an obelisk was measured at the same time. Although the distance between the measuring points was difficult to define he arrived at a calculation – partly through good luck – with astonishing accuracy. Later

scholars in the Hellenistic period estimated the size of the earth to be much smaller. Columbus based his calculations of the earth's circumference on the latter, with consequences that are well-known.

The earth's axis is inclined at an angle to the plane of the planet's orbit around the sun. This plane of the ecliptic explains the difference between the seasons. The further north we are, the sharper the change. The people of the north can thank the ecliptic for the darkness of winter and the lightness of summer. The astronomers and seafarers of ancient times knew how to make allowances for the effect of the ecliptic on the elevation of a heavenly body.

Various kinds of instruments have been used throughout the ages to measure true

132 *The cross staff was one of the earliest instruments for measuring angles. By supporting the staff on the cheekbone and moving the crosspiece on the staff's scale in such a way that the lower edge of the crosspiece 'rested' on the horizon and the upper edge touched the heavenly body to be measured it was possible to read the angle of elevation from the scale. This gave the degree of latitude. According to the altitude the navigator selected a suitable crosspiece. The cross staff was also called the Jacob's staff. In the 16th century a variation of it was developed and called the Davis quadrant after the sailor of the Northwest Passage.* (Maritime Museum of Finland)

133 *In the 18th century, the octant was the instrument most commonly used to measure latitude. It was possible to reach an exactitude of a fraction of a degree. This instrument is made of ebony. The altitude of celestial bodies is measured to determine a ship's position by turning the brass shaft on the ivory scale. At the top of the scale is a system of mirrors that reflects the horizon and heavenly body side by side.* (John Nurminen Foundation)

134 The Kendall K2 chronometer has a colourful history. The Admiralty tested the timepiece on Phipps' Arctic voyage, which attempted to cross the North Pole by sea starting from Spitzbergen. The sailors were stopped by ice, but the clock helped to reliably measure longitude. The K2 was one of the first clocks that was as accurate as a chronometer. Following the 1773 Spitzbergen attempt, the Kendall K2 was next used on the ill-fated BOUNTY, *commanded by Captain Bligh in 1787. After a mutiny broke out on the ship, the chronometer found its way to a desolate South Sea island with the mutineers, who ultimately perished there. The Navy eventually came across the clock and it was returned to ship's service in 1792.*
(NATIONAL MARITIME MUSEUM, LONDON)

elevations. The scientists of ancient times called the tool used for measurements based on shadows cast by the sun a "gnomon". This was a stick, rod or pillar whose shadow in relation to its height was used to calculate the elevation of stars and other heavenly bodies.

Pytheas calculated the latitude of his port of departure, Massalia, with considerable accuracy using a pillar erected in the town square as a gnomon. On his journeys he might have employed smaller instruments, such as a staff. He would perhaps also have used his arm, hand and fingers to measure the sun's elevation, as indeed seafarers and astronomers sometimes still do. In winter, when the sun is low in the sky, it is easy to measure its approximate angular distance from the horizon with the palm of the hand. When defining a degree of latitude Pytheas also measured the time the sun spent above and below the horizon. The short period of light at the winter solstice in relation to the number of hours in the day gave a direct latitudinal reading.

The Irish monks and Vikings who navigated the waters of the north at the end of the first millennium also observed the heavenly bodies to find out their north-south position. Portuguese seafarers were measuring the altitude of heavenly bodies with a quadrant as early as the 14th century. This was a device which was kept in a vertical position with the aid of a plumbline. The sun cast a shadow on its perimeter from which the elevation could be read. In this way sailors could find out, for example, how far south they had progressed along the African coast.

Towards the end of the Middle Ages seafarers had more effective devices for measuring angles at their disposal. The marine astrolabe, a modification of the Arabian astronomical astrolabe, was in use until the 18th century. Similarly, the inexpensive and simple cross staff was a popular navigational tool for many centuries. Among travellers to the north, it is known that Barents, at least, calculated his degree of latitude with both instruments. Those who used the cross-staff, or Jacob's staff, had to contend with the glare of the sun. The Davis quadrant, which took advantage of the shade, solved this problem, as measurements could be taken with the user's back to the sun. The navigator Davis developed this instrument on his voyages in the north.

The mirror technique developed in the 17th century brought about a revolution in angular measurement. This gave birth to the octant, the main instrument used on many voyages, from Cook to Nordenskiöld. When the wooden octant was replaced by brass and it was fitted with additional optical equipment and a nonius, and its arc was enlarged to one sixth of a circle, the result was a sextant, which meets the precision requirements of today. For 19th and 20th century polar explorers the sextant was an essential piece of equipment. It made it possible to measure not only the sun's angle of elevation but also the altitude of the stars, and in favourable conditions it was accurate to one minute of a degree. The records for the northernmost points achieved by all Arctic explorers of the 19th and 20th centuries were measured with either an octant or a sextant.

Whereas geographical latitude could already be accurately calculated from the stars in ancient times, defining geographical longitude was more problematic. The stars alone were not enough to define a position on an east/west axis, and extremely accurate measurement of time was also necessary. In order to calculate the longitude of their position, sailors and mapmakers have to know the difference in time between their position and a reference position of known longitude. This perplexing problem was only solved in the 18th century by a British carpenter named Harrison. He designed and made a clock which kept time for months, and withstood difficult conditions on land and sea as well as changes in temperature and humidity. These precision instruments, which were called chronometers, gradually became available to explorers in the late 18th century. James Cook was among the first to use a chronometer. After the Greenwich meridian was made the zero meridian in 1884, sailors began to synchronise their clocks with Greenwich time. Measuring the longitude, or meridian, of a given place was now relatively simple. When the mid-day point was determined with the aid of the sun, local time was compared with Greenwich time on the clock and converted into degrees. The conversion scale could easily be found from the simple fact that the earth turned a complete revolution in 1 440 minutes. Later, when Greenwich time could later be heard on the radio, it was possible to check the chronometer, and defining a position on an east/west course was easier than ever.

135 Nordenskiöld took two precision chronometers on his voyage. The primary one was a Frodsham 3194 and it was kept strictly in the expedition leader's cabin. The other, a Frodsham 8872 could be taken on the deck. In order for the longitudinal position to be measured with accuracy, the clocks had to run reliably for long periods. The primary clock was only five minutes late off the mark on the Arctic voyage, which lasted over a year. This was verified in Yokohama, where there was a telegraph even then and where Greenwich time could be obtained. The clock functioned better in the cool northern climate than on later, warmer stages of the trip. Once the VEGA entered the tropics, the timepiece went wild.
(KUNGLIGA VETENSKAPSAKADEMIEN)

EAST AND WEST MEET IN ALASKA

AFTER BERING'S SECOND VOYAGE (1733-1743) THE FOCUS FOR RUSSIAN FUR-HUNTING SHIFTED FURTHER EAST, TO THE ALEUTS AND ALASKA. ALTHOUGH PETER III'S SUCCESSOR, CATHERINE II, DID NOT WANT TO COMMIT MEN, SHIPS AND MONEY TO THE CONQUERING OF NEW LANDS, SHE RECEIVED THE RESULTS OF EXPANSION WITH SATISFACTION. AS LONG AS FURRED ANIMALS COULD BE FOUND, THEIR HUNTING SERVED AS A SOURCE OF IMPERIAL POWER.

The results of Bering's mapping and that of his successors were never published because the Russian Navy classified charts of the area as secret. Neither did the information reach the Russian Academy, whose maps were used by European explorers.

Interest in the west coast of America and Alaska increased after the mid-18th century. The area interested Spain since, under the agreement between Spain and Portugal, it belonged to Spain. The British interest was aroused because the Russians were nearing their sphere of influence in North America. With the coming of independence to the United States a new interested party was born. France had not completely forgotten the northern Pacific Ocean either.

COOK MAKES THE OPENING MOVE

Great Britain had long been interested in the South Pacific. In 1776, James Cook's instructions for his third voyage were to seek a Northwest Passage from the Pacific Ocean. Cook was instructed to sail via the Cape of Good Hope, New Zealand and Tahiti to the coast of America but carefully to avoid Spanish controlled areas. He was ordered to seek a passage at latitude 65° which would lead to Hudson Bay or Baffin Bay. The British knew that a Spanish expedition had reached about latitude 58°. Therefore Cook received the order to sail straight to his destination. His journey was an historic one since he had the use of the Harrison chronometer for the first time. It was partly thanks to this that Cook was able to specify longitudes with greater accuracy than before.

The Sandwich Islands (Hawaii) became the main achievement of the voyage, however. On 18 February 1778 Cook discovered a group of islands, the five largest of which are known as Hawaii, Maui, Molokai, Oahu and Kauai. He continued his voyage and at the end of March arrived at Nootka Sound situated off Vancouver Island. Here repairs were made

to the ships the *Resolution* and the *Discovery*, and goods were bartered with the local inhabitants. From the two silver spoons of Spanish origin bought from the local people Cook could assume that the Spanish had already reached Nootka. John Ledyard tells in his travel journal of furs which Cook's men bought from the indigenous people for a few worthless ornaments. In Canton the same furs fetched one hundred dollars each from the Chinese. This quickly attracted American fur traders to the north-west coast of America.

Cook followed the coast north and marked a few islands, mountains and Cross Sound on his chart. He also identified Mount St. Elias, which Bering had named. Cook showed his

136 Admiral Nageaev was a key figure in Russian nautical measurement. From 1765 onwards he collected material on the North Pacific area to form the basis for mapping work. One of his most important sources was a map by the educated Chukchi Nikolai Daurkin. It was drawn in traditional Russian style and was based on Daurkin's voyages to the Diomede Islands and Alaska. A wide strip of the Alaskan coast can be seen for the first time. Ethnographically the map is a rich source of information, and on it the original names of Eskimo villages such as Tikega, Okivuk and Kyng-Myn appear; these places were known before Cook's voyages. An Eskimo dwelling surrounded by a wooden defensive wall has been drawn on the banks of the Kheuver River. This is depicted in more detail in the map's explanatory text.

The Eskimo fortifications are believed to be a reference to a Russian legend, which asserted that men who had disappeared on Dezhnev's voyage had established a colony in America in 1648. Thus legend had it that there was a Russian town in America; a supposition apparently corroborated by archaeological discoveries in the 18th century. The town was called the lost colony of Novgorod. The belief has nowadays been shown to be pure fable. Daurkin's map has not previously been published in its original form.
(RUSSIAN STATE ARCHIVES)

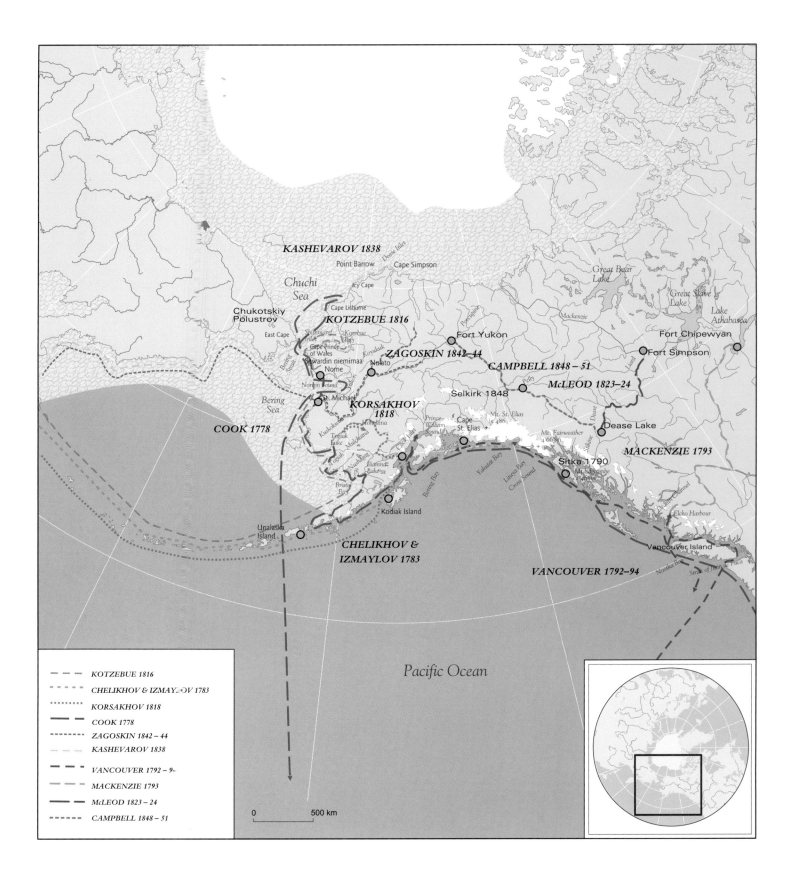

KASHEVAROV 1838

Chuchi
Sea

Chukotskiy
Polustrov

KOTZEBUE 1816

COOK 1778

Bering
Sea

ZAGOSKIN 1842–44

CAMPBELL 1848 – 51

McLEOD 1823–24

Fort Yukon

KORSAKHOV
1818

Selkirk 1848

Cape
St. Elias +

Sitka 1790

Dease Lake

Fort Chipewyan

Fort Simpson

MACKENZIE 1793

Kodiak Island

Unalaska
Island

CHELIKHOV &
IZMAYLOV 1783

Vancouver Island

VANCOUVER 1792–94

Pacific Ocean

- – – – KOTZEBUE 1816
- · · · · CHELIKHOV & IZMAYLOV 1783
- · · · · · · · · KORSAKHOV 1818
- — — COOK 1778
- - - - - ZAGOSKIN 1842 – 44
- – – – KASHEVAROV 1838
- – – – VANCOUVER 1792 – 9–
- – – – MACKENZIE 1793
- — – McLEOD 1823 – 24
- - - - - CAMPBELL 1848 – 51

0   500 km

137 The extent of Cook's voyage to the Alaskan coast and Bering Sea is made clear on the map. Cook sailed along the coast and explored every bay in his search for the Northwest Passage. The ice stopped his progress at Icy Cape on the north coast of Alaska. Simultaneous expeditions into the interior made by Mackenzie, McLeod and Campbell among others are also marked on the map. (PATANEN)

respect for his predecessor by naming a bay close to Bering's landing place, Bering Bay.

He had to sail as far as Prince William Sound before finding a possible entrance to a Northwest Passage. In May, after three days of exploration, the waterway turned out to be a dead end and Cook continued his voyage. He soon found another promising bay. Neither did Cook Inlet, as Vancouver was later to call the strait, prove to be a passage through the continent. Cook was forced to sail south-west along the Alaskan peninsula.

138 James Cook was one of the greatest explorers in history. His voyages stretched from the Pacific Ocean to the Antarctic and Arctic. The aim of Cook's third voyage was to sail the Northwest Passage from Bering Strait to Europe. The ice stopped him. When in 1779 he returned to spend the winter at the Hawaiian islands he had discovered, the indigenous people killed him.
(THE NATIONAL MARITIME MUSEUM, LONDON)

In August Cook at last found a strait and was able to sail north again. He proved Müller's and Stählin's maps to be absurdly inaccurate. Because of bad visibility, charting the foggy Bristol Bay proved impossible. Off Kuskokwim Bay he sailed into another belt of fog behind which were hidden Nunivak Island and the Yukon delta.

Having passed Nome, Cook progressed to the Bering Strait, mapped the westernmost cape of the American continent, Cape Prince of Wales, and sailed north-east along the coast of what is now Alaska until ice blocked his way at around latitude 70°. He turned back to the south and continued west, but came up against a belt of solid ice there too. Cook returned from a cape he named Icy Cape to the coast of Asia and named the continent's easternmost peninsula East Cape. Near the cape the weather cleared up and – unlike Bering – he saw America as well as the Asian coast.

Cook returned to America along the coast and found that Cape Prince of Wales was, contrary to Russian maps, part of the continent and not an island. He also explored Norton

Sound. Autumn had arrived and Cook was obliged to sail back towards the south.

In October, on his return journey, Cook met Russians for the first time on Unalaska Island. Captain Gerasim Izmaylov, the most experienced sailor of his time to sail the Bering Sea, arrived to greet him. Izmaylov gave Cook two hand-drawn maps to copy and agreed about the mistakes on Müller's and Stählin's maps which Cook had observed. Izmaylov erased one third of the islands on the maps and claimed that they did not exist. The Russian researcher, Aleksey Postnikov, suspected that Izmaylov did not want to reveal the rich treasure of furs to a foreigner, which is why some of the Aleutian Islands were missing from Cook's map. Cook was favourably impressed by Izmaylov, however. He was able to handle the Hadley octant, new to him, and showed himself otherwise a master of the art of charting.

Both parties benefited from their discussions. The Russians acquired the new information on the American coast before the British Admiralty. The first Russian chart to make use of the information supplied by Cook was drawn up as early as the following year, that is to say 1779.

Cook accomplished what might have been expected of Bering. He presented the first reliable overall view of the Bering Strait area and of the coast of Alaska all the way from Nootka to its northern reaches. Although to a certain extent Cook's work was superficial, his achievements were very significant and his calculations precise. When Cook was killed in an attack by the indigenous people of the Hawaiian Islands, Charles Clerke twice attempted to sail further the following summer, but on both occasions was forced to turn back when the ice closed his passage at around latitude 70°.

On his return journey Clerke called in at Petropavlovsk and the exchange of information between the Russians and the British continued. Prince William Sound and its rich hauls of fur were described to the Russians. Cook's men brought hard proof with them: in Macao, China, they received £2000 for their catch.

THE SPANIARDS
CONSOLIDATE THEIR POSITION

Spain had sent its first expedition to Nootka as early as 1774, four years before Cook. Juan Pérez sailed the waters of Vancouver Island but did not go ashore. His task was to find out how far along the American coast the Russians had advanced. Peres saw no sign at all of the Russians. An expedition sent out the following year reached the vicinity of Mount Edgecombe and took 'possession' of the coast for Spain.

The third Spanish expedition was sent north in 1779, one year after Cook's voyage. The expedition found no signs of Cook or of other European voyages.

News of the riches of America's north-west coast had spread among the British in Canton, and they began to arrive on the American coast from Macao, Bengal, Bombay and before long from England too. Initial successes heightened their

139 James Cook's journey to the Bering Sea revealed the extent of the area's fur stocks. Cook's men exchanged trinkets and small ornaments for furs with the indigenous people and sold them for high prices in Canton. The area's most important fur-bearing animals were the sea cow, which became extinct, the sea otter, which almost disappeared before it became a protected species, and the seals and walrus that Cook's men are hunting in the picture. (B. & C. ALEXANDER)

COOK'S COLLIERS – THE WORKHORSES OF THE SEAS

Captain James Cook made his three voyages on what can truly be described as the workhorses of the seas. The *Endeavour*, on which he made his first journey, and the *Resolution*, the *Adventure* and the *Discovery* were all former coal ships or colliers.

Cook began his seafaring career as a sea apprentice on a collier belonging to a man named John Walker. He placed his trust in these sturdy toilers when he embarked on his historical voyages by order of the Admiralty in 1771.

For over two hundred years colliers were a familiar sight in Europe's northern waters. Originally rigged as brigs, they hauled coal from Britain's northeastern ports to London especially, but also elsewhere in Britain and abroad, particularly Scandinavia.

Indeed, it was from Scandinavia – Norway – that the design of Cook's ships originated. They were "cat-ships" built in Whitby and rigged as three-masted barks. The foremast and mainmast had topgallant sails as well as topsails and mainsails. The mizzenmast had one square sail above its gaffsail and, supported by the bowsprit, two jibs and spritsails. Whitby cats could hold up to 600 tonnes of cargo or nearly twice as much as a coal brig.

Colliers were easily recognized by their blunt bows, which typically lacked a figurehead or other emblem. This was unusual, since even the most humble vessel's bow was usually decorated by at least some kind of ornament in those days. *Resolution's* rigging caused continuous problems on its last journey. The trouble was caused by mistakes made, for example, in the choice of materials used when the ship, which was damaged on its second voyage, was being fitted out for the third. Similar problems were noted on the *Discovery*. The return to Hawaii, necessitated by the breaking of *Resolution's* foremast, led to Cook's death in a fight with the islanders in February 1779.

The *Resolution* was 110 feet long, 35 feet wide, had a draught of 13 feet and a carrying capacity of 462 tons, some 100 tons more than the *Endeavour*. Both ships' length-to-width ratio was about 1:3 at a time when the rule-of-thumb was 1:4. The collier was obviously a beast of burden, designed to carry bulk cargo in the heavy weather of the North Sea. Speed and manoeuvrability were of secondary importance.

Cook would have liked to have been able to take the *Endeavour* on his second voyage too, but it had already been sent to the Falklands to serve as a warehouse ship. The *Resolution's* end was equally inglorious. After its legendary journeys it was assigned for transport duty in the Caribbean, where it was captured by a French buccaneer.

enthusiasm. The Spaniards also became more active, and they were worried about the voyage of the Frenchman La Pérouse in 1786, the aim of which, it had been announced, was to establish French trading posts on the coast. La Pérouse sailed to the latitude of Yakutat Bay and was probably the first to discover this bay which was located to the south of Mount St Elias.

After reading his narrative, which appeared in 1784, the Spanish held Cook's voyage in great esteem. They did not, however, appreciate the commercial consequences of the voyage. Only in 1788 did the next Spanish expedition arrive at the North Pacific. The leader of the expedition, José Martínez, had been in contact with La Perouse and he had a clear vision of Spain's role in the area. He found out that the Russians had established several trading stations in what is now Alaska and that

the British were involved in fur trading in the North Pacific.

Martínez was ordered to take control of Nootka and to stop the Russian advance. He wanted to establish a Spanish trading company specialising in furs which would gain a monopoly in the fur trade. The Spanish viceroy of New Spain was not inspired by the affair, the Spanish had become less inclined to take risks. They were only interested in carrying out research among the Indians of the area in which Spain had staked most.

José Mariano Moziño published the best study on the Indians and their way of life, *Noticias de Nutka*. He took part in Bodega y Quadra's voyage of 1799 and his research caught the attention of Alexander von Humboldt. The study was forgotten, however. A condensed Spanish-language edition was published as late as 1913 and an English-language edition in 1970.

140 The RESOLUTION was a coal ship that was refitted for naval use. Coal ships and their modifications were stable and safe vessels in even the harshest conditions. The RESOLUTION served the Royal Navy on several Arctic expeditions. She was the first vessel to cross the Antarctic Circle on 17 January 1773, and later again accomplished the feat twice. She also crossed the Arctic Circle twice.

The RESOLUTION and the DISCOVERY departed on Cook's third expedition in 1776–1779. The main objective was to chart the Northwest Passage starting from the Pacific. After Cook, the RESOLUTION ended up in the hands of French buccaneers.

The RESOLUTION was 33 metres long and 10.5 metres wide, with a draught of about 4 metres. She was extremely well equipped, with, among other items, a George Azimuth compass, ice anchors, 12 ship guns, 12 swivel guns and the most modern evaporator available, used to obtain drinking water from the sea. It is recorded that Cook paid from his own purse for brass doorknobs to be installed in his ship's parlour (JOHN NURMINEN FOUNDATION)

Moziño's research considered the possibility of Spain's preserving its supremacy in the Pacific very questionable. The contest for the Arctic areas of the Pacific was being fought between Russia, Great Britain and the newly formed United States.

THE RUSSIANS TIGHTEN THEIR GRIP

The struggle for power by Russia's trading companies in America took fur trading out of the hands of individual enterprises and put it into the control of the bigger companies. Grigory Ivanovich Chelikhov was a pioneer of this change. He had earlier operated in Siberia and his attention had been drawn to the opportunities that fur trading in America offered. The first commercial journeys were very profitable, and in 1781 Chelikhov and Ivan Golikov founded a joint venture to carry out fur trading in the area.

In 1783 Chelikhov equipped three ships for an expedition and sailed east with his wife. Their first winter was spent on Bering Island, from which they continued their journey to Unalaska and Kodiak. Chelikhov built four forts to secure the position of his trading post, two on the islands and one each at Cook Inlet and the St Elias Peninsula. The commander of one of his ships was Izmaylov, whom Cook had met. Izmaylov found signs of European fur traders. Chelikhov returned to Kamchatka after three years. The ground had been laid for the Trading Company of Russian America.

Chelikhov returned to St. Petersburg to organise a trade monopoly in Alaska for his company. He could see that unlimited competition would quickly deplete the fur stock and that international competition was already under way. British traders would also bring Britains naval forces to the waters. Nor could the Spanish be ruled out. Chelikhov needed the support of his ruler for his operations. Catherine did not warm to his suggestion. However, as a gesture of gratitude, she gave him a silver sabre and gold medal on which was engraved: "For services to mankind".

Chelikhov was not discouraged, but strengthened the leadership of the trading company. He managed to persuade Alexandr Baranov to take on the job. Baranov's own business operations had failed in Anadyr and Irkutsk. In 1790 Baranov arrived on Kodiak Island and as "Governor" of Russian America led Russian explorations and oversaw the establishment of trading posts in the interior until 1818, when he set out to return to Russia but died on the journey home.

Following Cook's voyage, Catherine asked the Englishman Joseph Billings, who had been on Cook's third voyage, to carry out further surveys in the Bering area. Billings' expedition set out from Okhotsk in 1786 and returned to St Petersburg only in 1794. Between 1790–1791 Billings sailed the waters of Unalaska and Kodiak but made no new discoveries. He also took with him the first Russian priest to go to Alaska. Billings did not paint a very flattering picture of the operations of Chelikhov's company, accusing him of cruelty towards the indigenous population.

Billings also mapped the Chukchi Peninsula. In his travel journals published in 1804, Billings' Lieutenant, Gavriil

141 When James Cook was killed in Hawaii in February 1779, Captain Charles Clerke decided to try once more to find the Northwest Passage. He sailed north by way of Kamchatka, stayed at St. Peter and St. Paul harbour (seen in the picture) in May and stocked up on food supplies, as well as sending a letter via Russia telling of Cook's death. Clerke was forced to turn back, however, when the ice stopped his progress. He decided to return to England but died on 22 August after his ships had just reached St. Peter and St. Paul harbour again. (JOHN NURMINEN FOUNDATION)

142 Before returning from Bering Strait to winter in Hawaii, Cook sailed past the Aleutian Islands and went to Unalaska. There he met some Russian traders and in particular Gerasim Izmaylov, with whom he traded information. The picture is of an Aleut man on this journey. (JOHN NURMINEN FOUNDATION)

143 The Aleuts that Cook met on the island of Unalaska were very friendly people. The Russian influence could be seen from the fact, inter alia, that one of the men took a picture of the crucifix from his breast and kissed it. Cook's men bought furs from the indigenous people and enjoyed the bread they baked. The picture shows an Aleut woman. (JOHN NURMINEN FOUNDATION)

Sarychev, described the lives of the Chukchi, Kamchadal, Yakuts and Aleuts. He also set out his theory which postulated that an unknown land was to be found north of the Kolyma River estuary.

Baranov pushed ever further into the American continent. He sent an expedition to explore the Copper River and subdue the indigenous population living at its estuary. A fort was built close to Sitka, which the local Koloshi destroyed once but which was re-built in 1804 to resemble the original fort.

Chelikhov's dream of a fur-trade monopoly came true at the end of the century. Chelikhov's son-in-law, Nikolai Rezanov, succeeded in creating good relations with Alexander I and his advisors. The reienforced Russian-American Trading company, which had also taken over the business operations of it competitor Mylnikov in 1797, gained an American trade monopoly in 1799. This made the expansion of the trading company still further to both Kuskokwim and Yukon easier, as the government now supported the trading company and sent its own expedition to the area.

It is not known who the first European to discover the great

rivers of Alaska was. This honour probably goes to the fur hunters who had heard of the riches of the river valleys from the indigenous population. Officially, the first to go there was Petr Korsakhov who, in 1818, travelled from Cook Inlet to Lake Iliamna, from there to a tributary of the River Nushagak at the upper reaches of Mulchatna, crossed the watershed and came down the River Hoholitna to the fork of the Kuskokwim. His travelling companion was Fjodor Kolmakov. The definitive exploration of the Kuskokwim area took place in the 1820s. In 1832 Kolmakov established a trading post at the fork of the Kuskokwim and Hoholitna and searched every corner of the remaining unexplored headwater areas.

At the turn of the 1820s and 30s, Ivan Vasilyev went up the River Nushagak and discovered the lakes between Bristol Bay and the River Kuskokwim. He continued west to Lake Togiak and returned down the River Togiak to the sea. In the 1830s the Russians also arrived in the Yukon district. First they built a trading post on Saint Michael Island at the mouth of the river, then pushed their way inland. In 1838 Vasily Malakhov went upstream all the way to the village of

144 *Antonio Zatta's map of 1776 shows what a colourful idea there was in Europe of the Bering Strait area prior to Cook's mapping work of 1778–1779. Thanks to Russian exploration the Asian coast is depicted relatively well. Zatta did not, on the other hand, know of Hearne's voyage to the mouth of the Coppermine River. In his imagination it was possible to get from Hudson Bay to both the Arctic Ocean and, by way of the Anian Strait, to the Pacific. Originally it was believed that the Anian Strait separated Asia and America. In 1592 Juan de Fuca claimed to have sailed north along the coast of California and via the Anian Strait to the Arctic. Admiral de Fonte also tells of going along the strait to the Great Lakes. Gama Island, which Bering did not find, is still on the map. Other islands in Bering Strait drawn by Müller haunt the map and divide the strait into two. Cook had Müller's map with him, and it was only then that the mistakes were corrected.*

(MATTI LAINEMA)

NEXT DOUBLE PAGE SPREAD 190–1
145 *Measuring a degree of longitude accurately required a sufficiently reliable clock. Although the Russians made competent cartographic measurements in the Bering Strait area at the beginning of the 18th century, it was only Cook who had sufficiently accurate equipment and methods to carry out measurements of longitude. For this reason it was only possible to properly chart the coasts and islands of the Bering Strait after Cook's last voyage. This can be first seen on the fine Roberts and Palmer map of 1794. At that time the Pacific coastal areas of Asia and America were relatively accurately charted. The Arctic edge of the American coastline remained a challenge to be tackled by explorers of the next century.*

(JOHN NURMINEN FOUNDATION)

NUOVE SCOPERTE
DE' RUSSI
al Nord del Mare del Sud
sì nell'ASIA, che nell'AMERICA

VENEZIA 1776.
Presso Antonio Zatta
Con Privilegio dell'Eccmo Senato.

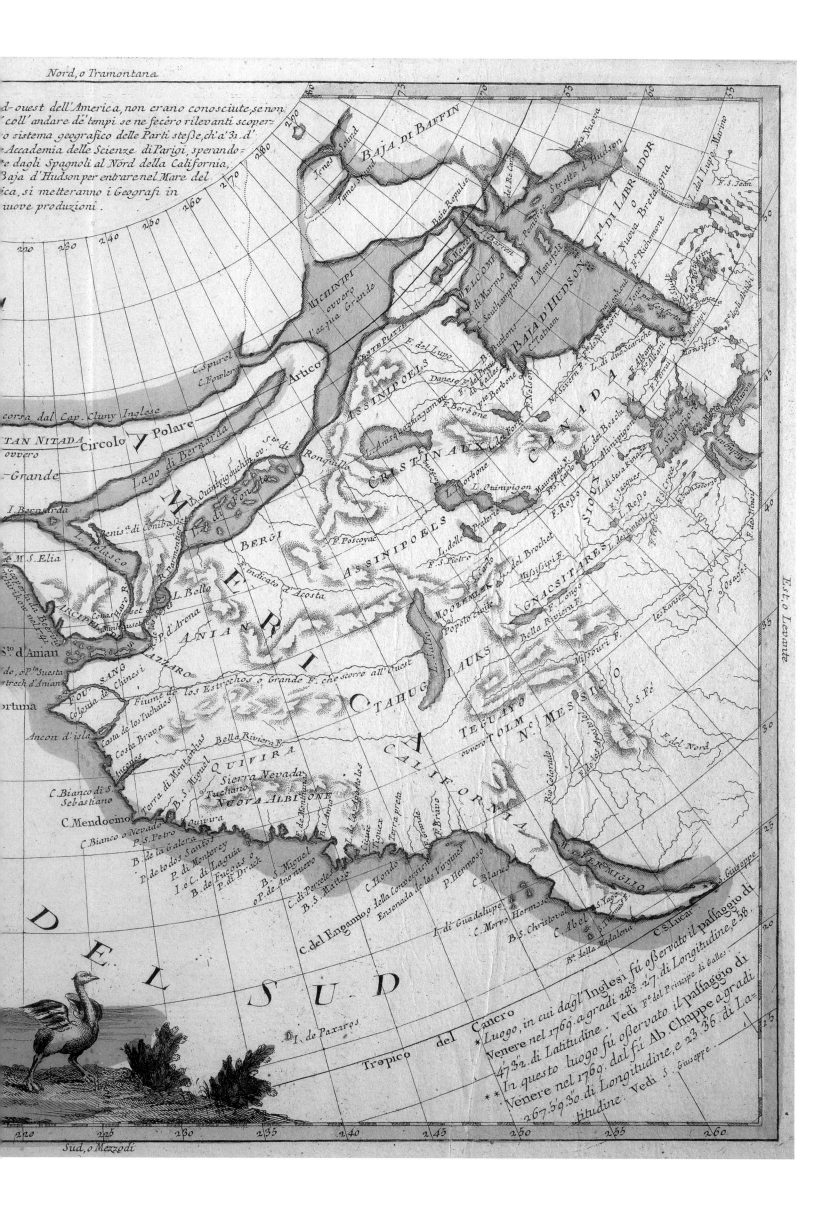

d-ouest dell'America, non erano conosciute, se non
coll'andare de' tempi se ne fecero rilevanti scoper-
o sistema geografico delle Parti stesse, ch'a '31.d'
Accademia delle Scienze di Parigi, sperando =
e dagli Spagnoli al Nord della California,
Baja d'Hudson per entrare nel Mare del
ica, si metteranno i Geografi in
uove produzioni.

290 280 270 260 250 240 230 220

275 270 265 260 255

BAJA DI BAFFIN

Jones Sound

James Sund

I. del Re Carlo

T.to Nuova

Svretto d'Hudson

T.ta DI LABRADOR

Nuova Bretagna

F. Richemont

P. del Lupo Marino

F. S. Jean

corsa dal Cap. Cluny Inglese

TAN NITADA
ovvero
Grande

Circolo Polare Artico

MICHINIPI
ovvero
l'acqua Grande

C. Spurel
C. Fowler

Lago di Bernarda

B. Quintrigouchin ov.
di Fonte

S.to di Ronquillo

ESTE PLATTE

E. del Lupo

ASSINIPOELS

Danese F. del Lupo
F. Pallas

WELCOME
I. di Marmo
I. di Marmo
Southampton

T. di Wager
Baren

Baja Repulse
B. Pistoleto

I. Mansfeld

BAJA D'HUDSON

C.to Tatnam

Pomponio

F. Bourbone

Ponchartrain

F. S. Giorgio
F. Nelson

N. Savern F. ti.
I. di due Scariche
F. Albani

F. Hood
F. Eschiscaul

Moose F.

Monsipi P.

Nuova

I. Bernarda

Benis.a di Conibas

L. Velasco

e M. S. Elia

Consenare R.

Minbiausko

P. d'Arena

BERGI

R. Parmentier

F. indicato d'Acosta

L. Bello

AMERIC

ANIANN

FOU-SANG
Colonia de Chinesi

Fiume de los Estrechos o Grande F. che scorre all'Ouest

Costa de los Tuchaios

Costa Brava

CRISTINAUX

F. Poscoyac

F. S. Pietro

L. delle Praterie

L. Borbone

L. Ouinipigon

L. Ouinipigon

Mauregas R.

Ps. Carlo

L. del Boschi

SIOUX

L. di Sera Kinava

L. Rosso

L. Superiore

F. di Tibwi

CANADA

F. Real

MOOZEMLEK
Popolo cuvili

Popolo cuvili

GNACSITARES
L. del Brochet

L. dei Pantani

F. Rosso

F. Lungo

Missipipi F.

Bella Riviera F.

Misisipi F.

le Kanzes

le Osages

F. del Nord

TAHUGLAUKS

TEGUAYO
ovvero TOLM

N.o MESSICO

S. Fe

Est, o Levante

Rio Colorado

F. del Nord

Ancon d'isla

Nicoles

C. Bianco di S.
Sebastiano

C. Mendocino

C. Bianco o Nevado

C. di Montanhas

Bella Riviera F.

QUIVIRA

Sierra Nevada
Tuchano
NUOVA ALBIONE

CALIFORNIA

MAR VERMIGLIO

S. Giuseppe

Terra di Montanhas

B. S. Miguel

B. S. Pedro

B. de la Galera

P. de todos Santos

P. di Monterey

I. e C. di Laquia

B. de Fucos o
P. di Drack

B. S. Miguel o
P. de Ano nuevo

Quivira

F. de Montana

B. S. Anna

Tiquex

Terra preta

F. Bravo

C. Hondo

C. del Engaño o
della Concessione
Ensenada de las Virgines

P. Hermoso

C. Blanco

I. di Guadalupe

C. Morro Hermoso

B. S. Christoval

C. Abel

C. S. Lucar

Ba. della Madalena

DEL SUD

I. de Paxaros

Tropico del Cancro

* Luogo, in cui dagl' Inglesi fu osservato il passaggio di
Venere nel 1769. a gradi 283.27. di Longitudine, e 58.
47.32. di Latitudine. Vedi F.te del Principe di Galles.
** In questo luogo fù osservato il passaggio di
Venere nel 1769. dal fù Ab. Chappe a gradi
267.5.9.30. di Longitudine, e 23.36. di Latitudine. Vedi S. Giuseppe.

220 225 230 235 240 245 250 255 260

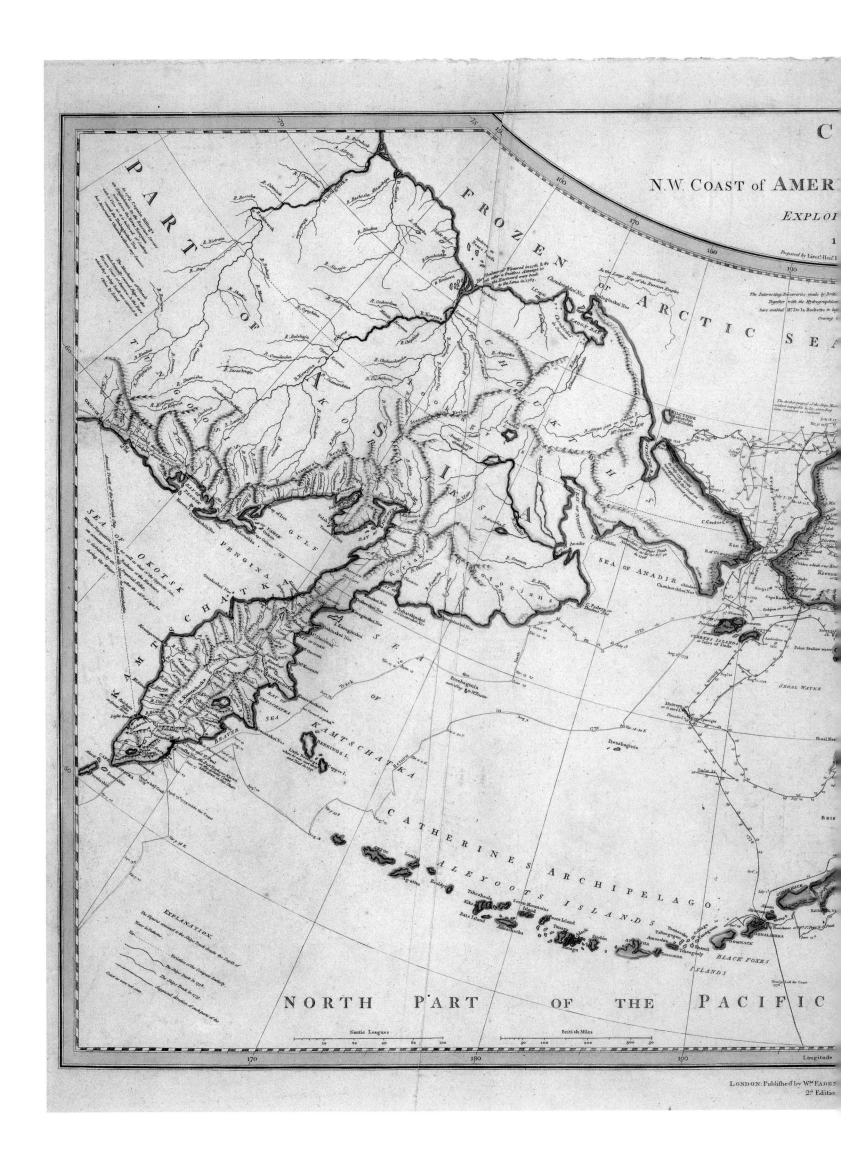

FROZEN OR ARCTIC SEA

PART OF

SEA OF OKOTSK

KAMTSCHATKA

PENGINA GULF

SEA OF ANADIR

CATHERINES ARCHIPELAGO

ALEYOOTS ISLANDS

BLACK FOXES ISLANDS

NORTH PART OF THE PACIFIC

EXPLANATION.

Nautic Leagues

British Miles

LONDON: Published by W.m FADEN
2.d Edition

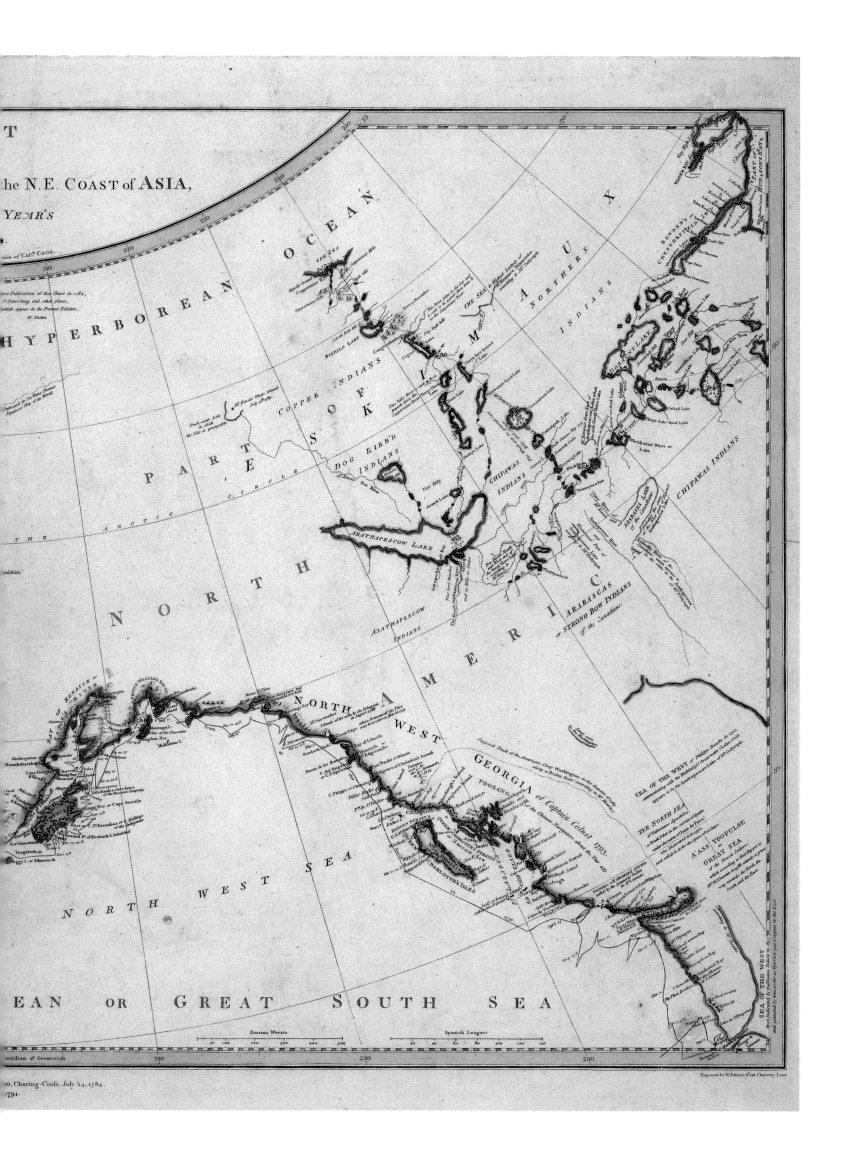

Видъ Верхнъ=Колымскаго Острога съ рѣки Асашны

Nulato and the Koyukuk estuary. A report and draft maps of the expedition were made for the trading company.

Great credit for the mapping of Alaska goes to Lieutenant Lavrenty Alekseyevich Zagoskin, who had studied at the Naval Academy and had spent eight years in the Caspian Sea navy. In 1838 he was granted permission to join the service of the Russian-American Trading Company. For two years he commanded a company corvette. Ilya Voznesensky, an assistant at the Arts Academy, who in his time was considered one of the central figures of American studies in Russia, went along on one of the journeys. He probably influenced the fact that Zagoskin applied for and was given permission to make voyages of exploration into the interior.

Zagoskin's journey began in December 1842 from Saint Michael at the Yukon estuary. His party, having made its way along the frozen river, arrived in Nulato, from which they proceeded to Koyukuk to seek a pass leading to Kotzebue Sound. On 8 May, when the ice broke on the Yukon, Zagoskin was in Nulato again. When the spring floods had subsided the group paddled their canoes to the upper Yukon. The expedition was made up of five hunters and one interpreter. The Indians told them of the Innoko River pass which

146 Grigory Chelikhov built four forts in the 1780s to protect his trading posts in the Aleutians and Alaska. The fort in the picture was built on Kodiak Island. Alexander Baranov arrived at Kodiak Island in 1790 and from there, as Governor of Alaska, he oversaw the building of Russian trading posts on the mainland.
(HELSINKI UNIVERSITY LIBRARY)

Kolmakov had reached when seeking the Yukon. After a couple of weeks their way was blocked by rapids and they returned to Nulato. In August 1843, having explored the area around Nulato, Zagoskin continued his journey down the Yukon, exploring its tributaries. By the time he had reached the river estuary he had mapped 435 miles of riverbank.

In November 1843 Zagoskin headed for the area between the Kuskokwim and the Yukon, and the Kuskokwim valley. The expedition returned to the Yukon estuary in June 1844 after a journey that had lasted one year and six months. Zagoskin's term of contract had finished and he returned to Russia in 1845. His diary was published in instalments in a periodical and as a book in 1848. This diary was the first account of the Alaskan interior. Zagogskin was later made a member of the Russian Geographical Society.

RUSSIAN MARITIME EXPEDITIONS

In 1815 the Russian navy sent an expedition, led by Otto von Kotzebue, to chart the Bering Sea area. Kotzebue's aim was to find a Northwest Passage from the Bering Strait. After reaching the Bering Strait, Kotzebue followed the coast of Alaska north-east, discovered Shishmaref Inlet and, in August 1815, a sound which had gone unnoticed by Cook. He thought he had already discovered the entrance to the Northwest Passage but soon realised his mistake. Unlike the Russians in general, Kotzebue named the areas he had discovered after his chiefs or members of his crew. He named the sound Kotzebue Sound. To an extent Kotzebue made the mapping of the Alaskan coast more precise, and his scientific aids compiled a wide-ranging report on the natural habitat of the Bering Strait and the Aleutians. He became aware of the fact that the British Admiralty was concentrating on the discovery of a Northwest Passage and that Russian expansion would be stopped.

Besides their mapping of the American coast, the Russians continued to chart the coastal waters of Eastern Siberia. In spite of the efforts of the second Great Kamchatka expedition, the easternmost coast had remained partly unexplored. Ferdinand Wrangel was sent to continue the work. His expedition was divided up into two independent groups. The second, which was led by Wrangel's subordinate, Petr Fjodorovich Anzu, completed the mapping of the New Siberia islands and coast. Wrangel's aim was to map the northern coast east of Kolyma. Dmitri Laptev, 1736–43, Joseph Billings, at the end of the 18th century, and Matvei Hedenström, 1808–1811, had preceded him in this work. After three years of exertion (1822–1824) Wrangel charted the coast between Cape Shelagsky and Kolyuchinskaya Guba more accurately than his predecessors. He heard stories of an island off the coast but did not find it. He was convinced of the island's existence and drew it on his map at almost the same place where Wrangel Island was discovered later.

Between 1819–1822 Mikhail Vasilyev and Gleb Shishmarev sailed first to Unalaska and then to Kotzebue Sound. The following summer Vasilyev explored Norton Bay and discovered Nunivak Island further to the north. Like Cook he managed to make his way into Icy Cape but no further. The expedition charted the Alaskan coast in greater detail than had Cook.

In 1821 the Finn, Arvid Adolf Etholen, charted the coast of Russian America north of Goodnews Bay and was also one of the first to make his way up the River Kuskokwim. He went to Nunivak Island immediately after Vasilyev. Except for a few expeditions Russian interest in what is now Alaska was diminishing.

Almost twenty years later (1838) the Russian-American Trading Company sent Alexandr Kashevarov to explore the north coast of Alaska. He left his ship the *Polifem* at Cape Lisburn and continued with six boats to Icy Cape and, with a smaller group, to Point Barrow and Dease Inlet. Eskimo hostility forced him to turn back. Kashevarov had arrived too late as Simpson and Dease had already mapped the coast east of Point Barrow the previous year from the Mackenzie. But Kashevarov compiled more information on the coast and the life of the Eskimos than had his predecessors .

One of the last expeditions carried out by the Russians was that made by Petr Doroshin to look for gold on the Kenai Peninsular. This, the first known expedition for gold to Alaska, took place almost 50 years before the great Klondike gold rush. Gold was found but this did not lead to the area being mined.

THE HUDSON'S BAY COMPANY AND THE BRITISH

The further the 19th century progressed, the more actively the British pushed their expeditions into the waters and wilderness of Alaska. While on the one hand the Navy was looking for a Northwest Passage, on the other they were making advances west into the interior, towards the Pacific coast.

The Hudson's Bay Company had not fulfilled the desire of the more enthusiastic imperialists for territorial expansion. The company underwent a change of attitude only when unbridled competition forced the Hudson's Bay Company and the North West Company to merge. The North West was a dynamic company whose men – particularly Alexander Mackenzie and Peter Pond – travelled to both the Arctic Ocean and the Pacific Ocean to seek new sources of fur.

The two companies merged in 1821 during the time of Franklin's first expedition.

Although the Hudson's Bay Company's young George Simpson was made overseas governor of the new company, most of its leading figures came from the North West Company. The spirit of enthusiasm at North West held sway in the new company too, and Simpson was not at all opposed to the expansion of the company. John McLeod made his way west of the Mackenzie River and discovered the Liard River, the Dease River and Lake Dease.

McLeod's second expedition was a failure, however, and the young Robert Campbell was given the job of building a trading post on Lake Dease. Campbell advanced to the headwaters of the River Stikine, where he met the Pacific Ocean Indians who had already traded with the Russians. Campbell continued his explorations, and was the first European to penetrate the upper reaches of the Yukon. In 1848 he founded a trading post at Selkirk, on the banks of the Yukon near the estuary of the River Pelly.

Two years later Campbell progressed to Fort Yukon. A trading station had been built there a few years earlier which became the Hudson's Bay Company's furthest outpost. The station was situated at the point where the River Porcupine and the Yukon converged on the Russian side of the border, but the Russians had not yet even got as far as the border.

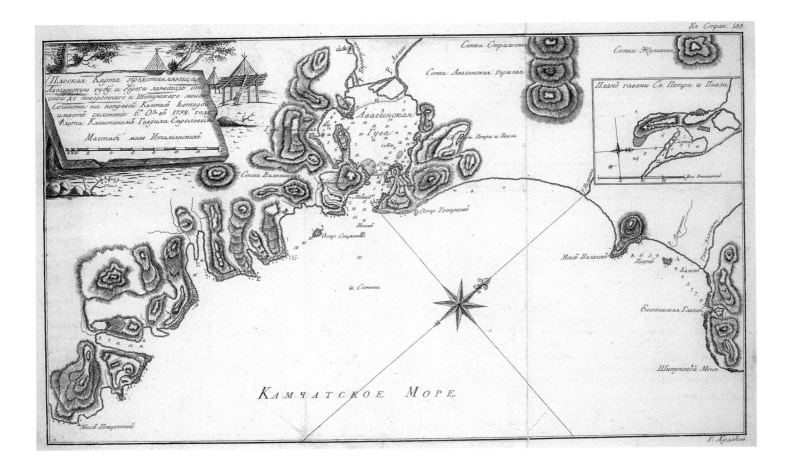

147 The Russians asked the Englishman Joseph Billings to lead an expedition from the Arctic Ocean to the Pacific. Billings knew the area to an extent, since he had been on Cook's last voyage. Billings was a distinguished sea charter and captain. His Lieutenant, Gavriil Sarychev, charted the eastern end of the Northeast Passage at the mouth of the Kolyma and in the Bering Strait. He also explored the Aleutian Islands and the coast of Kamchatka. Written on this map of Kamchatka is: "Avachinskaya Bay and its beach, up to where it turns and as far as the Shipunsky spit. Drawn with the aid of a compass, with a declination of 6 degrees East, in 1792 by the fleet commanded by Captain Gavriil Sarychev. Italian mile used for scale". Attention is drawn by the precision of Sarychev's description of the coast and his hydrographical measurments; Avanchinskaya Bay has been thoroughly sounded. The unit of measurement is the fathom. The topography of the coast is also depicted graphically in a creditable manner.

(Helsinki University Library)

They were obliged to move the station in 1869 when the Americans arrived there and discovered that it was located in their area. The move was made with a certain amount of latitude, however, because in 1890 it was still found to be twelve miles inside the American area.

Although James Cook had found several mistakes on maps of the North Pacific Ocean, he had not had time to explore the coast more thoroughly. Belief that a Northwest Passage could be found south of the Bering Strait had not died down. Although Cook had explored Cook Inlet he had done it in a hurry. An entrance to the Northwest Passage might still be found there or on the coast. George Vancouver, who had been with Cook for the first time as a 14-year-old midshipman, was sent to explore the coast once more. He set out on his journey from England and sailed by the way of the Cape of Good Hope in autumn 1791.

Vancouver sailed directly to the Strait of Juan de Fuca, which lay between Vancouver Island and the American mainland. There he encountered some Spanish ships with whose commander he made an agreement to co-operate. The Spaniards, however, did not like Vancouver's men checking everything that they had already done. Vancouver showed that Vancouver Island was not part of the continent.

The second summer Vancouver continued charting the coast to the north of the point at which he had ended his work the previous summer. The following summer he began work at Cook Inlet, which to his disappointment proved to be a dead end. At the same time Vancouver gave the bay its present name. On the third summer he proved that a Northwest Passage was not to be found from the Pacific coast.

On 4 June, during his final summer (1793), he arrived at Elcho Harbour, a small cove on the banks of the Dean Channel. Six weeks later, on 22 July, Alexander Mackenzie arrived at the same cove, having travelled for nine months from Fort Chipewyan to the Pacific coast. As proof of his voyage he carved the date and the words 'Alexander Mackenzie, from Canada, by land' into the cliff where he had sheltered the previous night. The Indians told Mackenzie that a great boat had come there and opened fire on them. The Indians' manner was so threatening that Mackenzie understood the precautionary measures taken by his predecessor.

The next British expeditions would involve either the search for a Northwest Passage or were connected in some way with the search for Franklin. First, F. W. Beechey sailed to the Bering Strait with the task of backing up John Franklin's second expedition. Franklin's aim was to map the north coast, west of the River Mackenzie, and to meet Beechey's men at Icy Cape. Beechey explored Kotzebue Sound and discovered Hotham Inlet, which had gone unnoticed by Kotzebue. He did not meet Franklin, who had had to turn back before achieving his aim.

The disappearance of Franklin's last expedition of 1845–48 caused a flood of expeditions focusing on the Arctic archipelago north of Canada. Prior to this the whaler, Thomas Welcome Roys, had heard of the whaling grounds of the Bering Strait from a Russian officer in Petropavlovsk. Roys acquired some sea-charts from the Russians and carefully examined Cook's narrative. In 1847 he sailed about 280 miles north of Bering Strait to the Chukchi Sea and returned to Honolulu the following year with his catch of eleven whales. News of Roys' journey spread, and over the next 50 years whale hunters sailing to the Arctic Ocean were fundamentally to change the lives of the inhabitants of the coast.

THE VACUUM IS FILLED

The ownership of the last Arctic wilderness was decided in 1867. That year the United States bought Alaska from Russia for a price of 7.2 million dollars. Why was a measure that would be inconceivable nowadays possible not much more than a hundred years ago?

The Russians had never conquered Alaska. There were, at the most, only 1000 Russians there; traders, hunters and priests. When the Crimean war broke out between Russia and Great Britain 1854–56, it would have been easy for the British to conquer Alaska and annex it to Canada, since Russian America was extremely vulnerable.

The Russian-American Trading company had also gone into decline. Although the company took unscrupulous advantage of the indigenous population, it was not profitable and needed the continuous support of the government. The company's licence had expired in 1862. The riches of Alaska attracted opportunists, the supervision of whom would have required more and different kinds of resources. Many Russians therefore were in favour of giving up the whole area.

Negotiations began as early as the 1850s after Zagoskin's voyages. In 1867 the area was surrendered to the Americans at Novo-Arkangelsk whose name was immediately changed to Sitka.

The exploration of Alaska began again. Some Russian expeditions and their results sank into oblivion. The Americans explored their new area with enthusiasm, but the exploration proper had already been made.

148 The Russians were not usually satisfied with simply mapping, and they often also collected information on the indigenous peoples and their cultures. Gavriil Sarychev served as a Lieutenant under Joseph Billings in the Bering Strait area between 1786 and 1794. He presented the theory of a land situated to the north of the estuary of the Kolyma River, and in his travel journals described the lives of the Chukchi, Kamchadaal, Yakut and Aleut peoples. (ARKTINEN MUSEO, PIETARI)

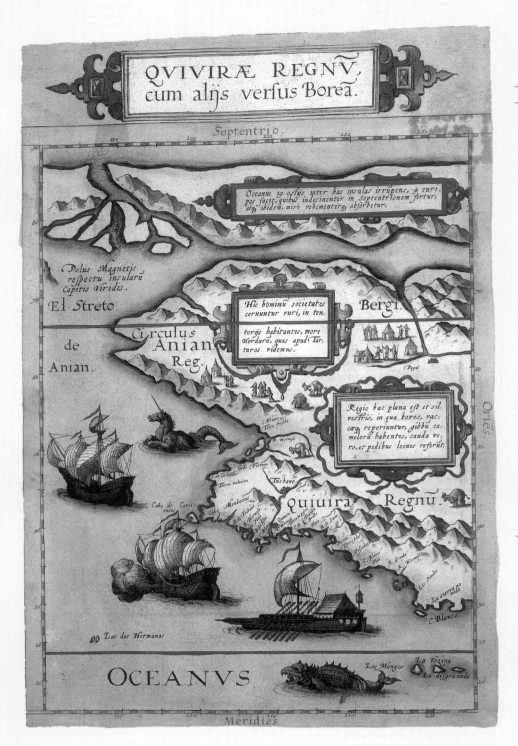

149 *Cornelis de Jode published an improved atlas based on the work of his father Gerard in Antwerp. North America was of particular focus. As far as is known, the atlas has the first printed map of Alaska (on the map the Ania Peninsula). In the north we can see "Mercator's" polar islands and in the south an area of California which appears as the Quiviran Peninsula on the map. Indians are depicted on the land and the sea is decorated with sailing ships and sea monsters. Europeans had not yet been to the area. So, despite his beautiful map, de Jode was not able to offer any better geographical information.*
(THE NEWBERRY LIBRARY)

150 *Russian interest in territories to the east began to grow in the 18th century. Vladimir Atsalov released information following his 1701 journey to Kamtchtka, which made references to a large land in the east. Ivan Kozyrevskii had taken part in a mutiny in which Atsalov lost his life. To redeem himself, Kozyrevskii was given the task of discovering new lands for Russia. He visited the Kurill islands in 1712–1714 and described them in detail. He made contact with Cossacks roaming the region and collected fresh geographical knowledge from them. When Bering was departing on his first voyage to Kamchtka in 1726 Kozyrevskii delivered the best knowledge on Russia's eastern parts. Included was a handmade map that clearly depicts Kamchatka as well as several Pacific islands. The map faces east. The sausage-shaped island in the upper left corner refers to the mythical land of Gama or the American continent.* (RUSSIAN NATIONAL ARCHIVES)

THE MEETING OF ASIA AND AMERICA

Europeans began to understand the proportions of the northern continents during the era of the great voyages of exploration. In the 17th century, the idea that the northern hemisphere consisted of two different continents began to take hold. But a more accurate picture of the location of and the relationship between Asia and America only became clear in the 18th century. It was then that sailors equipped with the most up-to-date measuring instruments arrived in the Bering Strait. This area of sea and the land adjacent to it, Alaska, the westernmost part of America, was the last of all the inhabited regions to be mapped.

The Russians were the first to arrive at the sea separating Asia from America. What lay beyond the sea only became clear during the time of Peter the Great, however. In the earliest Russian descriptions of Siberia, Asia was, quite correctly, surrounded by water to the northeast. On Russian maps from the end of the 17th century onwards there are suggestions of a land connection to America. They often depict a peninsula with an indeterminate tip pushing into the northeast. Some maps show several peninsulas. At the time the maps were being made in the 17th century, Dechneyov had already sailed round the Chuchki Peninsula, but his reports were buried in the Yakutsk archives. Later, one of Bering's contemporaries, the German Gerhard Friedrich Müller, found them and showed that at least some Russians knew that a navigable waterway led round Asia.

The Asian Chuchki had always been in contact with the Eskimos of Alaska, making trading trips across the strait in their kayaks and umiaks. It is possible that the nature of these contacts were misinterpreted. Mapmakers might have believed that the dwelling places and hunting grounds of the Chuchki and Eskimos were connected by a land bridge. According to Bagrov, the pioneer of Russian cartography, the Jesuit Gerbillion who had taken part in border negotiations between the Russians and the Chinese, propagated the idea that Asia and America were joined. There are also suggestions of a land bridge on Remizov's and Godunov's old maps. This idea travelled to Western European scientific communities. The well-known mapmakers Nicolaas Witsen, Evert Isbrand Ides, Johan Baptist Homann (1664–1724), Guillaume Delisle and John Thornton strengthened this idea in Europe.

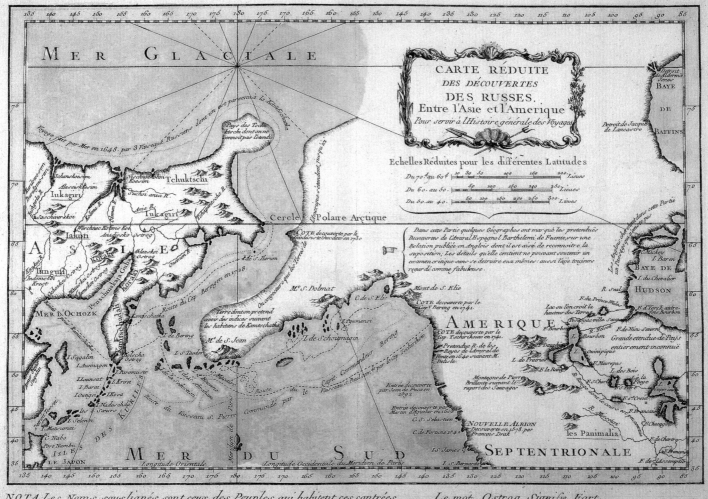

151 *The observations of the Aleutian Islands made from Bering's* St. Peter *were wrongly interpreted by his men Sven Waxell and Sofron Kchitrovho in the map they made. The so-called parrot's beak that exaggerated the American continent was passed on to European maps by Müller. The prolific Frenchman Jacques Nicolas Bellin also adapted this ludicrous Alaska-extremity in his description of America. His 1764 map also shows a bulge on the Chuchki peninsula that depicts a continental continuation – an old reference to a northern connection to a continent or islands. Such illusory mistakes in maps were not corrected until after Cook's voyage.*
(JOHN NURMINEN FOUNDATION)

With Vladimir Atlasov's journey to Kamchatka in 1701, new information spread on the islands, archipelagos and "great lands" to the east of the Chuchki Peninsula. The Russian mapmaker Lvov drew a land projecting north from the Chuchki Peninsula and added some islands to the east of the Asian continent and, beyond them still, a sizeable land area pushing from north to south. Kamchatka was often depicted as being separated from the Chuchki Peninsula. These mistakes were only corrected after Bering's journeys.

Bering made no contact with America on his first journey in 1724. Sketches made by Pjotr Tshaplin on this journey show the real shape of the Chuchki Peninsula. Tshaplin's finds were kept secret, however, and it was not until 1733 that

the Russian Ivan Kirilov's atlas finally quashed the belief in a land bridge between Asia and America. In western Europe the cartographers Du Halde and d'Anville confirmed Kirilov's claim in publications of their own.

In 1732, a two-vessel expedition set out from Ohotsk to explore the great land to the east. One of the vessels was shipwrecked, but the *Svayatoi Gavriil*, with its commander Mihail Gvozdev and navigator Ivan Feorov, discovered the Diomede Islands in the midst of the Bering Strait and arrived at Cape Prince of Wales at the northeastern tip of Alaska. This was the first known contact with America by Europeans arriving there from the west. Gvozdev's maps have not survived, but a little later his discoveries were marked on Spangberg's and Jeffrey's maps.

The Frenchman Joseph Nicolas Delisle, Guillaume Delisle's younger brother, compiled a map for Bering's second expedition. The map depicted the imaginary islands of the North Pacific – Terro de Jeso, Companyland and Gamaland – mistakes that were to hamper Bering's expedition, which eventually met a harsh fate. The commander of one of Bering's ships, Alexei Chirikov, made corrections to the map of the Bering Sea. He did not explore the American mainland, but he located many of the Aleutian Islands. Two members of the expedition, the cartographer Ivan Elagin and the explorer Sven Waxell, made further improvements to the map. On the basis of this information the German cartographer, Müller, presented his own incorrect view of the Aleutians. The enormous

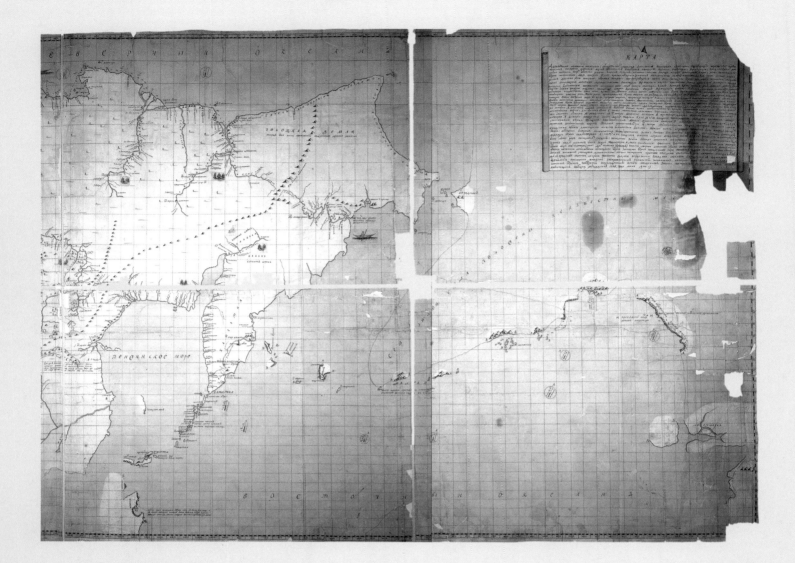

152 The St. Peter *and* St. Paul *were Bering's ships on his second expedition. Bering captained the former and Aleksei Chirikov the latter. The ships' crews made their own interpretations of their observations and accordingly the maps they made differed from each other a good deal. Navigational Officer Ivan Elagin made this map, which was approved by Aleksei Chirikov. The map's description of the Aleutian Islands and parts of the American continent are relatively correct and leave little room for speculation.* (Russian National Archives)

turtleneck stretching to the west from America which he 'invented' appears for the first time on a map made by the Englishman Truscott.

In St Petersburg, Catherine the Great was showing an interest in the eastern extremity of her country and sent a two-vessel expedition to explore the area. Sind, who commanded one of the vessels, misinterpreted observations made on the journey, which caused Stählin to place large islands between the continents on his map. Later, Admiral Nagayev was ordered to continue the mapping work. With the Chuchki, Nicholas I. Daurkin and fur hunters as his sources of information, he compiled a map which also shows part of America. Although the information found its way to St Petersburg slowly, the Admiralty gradually formed a more accurate picture of Russia's coast and general outline.

When he was sailing the Bering Strait in 1778, James Cook found Müller's and Stählin's new maps to be inaccurate. Having anchored off Unalaska he met the Russian pilot Gerasim Grigoryevich Izmaylov, who had been educated at the Irkutsk School of Navigation. Izmaylov made substantial corrections to Cook's maps. Cook trusted him and presented him with a valuable Hadley octant. James Clerke brought the information gained on Cook's journey to Europe, where it was published. The Bering Strait was now given its proper place on the world map.

The German naturalist Peter Simon Pallas made great strides in reforming the cartography of the North Pacific. He published the information collected by the Russians, which the Englishman William Cox later distributed in Europe. The Russian Admiralty was also developing its sea charts and the Spanish were mapping the Pacific coast from the south.

The Englishman Joseph Billings, who had served on Cook's journey, was ordered to lead an expedition around the Chuchki and Kamchatka Peninsulas in 1785. His navigator, Gavriil Sarychev, made an important contribution to the mapping of the area. Sarychev's maps are also of high hydrographic quality. The final great areas missing from the map of Alaska were filled in after Krusenstern's and Kotseby's sea voyages and Vancouver's inland expedition. Making the map of the north coast of Alaska more precise would have to wait until the coming of the polar explorers in the 19th century.

THE ROYAL NAVY SAILS TO THE ARCTIC OCEAN

THE FIRST EXPLORERS – CABOT, CORTE-REAL, BARENTS, FROBISHER, DAVIS, BAFFIN AND MANY
OTHERS – WERE BOLD MEN WHO SET OUT TO FIND SOMETHING NEW AND BETTER. THEY OFTEN
FOUND SOMETHING NEW BUT NOT ALWAYS WHAT THEY WERE LOOKING FOR. THE VISION, COURAGE
AND SKILL OF THE CAPTAIN WAS DECISIVE IN DETERMINING WHETHER THE BRAVE SAILORS EVER
REACHED THEIR DESTINATIONS AND RETURNED HOME.

EXPEDITION TYPOLOGIES

From the end of the 18th century onwards expeditions could
be broadly divided into three types: the co-operative, the naval
and the scientific. The first – in which the expedition leaned on
the support of the indigenous inhabitants – were few in number and were undertaken at the interim stage when explorers
were still learning about conditions in the Arctic. Samuel
Hearne was completely dependent on the co-operation of the
local Indians. He was continuously forced to make compromis-
es. He could never be sure if those under him wanted or were
able to do what they had promised.

In one respect John Franklin's first overland expedition be-
longs in the same category. It too was crucially dependent on
outside help since, without it, the expedition would never have
accomplished its objective or made it home alive. Unlike
Hearne, Franklin did attempt to preserve the illusion of independence and self-determination. He never actually led the
voyageurs and Indians, however, and it was their decisions to an
extent that determined the fate of the expedition.

On the other hand, Franklin's expedition was an example of
the naval type, the kind which was a typically Russian phenomenon during the 18th century and which the British, too,
adopted at the end of the 18th century. At the heart of the
expedition was a naval unit which was reinforced – both spiri-
tually and materially – to be better suited to the Arctic
environment. Apart from whalers who participated as pilots,
such expeditions were manned by sailors with virtually no experience of Arctic conditions. Bearing in mind their "starting
point" the best leaders fared well. But the kind of military

154 In his painting Stephen Pearce has depicted a group of distinguished persons, and has given them the name of the Arctic Council. The Admiralty invited these veterans, that is to say George Back, Edward Parry, James Clark Ross, Francis Beaufort, Edward Sabine and John Richardson, among others, to consider measures to rescue Franklin's expedition. In spite of the expertise of its members, decisions were delayed. The Council did not listen to Richard King, who several times suggested the sending of an expedition to the mouth of the Back River. When measures were finally taken the rescue expedition were unable to clear up the chain of events that had caused the loss of the expedition.
(NATIONAL PORTRAIT GALLERY)

153 On his third voyage Parry again made for Lancaster Sound and attempted to go south from Prince Regent Inlet. The ice stopped his vessels the HECLA and the FURY in their tracks. In the picture the vessels are in a gentle wind off the southern tip of Prince Leopold Island waiting for the ice conditions to improve.
(JOHN NURMINEN FOUNDATION)

organisation in which only one individual concentrates on the "thinking" while the others wait passively, will fail to develop into an expedition capable of functioning in Arctic conditions. The problems increased considerably when the navy left the sea and went ashore.

A better solution was already being developed. Alongside Thomas Simpson, John Rae was among the pioneers of this new approach (not forgetting Alexander Mackenzie, Peter Pond and Samuel Champlain). The unit was small, rarely comprising more than a dozen men, but it could draw on the support of a larger group at its base. Each member of the team, including the leader, had several areas of competence at his command. He was able not only to think but also to hunt. The expedition could also be divided up flexibly into smaller groups that were able to perform all the necessary functions. Because the group's activities were not limited by any rules or regulations it could decide itself on the best tools and skills to employ in order to achieve its aims and to meet the requirements of the task in hand. This was how, from the end of the 19th century onwards, almost all the great expeditions were carried out. But each leader was an individual in his own right.

The first British naval expedition took place in 1676, when the Admiralty sponsored Wood's attempt to find a Northeast Passage. After this, trading societies and whalers would again be responsible for expeditions for a century to come.

At the beginning of the 18th century the politician Arthur Dobbs severely criticised the Hudson's Bay Company and demanded that it take a more active role in exploring Hudson Bay and the passages leading west from it. Christopher Middleton had sailed on Hudson's Bay Company vessels for twenty years and, in 1741, at Dobbs' suggestion, the Admiralty selected him to lead an expedition. Middleton reached and named Repulse Bay, but reported that a Northwest Passage could not be found from either Wager Bay or via Rae's Welcome Sound.

On the third occasion in which the Admiralty participated in an expedition, its affairs were decided upon by a credible outside party. Daines Barrington was a judge and amateur scientist, one of the first proponents of the open polar sea theory. He persuaded the Royal Society to suggest to the Admiralty the exploration of a route leading from Spitsbergen, a proposition to which the Admiralty agreed in spite of the fact that the experiences of some whalers were in conflict with the theory. Constantine John Phipps, a naval Captain,

155 and 156 During the time of the great expeditions of the 16th century and early 17th century, Europe took an interest in areas to the north. The worldview of the north also expanded substantially. The Arctic area of Russia received a more precise shape in the 18th century, although northern parts of America still remained unknown. At the end of the 18th century the Arctic Ocean was reached for the first time along America's inland waterways. Only in the 19th century, when the British Navy sailed to the north, did the blank areas begin to be filled in.

Of the two maps shown, Beaurain's map (p. 202) was printed in Paris in 1782. The other (p. 203) was printed by the Whittle & Laurie company in London in 1802. Beaurain's map depicts James Cook's and John Phipps' voyages, among others. It presents the same imaginary Northwest Passage across North America, which is already known from Champlain's map. Whittle & Laurie's map depicts North America more realistically, even though the map asserts that it is impossible to sail north-west from Davis Strait or Baffin Bay. The charting of these waters began when the British Navy sailed to the Arctic. (JOHN NURMINEN FOUNDATION)

was to lead the expedition. Phipps was given the order to sail to the North Pole or at least find out how far in the direction of the Pole it was possible to sail. Although Phipps broke a new record in reaching latitude 80° 28', his voyage revealed little new geographically but a great deal scientifically. He pursued his objective with determination and nearly lost both of his ships, the *Racehorse* and the *Carcass,* to the jaws of the pack ice. The expedition went down in history as the second attempt (after that of John Davis) to sail to the Pole.

It can be mentioned in passing that a fourteen-year-old midshipman by the name of Horatio Nelson taking part in Phipps' expedition went on a bear hunting expedition without permission and, defying an order to retreat, marched alone towards an oncoming polar bear. When he had run out of ammunition for his musket he decided to kill the bear with the butt of the weapon. To his good fortune the bear was frightened away by a shot fired from the ship. That significant shot possibly decided the outcome of the Battle of Trafalgar thirty-three years later.

JOHN BARROW, SECOND SECRETARY TO THE ADMIRALTY

The British Navy's interest in the Arctic region increased early in the 19th century. One reason for this was the Admiralty's Second Secretary John Barrow, who as a young man had taken part in a whaling voyage to the Arctic Ocean. In 1818 Barrow published a history of Arctic exploration, and he played an important part in deciding who would be chosen to command an expedition at any given time.

In 1772, Samuel Hearne had shown that the River Coppermine flowed into the sea much further to the north than the latitude of Hudson Bay, which meant that the Northwest Passage should be sought to the north of Hudson Bay. The Russians had already advanced across the Bering Sea to Alaska. In 1778, James Cook had tried to find a Northwest Passage by way of the Bering Strait but had been turned back when the ice barred his passage.

Napoleon and France had been defeated in 1815 and the

CAPTAIN ROSS.

THE THIRD WINTER IN VICTORIA HARBOUR.

157 John Ross was courageous, stubborn, impatient and vain. It was difficult for a man like this to endure the kind of humiliation caused by his imagining the Croker Mountains in the far corner of Lancaster Sound. But Ross's stubbornness and courage saw him returning to the Arctic between 1829–1833, when he achieved the best result after Parry's first expedition. When he returned from this expedition he was 56 years old, but this did not prevent him from participating in the search for Franklin in 1850–1851.
(JOHN NURMINEN FOUNDATION)

Royal Navy free to look to new challenges. The Russians were clearly advancing towards the east. Otto von Kotzebue's voyage to the Bering Strait was a new indication of their interest in that direction. Changes in the natural environment of the area also favoured directing more resources towards the north. In 1817, William Scoresby Jr. made the announcement that for the first time during his lifetime the east coast of Greenland was free from ice between latitudes 74° and 80°. At the same time he applied to lead an expedition. He met John Barrow who, in spite of Scoresby's obvious qualifications, was not willing to entrust the command of a naval vessel to an outsider.

In 1818 the decision was made to send four ships to the north. The Admiralty made careful preparations for the expedition. The ships were reinforced with oak balks and iron plates for navigation. Warm clothing was designed for the cold conditions. Preserved meat, sauerkraut, potatoes, vegetables and lemon juice were taken along to prevent scurvy.

One of the two-ship expeditions was led by Commander John Ross, the other by Captain David Buchan. Parliament supported the programme by increasing the monetary rewards for Arctic expeditions, including £20,000 sterling for whoever discovered a Northwest Passage. Intermediary goals were also to be rewarded: reaching 110° West was valued at £5000, reaching 130° at £10,000 and reaching 150° at £15,000. But progress towards the North Pole was also to be rewarded. Crossing 83° North merited £1000. The sum was gradually increased, rising to £5000 upon reaching a latitude of 89°.

THE ROSS AND BUCHAN EXPEDITIONS, 1818

The two-ship expedition led by Captain David Buchan, like that of Phipps, was given the task of sailing between Greenland and Spitsbergen as far as possible in the direction of the North Pole. They were ordered to continue their journey from the Pole to the Bering Strait. Buchan was in command of the mortar ship *Dorothea.* His subordinate, Lieutenant John Franklin, was in command of the *Trent.* Buchan achieved less than Phipps, however, and barely made it back from the grip of the ice and fog.

Buchan failed because the task he had been given was hopeless. John Ross was given an altogether more interesting assignment: he was to find out from which of the three sounds discovered by Baffin – Smith, Jones or Lancaster – there was an entrance to the Northwest Passage in the direction of the Bering Strait. He was then to sail through the strait in question and leave a report at Kamchatka to be dispatched by land to both St. Petersburg and London.

Ross's expedition, with himself at the command of the *Alexander* and a young Lieutenant by the name of Edward Parry at the command of the *Isabella,* sailed north along the west coast of Greenland to the remotest corner of Baffin Bay, Smith Sound.

On the voyage Ross charted, if only perfunctorily, the Greenland coast. Although, because of the ice, he was obliged to sail relatively far out from the coast he drew the furthest reaches of the bays in great detail. So it was that Ross's subordinate, Lieutenant William Robertson, wrote the word 'unknown' in the margins of Ross's book which he had received as a present and which dealt with Wolstenholm Bay and Whale Bay.

The ice prevented Ross from reaching Smith Sound. In his assessment of the Strait Ross wrote: "Even if it be imagined by those who are unwilling to concede their opinions while there is yet a single yarn of their hypothesis holding that some narrow strait may exist through these mountains, it is evident that it must for ever be unnavigable..." Once again Robertson commented bitterly: "...that land apparently continuing is no argument that there is no opening..."

158 Lancaster Sound from John Ross's voyage in 1818. The Northwest Passage opens from the sound but Ross did not discover it. As he saw it, the Croker range seemed to close the sound although his men, including the young lieutenant Edward Parry, were unable to see the mountains. Indeed, Ross himself sailed through the sound ten years later without being hindered by them.
(JOHN NURMINEN FOUNDATION)

Ross is best remembered for the Croker Mountains. He saw these mountains in the furthest corner of the open Lancaster Sound and named them after the First Secretary to the Admiralty, John Croker. These mountains did not in fact exist. Not all of Ross's officers saw them, and nor was John Barrow convinced of the matter. Discussions with Ross's officers, particularly with Parry, confirmed his belief that Ross had turned back at the entrance to the Northwest Passage.

Although Ross did not succeed in his main objective, he charted long stretches of the coasts of Greenland and Baffin Island and confirmed William Baffin's discoveries, which many cartographers had removed from their maps. Ross was the first to describe the Eskimos of the north-west coast of Greenland, of whose lives a great deal of detailed information was obtained with the help of the Eskimo interpreter John Sacheuse. Ross fell out of favour with the Admiralty, however, and the Admiralty was largely John Barrow, who held his position for 40 years (1804–1844).

PARRY GETS HIS CHANCE

John Barrow invited Parry and a few other officers to discuss discrepancies concerning Ross's and Parry's Lancaster Sound. The discussions led to the sending of another expedition. Parry was chosen to command the expedition although he was still a Lieutenant. He was given the *Hecla* and the additional help of the *Griper* commanded by Lieutenant Matthew Liddon. Many of the officers had been members of Ross's crew, including James Clark Ross, who eventually became the most experienced of all the "Arctic officers" of the Royal Navy.

Parry's orders were explicit. His main task was to explore Lancaster Sound. If it turned out not to be a sound he was to seek a Northwest Passage elsewhere. His further orders were the same as those given to Ross; to advance into the Bering Strait and return to Europe by way of the Pacific Ocean.

In summer 1819 both the weather and the ice conditions favoured Parry. He was also the right man to take advantage of them. He proceeded west along Lancaster Sound – it was in fact a sound and not a bay – and named the pocket pushing into the north after the entrance to the sound, Croker Bay. The Admiralty's First Secretary could not allow himself to disappear into thin air along with the mountains named after him. The area of sea between Baffin and Somerset Islands was given the name Prince Regent Inlet because Parry was not able to determine whether this was a bay or a sound.

The ice stopped Parry in his tracks south of Prince Regent Inlet and he turned back and continued to travel west along Barrow Strait. He sailed to Viscount Melville Sound at the south of Cornwallis and Bathurst Islands. The Wellington Channel led northwards before Cornwallis Island was free of ice, but in Parry's view it led in the wrong direction. A narrow channel remained between the ice and the south coast of Melville Island, along which Parry advanced as far as was possible. On 20 September he was forced to retreat to winter quarters at the far corner of Hecla and Griper Bay, which was named Winter Harbour. His ships were towed on shore by cutting a passage into the thickening ice. On 26 September everything was made ready to spend the winter.

Parry was convinced that discipline, mental agility and good food would ensure the success of their winter stay. Discipline was not to be achieved by punishment, although this too was needed on one occasion. In February two of the *Hecla's* naval seamen were punished for being drunk. Every second week a play was performed. Parry, who in his youth had been interested in the theatre as well as music, performed in these himself. When the supply of plays had been exhausted he set about writing new ones.

Captain Edward Sabine, who was responsible for scientific observations, published a newspaper. They made expeditions into the surrounding countryside and hunted until the depth of winter made outdoor activities impossible. Every day the

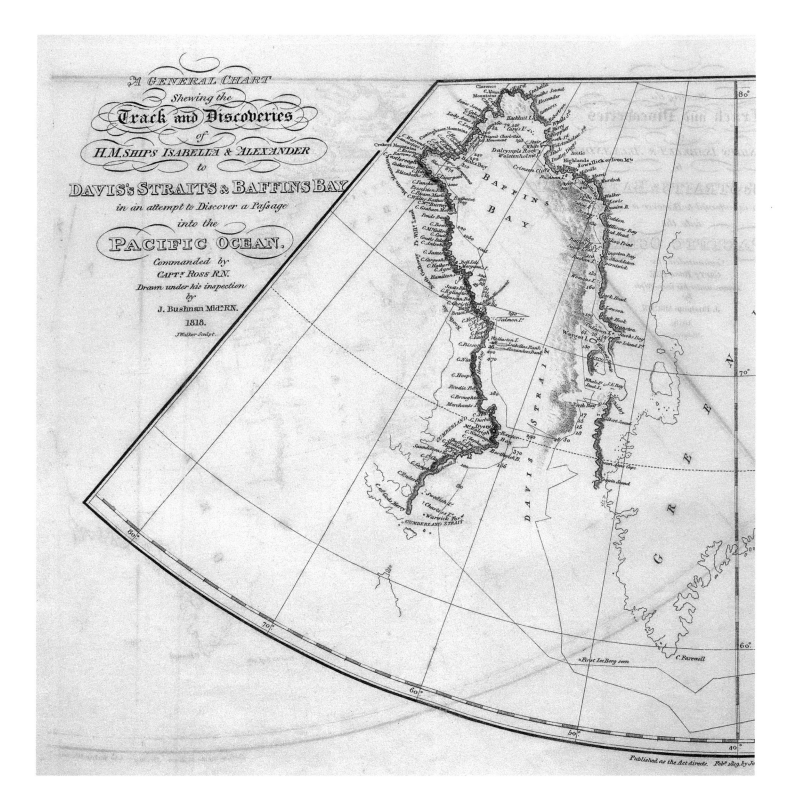

men were given one ounce (28g) of lemon juice mixed with sugar. Every man had to drink his daily dose in the presence of an officer. Each week every man was given a medical examination, with particular attention being paid to the state of his gums.

The first case of scurvy was observed in early January and surprisingly it was an officer who came down with it. He was fed on mustard and cress which Parry grew in his cabin. In nine days he was already up and walking. The same treatment was given to the next patients who were admitted to the sick bay in March. Hunting meant that the sick could also be provided with fresh meat. They got through the winter without serious setbacks. In May the ice was cut free from around the

ships. The *Hecla* rose considerably in the water since a great deal of her provisions and fuel had been used during the winter.

At the beginning of July they began to explore Melville Island. Parry was the first to make use of sledge parties. He and Sabine set out north with ten men. After a full week the men arrived at the shore of a sea. The land visible to the north, which was in reality the Melville Peninsula, was dubbed Sabine Island. The party continued south-west and crossed a deep bay which was named after Liddon. On the journey they saw signs of Eskimos, although they had not been seen during the winter. In June they bagged seals as well as caribou. Fishing, too, increased the amount of their fresh food.

159 In 1818 the Admiralty sent John Ross to find out whether a Northwest Passage opened up from Smith, Jones or Lancaster Sounds, which Baffin and Bylot had discovered but left unexplored more than 200 years earlier (in 1616). The ice prevented Ross's progress to Smith Sound and he doubted the sound's continuation. Ross mapped Coburg Island in the mouth of the Jones Strait but saw mountains shutting off the strait. Ross placed the Croker Mountains, the existence of which his young subordinate Edward William Parry did not believe in, at the far end of Lancaster Sound. In spite of its failings Ross's map tempted whalers to the Davis Strait and Baffin Bay, which gradually became a whaling centre. (JOHN NURMINEN FOUNDATION)

160 In winter 1822 Parry asked his Eskimo wife Iligliuk to draw a map of the coast that continued north from their winter quarters to a region they had not been to yet. On the bottom left hand corner of the map is Winter Island where Parry had established a winter camp. In the centre of the map is a strait to which Parry later gave the name the Fury and Hecla Strait after his ships. (JOHN NURMINEN FOUNDATION)

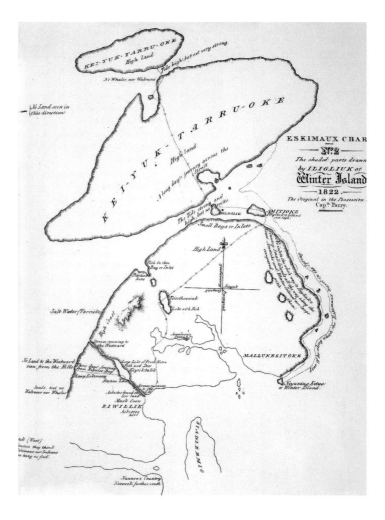

At the beginning of July the ice had thinned out to a little more than half a metre. The coastal waters were melting and it was possible to move about by boat. On 20 July they were floating free in the harbour but the ice still blocked its exit. During the last days of July it too disappeared, and on 1 August Parry's expedition sailed once more towards the west.

For a month they did not succeed in progressing to the point where they had turned back the previous autumn, which went beyond the first of Parliament's intermediary targets of longitude 110°. Parry feared that the second winter would be considerably worse than the first. There was little lemon juice left. He asked his officers to consider the expediency of a second wintering and, on 26 August, heard that they were unanimous in their wish to return home. They set sail towards the east. The Wellington Channel was once more free from ice but they did not sail into it this time either. On the return journey Parry completed the charting of the east coast of Baffin Island which had been begun by Ross. It might have been possible to find a new passage west there too.

No new passage was found from Baffin Bay. Parry came to the conclusion that the northern part of Hudson Bay was another likely opening to the Northwest Passage. Since westerly winds blew in the area throughout almost the entire summer it was natural to sail though the Northwest Passage from the Bering Strait. On the other hand the long journey to the Bering Strait made servicing and the access to fresh supplies more difficult. For this reason Parry suggested seeking a Northwest Passage at the north of Hudson Bay.

PARRY'S SECOND VOYAGE

Parry became a national hero. His appeal was increased by the fact that he had found no time to be married yet. And there was no time to seek a wife now.

In May 1821 Parry set sail for Hudson Bay. He took command of the *Hecla's* sister ship the *Fury*, which replaced the *Griper*. The *Hecla's* commander was George Francis Lyon, who had a voyage of exploration to Africa behind him. The crews were made up of volunteers from the previous voyage. Still a midshipman, James Clark Ross was embarking on his third voyage.

Parry had made improvements based on the experience of his previous voyage. Insulation was added to make heating more efficient and to ward off damp. Snow was melted with the heat of flue gas to make drinking and washing water. 35% proof liquor was taken onto the boat and was diluted before serving. This meant a 40% saving on storage space.

Salted beef was replaced by pork, whose flavour lasted longer. Instead of ship's biscuits they took along flour, and bread was baked on board the ship. Because lemon juice bottles broke in the cold they were replaced by five-gallon drums. Rum was added to the juice, which preserved its liquid state at low temperatures. Although on the earlier voyage they had managed to ward off scurvy, preserved carrots and cranberries were also taken along.

The Admiralty ordered Parry to sail north from the Repulse Bay region, along the American coast and then west towards the Bering Strait and the Pacific. At the same time Franklin's first overland expedition was making its way to the mouth of the Coppermine and the coast. Both expeditions were to leave messages for each other. Parry was ordered to take Franklin's men with him when they met, if the men were willing.

Parry believed Middleton's report and did not consider Wager Bay to be the entrance to the Northwest Passage. He sailed directly to the Frozen Strait at the north of Southampton Island, which according to Middleton was the shortest route to Repulse Bay. At the end of August Parry pushed his way into the unfrozen Repulse Bay. But he did not find a passage to the west there. During the autumn he charted the coast while making his way north and wintered on Winter Island to the west of Foxe Channel. The results of the first summer were slim. Only 185 miles of coast had been charted.

Winter passed as it had on the previous voyage but the men, and particularly the officers, found a new and interesting

161 A map of Fury and Hecla Strait made after Parry's second voyage of 1821–1823. Marked on the map are the routes of both Parry's ships and expeditions made onto the mainland. The shape of the west coast of Melville Peninsula is based on accounts by the Eskimos since no European charter had been there yet.
(JOHN NURMINEN FOUNDATION)

pursuit in getting to know the Eskimos. Parry had already met the Hudson Strait Eskimos during the early stage of the voyage. In his opinion, during the space of a hundred years they had learned all the bad ways of the Europeans but had managed to avoid those virtues that made the civilised world happy. Now he was confronted with Eskimos that had lived in almost complete isolation. Although Parry was offended by the fact that the Eskimos showed no gratitude for anything, he went among them without reservation. He took part in a hunting trip, tried out their kayaks, lived in their igloos and gave them food when their hunting was unsuccessful. He took care of their sick and even tried to influence the way they buried their dead. In all this he found an excellent companion in George Lyon, whose published diary provides exceptional documentation of the Eskimos' lives, dress, hunting, tools and weapons, even of their family life and beliefs.

In summer 1822 Parry made his way north to the mouth of a strait leading from the Gulf of Boothia which he had heard of from the Eskimos. Although Parry retained some of the Eskimo names, the strait was named the Fury and Hecla Strait. It was frozen over and Parry stayed to winter off Igloolik Island with the Eskimos. During the winter a sledge party explored the strait and the areas surrounding it. Although Parry had designed the men's clothing according to the Eskimo model he did not adopt the use of their light sledges. They bought fresh meat from the Eskimos and Parry's men went hunting. In the

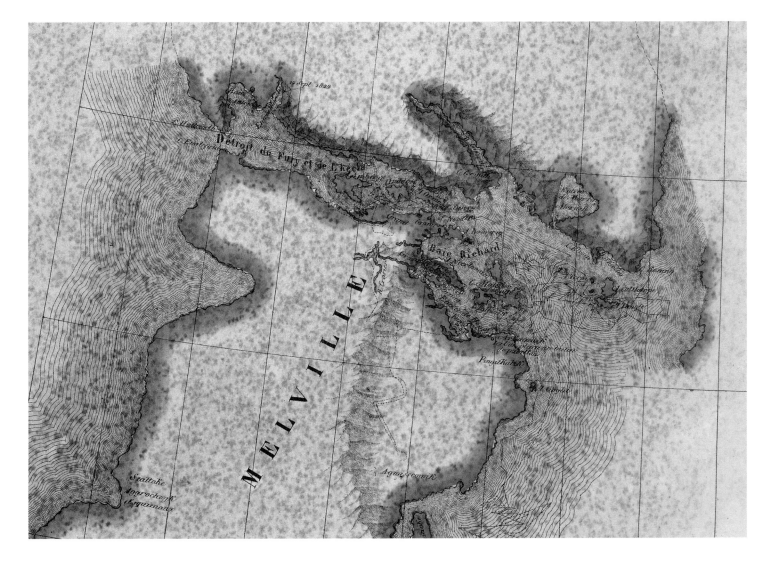

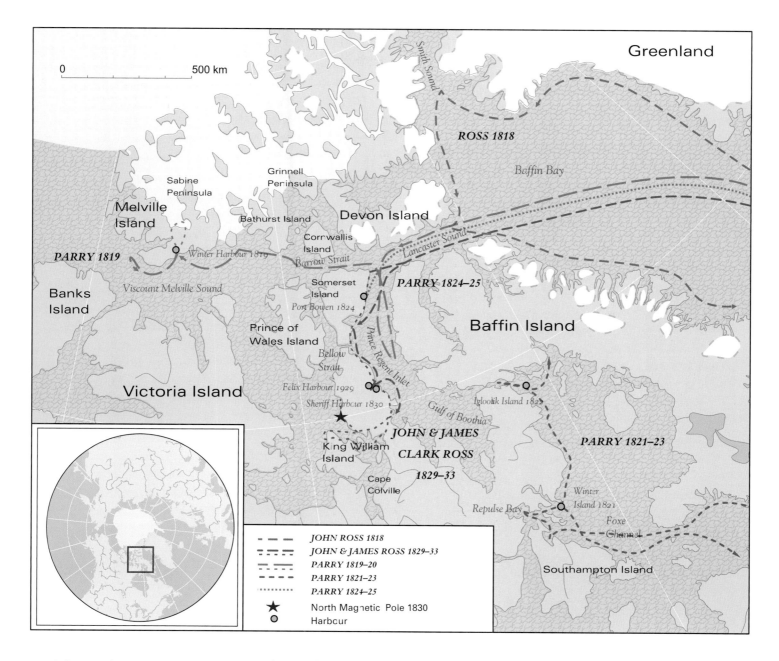

0   500 km

Greenland

ROSS 1818

Baffin Bay

Sabine
Peninsula

Grinnell
Peninsula

Melville
Island

Bathurst Island

Devon Island

Cornwallis
Island

Barrow Strait

Lancaster Sound

PARRY 1819

Winter Harbour 1819

Banks
Island

Viscount Melville Sound

Somerset
Island

Port Bowen 1824

PARRY 1824–25

Baffin Island

Prince of
Wales Island

Bellow
Strait

Prince Regent Inlet

Felix Harbour 1929

Igloolik Island 1822

PARRY 1821–23

Victoria Island

Sheriff Harbour 1830

★

Gulf of Boothia

King William
Island

*JOHN & JAMES
CLARK ROSS
1829–33*

Cape
Colville

Winter
Island 1821

Repulse Bay

Foxe
Channel

Southampton Island

- – – – *JOHN ROSS 1818*
- = = = *JOHN & JAMES ROSS 1829–33*
- – · – *PARRY 1819–20*
- – – – *PARRY 1821–23*
- ······· *PARRY 1824–25*
- ★ North Magnetic Pole 1830
- ◎ Harbour

162 The Royal Navy's most important expeditions, that is to say that of Ross in 1818, Parry's extremely successful expedition in favourable ice conditions of 1819 and his less successful expeditions are marked on the map, as are their winter harbours. The course of Ross's independent expedition of 1829-33 is also shown. On this expedition James Ross and James Clark Ross found the Magnetic North Pole and spent four winters in the Arctic without major losses. (PATANEN)

spring scurvy began to bother them again. The ships were still beset in the ice at the beginning of August and Parry only managed to leave Igloolik on 12 August by sawing a passage out of their winter harbour. He sailed straight for England.

The second voyage was a disappointment. The Fury and Hecla Strait could not be considered a navigable entrance to a Northwest Passage, although a way forward might indeed have led from the Gulf of Boothia. Parry believed, after all, that a Northwest Passage could be found from Prince Regent Inlet, from which his first expedition had turned back.

THE ROYAL NAVY
PREPARES FOR A BREAKTHROUGH

The Admiralty and John Barrow had decided to solve the mystery of the Northwest Passage. From 1818 to 1837 the Navy carried out twelve Arctic explorations. Two, the Franklin and Richardson expeditions, were accomplished overland to the Arctic coast of North America in co-operation with the Hudson's Bay Company; after Parry's second expedition Clavering carried out what were mostly geographical and magnetic surveys together with Sabine in the waters of Spitsbergen and Greenland in 1823. In 1824, Lyon, who had taken part in Parry's second expedition, was sent to the American coast to chart the stretch between the west coast of the Melville Peninsula and Turnagain Point, the point at which Franklin's first overland expedition had turned back. But he was forced by storms and battered by ice to return from Hudson Bay. Next it was the turn of Parry once again.

At the same time as Lyon was trying to progress west by way of Hudson Bay, Parry was sailing to Prince Regent Inlet. He believed he would find a Northwest Passage at roughly the

ROYAL NAVY BOMB KETCHES PUSHING THROUGH THE POLAR ICE

Many ships used on Arctic expeditions were originally built for other purposes and adapted to meet the new demands before setting off. The British often used merchant ships for their expeditions, such as colliers built in Whitby in northern England. The ships used on all three of James Cook's voyages were colliers. George Vancouver, too, sailed a collier.

Some expeditions were already using whalers at the beginning of the 19th century, but it was only during the time of George Nares in the 1870s that the British put their complete faith in them, because of their excellent sailing qualities. Nordenskiöld's *Vega*, which was the first ship to sail the Northeast Passage, was also a whaler.

Sturdiness of build had long been the most important factor when choosing a vessel. Thus it was that, at the turn of the 18th and 19th century, it was a warship, the bomb ketch, that became the principal vessel for expeditions organized by the British Royal Navy. Because of its broad, almost barge-like hull, its blunt-

nosed bow and the fact that it was under-rigged, the bomb ketch was modest as far as navigability was concerned but its sturdy hull withstood the pressure of the ice all the better for that.

The bomb ketch was only able to ram the ice, however, and could not break through it. The idea of a bow which rode up over the ice had not yet been conceived. Originally the bomb ketch was a merchant ship of the Dutch galliot type, which the French adapted to fire on coastal fortifications by mounting a cannon in the bows. There was enough room in the bows for a heavy mortar because the vessel only had two masts – a main mast and a mizzen mast. The final version of the vessel, which all the sea powers used, had two heavy cannon able to fire a 200-pound missile at coastal fortifications from close range. Because of the cannon's recoil the bow had to be extremely wide and strong. The ship's displacement also had to be shallow enough to allow it to get within range of the coast. These two features were also the vessel's

great assets when sailing the polar seas. Their value became particularly apparent in the search for the Northwest Passage.

In the 1820s, William Parry made four voyages in search of the Northwest Passage, all of them in bomb ketches. HMS *Hecla*, which took part in all four voyages, was the expedition's flag ship on three occasions and HMS *Fury*, which participated three times, took the lead once. These were 110–120 feet long and about 30 feet in the beam. The 377-ton *Fury* was launched at Rochester in 1814 and the 375-ton *Hecla* in 1815 at North Barton. Both originally had three masts and square rigging. They were converted into bomb ketches by removing their foremasts and reinforcing their foredecks with crossbeams. On her fourth voyage, the *Hecla* achieved a new northerly record of 82° 45'. The *Fury* was shipwrecked on her third voyage.

John Franklin used two bomb ketches on his fateful expedition in search of the Northwest Passage. Both of them, the *Erebus* and the *Terror*, were lost without

163 HMS GRIPER *and* HMS HECLA *were navy vessels with specially reinforced hulls, and were equipped with two heavy mortars. The reinforced hulls improved their ability to sail in Arctic waters and especially to withstand the crush of the pack ice.* (JOHN NURMINEN FOUNDATION)

Departure of South West Division

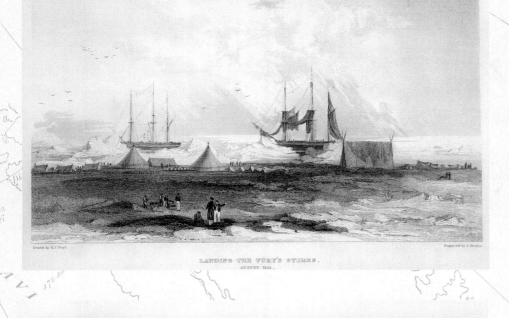

Drawn by H.N.Head

Engraved by E.Finden

LANDING THE FURY'S STORES.
AUGUST 1825.

Drawn & Engraved by W.Westall,A.R.A. from a Sketch made on the spot by Lieut Hoppner.

Situation of H. M. Ships Hecla & Griper
from the 17th to the 23rd of Augt. 1820

trace in 1845, in all probability having been crushed by the ice. Other bomb ketches used in northern waters include the HMS *Racehorse* and the HMS *Carcass*, on which Constantine Phipps set out to seek the Northeast Passage in 1773. North of Spitsbergen the ships were forced to turn back, prevented from going on by the ice.

The story of the *Racehorse* is interesting in terms of maritime history. The ship was originally a French privateer, the *Marquis de Vandreuil*, which the British captured in the Seven Years War. After service on polar voyages she was captured by the American *Andrea Doria* in the American War of Independence. The story ends when the Royal Navy destroyed the vessel in Delaware Bay.

The *Carcass* too played a role in maritime history; a certain midshipman by the name of Horatio Nelson served on her under Constantine Phipps.

164 *Sledges and boats designed for the expedition proved to be too heavy to pull. When the weather allowed it a square sail was used to lighten the burden, but progress in calm weather and on areas of pack ice required good physical condition and a sufficiently nourishing diet.*
(JOHN NURMINEN FOUNDATION)

165 *On Edward Parry's third voyage in August 1825* HMS FURY *was damaged in the ice and sprung a leak in her hull. In spite of several attempts the damage could not be repaired and the vessel's supplies and equipment had to be salvaged ashore. The ship had to be abandoned. The British were still taking advantage of the camp's stores in 1859 when McClintock was looking for Franklin's expedition.* (JOHN NURMINEN FOUNDATION)

166 *The progress of the vessels took place largely along open channels in the ice field. The men were often obliged to saw or blast a channel through the ice, which could be metres thick. The channels were opened up at random and could freeze over quickly, shutting off the vessels in the middle of the ice. Progress along the passages was made using either a sail or a kedge, an anchor transported to a distance and secured to the ice.*
(JOHN NURMINEN FOUNDATION)

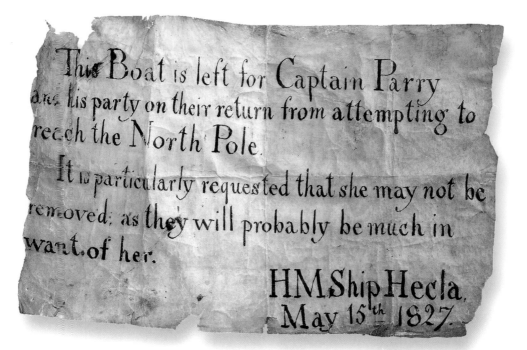

This Boat is left for Captain Parry and his party on their return from attempting to reach the North Pole.

It is particularly requested that she may not be removed; as they will probably be much in want of her.

HM Ship Hecla, May 15th 1827.

same degree of latitude as that of the River Coppermine estuary.

Fortune no longer favoured Parry. The ice was already making progress difficult at Baffin Bay. The expedition reached Lancaster Sound, however, and pushed its way – as late as 27 September – into Prince Regent Inlet. It was no longer possible to sail south, and Parry wintered at Port Bowen, which he had discovered in summer 1819.

The ships broke free from the ice on 20 July, but the summer was difficult. As early as August 1 the ships became stuck in the ice and the *Fury* was badly damaged. She was towed to safety but a storm interrupted repair work and also endangered the *Hecla*. They were forced to abandon the *Fury,* and a great deal of their food supplies were deposited on Fury Beach on Somerset Island. Parry was forced to return home. His third voyage had been almost a complete failure. Whereas the ice and weather conditions had been in his favour on his first voyage they were now against him.

The meeting to have taken place between Parry and Franklin's second overland expedition was not accomplished. William Beechey, Parry's Lieutenant on his first voyage, had been sent to Bering Strait. Beechey's mission was to meet up with Franklin's second overland expedition journeying west from the Mackenzie River estuary, the aim being to complete the chart between Cook's turning point, Icy Cape, and the Coppermine.

In July 1826 Beechey arrived at Kotzebue Sound. The ice forced him to turn back before Icy Cape and the ship's boat was sent to explore the northern coast of Alaska. The coast was charted all the way from Icy Cape to Point Barrow, a good 60 miles stretch. Beechey charted Seward Peninsular and the coasts of Kotzebue Sound and discovered Hotham Inlet by way of which the Rivers Kobuk and Noatak flow into the Chukchi Sea.

Beechey asked the Kotzebue Sound Eskimos to make a

167 Edward Parry attempted to reach the North Pole in a specially built sledge boat. The Hecla *had a spare boat for Parry's men, which was left at Spitsbergen as back up. The boat contained the message shown in the picture. The boat was never needed, however, since on 21 August 1827, after 61 days away, Parry arrived back at the vessel having achieved a new record of latitude 82°45' North. This narrowly beat the previous record made by Scoresby Sr.* (NATIONAL MARITIME MUSEUM, LONDON)

map of the coast, and they drew it in the sand on the beach. The coastline was drawn with a stick, and distances were estimated as day's journeys. Hills and mountain ranges were depicted by building them with sand and stones. Islands were marked with small stones corresponding to their shapes. As the work progressed other members of the group suggested changes. The map depicted the Seward Peninsula and the coast of Kotzebue Sound as far as Cape Krusenstern and included a couple of rivers that Beechey had not been aware of.

Parry had been married in autumn 1827 and he was appointed Hydrographer of the Navy by the Admiralty. This took him away from exploration, but he carried out one more expedition. John Franklin had proposed a journey to the North Pole in specially made sledge boats. Parry was assigned to lead the expedition. He sailed with whalers to Spitsbergen, found a harbour for the *Hecla* and set out on a journey across the sea ice at the beginning of June. Parry had built two boats. Steel runners had been fitted to their keels according to Parry's precise specifications. The crews of both boats comprised two officers and five men. One of the boats was commanded by Parry and the other by James Clark Ross.

Their departure was delayed for three days by the ice. The reindeer they had taken with them were left on board the ship to supplement their food, since they were not suitable for pulling the heavy sledges. Progress was painfully slow. Now and again all the men were needed to move one boat through or over the pack ice, and because of the ice shifting south they often wasted half the day's journey. They did not find solid ice throughout the entire journey. The northernmost degree of latitude reached was 82° 45'.

William Scoresby, even though he was a sailor, criticised Parry's decisions. The sledges were altogether too heavy. Scoresby suggested replacing them with Eskimo umiaks or dog teams. Scoresby compared Parry's rate of progress with that of the Cossack Alexei Markov, who covered an almost 800-mile journey in the River Yana delta by dog-pulled sledges in 24 days. Scoresby believed that the Pole could be reached from Spitsbergen with dog teams, but that the journey should be begun in early April. He had first made the proposal in 1815 when writing of the Greenland and polar ice. The Admiralty did not listen to him, however.

JOHN ROSS RETURNS

The Admiralty's enthusiasm waned after Parry's last unsuccessful polar expedition. The most significant achievement after Parry's first voyage was not accomplished at John Barrow's instigation. John Ross wanted to make up for his failure in 1818 and found a private sponsor for his voyage. Felix Booth was the owner of a gin distillery and former Sheriff of London. When, in 1828, Parliament discontinued its policy of rewards for discovering a Northwest Passage, Booth was able to take up exploring in the safe knowledge that nobody would think his aim mercenary.

In 1829 John Ross and his nephew James Clark Ross – who was now embarking on his sixth voyage – made their way in their vessel the *Victory,* which was fitted with a steam engine, to Prince Regent Inlet, which in spite of Parry's failure they considered the probable entrance to the Northwest Passage. Ross sailed south, got as far as Fury Beach, but was unable to go ashore. He returned once again and found that the reserves of food left by Parry were still there.

Nevertheless Ross passed Somerset Island and Boothia Felix, that is to say the Bellot Strait, which ran through the Boothia Peninsula, without noticing it, and progressed to Lord Mayor's Bay on the east coast of the Boothia Peninsula, considerably further than had Parry. In Felix Harbour Ross found a winter harbour for the *Victory.* The following summer the ship was freed from the ice but Ross only managed to travel three miles to the north-east. The next summer was difficult too and after some distance the *Victory* became stuck in the ice again. Ross was obliged to stay in the Arctic for a third winter – the first expedition to do so.

168 John Ross's second voyage of 1829–1833 was a great success. He made his way deep into Prince Regent's Inlet and was forced to stay there for three winters because his vessel the Victory, *shown in the picture, was beset in the ice on the east coast of the Boothia Peninsula. Ross and his crew pulled their boats to Fury Beach and survived thanks to the stores of food they found there. Ross and his men spent a fourth winter in the area before sailing to Lancaster Sound, where they were rescued by whalers in 1833.*
(JOHN NURMINEN FOUNDATION)

169 The English developed ships for wintering that were as homely as was at all possible. Heating and insulation were made more efficient. The mental agility of the crew was also important. Plays were performed and newspapers delivered. Their minds were also warmed by regular liquor allowances in the best navy tradition. The picture shows the ENTERPRISE *in 1848 at Port Leopold on the coast of North Somerset in the dimness of the midday December sun.* (JOHN NURMINEN FOUNDATION)

The Rosses, James Clark Ross in particular, made several journeys of exploration. During the first spring, J. C. Ross crossed the Boothia Peninsula with three companions. He explored the coast and tried to find a strait which the Eskimos had told him of. He did not proceed far enough to the north, however, and thus fell short of discovering the Bellot Strait. He made his way across the peninsula again and crossed the James Ross Strait separating the Boothia Peninsula and King William Land, later Island.

Ross explored the north coast of King William Land all the way to Victory Point on the south west coast. He did not, however, realise that the land was an island, but thought it to be part of the mainland, a fact that might have been of significance in regard to the choices of subsequent expeditions. John Ross also crossed the peninsula and travelled south to Lake Netsilik. In the course of the summer both Rosses fished with the Eskimos.

In spring 1831 John and James Ross made a new journey to the southern part of the peninsula to make sure that no strait ran across it. The most important achievement of the second spring was James Ross's expedition to the North Magnetic Pole which he reached on 1 June 1831.

During the third winter Ross abandoned the *Victory,* whose steam engine had not withstood the strain of the Arctic. In the spring he and his companions set out to tow the boats across the ice. When they got near to Fury Beach, where they found the supplies left by Parry and the almost serviceable boats of the *Fury,* they left their own. They attempted to sail home in August 1832. The ice forced them to return to Fury Beach and to spend their fourth winter there.

Only on 15 August 1833 did the expedition sail east. Eleven days later the whaler *Isabella,* Ross's former vessel on the 1818 expedition, plucked them from Lancaster Sound. It was a close thing, since they only managed to row to the vessel when the wind changed direction.

Ross's voyage was the most important since Parry's first expedition. This time Ross had luck on his side, as the first summer was warm and the ice obstacles were smaller than usual. Ross crossed Baffin Bay in nine days, whereas Parry, on his second voyage, had taken two months.

Ross demonstrated that Prince Regent Inlet was not the entrance to the Northwest Passage. The discovery of the Magnetic North Pole was an interesting scientific achievement. James Clark Ross used sledge dogs and Eskimo guides on his journey and even spent nights in igloos. His main means of transport was still the man-hauled sledge, however. The

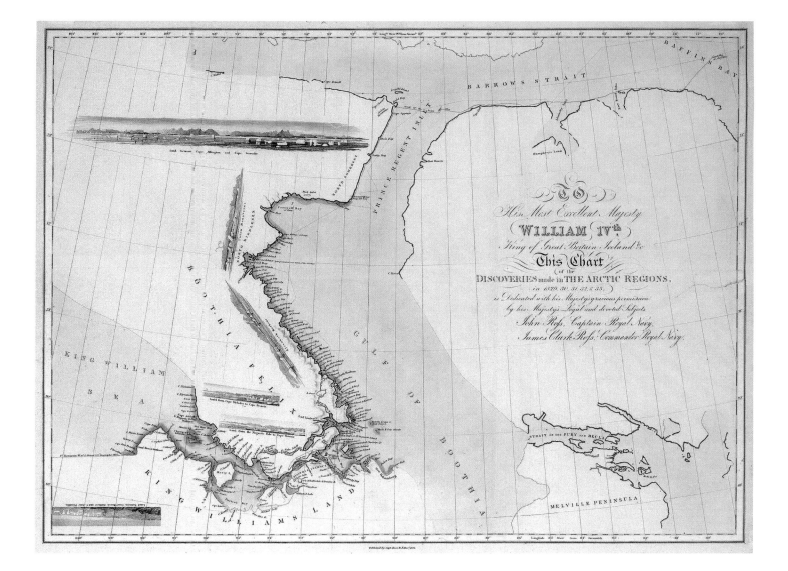

170 John Ross's map of Prince Regent Inlet and the Boothia Peninsula. The map is based partly on John Ross's sailing along the east coast of the peninsula to Felix Harbour, partly on James Clark Ross's sledge expeditions of 1829–1832. James Ross was the first to find King William Land, but he thought it to be part of the mainland. The Rosses mapped the peninsula in an attempt to find a passage west hinted at by the Eskimos, but they did not recognise the Bellot Strait, which started from Brentford Bay.
(JOHN NURMINEN FOUNDATION)

Eskimos helped the expedition survive. From them they got fur clothing, food and female company which helped them stand the monotonous winters. When they reached Fury Beach the expedition members were close to starvation and without the supplies left by Parry they would have perished. The expedition's survival was helped by the fact that it consisted of only 23 men, of whom 20 made it back home to England.

Ross's reputation soared among the public but Sir John Barrow did not consider the expedition of any value. Neither were its lessons recorded in writing. The sponsor of the voyage, however, was satisfied. The Boothia Peninsula and the Gulf of Boothia were named in his honour. The names of the

winter harbours too remind us of who paid the fiddler. The stage for the next Arctic episode, the northernmost point of King William Island, would be called Cape Felix.

THE ADMIRALTY
ATTEMPTS A BREAKTHROUGH

In 1835 George Back returned from the mouth of the Great Fish River, that is to say the Back River estuary. He had charted only a little of the Arctic coast, because he wanted to carry out his instructions to the letter. The ice had blocked his way to the west and, in spite of Richard King's recommendation, he had not wanted to go east. The following year Richard King suggested exploring Boothia Felix by land. But the Royal Geographical Society was unenthusiastic. The Admiralty sent Back to Wager Bay on the north-west coast of Hudson Bay with almost the same instructions they had given to Lyon. From there he was instructed to take his boat across the isthmus and complete the mapping of the northern coast of America from the Fury and Hecla Strait all the way to Turnagain Point.

Back's voyage was a failure. His bomb vessel the *Terror* – with almost twice the tonnage of Ross's *Victory* – became stuck in the ice in the summer of 1836 before he reached the

Frozen Strait. She was freed only the following summer and stayed afloat with difficulty until she reached the shallows off the coast of Ireland, where her journey came to an end.

The voyage did not paint a very good picture of Back as a leader. John Ross had realised the importance of fresh fish and meat as a way of warding off scurvy, but Back stuck to the Navy's outdated remedies: lemon juice, preserved vegetables and cranberries. During a single winter three of Back's crew fell to scurvy; John Ross had lost only one man during a voyage which spanned four winters. In spite of Barrow's scorn, as leader of an Arctic expedition John Ross had surpassed the navy.

Before he left his post in 1844, Sir John Barrow presented a plan for a new attempt to sail the Northwest Passage to the First Lord of the Admiralty. Success, in his opinion, was at last within arm's reach. The route suggested by Barrow ran from Barrow Strait to Cape Walker, from one side or another, to the coastal passage that Franklin's, Richardson's Dease's and Simpson's expeditions had charted.

Barrow believed the voyage could be done with only one wintering, although a great many experts doubted it. He recommended two ships to carry out the task, *Erebus* and *Terror,* which J.C. Ross had brought to England from his voyage.

In 1844 Prime Minister Robert Peel asked for clarification as to the scientific grounds for the expedition and the opinions of experts on its chances of success. John Barrow put forward the names Parry, Franklin, Back, James Ross and Beechey as experts. Although the Royal Society was not as enthusiastic as John Barrow regarding the scientific aspect, it did think that making magnetic measurements would be worthwhile. The experts supported Barrow's plan and made useful suggestions for improvements. Both Franklin and Parry agreed with Barrow's view according to which a Northwest Passage would be found between 'Banks Land' (Banks Island) and Cape Walker.

James Clark Ross would have been the natural choice to lead the expedition, but he considered himself too advanced in years for the job; he was after all 44 years old. In addition he had married and had promised his bride on his return from the Antarctic that he would not become the leader of the new expedition. Barrow's favourite, James Fitzjames, had no experience of the Arctic. Franklin wanted to go on the voyage, in spite of being 59 years old, to make up for his ignobly terminated period as Governor of Tasmania. Edward Parry's recommendation decided the matter. According to Parry, Franklin was better qualified than anybody else. He added "If you do not select him, he will die of disappointment". Captain Francis Rawdon Moira Crozier, who had already been with Parry and James Ross, was to command the *Terror,* while Commander James Fitzjames was assigned the *Erebus.*

The expedition consisted of two large vessels and 134 men, five times as many as on John Ross's expedition. They were chosen from the navy's best. Crozier had been on four expeditions – of the officers, seven had participated in Arctic explorations, as had many of the non-commissioned officers.

Both ships were large, more than 300 gross registered tons. Ross's *Victory* was originally an 85-ton vessel, but improve-

ments had doubled its capacity. The capacity of Amundsen's *Gjøa,* the first ship to sail through the Northwest Passage, was 47 gross registered tons. At Edward Parry's suggestion Franklin's ships were fitted with steam engines and screws.

Although Barrow believed one year to be sufficient, John Ross's experiences meant equipping the vessels for a three-year voyage. Sir John Franklin was concerned about the spiritual well-being of his men and asked the Admiralty to send a hundred Bibles and prayer books to the ships. With enough private donations, it was possible to return the Admiralty's books, which it had been intended should be sold to the men at half price. Hand-played organs were also acquired for both ships.

Franklin's orders were to sail directly to Barrow Strait within reach of Cape Walker. From there he should proceed south-west or west towards Bering Strait. If the southern passage was blocked by ice he was ordered to explore the Wellington Channel, which ran north between Cornwallis Island and Devon Island. It had been open in 1819 and 1820 when Parry had passed it. John Franklin thought that if the expedition reached Simpson Strait the mission would be as good as accomplished. The inexperienced Fitzjames believed in the Wellington Channel; he was probably not the only officer who was of this opinion.

On Thursday 8 May 1845, Lord Harrington, First Lord to the Admiralty, organised a reception in honour of Sir John Franklin, Captain Crozier and Commander Fitzjames. Sir John Barrow, Sir Edward Parry, Sir James Ross and Sir George Back were among those who took part in the celebrations. The expedition set off from the Thames on 19 May. The British public watched the departure with pride and confidence.

The voyage across the Atlantic was stormy but otherwise uneventful. The ships took on more supplies at Disko Island, off the west coast of Greenland. The members of the expedition had their last opportunity to send letters to England. The following post would be only when they reached Kamchatka in Petropavlovsk, to which relatives had been asked to address their letters if nothing had been heard of the expedition before June 1846. In his letter to the Admiralty Franklin wrote that spring in Greenland had been normal and that they were expecting the passage to Lancaster Sound to be open. All the expedition's officers and men were well and confident.

Franklin continued his voyage. At the entrance to Lancaster Sound he had to wait for the pack ice to disperse. Two whalers were in close proximity to Franklin, *the Enterprise* commanded by Captain Martin and Dannett's *Prince of Wales.* Martin told of speaking with Franklin and his pilot. He learned that the expedition had food for five years but that it could be enough for seven if they hunted game.

A few days later some of the ships' officers dropped in on Martin, who told him the voyage would take several years, possibly as long as six. On 26 July Dannett also met Franklin's officers and received an invitation to dine with Sir John Franklin. He could not accept the invitation because, with the wind getting up, he wanted to set sail. The captains and their crews were the last Europeans to see the members of Franklin's expedition alive.

THE MAGNETIC NORTH POLE AND THE COMPASS

The compass was known in China more than one thousand years ago. The first descriptions of its use in Europe date from the end of the 13th century. It is known that Mediterranean sailors were using the compass fairly regularly during the 14th century. Columbus calculated his direction and location with a compass. Declination, a phenomenon which affected the compass needle, was also familiar to the discoverer of the New World. Columbus even observed changes in the declination as his vessel travelled further and further from Europe. The first Europeans to discover America, the Vikings, did not use a compass. For later sailors of the north, such as Verrazano, Cabot, Davis and Hudson, the compass guided them through the misty Atlantic to new shores.

In the 16th century it was believed that a northern magnetic mountain attracted the needle of the compass. On his map of the polar region, the master mapmaker Mercator located that mountain somewhere in the north of the Chuchki Peninsula, close to what he assumed to be the Anian Sound, later named the Bering Strait.

Sir William Gilbert, court physicist to Queen Elizabeth I, later presented the theory that the earth was a giant magnet and that the force that turned the needle of the compass came from inside the earth itself. He even demonstrated the matter using a magnetic stone, showing that the earth had two poles at which the magnetic needle pointed in a vertical direction. This kind of magnetic stone, or lodestone, was used to 'charge' the magnetic threads of ships' compasses. Gilbert's theory later proved to be correct. In the 19th century, the magnetic North Pole was defined as the place where a vertical magnetic needle turned at a 90° angle to the earth's surface. An instrument known as a vertical compass or inclinometer was used for measuring the vertical magnetic fields, and was a standard piece of equipment for every polar explorer.

The compass rose with its 32 points, which was based on the ancient wind rose, was still common on ships in the 19th century. The modern compass is divided into 360 degrees. The early compass was difficult to use because the small paper disk and its iron wires which functioned as the compass card was pivoted freely in the air, and moved freely and restlessly. When the idea of adding liquid damping to a compass was invented, the needle's movement became steadier and maintaining course was made considerably easier.

The reasons for declination were discovered in the 16th century, and sailors soon learnt to take it into account. Declination is caused by the fact that the Magnetic North Pole is not in the same place as the Geographic North Pole. Because the magnetic pole moves, declination changes with time. Declination is also of different magnitude in different places. Sailors in the North Atlantic observed that declination increased as they approached America. In order to be able to steer the vessel in the right direction it was important for mariners to know the declination for

171 The compass became more and more common on ships during the Renaissance. Before the advent of hydraulic dampening in the 19th century the helmsman would have to take his readings against a quivering paper card that rested on a sharp-pointed spindle attached to the bottom of the bowl. This type of dry compass was common on British naval vessels in the 19th century. An Azimuth bearing-device has been attached on top of this compass. (JOHN NURMINEN FOUNDATION)

currents in the upper atmosphere, and these bring about disturbances in the earth's magnetic field. The sun thus contributes to the fact that the magnetic poles move.

In addition, a ship's compass will be affected by deviation. At the time of the great voyages of exploration, deviation caused by a vessel's own magnetic field was already recognised as a disturbance. This kind of disturbance was particularly strong on great warships which carried a lot of cannon. 19th century steel-hulled ships caused such powerful magnetic fields that deviation had to be reduced by building iron compensation structures around their compasses.

Using the compass in the north is difficult on long and short journeys because of the fluctuating declination. This change may be greater than a degree per mile travelled. The way a compass functions can also be disturbed near the Magnetic Pole by a powerful inclination of the needle called 'dip'. Thus it is virtually impossible to use a compass there. Polar explorers must steer a course and define their position by other astronomical means.

173 The red line shows the change in location of the North Magnetic Pole in 1831–1998. (PATANEN)

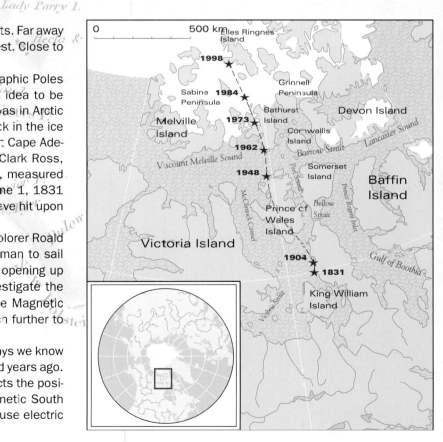

each given place. Nowadays it is given on all sea charts. Far away in the north the compass begins to vacillate in earnest. Close to the North Pole, declination can exceed 90°.

Gilbert believed that the magnetic and the geographic Poles were in the same place. Observations proved this idea to be wrong and indicated that the magnetic North Pole was in Arctic Canada. In 1829 John Ross's vessels became stuck in the ice on the southwest coast of the Bothnia Peninsula. At Cape Adelaide, on the west coast of the peninsula, James Clark Ross, John's nephew, who was on the same expedition, measured that his magnetic needle inclined to 89° 59' on June 1, 1831 during a sledge ride. He was the first European to have hit upon the Magnetic North Pole.

70 years after John Ross, the Norwegian polar explorer Roald Amundsen, in his ship the *Gjøa*, became the first man to sail round the American continent by way of the north, opening up the Northwest Passage. His intention was to investigate the magnetism in the Arctic area and to try to find the Magnetic North Pole again. He did find it, but at a place much further to the north than that measured by Clark Ross.

Why does the Magnetic North Pole move? Nowadays we know more about the matter than Amundsen did a hundred years ago. The slow movement of the earth's molten core affects the position of both the Magnetic North Pole and the Magnetic South Pole. In addition, charged particles from the sun cause electric

H. M. S. *Ships Erebus and Terror*
{ Wintered in the Ice in

28 of May 184 7   Lat. 70° 5' N Long. 98° 23' W

Having wintered in 1846—7 at Beechey Island
in Lat 74° 43' 28" N. Long 91° 39' 15" W After having
ascended Wellington Channel to Lat 77° and returned
by the West side of Cornwallis Island.

                     ~~Commander.~~

Sir John Franklin commanding the Expedition

All well

WHOEVER finds this paper is requested to forward it to the Secretary of the Admiralty, London, *with a note of the time and place at which it was found:* or, if more convenient, to deliver it for that purpose to the British Consul at the nearest Port.

QUINCONQUE trouvera ce papier est prié d'y marquer le tems et lieu ou il l'aura trouvé, et de le faire parvenir au plutot au Secretaire de l'Amirauté Britannique à Londres.

CUALQUIERA que hallare este Papel, se le suplica de enviarlo al Secretario del Almirantazgo, en Londrés, con una nota del tiempo y del lugar en donde se halló.

EEN ieder die dit Papier mogt vinden, wordt hiermede verzogt, om het zelve, ten spoedigste, te willen zenden aan den Heer Minister van de Marine der Nederlanden in 's Gravenhage, of wel aan den Secretaris der Britsche Admiraliteit, te London en daar by te voegen eene Nota, inhoudende de tyd en de plaats alwaar dit Papier is gevonden geworden.

FINDEREN af dette Papiir ombedes, naar Leilighed gives, at sende samme til Admiralitets Secretairen i London, eller nærmeste Embedsmand i Danmark, Norge, eller Sverrig. Tiden og Stœdit hvor dette er fundet önskes venskabeligt paategnet.

WER diesen Zettel findet, wird hier-durch ersucht denselben an den Secretair des Admiralitet in London einzusenden, mit gefälliger angabe an welchen ort und zu welcher Zeit er gefundet worden ist.

Party consisting of 2 Officers and 6 Men left the Ships on Monday 24th May 1847

Gm Gore —
Charl F. Des Vaeux

FRANKLIN AND THE MYSTERY OF
THE NORTHWEST PASSAGE

THE FAILURE OF JOHN FRANKLIN EVENTUALLY LED TO THE ACHIEVEMENT OF THE EXPEDITION'S ORIG-
INAL AIM. THOSE SEEKING HIM AND THE EXPEDITIONS SET UP UNDER COVER OF SEEKING HIM WERE
INTERESTED IN FINDING THE ANSWER TO THREE QUESTIONS: WHY AND HOW DID FRANKLIN'S EXPEDI-
TION PERISH, AND WHERE COULD THE NORTHWEST PASSAGE BE FOUND? MOST NO LONGER BELIEVED
THAT THEY WOULD FIND THE EXPEDITION'S MEMBERS ALIVE.

Two stubborn, troublesome men, underestimated by their contemporaries, had weighed up Franklin's chances even before the Admiralty began to feel concerned about the fate of the expedition. The first was John Ross. Although the Admiralty had not selected him as an expert he had discussed the organisation of the voyage with Franklin. Ross suggested that Franklin leave a store of food and boats at a suitable place in case they should become shipwrecked. He also suggested planning a rescue party in case Franklin ran into difficulty. Neither of these were considered. Ross volunteered to go and look for Franklin if nothing were to be heard of him before February 1847. Franklin was not interested in his proposals.

Nobody listened to Richard King, the other dissenting voice, either. King did not believe in maritime or large-scale expeditions but recommended looking for a Northwest Passage by sending an expedition along the Back River to the Arctic coast. King maintained that the seven expeditions organised by Barrow had failed, and predicted that the next expedition would leave a blot on the history of exploration.

174 In spring 1859 Lieutenant William Hobson found a cairn at Point Victory on King William Island from which this partly blackened message was taken. According to the words of First Lieutenant Graham Gore (28.5.1847) written at the top, the affairs of Franklin's expedition were still in good shape. Written in the margin one year later (25.4.1848) was the news that the expedition had left the ships and that 24 men, among them Sir John Franklin, were dead. This message was signed by expedition leaders Captain F.R.M. Crozier and James Fitzjames.
(NATIONAL MARITIME MUSEUM, LONDON)

WHERE IS FRANKLIN?

The Admiralty had decided, in all secrecy, to send a rescue party if nothing had been heard of Franklin by the end of 1847. The first expedition would then reach Franklin as late as three years after his departure. We now know that some of the men could have been saved if the expedition had been able to choose the best direction to start looking immediately.

Like King, Captain Beechey suggested sending a rescue party to the Back River estuary. This boat party was to explore the coast east of the river estuary in the direction of Prince Regent Inlet. The proposal was that the party would be supported by ships sailing to the Barrow Strait and Cape Walker. This suggestion was not accepted either. The Admiralty ordered three rescue parties to set out on a journey: one by way of the Bering Strait, one by land to explore the coast between the rivers Mackenzie and Coppermine and one, led by James Clark Ross, to Lancaster Sound, where Franklin had last been seen.

The expedition to the Bering Strait found no trace of Franklin but continued charting the coast. No sign of Franklin was found in summer 1848 either by Franklin's earlier travelling companion John Richardson or by John Rae, whose skills were much admired by Richardson. Richardson was one of Franklin's closest friends and, despite his age, volunteered to take part in the search. Their expedition combined the skill of the British navy with Rae's experience of the Arctic. The men liked each other's company and Richardson gave Rae the task of continuing the search the following summer east of the Coppermine on the south coast of Wollaston Peninsula and Victoria Island. The weather was bad and Rae could not make his way very far east of the Coppermine. Neither did he hear anything of Franklin's men from the Eskimos.

175 There is only a period of a few weeks in the Arctic after the ice has melted when it is possible to sail to one's destination or back home. Every day gained is important. Expeditions learned how to saw a passage through the ice to get their ships into open water or more quickly to safety. The picture shows a more advanced method from the 1870s. (JOHN NURMINEN FOUNDATION)

176 John Rae took up a position as doctor on a Hudson's Bay Company ship and stayed in Canada. He worked as the company's doctor for ten years until George Simpson chose him to be Thomas Simpson's successor. Rae – an excellent and pertinacious explorer – received a scientific education, and between 1846–1854 made four expeditions to the area between the Boothia Peninsula and the Coppermine River delta. A pioneer of the modern, light and mobile explorer generation, Rae was the first to find proof of the fate of Franklin's expedition. (NATIONAL PORTRAIT GALLERY)

177 Thanks to Franklin's expeditions the fund of knowledge on the north of Melville Strait increased. The map in the picture is from 1864. Robert McClure, who claimed to have found the Northwest Passage between Melville Island and Banks Island, is mentioned as its other compiler. He walked part of the journey, however, and it has not been possible to sail this part afterwards except by icebreaker. The upper map gives a good picture of Prince Patrick, Melville and Bathurst islands, but the islands located to the north of them were discovered only at the beginning of the 20th century. The purpose of the map was to tell of the achievements of northern exploration and Arctic conditions, which is why the map is decorated with beautiful drawings. (JOHN NURMINEN FOUNDATION)

Later in the autumn, Rae met a boat patrol from HMS *Plover*, which had sailed to the Bering Strait. Under the leadership of Lieutenant William Pullen, it had made its way west from Point Barrow to the Mackenzie River. Pullen arrived at Fort Simpson in October 1849, where John Rae was co-ordinating operations, having made his way up river with seven men. He had seen no trace of Franklin. If Franklin had got as far as the American continent he had never reached the Coppermine.

James Clark Ross returned in the autumn of 1849. He had command of two ships, the *Enterprise* and the *Investigator*. By August they had only reached Lancaster Sound. Since both Barrow Strait and Wellington Channel were blocked by ice, Ross set up his base at Port Leopold at the north-east corner of Somerset Island. The Second Lieutenant of *Enterprise* was F. L. McClintock, one of the explorers who would rise to the rank of Admiral. The expedition searched the north and west coasts of Somerset Island as far south as the region of latitude 73°. Although Prince of Wales Island could be seen across Peel Sound they did not go there. The west coast of Prince Regent Inlet was explored as far as the southern half of Cresswell Bay.

The summer of 1849 was late in coming and the ships were only freed from the ice on 29 August. Barrow Strait was still blocked by ice, however. The expedition had no other choice than to return to England. Although it had

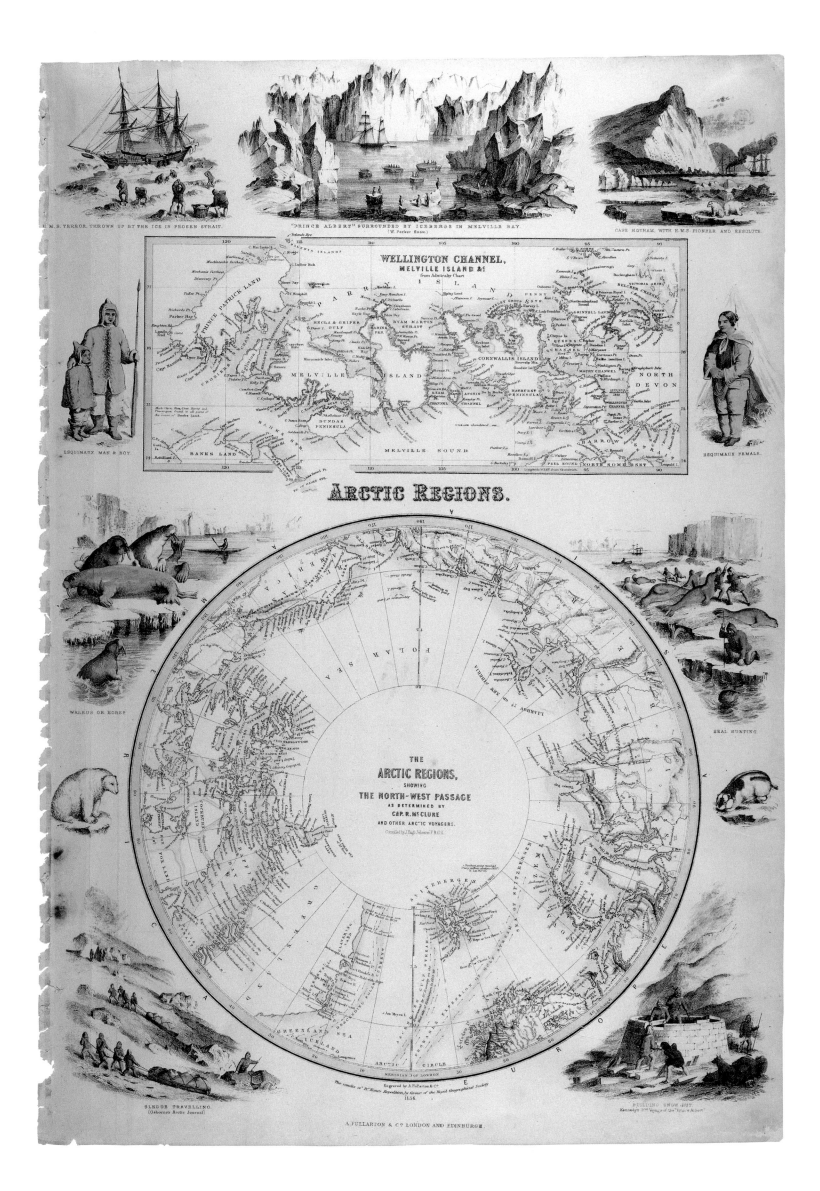

H.M.S. TERROR, THROWN UP BY THE ICE IN FROZEN STRAIT.

"PRINCE ALBERT" SURROUNDED BY ICEBERGS IN MELVILLE BAY.
(W. Parker Snow.)

CAPE HOTHAM, WITH H.M.S. PIONEER AND RESOLUTE.

ESQUIMAUX MAN & BOY

ESQUIMAUX FEMALE.

WELLINGTON CHANNEL, MELVILLE ISLAND &c.
from Admiralty Chart

ARCTIC REGIONS.

WALRUS OR HORSE

SEAL HUNTING

THE
ARCTIC REGIONS,
SHOWING
THE NORTH-WEST PASSAGE
AS DETERMINED BY
CAP. R. M'CLURE
AND OTHER ARCTIC VOYAGERS.

SLEDGE TRAVELLING.
(Osborne's Arctic Journal)

BUILDING SNOW HUT.

A. FULLARTON & Co. LONDON AND EDINBURGH.

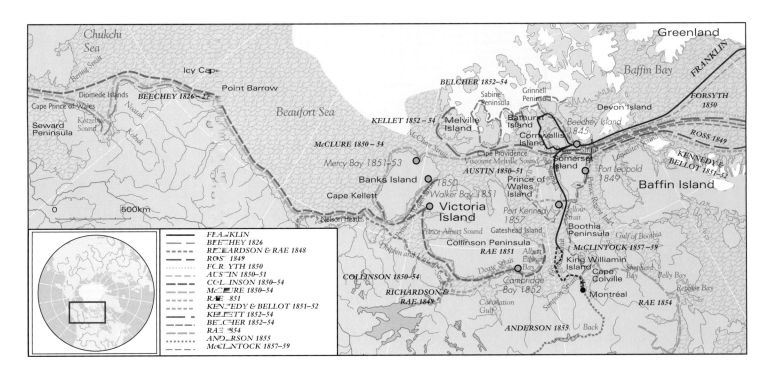

178 The journey made by Franklin's expedition first to Beechey Island and then around Cornwallis Island to Peel Sound and Victoria Sound near to the west coast of King William's Land where the expedition abandoned their vessel and began the trek towards the mouth of the Back River is shown on the map. The routes and winter harbours of the most important expeditions looking for Franklin are also marked. It is easy to see how short the journey between Collinson's Cambridge Bay and Franklin's position was on the one hand, and between McClure's Mercy Bay and Parry's Winter Harbour on the south coast of Melville Island was on the other. (PATANEN)

charted 155 miles of the Arctic coast it had found not a single trace of Franklin.

Franklin's disappearance aroused concern not only in England but throughout the world. Interest in the Arctic grew and books dealing with the area sold well. At Lady Franklin's suggestion prayers were said in sixty churches for the safety of the expedition. For a long time she believed her husband to be alive and, even when she was forced to give up hope, she did all she could to discover his fate.

When Ross returned, Franklin had been gone for more than four and a half years and hope was no longer held out that the expedition had survived. There had only been enough food for three years, and such a large group would not have been able to support itself by hunting. It was still not known in which direction Franklin should be sought. Many assumed that the expedition had become prisoner to the ice further to the west, on the coasts of Melville Island or Banks Island. If Franklin had been forced to stop earlier he would have left word either at Fury Beach or the Barrow Strait. No message of this kind had been found. If Franklin had made it further to the west it would be just as easy to find his expedition by way of the Bering Strait or Baffin Bay. A reward was offered for finding Franklin or discovering his fate.

THE FIRST SIGNS

Next, six new expeditions were equipped, one to the Bering Strait and five to Lancaster Sound. The Admiralty ordered Captain Richard Collinson's *Enterprise* and Robert McClure's *Investigator* to the Bering Strait. The expedition was led by Collinson, who at no time during the voyage made contact with McClure.

The Admiralty sent two sailing vessels and two steam ships under the command of Horatio Austin, as well as two vessels under the leadership of the experienced whaler Captain Penny to Lancaster Sound.

The United States government equipped two ships, commanded by Lieutenant E. J. De Haven, for a search mission to Lancaster Sound. The Hudson's Bay Company and private parties sent two small vessels under the leadership of Sir John Ross, while Lady Franklin and her friends sent a sailing vessel commanded by Charles C. Forsyth.

In summer 1850 Forsyth's *Prince Albert* got no further than Fury Beach, as Prince Regent Inlet was cut off by ice. On returning to the Barrow Strait, Forsyth called in at Devon Island, where he heard that Austin's expedition had found signs of Franklin. Forsyth also met De Haven, who knew that Franklin's winter quarters had been found on nearby Beechey Island.

Forsyth was of the opinion that the news was so important that it was worth taking to Lady Franklin without delay, and he sailed straight home. Soon after this De Haven's vessels became stuck in the ice and were gradually driven through Lancaster Sound to Baffin Bay. De Haven, too, was forced to give up the search. His expedition's greatest contribution was that its doctor, Elisha Kent Kane, became interested in Arctic exploration.

Austin's four ships reached Lancaster Sound in mid-August, 1850. The *Assistance,* Captained by Erasmus Ommanney, explored the north coast of the Barrow Strait. On August 23 Ommanney found some ropes and beef bones which were believed to have been left by Franklin's expedition.

Within a few days his winter quarters of 1845–1846 were found on Beechey Island to the south-west of Devon Island.

Austin's ships found no sign of Franklin at the south of Wellington Channel nor on the west coast of Peel Sound. Since the strait was open, Penny was convinced that Franklin had sailed along Wellington Channel. He was strengthened in his conviction by the fact that he had found a piece of English elm on Baillie-Hamilton Island in the Wellington Channel to the north of Cornwallis. Sir John Ross took part in the search of Beechey Island and wintered on Cornwallis Island with Penny's expedition.

In the spring Austin's expedition charted wide tracts of the coasts of Prince of Wales and Cornwallis Islands. The ships broke free from the ice on 8 August 1851. Penny tried to borrow one of Austin's steam ships to continue searching Wellington Channel. Austin did not agree to this and decided to set off home. Penny followed him.

In 1850 the British government asked the Hudson's Bay Company to send John Rae to explore the coast again. He began to prepare for the voyage in 1850. He had two boats built according to plans he had drawn up himself, the rigging for which he made by his own hand. The boats were carved out of birch and were durable and light as well as being excellently suited to sailing shallow waters.

In February 1851 Rae left Fort Confidence and gave instructions to bring the boats down the Coppermine River later in the spring. There were four men and three dog teams with their sledges in the advance group. By 2 May Rae had arrived at the mouth of the Coppermine with two men. He continued north-east, crossed Dolphin and Union Strait and went up the Wollaston Peninsula. Rae followed the south coast of Victoria Island east, discovered a new island group, named them the Richardson Islands and turned back to the west. He travelled along the south coast of the Wollaston Peninsula to the entrance to Prince Albert Sound from which he turned back south and, on 15 June, met the group bringing the boats. Rae had travelled about 800 miles on foot mapping and looking for signs of the lost expedition.

179 For a long expedition to succeed it was necessary to leave food stores along the planned route. In this way it was possible to lighten the load of the sledges and broaden the range of activities. The picture shows the arrival of the advance parties of Lieutenants Robinson and Brown from the expedition of James C. Ross at the southern food store in the Prince Regent inlet area in 1849.
(JOHN NURMINEN FOUNDATION)

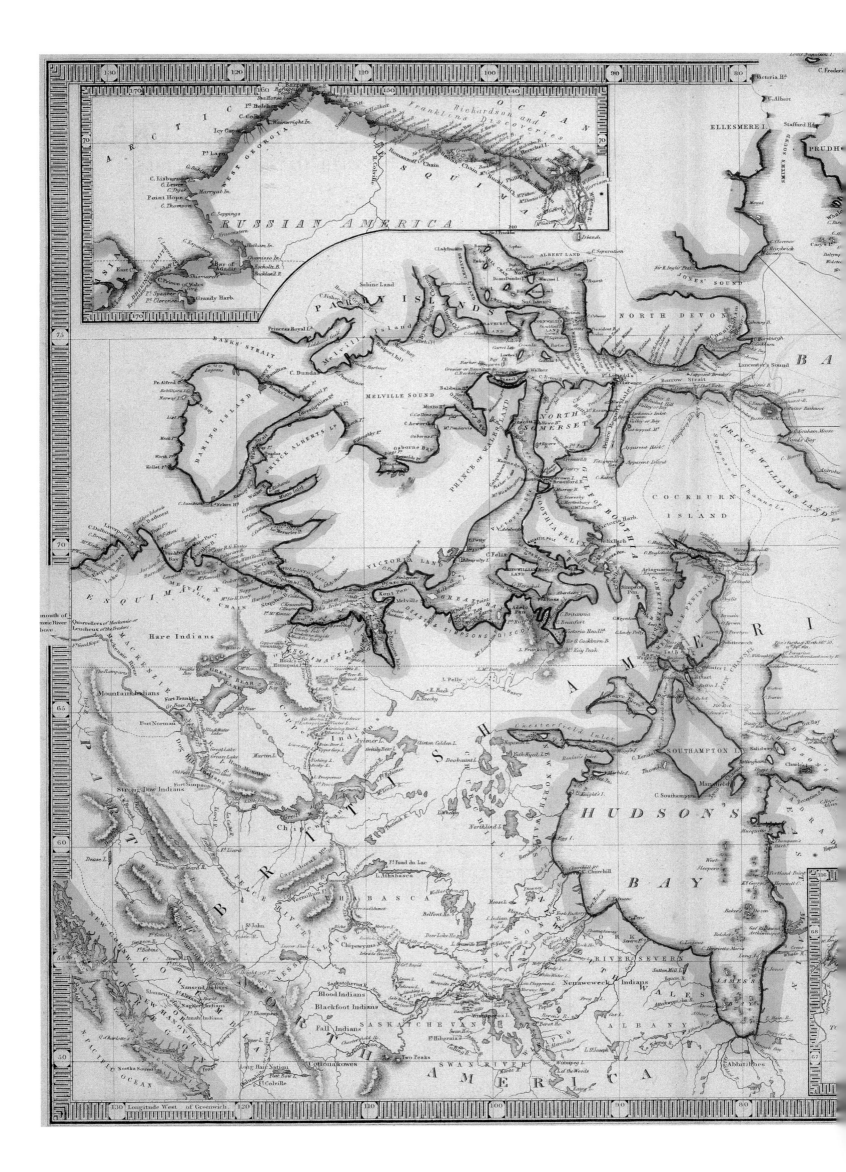

180 The map contains most of the discoveries by expeditions looking for Franklin in the area south of Melville Island. Prince of Wales Strait, discovered by McClure, separates Banks and Victoria Island. On the other hand Prince of Wales Island is still thought to be an eastern peninsula of Victoria Island. McClintock and Hobson charted the west part of the island and the McClintock Strait only a few years later. The north-west and west coasts of Baffin Land are still unmapped. The prerequisites for sailing the Northwest Passage exist because King William Land is now recognised as an island. George Philip's map contains most of the finds of Franklin's expeditions in the regions to the south of Melville Island. (JOHN NURMINEN FOUNDATION)

On 5 July Rae again sent his boats off towards the mouth of the Coppermine. An open passage led east along the Kent Peninsula. At first following the peninsula, Rae crossed a sound and continued east along the coast of Victoria Island, explored Albert Edward Bay on the east coast and, with the ice blocking the waterway east, went ashore on its northern shore. He travelled over difficult terrain to Cape Pelly. On returning to the boats Rae left a message for those coming after him telling of his route. He attempted to cross the Victoria Strait and reach King William Island, but the ice prevented his progress. Rae unfortunately turned back just on the point of finding signs of Franklin's expedition.

On the return journey Rae found two pieces of wood. One seemed to be an oak stanchion, the other, a piece of a pinewood, appeared to be the butt end of a small flagstaff on which were inscribed the letters "S.C." A white line which contained a red thread had been tacked on it. The fragment was assumed to have come from a British naval vessel. The finds were sent to England and examined. Although they were not successfully identified they were probably from Franklin's ships. Rae presumed the pieces to have come from the north with the ice between Victoria Island and Somerset Island. He was convinced that Franklin's expedition had never reached the western part of Queen Maud Gulf. The area to be searched narrowed, although it was not yet clear whether Franklin had continued west or south from the Barrow Strait. If the pieces were assumed to have come from the expedition's vessels, Rae had found a clue as to the direction they had taken.

While Rae was exploring the southern coast, Lady Franklin had sent the *Prince Albert* off on another expedition. William Kennedy, a Canadian fur-trader with Indian blood in his veins, was an unconventional choice to lead the expedition. He was at sea for the first time. Joseph-René Bellot – Kennedy's assistant – was a 25-year-old French naval lieutenant who was in the Arctic area for the first time. Kennedy's mission was to explore the southern part of Prince Regent Inlet and the lands to the west of it. He spent the winter in Batty Bay on the east coast of Somerset Island and, with Bellot, travelled south along the coast of the island by dog sledge. He discovered a strait separating Somerset Island from the northernmost tip of the American continent, the Boothia Peninsula. Kennedy named the strait Bellot Strait after his companion.

Paraselena, Nov 30th Northumberland Sound

181 *A detachment led by Edward Belcher, which included the ships* ASSISTANCE *and* PIONEER, *looked for Franklin in the Wellington Channel and Melville Island area. In autumn 1852 the vessels wintered in the Northumberland Strait, as shown in the picture. Although the ships broke free they became icebound again in Wellington Channel, where Belcher abandoned them in summer 1854. He also ordered Kellet to abandon his vessels the* RESOLUTE *and the* INTREPID. *Belcher was accused of bungling, and the accusation is not perhaps quite without grounds, since the abandoned* RESOLUTE *drifted to the Davis Strait where some American whale hunters found it undamaged in spring 1855.* (JOHN NURMINEN FOUNDATION)

Kennedy and Bellot crossed Peel Sound and continued to Ommanney Bay across Prince of Wales Island. They returned by way of Cape Walker and then made their way partly through the same country that James Clark Ross had travelled three years earlier. Their sledge journey was 1100 miles long, one of the longest to be made during the years of the search for Franklin.

Those who were involved in the search were perplexed. Where had Franklin gone from Beechey Island? Many believed him to have proceeded south from the west of Cape Walker according to the orders he had received, but explorations of Ommanney showed that they he had not progressed to the west coast of Prince of Wales Island. No sign of the expedition had been found on the west coast of Peel

Sound nor on the east coast of Melville Island. More and more people believed, like Penny, that Franklin had made his way up Wellington Channel.

THE RACE FOR THE BEAUFORT SEA

The Bering Strait expedition left London on 20 January 1850. Collinson's *Enterprise* and McClure's *Investigator* parted ways during the journey. The Irishman McClure did his all to reach the Bering Sea before his Captain, Collinson. McClure did not follow Collinson from Honolulu to Petropavlovsk, in Kamchatka, but sailed north along a more dangerous route through the Aleutians to the Bering Strait without waiting for Collinson.

The *Investigator* arrived at Kotzebue Sound in July 1850 and continued east along the coastal waters of Alaska. McClure rounded Point Barrow at the beginning of August. On 7 September he passed the south-east corner of Banks Land.

McClure did not recognise the island as Parry's Banks Land. He pushed his way up the Prince of Wales Strait between Victoria Island and Banks Island and sailed to its northern reaches, only 35 miles away from Viscount Melville Sound. The ice blocked his way only 93 miles away from the place where Parry had turned back in 1820. The ice pushed the *Investigator* south and the ship was forced to spend a dangerous winter in the middle of the sound.

A sledge party made up of McClure's officers mapped the northern part of the Prince of Wales Strait west from the north coast of Banks Island and east from Victoria Island. One member of the party reached Prince Albert Sound, 47 miles from the south coast of the Strait. John Rae made his way there ten days later from the opposite direction. With his interpreter, J. A. Miertsching, McClure made contact with the Eskimo from whom he heard that the Wollaston Peninsula (Wollaston Land) was part of Victoria Island.

The ship began to make its way through the ice in mid-July. McClure was still trying to go north towards Melville Sound. The ice blocked his way and on 16 August he decided to turn south and sail to Melville Sound from the west – from the north of Banks Island. McClure was taking quite a risk, as the northern coast of the island was unexplored. Another alternative would have been to follow the coast of America, almost all of which had been charted.

McClure was so close to a solution to the Northwest Passage question that he considered the risk worthwhile. The following day the *Investigator* passed Nelson Head, the southern tip of Banks Island, and on 18 August the western cape, Cape Kellett. The ice grew thicker and a couple of days later the *Investigator* was stuck. One month later the ice began to move again and McClure sailed first east and then east-south-east having rounded the north-western tip of Banks Island. On 22 September the ship was driven onto a sand bank. When it was freed McClure saw a suitable harbour and headed there for the winter. Now McClure chose the 'safe' alternative since, the *Investigator* might have been able to make it to Melville Sound although not necessarily to Melville Island, where Parry's Winter Harbour was located.

McClure knew that the island was Parry's 'Banks Land'. As J. A. Miertsching testifies in his diary, McClure had already found two Northwest Passages. It was not until 1944 that a Canadian, Henry Larsen, with his scooner the *St. Roch* was the first to sail through the Prince of Wales Strait. The following summer 1851 would show whether the strait to the north of Banks Island, McClure Strait. was a better passage.

Richard Collinson passed Point Barrow at the end of August, a good two weeks later than McClure. The ice had already shut off the route and Collinson returned to Hong Kong for the winter. The following summer Collinson had passed Point Barrow by 25 July and, one month later, sailed up the Prince of Wales Strait, which McClure had left ten days earlier to circumnavigate Banks Island.

Collinson found evidence that the *Investigator* had wintered in the strait. He, too, tried to sail north but the ice barred his way before he had reached Melville Sound. Like McClure, Collinsen set out to circumnavigate Banks Island, but after Cape Kellett he was brought to a halt by the ice. There, too, he noticed that he had followed in the wake of the *Investigator*. Turning back he found a winter harbour at Walker Bay on Victoria Island.

During the winter, reconnaissance parties sent out by Collinson made journeys south to the Wollaston Peninsula and north to the entrance to the Prince of Wales Strait. One of the sledge parties crossed Viscount Melville Sound and pushed on to Cape Providence on Melville Island. The

Enterprise broke free from the ice at the beginning of August 1852, and Collinson sailed south and explored Prince Albert Sound, which proved to be a bay. He continued east to the Dolphin and Union Strait and from there to Coronation Gulf and Dease Strait. At Cambridge Bay he found the harbour that Rae had noted. Collinson wintered there.

In spring 1853, one of Collinson's patrols explored the east coast of Victoria Island and found Rae's record left there in 1851. Collinson continued on further than Rae and only turned back at Gateshead Island midway between Prince of Wales Island and Victoria Island. Collinson found a piece of doorframe and a piece of metal bolt which were later linked to Franklin. The *Enterprise* was freed from the ice at the beginning of August and Collinson sailed west towards the Bering Strait. He spent one more winter on the north coast of Alaska, passed through the Bering Sea and returned to England in autumn 1854.

Collinson made the same mistakes as McClure, Simpson and Rae had made before him. In exercising caution – and in paying no attention to the opinions of his officers – he lost a whole year, during which time the bold McClure had come close to Melville Bay. In skilfully sailing along the coastal passage almost as far as King William Island, Collinson had made the right decision. A bolder man would have pushed further east upon finding Rae's message. A more open man would have taken great interest in the door bolt he had found and asked himself what the discovery signified if it had come from Franklin's ship.

THE FIRST WALK
THROUGH THE NORTHWEST PASSAGE

In the spring of 1852, McClure made a sledge journey with seven men to Winter Harbour on Melville Island where Parry had wintered. He left a message about the *Investigator's* position and wintering place. He had found a metal cylinder on Melville Island which contained a record concerning a search by seven English and two American ships in summer 1850. The information had been left by McClintock's search party sent out from Austin's ship the *Resolute* on his return journey to Mercy Bay, his winter quarters. McClure informed his crew that it was essential that some of them should go the following spring to the Mackenzie River and Port Leopold where Sir James Ross had left a food supply. On 26 October 1852, McClure gave his men a meal and an extra grog from his own reserves in honour of finding the Northwest Passage. In January 1853 McClure organised a sledge party and divided the men up into those who would remain with the ship and those who would leave. Many of the crew had fallen sick with scurvy and all were in a weak condition.

McClure decided to send so many of the ship's crew away that the rest would survive until spring 1854 with the food that remained. Four officers, one of whom was deranged, were given the order to set off with 26 men to Port Leopold on Somerset Island, 620 miles away. They took with them

ARCTIC FAUNA

Life in the Arctic is often viewed as being particularly bleak, and the species of animal that inhabit it as endangered. It is hardly that simple, however. Few species permanently inhabit the Arctic, but they often have very large populations. The Arctic and Antarctic waters support more plankton than any other. This is why the largest populations of whales are to be found there. Herds of caribou are numbered – or at least they used to be numbered – in their tens, or even hundreds, of thousands. The largest salmon, seal and walrus grounds are also found there.

The Arctic environment demands a considerable amount of adaptability from the species – such as polar bears, foxes, hares, seals, walruses and Greenland whales – that make the north their permanent habitat. The long, dark winter and the permafrost combined with the short seasons of spring, summer and autumn force other species – migratory birds, brown bears and wolves – to dwell further south. When the chances of survival improve in the summer, species must be able to take advantage of improved conditions rapidly. The longest day of the Arctic summer sees more daylight than the Equator. A young harp seal is capable of increasing its body weight four-fold in ten days.

Coping with northern conditions requires an appropriate size or shape of animal. It can keep out the cold with either a thick, double-layered fur or a sufficient amount of fat. Shedding excess heat in summer requires flippers, tails, fins or ears. It is possible to move on the snow rapidly if the foot resembles a snowshoe. Enzymes that are able to function in low temperatures and agents that prevent the blood from freezing boost the body's functions. Also the behavioural patterns of species have an impact on its survival. The caribou migrate throughout the year to where conditions are most favourable. The animals' territories are so large that random fluctuations in conditions do not pose an immediate threat to their survival.

The Arctic fauna forms a whole in which the different parts are dependent on each other. The lowest layers are formed by the lichen in the tundra and the plankton in the sea. The second layer is populated by the caribou that eat the lichen and the krill that consume the plankton. They in turn provide carnivores such as wolves and baleen whales, which sift enormous amounts of krill for nourishment, with an opportunity to survive. The animals and plants of the fourth stage survive on the waste of the previous ones and transform it into nourishment that feeds the next cycle. Sometimes this chain of events can be extremely dramatic. The salmon come from the Pacific to the river where they were born to spawn and then die. Their remains provide, directly or indirectly,

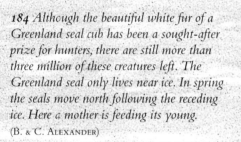

184 Although the beautiful white fur of a Greenland seal cub has been a sought-after prize for hunters, there are still more than three million of these creatures left. The Greenland seal only lives near ice. In spring the seals move north following the receding ice. Here a mother is feeding its young.
(B. & C. ALEXANDER)

185 Curiosity and fearlessness are characteristics that define the polar bear, a permanent resident of the Arctic region. It mainly hunts in the ice-covered sea and can wander hundreds of miles from the continent. Its most important source of food is the seal, which it often stalks above breathing holes in the ice. A polar bear will also attack a pack of walruses. The creature builds a den for the winter, either on land or in stacks of ice. A layer of snow helps to insulate the dwelling and the female can give birth during the winter. The young follow their mother for two years before they become independent. (DEREK FORDHAM)

nourishment for their progeny improving, its chances of survival.

Life can also be found in some rather surprising places. The cracks and fissures in the underwater surface of the ice that covers the sea are home to many communities: protozoa, crustacea, worms and especially diatoms that can grow with almost no light. Their significance to life in the Arctic seas is crucial. Also the ice is an essential habitat for many animals: polar bears, walruses and some species of seal. A young seal can only survive on the ice for the first weeks of its life. Bears and foxes broaden their hunting territories by venturing to sea on the ice.

The Arctic life cycle and especially the mammals in it have provided the historic basis for human survival. The Eskimo cultures were dependent on certain species of game. The earliest culture, the Paleo-Eskimos, hunted musk ox, polar bears and small game. The Dorset culture relied on hunting seals and the wealth that it created. The superiority of the Thule culture was shown in their ability to hunt whales, too; beluga, narwhal and Greenland whale were all hunted.

Game and nourishment were also motivating factors behind voyages of exploration. Walruses and seals have been hunted since the Viking era; whaling began to proliferate in the 17th century. Russian fur hunters followed the sable over the Urals to Siberia and the sea otter to the Bering Sea and the North-American coast. Fishing remains an important source of income for the peoples of the Arctic. The teeming life in the Arctic seas is an important part of the global food chain, perhaps even more important than we think.

186 Frederick Schwatka's five-man expedition looked for traces of Franklin's expedition from 1878–1880. They travelled over 3000 miles by dog sledge, which was a new record. Schwatka's expedition found some of Franklin's effects. The members of the expedition are seen at midday break. (JOHN NURMINEN FOUNDATION)

food for 45 days. At Port Leopold they should find a small sailing vessel with which it was possible to sail to Baffin Bay to meet whalers. Two officers, one of whom was the interpreter Miertsching, were ordered to make their way south with six men to the Prince of Wales Strait where the expedition had left a store of food and a boat, and to sail from there to the Mackenzie River and from there south to the Hudson's Bay Company's trading post.

The Captain, surgeon, second mate, clerk and the strongest men remained on the ship as planned, to wait for spring. By 11 March, sixteen of the men ordered on the journey had become sick. From the 16th onwards a full day's ration was shared out to all the men. By the end of March all the men had come down with scurvy.

On 7 April, McClure wrote letters addressed to the Admiralty, which he gave to those who were leaving. Just as the Captain was giving out the letters, one of the sailors declared that a moving black spot could be seen on the ice. Soon another man came running and shouting of men approaching with a sledge. The first man to reach the *Investigator,* dressed in Eskimo clothes, announced himself to be Lieutenant Bedford Pim from the HMS *Resolute,* which was in winter quarters on Melville Island. The *Resolute* was under the command of the very same Captain Kellett whose instructions to wait for Collinson McClure had ignored off the Alaskan coast.

McClure's 'survival plan' could therefore be torn up. On 9 April, he set out with Pim to draw up plans on how to proceed. Over the next nine days three of the men who had been ordered out on the journey died. On 15 April, four officers and 26 men set out across the ice for the *Resolute.* The party reached their destination on 2 May. Twenty-two of the men were hospitalised on board the *Intrepid,* which was wintering near the *Resolute.* McClure asked for volunteers to stay with him on the *Investigator* for a further year to wait for the ship to break free from the ice. Only three men signed up.

The last of the *Investigator's* crew arrived at Melville Island on 17th June. At mid-day they were still 3 miles from the ship. It took the sick and exhausted men four hours to cover the last leg. All four of their sledges carried two sick men.

When, in 1855, the rescuers and the rescued had returned to England, a Parliamentary Committee was set up to decide to whom the reward for discovering the Northwest Passage should go: McClure, his superior Collinson or Captain Kellett who had rescued him. Collinson generously insisted that McClure had not acted against his orders in his haste to reach the Beaufort Sea.

McClure maintained that the assistance of Captain Kellett and the *Resolute* had not been necessary; they would have been able to survive according to his plan. He had left the *Investigator* on Kellet's order and would not himself have done so. Since McClure had not brought the promised officers' diaries from the *Investigator* – the officers had been ordered to leave them on board – there was no evidence to the contrary. The committee decided to award the prize of £10,000 to McClure and his crew.

Did McClure discover the Northwest Passage?

If the Northwest Passage is defined as a navigable sea route McClure did not find it. The world's first tanker modified to sail through the ice, the *Manhattan,* could not break through it in 1969 and only with great difficulty managed to force a passage through the six-metre-high mass of ice of the Prince of Wales Strait. A navigable but shallow Northwest Passage runs along the coast of America, and it had not yet been navigated in 1855. But McClure's crew did deserve the reward for the first traverse of the Northwest Passage. The first to do so was a Lieutenant S. G. Cresswell, with the *Investigator,* who returned to England before the others in 1853 with the supply ship the *Phoenix.*

THE FRANKLIN MYSTERY IS SOLVED

In spring 1852, the Admiralty sent a squadron of five ships, under the leadership of Captain Sir Edward Belcher, to explore the Wellington Channel. The fleet consisted of three sailing vessels and two steam ships. One was left at Beechey Island as a supply ship. Belcher sailed to Wellington Channel with two ships and sent Captain Kellett with the *Resolute* and the *Intrepid* to Melville Island, where Kellett's task was to look for Franklin and to leave supplies for Collinson and McClure.

Belcher sailed through Wellington Channel and charted the Grinnell Peninsula to the north of Devon Island. During a boat voyage in autumn, two islands in the Belcher Channel and the southern part of Cornwallis Island were charted. In winter the islands off the north of Bathurst Island were discovered. Belcher did not succeed in returning to Lancaster Sound the following summer, but had to winter once again off Devon Island. In summer 1854 he felt obliged to abandon his ships and to move with his men to the supply vessel, *North Star,* stationed at Beechey Island.

Kellett's ships the *Resolute,* and the *Intrepid* which was commanded by Francis Leopold McClintock, sailed to Dealy Island off the south coast of Melville Island slightly to the east of Parry's Winter Harbour. During the winter a sledge party explored Eglinton, Prince Patrick and Emerald Islands to the north of Melville Island. McClintock's and G. F. Mecham's sledge journeys covered over 1100 miles. No trace of Franklin was found. One member of the party went to Winter Harbour and found the message left there by McClure. Lieutenant Pim then set out with the *Resolute's* surgeon, Dr D. T. Domville, for Mercy Bay in March and found the *Investigator.*

In summer 1853 Kellett attempted to sail to Lancaster Sound but the ice prevented him. The ships spent the following winter at Bathurst Island. In spring 1854 Mecham made a long sledge journey to Prince of Wales Strait and looked for signs of Collinson's *Enterprise.* Meanwhile Belcher had or-

187 One of Captain Austin's four ships looking for Franklin in 1850 was the ASSISTANCE *commanded by Captain Ommanney. Austin looked for Franklin in Lancaster Sound and indeed found his camp on Beechey Island. The* ASSISTANCE *survived the winter well in the grip of the ice; it was, in the words of midshipman Clements Markham, 'the best administered and happiest ship that ever crossed the Arctic Circle.'*
(NATIONAL MARITIME MUSEUM, LONDON)

dered Kellett to abandon his ships and lead his own crews and that of the *Investigator* to Beechey Island. Kellet objected since his ship was in no immediate danger, but had to give way. The crews were transferred to the *North Star* where Mecham, too, arrived later. Mecham's sledge journey covered as much as 1535 miles. Although they did not find Franklin, a further tragedy was prevented by the rescuing of McClure and his crew, most of whom would have surely perished.

Kellett had been right that his ships had not been in danger. In 1855 one of Kellett's two ships, the *Resolute,* floated out of Melville Sound without a crew through Lancaster Sound to the Davis Strait, where she was found by the crew of an American whaler, the *George Henry.* Even the glasses from which Kellett and his officers had drunk their farewell toast were found unbroken on the cabin table where they had been left.

A few weeks after the officers and men under Belcher's command reached London came the first news of the fate of Franklin's expedition. It was brought by Dr John Rae, who had arrived from a survey expedition which had been exploring the Boothia Peninsula. Rae had been convinced that the search for Franklin should concentrate on the southern and western areas from Cape Walker, not to the north of Melville Sound and Barrow Strait. In spring 1852 he had suggested an expedition the aim of which was to chart the last unmapped area to the west of the Boothia Peninsula. Rae was critical of the fact that the Admiralty had not accepted his evidence that Boothia was a peninsula.

Rae set out on his journey from York Factory on Hudson Bay in summer 1853. The expedition consisted of two boats and thirteen men. First Rae attempted to make his way from Chesterfield Inlet across an isthmus to the estuary of the Back River, but the route was too difficult and he returned to Hudson Bay. Some of the party were sent back to Churchill and Rae proceeded to Repulse Bay.

In spring Rae left Repulse Bay with four men and provisions for 65 days. He carried 100 lbs of supplies on his sledge, the others over 160 lbs. In April they came across a large group of Eskimos at Pelly Bay. Rae tried to persuade them to join him but they all refused and tried to get Rae to give up his intentions. A couple of days later they were joined by a solitary Eskimo whose tale Rae recorded in his diary as follows:

"Met a very communicative and apparently intelligent Eskimo; had never met whites before but said that a number of Kabloonans, at least 35–40, had starved to death west of a large river a long distance off. Perhaps about 10 or 12 days journey. Could not tell the distance, never had been there, and could not accompany us so far. Dead bodies seen beyond two large rivers; did not know the place, could not or would not explain it on a chart. Had seen a pile of stones that had been built by whites near a small river. Top of pillar had fallen down; suppose Dease and Simpson's cairn at Castor and Pollux Rivers."

Rae did not wish to continue on the basis of such uncertain information. He bought a golden cap-band from the Eskimos and asked all Eskimos in possession of information or items to come to his camp at Repulse Bay. Rae continued his journey across the Boothia Peninsula to the sea and went on to the cairn erected by Dease and Simpson on the Castor and Pollux River. He observed that the top of the cairn was broken but found no message there.

Rae journeyed north to Shepherd Bay and Cape Colville but was forced to turn back because of the difficult conditions. He set out on the journey home at the beginning of May and again met the Eskimos at Pelly Bay. He bought some more of the relics from Franklin's expedition, some of which were brought to him later at Repulse Bay. There Rae also received more information on the fate of Franklin's expedition.

In spring, four years earlier, the Eskimos had met a group of about 40 white men while hunting seals on the north coast of King William Island. The men were travelling south and were pulling a boat and sledges. They were thin. Later the same spring the Eskimos found some graves and the bodies of 30 men on the mainland and five on an island one day's journey from a large river.

Rae recognised the river as the Back and the island as Montreal Island. None of the Eskimos he spoke to had been to the place themselves but had heard stories and acquired objects from those who had been there. There was no doubt that at least one of the objects was Franklin's own: the words 'Sir John Franklin KCH' were etched on a round silver plate.

Rae arrived back in Churchill on 28 August and immediately set out for England. He had demonstrated that Boothia was a peninsula and that 'King William Land' was an island which was separated from Boothia by the Rae Strait. Rae wanted recognition from the Admiralty, which had doubted his discovery. He also wanted to make sure that the names he had given to the features on the east coast of Victoria Island a year before Collinson's expedition were put on the chart. Rae further wished to present the results of his new journey.

Rae presented his report, giving the first evidence of the fate of Franklin's expedition, nine years after it had set out, to the Admiralty on 2 October 1854, and it was published in *The Times* newspaper the following day. It included the following: "From the mutilated state of many of the corpses and the contents of the kettles it is evident that our wretched countrymen had been driven to the last resource – cannibalism – as a means of prolonging existence." Those who had been in the north and knew the area believed Rae's conclusions, but the report caused heated debate. Rae was considered too gullible in accepting the Eskimos' stories at face value. He was also seen to be accusing the ship's officers and crew of cannibalism. In addition he had neglected to confirm the Eskimos' claims, and was thought to have hurried back to England to claim the very large reward for his discovery.

Rae replied that he had accused nobody of cannibalism, but had only reported what the Eskimos had said. In addition not only had he had a good Eskimo interpreter but he knew the Eskimos and their ways. He had already been in the north for twenty years and there were Eskimos travelling with him. Rae had confirmed the story by talking to them a number of times. He knew the ability of the Eskimos to draw accurate maps of the regions they knew, but also of their desire to please those questioning them.

Why had Rae not continued his journey to the scene of the tragedy?

It was only at Repulse Bay on his return journey that Rae had received most of his information, and according to the Eskimos the 'Kabloonans' had already been dead for four years. In addition it was winter – Richard King attacked Rae on the grounds that he had made his journey in winter when the terrain was covered in ice and snow and when finding bodies and remains would have been difficult. And the expedition had not, in fact, been seeking Franklin's fate. For this reason – as Rae suggested – another expedition should be set up.

In summer 1855 the Hudson's Bay Company sent a new expedition to confirm Rae's information. Under the leadership of James Anderson, the party went down the Back River by canoe and explored Montreal Island and the west coast of the estuary. A broken boat and certain articles from the *Erebus* and the *Terror* were found on Montreal Island. It was not possible to question the Eskimos because Anderson

188 Francis Leopold McClintock developed the Arctic skills of the English Navy to a greater extent than anybody else. He was with James Ross as a young Lieutenant in 1849 and took part in an expedition for the first time as Ommanney's First Lieutenant in 1850–1851. He was the Commander of the Intrepid *from 1852–1854 and of the* Fox *from 1857–1859. He developed sledge technology, experimented with dog teams, made the longest sledge trips and cleared up the last stages of Franklin's expedition. As a Vice Admiral McClintock was broad-minded and unconventional, and was one of the few men to encourage Nansen when he presented his plan in London for crossing the polar sea.*
(National Maritime Museum, London)

unfortunately had no interpreter with him. On receiving Anderson's report the Admiralty handed the reward to Rae and his men although, according to Lady Franklin, Rae had not ascertained the fate of her husband and his shipmates and his report concerned only some of them.

The bearer of such unpleasant news became the centre of controversy. Later investigations showed that everything Rae had related was borne out by fact. In an era when almost every Arctic leader was knighted – even Back and McClure – one of the most remarkable men of his time went without recognition.

McCLINTOCK INVESTIGATES

In giving John Rae the reward, the Admiralty had washed its hands of the matter. But Lady Franklin considered Rae's discovery only a starting point, not a definitive explanation. She

recommended further exploration. Although the Prime Minister regarded Lady Franklin's proposal favourably the Admiralty persuaded him to give up the idea. Lady Franklin equipped one more expedition and, with private support, bought the steamship the *Fox*. She persuaded McClintock, who had been on James Ross's, Austin's and Belcher's expeditions and who, with Mecham and others had developed the art of sledge travelling, to command the expedition, which set off from Aberdeen on 1 July 1857

Her choice was a fortunate one. Although the *Fox* was stuck in the ice of Baffin Bay for 250 days in the summer of 1857 and drifted with the ice for over 1200 miles or 2000 kilometres, McClintock did not give up on his task. On the ship's becoming free from the ice he procured more supplies in Greenland and replenished his reserves of coal and provisions at Beechey Island, Port Leopold and Fury Beach.

McClintock tried to make his way into Peel Sound but was forced to turn back. He sailed to Prince Regent Inlet and onwards to the Bellot Strait which joined Peel Sound more than 155 miles south of the Barrow Strait. He reached the strait but could not sail through it. The strait was only 25 miles long but its western part was frozen over throughout the summer. McClintock decided to send a sledge party from Kennedy Harbour in the Bellot Strait to his destination .

In autumn a sledge party brought food supplies for a spring expedition. McClintock had taken along 22 Greenland sledge dogs and three drivers, the Danish interpreter Carl Petersen, who had been on earlier expeditions, and two Greenland Eskimos. Each of the *Fox's* sledge parties had both a man-drawn and a dog-drawn sledge. In spring 1859 they also had five pups with them, that is to say a fourth team, which McClintock trained himself. McClintock and his companions lived in igloos, some of which the Eskimos were paid to build.

Lieutenant William Hobson and McClintock set out at the beginning of April, with Captain Sir Allen Young, who had volunteered, joining them later. Young was to search the partly unexplored coasts of Prince of Wales Island and Hobson the north coast of King William Island. McClintock chose the east coast of King William Island, the Great Fish River or Back River delta, Montreal Island and the west coast of King William Island as his target areas. They bartered with the Eskimos for many articles originating from Franklin's expedition. On Montreal Island McClintock found more items from Franklin's expedition but no trace of the men.

At Cape Herschel on the south-west coast of King William Island, McClintock examined a one-and-a-half metre, or five-feet high cairn but found no messages on it; the cairn had probably been built by Simpson. On 25 May McClintock found a skeleton on the west coast of the island. Judging from the neckerchief the young man had probably been a steward; he was dressed in English clothes and beside his body they found a clothes-brush and a comb. Judging from his position the man had fallen to the ground on his face in exhaustion and died of starvation. McClintock recalled the words of an old Eskimo: 'They fell down and died as they walked along'.

YANKEE BOAT
– AN UNBEATABLE WHALER

"A short whizzing sound came from the boat – *Queequeg* had thrown a harpoon. After this all was complete confusion and commotion: something bumped into the boat's stern and it was as if the bow had hit a cliff face. The sail folded with a bang, a warm pillar of steam flew into the air nearby and something rocked and rolled beneath us just like an earthquake. The effects of the storm, the whale and the harpoon all intermingled to create chaos. The whale, which had barely been nicked by the projectile, made a getaway."

Whaling was undoubtedly one of the greatest challenges facing sailors in the era of sailing ships. Herman Melville describes it in his classic *Moby Dick*, from where the above passage is taken.

American whaling ships and boats were considerably more advanced than those in traditional whale-hunting countries. The Americans made a later start in whaling (and also gave it up earlier) but they were broad-minded in their development work and made their whaling fleet very effective.

189

Painting by John Stobart

The American whaleboat was the world's fastest, most seaworthy and agile – until others copied its characteristics. Many of its innovations were later adapted for other kinds of ships, too.

The model was developed from the Indian canoe, from where it got its light structure, flat bottom, and sides that narrowed towards the stern and bow. This made it both an excellent sailboat and a fine vessel in surges near the shores, which suited the American practice of beginning the hunt from ashore. With time, the whaleboats became ever larger and needed to be taken out to sea with ships. It was precisely because the whaleboat was capable of sailing in surging water so well that it later became so popular as an all-purpose boat. It was especially in the southern ocean areas that landing ashore in rough seas required a special boat.

Whaleboats were equipped with sails even before the American contribution to their development. When whaling reached its peak, the Americans equipped their boats with efficient rigging; a bow-jib and a large gaffsail that reached higher than the top of the mast. The lifting keel or center-board, also developed by the Americans in the early 19th century, greatly improved the sailing characteristics of hunting boats. For a long time Yankee boat was completely clinker-built, but its bottom later became carvel-built.

An American whaleboat always had a crew of six. The harpooner sat at the bow and the helmsman sat at the stern. The other four were seated each on their own seat on the opposite side to the oar they were rowing. This made the special long oars lighter to row.

The boat only weighed a couple of hundred kilos. Because of its light structure, it was incapable of withstanding the weight of the harpoon ropes and other equipment when it was being raised or lowered. So the equipment was lowered into the boat in wooden boxes when it had already taken to the water. With six fully equipped men onboard, the boat's light frame would have to support a one-ton load.

In C.W. Ashley's opinion the American whaleboat was by far the best water transport then available. He is speaking of the time, in the middle of the 19th century, when the fleet residing in the New Bedford whale-hunting centre was over 400 ships strong and thus comprised two or three thousand whaleboats.

190

At Point Victory Hobson found a cairn in which was hidden a two-part message. The first was left by Lieutenant Graham Gore, whose eight-man party had carried out explorations on King William Island. His message read as follows: "28 May 1847 H.M.S. ships Erebus and Terror wintered in the Ice (Lat.) 70° 5' N. (Long.) 98° 23' W. Having wintered in 1846–7 at Beechey Island in Lat. 74°. 43'. 28". N. Long. 91°. 39'. 15" W., after having ascended Wellington Channel to Lat. 77°, and returned by the west side of Cornwallis Island. Sir John Franklin commanding the Expedition. All well. Party consisting of 2 officers and 6 men left the Ships on Monday 24th May, 1847. Gm. Gore, Lieut. Chas. F. Des Voeux, Mate." There was a error in this message since the expedition had already wintered in 1845–1846 at Beechey Island.

A year later the following was added in the margin of the message left by Gore at Point Victory: "25th April, 1848. HMS ships Terror and Erebus were deserted on 22nd April, 5 leagues (24 kilometres) NNW of this, having been beset since 12th Septr. 1846. The Officers and the Crews consisting of 105 souls – under the command of Captain F. R. M. Crozier landed here... Sir John Franklin died on 11th June 1847 and the total loss by deaths in the expedition has been to this date 9 Officers and 15 Men. F. R. M. Crozier James Fitzjames Captain and Senior Offr. Captain, HMS Erebus and start on tomorrow 26th for Backs Fish River."

A third message still was written on the paper: "This paper was found by Lt. Irving under the cairn supposed to have built by Sir James Ross in 1831... where it has been deposited by the late Commander Gore in June 1847. Sir James Ross' pillar has not however been found, and the paper has been transferred to this position, which is that in which Sir J. Ross' pillar was erected."

Hobson and McClintock found many traces of Franklin's expedition's march towards the Back River but also evidence of the fact that some of the crew may have returned to the ships. At Erebus Bay, more than sixty miles or a hundred kilometres from the ship, a heavy sledge was found which was loaded with an even heavier boat. McClintock calculated their combined weight to be 1400 lbs, over 500 kilos, which would have been an exhausting task for seven men to pull. Two skeletons were found in the boat. The men had apparently been sick and the other men dragging the sledge had left them behind.

The most astonishing thing was the abundance of useless items which were in McClintock's words "a mere accumulation of dead weight, but slightly useful, and very likely to break down the strength of the sledge-crews". Books were found in the sledge, from the Bible to Oliver Goldsmith's novel The Bishop of Wakefield. In addition, five clocks, seven boots, 26 pieces of silver cutlery engraved with the initials of various officers and a great deal more were found.

Discarded articles were also discovered close to the landing place at Back Bay; four heavy boat stoves, spades, medicines, a sextant and a pile of clothes over a metre high.

According to later Eskimo accounts, one of the ships in which five men had been living was still afloat in 1849. The other, it seems, had drifted to and beyond the Simpson Strait and was shipwrecked on the east coast of King William Island.

McClintock had been given three tasks by Lady Franklin. He was to rescue all those still alive, to find the expedition's written records and, above all, to find evidence to support the supposition that Franklin's expedition had found the Northwest Passage. The last survivors of the expedition, the hardiest of the explorers to have reached the Back river, had died in autumn 1850 at the latest. Retrieving the documents might have been possible two or three years after the death of these men, before the papers, which the Eskimos had procured, had blown away or disintegrated.

McClintock fulfilled Lady Franklin's last wish by demonstrating that some had reached the Simpson Strait and thus discovered the last remaining link in the Northwest Passage. The expedition had been destroyed because it chose a passage through the sound to the west of King William Island blocked by the ice drifting from the north. This was confirmed by Rae and Collinson, both of whom gave up trying to cross the Victoria Strait because of difficulty in negotiating the ice.

McClintock was also able to demonstrate that the most likely southern Northwest Passage would be east of King William Island through the James Ross Strait and the Rae Strait to the Simpson Strait and then along the north coast of America to the Bering Strait, a route that Collinson had already sailed.

FRANKLIN'S EXPEDITION MAKES ITS FINAL VOYAGE

The various stages of Franklin's expedition were investigated and explained as precisely as was possible. During the first summer of 1845 Franklin had sailed from Lancaster Sound to Barrow Strait and, as Penny had assumed, proceeded north along Wellington Channel all the way to latitude 77°. He must have discovered the Grinnell Peninsula and also charted the east coast of Bathurst Island. More fortunate than Belcher, he sailed the length of Crozier Channel and back to Barrow Strait between Bathurst and Cornwallis Islands the same summer. Only after this did the expedition return to winter on Beechey Island, where three of their number died.

The following summer they sailed south. There is evidence to suggest that during the time of the expedition Peel Sound was open only once every five years. In 1846 it was open, and this is the route that Franklin took to sail south. After sailing through the sound Franklin had to decide how to continue. Both Simpson and James Ross, whose travel journals Franklin had on his shelf, appear to have assumed that King William was not an island but was connected to the Boothia Peninsula.

This is probably why Franklin progressed to the Victoria Strait, where his ships ended up on 12 September 1846. The strength of the pack ice in the Victoria Strait can be seen from the fact that at places on the north-west coast of King William Island the ice had pushed half a mile inland when James Ross went there in 1830.

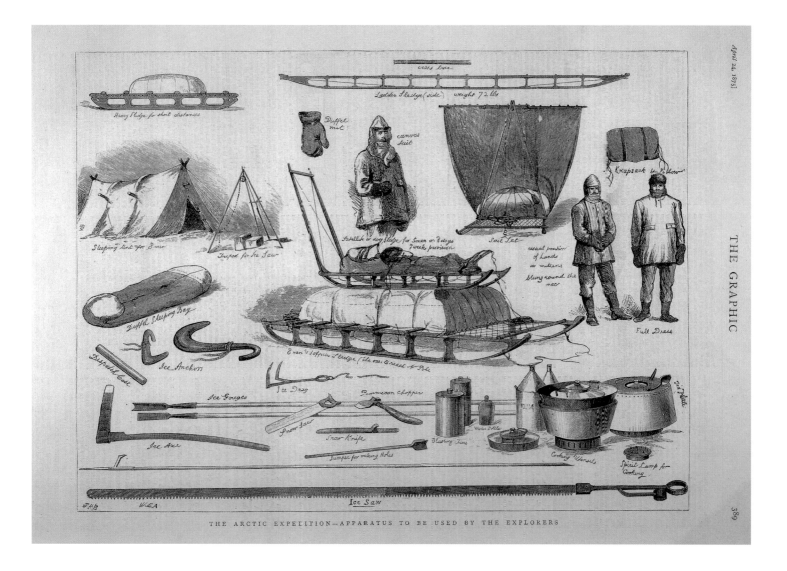

THE ARCTIC EXPEDITION—APPARATUS TO BE USED BY THE EXPLORERS

A year after having being trapped in the ice Franklin sent Gore's party to try to find out how the Northwest Passage continued. It was on this journey that Gore left his first message. A great deal happened after this. Franklin died within a month of what Gore described as all being well. Many officers also died, including Gore. There was a higher death rate among the officers than among the crew.

During the winter, conditions changed so drastically that the officers lost hope that the ships would ever be freed from the ice and, abandoning them, made their way towards the Back River. In spite of having waited for two years the expedition set off very ill-equipped. In addition, it looks as if Crozier chose to set out too early in the spring and the men had to pull their heavy boats instead of being able to sail along the coastal waters later in summer.

Why did one of the three sledge crews appear to have turned back after advancing a considerable way? Did the members of the expedition die of hunger or of scurvy? Why did the expedition set off so early in the spring? Why did they set out for the Back River, which was difficult to negotiate? Why did they not set off north for Fury Beach where they must have found provisions and from which they would possibly have come across whalers within ten days? Why was the mortality rate higher among the officers than among the

191 The picture shows equipment for Arctic exploration which in the opinion of the English in 1875 was the best possible. The sledge is a McClintock man-hauled type, but Thomas Simpson and John Rae as well as the Americans had already started to use lighter dog-pulled sledges before this. Many had at this stage already learned that Eskimo fur clothing was incomparable winter wear. Over the next fifty years the equipment was developed at a dizzying pace. Peary's sledges weighed only one third of the McClintock type. (JOHN NURMINEN FOUNDATION)

crew? Did a member of James Anderson's expedition see one of the ships as it drifted eastwards along the Northwest Passage through the Simpson Strait?

THEORIES AND GUESSWORK

The fate of Franklin's expedition has been puzzled over to this day. Citing some of the most critical writers may easily create the impression that the author has a fierce anti-Franklin and indeed anti-Royal Navy bias.

The first controversy was created by Dr John Rae, who

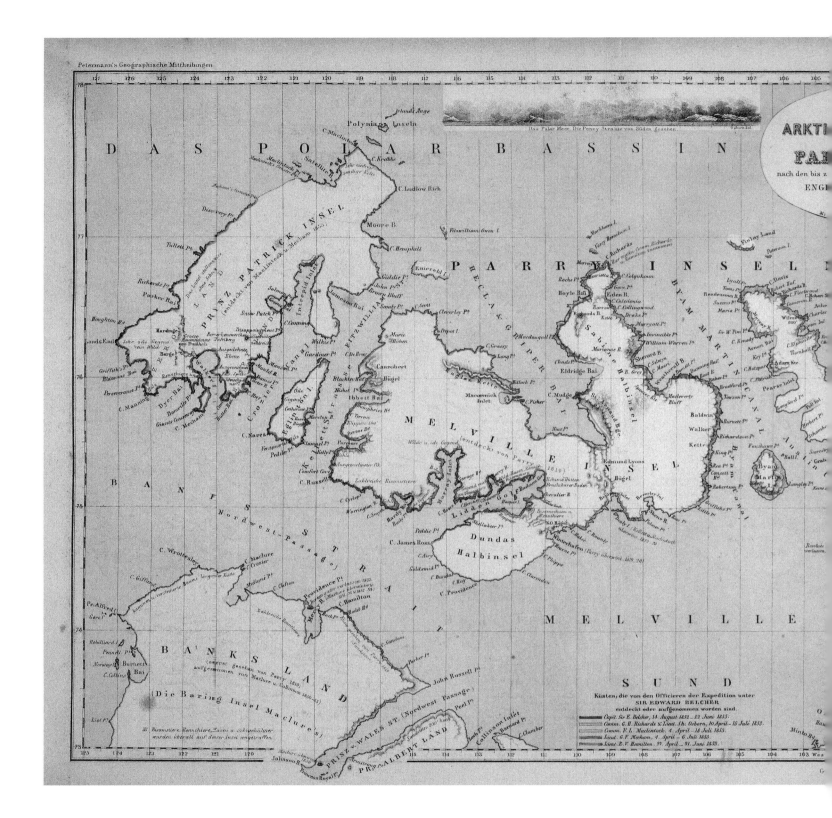

192 A chart of Parry's islands, made following the major searches for Franklin in the 1850s. Austin's and Penny's expeditions had charted the area between North Devon and Bathurst and found out that Bathurst and Cornwallis Islands were separated by a strait. Belcher's expedition mapped Cameron, Helen and Sherard Osborn islands to the north of Bathurst. Kellet's sledge parties charted the south coast of Melville Island and the area between Melville and Prince Patrick islands. Jones Sound and Ellesmere Island in the top right corner are still uncharted. Since the waters in these northern areas are covered by ice for most of the year the majority of mapping journeys were made by sledge during winter.
(JOHN NURMINEN FOUNDATION)

mentioned the possibility of cannibalism "as a means of prolonging existence". Charles Dickens then attacked the source of the information, the Inuit, and regarded them to be "covetous, treacherous and cruel...with a domesticity of blood and blubber". Owen Beattie examined the remains of Franklin's expedition in the 1980's and found on the coast of King William Island some bones which appeared to have been violently removed from their bodies. There were signs of cuts on the bones that suggest the use of a knife or some other sharp implement. This may, however, be explained by pointing out that Eskimos, tempted by the riches which officers and men carried with them, murdered the last surviving men.

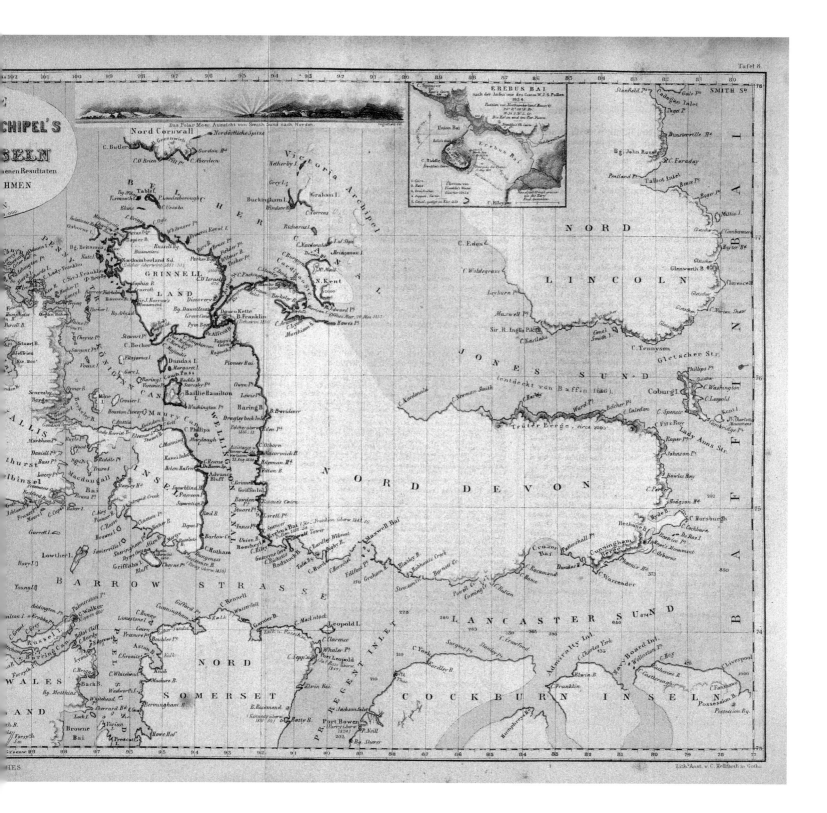

But a much more interesting question is why did Franklin's expedition perish? Owen Beattie made another interesting observation. The bones of Franklin's companions had a very high lead content. According to Beattie lead poisoning increases the effect of scurvy and the incidence of death. Because lead can be absorbed into the bones over years Beattie dug up three of the bodies buried on Beechey Island and carried out tests on their remains.

The hair of the bodies had an extremely high lead content, which indicates that the lead was absorbed slightly before death. Beattie thought it possible that the tin cans containing preserved foods were the cause of lead contamination because the side seams of some of the tins were incomplete. However, some researchers say that lead soldering will not enter the can unless it is highly acidic, as some fruits are. On the other hand the men were already dead as early as 1846, and Lieutenant Gore wrote in his record for May 1847 'all well'. The record for 25 April 1848 informs us that 'the total loss by deaths in the Expedition has been to this date 9 Officers and 15 Men'. If lead from tins on Beechey Island and before had been the reason for illness and deaths, shouldn't more men have already died within the first year after leaving Beechey Island?

The Eskimos gave quite consistent information about Franklin's men who were marching south along the coast of

King William Island. They had noticed an abnormal condition of the mouth and gums in the white men. According to Richard J. Cyriax an outbreak of scurvy is a very possible explanation. Although Franklin was furnished with real lemon juice, which is an effective antiscorbutic, insufficient fresh food and progressive diminution in the antiscorbutic property of the lemon juice lowered the resistance of the men against scurvy.

John Ross had proved the importance of hunting fresh food by surviving four winters from 1829–1833. He had, however, been assisted in hunting by the Eskimos. The prospects of obtaining fresh meat in the ships of Franklin's expedition were poor. McClintock observed in 1859 that the west shores of King William Island were devoid of game during April and May although Schwatka found plenty from June to November. In addition the Eskimos later remarked that the winters of 1846–1848 had been very cold and that they found very few caribou and seals. And considering the number of officers and men, they had a very slight chance of getting enough fresh food even under better conditions.

Why did the expedition leave the ships so early in the spring? Captain Crozier certainly had enough provisions to remain on board until summer 1848: they were originally calculated to suffice for about three years. Even if the summer thaw had not freed the ships, he could have hauled the boats close to the shore where there was most probably open water for sailing southwards. Waiting passively for the deaths of many and the disablement of many more was certainly awful, but putting men weakened by scurvy to haul heavy sledges would have killed them sooner. Or were they compelled to abandon the ships? If so, why?

Why did they leave for the Back River? According to Cyriax, Crozier failed to take the route which other Arctic explorers expected him to, but took the very one which they declared to be the most impracticable. An attempt to go to Fury Beach may have been considered too risky because there was not much game to be had, only preserved and dried provisions. The Back River, on the other hand, promised supplies of fresh food as George Back had seen plenty of caribou and musk-ox in 1834 as had Dease and Simpson on the south coast of King William Island five years later. John Richardson believed that Crozier went to the Back River to find caribou, fish and fowl. He may have intended to travel later in boats along the coast to the Mackenzie River.

After his disappearance Sir John Franklin became one of the greatest, if not the greatest, figures of Arctic exploration. Was he that or simply a romanticised hero?

Franklin's first overland Arctic expedition was a disaster in terms of men lost. There was nothing remarkable about the second voyage, although it does show Franklin's ability to learn from his mistakes. Franklin's best achievement was to be the first to sail through Wellington Channel and Peel Sound. These voyages were carried out when Franklin was still alive and leading the expeditions. The real acid test, however, began only after this.

Franklin did not choose the ships the *Erebus* and the *Terror*, which were quite big for the waters of the Northwest Passage. Amundsen had difficulties in sailing through the passage with the *Gjøa*, a much smaller vessel. However, he did not have problems when crossing the North Atlantic. Big ships required more men, and this increased the number of officers and crew to such an extent that subsistence hunting in an emergency situation would not be easy.

Perhaps the most serious criticism should be directed at the British social and naval traditions they took to the Arctic. The only weapons found by Hobson were shotguns. Based on Eskimo testimony Hall, Schwatka and Knud Rasmussen report that Franklin's men shot birds and followed the tradition of English sportsmen. Pierre Berton, a Canadian, writes in *The Arctic Grail* that "John Franklin and his officers dined in Victorian splendour, the brass buttons of their dress uniforms carefully polished by their servants, their tables set with linen, their salt meat carved with silver-plated, crested knives". Vilhjálmur Stefánsson, one of the greatest Arctic explorers of the 20th century, summarised his analysis of Franklin's fate thus: "the crews of the *Erebus* and *Terror* perished as victims of the manners, customs, social outlook and medical views of their time". The legend of Franklin and his companions is based on how they met their fate: "They perished gloriously".

One of the lessons of Franklin's story is that a man for whom being chosen for the mission itself is the most important thing in the world should not be chosen for the task. When Franklin was chosen he had already achieved his aim. The best leaders are often those for whom the task at hand is a challenge and its accomplishment a step towards the next even more ambitious mission.

according to Petermann's theory, unlikely. The search for Franklin was more a way of arranging funding than the main aim of the expedition, although Kane genuinely believed Franklin's expedition to have got lost its way through the Wellington Channel to the polar sea.

Before setting off, in the spring of 1853, from mid-April to mid-May Kane had been confined to his bed. This was reflected in his choice of equipment and personnel. Only a few of the crew members had any experience of the polar region. Kane's deputy and expedition doctor, Isaac Israel Hayes was 21 and had only recently graduated. Two crewmen who were enrolled at random at the harbour were to cause problems on the voyage. The Dane, Carl Petersen, who was signed on in Greenland, had been with Penny while seeking Franklin. He was an experienced and capable man but was also aware of his own worth and supercilious as a result. Upon boarding the ship, Petersen declared that half the crew had never served on a ship before and that the others lacked experience of the polar region. In his opinion the ship's crew was not up to scratch, and he did not think highly of Kane either.

Kane succeeded in navigating Smith Sound and found a winter harbour for his vessel the *Advance* at Kane Basin on the south-east coast which he named Rensselaer Harbour after his parents' summer residence. At the very beginning almost all of the expedition's dogs died. The sledge designed by Kane proved to be too heavy when loaded with a boat, and even without a boat brought the men difficulties. To begin with Kane was inexperienced and ordered his men to carry out tasks that were far too demanding.

The ice did not release the *Advance* from its grip in summer 1854. The expedition had to spend a second winter in the polar region. But with the coming of autumn eleven of his men wanted to leave for Upernavik in the south and leave Kane and the sick men on the vessel. To Kane's disappointment those leaving were joined by four of his officers, including Hayes and Petersen. Kane urged them to choose a leader and gave two boats, food and other equipment to the eight men setting off for the south. Along with the ten remaining men Kane prepared to spend a second winter in his ice-bound ship.

In postponing his departure until the spring Kane had made the right decision. Those who had left failed in their aim to reach Upernavik. They stayed alive and were able to make it back to Kane only with the help of the Eskimos at the village of Netlik. It would probably not have been possible to survive the winter at Rensselaer Harbour either without the co-operation of the Eskimos. Kane managed to gain the trust of the Eskimos. It is perhaps thanks to him that co-operation between the Americans and the Eskimos went well later too. Kane stayed in good health because he was the only member of the expedition to eat the domestic animals of the *Advance*, rats. The fresh meat kept scurvy at bay.

Kane planned his departure meticulously. His journey began at the end of May. The boats were towed into open water with the aid of sledges. Three sledge-crews pushed their way forward, sometimes squeezed by the ice, sometimes brought to a stop by it. They succeeded in crossing Melville Bay – occasionally dragging the boats over the ice – by the beginning of August. Near Upernavik Petersen met a familiar Eskimo who informed him that his wife had declared that her husband was dead. At the beginning of August 1855 a patrol boat out of Upernavik picked up the members of the expedition.

Kane was an American polar hero, in part because of his youthful enthusiasm, and in part thanks to two well-written books, which made light of the difficulties he experienced. Kane's expedition charted several hundred miles of the coast of Kane Basin. The party also discovered the Humboldt Glacier and thought they had found an open polar sea in the north; one of the members, William Morton, probably saw a mirage, his eyes bewitched either by a distant shimmering area of open water, a polynya, or by Kane's suggestive enthusiasm. Thanks to his discovery, Kane guided the Americans to Smith Sound and thus, in Adolphus Greely's words, defined the "American way to the North Pole". Kane died of his illness in 1857 in Havana, Cuba, almost immediately after writing his second book. Many readers were to be inspired by this book, which became a great success. Among these impressionable readers was a certain six-year-old boy. The year was 1862 and the boy's name was Robert Peary.

THE SINGULAR CHARLES FRANCES HALL

The first to follow in the footsteps of Elisha Kane was his doctor Isaac Hayes, who on Kane's expedition had crossed Kane Basin and reached Grinnell Land on what is now Ellesmere Island and had advanced to around latitude 80°. He was given funds to carry out his own plans on how to continue and sailed to Smith Sound in summer 1860.

Hayes too was looking for an open polar sea. He was not to see it either. Only with difficulty did he cross Kane Basin with his two companions. Hayes claimed to have reached latitude 81° 35', but the map he made does not lend support to this. His depiction of the west coast of Kennedy Channel did not agree with the observations of later explorers and he was not believed to have in fact progressed beyond latitude 80° 14' north.

Charles Francis Hall was the most important of Kane's successors. Hall was a real man of the people compared with the fashionable Kane or the many British naval officers. Hall's educational background was insignificant. He earned his living as a blacksmith and later developed hot-air machines, then learned to engrave and draw and finally became a newspaper publisher.

Efforts to ascertain Franklin's fate increased knowledge of the Arctic and inspired people to try to reach it. Hall, too, decided to set out to look for Franklin. McClintock's discoveries led him to believe that some of Franklin's men could still be rescued.

Hall received the support of the merchant Henry Grinnell and was given the opportunity to present his ideas to the American Geographical Society. For an explorer he was lacking a number of the basic skills; among other things he did not master the techniques of navigation at sea or on land. But he had qualities that may have sometimes been lacking in the better educated. He was strong, resilient, good-natured and friendly. Since Hall had little money he travelled from one area of the polar region to another with little fuss; he lacked both silver spoons and servants.

202 Charles Francis Hall earned his living as a smith, engraver and newspaper publisher. He also wanted to set out to look for Franklin. Lacking sponsors, he made his first voyage modestly as a passenger on a whaler. He gained experience on Baffin Island and looked for remains of Frobisher's voyage. He learnt the Eskimo ways and lived like one of them. Hall's third voyage on the vessel POLARIS *made its way towards Kennedy Channel. He died in the autumn of 1871 of what later investigations proved to be arsenic poisoning.* (JOHN NURMINEN FOUNDATION)

The budget for Hall's first voyage was $1000, but he received additional equipment from private companies and his friends. He was offered a free passage to Baffin Bay on a whaler and, on 29 May 1860, he sailed north as a passenger on the *George Henry,* commanded by Sidney Budington. An Eskimo named Kudlago whom Budington had brought south with him was among the passengers. Pining for his home, Kudlago died on the journey, his last words being "Can you see ice?"

In Baffin Bay, Hall made the acquaintance of an Eskimo by the name of Tookoolito and her husband Ebierbing, otherwise known as Hannah and Joe. They had both been to England and spoke English. They were to follow Hall on his travels – all the way to America.

U. S. S. Polaris.   C. F. Hall, Commander.

May 31st 1871.

Bureau, Engraving & Printing.

203 *Charles Francis Hall set out on his last expedition in 1871 in the* POLARIS *captained by Sidney Budington, who had also captained him on his first expedition on a whaler. The* POLARIS *pushed her way deep into the Kennedy Channel, where she wintered. On the return journey – with Hall already dead – the* POLARIS *sailed south and drifted with the ice. In spring 1873 all the men left on the ship abandoned her. The* POLARIS *was a sailing vessel equipped with a steam engine.* (JOHN NURMINEN FOUNDATION)

Hall travelled about Baffin Island and Frobisher Bay collecting relics and recording the Eskimos' oral history associated with Martin Frobisher's voyages of 1576–1578. He showed the Frobisher Strait to be a bay, and also showed that it was not connected to the Hudson Strait as had been believed.

Two years after returning on the *George Henry*, Hall began to plan a new journey. In spring 1864 he travelled north with Joe and Hannah on the whaler *Monticello*. He spent all of five years in the north.

Hall went ashore in the region of Wager Bay off Hudson Bay, travelled from there to Repulse Bay, wintering at Fort Hope which had been built by Rae. Although Hall made regular contact with the whalers, he lived like an Eskimo. He travelled with the Eskimos and acquired a great many items from Franklin's expedition. He heard from the Eskimos of white men and set out once more for Fury and the Hecla Strait but found no trace of them.

On his journey to King William Island in 1869 he found some graves of Franklin's men, and confirmed once and for all that none of the expedition members was still alive. On his travels he refined the maps of Melville Peninsula and proved that a white man could live like an Eskimo if he accepted their way of life.

When, in 1871, Hall set out on his third expedition, he was an expert on the polar region whose ability to survive in the Arctic was in no doubt. This voyage was financed by the United States government and its aim was to reach the North Pole by way of Smith Sound. The *Polaris,* which was made available to Hall, was commanded by his old acquaintance Captain Budington.

In August the *Polaris* made its way deep into Kennedy Channel and, on 29 August 1871, set a new record of latitude 82° 11' North. This broke the record of 81° 42' set by the Finnish Swede A. E. Nordenskiöld's vessel the *Sofia,* which in her time had broken Scoresby's record. Hall sailed to the area where Morton had seen the open polar sea. But the ice prevented the *Polaris* from sailing further north. He sought a winter harbour to the south of what is now Hall Basin.

Hall made a sledge trip to latitude 82° as late as October. Everything was set for a spring expedition, and Hall could

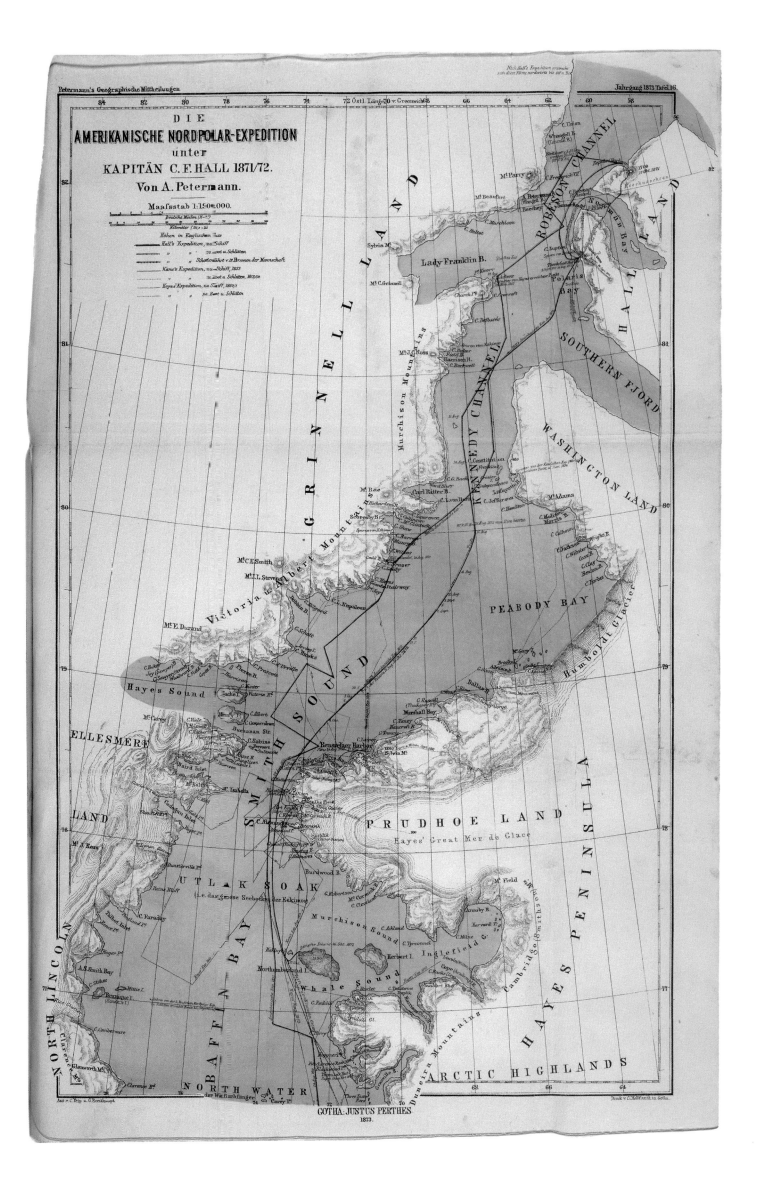

204 Charles Hall's POLARIS *expedition of 1871-1872 attempted to reach the North Pole by way of Smith Sound. The* POLARIS *achieved a new northerly record for ships, but Hall hardly had time to properly begin mapping work before dying of poisoning. He crossed Kane's and Hayes' northernmost turning points and charted Hall Basin, Lady Franklin and Newman fjords and began mapping the north-east corner of Ellesmere Island.*
(JOHN NURMINEN FOUNDATION)

205 When the POLARIS *was sailing south in autumn 1872 she became icebound and the crew prepared to abandon her. Eleven members of the crew were on an ice floe making ready for the change when the floe broke free and drifted away from the vessel. Some Eskimos saved the men on the ice floe but they only got off the ice in April 1873 (after six months) when the Eskimos had caught enough prey and returned to land. Two of the ship's boats and two kayaks stayed on the ice floe. The Eskimos in the party, Joe and Hans, hunted seal. In March they killed a polar bear, just when they had run out of food. In the last weeks they drifted in the whaleboat, commanded by G. E. Tyson, until they were rescued by the* TIGRESS *in April 1872, after six months.*
(JOHN NURMINEN FOUNDATION)

hardly have found a better base. It was further to the north than either Kane's or Hayes' expeditions had managed to reach.

No sooner had Hall returned to the ship on 24 October than he was obliged to take to his bed. He had some kind of stomach ailment and was vomiting. His condition worsened and he died on 8 November 1871. Before his death Hall claimed to have fallen ill after drinking coffee. The coffee had been too sweet and Hall believed that somebody had poisoned him.

Hall's death is one of the mysteries of Arctic exploration. He was probably right about the cause of his death. When, in 1965, his frozen body was exhumed and examined, it was shown from his hair and nails that he had received a large amount of arsenic before his death. Both Hall and the

expedition's doctor, Emil Bessels, had access to arsenic. It is difficult, however, to believe that Hall had taken it himself by mistake. There had been friction between Hall, Budington and Bessels. Bessels, who had nursed Hall, would easily have been able to poison him.

After Hall's death the expedition members lost all their enthusiasm for exploring. When the vessel was freed from the ice they headed south. The *Polaris* became beset in the pack ice and, fearing her loss, some of the crew and some equipment was later transferred onto an ice floe. When the floe suddenly split, the *Polaris* was cast adrift and most of the group remained on the floe with the boats and plenty of equipment. After some colourful adventures both groups were rescued.

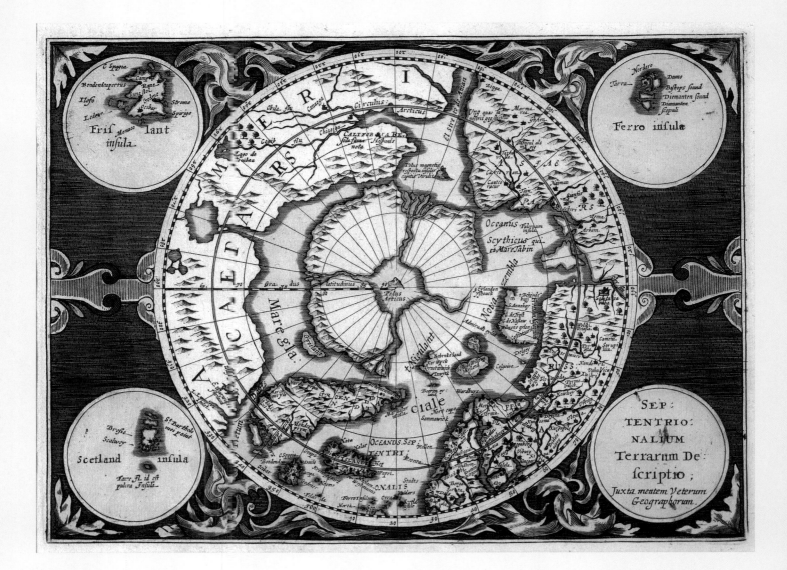

THE OPEN POLAR SEA

206 Mercator's view of the polar region, its islands and seas had a significant effect on geographical knowledge of the north until the 18th century. This beautiful draft from the miniature atlas displays Zeno's phantom islands and the mythical polar islands. The Pole is in the middle of the islands and the Magnetic North Pole is in the upper right corner. Water flows in the polar rivers and the northern sea is connected to the interior by whirlpools. According to this map it would have been possible to sail to the Pacific from the Atlantic through either the Northeast or Northwest Passages or even directly over the Pole. (JOHN NURMINEN FOUNDATION)

At different times in history people have had the most extraordinary ideas about the Arctic, the last area of the world to be mapped. From ancient times until the 20th century it has been imagined that islands, continents with their mountains and rivers, glaciers, areas of open water and even settlements could be found there. Myth, fantasy and observation became confused. Imagination influenced the maps, which in turn affected our image of the world.

Man went to the North Pole for the first time in 1909. During the first half of the 20th century various types of aircraft flew over the polar region and in the 1950s a submarine sailed beneath it. It was at this time that commercial passenger flights began to cross the area and the polar region

was opened to international civil aviation. We could see the first satellite picture of the polar region in the 1960s. It was only then that we were able to comprehend the enormous expanse of ice there.

During the time of the great voyages of exploration, the southern trade routes between Europe and the Far East were controlled by the Spanish and Portuguese. The English and the Dutch were obliged to look to the north. In 1527 the English merchant, Robert Thorne, who lived and worked in Seville, made the bold proposal of seeking a new trade route to China and Japan via the north. This was based on the belief that the northern polar sea was not frozen. Gradually, the idea of several northern sailing routes – the Northeast Passage, the Northwest Passage and a route

running straight through the polar region – gained a foothold in nautical circles.

In 1507 Martin Waldseemüller published a map in Strasbourg on which America was already taking shape. It was based on the Ptolemaic concept of the polar region and suggested the possibility of sailing via a number of northern routes to the Far East. The belief in open passages in the polar sea was strengthened decisively by Mercator's map published in 1569, to which was attached a separate map of the Northern Calotte. This positively invited explorers to sail across the polar region and onwards by way of the imaginary Anian Strait to China.

Petrus Plancius was already trying to find a scientific explanation for an open polar sea in the 16th century. This clergyman, navigation teacher and cartographer had a powerful influence on Dutch polar exploration in particular. He wrote: 'Although [the sun's] rays are weak, yet on account of the long time they continue, they have sufficient strength to warm the ground, to render it tempered, to accommodate it for the habitation of man and to produce grass for the nourishment of animals.' An open polar sea would be brought about, then, by the warmth of the long light days of summer.

In times gone by it was believed that ice could only be formed from sweet water – the melted water from icebergs and pack ice was, after all, saltless. Thus sea ice could only be formed in coastal estuaries. Barents' observations of the movement of the pack ice seemed to support this idea. His supporter, Plancius, believed in fact that the further north one went, the more certain one would be of finding open water.

In the 1770s, the Englishman Daines Barrington confirmed the British belief in an open polar sea in his publications. He argued that the North Pole was surrounded by a pack-ice zone in the middle of which was an unfrozen sea. Barrington's enthusiasm influenced the setting-up of Phipps' expedition, which attempted to cross the Pole but was confronted with an impenetrable ice barrier north of Spitsbergen.

The concept of sea currents also fed belief in an unfrozen polar sea. The supporters of the open sea explained that the Gulf Stream and the Japan Stream pushed warm water under the ice zone to the North Pole, so the water there always remained unfrozen. Scoresby, who made reliable observations of polar conditions on his whaling trips and published them in books and articles, had evidence to the contrary, however.

In the mid 19th century the American Elisha Kent Kane led an expedition to the north-east coast of Greenland. It reached the northernmost point that man had hitherto achieved and it was here, at Kane Constitution, that he observed that the unfrozen water stretched far into the north. Thus the open-sea theory was given a new lease of life.

207 Phipps' goal in 1733 was to sail through the ice to explore the imaginary stretch of open water in the polar sea. North of Spitsbergen the edge of the pack ice prevented sailing further on. Phipps' travel log's map graphically displays the movement of the RACEHORSE and the CARCASS through the ice sheets and the pack ice that prevented the ships' further progress north. The two made it as far as the Seven Islands, where is written on the map: 'From this mountain no land or water is visible due north. The ice appears unbroken and even.' (JOHN NURMINEN FOUNDATION)

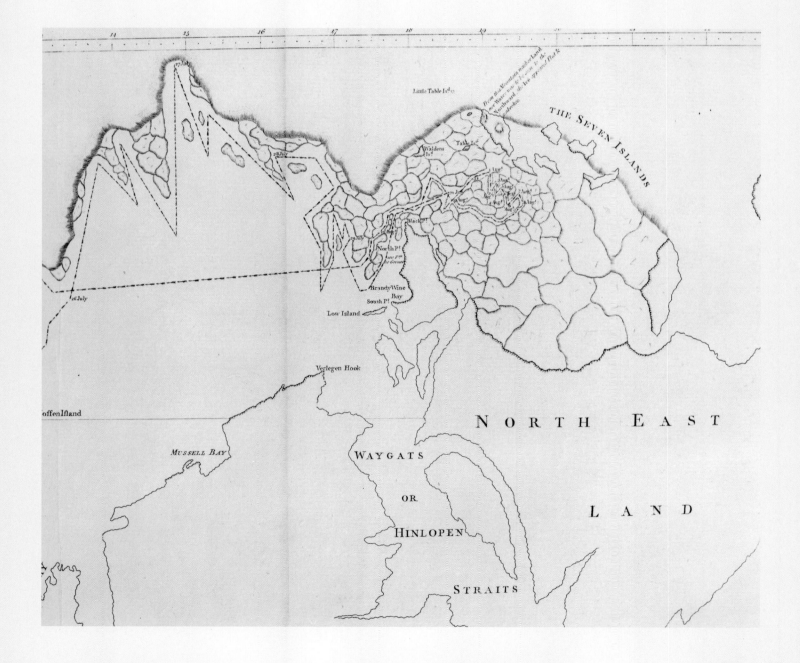

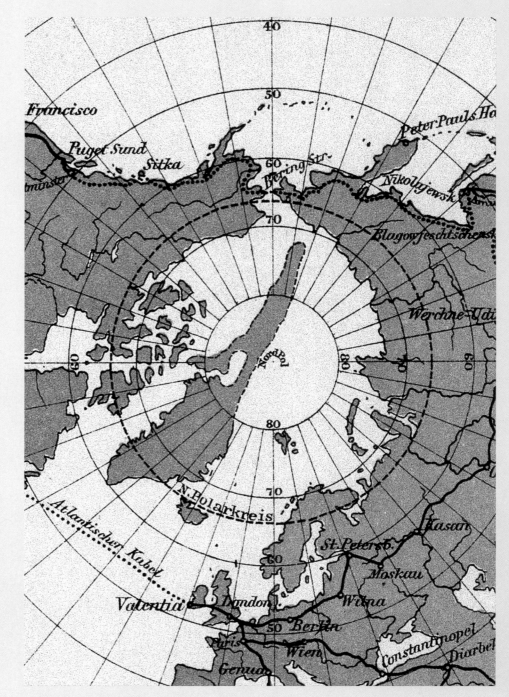

208 Petermann was a staunch believer in the open polar sea theory. According to his map Greenland continued over the polar region towards the Bering Straight. A similar theory was presented to the St Petersburg Academy by Mihail Lomonosov as early as the 18th century. A gigantic ridge that lies under the Arctic Ocean was later named after this geographer from the then Russian capital. It is possible that Petermann drew material from Lomonosov's theses for his own description of the polar region. Both men were interested in the possibility of opening the way north for seafarers. Petermann did not have faith in Nansen's plan to drift with the ice through the polar region. Nansen completed his voyage but found no sign of an open polar sea.
(HELSINKI UNIVERSITY LIBRARY)

The German geographer August Petermann was interested in polar exploration. He was a passionate supporter of the open polar sea. He believed, like Barrington, that there would be unfrozen sea to the north of an ice zone that was a few degrees wide. The best route across the Pole, he argued, would be found to the east of Spitsbergen. Petermann's *Geographische Mitteilungen* published some interesting maps of the Arctic Ocean. They depicted a Giant Greenland which extended across the Arctic Ocean as far as Wrangel Island.

Petermann played a part in motivating German and Austrian expeditions. One of these was the voyage of Weyprecht and Payer in 1872–74 in their vessel the *Tegethoff*, a voyage which ended in ship-

wreck. The expedition did not find an open sea but they did find Franz Josef Land. The men were rescued by way of Novaya Zemlya, after two winters in the north.

Nordenskiöld diligently gathered information on Arctic navigation from both old sources and the latest travel journals. He was particularly interested in navigating in icy conditions. He obtained new information from whale and walrus hunters, amongst other sources, and he made careful note of Payer's experiences. Nordenskiöld disagreed with Petermann. He did not believe that open water would be found to the north of Spitsbergen. He planned his Northeast Passage voyage to closely follow the Siberian coast after the Kara Sea, as he believed that he would find open water there. The voyage of the

Vega in 1878-79 proved him to be right.

Nordenskiöld and Nansen understood where the driftwood found on the coast of Iceland originated. They knew that the ice brought it from Siberia across the polar area. It was later possible to establish the speed of the ice current from the remains of the wreckage of the *Jeannette*. Once Nansen's *Fram* had travelled, stuck in the ice, across the polar region, and Nansen himself had skied from the *Fram*, first towards the Pole and then south to Franz Josef Land, the ice conditions in the northern sea were finally understood. The area is constantly changing shape and is covered by a thick layer of ice, but in summer there are places of melted water, too. The *Fram's* movement with the ice sounded the death knell for the open polar sea theory.

THE GERMANS AND AUSTRIANS
ENTER THE STAGE

August Petermann still wished to prove his theory right, and wanted to put a German expedition together to carry out the mission. He managed to get a German scientific society to provide the funds for the expedition.

In 1868 an expedition led by Karl Koldewey sailed to Greenland with the aim of following the east coast, charting it north from latitude 75°, but the ice prevented them from getting close to the coast. In the waters of Spitsbergen, however, they succeeded in crossing latitude 80°. The voyage was disappointing, but its cheif aim had in fact been to prepare for the main expedition the following year.

In 1869 two vessels were sent to the east coast of Greenland under Koldewey's leadership. The vessels immediately became separated. The *Hansa* was shipwrecked and the men took to an ice floe, spent the winter on the ice and finally reached the safety of a Danish settlement on the south-west coast. The *Germania* reached the coast but the ice blocked her way to the north. After wintering further south, she returned. A sledge party charted the east coast of Greenland all the way to latitude 77° and named the coast it had explored after Kaiser Wilhelm.

Petermann swallowed his disappointment and did not lose faith; reaching the polar sea would succeed from the Barents Sea between Spitsbergen and Novaya Zemlya. Since Germany and France were at war and Petermann believed in the Germans with all his heart, he sought new co-operation partners from Austria-Hungary. Expedition leaders Karl Weyprecht and Julius von Payer carried out a reconnaissance trip once more before the main expedition, which was put together in 1872. Its aim was to sail to the Pole. Once again it failed.

Weyprecht and Payer came up against the ice as early as latitude 74°. They found a passage leading north from the west coast of Novaya Zemlya. In August their vessel the *Tegetthoff* became stuck in the ice and was carried northwards with it. At the beginning of October their position was 77° north. They continued to drift for the entire winter, spring and summer. In August 1873 they saw land in front of them. Franz Josef Land was located at latitude 79° 43' north.

In spring 1874 Payer led three sledge parties to Franz Josef Land. He made his way to an island in the north, Rudolph Island, and calculated the location of Cape Fligeli to be latitude 82° 5' north. From the tip of Cape Fligeli he thought he saw open water to the north, but what he saw were in fact areas of open water surrounded by old ice, polynyas created by the winds. Payer saw not a sign of an open polar sea. To the northeast and north there were bluish mountain peaks. He believed these to be part of two islands, which he named King Oskar Land and Petermann Land.

The names were an omen. The islands were later to disappear into thin air along with Petermann's open-polar-sea theory. Although the scientific results of the Austro-Hungarian expedition were considerable, the return of Petermann's expedition brought disappointment. Petermann was forced to give up his theory. He was in despair, and along with his

Payer,   Weyprecht,
die Führer der „Tegetthoff"-Expedition.

209 In 1872–1874 Julius Payer, with Karl Weyprecht, led an Austro-Hungarian expedition whose task, after the failure of Koldeway, was to show that Petermann's claim of an open polar sea held good. But the journey proved the theory to be incorrect. The expedition did not reach the Pole but it did discover the Franz Josef Islands. Julius Payer led a sledge trip, which mapped the eastern part of the archipelago. Payer and his companions saw peaks on Rudolf Island which they presumed to belong to King Oscar and Petermann Lands. These lands have never been found. (JOHN NURMINEN FOUNDATION)

theory he lost his will to live. Serious depression led to his suicide in 1878, four years after the expedition's return. His influence did not end with Weyprecht's and Payer's expedition, however, but was later to influence George Washington De Long and through him Nansen too.

In the 1870s a tough Finn by the name of Adolf Erik Nordenskiöld, who had moved to Sweden, was also enthusiastically trying to reach the North Pole. On his first voyage he succeeded in breaking the record previously held by Scoresby by sailing to latitude 81° 42' North. He first tried to reach the Pole in his vessel the *Sofia* by setting out from Spitsbergen. This was followed by another attempt four years later in 1874. An interesting technique was employed on the latter of these voyages; reindeer-drawn sledges. With one exception, however, the reindeer escaped. Nordenskiöld's journey provided him with the experience to make it possible for him to sail the Northeast Passage.

THE BRITISH ONCE MORE

Clements Markham – an English geographer and writer on the Arctic – suggested to the experienced explorer Sherard Osborn the exploration of Smith Sound and the coast of the

210 Payer's and Weyprecht's vessel the TEGETTHOFF *in the embrace of the ice at the start of the long night of the second winter on the coast of Franz Josef Land. The polar bear in the picture also went into hibernation. The vessel could not be freed the following spring either, and the men were saved by pulling the vessel's four boats over the ice. They were rescued by Russian fishermen on the west coast of Novaya Zemlya.* (JOHN NURMINEN FOUNDATION)

polar sea beyond it. Both were convinced of the error of Petermann's open-polar-sea theory.

As a young Lieutenant, Osborn, like Markham, had taken part in the search for Franklin, and was afraid that the Navy's hard-won Arctic know-how would disappear unless a new expedition was sent off. Markham even wrote a book in support of the idea. Eventually it was decided to equip, at government expense, an expedition to Smith Sound, the aim of which was to explore the area surrounding the Pole, particularly the north-west corner of Greenland and Ellesmere Island, but also to proceed to the North Pole.

The expedition set out from Portsmouth in spring 1875. The two vessels were commanded by George Nares, later Sir George Nares. His vessel, the *Discovery,* remained at her winter quarters on the coast of Ellesmere Island at Lady Franklin Bay while the *Alert,* commanded by Nares, sailed north to Robeson Channel, achieving a new maritime record by reaching latitude 82° 28' north. Nares managed to find a

secure winter harbour for his ship. Autumn was spent in traditional fashion by leaving deposits of food needed on the sledge journeys at Cape Joseph Henry.

In April Nares sent out three sledge parties, one towards the North Pole, one to Ellesmere Island and one to the north coast of Greenland. The sledge party making for the Pole was led by Clements Markham's cousin, Commander Albert Markham – himself a distinguished author.

Dragging heavy sledges over the hummocky pack ice was exhausting work, but in spite of the appearance of scurvy, Markham's group succeeded in reaching a new record of 83° 20'. They had only advanced to within 30 miles of Cape Joseph Henry after a journey lasting a month. This says everything that needs to be said about how difficult it was to get through the sea ice surrounding the North Pole.

The experiences of Nares' expedition showed that, regarding skill and techniques, the British were fundamentally lagging behind the Americans and the underrated John Rae. The men were troubled by scurvy from the outset and most of the crew were unable to work at the end. It is indeed a wonder that the sledge crews lost only three men.

With the men falling sick Markham was forced to do without two of the boats. If Lieutenant Parr had not hurried back to Nares in advance and raised the alarm, the party would have perished on its return journey. On reaching the ship only three of Markham's fifteen men were able to walk unaided.

Nares was a sea captain who went where he was ordered. Although – or perhaps for the very reason that – he had

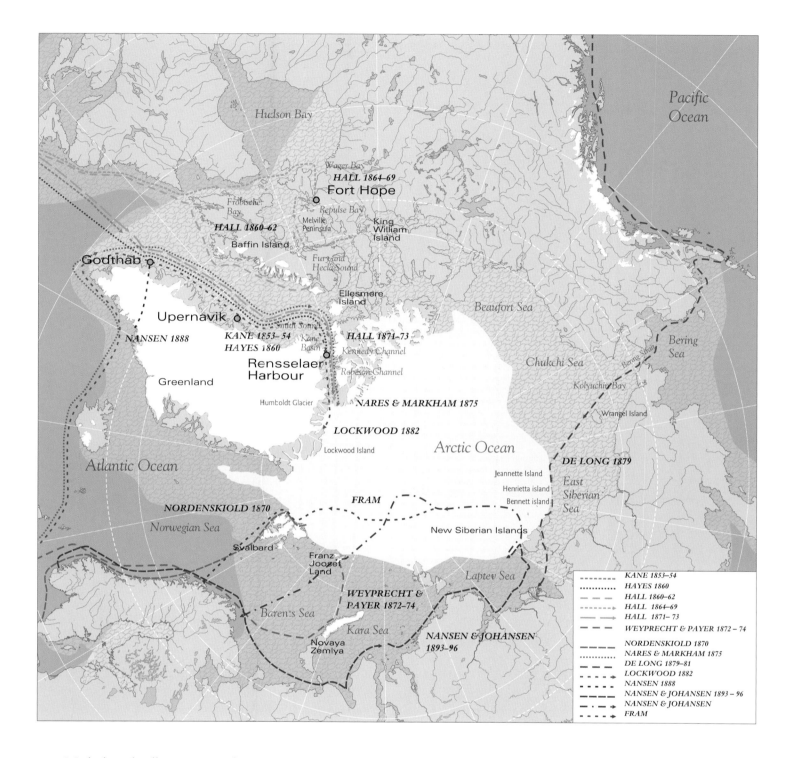

211 Marked on the illustration are the most important expeditions trying to reach the Pole and their routes before Peary and Cagni. The other most important expeditions of the age are also marked. De Long and Nansen attempted to sail to the Pole with the ice floes, Weyprecht and Payer discovered Franz Josef Land, Kane, Hayes, Hall and Nares attempted to go north by way of Smith Sound. (PATANEN)

served as mate on HMS *Resolute* under Kellett from 1852–1854 and had taken part in the sledge party that found McClure's message on Melville Island, he was not inspired by the Arctic. The polar region was, in his view, a miserable and unhealthy place.

As a realist Nares understood the situation and sensed that two other sledge parties, that of Aldrich exploring the Ellesmere coast and that of Lewis Beaumont on its way to Greenland, might also have run into trouble. The relief party sent out by Nares met Aldrich's group, which had explored the north coast of Ellesmere Island when only its leader and three of its men were able to pull a sledge.

The north Greenland party led by Beaumont had also run into difficulty. At their most desperate point Beaumont threw his knife into the snow because he could no longer be bothered to carry it. He and his men were only saved thanks to a party sent out to help. The party's central figure was the Eskimo Hans-Hendrik, who had served on Kane's and Hayes' expedition, and whose dog team and fresh meat were needed to save the exhausted men. Because scurvy had begun to appear in the crew of the *Alert*, Nares decided to call off the expedition, which had taken two years to plan, and began to make preparations to leave.

The symbol of Arctic exploration, Lady Franklin, had died in 1875, two months after the expedition had set out. Although the expedition had conducted itself in the best tradition of the Royal Navy and, with the exception of its leader, its officers were promoted upon their return, its results were considered disappointing. Disappointment was vented on Nares. He was blamed for the fact that he had not ordered lemon juice to be taken on the sledge journeys. The real culprit was the Navy's lack of scientific knowledge and the experts who had believed that the expedition could have safely spent another winter in the Arctic. Not a single sledge party had previously taken lemon juice on its sledges because it was impossible to prevent the juice from freezing and the glass from breaking.

The Navy's Arctic specialists were still ignorant of how to prevent scurvy with fresh meat, although every American explorer had learnt how to avoid it by copying the Eskimos. Time had passed the Royal Navy by. It was only in the 1930s that the next British expedition would arrive in the area.

The scientific results of Nares' expedition were comparable to those of his predecessors. In addition to charting the north coasts of Ellesmere and Greenland, the voyage collected a lot of scientific data. Nares was wrong, however, in his claim that it was not possible to reach the Pole by way of Smith Sound. Reaching the Pole did, however, mean concentrating on only one matter; all others had to be blocked from the mind.

THE *JEANNETTE* AND ADOLPHUS GREELY

A new phase in the history of Arctic exploration began with George Washington De Long's voyage: newspapers became interested in expeditions for their news value and because they increased their circulation. The newspaper magnate James Gordon Bennett had sent Henry Morton Stanley to Africa to look for Livingstone and took a favourable attitude to De Long, who was a naval Lieutenant and had taken part in the search for Hall's third expedition. De Long was a staunch believer in the open polar sea theory. Before his death Petermann convinced Bennett and De Long that by following the Kuroshio, a warm current flowing north from the Bering Strait, it was possible to reach the North Pole. Bennett promised to finance the project because he valued De Long as a leader. The vessel acquired for the project was christened the *Jeannette* after Bennett's sister, and the crew was joined by two reporters from the *New York Herald* which Bennett owned. The United States Navy selected De Long's crew from among its ranks and made available the necessary equipment.

The Navy ordered De Long to proceed to the North Pole. Bennett added the task of searching for Nordenskiöld, who was sailing the Northeast Passage, to their duties. Not for the reason that Nordenskiöld was missing, but to create more excitement and to make use of the reporters sent along on the voyage. Livingstone was not actually missing either when Bennett sent Stanley to Africa.

212 The last great English polar expedition, to Smith Sound, was led by the experienced George Nares, who as a lieutenant had taken part in the search for Franklin in 1850–1852. The expedition failed. The men fell sick with scurvy because the leadership had learned nothing from Rae or the Americans. The vessels were too large, there were too many men and the sledges were too heavy. Neither did a daily grog ration help it to succeed. In fairness to Nares it must be said that he terminated the expedition after one year. (JOHN NURMINEN FOUNDATION)

213 Although the British expedition of 1875–1876 led by George Nares did not fulfil its aims it continued the mapping work begun by Kane and Hall in the areas of both the north-east corner of Ellesmere Island and the north-western tip of Greenland. Markham's sledge party was only able to progress 30 miles from the Joseph Henry Peninsula on its journey to the North Pole. On the other hand, Aldrich's party mapped 250 miles of the coast of Ellesmere, and Beaumont's party charted the north coast of Greenland all the way to the Sherard Osborn fjord. Markham did however achieve a new northerly record. (JOHN NURMINEN FOUNDATION)

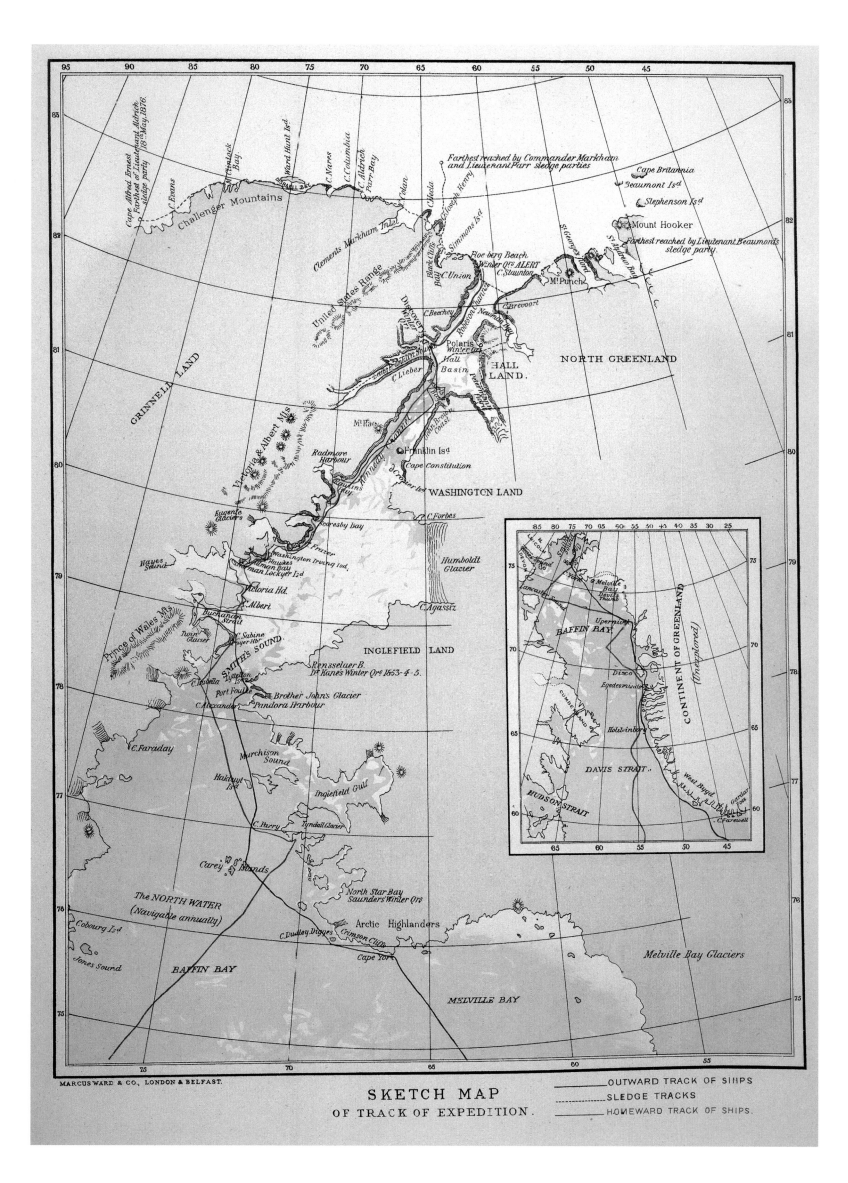

SKETCH MAP

OF TRACK OF EXPEDITION.

_____ OUTWARD TRACK OF SHIPS
- - - - - - SLEDGE TRACKS
_____ HOMEWARD TRACK OF SHIPS.

MARCUS WARD & CO., LONDON & BELFAST.

214 Nares' expedition's vessel the ALERT was able to sail along Robeson Channel between Ellesmere Island and Greenland as far as latitude 82° 28' north. No ship had ever got this far before. The picture shows the ALERT on a March night in 1876. Because it was feared that the ice would take the ship with it, the ALERT is anchored to the shore by a chain. The purpose of the barrels was to prevent the chains from becoming frozen to the ice. In summer 1876 the ALERT broke free and sailed back to Portsmouth.
(JOHN NURMINEN FOUNDATION)

De Long sailed from San Francisco in July 1879 and after passing through the Bering Strait continued north-west along the coast of Siberia. At Kolyuchinskaya Guba De Long learnt that Nordenskiöld had wintered there the previous winter. The *Jeannette* continued north and on 4 September its crew saw an island which was given the name Herald. They did not manage to go ashore to winter on the island, but drifted towards the north-west.

Towards the end of the year they approached Wrangel Island. The island was still visible in January when the ship was imprisoned in the ice and could only stay afloat with the aid of pumps. The spring and summer of 1880 brought no relief, as the ice kept its firm grip on the *Jeannette*. The current changed direction and in November 1880 they were in the same place as they had been in spring. They were trapped and losing hope of reaching open water.

In spring 1881 the *Jeannette* approached the New Siberian Islands. The first island was named Jeannette Island. A few days later they saw Henrietta Island. On 12 June the *Jeannette* was crushed by the ice off the north of the island. De Long abandoned the ship, which sank the following day. The men escaped onto the ice, which was drifting north. Dragging sledges and boats, they travelled south and in July reached the third of the New Siberian Islands. They went ashore on the island, which is now known as De Long Island, and, at the beginning of August, sailed south from there towards the River Lena delta in three vessels – two cutters and a whaler.

On 12 September a storm broke out and De Long lost sight of the other boats. One of the cutters sank and nothing was ever heard of her again. After two weeks the whaler, commanded by an engineer, George Melville, reached the Lena estuary, where the group were rescued by local hunters. De Long's cutter had already reached the Lena delta two days earlier, but fortune did not favour them. Most of the men died of hunger and exhaustion. De Long sent out a two-man advance group to seek help, but the Tungus did not understand what the men wanted.

Only when those seeking help arrived at Bulun and met Melville was a rescue party sent north. The help came too late. De Long died on 30 October after making the final entry in his diary. Twenty of the *Jeannette's* 33-man crew died.

In 1875 Karl Weyprecht suggested an international polar year, an idea that was implemented seven years later. The year was held between 1 August 1882 and 1 September 1883. New Arctic scientific stations were set up and exploration expeditions were organised as part of the programme.

One of the expeditions was that financed by the United States government and led by Adolphus Greely to Lady Franklin Bay on the east coast of Ellesmere Island in August 1881. The *Proteus* left 25 men at a cove to build the Fort Conger research station at Discovery Harbour. The expedition planned a research programme and sledge journeys to Ellesmere island and the north coast of Greenland.

Lieutenant James Lockwood's party set out for the north, broke Markham's record and progressed to Lockwood Island, located at latitude 83° 24' north. It exceeded Markham's northernmost point by 90 miles. Others of Greely's parties charted Ellesmere Island in the springs of 1882 and 1883.

The supply ship, the *Neptune,* which was ordered to bring fresh supplies to the expedition, did not succeed in reaching Lady Franklin Bay in summer 1882. Neither was the vessel sent to pick up Greely successful in sailing to Fort Conger the following summer. In August 1883 Greely made his way, as instructed, towards Smith Sound. On reaching the sound he wintered at Cape Sabine and looked for the supplies left by the supply ship and relief party, but found only one small container. Supplies ran out during the winter and hunting trips were so unsuccessful that 16 men died of hunger and scurvy, one committed suicide and one was executed for continuously pilfering food. Only seven men were alive when Winfield Schley's expedition reached them at the end of June 1884, after having found a message left by Greely on one of the islands.

NANSEN – SCIENTIST AND ADVENTURER

Hardly a single Arctic explorer has been as versatile as was Fridtjof Nansen. He was a combination of scientist, writer and statesman, but also a bold adventurer who was prepared to take great risks. By training he was a zoologist. As a 21-year-old, Nansen took part in a seal-hunting voyage in Arctic waters and got to know both the Arctic and its fauna. A good hunter, he enjoyed the voyage even though the vessel the *Viking* was occasionally beset off the east coast of Greenland – or perhaps for that very reason.

On his first expedition Nansen observed things that would later affect his actions. Branches and trunks of trees had stuck in the ice drifting with the current past the coast of Greenland. Where had they come from? No forests grew in Greenland, Iceland or Spitsbergen. The forested northern coasts of Scandinavia were free of ice, and the driftwood that had ended up in the sea could not have come from there to the east coast of Greenland or the north of Spitsbergen where Nansen had found them. The wood must have come from the rivers of Siberia. If they had come from Siberia they had travelled through a polar sea. The earth that was stuck to the ice could perhaps tell of their origin.

Greenland's peaks had enchanted Nansen. He wanted to be the first to travel across Greenland. He believed that the best route ran from east to west; from the difficult-to-access east coast to the inhabited west coast.

One autumn evening in 1883 Nansen read in a newspaper that Nordenskiöld had found wide snowfields in Greenland's interior, over which the Lapps with him had been able to ski effortlessly. Nansen decided to cross Greenland on skis. And when the bleak and inaccessible east coast was behind him and in front of him were 'the fleshpots of Egypt' as Nansen put it, the plan would work. The participants would set out on a full-blooded advance, in contrast to their approach when travelling from the west to the east.

Christiania (Oslo) University unsuccessfully recommended the financing of the expedition to the Norwegian government, but it had no wish to support the expedition. Nansen received funds from Denmark and he set out in spring 1888. On reaching the east coast Nansen used up more time than he had calculated, having been driven almost 300 miles south of the place from which it had been decided to begin.

The expedition endeavoured to make its way along the coast to the north for two weeks and only reached the coastal mountains in mid-August. To avoid a northerly head wind – they were still considerably further south of the place from which the journey was due to start – they changed plans and made for Christianshåb instead of Godthåb. The change shortened the distance they had to cover, but did not make up for the weeks lost.

Nansen's decision proved successful. The light but fully loaded sledges pulled by the men withstood the strain of the journey, and skiing on the high ice sheet was easy. The most difficult part was to climb the eastern mountains and descend to the west coast. On the coast they built a boat from willow branches and pieces of their equipment, since it was impossible to reach Godthåb overland. In the leaking willow boat, sewed together with tent canvas, Nansen and Otto Sverdrup – who was also to become a polar explorer of note – rowed with willow-branch oars for six days to Godthåb. There they heard that they were too late for the last ship of autumn. Nansen and his companions were now given the opportunity to learn the Eskimo way of life for a whole winter before returning to Norway.

Nansen had got the idea for the next expedition before he had conceived the notion of skiing across Greenland. He relates having read Professor Mohn's article in *Morgenbladet*, in which he told of coming across parts of the wreckage from De Long's *Jeannette* on Greenland's south-west coast. Nansen wrote of the occasion thus: "It immediately occurred to me that here lay the route ready to hand. If a floe could drift right across the unknown region, that drift might also be enlisted in the service of exploration – and my plan was laid. Some years, however, elapsed before, on the 18th of February, 1890, after my return from the Greenland Expedition, I at last propounded the idea in an address before the Christiania Geographical Society."

Nansen decided to take advantage of the forces of nature rather than struggle against them like many explorers before him. There was a favourable ocean current to be sailed. True, the voyage would be slow. The *Jeannette* had first drifted for two years from Wrangel Island to New Siberian Island before being shipwrecked. The remains of the wreck were still to be found on the west coast of Greenland three years after the shipwreck. There can be no doubt about the origin of the find, since a list of provisions signed by De Long was found among the effects. Both Nansen and Professor Mohn came to the conclusion that the articles had travelled across the pole. After the shipwreck they had travelled an average of a good 2.6 miles a day. This speed corresponded fairly accurately with that of the *Jeannette* before it was shipwrecked.

The *Jeannette* was not the only evidence of a polar current. A wooden Eskimo sling, which must have drifted from the Bering Strait region of the Alaskan coast, was found near Godthåb. The Eskimos of the west coast of Greenland also used this type of sling to fire arrows at birds, but these were different from the one found in the sea. The driftwood observed on Nansen's first voyage must have travelled with the same polar current, because some of it was identified as a species of tree which grew in Siberia. In addition, small creatures and minerals originating either in Siberia or the Bering Strait region were found in the mud of icebergs on the Greenland coast. In other words '...a current flows at some point between the Pole and Franz Josef Land from the Siberian Arctic Sea to the east coast of Greenland."

Nansen decided to build a vessel which was small and strong but big enough to take food and coal for a dozen men for five years. The ship was fitted with both a powerful engine and sails. Above all, the ship had to be able to withstand the pressure of the ice. Therefore it was built with such slanting sides that if squeezed by the ice it would be lifted up. No great changes were needed, as the *Jeannette* had withstood the pressure of the ice for two years. It was intended to edge through the current by sailing from the Bering Strait to the New Siberian Islands. The sturdy ship was able to sail with the current for as long as there was enough open water. The most important requisites, according to Nansen, were warm clothes and plenty of food. If, unexpectedly, the ship were to sink, the crew had to have enough time to move onto the ice with their equipment. They would continue sailing south on the ice floe.

Scurvy was a bad threat – Nares' expedition had experienced its dangers a few years earlier. Nansen decided to ward off scurvy with a varied diet and he believed he would be able to supplement the diet, with fresh meat, particularly seal and polar bear, which were found well to the north. In an emergency, said Nansen, who was a doctor of zoology, they could catch small sea creatures.

Nansen hoped that he would drift with the current to the Pole, but he considered the journey's scientific contribution

just as important, even if he were to miss the Pole by a degree or two. At first his plan found favour in Norway. Colleagues and authorities from abroad on the other hand 'declared more or less directly, that it was pure insanity'. A year before setting out Nansen presented his plan at a meeting of the Royal Geographical Society in London. It caused a heated debate. Admiral Sir Leopold McClintock opened the discussion with the remark: "I think I may say that this is the most adventurous programme ever brought under the notice of the Royal Geographical Society." McClintock doubted that any ship could resist the pressure of the ice in the winter months.

216 Three routes are drawn on this map of the Arctic Ocean, which was originally an appendage to a book telling of the voyage of Nansen's FRAM. *Crosses mark the route along which the remains of De Long's* JEANNETTE *are assumed to have drifted to the coast of Greenland. It was this evidence which led to Nansen's conclusion that the North Pole could be reached by ship in spite of the ice. The* FRAM's *route to the mouth of the Olenek and the drifting ice is marked with a broken line. The dotted line shows the route of Nansen's and Johansen's skiing expedition towards the Pole and rescue on Franz Josef Land.*

(NASJONAL BIBLIOTEKET, OSLO)

215 Nansen drew this 'map' with his own hand immediately after his voyage. Its purpose is to describe, in simplified form, the idea of sailing with the ice. Nansen also presented the theory that the FRAM *rose up, like a piece of soap, when squeezed by the ice because of its round bottom, and was not crushed.*

(NASJONAL BIBLIOTEKET, OSLO)

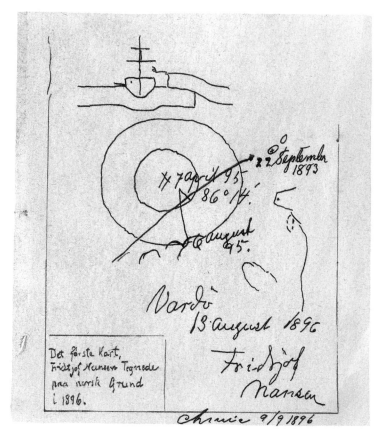

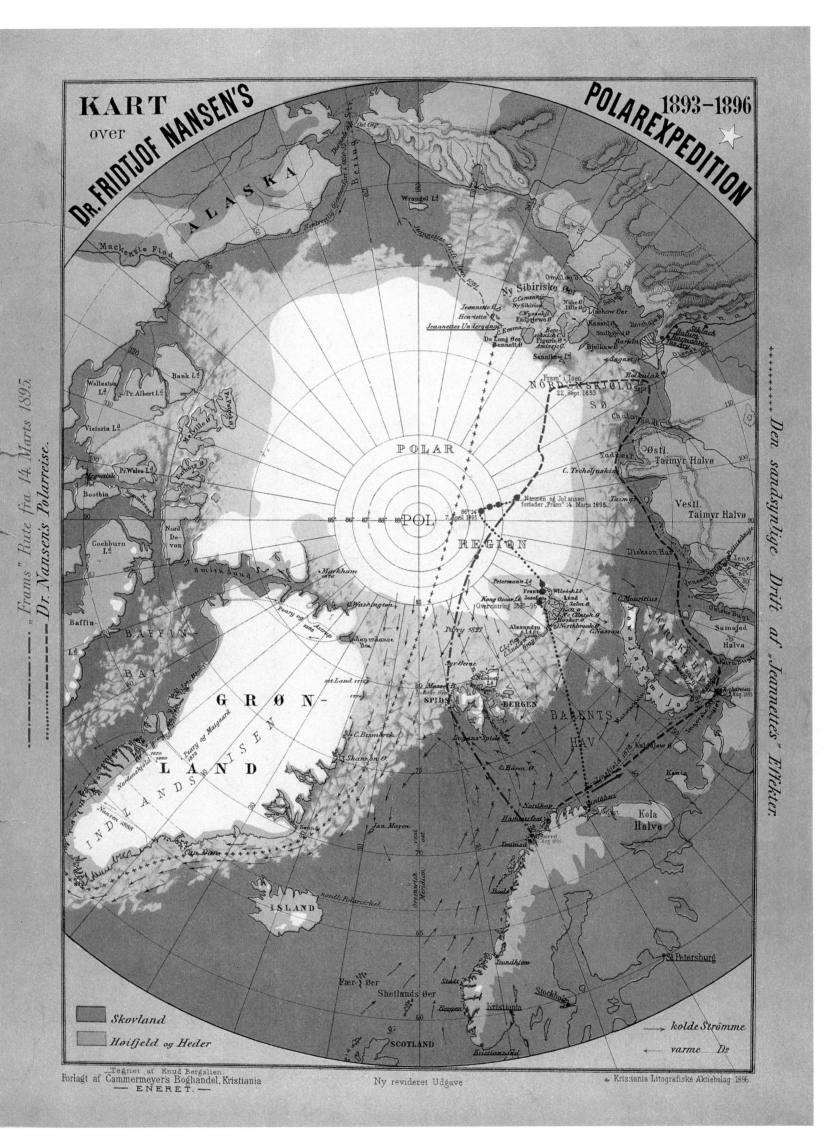

KART
over
Dr. FRIDTJOF NANSEN'S

POLAREXPEDITION
1893–1896

Skovland
Høifjeld og Heder

kolde Strömme
varme Dº

"Frams" Rute fra 14. Marts 1895.
Dr. Nansen's Polarreise.

Den sandsynlige Drift af "Jeannettes" Effekter.

Tegnet af Knud Bergslien.
Forlagt af Cammermeyer's Boghandel, Kristiania
— ENERET. —

Ny revideret Udgave

Kristiania Litografiske Aktiebolag 1896.

THE GRAPHIC

AN ILLUSTRATED WEEKLY NEWSPAPER

No. 1,398—VOL. LIV.
Registered as a Newspaper

SATURDAY, SEPTEMBER 12, 1896 WITH EXTRA FOUR-PAGE SUPPLEMENT
"The Riots in Constantinople"

Price Sixpence
By Post 6½d.

Mr. Harry Fisher, the botanist of the Jackson Expedition, who has returned home in the *Windward*, thus describes Dr. Nansen's appearance when met by Mr. Jackson on the ice near Cape Flora:—" Now we had time to look at Nansen, and it is certain his nearest relation would not have recognised him. He was absolutely black from head to foot. His light hair and moustache were jet black, and there was not a speck of white about his face or hands. He looked for all the world like a nigger, and the brightness of his eyes was accentuated by the grime of his face, which had been blackened by the blubber-smoke. His clothes—the one suit he had worn for fifteen months—were stiff with blood and oil with which his face and hands were also covered." As soon as ever the first greetings were over, Dr. Nansen and Lieutenant Johansen enjoyed what was to them a great luxury, namely, a good wash.

DR. NANSEN AS HE APPEARED WHEN MET BY MR. JACKSON IN FRANZ JOSEF LAND

217 Many Arctic explorers were adventurers who presented the reasons for their journeys as the carrying out of scientific research in order to gain funding. Fridtjof Nansen was first and foremost a scientist, but he too was drawn by adventure. In 1888 he was the first to ski across the Greenland continental glacier, and surrendered to the attraction of the polar sea in his vessel THE FRAM *between 1893–1896. When* THE FRAM *was driven past the Pole, Nansen attempted to ski there and set a new record. Nansen and Johansen had a way of miraculously surviving dangerous situations. Nansen later concentrated on science and the peace movement. He received the Nobel Peace Prize for his work in 1922. The picture is of Nansen on Franz Josef Land. It was taken by Frederick G. Jackson, in front of his hut.*

(JOHN NURMINEN FOUNDATION)

Vice Admiral Sir George Nares maintained that Nansen disregarded the adopted axioms of Arctic navigation. According to him, no ship stuck in the pack ice had ever succeeded in disengaging itself from the ice. In Nares' opinion the winds would have more influence on the way the ship drifted than would the sea current. However, Edward Inglefield, who had sailed in the region of Smith Sound, and the head of England's Hydrographic Office believed in Nansen's plan. The most crushing opinion was presented by Adolphus Greely, who had experienced how even a well-planned expedition could fail in difficult ice conditions. According to Greely "Dr. Nansen has had no Arctic service", his crossing of Greenland was no more polar work than the scaling of Mount St. Elias. Not a single one of Nansen's conclusions held good, and Greely predicted that his ship the *Fram* would end up in pieces, crushed by the ice.

To defend his plan in front of such an eminent body, a man had to have strong faith in himself and his research. He also had to be a good leader in order to get his men to follow him. Nansen had wanted only bachelors on his Greenland crossing, although one of the Lapps later turned out to be the father of five children. Volunteers came from all over the world, however, but only Norwegians were taken. The Master of the *Fram* was Otto Sverdrup, who already had a wife and one child. The *Fram*'s first engineer had seven children. Since there were several fathers of four among the men, Nansen must have had a greater belief in his success this time than he had in his Greenland days.

In addition to Nansen, the shipbuilder Colin Archer participated in the designing of the *Fram*. Because the ship's most important function was to withstand the pressure of the ice, she was built to meet this aim in spite of the fact that this would mean less speed and fewer sailing qualities. The vessel eventually became twice as big as Nansen had originally planned. The *Fram* was to "slip like an eel out of the embrace of the ice". To save fuel, in addition to a steam engine the *Fram* had a sail capacity of 600 square feet. Her interior was designed for wintering. The ship's bunks surrounded a saloon and she was equipped with more efficient insulation than was

usual. For lighting, an electrical generator was driven by steam when the ship was in motion and by a windmill when it was immobile in the ice. There were innovations in Nansen's menu too. In place of salted or smoked food, the *Fram*'s store of provisions contained fish, meat, vegetables and fruit preserved in hermetically sealed packs.

THE *FRAM* GOES FORTH

The *Fram*'s voyage was both a serious expedition and an exciting adventure. Many of those opposed to the voyage considered the adventurous aspect unsuitable for scientific work.

At first the journey went according to plan. The *Fram* sailed across the Barents, Kara and Laptev Seas to the New Siberian Islands, close to the place where the *Jeannette* had been shipwrecked thirteen year earlier. In September 1893 the ice locked the *Fram* into place; everything was going as Nansen had predicted. Under the pressure of the ice the *Fram* rose up. She drifted peacefully north and the crew immersed themselves in scientific research.

Nansen had time to think again. On 15 January 1894 he wrote in his diary: "The longer I wander about and see this sort of ice in all directions, the more strongly does a plan take hold of me that I have long had in mind. It would be possible to get with dogs and sledges over the ice to the Pole, if one left the ship for good and made one's way back in the direction of Franz Jozef Land, Spitzbergen, or the west coast of Greenland. It might also be called an easy expedition for two men."

"But it would be too hasty to go off in spring... and as I think it over, I feel doubtful if it would be right to go off and leave the others. Imagine if I came home and they did not! Yet it was to explore the unknown Polar regions that I came... and surely my first duty is to do that if I can."

Nansen was overcome with restlessness. He could not concern himself with the monotonous lives of the scientists when the polar ice sheets were waiting for adventure. He was not held back by fear but by a feeling of duty towards his men. When, on occasions, the *Fram* moved south, his mind was torn with disappointment. His main goal was even further away than before. He tried out a dog-team on the ice and found driving it a lot easier than he had believed. Skiing too was easy there. In five months the expedition had gained only one degree of latitude to the north, and in February its position was only slightly more than 80° North. Nansen calculated that in the worst scenario it would take him eight years before he got home.

In autumn Nansen's mind was clear. On 6 September the *Fram*'s position was 81° 14' North. Nansen wrote: "Why should not this winter carry the *Fram* west to some place north of Franz Josef Land?... and then my time has come, and off I go with dogs and sledges – to the north. My heart beats with joy at the very thought of it. The winter shall be spent in making every preparation for that expedition and it will pass quickly... If she (the *Fram*) could just reach 84° or 85°, then I should be off at the end of February or the first days of

March, as soon as the daylight comes... and the whole would be like a dance."

Nansen and Fredrik Johansen first left the ship on 28 February 1895. The *Fram* had by then already achieved a new record of 83° 47' North. She had also crossed Lockwood's northernmost point. But Nansen was twice forced to return to the ship. When, on 14 March, Nansen and Johansen finally left the *Fram,* she had already crossed 84° North. Nansen calculated that they could travel by dog team for 80 days if they fed the dogs to each other as food. The men had enough food for 100 days.

The journey took longer than Nansen had calculated. At the beginning of February the men had crossed 86°, but both they and the dogs were exhausted. The ice got worse than ever and Nansen was forced to give up his revised goal of 87°. According to Nansen's calculations, the journey to Petermann Land, as noted by Payer, was 260 miles; he did not know that Petermann Land did not exist. It was in fact over 220 miles to Cape Fligeli on Rudolf Land. On 8 February, Nansen and Johansen ate a banquet and turned back towards Franz Josef Land. The new record stood at 86° 13'.

On the return journey the ice conditions improved but they were slowed up by open leads. Nansen went the way of many of his predecessors: the ice drifted north and increased the length of the journey. On several days he calculated the actual distance travelled to have exceeded 20 miles. At the beginning of May the ice deteriorated again. The dogs were tired and hungry.

The pair drifted back and forth with the ice. The further south they reached, the more signs of life they saw: foxes, whales, fulmars and bear footprints. They did not find Petermann Land. At the end of May in front of them were only open channels. Progress was difficult and there were only seven dogs left. Nansen calculated the latitude as being a good 82°, but there was no land in sight. They made repairs to their kayaks since the amount of open water was increasing. They were forced to ration their food. They got fresh meat for the first time on 7 June when Johansen shot a gull.

On 22 June, as if from nowhere Johansen shot a seal and there was again sufficient food.

There were only two dogs left – both pets – when they saw land for the first time on 7 August. They were no longer able to feed the dogs. Johansen shot Nansen's dog and Nansen reciprocated by shooting Johansen's – previously they had not wasted ammunition on killing the dogs.

Clive Holland, who compiled a wide-ranging encyclopaedia of Arctic expeditions, considers Nansen's and Johansen's expedition a foolhardy adventure from which both survived with their lives thanks to extremely good luck.

In Holland's opinion Nansen should never have left the *Fram*. It was partly due to their carelessness and partly their misfortune that a fortunate coincidence led to their being saved on Franz Josef Land.

Discovering land was no guarantee that they were safe. Ahead of them was a long gloomy winter. They built a winter shelter, half underground, from a piece of timber, walrus

tusks, two walrus skins and six bear skins they had found. By hunting they got a great amount of fresh meat and planned to hunt more bears as the winter went on.

In winter, foxes gnawed through the skin roof of the shelter. In spring the bears returned, bringing a change of diet. There were 100 cartridges left for both the rifle and the shotgun. According to Nansen they would suffice for several winters still if necessary.

The men continued their trek south on 19 May 1896. They left an account of their journey and their plans at the shelter. On 24 May Nansen sank into the ice. Since he had skis on his feet and had hold of his harness he was able to strike his icepick into the ice and wait for Johansen to help. Johansen did not hear him and he began to shout as he sank ever deeper, frozen to the waist. Only then did Johansen notice that he had fallen and pulled him out.

A few weeks later their carelessly moored kayaks broke

218 The most dangerous and disputed question associated with Nansen's voyage was the ability of THE FRAM *to withstand the crushing of the polar sea ice. Some prestigious experts questioned Nansen's assumptions. Admiral McClintock believed* THE FRAM *would withstand the ice during the summer but not in the winter. Another explorer, George Nares, said that the form of the ship would no longer have any significance once the ship was gripped by the ice. The picture shows that Nares' prediction did not come true. A windmill turned the vessel's electric generator, producing energy while the ship's engine was not in use.*
(JOHN NURMINEN FOUNDATION)

my hat; we extended a hand to one another with a hearty: 'How do you do?' Above us a roof of mist, shutting out the world around... on one side the civilised European in an English check suit and high rubber water boots, well shaved, well groomed, bringing with him a perfume of scented soap, perceptible to the wild man's sharpened senses; on the other side the wild man, clad in dirty rags, black with oil and soot, with long, uncombed hair and shaggy beard black with smoke, with a face in which the natural fair complexion could no possibly be discerned ..." After a short conversation Jackson stopped and looked at the stranger with sharp eyes and asked: "Aren't you Nansen?"

On 26 July a ship arrived bringing fresh supplies for Jackson. Nansen and Johansen travelled with it to Vardö Harbour in northern Norway. From there Nansen sent telegrams to his wife, to Johansen's mother, to the relatives of comrades left on the *Fram*, to the King and to the Norwegian government. After a week he received a telegram in which Sverdrup informed him that the *Fram* had arrived at its destination. The vessel had continued to drift after Nansen had left her and, in November 1895, had reached its northernmost position of 85° 55'. In August 1896 the *Fram* had broken through the ice north west of Spitsbergen and set sail for Norway. By then her journey had lasted for three years.

Nansen made no more Arctic expeditions, but his scientific career continued. His unsurpassed historical work on Arctic exploration *In Northern Mists* appeared in English in 1911. Nansen later dedicated himself to the peace movement. Between 1920–1922 he served as a League of Nations commissioner and after the First World War arranged the repatriation of 400 prisoners. In 1922 Nansen was awarded the Nobel Peace Prize. If, as Clive Holland speculates, a Godly hand saved Nansen from his own madness, he used the extra days of his life for the good of man.

loose and were drifting quickly away. The kayaks had already drifted a great distance and the wind was driving them further when Nansen plunged into the icy water and swam after them. By the time he had at last caught up with one of the two kayaks, which were tied together, Nansen was so stiff with cold that he hardly could climb onto them.

On 17 June 1896 Nansen said he had heard a dog bark and decided to go and look, since he had heard two reports the previous day which could have been gun-shots. He followed the fresh tracks of what he thought now to be those of a dog, now of a fox, until he thought he heard voices. In a moment he had made out a black point, a dog, between the ice floes, followed by a larger creature – a human being.

Nansen thought that the man might be the Englishman Frederick G. Jackson, who had planned an expedition to Franz Josef Land: "...as I drew nearer I thought I recognised Mr. Jackson, whom I remembered once to have seen. I raised

THE *FRAM* – ONE OF A KIND

The Fram, affectionately referred to as "Norway's own ship", was the best polar ship of its time, the only one designed to be surrounded by the ice and move with its flow. Its design was ground-breaking, at least in comparison with Western ships built up to that time. The ship's creators, polar explorer Fridtjof Nansen and legendary shipbuilder Colin Archer, together with Otto Svedrup, who had gone to sea when still a young lad, followed guidelines based on the experience of native peoples in the ship's design: it is pointless to resist the forces of nature, one should rather adapt as best one can.

In the magazine 'Naturen' in 1890, Nansen made public for the first time his plan to travel to the North Pole using a ship that would be riding the sea currents attached to the ice.

This ship would have to meet many requirements. Its hull below the waterline should be rounded and tapering, and the planking carvel-built. Moreover, the ship would not be too heavy because it should have to be capable of 'sliding' upwards under the pressure of the ice. A large, heavy ship would not be able to sail the channels in the ice. In addition, it should also have simple, easy-to-handle rigging and an engine. It would have to accommodate 12 men and all the food and gear they would require for five years. Nansen made no mention of a piano, but one was acquired for the *Fram*'s second voyage; Svendrup's voyage north-west from Greenland. The ship ended up quite a bit larger than Nansen had envisaged: her carrying capacity had grown to 402 net register tonnes when the *Fram* was launched in Larvik in 1892. This was well up from the 170 tons of the preliminary design.

In Nansen's opinion it was not reasonable to expect a round-bottomed ship to be able to ride the waves very well, so he gave up on those properties. "It is better to roll the waves on open waters and possibly suffer some seasickness than to perish in the ice on the Arctic Ocean", he said. His ideas of speed and beauty were equally bleak.

Archer was the right man for the job of designing the sturdiest wooden ship so far built. He stated, however, that it was nec-essary to pay attention to form as well as structure. "It is sometimes expedient to dodge a blow rather than catching it."

The *Fram*'s strength was startling: the three-layered side planking was 32.5 centimetres thick on the waterline (7.5 cm + 10 cm of oak and 15 cm of greenheart), but with the pitch pine insulation between the layers and the oak ribs that were 25–28 centimetres thick, all in all the sides were 70–80 centimetres thick. The ship's stem was assembled from three oak logs and was 1.25 metres thick, and the double oak frames were 56 centimetres thick. The 3–4 cm gap between the frames was filled with a mixture of pitch and sawdust.

The saloons and cabins had roofs that were 40 centimetres thick. In order to ward off the cold and moisture, the roofs were built of sandwich construction: a 10-centimetre-thick layer of oak on top and, below it, air, felt, spruce panelling, linoleum, reindeer fur, more spruce panelling and linoleum, air and yet more spruce. Ten layers in all (or eleven if you count the white paint on the ceiling).

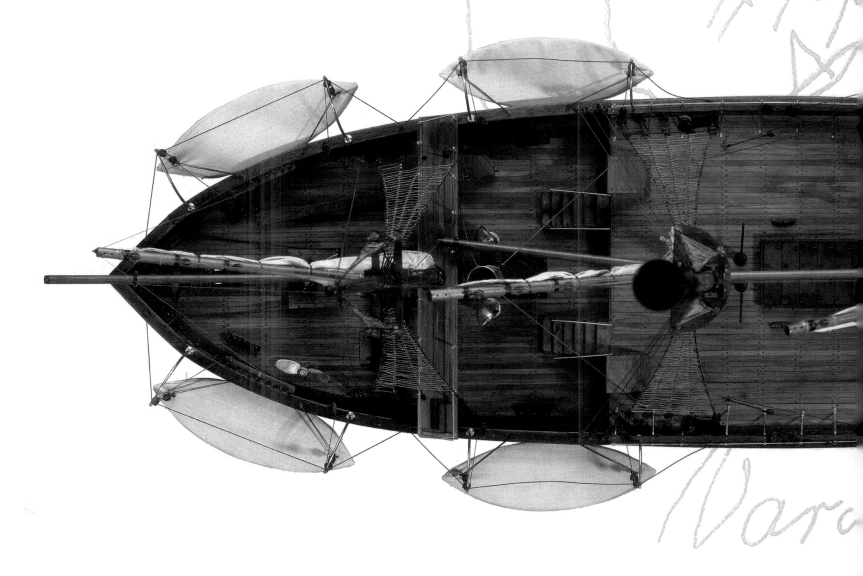

Archer's meticulous planning was evident in every detail. Not one bolt penetrated the entire depth of the sides, because that would provide a conduit for cold and damp to enter the ship. The greenheart 'ice-skin' was attached with nails and hook bolts and could be torn off without causing damage to the hull proper.

Because conditions were harsh and the crew small, the rigging had to be as simple to use as possible – which meant that it had to be manageable from the deck. Archer decided that the rigging master Christian Jensen should rig the *Fram* as a fore-and-aft sail schooner. The foremast carried two square sails that could be moved up and down with Archer's personal version of a Dutch snaumast. The main topmast could be lowered – probably also a Dutch idea. Using this feature it was possible to decrease the sail area when the wind grew in force and increase it again when the weather calmed down. The lookout, or crow's nest, was perched 32 metres above sea level at the top of the mast. The mizzenmast was a 'polemast' made of a single tree trunk.

The *Fram*'s main measurements were: overall length 39 metres, waterline length 34.5 metres, length of keel 31 metres, beam at the waterline 10.4 metres, maximum beam 11 metres, average depth 5.25 metres, draught 3.75 metres (with a displacement of 530 tonnes), draught 4.75 metres (with a displacement of 800 tonnes), weight 420 tonnes, maximum cargo 380 tonnes, net register tonnage 402, sail area 600 square metres. She had a 220-horsepower steam engine.

Nansen thought that the stern was the weak spot of polar ships as the rudder and propellers were prone to be damaged in the ice. The *Fram*'s rudder and propellers were designed to be easily raised onto the deck for safety or repairs into what were called wells. A windmill was built on the deck to turn the generator (when there was no wind, manpower was used). The voyage lasted for three polar winters, so there was a need for months of electric lighting. When the ship reached open water on 14 August, 1896 it was already summer and the sun was shining in the polar region day in, day out.

219 and 220 Explorer Fridtjof Nansen's vessel was the best polar ship of its time. Colin Archer had taken into account the extreme cold of the region in its design, suitability for drifting with the ice being the number one criterion. The hull of the FRAM *was reinforced. Due to its hull's convex shape and evenly-boarded surface, the ship would slide upwards when squeezed by the ice. It made three successful voyages to the polar region.*
(JOHN NURMINEN FOUNDATION)

DARKNESS FALLS
ON THE NORTH POLE

AFTER NANSEN THE NATURE OF THE RACE FOR THE NORTH
POLE CHANGED. REACHING THE POLE WAS NO LONGER AN
INTERESTING ADDITIONAL CHALLENGE BUT AN END IN ITSELF.
NEW TECHNOLOGY ALSO BECAME A FACTOR.

ANDRÉE'S FLIGHT

Salomon August Andrée, a Swedish engineer, had decided to
conquer the North Pole by flying there by balloon. The dangers involved were no less than those of Nansen's journey. The
advantage of a balloon was that it made it unnecessary to cross
the almost impassable ridges and furrows of the polar ice. But
there were many dangers to counterbalance this single advantage.

The winds of the Arctic are fierce and capricious, and neither of these characteristics makes travelling by balloon any
safer. Reaching the North Pole required taking advantage of
a south wind and a north wind getting back. The only com-
fort was that at the North Pole all winds blow from and to the
south. Andrée could not have known where he would drift
upon reaching the Pole.

A balloon's airworthiness is reduced by the formation of ice
on its surface or on its basket. The length of the journey too
– from Spitsbergen to the Pole is about 600 nautical miles or

*221 In 1885 the German Justus Perthes published a beautiful
polar map of high standard; on it is collected the geographical
knowledge of that time. Later the east coast of Greenland was
drawn more precisely, as were the western regions of Elles Sea
Island. The later discovered Svernaja Zemlja in the north of the
Taimyr Peninsula is completedly missing. The routes of important
Arctic expeditions are marked on the map.*

(JOHN NURMINEN FOUNDATION)

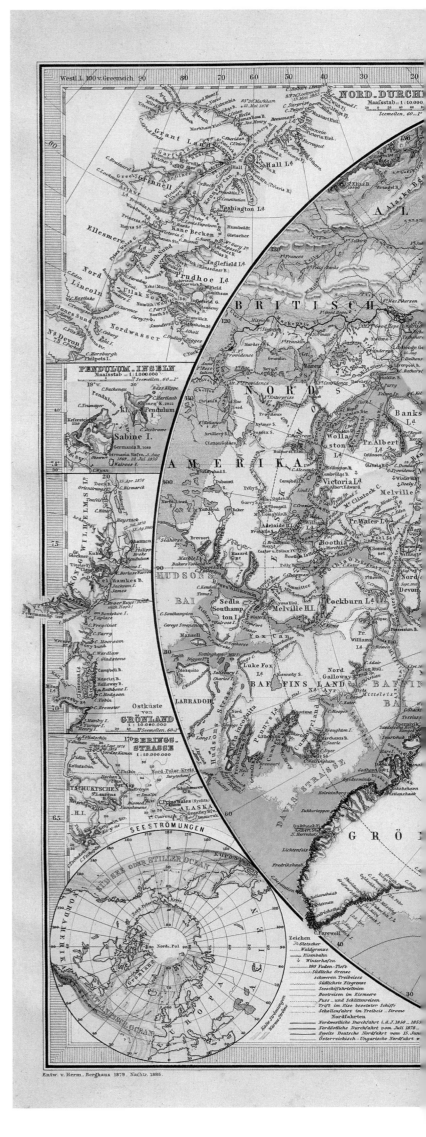

NORD-POLAR-KARTE
Breiten-Maafsstab 1 : 20.000.000

GOTHA: JUSTUS PERTHES.

Die Beobachtungs-Stationen f. d. J. 1882/83 sind farbig unterstrichen.

Gest. v. H. Eberhardt u. A. Kramer.

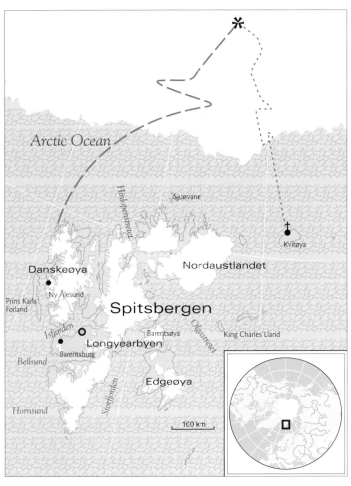

222 On 11 July 1897 Andrée gave the order to cast off the ropes and the journey by air balloon to the North Pole began. Three days later the ÖRNEN made an emergency landing on the ice. For the next three months Andrée, Strindberg and Fraenkell trekked over the ice and ended up at Kvitøya, where 33 years later the men's last camp and their bodies were found. (ANDRÉE MUSEET)

223 Andrée's flight was a bold, even reckless attempt that ended in tragedy. After their flight the expedition made it to White Island, where they perished, probably of an illness brought on by trichina. (PATANEN)

over 622 miles – increases the risks. Neither are there many options with regard to a forced landing place when a balloon loses its airworthiness. In the worst case, landing in the middle of a desert of ice would mean a walk of hundreds of nautical miles, difficulties of which Andrée was well aware, having read his predecessors' journals.

Andrée attempted the journey for the first time in summer 1896 from Spitsbergen. While he was waiting for a favourable wind, Sverdrup's *Fram* returned from the Arctic Ocean. A few days after Sverdrup's arrival Andrée was forced to give up the idea. He decided to return the following summer, however.

In spite of the risks Andrée succeeded in finding enough patrons, among them Alfred Nobel, King Oscar of Sweden and A. E. Nordenskiöld, who had sailed the Northeast Passage. All he sought from the Pole was fame. There were no scientific aims attached to the expedition. Indeed Andrée had had no scientific training.

At the end of May 1897 Andrée returned to the north-west coast of Spitsbergen, to Danskoya. On 11 June he, Nils Strindberg and Knut Fraenkel took to the air in their balloon the Örnen (eagle). The balloon rose with difficulty to the height of less than one hundred metres. Its drag lines, intended to control the height and steer the balloon, came off and it rapidly lost height and brushed along the surface of the sea. The crew succeeded in getting it to rise again by throwing out 200 kilos of ballast. After this the balloonists were completely at the mercy of the wind, unable to steer. Once the Örnen had disappeared, with the exception of a message brought by a carrier pigeon, nothing was heard of it for over 30 years. According to the message everything was going well.

In 1930 a Norwegian expedition reached Kvitøya or White Island, about 62 miles north-east of Spitsbergen. The group went ashore and discovered the remains of a camp, a canvas boat and, at the bottom of the boat, a diary. On the book's flyleaf was written: "Sledge journey 1897." Ten metres from the boat lay a body and a coat in whose pocket was Andrée's diary. Later searches also found the remains of other members of the expedition and all the diaries telling of its various stages. A film from the expedition's camera was successfully developed.

At first the balloon had drifted north-east. The travellers sent out carrier pigeons, the first four of which never reached their destinations. Although the crew threw out more ballast, the balloon was tending to lose height. Cold winds compressed it and reduced its carrying capacity. The next day, with the wind becoming calmer, the balloon fell to a height of 30 metres. An easterly wind rose and carried it slowly west, and the basket began to trail along the ice. Lightening the balloon no longer lifted it and, with the wind subsiding, it landed for the night. The next day the warmth of the sun lifted the balloon into the air again, but the flight came to an end on the ice on 14 June in spite of the fact that Andrée and company had already thrown out their equipment. Their location was slightly beyond latitude 82°, mid-way between Spitsbergen and Franz Josef Land. The flight had lasted for 65 hours and taken the balloonists more than 185 miles north-east of Danskoya.

The expedition members gathered up their equipment and began the trek east towards Franz Josef Land and Cape Flora, where Jackson had left a shelter and some food. Their equipment was good but they themselves were inexperienced. Their sledge was so heavy that it required all three men to haul it. For this reason they were obliged to abandon some of their equipment and food. The ice carried them west faster than they could make their way east. At the beginning of August, after thirteen days of trekking, they were forced to give up

their aim of reaching Cape Flora. They struck out west for the Seven Islands, an island group to the north of Spitsbergen. Their progress became more difficult and they were forced to discard more of their equipment; they did not yet have the heart to do without their port wine. Although the men were tired and suffered from sundry complaints, thanks to bears they had enough food. The weather grew colder. With land getting closer both the amount of open water and game increased.

In September their diary entries became fewer. The ice carried them south and it was no longer possible to get to the Seven Islands. It was already beginning to look as if they would have to spend the winter on the ice when, on 17 September, White Island appeared on the horizon. Its coasts looked so sheer, however, that they did not think they would be able to get ashore. They built an igloo on the ice and in addition to bears they succeeded in hunting seals in such number that their food would suffice until the following spring.

As September turned into October the ice-floe drifted to the shore of the island and the igloo was flooded with water. They were obliged to move their camp onto land. After this it is impossible to read Andrée's diary as the water had ruined the new entries. According to Strindberg they moved to live in a tent under the rocks. Strindberg's last entry on 17 October 1899 reads as follows: "At home, morning 7.05 am".

Strindberg must have been the first to die since only he was buried. Andrée and Fraenkel probably died at the same time as their bodies were found side by side in the tent. When, on 18 August 1898. A. G. Nathorst arrived in the waters of White Island in his vessel the Antarctic to look for Andrée's expedition, there were no signs of life on the island. Nathorst went ashore with two companions, but the recent snow had covered the signs and, with the onset of winter, they had no time for more thorough explorations.

It is still not certain what Andrée and his companions died of. Various theories have been put forward. Those who found their bodies suspected that they had died from cold. They had been sleeping in the same three-man sleeping bag. They had perhaps also lost all hope of surviving, which would have increased their susceptibility to the cold.

Vilhjálmur Stefánsson, one of the most noteworthy explorers of the 20th century, did not believe in this assumption. In his opinion, Strindberg had drowned and Andrée and Fraenkel had died of carbon monoxide poisoning soon after. In addition, Stefánsson believed the end to have come before 10 October. According to a Swedish analysis the above quotation from Strindberg's diary was written before the journey, not on White Island. Strindberg had believed that they were at home again on 17 October.

Later Swedish research has been able to identify the calcareous crust on the remains of polar bear flesh, which proves that the bears shot contained trichinae. Trichinae do not die if the flesh is raw or undercooked. The symptoms of trichina are diarrhoea and fatigue, ailments which, according to the diary, afflicted the men on Andrée's expedition. Trichina can

224 *Robert Peary had a will and a physique of iron. Between 1886–1909 he made eight separate expeditions to Greenland and the North Pole area. He had only one aim: to be the first to reach the North Pole. He developed a system by which (at the age of 53) he succeeded even though he had had seven toes amputated. A few days before his achievement Peary wrote of how he would like people to see him: "a portrait of me in deer or sheep coat… face unshaven… Have Foster color a special print of this to bring out the grey eyes, the red sun burned skin… frosted eyebrows, eyelashes, beard."* (JOHN NURMINEN FOUNDATION)

225 *and* 226 *These two maps depict both Peary's voyages and his disputed discovery, Peary Land. Although Peary's most celebrated achievement was the conquering of the Pole, his most noteworthy accomplishments are concerned with the mapping of North Greenland and the north coast of Ellesmere Island. On his expedition of 1892, Peary tells of discovering a channel running through the north-east tip of Greenland. Although incorrect, the observation was not surprising. Lauge Koch's beautiful four-colour map shows that there is a lake in Wandel Valley, which lies between Independence fjord and J. P. Koch fjord, which pushes inland from the west. Only narrow isthmuses lie between the lake and both fjords. As the route map shows, Peary never descended the mountains to explore the valley but came to his conclusion without exploring the terrain. The route of his later journey went even further from the supposed Peary Channel, so it is completely understandable that he was not able to correct his mistake then.* (MATTI LAINEMA)

lead to death; under the conditions experienced on White Island its effect was probably fatal.

In addition to Andrée, the American journalist Walter Wellman attempted to reach the Pole five times without success. He made his first attempt by dog sledge in 1894 from Spitsbergen but, because of a late start, he only got to about latitude 81°. He made a second attempt four years later. For his third attempt Wellman chose an airship equipped with an engine, even though before Andrée's failure he had decided on a balloon. According to Wellman, Andrée knew after his first attempt that his balloon was not good enough. In spite of this, pressure from the media forced him to save his reputation and set out on a new journey.

Wellman tried to get to the Pole in an airship three times; in 1906, 1907 and 1909. The first time he could not even take off. The second attempt from Spitsbergen ended in a forced landing on the sea ice. The aim of the third attempt was the North Pole, but when the airship's stabilisers were broken Wellman and his companions were forced to return to Spitsbergen.

PEARY STEPS ONTO THE STAGE

When Robert Peary announced his intention of conquering the North Pole in 1898 he had already made three journeys to the Smith Sound area in north-west Greenland. Peary was an engineer by training and he had been fascinated by the Arctic since childhood. On reaching the age of 23 he found employment at the United States Coast and Geodetic Survey Bureau. A year later he wrote to his mother: "I do not wish to live and die without accomplishing anything or without being known beyond a narrow circle of friends."

Peary joined the navy and took part in the planning of the proposed canal across Nicaragua. This endeavour remained in the shadow of the Panama Canal project and Peary concentrated on Arctic expeditions. He wanted to be the first man to cross Greenland's inland ice. His first expedition in 1886 was still a reconnaissance.

Peary travelled to Greenland alone. At first he had language difficulties, but he managed to get hold of an umiak to transport his equipment from Godhavn on Disko Island to

MEDD. OM GRØNL. BD. 130. NR. 1. [LAUGE KOCH].

Pl. 17 A.

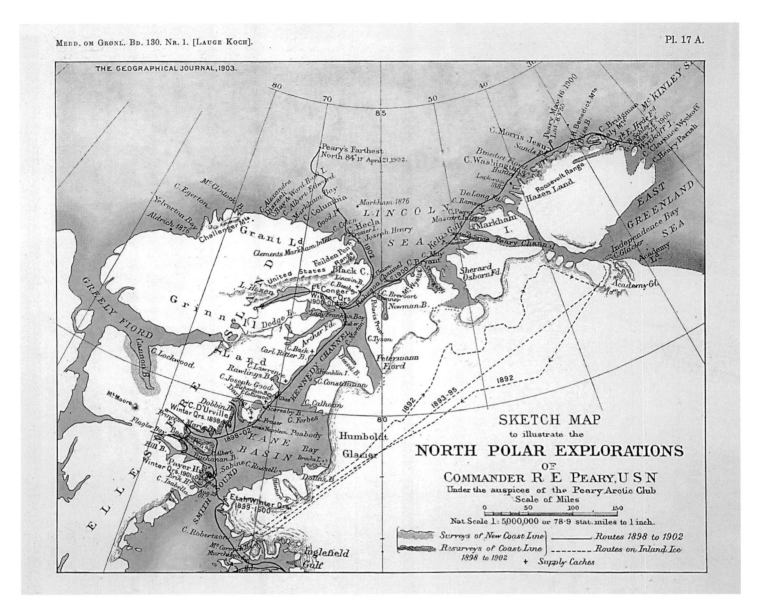

THE GEOGRAPHICAL JOURNAL, 1903.

SKETCH MAP
to illustrate the
NORTH POLAR EXPLORATIONS
OF
COMMANDER R E PEARY, U S N
Under the auspices of the Peary Arctic Club
Scale of Miles
0   50   100   150
Nat Scale 1: 5,000,000 or 78·9 stat. miles to 1 inch.

Surveys of New Coast Line ———— Routes 1898 to 1902
Resurveys of Coast Line -------- Routes on Inland Ice
1898 to 1902 + Supply Caches

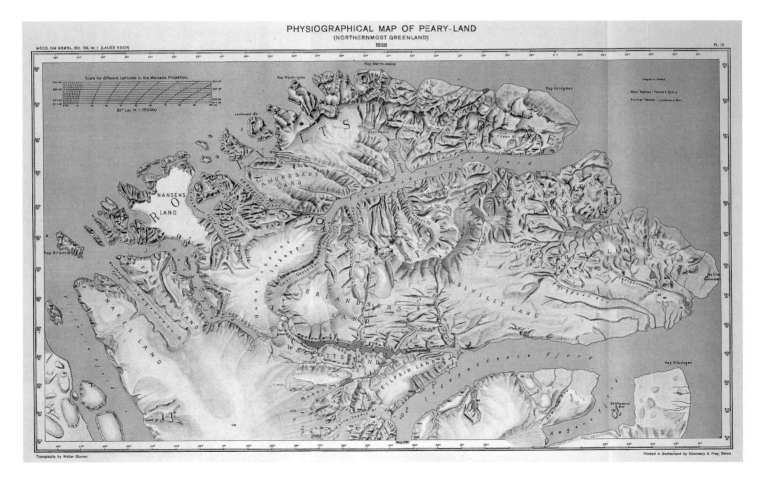

PHYSIOGRAPHICAL MAP OF PEARY-LAND
(NORTHERNMOST GREENLAND)
1938

MEDD. OM GRØNL. BD. 130. NR. 1 (LAUGE KOCH)

Pl. 13.

Topography by Walter Blumer

Printed in Switzerland by Kümmerly & Frey, Berne

The Northern Lights are a colourful natural phenomenon peculiar to polar regions. They are most clearly visible in a zone a few hundred miles wide, 1200–2000 miles from the magnetic Poles. It is here that the Northern Lights form elliptical rings at a height of 62–200 miles. These oval lights can only be seen in their entirety from a satellite; they cannot be seen by the human eye during the daytime, and at night, too, they are only partially visible.

To the north of the Arctic Circle the Northern Lights blaze for 200 days a year. The best time to see them is late on cloudless nights in February-March. Further south the lights are rarely seen; in the Mediterranean, for example, they can only be seen a couple of times a decade.

In Asia there are written descriptions of the Northern Lights dating from about 2600 BC. The Bible also speaks of them. They were given their scientific name, *aurora borealis* (*aurora australis* in the southern hemisphere), in the 17th century. After 1621 they were hardly seen at all for a hundred years. During that time there were no observations of sun spots, either. Coincidence or not, the earth's weather was also a little confused at that period. The well-known time known as the Maunder Period ended in a spectacular display of the Northern Lights on March 17, 1761.

The Northern Lights have religious connotations for all the peoples of the north – Scandinavians, Finns, Eskimos, Indians, the peoples of Siberian Russia and the Baltic countries, and even the Mongolians.

The Finnish word for the Northern Lights, *revontuli*, means "fox fire". According to folk tales, a fire-fox running in the north rubs its side against a Lapland fell, causing sparks to fly off into the sky to form the Northern Lights.

Although the Northern Lights have been explained as being the tail of a fox or the spout of a whale, and caused by icebergs or volcanoes, explanations connected with the spiritual world are even more common. The Eskimos considered them to be guiding lights which the spirits used to lead the dead to heaven. They called the flashing lights the "dance of death". They also believed they could hear the Northern Lights. The Greenland sagas tell that the sound they make comes from the spirits as they trample down the hardened snow in the sky. Imitating the sound by whistling draws the lights closer. Unlike the Eskimos, the Sami people feared and respected the Northern Lights and considered whistling to them dangerous.

The first scientific explanation for the lights was put forward in the 18th century by the astronomer Sir Edmund Halley, who is best known for the comet named after him. According to Halley the strands of the Northern Lights are formed by par-

ticles reacting with the earth's magnetic field, causing them to stream along the field's lines of force. The vault-like effect is caused by perspective. In 1741, the Swedish astronomer Anders Celcius also believed the Northern Lights to be connected with the earth's magnetic force.

Polar expeditions have supplied a great deal of information on both the climate and magnetism, and have played a key role in investigating the Northern Lights. Nordenskiöld observed the lights in northeastern Siberia while wintering on his ship the *Vega* in 1878–79. During the first Polar Year (1882–83) they were investigated systematically at a number of measuring stations in the Arctic area.

At the beginning of the 20th century the Norwegian professors Kristian Birkeland and Carl Störmer revolutionised the whole field of research into the Northern Lights. According to Birkeland, the lights involve the system of electric currents extending into near space. In the area where the Northern Lights are seen, electricity flows both horizontally and along the earth's magnetic lines of force. The lines of force of a magnetic field are nowadays called the Birkeland Lines. In the late 1950s it was ascertained that the particles flowing through the system are mostly electrons.

Simply explained, the Northern Lights come into being when the earth is bombarded with electrons. When they reach a denser atmosphere they collide with oxygen and nitrogen atoms and release some of their energy to charge them. Once the atoms' charge becomes lower, their energy is converted into light, similar to the neon molecules in fluorescent strip lighting.

The colours of the Northern Lights are the result of different properties of the particles in the earth's atmosphere. Their precominantly yellow colour and the deep red of their upper extremities are caused by oxygen molecules, while the nitrogen molecules in the air are responsible for the crimson at their lower edge and the scarcely discernible areas of violet.

227 Southern Finland witnessed a performance several hours long and of exceptional beauty in autumn 1999. The northern spectacle covered the entire sky around two in the morning. The Aurora Borealis took on an arc-like shape, imitating a brightly-glowing crown in the heavens. The powerful crimson illumination was a rare occurrence, coming about from changes in the excitation states of nitrogen atoms in the atmosphere. (Pekka Parviainen)

228 The best places to see the northern lights are close to and north of the Arctic circle. Usually they perform a shadow-like dance across the sky in a greenish, phosphorescent glow. (Matti Rikkonen)

Pakitsoq Fjord on the mainland. From there he climbed onto the ice sheet with the Dane Christian Maigaard. Within two weeks they had pushed their way 100 miles inland and to a height of 7500 feet above sea level.

In spite of its brevity the expedition gave Peary an inkling of the difficulties involved on Arctic journeys. With the exception of A. E. Nordenskiöld's skiing expedition three years earlier, which he made with his two Lapp companions and whose length was questionable, this was the longest expedition onto the Greenland ice sheet so far. Peary's experience grew. He learned the advantages of small scale expeditions and of using snow-shoes and skis.

Peary continued his canal research in Nicaragua 1887–88. An important event from the point of view of his career was his engagement of the black American Matthew Henson as his servant. Peary found Henson in a hat shop when buying a sun helmet in 1887. Henson was working as an assistant in the shop, but prior to that he had had six years' experience at sea. After this Henson was with Peary on all of his journeys.

Nansen was the first man to cross the Greenland ice sheet. Peary heard of the matter in Nicaragua and it upset him. Nansen had already planned his expedition in 1883, in other words before Peary's first journey, but in Peary's opinion that was of no significance. He wanted a monopoly of his chosen challenge. Nansen's success changed his plans, and his next journey of 1891–1892 was into northern Greenland, whose coast was still largely unexplored.

Peary financed the first journey himself. The American Geographical Society and other foundations as well as private persons were responsible for equipping the second. A research group from the Philadelphia Academy of Natural Sciences took part in the expedition. On the basis of his predecessor's experiences, Peary decided on a small group helped by Eskimos. The model became just as American as had the American route to the Pole from Smith Sound. Peary left Spitsbergen and Franz Josef Land to the British, Germans and Austrians.

The expedition headed for the Thule area of northern Greenland, and its aim was to explore both the north and north-east coasts. To Peary's mind his journey was more important than his civilian work. He wrote to his mother that he was seeking "...an enduring name and honour...social advancement... and make powerful friends...I want my fame now while you too can enjoy it" The expedition consisted of seven people. Along with Peary were his wife Josephine, Eivind Astrup, a young Norwegian (a good skier), Doctor Frederick A. Cook and Matthew Henson.

Their first destination was Inglefield Bay in North Greenland, north-east of Smith Sound. On the sea voyage, Peary broke his leg, and it took weeks for it to mend.

Small-scale journeys were made during the winter, and the expedition proper began in May 1892. Peary's only companion was Eivind Astrup. When the escort group returned they had three sledges and 14 dogs. Peary and his companion continued towards the north-east. At the beginning of July they arrived at a mountain on the east coast, from which they could distinguish a frozen bay. Peary named it Independence Bay (nowadays Independence Fjord) in honour of 4 July.

Peary mapped the terrain to the north, from the top of Navy Cliff. He thought that the fjord stretching to the east from Robeson Channel continued through Greenland to the mouth of Independence Fjord. However, this channel, named Peary Channel, did not exist. This misleading information was later to surprise those who had believed it. In his own book Astrup makes no mention of it. Peary did not complete his crossing of Greenland because he did not continue to the coast but turned back having seen it. Peary's entire journey was 1100 miles, however – more than four times longer than Nansen's. Peary also took twice as much time on his expedition.

Peary and Astrup hunted musk-ox and secured a supply of food for the return journey. This was probably Peary's most valuable journey in terms of scientific results. Nansen too – who would scarcely have considered himself Peary's competitor – sent Peary a telegram congratulating him signed "Your admirer, Fridtjof Nansen."

In spite of the prestige that the expedition brought Peary, he lacked a financier for the next journey. He raised the greater part of his funds from lectures, which he gave dressed up in his furs while Henson cracked his whip above the heads of five Eskimo dogs in the background. Peary returned to Greenland the very next year with his wife Josephine, Astrup, and Henson. Frederick Cook had promised to go, but he backed out when Peary refused to give him permission to write ethnological articles based on the experiences of the previous journey. The expedition's base was Anniversary Lodge which Peary had built on the coast of Inglefield Bay. It was there that Jo gave birth to Peary's daughter Marie.

The expedition to the north of Greenland began in spring 1894, but Peary was forced to cut it short. Meanwhile Astrup, who had recovered from an illness, set out without Peary's permission to explore the unknown coastal areas of Melville Bay. As far as exploration is concerned this remained the best contribution. Peary wanted to ensure that his supporters still had faith in the future, and set out to look for the 'iron mountain' which John Ross had described and from which the Eskimos had made their knives and harpoon tips for generations. Most of the group returned to the United States in August but Peary and Henson remained for a further year.

The expedition of spring 1895 was a dress rehearsal for the method Peary was developing. Along with Peary and his two companions there were six Eskimos and 60 dogs. The Eskimos, who were functioning as a support party, returned after six days. After five weeks Peary reached Independence Fjord. When they arrived they had only nine dogs and food for 14 days left. The time was to be used primarily for the acquisition of food. Nothing new was discovered during the journey. Returning home was a race against death. They returned after a three-week struggle with just one dog.

Peary returned home with two meteorites – part of the Eskimos' "iron mountain" – six live Eskimos and the remains of a few Eskimos dug up from the ground. He sold the meteors and the bodies of the Eskimos to the American Museum of Natural History. Peary had brought the live Eskimos at the request of the famous anthropologist Franz Boas – Boas had in fact only asked for one. The Eskimos were a great exhibit in New York until all but two fell ill with pneumonia and died.

PEARY'S FIRST ATTEMPT AT THE POLE

In 1898 Peary set out for Greenland again at the expense of his wealthy patrons, the Peary Arctic Club. His expedition had two ships, the *Windward* and the *Hope*. After the *Hope* had returned home, the *Windward* succeeded in making her way into Smith Sound, along Ellesmere Island to Cape D'Urville. This time Peary stayed in the Smith Sound region for four years. During his first winter he went north to Fort Conger, Greely's former base. Peary saw Sverdrup, who had arrived at Ellesmere Island, as a new competitor. Perhaps this is why he timed his journey for the coldest time of winter and got his toes frozen, seven of which had to be amputated.

In spring 1900 Peary made his way north-east with Henson and one Eskimo, following the coast of Greenland. He passed the point at which Lieutenant J. B. Lockwood had turned back on Greely's expedition and continued for more than 155 miles. Greenland's northernmost peninsula became Cape Morris Jesup, after Peary's most important patron. This journey was Peary's second important achievement in exploration. He could return to Fort Conger a satisfied man, to make preparations for his new attempt towards the North Pole.

The departure from Fort Conger took place in April 1901. Neither the men nor the dogs were in very good condition, and after an eight-day march Peary turned back. Six of the Eskimos that Peary had taken with him died during the following winter. The doctor had resigned his post as the result of a quarrell and Peary did not permit him tend to the Eskimos. In spite of the incident Peary managed, with Henson's help, to persuade four Eskimos to go on the journey to the Pole.

A new attempt began in April 1902. It was just as difficult to cross the sea ice as it had been in Markham's time in 1876. For sixteen days Peary and Henson fought for every mile with the Eskimos. Their northernmost point was latitude 84° 17' north. The expedition covered only some five miles a day. At their turning point they were still 400 miles from the Pole. At that rate they would still have needed 150 more days to get to the Pole and back.

Peary was despondent. He wrote in his diary: "The game is off. My dream of sixteen years is ended... I have made the best fight I knew. I believe it has been a good one. But I cannot accomplish the impossible." Peary was already 46. Edward Parry had ended his career as an explorer at the age of 37. On the other hand John Ross was still looking for Franklin at the age of 73. Franklin was 62 when he died. Both Ross and Franklin, however, concentrated on leading their expeditions.

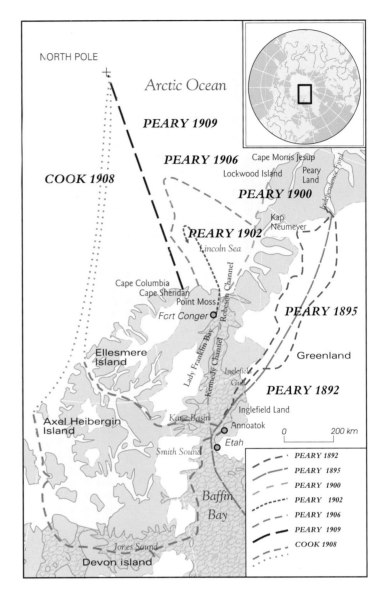

229 Marked on the map are Peary's most important expeditions to the north-east and north coast of Greenland, his attempts in 1902 and 1906, and his last expedition in 1909, when he probably got to within 60 miles of the North Pole. The route Cook claims to have taken to the Pole is also marked. (PATANEN)

THE DUKE OF ABRUZZI AND UMBERTO CAGNI

During the two years that Peary had been making preparations, he had gained a new competitor who nevertheless respected Peary's 'monopoly', and chose Franz Josef Land as his base. Luigi Amadeo di Savoia, Duke of the Abruzzi, was the first Italian Arctic explorer after Giovanni da Verrazzano who had sailed the waters of Newfoundland in 1524. The Duke was an experienced mountaineer, and his group consisted of Italian army officers and men accustomed to conditions in the Alps. The crew of the *Stella Polare* were Norwegians.

The journey started from Rudolph Land, an island to the north of Franz Josef Land. The *Stella Polare* succeeded in passing latitude 82° but sprang a leak in the autumn of 1899. The crew and equipment were landed. The Duke's hands were

frozen and two of his fingers had to be amputated. He named Umberto Cagni leader of the polar party. The bad luck continued, as Cagni was forced to return from his first attempt after two days, having sunk through the ice.

On 11 March 1900 ten men, thirteen sledges and 102 dogs set out; there were no Eskimos with them. The Duke of the Abruzzi accompanied Cagni for a while. Two support parties turned back at the end of March and only four men continued the journey. The problems were familiar: open leads, pressure ridges, snowstorms and fatigue. Now and then they cut their way with axes through the ridges formed from ice floes, but time went by and their supplies were dwindling. Cagni eventually lowered his aim to 86° 30'.

On April 25, after toiling for 46 days, they reached their goal. With tears in his eyes, proud of his accomplishment, Cagni erected a bamboo pole with a flag at the turning point. "Long live Italy! Long live the King! Long live the Duke of the Abruzzi!" Cagni placed three tin tubes in the snow, each containing a paper and information on his final degree of latitude: 86° 31', which after checking improved to 34'. The party had food for 30 days left.

The return journey took the tired men almost 60 days. By the time they had reached their camp they had only seven of their 49 dogs left. They had averaged about six miles a day, slightly more than Nansen and Johansen. They arrived back in good health but were told that their first support party had disappeared. Cagni and his companions broke the record

230 The picture shows Peary and his companions making soundings five miles south of the Pole. Peary's soundings extended to a depth of 1500 fathoms or almost two miles, without reaching bottom. The value of Peary's sea-bed soundings has been questioned. THE NATIONAL GEOGRAPHIC did however take the soundings as proof that Peary reached the Pole. The depth of the sea bed could only be measured reliably with the coming of submarines, and more easily with the aid of satellite technology.
(JOHN NURMINEN FOUNDATION)

previously held by Nansen and Johansen by a good half a degree, but they never returned to the race. Peary only heard of Cagni's record when he returned home. He still had – as one of Peary's biographers said – the northern record for the western half of the globe in his possession.

BACK INTO THE FRAY, WHATEVER THE COST

Peary returned to the army. His contemporaries had already forgotten him and the younger generation considered him a man who in his youth had had an unfulfilled dream. Some of Peary's supporters had also lost faith. As businessmen they were afraid that they would 'throw good money after bad'.

Peary was ordered to make a study of the European style of military barracks. He arrived in Europe when Scott was breaking new records in the Antarctic. On his return journey Peary began to plan a new expedition. He lacked both time and money. Sponsors had interpreted Peary's journals to mean that reaching the Pole was improbable. But two backers promised him $100,000 in all to build the kind of ship that would help him to move the base further to the north. Peary appealed to a sense of national pride by naming the new vessel the *Roosevelt*. Theodore Roosevelt was happy to accept the honour.

Peary thought talk of linking scientific exploration with polar expeditions to be nonsense. He did not believe that anyone would care about scientific achievements if the alternative was being the first to reach the Pole. Peary did not understand Nansen or Sverdrup. He considered others to be like him and expected them to pursue the same goal. Peary wanted to be the first. His associates were the tools for him to pursue that aim. Perhaps this is why many came into conflict with Peary. But his firm resolve and staunch belief appealed to others.

Peary's new attempt was again to be his last. He no longer believed that a small group could reach the goal. Peary's method resembled the Italian model but was considerably more complicated. Advance parties were to open up a way forward and many men and dogs were required to take care of the supplies. It was difficult to increase the speed signifi-

cantly above the ten miles a day that the Italians achieved on their best stretches. Instead it was essential to be able to extend the travel time.

Peary had acquired new travelling companions. The captain of the *Roosevelt*, Robert Bartlett, his confidant, had experience of Arctic navigation. Henson's role would be more important than before since, in addition to Bartlett, there were only three other members of the expedition with Arctic experience. Ross G. Marvin was Peary's new assistant.

The *Roosevelt* set off from New York in July 1905 and at Etah took on 40 Eskimos and 200 dogs. As expected the ship was able to navigate as far as Cape Sheridan at the north-east corner of Ellesmere Island, on the very edge of the polar sea.

During the winter a disease, apparently caused by poisonous whale meat, killed 80 of the dogs. Hunting went well and 73 musk-ox and 27 caribou were shot for food on the expedition. Peary left Cape Sheridan as early as 21 February.

231 Although Peary's sledges had been designed to cross the ice fields and ice blocks, pulling an over-200 kilo (500lbs) sledge over ridges demanded a great deal of exertion of both the men and the dogs. In addition to the ridges of ice they also had to contend with leads which slowed down their progress. At its worst Peary's average speed was only five miles a day; at its best, according to Peary, thirty miles. (John Nurminen Foundation)

Twenty-eight men and 120 dogs pioneered a route and supported Peary's main group, which would continue alone to the Pole. Peary estimated that he would need 100 days for the entire journey. From Point Moss, Ellesmere's furthermost headland, it was 422 miles to the Pole. Their aim was an average speed of ten miles a day, twice as much as in 1902.

The complex system could easily be upset. Henson told Peary that the journey would succeed if "God, wind, leads, ice, snow and all the hells of this damned frozen land are willing". Henson was usually the one breaking a trail. The ice hummocks were, if possible, higher than ever. Other parties followed to smooth the path for Peary when he, the last to set out, left Point Moss on 6 March. All the parties would spend the night in igloos built by the spearhead party. This saved on both equipment and time. When he arrived, Peary's overnight accommodation was ready.

On 26 March 1906 Peary caught up with the party in front of him, which had come to a stop at a big lead. Although the expedition had passed latitude 84°, it had drifted too far to the west. Peary believed this to stem from Henson's tendency to go to the left when negotiating leads and rough ice. Wally Herbert suspected that the mistake was due to the fact that the expedition had been heading out from Point Moss using the Cape Sheridan magnetic variation. Whether it was a mistake or overcompensation for the drift, the error was probably Peary's. The journey was again taking longer than Peary had estimated. The average speed of the early stages of the journey was only five miles a day – as in 1902.

On 2 April, after waiting for a few days, Peary crossed a lead even though the ice covering it was very thin. He was followed by Henson and the Eskimos. Those who could have confirmed Peary's coming achievement were left on the other side of the lead.

The seven-day delay was a blow to the men, whose time was running out. After two days a blizzard broke out and stopped further progress. On 12 April Peary was able to calculate his position again. The party's latitude was slightly more than 85°, but the storm had driven them sixty miles east, that is to say to the longitude of Cape Sheridan again. Peary knew he had lost his chance of reaching the North Pole, but he desperately needed to set a new northerly record. Without it his chances of returning once more were slight. In order to break Cagni's record Peary would have to advance ninety miles to the north of his Storm Camp.

Peary was not in the habit of conceding defeat. He continued north. Everything turned for the better. The storm had levelled out the surface of the ice and the wind bludgeoned the ridges into terraces. There are no entries in Peary's diary for these days, but he claimed to have made at least sixty miles progress in two days. On the third day he covered 20 miles.

On the fifth day Peary, having calculated his latitude, announced that they were very close to Cagni's record. This means that he had either overestimated his mileage or that the drifting ice had eaten away some of the journey. On the sixth and seventh days they were forced to cross leads. On the next day, 21 April 1906, Peary informed his men that they had

232 Luigi Amedeo di Savoia, Duke of the Abruzzi, was a 26-year-old naval lieutenant when, in 1900, he equipped an expedition whose aim was to conquer the North Pole. The Duke was an experienced mountaineer, who developed the spearhead party technique later to be used by Peary. He also planned to use balloons to make the sledges lighter, but had to abandon the idea, as he had to give up command of the expedition due to frost bite.
(JOHN NURMISEN FOUNDATION)

reached 87° 06'. He had beaten Cagni by less than a degree. Immediately after the measurement had been made, Peary set out on the journey back to the previous night's camp.

Some doubted Peary's achievement from the outset. At the leads Peary had declared the latitude to be 86° 30'. He gives no information on the mileage of the last three days' journeys. In his book *The Noose of Laurels* Wally Herbert elaborated his suspicion that Peary would not have been able to cover the roughly 40 nautical miles, more that 70 kilometres, from his camp to the turning point and back on his final day, particularly because negotiating the barriers would normally increase the mileage by 20–25%. Herbert believed Peary to have created a new record, but not to have reached the latitude he had declared.

The return journey was difficult. The expedition arrived at Cape Neumeyer on the north coast of Greenland on 12 May, that is after 52 day's travelling. The return journey had thus lasted five days longer than the journey there. Again they had to fight against pressure ridges and leads. A westerly wind drove them further east. Peary realised that they had come to that part of north coast of Greenland that he had mapped in 1900. Their food was running out but they managed to catch some game. They also rescued one of the parties driven to the coast not knowing its position.

After a week's rest Peary set out to explore the still-unmapped north coast of Ellesmere Island. Lieutenant Aldrich of Nares' expedition had charted much of Ellesmere's north coast in 1876, and Sverdrup the west coast in 1900. Peary wanted to fill in the blank area left in between. He took three Eskimos with him. The coming of spring made the journey difficult, and after Cape Columbia the party wandered about the slopes covered in a blanket of mist.

At the end of June Peary arrived at the coast which separated Nansen Strait from Sverdrup's northernmost point, Thomas Hubbard Peninsula, at the tip of Axel Heiberg Island. A high island which Peary named Cape Colgate was seen off Grant Land, the northern part of Ellesmere Island. From its peak he saw land to the north-west which he christened Crocker Land. At his turning point he wrote: "With my feeling of satisfaction is a feeling of sadness and regret that this may be the end of my Arctic work … Twenty years last month since I began, and yet I have missed the prize."

At the end of July Peary arrived, tired and wet, at Cape Sheridan, his clothes and shoes in tatters having waded back through the melted waters – not easy for a man without toes. The next day Peary told Bob Bartlett, who was worried because the *Roosevelt* had been driven onto the ice, lost one of her propellers and damaged her rudder: "We have got to get her back, Captain. We are going to come again next year".

Nobody has ever seen Crocker Land after Peary. His discovery went the way of John Ross's Croker Mountains. Peary was mistaken a second time, since Peary Channel did not exist either. Another strange thing about Crocker Land is that Peary does not speak about it in his diary, in his record hidden in a cairn, nor in the telegrams he sent home and to his backers. It only comes to light in an article Peary wrote after his February journey and in his book *Nearest the Pole*. It may have been that Crocker Land was needed to increase the dramatic effect so that Peary could make one more attempt.

THE POLE AT LAST?

Peary returned in summer 1908 to prepare for his final attempt. He had 21 Eskimos with him, but when the wives and children who followed them are included their number grew to fifty. Almost 250 dogs were taken along. The *Roosevelt's* captain was Bob Bartlett. Others included Matthew Henson and Ross Marvin, Peary's assistant, as well as two new members, Donald MacMillan and George Borup. For MacMillan the journey was his first but not his last Arctic expedition.

Peary had refined his system. The expedition was divided into seven parties, of which six were auxiliary. The task of the supporting parties was to open up the trail, carry the food and provide other necessary help. The main party led by Peary would be the last to follow the marked trail. At the point when less than 200 miles of the journey remained, the pioneer party would set out on their lonely final push towards the North Pole. The auxiliary parties would set out on their return journey at five-day intervals, making sure that the return trail remained open. Their best dogs would be given to the parties that continued, and when necessary the men would also be replaced by fresher individuals. Six of the parties were led by white men, the seventh by Henson. Every party had the assistance of two or three Eskimos, each of whom drove an eight dog team.

Peary was the only explorer who took full advantage of the centuries of knowledge accumulated by the Eskimos. Peary used animal furs as clothing like the Eskimos. Peary's men did not carry sleeping bags, but slept in their warm fur clothes. The igloo was more suited to the weather than tents. Peary's sledges were developed further from Eskimo sledges and they were driven by the best professionals, the Eskimos themselves.

On 28 February Bartlett set out with his team to open up the trail. He was followed by Borup. The other parties, Peary among them, followed a day later. The first party was opening a track and dictating the speed; for this reason more was demanded of them. After Bartlett it was Henson's task to break the trail, then Marvin's. On 4 March the main party caught up with Bartlett's team, which had come to a halt in front of a wide expanse of open water. The expedition waited for six days before the water froze over and they dared to cross it. Information on their progress was given to Marvin, who was on a visit to Cape Columbia.

Soon Dr. Goodsell returned and, following him, MacMillan, whose heel had been frozen and required treatment. When Borup left he had travelled, according to Peary, just as far as Nansen had done in making his way from his vessel the *Fram*. Nobody wanted to be the first to return. Everyone wanted to reach the North Pole, especially Bartlett, whom Peary had taken along with the promise of accompanying him to the Pole.

After Borup it was the turn of Marvin, who had exceeded Cagni's earlier achievement. Peary and his companions were never to see Marvin again. The Eskimos informed them that he had drowned. The truth was revealed only years later. Marvin's Eskimos had taken offence at his orders and killed him. One of the Eskimos confessed to the murder when he was converted to Christianity. When Marvin had left, Bartlett was again breaking the trail, his goal being to reach latitude 88° within five days.

Because of the light nights it was possible to change the plan of operations. The first party built an igloo, spent the night in the shelter and started moving only when the main party had caught up with it. The men arriving went to sleep in the igloo. The system facilitated the flexible distribution of resources; it was simple to provide the spearhead party with an undamaged sledge or a fresh man.

On 28 March Peary caught up with Bartlett after an unusually short period. Before them was more open water. A crack in the ice floe opening up nearly destroyed the expedition. Only by dashing out of the igloos and abandoning their camp did they avoid being hurt. The water froze over in two days and they continued their journey. On the last day of March, one day before Bartlett's departure, a north wind got up. The wind blew the ice south and ate into the distance covered.

On the morning of the first day of April Bartlett walked north in the hope of reaching latitude 88°. He was disappointed to find that his measurement showed the latitude to be only 87° 47'. He had been breaking the trail for 19 days, Henson for four and Marvin for only two.

Peary took Henson with him on the last stage of the journey: "He has... always been with me at my farthest north... Henson was the best man I had with me for this kind of work, with the exception of the Eskimos, who, with their racial inheritance of ice technique and their ability to handle sledges and dogs, were more necessary to me... Henson was almost as skilful as the Eskimos... The second reason [for taking him along] was that Henson... would not have been so competent as the white members of the expedition in getting himself and his party back to land." Some of Peary's severest critics have stressed a third reason still. With Bartlett, his last reliable witness, gone, only Peary was competent to judge the position of his turning point.

After Bartlett had turned back the distances that Peary covered daily grew longer. On the second day of April Peary believed he had travelled some thirty miles although "to be conservative" he estimated it at twenty-five. The next day he covered twenty miles, but then the conditions improved and he made twenty-five miles again. Peary now calculated his position to be nearly at latitude 89° and, in his diary, hoped for three good days' journeys.

Peary was so sure of his success that he was already dreaming of what the victory would bring. He wanted a portrait of himself in his furs, face unshaven. To increase the effect he wanted the picture "to bring out the grey eyes, the red sun burned skin, the bleached eyebrows and beard, frosted eyebrows, eyelashes, beard". Kane had received $7500 for his book, Nansen $50,000. Peary imagined his book, magazine articles and pictures bringing him $100,000. He decided to name his last camps after his predecessors and the members of the Peary Arctic Club. The northernmost should be named Camp Jesup. He even thought about his mausoleum. He hoped to be given the rank of Vice Admiral and the pension that went with it. England, he wrote, knighted its heroes, and gave them considerable rewards.

In his book Peary wrote that on 5 April he took a sun sighting which gave a latitude of 89° 25'. There is no mention of this in his diary or papers. Henson made no mention

of it either. At a Congressional Subcommittee Peary denied having made a measurement that day.

The following night the party set out with Henson walking ahead, breaking a trail. The Eskimos followed. According to Henson, Peary rode in a sledge even though he was often the first to start walking in the mornings. Normally within an hour, Henson had caught up with Peary and took the lead. At 10 o' clock on the morning of 6 April the tired

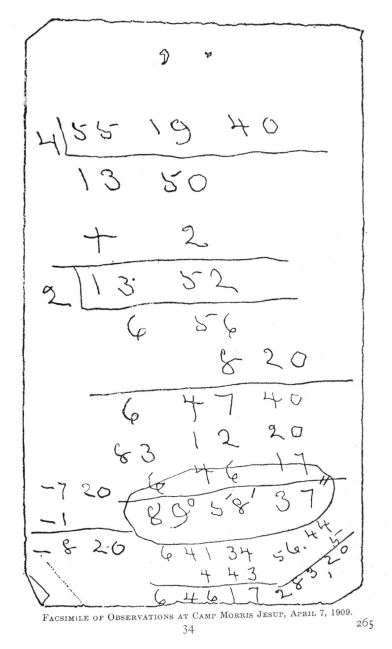

FACSIMILE OF OBSERVATIONS AT CAMP MORRIS JESUP, APRIL 7, 1909.
34   265

233 The calculation was an addenda to Peary's book. This has, as he puts it himself, readings of the degrees of latitude at Camp Jesup. The series of figures show how Peary, on the basis of four readings, calculated his position, made allowances for the deviation and arrived at the reading 89°58'37". The calculation has not convinced any of Peary's critics of the fact that he reached the North Pole, let alone that he measured the attached readings.

(JOHN NURMINEN FOUNDATION)

234 Peary and his companions at the North Pole. The picture was probably taken at Camp Jesup which was about 4 miles from the Pole since, according to Henson, he was not with Peary on the final measuring leg outside the camp. From left to right: Ooqueah, Ootah, Henson, Egingwak and Seegloo honouring the stars and stripes while Peary takes the picture.

(JOHN NURMINEN FOUNDATION)

Henson stopped, realising angrily that Peary did not intend taking him to the Pole. He even had time to build an igloo before Peary arrived at Camp Jesup. Peary measured the position of the camp as 89° 57'. The journey to the Pole was only three nautical miles, six kilometres.

In the evening Peary set out to make more measurements with the Eskimos. He returned to Camp Jesup at 6 o'clock on the morning of 7 April, took another set of observations at the camp, and set off again, returning to Camp Jesup at mid-day to make his final observations. The atmosphere was described by Henson in an interview in 1910:

"In about an hour the Commander returned. His face was long and serious. He would not speak to me. I quietly learned from the boys accompanying him that he had made observations a few miles further on.

'Well, Mr Peary,' I spoke up cheerfully enough, 'we are now at the North Pole, are we not?'

'I do not suppose that we can swear that we are exactly at the Pole,' was his evasive answer.

'Well, I have kept track of the distance and we have made exceptional time,' I replied, 'and I have the feeling that we have now just about covered the 132 miles since Captain Bartlett turned back. If we have travelled in the right direction we are now at the Pole. If we have not travelled in the right direction then it is your fault'."

Peary made no reply to this. Henson also describes his attempt to congratulate Peary. Peary did not grasp Henson's bare extended hand but instead lifted his own hands to protect his eyes, and gave instructions to be awoken in two hours.

Henson believed Peary to be angry because Henson was the first to arrive at Camp Jesup. Peary's behaviour might also have stemmed from tiredness. On arriving at Camp Jesup, Peary had been travelling for ten hours. After two or three hours sleep he travelled about 40 miles to make observations with the Eskimos. Peary must have been close to a mental and physical breakdown, particularly if the expedition was in fact farther from the North Pole than they should have been on the basis of the distance they had travelled.

Gordon Hayes wrote in his book *The Conquest of the North Pole* published in 1934 as follows: "There have been many critics of Peary's claims, on both sides of the Atlantic, and all disinterested inquirers have come to the same conclusion – that he did not reach the Pole; by this it may be understood that he was never within 50 or more miles of its position...Peary said that he returned from his camp at the Pole to latitude 87° 47' N in not more than 56 hours. This is a distance of 150 st. (130 geog.) miles, apart from deviations over the pack ice and the drifting of the floes. Hence a man 53 years old either walked considerably more than 75 m.p.d. for 2 days ... or he never came near to the Pole".

Wally Herbert, who was the first to cross the Arctic Ocean from Point Barrow in Alaska to Spitsbergen with a dog team, tried, in his own analysis, to take the effects of the winds and sea currents into account, and came to the same conclusion as Gordon Hayes. Whereas Peary claimed to have travelled – without taking observations – the whole time along longitude 70°, which runs by way of Cape Columbia, Herbert estimates him to have, in fact, been carried by the ice drift to the west and to have reached to within about one degree of the Pole at best. Camp Jesup's longitude was thus 135° West. The camp was then 55 nautical miles, or less than one hundred kilometres, from the Pole.

This is also suggested by Henson's statement about the position of the sun "at the North Pole" in an article in 1910: "The sun in that latitude does not cross the sky by travelling overhead. It goes around the horizon in a circle, starting low down and gradually rising for a little distance, and then sinking back towards the horizon, but never reaching it." This description, however, corresponds to the motion of the sun about a degree away from the North Pole. In fact, at the North Pole the sun's distance from the horizon is the same for the entire period of 24 hours.

235 The sextant was the basic tool for ascertaining one's location. The instrument could be described as the more advanced cousin of the octant. Sextants made in the latter half of the 19th century were technically and optically very precise. In favourable conditions, latitude could be measured to the minute of a degree. The closer one got to the pole, however, the more difficult it was to use, as the variations in the height of the sun were small and difficult to measure.
(JOHN NURMINEN FOUNDATION)

NAVIGATING ON THE ROOF OF THE WORLD

Sailors in the North Atlantic had recourse to goniometry, i.e. angular measurement of heavenly bodies, to determine their position. As early as the 16th century, Barents measured his degree of latitude with an astrolabe and cross-staff to an accuracy of about one degree. Defining a longitudinal position was difficult until the end of the 18th century, when Harrison's chronometer solved the problem. Ever since the Renaissance, ships had been steered with the help of a compass. Position was estimated on the basis of direction and distance covered. When sailing the remotest corners of the northern seas, Hudson Bay or Baffin Bay, for example, navigators came up against a new problem; declination, i.e. the compass variation from true north due to the proximity of the magnetic North Pole.

The further east or west one progressed and the longer the journey lasted, the more difficult it became to determine lon-

gitude. The first men to sail the Bering Strait, from Dechnyov to Tsirikov, could only estimate longitude, and it was only with Cook, and his chronometer, that it was possible to locate the point where America and Asia met with any accuracy. On long and cold voyages clocks needed to be accurate and reliable. Nordenskiöld had several chronometers with him on his ship the *Vega*. On the leg between Tromsa and Yokohama, which including wintering for more than a year, his main timepiece, the Frodsham 3194, lost only just over five minutes. Although the coast of Siberia had been mapped before the voyage of the *Vega*, there were still some longitudinal errors on Russian maps. Measurements carried out on the *Vega* corrected most of them.

At the beginning of the 19th century, Arctic exploration gained a new dimension – the race for the Pole had begun. Expeditions were no longer by sea but on foot

across the frozen sea. Technical aids for determining position – the chronometer, the sextant and the artificial horizon – had developed into precision instruments. When Nansen left the *Fram* on his bold trek across the ice, during which he achieved a new northerly record of 86°, he placed his trust in chronometers and sextants. On the return journey to Franz Josef Land, it is true, he was plagued with doubts about finding the island because he had forgotten to wind one of his two chronometers and he did not have complete faith in his longitudinal calculations. Peary, too, put his trust in chronometers.

Polar explorers had a lot to contend with on the expanses of ice in the north. Almost insurmountable obstacles in the shape of huge blocks of ice meant that the way forward was full of twists and turns. It was necessary to go around fissures and large areas of open water. Staying on course was difficult. Fog, snow-

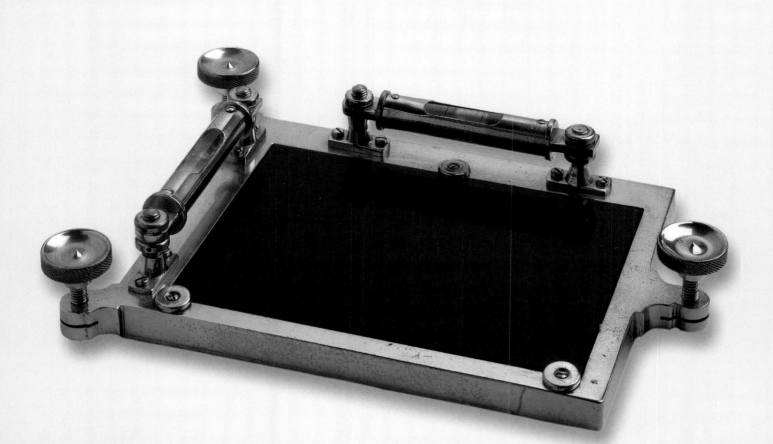

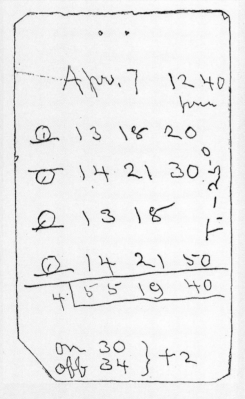

237 On a glacier, it is often difficult to make out the horizon. This is a problem when attempting to measure angles with a sextant, for the solving of which an artificial horizon was developed. It was based on the idea that the image of the sun reflected by the instrument was as far below the horizon as the sun was above it, as long as the mirror was horizontal. Mercury was used as the reflecting surface, or alternatively a sheet of glass that was set horizontal with spirit levels. This artificial horizon's glass sheet was darkened to cut down glare. When using a sextant to measure the altitude of the sun, the polar explorer would place the artificial horizon horizontally on the ice in front of him. The angles of the two suns appearing in front would be divided in two and the result would give the sun's elevation. (John Nurminen Foundation)

236 Peary's calculations made near the pole indicate that he studied the position of the sun in relation to the horizon. Without a sextant, he was able to deduce the correct direction to take due north by timing the rise and setting of the sun. (John Nurminen Foundation)

storms and mirages made observations difficult. Because it was almost impossible to see the horizon on an uneven glacier it was necessary to use an artificial horizon when measuring the altitude of the sun with a sextant. This could be a basin filled with mercury which reflected sunlight. It was possible to measure the elevation of the sun from the double image produced. A sheet of black glass which functioned as a horizontal mirror using spirit levels performed the same function.

The closer one gets to the Pole and the smaller the distance between the meridians of longitude becomes, the more difficult it is to take one's bearings. Both Peary in the north and Amundsen in the south faced the same problem. At the equator, the degree of longitude is about 60 nautical miles, whereas 125 miles

from the Pole it is just less than 2.5 nautical miles. It is almost pointless to try to measure one's longitudinal position near the Pole. A compass cannot be trusted there either. On Peary's trek from Cape Colombia to the Pole, his bearing error was at times as much as 90° West. Close to the Pole, a compass is almost useless. In actual fact, at the North Pole the compass needle points south!

The position of true north is usually obtained by measuring the shadow cast by the sun at midday. With a sextant it is possible to determine the highest position of the sun. The sun is at its highest at midday, and this can be calculated with a sextant. The difference between local time and the comparative time given by a chronometer shows the degree of longitude. By comparing the direction shown by the compass with that indicated by a shadow cast by the sun at midday, one can calculate deviation. At midday the shadow points north, exactly where the polar explorer is headed. As long as the sun is higher in the sky at midday than it is at other times of the day, the journey should be continued in a northerly direction. When the angle measurement shows that the sun is at the same altitude for an entire period of 24 hours, the Pole has been reached. There, the shadow cast by a rod erected by the explorer is exactly the same length throughout the 24-hour period.

Very close to the North Pole, the explorer is confronted with a new problem: the precise moment of midday can no longer be measured. The sun rises and falls extremely slowly and at midday seems to remain at the same height, and other ways must be found. It would seem that this is what Peary did when, with his companion Henson, he was the first to arrive at the roof of the world in March 1909.

Peary's navigational methods have provoked a great deal of argument to this day. Unlike Amundsen at the South Pole, he rarely used a sextant. Wally Herbert and Dennis Rawlins, who view Peary critically, are of the opinion that he strayed from his northerly direction and did not actually reach the Pole. William E. Molett, an expert on navigation in the north who has made many flights over the polar region, has presented the convincing argument that Peary did not need to use the height of the midday sun to find a reliable course to the Pole. He used a simpler method: he

determined his longitudinal position by comparing the height of the sun in the morning with that in the evening. According to Molett, it would not have been worth wasting several hours determining midday with uncertain results. Reaching the Pole along the same meridian line could be guaranteed by the simple method of ensuring that the sun was at the same height at six in the morning and six in the evening and if not, correcting the course accordingly. Arthur R. Hinks has developed an even better method of determining one's position in the proximity of the Pole, but this was not available to Peary or Amundsen.

Peary also measured the depth of the sea. The results of his soundings have been compared with what is now known of the sea bottom in order to find out if he really reached the Pole. The results have been interpreted both for and against. Thomas D. Davies points out that Peary's soundings at longitude 70° are very like those that are known today. Wally Hebert takes a different view; according to him, Peary strayed considerably from that position because of ice shifts. Dennis Rawlins, in turn, claims that Peary's soundings were inadequate. At some points his sounding line even broke.

The latest claim on behalf of Peary's success is perhaps that put forward by Davies, based on photogrammetry. The height of the sun can be measured comparatively reliably from the length, direction and proportions of the shadows of the people, objects and natural formations

seen in Peary's photographs. On the basis of this analysis, Peary was very near the Pole.

It is clear that the conditions for navigating near the Pole are exceptional and that not all those writing on the subject have understood this. We may never get a final answer to the question of whether or not Peary reached the Pole. It is certain, however, that he was near the Pole, and for this achievement he deserves full recognition. Let the critics argue over a foot or mile.

Scott's and Amundsen's measurements at the South Pole have not been thrown into question with the same enthusiasm as Peary's claims about the North Pole. This is perhaps not quite justified when we take into consideration the differences in their general circumstances. All those who have conquered the Poles have travelled over the ice. Scott's and Amundsen's ice was miles thick and firmly attached to the earth's surface. Peary, on the other hand, navigated on shifting sea ice that was only a few metres thick. The variables affecting the measurement of position were greater in the north than in the south.

238 In the extreme north differences of the angles of elevation of the sun are small. Near the Pole the sun always seems to be at the same height through the day and night. It is difficult to make out the horizon clearly.
(B. & C. ALEXANDER)

PEARY OR PEARY AND HENSON?

Peary's achievement cannot be disputed even if he had not made it exactly to the North Pole. We must admire the deeds of Peary and his companions, although we cannot admire a man whose will to succeed is greater than anything else. Peary was the only member of the expedition who knew that he had fallen short of his aim.

Matthew Henson followed Peary on all his expeditions with the exception of the first. To begin with he was a servant, but on the last journey his role was different. Donald MacMillan, who was with Peary only on his last expedition, describes Henson as follows:

"Matthew Henson first went north with Peary in 1891. He was with him on his long trip over the Greenland Ice Cap in 1893. He was with him when he rounded the northern end of Greenland in 1900. He was with him off Cape Hecla in 1902. He was with him when he broke the world's record in 1906. He was the most popular man aboard the ship with the Eskimos. He could speak their language like a native. He made all the sledges that went to the Pole. He made all the stoves. Henson, the coloured man, went to the Pole with Peary because he was a better man than any of his white assistants..."

Peary used the Eskimos more effectively than any before him; he boasted of this himself. He bought the service of the Eskimos cheaply, but he kept the promises made to them even when they complicated his journey. The Eskimos respected and feared Peary, but they loved Henson. Both men lived among the Eskimos and took part in their lives – both also had children with the Eskimos – but Peary never learned more than a few key words of the Eskimo language. Henson spoke their language fluently. He was such a skilful dog-team handler and hunter that only the best Eskimos could match him. Henson was one of them even when he was singing them the songs of his youth accompanied on an accordion.

Henson was irreplaceable but he never made much of himself. MacMillan tells of their first meeting as follows: "We sat on the caplog and he talked about the Arctic, of which I could not hear enough for what he already knew so well I was just beginning to learn. Since he was modest it took me much longer to learn what his true role had been..."

When the *Roosevelt* arrived at Etah, Henson exchanged guns, ammunition and kitchen utensils with the Eskimos for dogs. He also chose the people to accompany Peary. In the winter of 1908–1909 Henson made 20 sledges based on Peary's designs. The Eskimos often watched as Henson was working. When he did a certain job the way they did, they said 'ajungilak', it's good.

Henson led the women as they worked making new fur clothes for the entire expedition. Henson and the Eskimos taught new members of the expedition how to make igloos. Those who admired Peary's leadership qualities, praised how quickly he trained new men such as MacMillan and Borup to become party leaders. In actual fact it was Henson who did this, not Peary. Henson taught them how to drive dog

239 *With the exception of Peary's first voyage to Greenland, Matthew Alexander Henson was an irreplaceable companion on his journeys. Peary said that: 'Henson... was almost as skilful... as an Eskimo.' Peary confessed to his friend Donald McMillan that he could not get along without him. Henson took charge of affairs with the Eskimos because he spoke their language fluently. He led the making of fur clothes and built all the sledges. He taught new members how to drive a dog team. He understood why the Eskimos lost faith. Without Henson Peary would not have succeeded. Peary and Henson 'discovered' the North Pole in 1909.* (The Explorers Club, New York)

teams. He also taught them what they would need on the expedition.

Henson's role was decisive when the Eskimos lost faith. A six-day wait at the open water frightened the Eskimos. They did not like the polar sea. The idea that they would be cut off on the other side of the water and never return to their wives and children horrified them. Perhaps it was bad spirits that were keeping the water from freezing.

Henson understood the situation and told of his worries to MacMillan. In his opinion the Eskimos might run away in a group and stop the expedition's progress. MacMillan thought about the problem and asked if the Eskimos held any contests. Henson knew that they liked fingerpull, wristpull and wrestling. MacMillan suggested that they hold the Arctic Olympics. It was an exciting day and the morale of the group rose. Although the Eskimos did not understand why they should run against each other, the prizes attracted them and the bad spirits were forgotten.

The expedition returned to Cape Columbia after a period of 16 days. According to Henson, Peary travelled the whole journey in a sledge. Upon arrival Peary wrote in his diary: "My life's work is complete." Bartlett had arrived three days earlier. Peary still did not want to celebrate his achievement. Henson, too, was worried by Peary's lethargy; he had not exchanged a word with him on the *Roosevelt* on the return voyage. Peary only spoke about the work in hand, not of their joint achievement. Perhaps Peary was overcome with the emptiness which often accompanies the fulfilment of a lengthy and long-sought ambition.

It was only on the 56th day after Peary had gone aboard the ship that he signed a statement which he had written about his accomplishment. This made no mention of the date when he had reached the North Pole.

COOK – A NEW THREAT

Peary had heard that his old travelling companion Frederick Cook had set out for the North Pole. Peary did not like the idea but did not let it disturb him. Perhaps he did not believe in Cook's chances. But Cook was no novice. He had been on an Arctic expedition for the first time with Peary in 1891–1892. Peary valued his contribution. He wrote of Cook in his book as follows: "...personally I owe much to his professional skill, and unruffled patience and coolness in an emergency. In addition to his work in his special ethnological field, in which he has obtained a large mass of most valuable material concerning a practically unstudied tribe, he was always helpful and an indefatigable worker." Cook's attitude was shown by the way he took care of Matt Henson's eyes. Henson lived with Cook for two months and Cook arranged for an eye specialist to attend to his eyes – without remuneration. Peary even asked Cook to join him on his next expedition.

Like Richardson, Rae and Kane, Cook was a doctor who returned to the Arctic. He was chosen as doctor on the Antarctic expedition led by the Belgian Adrien de Gerlache after its physician resigned for 'family reasons'. He also wrote a book about the voyage. The most interesting appraisal of Cook is found in the memoirs of his shipmate Roald Amundsen. According to Amundsen, Cook was "the one man of unfaltering courage, unfailing hope, endless cheerfulness, and unwearied kindness... And not only was his faith undaunted, but his ingenuity and enterprise were boundless." Amundsen extolled Cook's practicality. Together they constructed a sledge and a tent, designed by Cook, which could be put up in five minutes. Amundsen wore sunglasses also designed by Cook during his expedition to the South Pole. When De Gerlache's ship the *Belgica* was beset in the ice their survival was largely due to Cook's initiative and optimism.

240 Frederick Cook is the great mysterious figure of Arctic exploration. His contemporaries described Cook as follows: Peary said that '... personally I owe much to his professional skill, and unruffled patience and coolness in emergency.' De Gerlache was impressed by '... his never-failing devotion to duty.' Amundsen said of his colleague 'I came to know Dr Cook intimately and to form affection for him and gratitude to him... He, of all the ship's company, was the one man of unfaltering courage, unfailing hope, endless cheerfulness, and unwearied kindness...' How would a man like this stoop to giving information on a polar expedition which did not in fact happen? Frederick Cook died in 1940 without ever having admitted his deception.

(FREDERICK A. COOK SOCIETY)

Cook returned to his profession without forgetting his passion. He wanted next to climb to the peak of Mount McKinley in Alaska, which had never been done before. His first attempt in 1903 failed, but his reputation as an expert on McKinley grew. Cook tried again in 1906 and, according to his account, succeeded in reaching the peak of Mount McKinley with his compatriot Edward Barrill. Cook's achievement was doubted from the outset, however. In New York, as one of the world's leading explorers, he was elected president of the Explorers Club after Adolphus Greely.

Eight months after Peary had returned from his penultimate expedition in 1907, Cook set out for Greenland. In Thule he had discussions with the Danish explorer Knud Rasmussen. Cook set up his winter camp at Annoatok to the north of Etah. He chose his men from volunteers, among them the young Rudolph Francke. Cook planned his expedition during the winter, build a sledge and had fur clothes made. He also polished his skills at driving dog teams and went to see Rasmussen again 125 miles away.

After he had heard of Cook's claim, Peary demanded sufficient evidence that Cook had reached the Pole. Before the journey he had written a letter to *The Times* accusing Cook of using his Eskimos and his dogs at Etah. At the same time Cook began his journey to the Pole with Francke and nine Eskimos. The sledges were piled high with food and other supplies. Cook had acquired 103 dogs. He planned to supplement his food by hunting. Hunting on Ellesmere Island was unsuccessful, however.

Fearing that his stores would be insufficient, Cook sent Francke and most of the Eskimos back to Annoatok. Two experienced Eskimos accompanied Cook on the sea ice for three days before returning with a letter from Cook to the awaiting Francke. Only two young Eskimos remained with him.

Like Peary, Cook was faced with open water. After a day's waiting the party managed to cross the lead. The pressure-ridges made the journey difficult. The Eskimos also began to worry. Cook managed to calm them by pointing out clouds on the horizon and by convincing them that there was land there.

On 30 March, eight days after they had crossed the lead, Cook saw land to his left which he described and named Bradley Land after his sponsor. Bradley Land was located roughly speaking at the same degree of longitude as the Crocker Land seen by Peary, but nearer the Pole. Cook did not see Crocker Land on his journey. He had no time to explore the land he had just discovered, but continued the journey to the Pole where he arrived on 21 April.

Cook wanted to make sure he was at the North Pole. At a certain point he measured the length of a standing Eskimo's shadow every hour and drew marks on the ice. After 24 hours the marks formed a circle. This test proved irrefutably that he had arrived at the Pole, because only there were shadows of equal length for an entire 24 hours. In his book, Cook wrote: "...although the Pole was discovered, it was not essentially discovered ... in the eyes of the world, unless we could return to civilisation and tell what we had done."

Peary and his friends did their best to discredit Cook's claims. They spoke to the young Eskimos who had been with Cook. The map drawn according to the Eskimos narrative shows that Cook turned back a few days' journey from the polar sea, passed the western coast of Axel Heiberg Island to the south-west corner of Ellesmere Island, crossed Jones Sound and spent the winter of 1908–1909 on Cape Sparbo on Devon Island and, in early winter, made his way along the east cost of Ellesmere Island back to the village of Annoatok.

There are many facts which prove that Cook did not reach the Pole. His story is, however, – perhaps for this very reason – considerably more lively than Peary's book or articles.

Not a single Eskimo believed that another Eskimo could be fooled into believing land to be near because of clouds. The Eskimos that had been with Cook told Peter Freuchen that they had never left the proximity of land. The pictures that Cook took have for the most part been shown to be misleading. Bradley Land does not exist any more than does Crocker Land. In spite of the wide range of evidence Cook never admitted his deception.

THE WAGES OF ENDEAVOUR

The public would have liked to believe Cook, who was friendly, modest and positive. Peary, on the other hand, was distant, self-centred and paranoid in his attitude towards his real and imagined competitors. Both men showed admirable self-confidence. Not a sign of discomfort crossed Cook's face when, in the middle of giving a lecture, he heard of Peary's return and suspicions. Peary's patrons, and in particular the Peary Arctic Club, did their utmost to throw doubt on Cook and to reject expressions of doubt aimed at Peary. The same criteria that Peary had demanded of Cook were never applied to Peary himself. *The Pittsburgh Press* also attacked Peary by publishing the results of an opinion poll. As many as 96% of those who replied believed Cook, and 76% of readers did not believe that Peary had been to the North Pole. Peary's position became stronger with time and he received the recognition he desired. The National Geographic Society was satisfied with the papers they received from Peary. Theodore Roosevelt praised his achievements. *Hampton Magazine* paid Peary $40,000 for a series of articles. He received an advance of $15,000 on his book, which was written by a ghost writer whose name is not mentioned anywhere in the book. Peary was paid as much as $7500 for giving lectures. In addition, the Civil Forum granted him a $10,000 reward. He received 22 gold medals, three honorary doctorates, the French Cross of Grand Officer of the Legion of Honour, and was finally promoted to the rank of Vice Admiral with its accompanying statutory pension, taking effect from 6 April 1909.

In 1917 Peary fell ill with pernicious anaemia, an ailment which Cook had already diagnosed in 1901 and for which Cook had recommended eating raw meat and particularly liver; only later research confirmed raw liver as a suitable remedy for the illness. Peary died in 1920 and appeared in public for the last time at an event held by the National Geographic Society at which he presented the Hubbard Gold Medal to Vilhjálmur Stefánsson for his achievements.

Matthew Henson was not invited to Peary's funeral. When he heard of the news, he was working as a messenger for the United States Customs House in New York. Henson wrote a book, *A Negro Explorer at the North Pole,* which was published in 1912, but it was not a success. Peary wrote the foreword, in which he gives Henson no greater recognition than he did in his own book, although he praises Henson for his adaptability and loyalty. The essence of Peary's thanks was

241 In summer the polar ice melts at the edges and wide areas of open water may appear in its centre too. (Derek Fordham)

that "Henson, a son of the tropics, has proven through the years his ability to withstand tropical temperature, and the fiercest stress of frigid climate and exposure..."

Like the commission of Vice Admiral given to Peary, Henson's letter of appointment was also signed by President Taft. The salary which Henson received from the U S Customs was small, and during his holidays he also worked for the Postal Office to augment his income. MacMillan worked for Henson's recognition. In 1937 Henson was elected to full membership of the Explorers Club and a dinner was arranged in his honour. In 1948 the Geographic Society of Chicago had a gold medal struck for Henson. Ten

years later President Eisenhower received Henson at the White House. In 1961 the first bronze tablet to be dedicated to an African American was unveiled in the state of Maryland, on which Henson was distinguished as "co-discoverer".

Peary's series of articles in *Hampton Magazine* as well as his book were reminiscent of Cook's account. The magazine articles were written by Elsa Barker, who received very little material from Peary; she had to seek additional subject matter from Cook's articles that appeared in the *New York Herald*. Cook's book *The Attainment of the North Pole* was published in 1911 at his own expense.

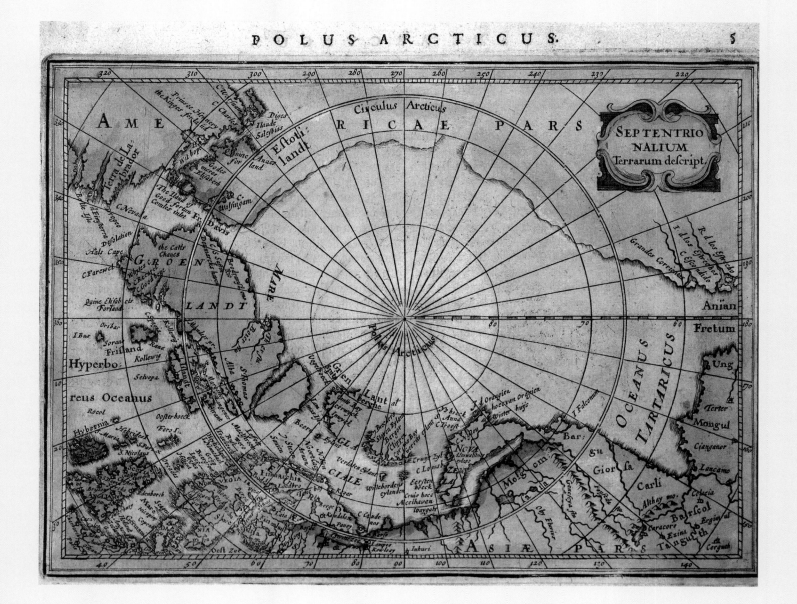

THE ISLANDS OF THE ARCTIC OCEAN

The strait between Asia and America became firmly established on the world map at the end of the 18th century. The coasts of the North Pacific were mapped relatively accurately at the turn of the 19th century. During the 19th century there were still many blank patches for polar explorers to fill in, in the northern part of the Bering Strait and along the coasts of Siberia and Alaska. There were thought to be several unexplored islands and even areas of mainland to the north of Siberia. It was believed that Greenland continued across the North Pole to the Bering Strait side of the Arctic Ocean. Nobody had yet sailed far along the north coast of Alaska. The search for the Northwest Passage led to new discoveries here.

Both the Chuchki and fur trappers told of seeing islands off various parts of the north coast of Siberia. As time went by, a whole group of islands was discovered in

*242 Mercator-Hondius. On his map of 1634 Henricus Hondius successfully depicts the islands of the Arctic Ocean. There is a separate island off north Greenland. The first explorers managed to break through the ice into the region only in the late 19th century. Of Spitzbergen, only the eastern part discovered by Barents was known. The islands east of that do not exist in reality. One possible explanation is that the edge of the pack ice had been interpreted as being land. On the maps, northern Novaya Zemlya is connected to a continent. This idea was taken from older maps and polar descriptions, and was in conflict with the results of Barents' charting work. He went around the northern peninsula there and wintered on the north-east corner of the island. Bering Sound (Anian Fretum) is placed in just about the right direction, only slightly too far to the west. When the map was printed, Northern Russia and the far north of the Americas was still unexplored territory. (*JOHN NURMINEN FOUNDATION*)*

the region. Some of the islands that were reported were never found, however, but the search for them attracted explorers to northern waters for a long time. Sometimes the reflections, known as polynyas, created over wide open channels, were probably misinterpreted as islands.

In the 18th century the Russian Stepan

Andreyev claimed to have discovered a large island or continent in the area of sea between the Lena and the Kolyma. There was talk of an Andreyev Land and a Sannikov Land. Many expeditions explored the area and found new islands. The largest of the New Siberian islands, Faddeyevski, in 1805, and New Siberia,

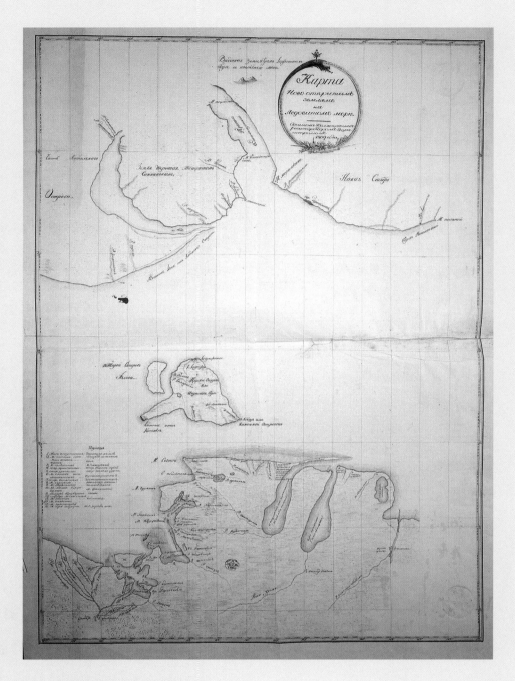

243 M.M. Hederström published an interesting map of the Siberian coast and the Arctic Ocean islands in 1809. It describes the mysterious Sannikov Land in detail. It is marked: land discovered by Sannikov. According to the map, Hedenstöm knew the islands, although he denied ever having been there. Local hunters would go far out to sea in winter, and their stories created geographical beliefs, some of them false. Hedenström was a distinguished scholar, but in the case of this map he relied too heavily on unverified information. Teams led by Anzhou and Wrangel respectively in 1820–1824 affirmed that there was no large land or islands to be found in the north. De Long later came across a previously unknown island further east and named it Wrangel Island in honour of his predecessor. (RUSSIAN STATE ARCHIVES)

244 An expedition led by Nordenskjöld landed on Bear Island in summer 1864. They performed measurements and based on them drew up a new map of the island that corrected earlier misconceptions regarding its size. The desolate, lonely and bleak island in the middle of the North Atlantic had previously been depicted as being much smaller. Nordenskjöld himself made many of the drafts. The island is measured in nautical miles. Out of the east rises the bleak Mt. Misery. (HELSINKI UNIVERSITY LIBRARY)

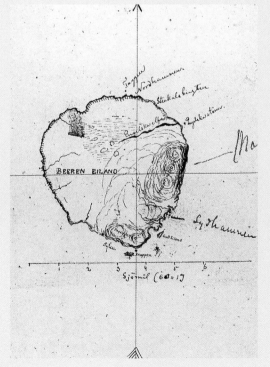

in 1806, were discovered to the north of the Lena delta. Wrangel Island, near which De Long's ship the Jeannette was shipwrecked, was discovered later. Many explorers, the most famous being Hedenström, Anjou and Wrangel, mapped the north coast of Siberia at the beginning of the 19th century. On the basis of incorrect observations, the tireless Arctic explorer Hedenström compiled a map of the mysterious Sannikov Land, which in fact does not exist.

Simpson and Dease mapped Alaska from the interior. After their journeys the north coast of Alaska began to take shape. Thanks to Franklin, cartographic knowledge of the lower reaches of the Coppermine increased. His map shows stretches of the Arctic Sea coast at the mouth of the river flowing from the south, surrounded by blank unexplored areas.

Franklin's intention was to progress

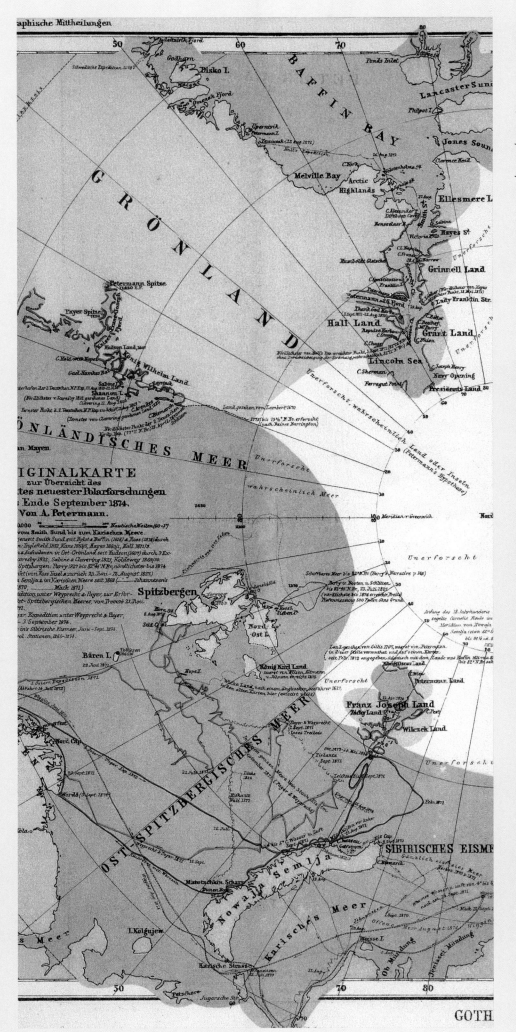

west of the Coppermine following the coast, and rendezvous with Beechey, who was making his way from the Bering Strait. The two explorers never met, however. Sailing towards the east, Beechey mapped a long stretch of the north coast of Alaska. At that time, rumours were circulating of islands off the north coast of Alaska. It was even believed that a land connection to Greenland could be found there. Beechey corrected these mistaken ideas, although it only became clear that there were no islands in the sea off Alaska in the 20th century.

The mapping of northern Russia continued throughout the 19th century. Vilkitskiy discovered Nicholas II Land north of the Taimyr Peninsula. After the revolution this was renamed Severnaya Zemlya, or the 'Northern Land'. This archipelago stretches further to the north than Spitsbergen, and only the most northerly islands of Franz Josef Land, the northernmost of which is Rudolf Island, reach closer to the North Pole. Nordenskiöld passed to the south of Severnaya Zemlya when he was sailing the Northeast Passage, and Nansen to the north of it while trekking across the glacier, but neither of them sighted it.

New areas of Greenland and Canada were still being discovered in the 20th century, and new coast lines were being drawn on maps and blank areas filled in. Measuring techniques became more precise in the 19th century and the quality of the new maps was good. Unconfirmed assumptions, such as that Greenland extended over the North Pole, were represented by a broken line. The last islands found their way onto maps during the 1930s.

THE RETURN OF THE VIKINGS

AT THE SAME TIME AS THE RACE FOR THE POLE WAS GOING ON, A LOT WAS HAPPENING IN ARCTIC EXPLORATION. ALMOST ALL THE COASTS AND ISLANDS OF THE ARCTIC OCEAN WERE CHARTED BEFORE THE FIRST WORLD WAR. THE NORTHEAST PASSAGE AND THE NORTHWEST PASSAGE HAD BEEN SAILED FROM BEGINNING TO END. A LOT OF ADVENTURE WAS ASSOCIATED WITH THESE CHALLENGES, BUT ALSO A GREAT DEAL OF SERIOUS EXPLORATION.

An interesting factor that almost all expeditions carried out between the end of the 1870s and the First World War had in common was the nationality of the men involved in them. The Americans wanted to achieve something great and they found a challenge in the North Pole. After the disappointment of Nares' expedition the British were concentrating on the Antarctic. The Vikings returned to spearhead Arctic exploration, especially if the concept of Vikings is widened to include Finns as well as Norwegians, Swedes and Danes.

THE SAILING OF THE NORTHEAST PASSAGE

The first of these new Vikings was the Finnish Swede, Adolf Erik Nordenskiöld (1832–1901). At the time of Nordenskiöld's birth, Finland was a Grand Duchy belonging to Russia and had three official languages: Finnish, Swedish and Russian. Nordenskiöld was a mineralogist who took his doctoral degree in 1855. Later, at a celebration, he gave a speech thanks to which he fell out of favour with the officials. Nordenskiöld moved to Sweden the same year, where he was appointed to an important post, and the very next year was

246 Originally a Finn who had moved to Sweden, Nils Adolf Erik Nordenskiöld was a geologist with Torrell's expeditions of 1858 and 1861. He led two expeditions of his own to Spitsbergen between 1864–1873. In 1868 in his vessel the SOFIA he broke the northerly record set by Scoresby Sr. Nordenskiöld tried to reach the North Pole in 1872–1873 using reindeers to pull sledges. His greatest achievement was to sail the Northeast Passage in his vessel the VEGA in 1878–1880, but he continued to explore Greenland after this. Perhaps Nordenskiöld's most significant achievement was his unique collection of geographical literature and maps now kept in Helsinki. (KUNGLIGA VETENSKAPSAKADAMIEN, STOCKHOLM)

invited to become a member of an expedition to Spitsbergen.

Nordenskiöld was to become the most famous Swedish explorer. On his fourth expedition in 1868, in his ship the *Sofia*, he broke the record for sailing north previously held by Scoresby. Two years later he made a voyage to Greenland and started to make preparations for an expedition to the North Pole.

On his sixth journey Nordenskiöld attempted to reach the North Pole but failed when his reindeer ran away before the journey had even begun. Nordenskiöld tried to prevent scurvy by taking along cloudberries mixed with lemon juice. Despite this the expedition suffered from scurvy, so the cloudberry was probably no better than lemon juice.

After this expedition Nordenskiöld began to take an interest in a Northeast Passage. He wanted to find out whether it was in fact possible to sail uninterruptedly from the Atlantic Ocean to the estuaries of the Ob and the Yenisey. At the time when Payer and Weyprecht sailed via Novaya Zemlya to Franz Josef Land, the sea south of Novaya Zemlya had not been frozen. They thought they could have sailed without obstruction to the Bering Strait.

Interest in the Northeast Passage was also aroused by a discovery made by a Captain Carlsen who was investigating the opportunities for fishing off Novaya Zemlya. Carlsen found Barents' winter camp of 1596 – 275 years later – almost in its original condition. The clock was even hanging on the wall of the hut. Carlsen collected the furniture and other items, and they can now be seen in the Rijks museum in Amsterdam.

Nordenkiöld's preparations were thorough. In 1875 he sailed across the Kara Sea to the Yenisey, up which he sailed, returning by way of Moscow. The following year he sailed to the Yenisey again and discovered a new island on the way. The *Vega* set out to sail the Northeast Passage from Karlskrona in Sweden on 22 June 1878. Nordenskiöld's vessel, the *Vega*, had been built as a whaler, had an auxiliary engine and was 357 gross registered tons. During the early stage she was

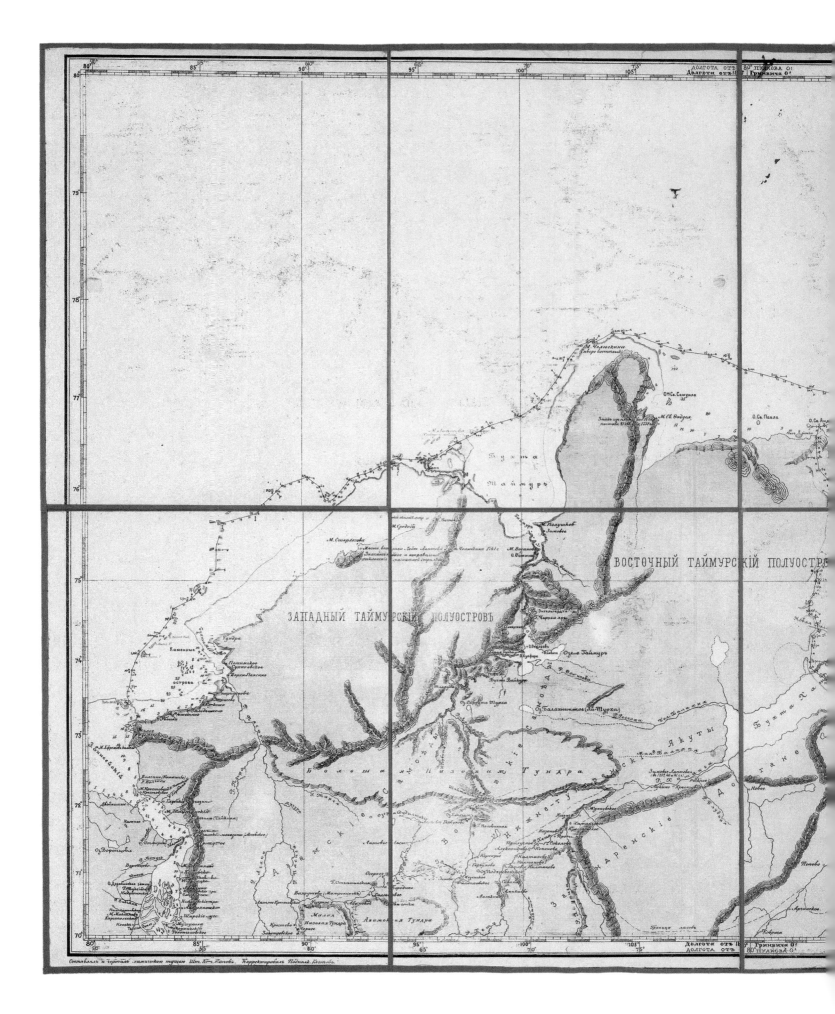

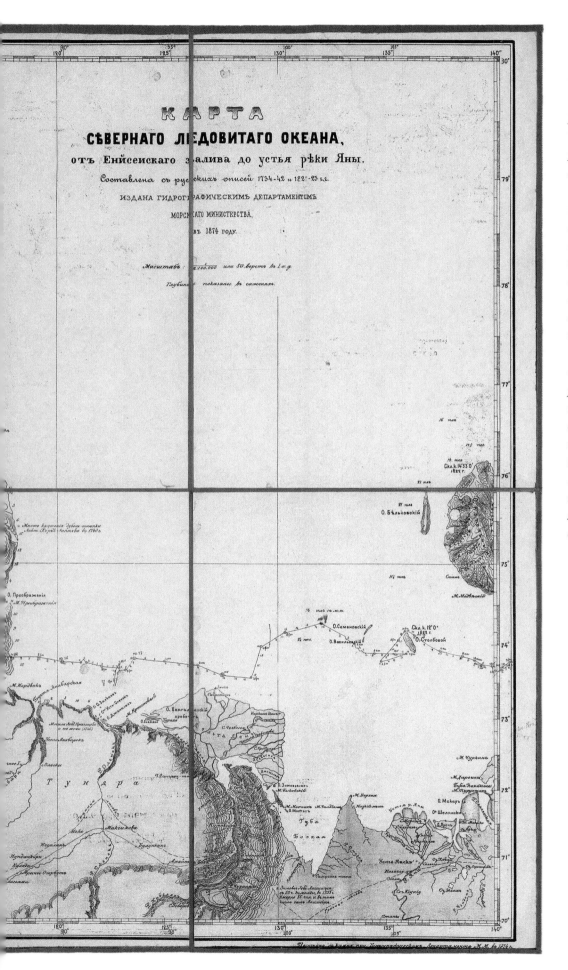

247 Nordenskiöld's expedition sailed first round the Taimyr Peninsula, which is the northernmost corner of Asia. Palander, who commanded the VEGA, had to navigate carefully. The ship was moving in previously unexplored and un-sounded waters which were very shallow in many places. The VEGA's steam-sloop was then sent out to sound a passage. Thanks to this, the bigger vessels were able to maintain a reasonable speed. Nordenskiöld had a map of Russian origin at his disposal, and the expedition's progress and information on sounding and wind direction was marked on it. Depths were expressed in fathoms. Previous mapping had been done partly in winter, and information from them was inadequate. The position of the coast in an east-west direction was also incorrect. Thanks to the precise chronometers on the VEGA's voyage it was possible to check the location of the extreme north coast of Siberia. The navigators of the Northeast Passage drew the coastlines in blue on the Russian map. Because of a mistaken longitude of the map it seems as though the VEGA had sailed part of the journey on dry land.
(JOHN NURMINEN FOUNDATION)

followed by three merchant ships carrying coal, and whose destinations were the harbours of the Lena and the Yenisey. Nordenskiöld himself boarded the ship in Tromsa in July.

During the journey the *Vega* made stops to gather scientific material. Nordenskiöld discovered some uncharted islands, later to be named after him, in the Kara Sea. In August the *Vega* arrived at Mys Chelyuskin, the northern cape of Asia, round which the ice had blocked off the Arctic sea route for several years. In 1878 it was possible to round the cape without difficulty. Louis Palander was captain of the *Vega*. He sent a sloop on ahead to find a passage through the continuously foggy and rocky seas.

The fog prevented Nordenskiöld from crossing the Laptev Sea, and he sailed along the coast charting the Taymyr Peninsula; according to charts in use at the time, the *Vega* was sailing on land. The first charts of this area were made by Bering's second great northern expedition. At that time the ice made charting difficult, and most of the work was done by sledge parties in winter.

At the end of August, the *Vega* and the *Lena* – which was still following the *Vega,* arrived at the Lena River. The *Vega* continued her voyage to the New Siberian Islands alone. The ice prevented anyone from going ashore. Only at the end of September did the ice, the darkness and the fog bring the voyage to a halt near Kolyuchinskaya Guba, only 120 miles away from the Bering Strait. A whaler, which was about 50 miles in front, made it to the Bering Strait that same autumn.

After just a few days some Chukchi arrived to greet the men. In the vicinity of the *Vega* there were several Chukchi villages, in which about 300 people lived. As a general rule visitors were not allowed below deck, but the deck of the *Vega*, sheltered by a canvas awning, became a meeting place for the local people.

The Chukchi did not behave like the Eskimos, and Nordenskiöld's crew did not lose a single weapon. The Chukchi had no reservations about begging, however. Because they had long had dealings with American whalers, they spoke better English than Russian. Nordenskiöld's Russian interpreter, a Lieutenant Nordquist, had little to do, but he did learn the Chukchi language. His ability to learn their language made such an impression on the Chukchi that they spoke of this wonder to the crew of De Long's *Jeannette* the following year.

Nordenskiöld wrote a lot about the Chukchi although – as the historian Richard Vaughan pointed out – he was not an ethnologist but a mineralogist. From the point of view of ethnology his observations were superficial. But the most valuable contribution made by the *Vega's* expedition was the ethnological, mineralogical and zoological data gathered, and its collection of old Japanese literature. Nordenskiöld's most significant scientific achievement is a collection of geographical literature and maps, which are preserved in Helsinki.

The *Vega* was freed from the ice on 18 July 1879 and within two days had entered the Bering Strait. Scientific material was gathered on both St Lawrence Island and the Commander Islands, and the *Vega* arrived at Yokohama at the beginning of September. Nordenskiöld returned to Europe in the spring of 1880.

Sailing the Northeast Passage was not Nordenskiöld's last expedition. In 1883 he returned to Greenland to explore the inland ice cap and look for signs of the old Viking settlements. A party led by Nordenskiöld climbed onto the inland ice and in three weeks had progressed 73 miles into the interior. Nordenskiöld decided to return but, urged the Lapps with him to continue east and to report on the ice conditions. The Lapps claimed to have progressed 140 miles in a little more than two days, finding nothing more than ice.

Later explorers, Nansen among them, assumed that the Lapps had exaggerated the distance they had covered, which according to Nansen had been 40 miles. From this Nansen got the idea for a ski journey across the ice cap. Prior to Nansen, Peary had made his way 93 miles from the coast on his first expedition, that is to say further than Nordenskiöld, but he probably fell slightly short of the Lapps' achievement.

EN MASSE TO THE KLONDIKE

When Alaska was sold to the United States of America, interest in the area increased, resulting in a great many expeditions being carried out through the initiative of the American government. Frederick Schwatka, an American lieutenant and experienced Arctic explorer who had contributed to clearing up the fate of Franklin's expedition at the end of the 1870s, was given the task of exploring the Yukon River. Schwatka sailed in the steamship *Victoria* from Portland, Oregon to Chilcat Bay, and from Chilcoot Pass up the Rocky Mountains. At the lake from which the Yukon flowed he built a raft and went down the Yukon all the way to the mouth of the Tanana River, from which he continued in a small schooner.

Almost all of the blank areas remaining on the map of Alaska were explored in the 1880s. In 1885 Henry Allen went up the Copper and Tanana Rivers, the latter being still unexplored. He continued his journey to the north of Alaska and to the Koyukuk River, which flowed from the Brooks Range. The other rivers of the Brooks area, the Kobuk, the Noatak, the Alatna and the Colville, which flowed into the Arctic Ocean, were explored in the years that followed. After this it was gold that attracted people to the area.

People had been looking for gold in Alaska for a long time, but as yet there had been no great finds. In the autumn of 1878 gold was discovered at a shore dig in the region of the town of Fairbanks, and more was found at Fortymiles on the Yukon. This became Alaska's first great gold field where, at its height, 300 prospectors were working.

Gold was also found a short journey upstream from Sixtymiles on the Yukon and soon after that at Birch Creek, around which Circle City grew up. At its greatest it had a population of some 500, and several thousand men panned for gold in the areas around it. At the height of its fame Circle City was the Paris of Alaska, where wages were five times higher than elsewhere in Alaska and in 1896, three years

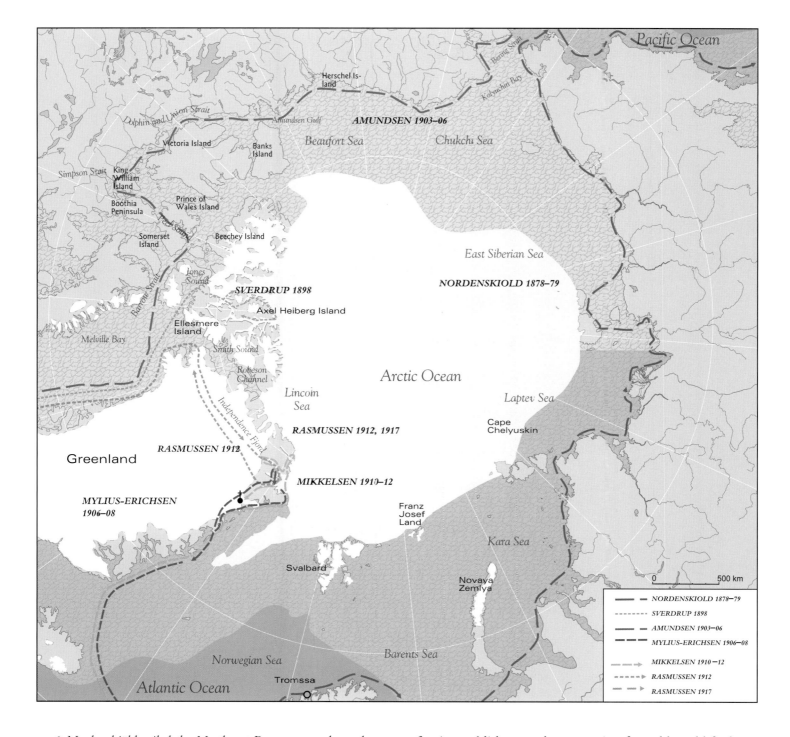

248 Nordenskiöld sailed the Northeast Passage as early as the 1870s. Amundsen sailed the Northwest Passage shown in the picture. There were other alternatives, as can be seen from the map. The ice prevented them from being sailed before the 20th century, when icebreakers opened up new Arctic routes. The north of Greenland was explored finally only in the 20th century. Sverdrup, whose work was completed by Stefánsson, explored the island group to the west of Ellesmere. (PATANEN)

after its establishment, those panning for gold could find entertainment at a music hall, two theatres, eight dance halls and 28 saloons. Being a saloon keeper or a prostitute was the most certain way to get rich at the gold field.

But it was the gold fields of the Klondike which created Alaska's fame. The Klondike was a tributary of the Yukon. Rabbit Creek flowed into the Yukon, on the banks of which George Carmack and his two Indian companions Skookum Jim and Tagish Charlie found four dollars-worth of gold in a single panful in 1896. At a time when a pan of eight to ten cents meant good prospects the discovery was astounding.

In the morning the friends staked out their claim. On the way to Fortymile to register their claim they told everyone they met of their find. These reacted to Carmack's news with disbelief until he showed them the great gold nuggets he had stashed into a Winchester shotgun shell. Once Carmack and his companions had staked their claim, Fortymiles became

VEGA – THE FORERUNNER OF MODERN POLAR VESSELS

In January 1877, Adolf Erik Nordenskiöld was dining in Stockholm as the guest of King Oscar II of Sweden. The gentlemen assembled there – Arctic researchers, their sponsors and seamen – were discussing northern exploration with the king, himself an expert on the subject. The king paid special attention to Nordenskiöld's opinions on sailing the Northeast Passage. The venture had often been tried and Nordenskiöld thought that it could now be accomplished with the aid of a modern ship, which should have an efficient rig and a steam engine. The stretch between the Jenisei and Chaun Bay had never truly been travelled with a genuinely seaworthy vessel, nor indeed with a steamer specifically fitted out for the ice.

Nordenskiöld considered the date of this dinner the birth of his Northeast Passage expedition. The king became one of three financial backers of the expedition and its most influential supporter. Thanks to him, the expedition's ship could be sent to the naval shipyard in Karlskrona, where it was fitted out to the last detail. The crew was comprised of volunteers, and Parliament decided that the men would be granted salaries equal to those of the Royal Navy.

The Vega was purchased in Gothenburg, hometown of the other main sponsor, wholesaler Oscar Dickson. The ship was the property of the Aktiebolaget Ishavet company, and had been built specifically for whaling in 1872–73 near Bremerhaven, Germany. Henrik Ramsay wrote that, "both whalers and Atlantic steamers were built in the region".

The Vega's overall length (length of the deck) was 43.4 metres, length of the keel 37.6 metres, beam 8.4 metres, depth of the hold 4.6 metres and cargo-carrying capacity 357 gross register tonnes or 299 net tonnes. At the time of the purchase, the ship was graded by Veritas as being first class for the next 12 years.

The finest oak had been used to build the ship. The masts were of Oregon pine and the rigging was supported by steel wire stays. An 'ice-skin' protected the hull from being damaged by the ice. It was a coating made from greenheart, an Indian hardwood that reached from the level of the chain plates above the waterline to below the waterline some one to one-and-a-half metres above the keel. After the Northeast Passage voyage the section of the hull below the waterline was fitted with a 'worm-shield' to protect her from the ravages of the tropical shipworm (teredo). The hold was also fitted with iron chests reaching from side to side. They were there to help compensate for the pressure of the ice. However, some were dismantled later in order to increase cargo space.

The Vega was rigged as a three-masted bark and Nordenskiöld mentions her good sailing characteristics, although she was certainly not as swift as a clipper. It was possible to reach speeds of 9 or 10 knots in favourable winds, however.

The Vega's manoeuvrability was considered excellent and it was further enhanced by the steam engine that was, in Nordenskiöld's opinion, essential for the successful completion of the voyage. The Wolff, a 60-horsepower engine fitted with a surface cooler, consumed 3 cubic metres of coal in an hour and powered the ship to a speed of 6–7 knots. The Vega represented the highest technology of her time. Equipment included a spare rudder and propellers as well as a little steam sloop with a two-horsepower engine used for reconnaissance sorties. The tent that was suspended over the deck proved invaluable when the Vega was forced to winter for ten months just a couple of hundred nautical miles from Bering Strait, which was the journey's destination.

249 The Vega was accompanied by three other steamers on its journey around Europe and Asia: the Lena, the Frasier and the Express. The latter two were there to take a shipment of European goods to the mouth of the river Jenisei and return with a cargo of grain. The other ships were also to carry coal for the Vega and the Lena. The steamer Lena continued to the mouth of the eponymous river, from where the Vega continued alone on its journey around Asia. The Vega was equipped with an uncovered steam-driven sloop, which when necessary would sound the way ahead of its mother ship. The expedition's commander was A. E. Nordenskiöld and the Vega's captain was the young lieutenant L. Palander, who was knighted after the voyage and received the title Palander af Vega.

(JOHN NURMINEN FOUNDATION)

Central-Tryckeriet, Stockholm.

deserted. Everyone rushed to Bonanza, as Rabbit Creek was now re-named.

By August 1897, one year after the find, the population of Dawson City, built at the mouth of the Klondike on the banks of the Yukon, had already risen to 4000. More and more people, driven by the thirst for gold, swarmed to the Klondike by way of Chilcoot Pass, which had been mapped by Schwatka. One year later the population of the town was almost 20 000. In addition, great numbers of people were out working their claims. The gold rush turned Alaska into an inhabited land.

OTTO SVERDRUP

Otto Sverdrup oversaw the building of Fritjof Nansen's vessel the *Fram* and was its captain when she was piloted through the Arctic Ocean to Spitsbergen. After Nansen set off with Johansen to ski towards the North Pole, Sverdrup took over the leadership of the expedition. When the *Fram* arrived in Norway, Sverdrup announced that he was ready for a new Arctic expedition. The Norwegians, proud of Nansen's achievements, arranged for the financing of a new expedition without delay.

Sverdrup decided to make his way by way of Smith Sound, Kane Basin and the Kennedy and Robeson Channels to the Arctic Ocean and the north coast of Greenland. From there he planned to travel along the north and east coasts. Sverdrup chose a fifteen-man crew, only one of whom, besides himself, had taken part in the *Fram's* previous voyage. The *Fram* arrived at Etah in mid-August 1898. After this the ice blocked her way and Sverdrup sailed to Pim Island off the coast of Ellesmere Island to look for traces of Adolphus Greely's expedition of 1883–1884. Nothing was found. The wind drove the ice west and the *Fram* sought refuge in Rice Sound between Pim Island and the mainland. They found winter quarters in the shelter of an island bay.

On 6 October two men approached the camp in an Eskimo sledge drawn by eight dogs. When Sverdrup went to meet the visitors, one of them asked if he was Captain Sverdrup. This was Robert Peary, whose vessel was beset in the ice further to the north. Peary did not even stay to drink a cup of coffee since he was expected for dinner and he did not like competitors. Sverdrup, however, did not consider reaching the North Pole worth the trouble.

In the spring the expedition went by sledge to Ellesmere Island. Sverdrup and Edvard Bay crossed the island to Bay Fjord. There they were the first Europeans to see and name Axel Heiberg Island.

At the end of July 1899 the *Fram* broke free from the ice and Sverdrup attempted to sail north. The ice stopped them once again and Sverdrup decided to concentrate on the area of Ellesmere. He sailed back further south and made his way into Jones Sound. The *Fram's* next winter harbour was found on the south coast of Ellesmere at Harbour Fjord.

William Baffin had been the first to identify Jones Sound in 1616. More than 200 years later John Ross turned back from

250 *Otto Sverdrup*

In the opinion of Nansen's brother the 33-year-old sea captain Otto Sverdrup was: "...solid as a rock, extremely agile, and afraid of nothing." Nansen took Sverdrup with him when he skied across Greenland. After this Sverdrup dedicated himself to Arctic exploration. He was Captain of the Fram from 1893–1896 and led an expedition to North Greenland between 1898–1902. Sverdrup mapped Ellesmere Island and the previously unknown islands to the west of it – the Sverdrup Islands. In 1914–1915, at the age of 60, Sverdrup was still leading an expedition to the Kara Sea which was looking for lost Russian explorers.

251 *A map drawn by Isachsen of exploration carried out by Sverdrup's expedition of 1898–1902. The brown colour depicting ground formation shows what a wide area the mapping work of Sverdrup and his companions covered. They mapped Jones Sound, the west coast of Ellesmere Island, Axel Heiberg Island and the islands to the west of it.* (FRAMMUSEEET, OSLO)

its mouth because he thought some mountains were blocking the sound. Captain Austin had explored the sound in 1851 when looking for John Franklin's expedition. The following year E. A. Inglefield sailed close to Harbour Fjord before turning back. The whole of Jones Sound from the *Fram's* winter harbour was still an unexplored area, although a British whaler had sailed down it for 150 miles not long before Austin's voyage.

In the spring three sledge parties set out led by Sverdrup. They explored the south coast of Ellesmere Island, progressed north along a strait between Devon and Ellesmere Islands

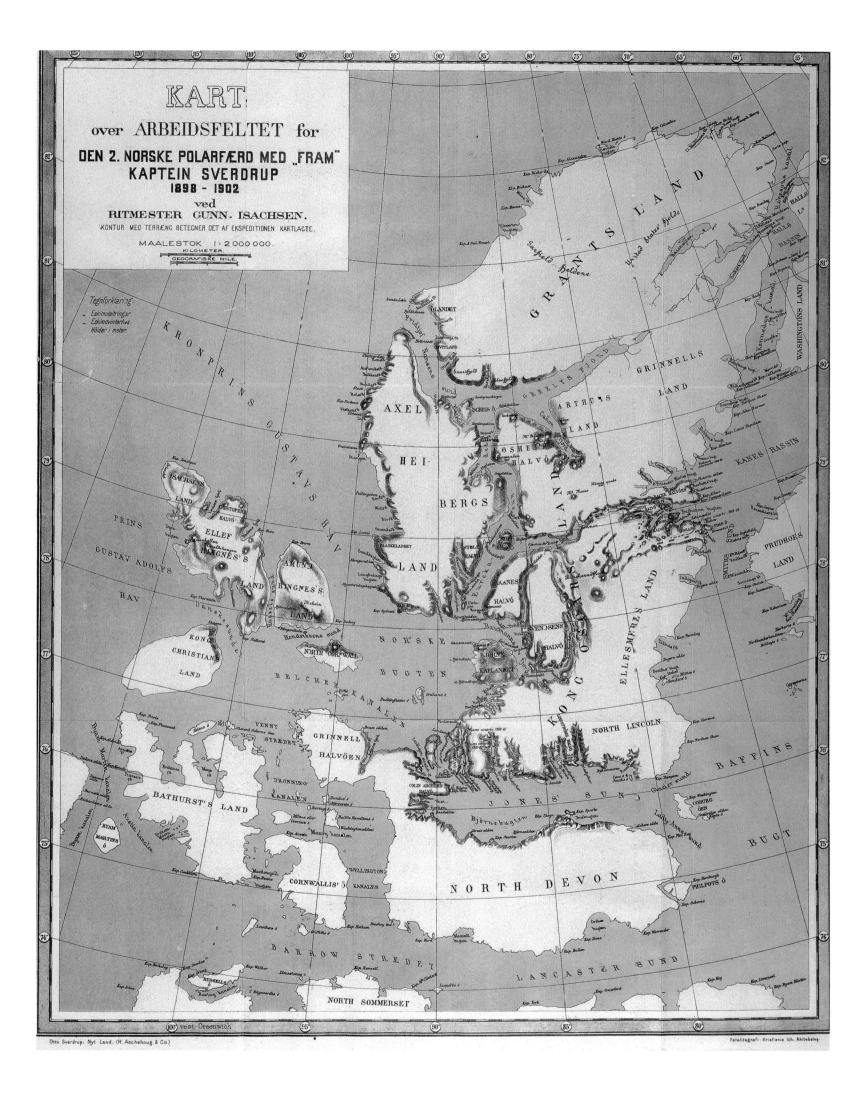

along Hells' Gate and continued along the west coast of
Ellesmere Island. Per Schei and Peder Hendriksen returned
to the ship from Goose Point at the entrance to Baumann
Fjord to stock up on food supplies, but they returned to
explore the islands of Norwegian Bay: North Kent, Buck-
ingham and Graham.

The other two parties continued from Goose Point to the
south coast of Axel Heiberg Island which, they followed to
the west. They discovered a new land in the west which Isachsen and Hassel set out to explore. The island was named
Amund Ringnes Island; the Ringnes brothers were brewery
owners who, with Consul Heiberg and the Norwegian government, had financed Sverdrup's journey.

Sverdrup and Ivar Fosheim made their way north along the
west coast of Axel Heiberg, almost reaching latitude 81° before returning to the ship. When Sverdrup arrived there on 4
July the other parties had already returned. The *Fram* broke
free from the ice on 9 August and Sverdrup sailed west
through Cardigan Strait between Devon and North Kent, but
returned to spend the winter in Goose Fjord on the south
coast of Ellesmere.

In the winter of 1901 Sverdrup continued to explore the
Ellesmere area. Sverdrup and Schei set out from the *Fram's*
winter quarters past Simmons Peninsula to Norwegian Bay,
explored Baumann and Vendon Fjords and travelled north
along the west coast of Ellesmere Island to the Schei Peninsula, which Sverdrup believed to be an island. Nansen Sound
and Greely Fjord met off the peninsula.

Gunnerius Isachsen's and Sverre Hassel's task was to explore
Ellef Ringnes Island. They crossed Hendriksen Sound, followed the coast of Amund Ringnes west to the southern tip
of Ellef Ringnes, turning north to follow the west coast. The
northernmost cape of Ellef Ringnes was named Cape Isachsen. From this cape they returned along the east coast of the
island, crossed Hassel Sound between Ellef and Amund and
returned to the *Fram* by way of the northern tip of Amund.

In the summer of 1901 Sverdrup did not succeed in sailing
out of Goose Fjord. He only managed to make his way 12
miles or so south, and had to set up quarters for one more
winter on Ellesmere.

The following spring Sverdrup and his men completed
their earlier explorations. Sverdrup and Schei extended their
expedition between Ellesmere and Axel Heiberg Islands
along Eureka Sound to Lands Lokk, the northern entrance to
Nansen Sound, and crossed latitude 81°. A three-man party
also set off south to Beechey Island. They found that stores
left there by the expeditions looking for Franklin were shattered, boxes of food and barrels were broken and cans
opened. Of the yacht *Mary* left by Ross all that remained was
a wreck.

The *Fram* was freed from the ice as early as July 1902, but
the vessel had to wait for three weeks at the entrance to Goose
Fjord before the wind opened up a passage in the frozen Jones
Sound and the *Fram* could make her way home.

Otto Sverdrup's expedition discovered and mapped Axel
Heiberg, Amund Ringnes and Ellef Ringnes Islands. They
were later named the Sverdrup Islands. Sverdrup and his men
also made some interesting discoveries about the ancient inhabitants of the islands. At Eureka Sound "the cape of the
ancient Eskimos" they found ruins of buildings as well as the
remains of tent-rings, store houses and traps.

On the 'bird island' of St Helena at the westernmost corner of Jones Sound, they found more Eskimo tent sites and
the same kind of stone eider nests which were built in Norway to attract eider ducks to places where it was easy to collect their eggs. In Vilhjálmur Stefánsson's opinion the stone
nests prove, that the Greenland Vikings had reached as far as
the corners of Jones Sound on their hunting trips.

On reaching Norway, Sverdrup demanded that King Oskar
take the islands he had discovered into Norwegian possession
in the same way that discoveries by British naval officers were
taken into the British Empire. Sverdrup repeated his demand,
when Norway became independent a matter which caused
concern in Canada. A number of Canadian expeditions set
out to the islands and declared them to belong to Canada.
Sverdrup was incensed by these measures and he even suggested sending the Norwegian police to the islands. When
the Canadian government heard that Knud Rasmussen had
been hunting musk-ox in the Ellesmere Island area, it pointed out that Rasmussen had neglected to seek a permit. Rasmussen reacted by saying that he considered the islands a
no-man's-land. The debate became heated again in the 1920s.
The Canadians could also see that Sverdrup's maps – till then
the only ones – were remarkably accurate.

In 1930–27 years too late – the Canadian government
granted Sverdrup a pension as a gesture of conciliation. Sverdrup died a few months later.

FRANZ JOSEF LAND AND THE SIBERIAN COAST

Norwegian walrus and seal hunters had probably been fishing
the waters of Franz Josef Land for a long time, although this
'Land' was discovered in 1873 by Payer and Weyprecht. The
next expedition, under the leadership of Frederick G. Jackson,
arrived at the islands in 1894 and stayed there until 1897. The
expedition was financed by a British newspaper publisher. Its
aim was to complete the work begun by the Austrians.

Jackson progressed beyond latitude 81° 19' north and, like
Nansen, found that neither Payer's and Weyprecht's King Oskar Land nor Petermann Land existed. He charted about 600
miles of coast and proved the land to be an archipelago. However, the last and easternmost of the Franz Josef islands was
only discovered in 1898. E. B. Baldwin, the meteorologist on
the American Walter Wellman's expedition, gave it the name
Graham Bell Island.

Russian interest in the northern areas increased once more
at the beginning of the 20th century. In 1912 three Russian
expeditions explored the Franz Josef archipelago and the areas east if it. The first was led by Lieutenant Georgiy Sedov.
He sailed in his vessel the *Svjatoi Foka* to the northern coast
of Novaya Zemlya, where he spent the winter. Some of the

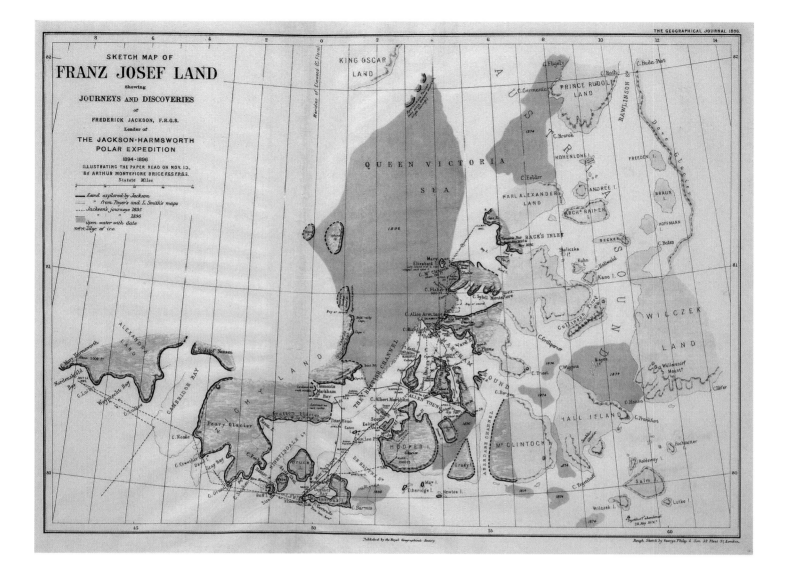

expedition's men had to be sent south because of scurvy. In summer Sedov tried to reach Franz Josef Land, but the ice prevented him from going ashore on Prince Rudolph Island, nowadays known as Rudolph Island. The expedition wintered on Hooker Island. In February 1914 Sedov began a journey towards the North Pole, in spite of the fact that he was weakened by scurvy. Three men and a dog-team advanced to Rudolph Island. At the beginning of March 1914 Sedov died and his comrades turned back.

The second expedition, led by Lieutenant Georgiy Brusilov, sailed in the *Anna* to the Kara Sea, and during the winter drifted with the pack ice along the east coast of Novaya Zemlya. The captain of the *Anna,* Valerian Albanov, was given permission to build kayaks after Brusilov had been dismissed from his post. In February 1914 Albanov and 13 men left the vessel. Three of them later returned to the ship, however. The members of the expedition had both sledges and kayaks, although only two of the kayaks were left when they reached the Franz Josef archipelago. The group was divided into two. The first tried to reach Mys Flora on skis, the second in kayaks. One of the kayaks was lost in a storm, and only the kayak of Albanov and the sailor Aleksandr Konrad reached their destination. They were rescued from Mys Flora by the *Svjatoi Foka* which, after Sedov's death, was heading south.

Before the Second World War two Russian icebreakers, the

252 Julius Payer drew the first map of Franz Josef Land in 1872–1874 when the Austro-Hungarian expedition discovered the island group. Payer identified two large islands in the north, which he named King Oscar Land and Petermann Land. Frederick Jackson, who drew the map above, continued Payer's work in 1894–1897 and discovered Franz Josef Land to be an island group. Petermann Land no longer appears on his map, but on the upper edge he still drew King Oscar Land. Nansen and Johansen attempted to reach the safety of Petermann Land in 1896, but were obliged to recognise that neither it nor King Oscar Land existed. They met Jackson on the western cape of Nortbruk Island at the lower edge of the map, which has the beautiful name of Mys Flora – Cape Flora. (JOHN NURMINEN FOUNDATION)

Taymyr and the *Vaygach,* explored the East Siberian coast from their base at Vladivostok. In 1913 they tried, under the leadership of Captain Vilkitskiy, to sail the Northeast Passage from east to west, in the opposite direction to Nordenskiöld. During this voyage the expedition discovered a number of islands in the coastal waters of Siberia. Their most important discovery was a new land situated about 30 miles north of Mys Chelyuskin, Asia's northern tip. Vilkitskiy gave the land the name Nicholas II Land, but after the Russian Revolution it became Severnaya Zemlya, the land of the North. The land extended 190 miles to the north, so that Nansen's *Fram* must have skirted it less than 100 miles to the north and Nordenskiöld to the south. Vilkitskiy went ashore on the island and left the Russian flag as a symbol of the right of possession. The attempt to sail the Northeast Passage failed, however.

In 1914 Vilkitskiy set out on another voyage with the intention of wintering. In August one of the icebreakers became ice-bound twelve miles or so east of Wrangel Island. In an attempt to help, the second of the icebreakers was damaged, and the icebreakers were unable to reach the *Karluk's* survivors, who waiting to be rescued on Wrangel Island. Once again Vilkitskiy discovered a couple of previously unknown islands, charted the islands of Severnaya Zemlya and, after some difficulties, made his way to his winter quarters in the proximity of Mys Chelyuskin

During the winter Vilkitskiy met Otto Sverdrup, who was taking part in the search for Bruslov's and Rusanov's Russian expeditions. Sverdrup also made contact with another expedition by way of the wireless telegraph for the first time in the history of Arctic exploration, giving instructions to Vilkitskiy. In winter Sverdrup, who was already 63 years old, went on board Vilkitskiy's vessel, and together they explored the mouth of the Taimyr River. In the summer of 1915 Vilkitskiy continued his voyage in spite of the war and arrived in Archangel in September. He was the first to have sailed the Northwest Passage from east to west.

The last discovery on the Siberian coast was made in 1930. A scientific expedition led by Professor Otto Schmidt advanced by way of Novaya Zemlya to the west coast of Severnaya Zemlya in the icebreaker Georgiy Sedov. A new island was discovered during the voyage, and was named Vize Island after a professor Wiese who was a member of the expedition.

Some other small islands were discovered, and the expedition remained to spend the winter on the west coast of Severnaya Zemlya. Most of the islands, which included three larger islands and numerous groups of smaller ones, were explored during the winter. A permanent research station was also established on Severnaya Zemlya. The northernmost cape of the island extended to latitude 83°. Only the northern coasts of Greenland and Ellesmere Island reach as far to the north.

THE FIRST SAILING OF THE NORTHWEST PASSAGE

In his youth Roald Amundsen read of the fate of Franklin's expedition. He was to become one of the most important explorers of the 20th century, who made groundbreaking expeditions in both the northern and the southern polar regions. In this respect he was, like James Clark Ross, an exceptional man among explorers.

Amundsen was about nine years old at the time of the search for Franklin's expedition. When Nansen set out to cross Greenland's inland ice, Amundsen was already a young man. He would have liked to have gone on Nansen's next expedition but he promised his mother that he would not leave yet. When his mother died he joined Adrien de Gerlache's Belgian Antarctic expedition, in which Frederick Cook participated as doctor.

When Amundsen returned from the Antarctic, he wanted to lead an expedition of his own. Financing it was difficult, and to arrange such a venture meant that the expedition had to have more serious aims than just adventure. When Amundsen realised that by linking magnetic observations at the magnetic north pole to the search for the Northwest Passage, the idea could be sold to financiers. He might have got the idea from his predecessor James Clark Ross, who reached the north magnetic pole in 1831.

Amundsen bought the *Gjøa,* a thirty-year-old herring boat, whose deadweight capacity was 47 gross registered tons; for the sake of comparison it is well to remember that Franklin's vessels the *Erebus* and the *Terror* had a tonnage of 370 and 340 respectively. Franklin led 128 officers and men, while in Amundsen's team there were seven. When Franklin set out on his expedition he was 60 years old, Amundsen was 31. Amundsen had a great deal more information at his disposal than his predecessor. Collinson had made his way into Cambridge Bay from the Bering Strait in 1852 and many had explored the waters to the south of the Barrow Strait and King William Island. It was clear that the best passage ran through the strait between the Boothia Peninsula and the east of King William Island. This strait had not been navigated from end to end.

Amundsen set out from Christiania, nowadays Oslo, in the summer of 1903. At the beginning of August he sailed to Melville Bay on the west coast of Greenland. He sailed through this notorious area in a little more than a week. At the entrance to Wolstenholme Fjord the ship was loaded with additional equipment and it was there that Amundsen met two of his colleagues, Ludvig Mylius-Erichsen and Knud Rasmussen. With her heavy deck cargo, the *Gjøa* sailed to Lancaster Sound where the expedition examined the winter quarters of Franklin's ships the *Erebus* and the *Terror* on Beechey Island.

On 24 August the voyage continued west of the Barrow Strait, making its way south along Peel Sound. Ice was encountered for the first time in the waters between Prince of Wales Island and Somerset Island. In the glittering sunshine it looked like solid ice, but upon closer inspection Amundsen and his companions saw open water between the floes.

The *Gjøa* passed the place where Sir Allen William Young had been forced to turn back from his attempt to navigate Peel Sound in 1875. Behind them lay the Bellot Strait through which McClintock had tried to sail several times in 1858. In these unknown waters their progress was slowed down by fog. In a storm they touched bottom but, apart from a few splinters from the keel, their passage was without incident. A fire which broke out in the engine room in the James Ross Strait threatened to stop them, but the fire was put out before it spread to the surrounding petrol drums.

253 As a 15-year-old Roald Amundsen read John Franklin's description of the polar area and decided to follow him. He hardened himself for the task from a young age, and as a 25-year-old he went along on de Gerlache's Antarctic expedition. As his second aim he chose to sail the Northwest Passage, which he succeeded in doing between 1903–1906. Amundsen was already fulfilling his plan to make his way to the North Pole with the ice current in his vessel the FRAM *when he heard that Peary had arrived there. Amundsen immediately set out for the South Pole where he arrived in December 1911, one month before Robert Scott. He continued his explorations of the north by both air balloon and aeroplane and was killed in 1928 while trying to save his colleague Umberto Nobile.* (NASJONALBIBLIOTEKET, OSLO)

The waters were extremely shallow. The *Gjøa* touched bottom again in the waters to the north of Matty Island. Luck no longer favoured them. They ran aground during a high tide.

A fresh wind turned into a storm. They set the sails. The sails and a high wave lifted the ship, which was slowly being driven towards some rocks beyond which the water was deeper. The keel was broken when the vessel was struck. Amundsen feared that the ship would disintegrate at any moment. Eventually they threw even the deck cargo overboard. Miraculously the vessel glided without further damage over the rocks. They reached deeper water, and Amundsen decided not to repeat the mistake which had led them into danger. He sent a lookout up the mast, and continuously sounded the water.

On Nansen's advice, Amundsen erected two cairns on the Boothia Peninsula, one of which contained a message. These stone pillars were easily visible from the sea. The *Gjøa* sailed south along Rae Strait and approached the south-eastern tip of King William Island and the Simpson Strait. It was already 8 September and time to find a winter harbour. They dropped anchor in a bay whose narrow entrance protected the vessel from the ice.

The Simpson Strait was still open and they would have perhaps been able to make good progress during the autumn; but they also had to make observations of the magnetic field. They therefore remained in the harbour. They immediately found fresh caribou footprints and signs of an Eskimo camp on the beach.

Amundsen and his men first built a shelter for the scientific apparatus. The ship was cleaned and put into winter condition. On their first hunting excursion they bagged 20 caribou and there was also an abundance of grouse. The best bag for one man in a day was 15 caribou. The animals were thin, perhaps because the summer had been hot and dry.

At the end of October the Eskimos paid a visit to the camp and Amundsen prepared for the worst. As the group carefully approached he shouted "teima" as his predecessors had advised. The Eskimos replied "manik-tu-mi", which, according to McClintock was a friendly greeting. They embraced and slapped each other on the back and Amundsen did not know "whose side's joy was the greatest".

In the winter of 1904 Amundsen made a sledge journey towards the magnetic north pole on the Boothia Peninsula. He met more Eskimos and was given presents of fur underclothes and outer wear. One of his presents was a caribou tongue, which the bearer licked clean before handing to him. He made arrangements for additional food supplies during the spring.

Amundsen had a high regard for the Eskimos' morals, but when spring came his illusions were shattered. The Eskimos offered their wives to the Kabloonas, the white men, but wanted needles, knives and other useful things in return. The Norwegians called the husband of three of the most beautiful women the 'butcher'. The name was undignified and did not respect the values of the Eskimo culture. Since there is no supply without demand the reproach should have perhaps fallen elsewhere.

The magnetic observations took time and the expedition

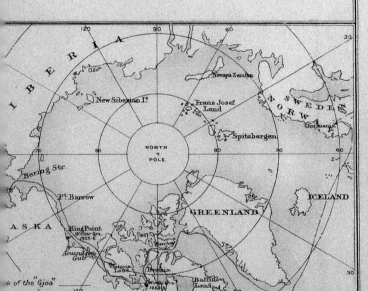

ARCTIC EXPLORATIONS
AMUNDSEN.

THE GEOGRAPHICAL JOURNAL 1907.

MAP

to illustrate the

VOYAGE

AND

ARCTIC EXPLORATIONS

OF

CAPT. ROALD AMUNDSEN.

From 'Surveys by
LIEUT. G. HANSEN.
(Royal Danish Navy)
1903 TO 1906.

KING WILLIAM LAND
NEUMAYER PENINSULA.

Scale 1: 125,000 or 1 inch = 1·97 miles.

△ Trigonometrical Point   & Observation Station

254 *Amundsen's sailing of the Northwest Passage in* THE GJØA *in 1903–1906 is marked with a continuous line. Amundsen was the first to sail from the James Ross Strait to the Deasen Strait's Cambridge Bay, from which Collinson had turned back. It would maybe never have been possible to make the voyage in Franklin's large vessels* THE EREBUS *and the* TERROR. *The sleigh journey in 1905 of Amundsen's mappers, Hansen and Ristvedt, is marked with a broken line.* (JOHN NURMINEN FOUNDATION)

spent a second winter in the harbour. The expedition members felt at home since the Eskimos brought them not only salmon but cod. In spring 1905 Godfred Hansen and Peder Ristvedt set out to chart the east coast of Victoria Island which neither Rae, Collinson nor McClintock had explored in its entirety.

At the end of June they returned. Victoria Strait was as difficult to cross as their predecessors had predicted. Charting the east coast was made difficult by the flat terrain and the ice. The expedition charted and named the islands between Victoria Island and King William Island.

Summer arrived all of a sudden. The harbour was free of ice as early as June. A north-easterly storm pushed the ice south, but it was only possible to sail the Simpson Strait a month later. On 12 August a north wind opened up passages of open water in the sound. They decided to set out at three in the morning. The Eskimos were there to wish them farewell. The departure was sad. Amundsen knew that the best he could wish for the Netsilik Eskimos was that "civilisation would *never* reach them".

As they sailed onward they sounded the water continuously. The *Gjøa* barely managed to navigate the narrow passages left by the ice. The shallows of the Simpson Strait brought them into difficulties with the ice blocking the deeper water off the south coast. Often the best route was open water in channels running along the coast, but there they found the most shallows and reefs.

The ice in Queen Maud Gulf, too, made it difficult to sail a southerly route, and in the north they had to thread their way between numerous islands and reefs. Hansen's and Ristvedt's charts were useful. They sailed to the south of Jenny Lind Island within sight of the southern coast of Victoria Island towards Cambridge Bay, from which Collinson had turned back to the Bering Strait. This was a moment to celebrate, since it meant that they had now sailed the missing part of the Northwest Passage. After this their progress was eased by Collinson's directions.

Their last challenge was to find the entrance to the Dolphin and Union Strait. A heavy current and magnetic disturbances made it difficult to take bearings, but they reached the strait and passed through it. To the south of Banks Island, in a sea now called Amundsen Gulf, they saw their first ship. The *Charles Hanson* out of San Francisco was one of the whalers still fishing these waters. Captain James McKenna's first

THE *GJØA* IN THE NORTHWEST PASSAGE
– WITH ONLY ONE INCH OF WATER UNDER THE KEEL

Although *the Fram* was undoubtedly the best polar vessel, *the Gjøa* probably holds a special place in Norwegian hearts. After all, it was an ordinary ship of the kind constructed by the country's most skilled shipbuilders in the 19th century to withstand the powerful winds on the North Atlantic coastline. The sloops built in Hardanger Fjord in western Norway were the small vessels best suited for herring fishing in the Arctic Ocean. This was known by all Norwegians, and the world was convinced when the *Gjøa* sailed the Northwest Passage with its seven-member crew led by Roald Amundsen.

In August 1905 the expedition sighted the American whaler *Charles Hanson*, coming from the west. The Norwegian skipper, sleeping on the off-duty watch, was still a young man at that glorious moment but his ship was getting old; both were 33 years old. The *Gjøa* was launched in 1872, the same year that her fourth owner Amundsen was born. When she rose to world fame as 'the brave little ship', many raised their hands in an attempt to share in the glory. Erroneous

information on the ship's origin and life abounded for many decades thereafter. It was only in 1981 that Hans Nerhus set the record straight in his study.

The *Gjøa* was built in Rosendal, west Norway. The master builder was Knut Skaale who, despite still being a young man, had already achieved a reputation as the builder of four similar vessels. He received the order for the ship from Asbjørn Sexe, a veteran skipper of northern waters. Skaale set out to build the fifth ship of his line, a first-class vessel with especially strong spars.

The wood for the ship was felled in nearby forests, and the biggest pines in the area were felled for the rig (which had to be replaced after the ship ran aground in 1882). The ship was built outdoors and the hours were long. Skaale teamed up with his young wife Anna to plane the keel. The ship was named after another hardy lady, Sexe's wife Gjøa, however. The shipowner himself was hammering out the stopper wedges prior to the launch when one of them suddenly hit him in the mouth. He spent a moment 'spitting out

his teeth', then grinned and bluntly stated that 'Gjøa has given me many a powerful kiss but never one quite this strong'.

Sexe ran the ship aground in 1882 and sold it off as a wreck. The buyer sold the derelict ship to famous a skipper, Hans Christian Johannesen from Tromsø, and he had the *Gjøa* repaired. Under Johannesen's command it fished off Greenland, Novaya Zemlya and Frans Josef Land. Polar researchers have great respect for Johannesen and say that it was 'he more than anyone who laid the foundations for Nordenskiöld's heroic feat'. It is indeed true that Nordenskiöld learnt a lot about northern conditions from him. Later, Johannesen was to become Nordenskiöld's friend and adviser. The *Gjøa* served science in Johannesen's time, too; for example in 1892, a Swedish researcher was on board the ship as a 'Vega scholar'.

Amundsen had become convinced that the most convenient vessel for the Northwest Passage would be a small, light, smooth-sailing, streamlined ship with a shallow draught. He believed he had found such a vessel when he bought the

Gjøa in 1901. And he was not disappointed; it sailed the Northwest Passage, sometimes with 'only one inch of water beneath the keel'. It would be half a century later before any vessel would accomplish the same feat – in 1954 two icebreakers, the *Northwind* and the *Burton Island* navigated the same route.

The *Gjøa* was 70 feet long and 20 wide, had a draught of 7.7 feet and carrying capacity of 47 net register tonnes. The ship was rigged as a yacht with a gaffsail and topsail and three jibs. In addition, the mast carried a square sail. Amundsen had a combustion engine installed, the first in the history of polar vessels. The experienced sailors considered this 'explosive' machine, a 13-horsepower Dan, more of a risk than the actual journey.

The *Gjøa* received a jubilant welcome when she arrived in San Francisco in October 1906. She almost became the first vessel to sail around North America. It was suggested that she should lead the inaugural squadron through the Panama Canal, but nothing came of the idea, and she was for a long time one of the sights of San Francisco. She returned to Norway in 1972 riding on the deck of the MS *Star Billabong*. There was no fee charged for this valuable cargo.

255 Roald Amundsen's intention was to sail the Northwest Passage from the Atlantic to the Pacific. With this in mind, he purchased the yacht THE GJØA in 1901. The vessel, built in 1872, was 70 feet long, 20 feet wide, had a draught of 7.7 feet and a net register tonnage of 27. It was yacht-rigged and Amundsen had an internal combustion engine installed. (NORSK SJØFARTSMUSEUM)

The main cartographic features of the northern Alaskan and Canadian coastline were already known when Amundsen started planning his voyage, but no one had succeeded in sailing the Northwest Passage. Many had gone that way earlier, especially when searching for survivors of Franklin's ill-fated expedition in 1845.

question to the captain of *Gjøa* was: "Are you Amundsen?" The old sea dog was moved to hear that his vessel was the first that Amundsen had met after sailing the Northwest Passage.

Amundsen was given a pile of newspapers by the captain; one headline startled him: war had broken out between Norway and Sweden. They came across more whalers in the waters off Cape Bathurst. The murky waters of the Mackenzie River swelled brown and muddy. Fog made sailing difficult and they were stopped by the ice again. On 9 September they realised that they would have to winter yet again. Twelve whalers had also been imprisoned in the ice, only three of which were equipped for wintering.

Amundsen and his crew wintered at King Point but were in continuous contact with the American whalers wintering at Herschel Island. Amundsen wanted to travel overland on the postal circuit from Herschel Island to Fort Yukon. He continued to Eagle City, where the nearest telegraph was. This winter journey went well and Amundsen returned to the ship in March.

In the spring Gustav Wiik died. He was the ship's engineer and the man who was responsible for making magnetic observations. The Eskimo boy Manni, whom Amundsen had taken along, fell into the water while hunting birds and drowned. The *Gjøa* got under way again in August. On 31 August 1906, after sailing through the Bering Strait, they arrived at their first port, Nome, Alaska.

THE CONQUEST OF GREENLAND

For twenty years or so the North Pole had been the main target for expeditions into the Greenland area. Peary made an expedition onto Greenland's inland ice to prepare for his final push. But he also wanted to achieve intermediary aims that would strengthen the faith of his backers. The Danes were not interested in the North Pole but in exploring the unmapped areas of Greenland which belonged to Denmark.

The Danish explorer, Ludvig Mylius-Erichsen, led his first expedition to Greenland in 1902–1904. The expedition members included the young Knud Rasmussen. The aim of Mylius-Erichsen's next expedition was to continue from where Peary had left off. After Peary had discovered the land bearing his name and the channel separating it from Greenland, no other explorers had yet made their way to the northeast corner of Greenland.

Both J. P. Koch and Alfred Wegener were members of the expedition. Peter Freuchen was one of two students participating. In June 1906 their vessel the *Danmark* sailed to Germania Land on Greenland's east coast. She wintered in Germania Bay, on whose coast the expedition built its base. In the autumn a sledge party left a store of supplies on the north coast for the spring.

In the spring of 1907 two parties set out for the north. The first, which included N. P. Høeg-Hagen and N. J. Brønlund, was led by Mylius-Erichsen, the second by J. P. Koch. According to the map based on Peary's and de Gerlache's

256 In 1900 Northeast Greenland was largely unexplored even though Peary had been to Independence Fjord and claimed that the Peary Channel ran through the island. In 1902–1904 Ludvig Mylius-Erichsen led an expedition which substantially increased knowledge of Greenland but ended tragically. Mylius-Erichsen and his friends took too many risks and they died of hunger and cold before help arrived. (ARCTIC INSTITUTE, COPENHAGEN)

findings, they would have perhaps needed to cover 250 miles to Independence Fjord. The coast was, in fact, anything but straight and the journey was twice as long as they had anticipated.

Once they had realised these errors, carrying out their original plan meant taking risks. Mylius-Erichsen decided that both journeys should continue, however, even though J. P. Koch suggested that he should go back and leave food stores for Mylius-Erichsen. Mylius-Erichsen headed off into a previously unknown area while Koch went to Independence Fjord.

Upon reaching Peary Land, Koch found a message in a cairn which Peary had built at the northernmost point reached by his expedition. Koch continued along the coast to Cape Bridgman, at the north-westernmost tip of Greenland. From there he and his companions returned to Independence Fjord.

257 Knud Rasmussen's maternal grandmother was an Eskimo. His Danish father worked as a missionary in Greenland and Knud learned the Eskimo language, how to drive a dog team and to hunt. He was with Mylius-Erichsen as a journalist but returned to his childhood home district and established the Thule trading station in 1910. Rasmussen explored North Greenland and the Arctic regions and cultures of Canada. He differed from many of his colleagues in that he was able to perform actions in the Arctic just as demanding as those of the best local inhabitants, and he was by nature first and foremost a Greenlander not a European.

(Arctic Institute, Copenhagen)

Because of their poor diet, Koch and his comrades fell sick. Some of their dogs were lost when they ran off to chase musk ox. The men recovered by eating musk-ox bone marrow, although they were not able to drink the animal's blood. On 27 May they met Mylius-Erichsen.

Once the parties had split up, Mylius-Erichsen's party set off west along the north coast of Christians Land. In a few days they had crossed a fjord and reached an area which would later be named Mylius-Erichsen Land. As the journey continued they mapped the 130 miles long Danmarks Fjord. They found signs of old Eskimo settlements in the area.

When he returned to Cape Rigsdagen and met Koch,

Mylius-Erichsen had food for only a few days. His intention was to return to the base with Koch, but he could not resist the unexplored areas hidden to the west and decided to stay for just a few more days. Koch divided up the supply of provisions and promised to leave some of the food supply for Mylius-Erichsen. Mylius-Erichsen left his account of the journey with Koch and announced that he was going on as far as Navy Cliff, but would return within six weeks.

When Koch arrived at Danmark Havn at the end of June he had covered more than 1 500 miles, of which almost half had been previously unexplored area. On finding Peary's message at Cape Bridgman he had proved once and for all that Greenland was an island. At the base they were already beginning to worry about the fate of the expedition when Koch arrived, tired but happy. The weeks went by but nothing was heard of Mylius-Erichsen. It was not possible to send out a rescue party in the summer, but on 23 September the first party made its way north with fully loaded sledges. Seven different parties left food depots. One of the parties reached Mallemuk Fjord but open water forced it to turn back. This same open water forced Mylius-Erichsen, coming from the north , to go inland onto the glacier. The party left a food supply and a message on the banks of the fjord and returned to the ship.

During the summer of 1907 the *Danmark* was still beset. Spending another winter where they were was unavoidable. Koch and Tobias Gabrielsen set out north at the beginning of 1908 with the aim of advancing to Cape York by way of Peary Channel, unless they found their leader and his men before they got there. When they reached a depot situated less than 200 miles from the base they found that it had been used. A hundred yards from the food store they found a piece of metal which they recognised as a sledge box lid. The lid led them to a small snow-covered cave. From this they first dug out Brønlund's body. In his lap Brøndlund held a loaded weapon and at his feet was a box in which were his diary and Høeg Hagen's sketch maps The diary was written in the Eskimo language and could only be read when it was taken to Denmark. The Danish-language instructions revealed where Mylius-Erichsen's and Hagen's bodies had been left. With his last strength Brønlund had made his way to a place where he would certainly be found.

No other remains were found. Brønlund's diary relates how Mylius-Erichsen's journey had progressed. The party had crossed Danmarks Fjord again and arrived at Hagen Fjord, which they had first thought to be Independence Fjord, and where they had probably arrived at the beginning of June. They mapped Academy Gletscher and Navy Cliff, which had been discovered by Peary. On 4 June the party had set out on their return journey. In the expedition's official report it is stated that Peary's draft map had played an important part in the party's fate. Later, however, Lauge Koch disputed the authenticity of this claim.

The return journey by way of Danmark and Hagen Fjords proved overwhelming. The men no longer managed to cross Danmark Fjord. They had to build a summer camp and to

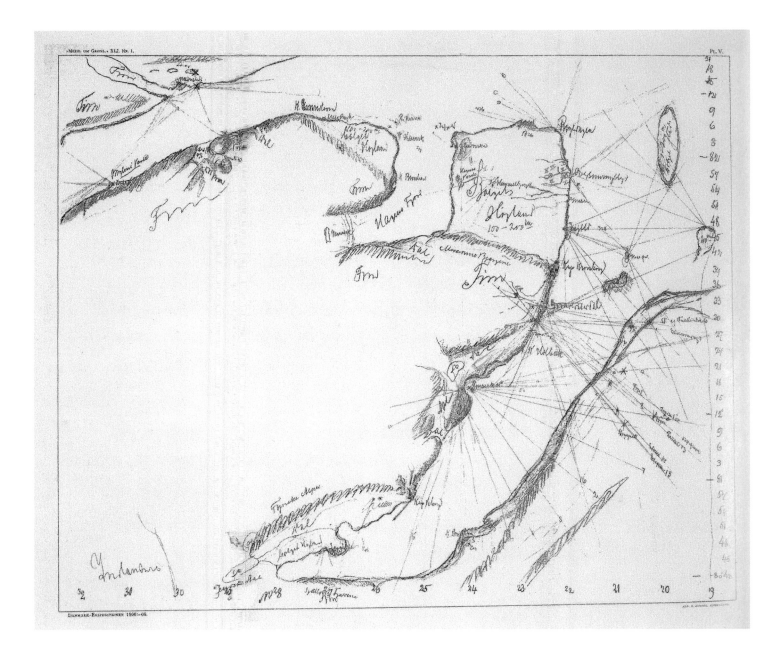

258 *Mylius-Erichsen's expedition perished in north-east Greenland in 1907. In addition to Mylius-Erichsen, the expedition included Höeg-Hagen and Brønlund. The expedition charted Independence Fjord, Hagen Fjord, and Danmark Fjord and was the first expedition to find out that the Peary Channel did not exist. The picture shows Hagen's map, which was made in summer, a few months before its makers' death.*

(OLE VENTEGOBT, DEN SISTE BRIK, 1998)

hunt to be able to last out the autumn and winter. As well as rabbits and geese, Brønlund, who was an excellent hunter, succeeded in shooting five muskox. These rendered no oil so they only had driftwood as fuel. The men's shoes fell to pieces. They tried to mend them with leather from the box containing the sextant. It started to snow in August. The men's health suffered further. The party's conditions were wretched because they could not warm themselves by a fire.

When the frosts came at the end of August there was little food left, but they had eight dogs, and that was enough. The severe weather and lack of food meant that they had to abandon all non-essentials.

They were only able to cross the fjord at the end of August. The next entry in Brønlund's diary was for 19 October. The men had managed to progress to the south, having found provisions at two coastal depots. Since Mallemuk Fjord was open they ascended the inland ice and did not encounter Koch and Gabrielsen. Their end was horrifying. At the beginning of November the sun disappeared. In their tattered clothes the men had trudged forward in the cold, with almost no food. Høeg-Hagen died on 15 November and Mylius-Erichsen could not manage to reach the depot in Lamberts Land. Gustav Thostrup's relief party had only left it at the end of October, just a couple of weeks before Brønlund arrived.

When Brønlund returned he found that Mylius-Erichsen had died. Brønlund took the expedition diaries with him and returned to the depot. The last entry in his diary was as follows: "I arrived here in the waning moonlight and could not go further for frozen feet and darkness. Bodies of the others are in the middle of the fjord off the glacier about 7 miles away, Hagen died on 15th November, Mylius ten days later."

MIKKELSEN TAKES OVER

The results of Mylius-Erichsen's expedition were scientifically valuable. In spite of this, a great deal remained to be done. Ejnar Mikkelsen took over where Mylius-Erichsen had left off. Mikkelsen had had his first experience of Greenland together with J. P. Koch on Georg Amdrup's expedition, which in 1900 explored the eastern coast of Greenland between Scoresby Sound and Angmagssalik.

Mikkelsen had also been assistant cartographer on Baldwin-Ziegler's expedition which attempted to reach the North Pole from Franz Josef Island. It was there that Mikkelsen got to know the geologist Ernest Leffingwell, with whom he made an expedition to the Beaufort Sea to find out whether there was land to the north of the Alaskan coast. The aim of Mikkelsen's expedition in 1909 was to search for Mylius-Erichsen and his party's diaries and papers.

Mikkelsen decided to sail to Denmark Harbour in 1909 and to winter at Mylius-Erichsen's base. The ice conditions were difficult and Mikkelsen's sloop the *Alabama* could not get through. He chose Shannon Island as a place to winter. Mikkelsen arrived at Danmark Harbour with two companions on 11 October and set about building depots for the spring.

At the end of October Mikkelsen arrived at Lambert Land, where he found Brønlund's body, which was re-buried. In spite of his efforts he did not find Mylius-Erichsen's or Høeg-Hagen's bodies or papers. On setting out on the return journey Mikkelsen and his companions had food for three days and the distance to their ship the *Alabama* was 250 miles. By making their way from one depot to another they eventually made it to Denmark Harbour at the end of November and to the *Alabama* in mid-December.

The main party, which included Mikkelsen and Iver Iversen, set out for the north again on 4 March 1910. They got onto the inland ice between Germania Land and Queen Louise Land. Progress proved difficult because of crevasses, and they were slowed down by storms. The expedition was forced to kill their first dog and go on half-rations. Two dogs died of fatigue even though in a month they only made 105 miles' progress.

They reached Danmarks Fjord in mid-May. After the ice cap the fjord seemed an Arctic paradise. There was grass and dwarf plants growing there, they found fresh tracks of musk-ox, rabbit, fox and wolf. On 23 May they found their first signs of Mylius-Erichsen. A note deposited in a cairn dated 12 September 1907 stated that they were on their way back to the ship.

When Mikkelsen and Iversen continued together on the journey north there were only seven dogs remaining. The expedition passed the remains of Mylius-Erichsen's summer camp. They found a report in a cairn saying that Peary Channel did not exist and Navy Cliff had a land connection to Heilprin Land. This message and the condition of the men changed Mikkelsen's plans, which had been to progress along Peary Channel to Smith Sound. They continued to Cape Rigsdagen and decided to return along the coast in the hope of finding Mylius-Erichsen's missing papers. Before them was a stretch of almost 600 miles and they only had enough food for 12 days for the dogs and 40 days for the men. The deep snow threatened to bring the expedition to a halt. They made the journey from one food depot to another. Because Mikkelsen was ill with scurvy, Iversen had to do almost all the work.

The thawed waters of Mallemuk Fjord eventually brought Mikkelsen to a stop too. They could not find the food depot there at first, but a few hares helped Mikkelsen's recovery. Iversen also hunted gulls. When they found the food depot the biscuits were mouldy and the chocolate had turned green. The men ate it, saying that after all mildew was a vegetable. In addition to cigars, cigarettes and clothes, they also found a map of the other depots along the coast.

When, on 5 July, they finally crossed the fjord, Mikkelsen was again in good health. They had only three dogs left. The sledge was often forced to travel through melt-water, the biscuits turned into dough and the tea tasted of salt. Once more there was a lack of food. They had no luck hunting. The seals they shot sank to the bottom, and instead of large game they got only ptarmigan. When they reached Lambert Land, the dogs were completely exhausted and Iversen had fallen sick. They had to make a dozen ptarmigan last for six days. They were forced to eat two of the three dogs. When they reached the next food depot they had only a few grams of food left.

They set out again on 4 September. The coming of winter helped their progress, as they no longer had to wade through melt-water. The next depot was found as planned, but the one after that was empty. So was the next. Mikkelsen had not ensured the condition of the depots, since he had thought they would return west by way of Peary Channel. There were only a few cans of food in the next two depots, but they were able to build fires from the boxes. The last thousand yards took one and a half hours. Supporting each other, they finally reached the hut built by Mylius-Erichsen, in which there was food, and they could rest at last.

But it was not all over. The *Alabama* was still 100 miles away. On 15 October, after resting for four weeks, they set out on their journey once again in the middle of a winter storm. Their progress was so slow that they were forced to turn round and go back for more food from the hut.

On 5 November they set out again. At the Danmark Harbour they saw only the *Alabama's* mast. The *Alabama* been crushed by the ice and sunk. The crew had built a hut for Mikkelsen and Iversen and had left as much food as possible there. Nobody had stayed there to wait for them.

Once again Mikkelsen and Iversen turned back to the hut. Worn out, they had also abandoned their diaries by the wayside. When they got back and retrieved them they found that Mikkelsen's diary had been eaten by a bear, but Iversen's was intact. Nor was this to be their last disappointment.

The following summer they waited in vain to be rescued. When they moved later in the autumn to another depot, they found a message informing them that the *Laura* had looked for them in vain. They had calmly been waiting a good 15 miles away but had left no messages. They were obliged to

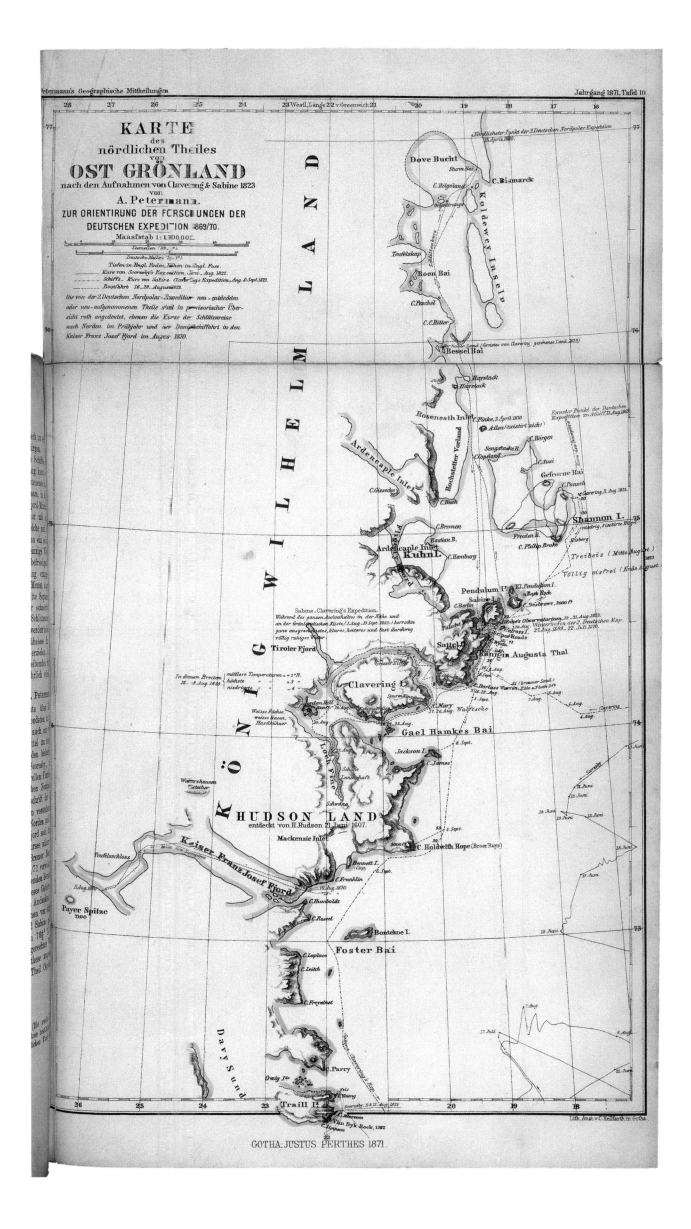

KARTE
des
nördlichen Theiles
von
OST GRÖNLAND
nach den Aufnahmen von Clavering & Sabine 1823
von
A. Petermann.
ZUR ORIENTIRUNG DER FORSCHUNGEN DER
DEUTSCHEN EXPEDITION 1869/70.
Maassstab 1 : 1,500,000.

Seemeilen (60 = 1°).

Deutsche Meilen (15 = 1°).

Tiefen in Engl. Faden, Höhen in Engl. Fuss.

Kurs von Scoresby's Expedition, Juni - Aug. 1822.

Schiff's - Kurs von Sabine Clavering's Expedition, Aug. & Sept. 1823.

Bootsfahrt 16.-29. August 1823.

Die von der 2. Deutschen Nordpolar-Expedition neu - entdeckten oder neu - aufgenommenen Theile sind in provisorischer Übersicht roth angedeutet, ebenso die Kurse der Schlittenreise nach Norden im Frühjahr und der Dampfschifffahrt in den Kaiser Franz Josef Fjord im Aug. 1870.

GRÖNLAND

KÖNIG WILHELM LAND

Dove Bucht

Sturm Bai

C. Bismarck

C. Helgoland

Koldewey Inseln

Teufelskap

Room Bai

C. Peschel

C. C. Ritter

Bessel Bai

Haystack

Haystack

Roseneath Inlet

Ardencaple Inlet

Hochstetter Vorland

C. Giesecke

C. Buch

C. Bremen

Bastian B.

Ardencaple Inlet

Kuhn I.

C. Hamburg

Shannon I.

Freeden B.

C. Philip Broke

Treibeis (Mitte August)

Völlig eisfrei (Ende August)

Pendulum I.

Kl. Pendulum I.

Sabine I.

C. Berlin

Falsche Bai

Pepper Roads

Sabel I.

Königin Augusta Thal

Tiroler Fjord

Clavering I.

Gael Hamkes Bai

Jordan Hill

C. Mary

Jackson I.

C. James

Loch Fyne

KÖNIG

HUDSON LAND
entdeckt von H. Hudson 21. Juni 1607.

Mackenzie Inlet

Kaiser Franz Josef Fjord

Teufelsschloss

C. Franklin

Bennett I.

C. Holdwith Hope (Broer Ruys)

Payer Spitze

C. Humboldt

C. Roscoe

Bontekoe I.

Foster Bai

C. Laplace

C. Leitch

C. Freycinet

Davy Sund

Craig I.

C. Parry

Traill I.

Van Dyk Rock

259 In 1869–1870 a German expedition led by Karl Koldeway attempted to prove the existence of an open polar sea, but the ice already cut off their path at latitude 75. The expedition concentrated on mapping that area of the east coast of Greenland later named King Wilhelm Land. (JOHN NURMINEN FOUNDATION)

spend one more winter in Greenland and only returned home in summer 1912.

Mikkelsen and his companion explored wide areas. Although they did not find the Mylius-Erichsen diaries, they were able to prove that Mylius-Erichsen was the first to discover that Peary Channel did not exist.

RASMUSSEN RETURNS TO HIS ROOTS

Knud Rasmussen was the first explorer of note to have Eskimo blood in his veins. His grandmother was an Eskimo and his father a Danish missionary who lived in Greenland for 28 years. Knud learnt the Eskimo language as a child, was given his first rifle at the age of 10, and was driving his own dog team by the time has was 12. Having graduated from Copenhagen University, Knud first wanted to become an actor, then a singer and, finally, a writer. He was with Mylius-Erichsen in Greenland in 1903 as a journalist. In 1910 he decided to return to the district of his youth and establish a trading post in the proximity of Wolstenholme Fjord, which he called Thule. He planned to explore Peary Channel, but heard that Mikkelsen had not returned after having set out to find Mylius-Erichsen.

Rasmussen's companion, Peter Freuchen, was to become perhaps the best known writer on Greenland and the lives of its Eskimos. In April 1912 Rasmussen went up Robertson Fjord to the ice cap with 35 sledges and 350 dogs. The support parties returned little by little, eventually leaving Knud, Peter and two of their Eskimo companions behind.

In a month the expedition went down Danmark Fjord and made their way north along the coast, hunting musk ox, seals and smaller game as they went. They were forced to kill some dogs to feed the others. They found Mylius-Erichsen's summer camp and continued southwest along Independence Fjord. They soon discovered that the Peary Channel drawn on Peary's chart did not exist. Peary Land and Heilprin Land were connected by an isthmus. Independence Bay was a fjord, as Peary had indeed described it in his notes. At that point Peary was not yet speaking of a channel.

In mid-July they found a cairn built by Peary and a bottle in which there was a message from 1892. They even saw Peary's footprints, which had been preserved remarkably clearly in the gravel.

When Freuchen had climbed Navy Cliff, they set out on the return journey and, at the beginning of September, arrived at Inglefield Gulf, from where they continued to Thule.

When they arrived they had only one sledge and 13 dogs left. Freuchen was in a bad state, but they had brought with them a great deal of scientific results and many specimens from the 1500 mile-long journey.

THE SECOND THULE EXPEDITION AND LAUGE KOCH

Much of northern Greenland remained to be explored after the first Thule expedition. Rasmussen's return, however, was postponed until 1917. The expedition was stronger and more versatile by then. Dr. Thorild Wulff, a botanist, and Lauge Koch, a geologist, were new members. The group was completed by Olsen, Rasmussen's assistant, and three more Eskimos. With 27 sledges, they set out at the beginning of April 1917. Before long the main party continued alone. They had with them provisions for two months and enough guns and ammunition for hunting.

From Thule they made their way to Etah, where they met Donald MacMillan, who had been with Peary. Their journey continued along the coast. They found Nares' depot on the coast of Kennedy Channel. A bear had eaten the sugar but the mutton they found tasted perfectly sweet. After Kennedy and Robeson Channels they turned east, following the north coast of Greenland. The expedition found Peary's 17-year-old message near Repulse Harbour. Peary had left a message of his own in place of a record by Lewis Beaumont. The original message left by Beaumont, who had led the sledge party sent out by Nares, was discovered at St George Fjord where it was hidden in 1876. The fjords to the east of this had never been explored before.

At the end of May, Wulff made his way with two companions to the edge of Peary Land, Cape Morris Jesup. Rasmussen and Koch continued to Independence Fjord. They named a fjord they discovered after Lauge Koch's uncle, J. P. Koch. Once again they ran out of food. Koch was having difficulties. The dogs fell ill but most of them recovered. The party explored most of Peary Land thoroughly. No channel was found between it and the mainland of Greenland.

The parties joined up and, in July, made their way west in the wet, slushy snow. They managed to shoot a few musk ox. They had only 18 dogs left. After Sherard Osborn and St George Fjords they could take advantage of the depot left there. When the party assembled after the hunting trip, Olson was missing. He had stayed behind to rest and was never seen again. They looked for him for three days but then they had to continue.

By mid-August they had nearly reached close to the Humboldt Glacier. Their food was again running out and the fog made progress across the crevasses and glacial streams difficult. Wulff fell down a crevasse and survived, but he fell ill. On 25 August Rasmussen set out with an Eskimo to find help at Etah, 125 miles away.

When Rasmussen had left, his comrades caught some hares, but Wulff was not able to eat his share. He talked of dying.

The men threw away most of their equipment and continued the journey with only their guns, some rugs and scientific notes. Wulff complained of his heart and of fatigue. Although he was not able to eat he continued his botanical research.

On 29 August the men left the exhausted Wulff, at his own request, lying in the shadow of a large rock in a valley. Wulff had dictated a few letters, his will and a botanical report to Koch. Koch and his companions shot a deer on 2 September. Wulff would perhaps have been able to eat some of it, but they did not believe him to be still alive. Ten days would have passed since Wulff's last meal if they had returned to where they had left him.

After two days' trekking they heard gun shots and they met Rasmussen and the rescue party. Koch sat on a rock, silently weeping. Wulff was later found dead. He had written the last line in his diary on the same day that he had been left alone: "I am half dead, but I found some Woodsia ilvensis. Lay down at 7 p.m. for I will not hamper the movements of my comrades on which hang their salvation."

Between 1921–1924 Rasmussen made his Fifth Thule expedition, which stretched from Greenland to Alaska. With him were Peter Freuchen, archaeologist Therkel Mathiassen and ethnologist Kaj Birket-Smith. The expedition camped on Denmark Island in Hudson Bay, to the north of Southampton Island. Rasmussen and his men collected an enormous amount of information on the life of the Netsilik Eskimos and charted the eastern part of Baffin Island, Melville Peninsula and Southampton Island.

Rasmussen also went to King William Island and gained information on Franklin's expedition, particularly on his ships, which the Eskimos had visited to gather useful articles. It had been dark in the hold of one of the two ships, so they had made a window by cutting the ship's side. But the window happened to be below the water line, so the ship sank and the Eskimos lost their treasures.

Laugh Koch made an important contribution to the exploration of northern Greenland. He returned in 1920 and in February 1921 he made an eight-month journey with three Eskimos, during which they travelled along the northern and north-eastern coasts of Greenland to Independence Fjord and then back along the west coast. The journey was demanding and dangerous. The hungry men barely made it back. As well as the charting he did, Koch brought back a collection of 4000 Palaeozoic fossils.

After this Koch made four more journeys of exploration from 1926 to 1934. His *Survey of North Greenland*, published in 1940, describes in great detail the history of the charting of northern Greenland.

VILHJÁLMUR STEFÁNSSON – THE LAST VIKING

Vilhjálmur Stefánsson learnt the Icelandic language from his parents. He spent his childhood in North Dakota and as a youth could already use a gun. This conceited and self-assured boy ran into difficulties at school with his teachers, but he got to Harvard where he succeeded in his studies. Stefánsson studied anthropology, made his first expedition to Iceland, and became interested in the fate of the Vikings who had moved to Greenland. He wrote an article on the subject and received the attention of Ejnar Mikkelsen and Ernest Leffingwell, who wanted to take Stefánsson along on their expedition to explore the Beaufort Sea. Stefánsson chose his own route and spent the winter of 1906–1907 under difficult conditions on Herschel Island completely separated from Mikkelsen and Leffingwell. On the island Stefánsson also met Amundsen, who was sailing the Northwest Passage.

Stefánsson became interested in the Eskimos and their ability to survive in the Arctic. A U.S./Canadian scientific expedition was sent to the Victoria Island area in 1908. The chief sponsors of the expedition were the American Museum of Natural History and the Canadian Geological Survey. The two-man expedition consisted of Vilhjálmur Stefánsson and R. M. Anderson, an ornithologist. Stefánsson's task was to carry out research on the Eskimos, Anderson's to collect zoological data.

The expedition took four years. Stefánsson made his reputation with two claims. He told of meeting 'blonde' Eskimos. Although he later claimed otherwise, he suggested that these were the descendants of Vikings lost in Greenland. This unfounded conclusion led many – among them Nansen and Amundsen – to question the validity of Stefánsson's claims.

Stefánsson's second claim caused at least as much confusion. According to Stefánsson the Arctic was a friendly environment in which a good hunter could live without trouble on the game he caught. Stefánsson was stating a fact that Rae and Rasmussen had already proved to be possible in certain conditions. Stefánsson lived on the mainland where there was plenty of game. He did not mention, however, that continuous hunting took some of the time that most explorers wanted to dedicate to their work.

Stefánsson's greatest achievements are associated with the Canadian Arctic expedition which he led in 1913–1918. The expedition was a sizeable enterprise, which exceeded its budget many times over. It also cost more lives than any expedition since Franklin. The expedition's geographical achievements were largely due to Stefánsson's courage and persistence, but he was also responsible for its failures.

Stefánsson bought the whaler *Karluk* to support the exploration of the Parry Islands. The captain of the *Karluk*, Bob Bartlett, had had a great deal of experience of the polar ice, having participated in Peary's polar expedition, and he considered the *Karluk* unsuitable for ice navigation. The *Karluk* did become a prisoner of the ice before she reached Collinson Point on the north coast of Alaska where Stefánsson's two parties were due to meet. Stefánsson became bored with life on board ship and set out to hunt in September 1913.

When Stefánsson had left, a storm drove the ice north and the *Karluk* disappeared from sight. He tried to find the vessel but gave up hope, explained the situation to the Canadian government who had financed the expedition and set out for

260 Vilhjálmur Stefánsson's parents moved from Iceland to Canada. Stefánsson studied anthropology, and one of his writings inspired Mikkelsen and Leffingwell to ask him to accompany them to the Beaufort Sea. This journey to the Arctic inspired Stefánsson to undertake new expeditions from 1908–1912 and 1913–1918, at which time he was leader of the Canadian Arctic Expedition. Stefánsson added to Sverdrup's findings, but his reputation was based to a great extent on his claims of a "friendly Arctic". Stefánsson was a visionary. His idea of flying over the polar region has been fulfilled, but many of his ideas were not successful. He was an excellent writer who both loved and received the limelight. (DARTMOUTH COLLEGE LIBRARY)

the north in the spring without the *Karluk*. The *Karluk* drifted to the vicinity of Wrangel Island and was shipwrecked on 11 January 1914. The men took refuge on the ice. Bartlett decided to make for Wrangler Island. One party of four men never reached their destination at all and another was overcome with exhaustion when trying to go straight to the Siberian coast. In March Bartlett too set out towards Siberia, which was a good 100 miles away. His aim was to organise a rescue expedition for the following summer. Pressure ridges and areas of open water made the going difficult, drawing out the journey, but Bartlett and his Eskimo companions succeeded in reaching the mainland.

Those who remained on the island experienced great difficulties. In spite of what Stefánsson had said, hunting was not easy. Three of the men died of hunger and exhaustion but the others survived, helped by an Eskimo family whose daughters were three and eleven years of age. The survivors hunted crows and gulls and, in summer, seals too.

Bartlett arrived in Alaska at the end of May. It was not possible to sail to Wrangel before the first open water. It was only in September that one of the rescue vessels reached the island and picked up the survivors, who would hardly have survived the following winter.

After having lost the *Karluk,* Stefánsson returned to the scientific party at Collinson Point led by R. M. Anderson. Stefánsson considered his own expedition to have priority, and came into conflict with Anderson and his scientists. Having received more equipment Stefánsson made for the north to the Beaufort Sea with Storker Storkerson and Ole Andreasen.

With ten month's provisions the men set out for the north with their dog teams on 22 March 1914. They made soundings until they could not touch bottom. Their supply of game rapidly diminished as they made their way over the sea ice further from the coast. Stefánsson's experiences did not lend weight to his own theories. In his work *The Friendly Arctic* Stefánsson admits to hurrying towards Banks Island in the hope that they would find seals near the island.

The men were on half rations when they reached the coast of Banks Island in May. Old boots and bed skins were fed to the dogs. There were only enough half rations for two days when two seals were shot in an open lead, both of which were lost. Occasionally the ice took the men west, further away from Banks Island. Only at the fifth attempt did they manage to secure a shot seal.

Although the journey to Cape Alfred on Banks Island was almost 120 miles, they found enough seals. With the coming of spring the birds arrived too. The wider open channels put the seaworthiness of the sledge-boats to the test. At the end of June 1914 they finally reached Norway Island near the Banks coast. They found that the Admiralty's charts sketched by McClure needed correction. When they reached the Banks mainland, Stefánsson was able to prove the validity of his theory: he shot six caribou with eight rounds from a distance of more than 200 yards.

The expedition built their winter camp on Cape Kellett, the westernmost cape of Banks Island. By February 1915 they had begun a new journey north to Prince Patrick Island. Stefánsson was the first to explore the area after the expeditions looking for Franklin. The drift ice took him and his three companions to the northwest. They discovered no new land and turned east towards Prince Patrick Island. In June Stefánsson found a message left by McClintock 62 years earlier to the day at the northernmost tip of the island.

Continuing their journey north, they came across an undiscovered island, which was named Brock Island after the head of the Canadian Geological Survey. Stefánsson did not wait to explore the island but began the return journey. The expedition made its way past Mackenzie King Island and along a strait between Prince Patrick and Melville Islands, and returned to winter quarters at Cape Kellett.

The following year Stefánsson set out as early as January. He made his way north by way of Mercy Bay, the last harbour of McClure's *Investigator,* to begin exploring Brock Island. From there he continued by way of Borden Island to Cape Isachsen, the northernmost tip of Elef Ringnes, where he arrived at the end of May. Stefánsson discovered Meighen Island to the north-west. He returned via Hassel Sound, which separated the Ringes Islands, passed King Christian Island and, in discovering Lougheed Island, revised the chart of the Findlay Group.

In 1917 Stefánsson returned to the north, but this journey resulted in nothing substantially new. When he returned home to the south he concentrated on lecturing and writing.

He inspired the Hudson's Bay Company to domesticate reindeer on Baffin Island. He also believed that the musk ox could give Canada a dominant position in the world's meat production. The reindeer project failed. The latter was brought to a halt by the fact that the muskox whose wool was gathered died of pneumonia after three weeks. This was a surprise for Stefánsson, who had previously had experience of muskox only after he had shot them.

Stefánsson was a visionary, but his projects often failed because of a lack of background work. He tried to force Canada to take possession of Wrangel Island by sending an occupying party there. The party's task was also to prove his theory of the friendly Arctic. In this they failed – three of the men died after leaving the island and going to Siberia to find better game. One of the men died of scurvy, and only an Eskimo woman who had gone with them was still alive when the rescue party arrived.

261 On an aerial photo taken of Northwest Greenland one can see how the icebergs have become prisoner to the new ice. When the temperature is low enough the calm sea freezes and new ice is formed on the top of the water. The ice shelf strengthens downwards in the frost. Pack ice is formed under the pressure of winds on the ice sheet when it breaks and piles up into heaps.
(B. & C. ALEXANDER)

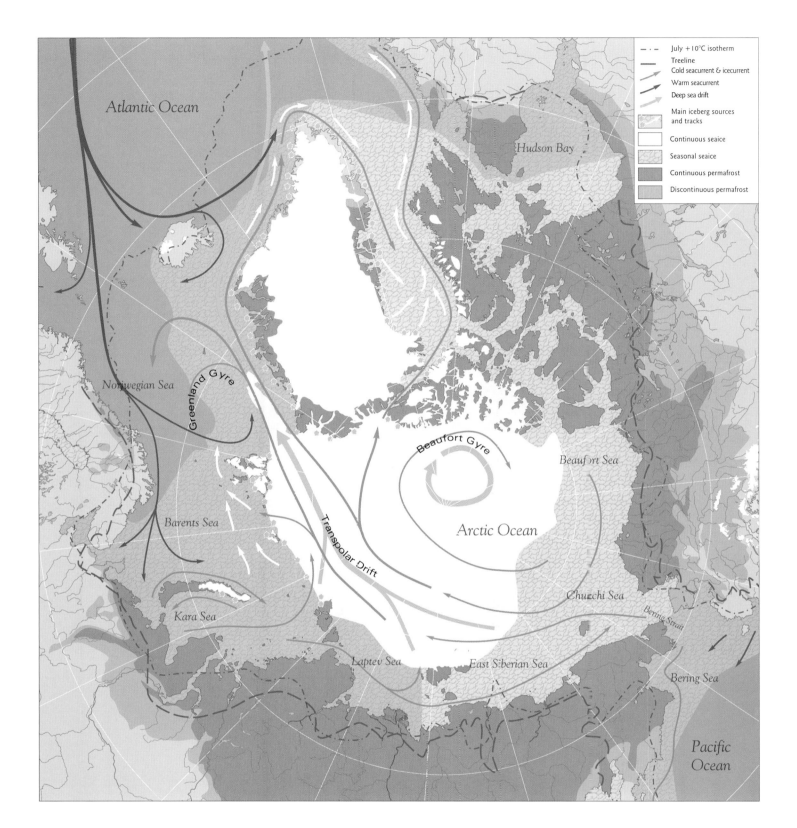

ICE, ICE STREAMS, GLACIERS AND ICEBERGS

Unlike the Antarctic, most of the ice in the Arctic is formed from the sea. In winter almost the entire polar sea is covered by a sheet of ice, which is often several metres thick. In places, fissures are torn open in it which freeze over quickly in the intense cold. The ice may also project downwards in the form of pillars many metres long. The winds take the ice with it, breaking it up and compressing it into piles. This is how wide mounds of pack ice more than ten metres high are formed. It is not possible to sail through them and they also make moving on foot, by skis and sledge, difficult. Research shows the northern polar ice to have become thinner over recent decades, from three metres to less than two metres.

The surface of the sea always freezes first. In calm weather, this freezing can

262 Both the winter and summer ice cover in the Arctic are marked on the map. The isotherm for July shows how much warmer the area surrounding Iceland and Scandinavia is compared to the Bering Sea area, where the isotherm moves much further south to the Pacific Ocean. The Arctic Ocean currents clearly show that Nansen's chances of sailing the FRAM to the Pole were very great. On the other hand success might also have caused the vessel to drift to the north coast of Greenland, from which it would not have perhaps survived in one piece. (PATANEN)

263 The finest glaciers and ice flows can be found in Greenland and Canada. This is where icebergs are created. Ice flows faster where the ice is most broken. The end of a glacier is constantly melting away, and small pieces of ice are carried by the water. This handsome flow was photographed in West Greenland. (B. & A. ALEXANDER)

be very fast. The freezing point of water gets lower as the salinity increases. Sea water can thus be colder than 0°C. With time the salt leaves the ice, so that it can be melted for drinking water, an important matter for those moving about on the ice sheet. Often, there is a layer of lightly compressed snow covering the surface of the ice.

In summer the ice cover thins out and its edge recedes towards the north. Very wide areas of melted water may form at the mouths of rivers. Nordenskiöld was able to sail almost the entire North-east Passage through these areas of open water. He had good luck in the Kara Sea, where ice conditions are often difficult even at the end of the summer. Amundsen had to use all his skill to navigate the Gjøa through the narrow labyrinths of ice of the Northwest Passage. He, too, found a navigable route near the mainland.

In summer, areas of melted ice can also be found on the ice sheet. These obstacles almost prevented Peary's sledge expedition from reaching the North Pole. Nansen crossed the unfrozen areas in a kayak, which he transported by sledge. He had some difficult experiences at

such places; once he almost drowned and once the kayak floated off into open water and he had to swim after it to retrieve it.

In the area affected by the Gulf Stream, the Arctic Ocean is open all year and the edge of the ice is further north than in other parts of the sea. Even though the Kola Peninsula extends to the north of the Arctic Circle, its coastline always remains unfrozen. Early sailors and whale hunters took advantage of these open waters.

The sea ice in the north is always on the move. In winter, too, it is alive. To the north of Canada the movement is circular, while on the Eurasian side the ice flows towards Greenland. Ice formed to the north of the Chukchi Peninsula melts in the North Atlantic, having travelled over 1250 miles north across the Arctic Ocean. Nordenskiöld deduced where Greenland's driftwood came from: the banks of the great rivers of Siberia. For three years it travelled across the polar region to Greenland in the same way as Nansen's icebound *Fram*.

Icebergs are always formed on land. The Swiss Louis Agassiz presented his ideas on the formation of glaciers in

1840. He argued that glaciers are formed from snow in cold areas which is compressed into dense masses over half-a-mile-thick and condensed into ice. The ice is elastic under great pressure and flows like dough towards the outer edge. Evaporation takes place at its upper surface and melting at its lower surface. As the ice stream pushes from the land out to sea, pieces split away from it to form icebergs, which float in the water. Approximately 80% of an iceberg is below the surface.

In the Arctic Ocean icebergs are formed in Alaska, Ellesmere Island, Greenland, Spitsbergen and Russia's Arctic islands. They can float far to the south before they melt. Icebergs are constantly being pushed from Baffin Bay to the south of Newfoundland. The phenomenon became widely known because of the fate of *the Titanic*. Although large table-like icebergs break free from the Ellesmere glacier, the real giants are found in the waters of the southern hemisphere. The largest known iceberg – 183 miles long and 23 miles wide – split away from the Ross glacier in March 2000. The area of this 'floating ice continent' was over 2800 square miles.

264 Large chunks separated by ice flows can, in a manner of speaking, have a long life. This iceberg in Northwest Greenland has become stuck to the bottom. The sea and trapped air erode the surface to form statuesque shapes. (B. & A. ALEXANDER)

EPILOGUE

The exploration of the Beaufort Sea archipelago was completed by Donald MacMillan and his companions, who looked for Peary's *Crocker Land* from 1913-15 without finding anything. It became apparent that there was nothing more than sea and ice to be found in that part of the North.

Aviation changed the nature of exploration. Roald Amundsen realised its potential and acquired his first aeroplane in 1914. He learned how to fly but was forced to give up his plans because of the First World War. He and his companions tried to fly to the North Pole in 1925, but the flight ended with a forced landing on the ice. Within three weeks they had built a runway on the ice from which Hjalmar Riiser-Larsen succeeded in taking off in one of the planes and flying back to Spitsbergen. In May 1926, Roald Amundsen, Lincoln Ellsworth, Hjalmar Riiser-Larsen and Umberto Nobile crossed the Arctic Ocean in the air ship *Norge*. They flew from Spitsbergen across the North Pole and landed near Nome in Alaska after a 70-hour flight.

A few days earlier Richard Byrd had flown in his Fokker aeroplane from Kings Bay in Spitsbergen to the North Pole and back, but his achievement was later to come under suspicion because the speed of his aircraft would not have been sufficient to fly to the Pole and back in 15.5 hours. Byrd based his speed on a following wind, but the critics claimed that a following wind would have meant a head wind on the outward flight, which would have slowed the journey down more than a following wind would have speeded it up on the return flight.

In 1926 Umberto Nobile came to believe that he had been in Amundsen's shadow and, in 1928, flew to the North Pole again in the air-ship *Italia*. On the return journey the *Italia* crashed on the sea ice north of Spitbergen. Six members were carried away by the air balloon, all the rest bar one were rescued. Nobile's reputation was tarnished because he and his lap-dog were brought to safety while his men waited for a long time before being rescued by the Russian ice-breaker *Krassin*. Amundsen was lost whilst flying to help Nobile.

G. H. Wilkins had been on Stefansson's expedition in 1913 but left to become a photographer in the First World War. He returned from the war to look for 'Keenan Land', which was believed to be located in the Beaufort Sea north of Barrow. Together with Carl Ben Eielson, Wilkins made several flights to the north without discovering anything. On one flight in 1927

they made a forced landing on the ice and only reached the mainland thanks to Wilkins' experience. The following year they were the first to fly over the Arctic Ocean to Spitsbergen. In 1931 Wilkins also tried to sail under the polar ice in a submarine, the *Nautilus*, but was forced to give up his attempt.

Gradually researchers replaced adventurers in the Arctic. The Russians had already been active before the Second World War. Otto Schmidt sailed in the *Sibiryakov* through the Northeast Passage in a single summer for the first time in 1932. In 1937 Schmidt established a camp at the North Pole led by Ivan Papanin.

Papanin's camp was built on an ice floe which drifted south. In one hundred days it drifted at a speed of 4 miles per day to latitude 87°. At the beginning of October it approached the north-east coast of Greenland and continued its voyage south at increasing speed to the Greenland Sea. Jostled by other floes it grew smaller and by February 1938 had already drifted to latitude 73°. The expedition's tent was torn down in a storm. The floe was on the point of breaking up on the east coast of Greenland when on 12 February they were rescued by the ice breakers the *Taimyr* and the *Murman*.

After the Second World War, between 1950-58, the Russians established six research stations on the sea ice. The men of one discovered the submarine ridge named Lomonosov Ridge which stretches from Ellesmere Island to the New Siberian Islands. The men of the American T-3 research station later discovered a second ridge, which was named after Ross Marvin who had died on Peary's last voyage.

The importance of the Arctic Ocean increased after the Second World War. The area was important from both a strategic and a civil-aviation point of view. The research stations and airfields built in the area made regular flights over the polar region possible. These began with the touchdown at Södre Strömfjord airfield in Greenland of an SAS flight in 1954 from Copenhagen to Los Angeles.

After the scientists came the adventurers once more. People wanted to discover their limits. Freya Stark, who as a twenty-year old had served as a nurse in the First World War, suggested dangerous journeys as a substitute for war, because they might bring forth virtues which there would otherwise be no opportunity to prove. Life should be heroic, but one can only prove oneself in dangerous circumstances. In the Arctic it was easy to find danger comparable to that found in

265

war. When the nuclear submarine the *Nautilus* commanded by W. R. Andersson made its way under the polar ice in 1958, this was a real adventure. Ten years later Ralph Plaisted made it to the North Pole by motor sledge, Naomi Uemura went there alone in 1979, and the first skiing party led by Dmitri Shaparo made it there one year later. Shinji Kazama drove to the North Pole on a motorcycle in 1987.

In 1969 a four-man expedition, led by Wally Herbert, became the first to cross the Arctic Ocean from Point Barrow in Alaska to Spitsbergen by way of the North Pole. They took advantage of drifting ice and spent more than six months of the dark winter in winter camps. If we assume that Peary did not reach the North Pole, Herbert was the first to get there under his own steam by dog-sledge. He received his food and supplies by air, however.

The threshold for Arctic voyages is being lowered continuously. Even the ordinary tourist can reach the Pole. In 1991 the Russian atomically powered ice-breaker *Sojus* took tourists to the North Pole for the first time.

The trek across Greenland attracts expeditions every year. Eight expeditions crossed the inland ice in 1988 in honour of the 100th anniversary of Nansen's expedition. The dangers are very real. One expedition was defeated by a snow storm in the early stages of its journey.

The bravest of us follow in the footsteps of the explorers to prove to ourselves and others that we would have been able to achieve similar accomplishments if we had only lived at the right time. Those of us who do not dare to venture into the loneliness of the Arctic are only left with the possibility of reading about such voyages of exploration. The English essayist William Hazlitt wrote: "The soul of a journey is liberty, perfect liberty, to think, feel, do just as one pleases. We go on a journey chiefly to be free of all the impediments and of all the inconveniences; to leave ourselves behind, much more to get rid of others." The truth, however, is just the opposite. It is not possible to go on an Arctic expedition alone. Nowhere is a person more dependent on his or her companions. Hardly anywhere could one be confronted with greater barriers and difficulties. In the Arctic a man must measure himself against the merciless forces of nature, and each member is guided only by the needs of the group. The Arctic expedition is a return to the past when people had to take responsibility for one another just as the Eskimos did hundreds of years ago.

THE RACE FOR THE NORTH POLE

The progress of Arctic expeditions can be described by following how the northernmost latitude reached approaches the North Pole over the centuries. The history begins with Pytheas, whether Thule was Iceland or Norway. The Vikings gradually pushed the record north. But there is no precise knowledge of how far north they got. Though their achievements are marked on the shore of Melville Bay, Greenland, the evidence discovered does not show how far north they got in Spitsbergen, where they sailed to hunt seal and walrus. Records can only be considered relatively trustworthy from Barents onward.

The first records were achieved by sailing as far north as open water permitted. Parry was the first to create a record by travelling over the ice.

320 BC	Pytheas	Iceland	63°–64°
1267	Vikings	Melville Bay	76°
1596	Barents	Spitsbergen	80° 11'
1607	Hudson	Spitsbergen	80° 23'
1766	Chichagov	Spitsbergen	80° 26'
1773	Phipps	Spitsbergen	80° 48'
1806	Scoresby sr.	Spitsbergen	81° 30'
1816	Munroe	Spitsbergen	82° 15'
1827	Parry	Spitsbergen, sledge	82° 45'
1876	Markham	Ellesmere	83° 20'
1882	Lockwood	Ellesmere	83° 24'
1895	Nansen	Framilta	86° 13'
1900	Cagni	from Franz Josef Land	86° 34'
1906	Peary	from Smith Sound	87° 00'
1909	Peary	from Smith Sound	90° 00'

After Scoresby northerly records improved as follows:

1868	Nordenskiöld	Spitsbergen	81° 42"
1871	Hall/Budington	Ellesmere	82° 11'
1875	Nares	Ellesmere	82° 28'
1896	Sverdrup	Arctic Ocean	85° 55'

The *Fram* achieved a record when Nansen went off with Johansen and a dog-team towards the Pole. The ship achieved the record independently, and it was not broken till icebreakers came along. In 1991 a Russian icebreaker took a group of paying tourists to the North Pole. The *Fram*'s record will always remain unbroken from the time when "ships were of wood and men were of iron".

266

LIST OF MAPS

New Haven 1967 (original at Yale University)

47. The sea routes of the Vikings. Jari Patanen, 2001

48. Ruysch, Johannes (k. 1533)
'Universalior Cogniti Orbis Tabula Ex Recentibus Confecta Observationibus.'
Ptolemaios, Klaudios, *Geographia*. 39.3 x 54.1 cm, Roma: Bernard Venetus de Vitalibus 1507-1508. (Helsinki University library/Nordenskiöld collection)

52. Mercator, Gerhardus (1512-1594)
World map 'Nova Et Aucta Orbis Terræ Descriptio Ad Usum Navigantium emendate accommoda.' A portion of the map.
Duisburg 1569. (Maritiem Museum, Rotterdam)

54. Frobisher, Martin (n.1535-1594)
Map of North Atlantic incl. Martin Frobisher's discoveries.
Beste, George, *A True Discours of the late Voyages of discovery, for the finding of a passage to Cathaya, by the Northweast, under the conduct of Martin Frobisher.*London 1578.
(The British Library, C.13.a.9.(1.)

55. Foxe (Fox), Luke (1586-1635)
'Part of China, ... Japon, Yedso', also known as 'North-West Fox' or 'Fox from the North-west passage'.
31.5 x 43.5 cm, 1635. (The British Library, C.32.e.8.)

57. Mercator, Gerhardus (1512-1594, & **Hondius, Henricus** (1597-1651)
'Septentrionalium Terrarum descriptio Per Gerardum Mercatorum Cum Privilegio.'
Mercator, G., & Hondius, H., *Atlas sive Cosmographicæ meditationes ...* 18 x 25 cm,
Duisburg 1595 / Amsterdam 1628 - Amsterdam 1630. (Juha Nurminen)

58. Borough, William (1536-1599)
The Scandinavian shield (Lappland o Norway, Sweden, Finland and Russia).
64 x 33 cm, n. 1578. (The British Library, Royal MS.18.d.III.fol.124)

59. Northern expeditions. Jari Patanen, 2001

60. The searchers of the Northeast Passage. Jari Patanen, 2001

61. de Veer, Gerrit (vaikutti 1594-1599)
'Tabula terræ Nouæ Zemblæ in qua fretum sinusq(ue) Waigats, item ora littoralis Tartariæ atq(ue) Russiæ ...'
de Veer, Gerrit (Gerardus), *Diarium Nauticum seu Vera Descriptio Trium Navigationum Adminandum ...*17 x 25.7 cm, Amsterdam 1598/99. (Juha Nurminen)

66. de Bry, Théodore (1528-1598, & **Gerritsz, Hessel** (1581-1632)
'Tabula Nautica, qua repræsenta(n)tur oræ maritimæ meatus, ac freta, noviter a H Hudsono Anglo ad C. rum supra Novam Franciam indagata Anno 1612.' Rev. ed. av Hessel Gerritsz.
de Bry, Théodore, *Petits voyages*. 5 x 33,5 cm, Frankfurt am Main 1613. (Juha Nurminen)

67. Ptolemeus ; Claudio (87-150) - Ruscelli, Girolamo (ca 1504-1566)
'Septentrionalivm Partivm Nova Tabvla.'
Ptolemaios, Klaudios, *La Geografia di Clavdio Tolomeo Alessandrino, Già tradotta di Greco in Italiano da M. Ger. Rvscelli.* 18 x 24.5 cm, Venetia 1574. (Juha Nurminen)

68. Plancius, Petrus (1552-1622)
'Europam ab Asia et Africa segregan Mare mediterraneum ...' sisältäen 'Descriptio Novæ Zemblæ ...' ca 1594. 39.5 x 54.5 cm, Amsterdam 1594. (Juha Nurminen)

69. de Jode, Gerard (1509-1591) & de Jode, Cornelis (1568-1600)
'Hemispheriu(m) ab Æquinoctial Linea, ad Circulu(m) Poli Arctici. - Hemispheriu(m) ab Æquinoctal Linea, ad Circulu(m) A(n)tarctici.'
de Jode, C., *Speculum Orbis terrae* 39.5 x 51.6 cm, Antwerpen 1593. (Juha Nurminen)

70. Unknown cartographer Atlas Arkhangel'skoj gubernii. 100 x 65 cm, 1797, vol. 1. (Russian State Archives of Military History, Fond 846, op. 16 # 18868)

71. Unknown cartographer
'General'noi plan Archangel'skago Namestnitjestva Mezenskago Uezda' Atlas Arkhangel'skago Namestnijesva 1787-92. 96 x 58 cm. (Russian State Archives of Military History, Moscow, Fond 846, op. 16 # 20680)

72. The charting of the Arctic Ocean coast. Jari Patanen, 2001

73. Keulen, Johannes van (1654-1715)
'Pascaarte vande Noord Oost Cust van Asia Vertoonende in sich alle de Zeekusten van Tartarien, Van Japan tot Nova Zemla alles op Wassende graaden geleght.', Keulen, J. van, *Zee-Atlas*. 51.7 x 59.4 cm, Amsterdam 1680. (Juha Nurminen)

74. Kurpakov, Ivan
'General'maja karta vsei Sibiri ... 1778.' Osa kartasta. 100 x 147 cm. (Russian State Navy Archives, Fond 349, op. 45 # 2361, Moscow)

77. Beringis second expedition. Jari Patanen, 2001

78. Homann, Johann Baptista (1663-1725)
'Geographica Nova et Oriente .. Mare Caspium, altera Kamtzadaliam seu Terram Jedso.' - 'Das Land Kamtzadalie sonst Jedso mit der Lamskisch od(er) Pensinskischen See...' 48.2 x 57.5 cm, Nürnberg: Homännische Erben 1759. (Juha Nurminen)

80. Bellin, Jacques Nicolas (1703-1772)
'Carte réduite des Parties Septentrionales du Globe, Situées entre l'Asie et l'Amerique. Pour servir à l'Histoire Générale des Voyages. Par M. Bellin Ingr de la Marine 1758.'
L'Histoire Générale des Voyages. [Publ. av] Abbé Antoine François Prévost. 21 x 34,5 cm, Paris 1759. T. XV, No 4. (Juha Nurminen)

83. de l'Isle, Joseph Nicolas (1688-1768), & **Buache, Philippe** (1700-1773) 'Carte des Nouvelles Découvertes au Nord de la Mer du Sud, tant à l'Est de la Sibirie et du Kamtchaka Qu´ à l'Ouest de la Nouvelle France. Dressée ... de Mr de l'Isle ... Par Philippe Buache.'
Après de Mannevillette, J.B.N D d', *Le Neptune Oriental*. 45 x 64 cm, Paris: J.A. Dezauche 1775/1780. (Juha Nurminen)

84. The charting of East Siberia. Jari Patanen, 2001

87. Gastaldi, Giacomo (ca 1500-ca 1565), & **Ruscelli, Girolamo** (ca 1504-1566)
'Carta marina nuova tavola.'
Ptolemaios, Klaudios, *La Geografia di Clavdio Tolomeo Alessandrino, Nuouamente tradotta di Greco in Italiano, da Girolamo Ruscelli.* 19 x 26 cm, Venetia: Vincenzo Valgrisi 1561 (Juha Nurminen)

88. Magini, Giovanni Antonio (1555-1617)
'Tartariae Imperium ... Auctore Ioan Antonio Magino Patavini.'
Ptolemaios, Klaudios, *Geographiæ universae.* 12.2 x 16.8 cm, Köln 1597. (Juha Nurminen)

89. Unknown cartographer
Map of Siberia, so-called Gudulov map. 95 x 80 cm, 1673. (Russian State Archives of Military History, Fond VUA # 20220, Moscow)

94. de Bry, Théodore (1523-1598) & **de Veer, Gerrit** (worked 1594-1599)
'Delineatio cartae trium navigatiorum per Batavos ad Septentrionalem plagem Norvegia, Moscovia et Nova Zembla.'
de Veer, Gerrit (Gerardus), *Diarum Nauticum seu Vera Descriptio Trium Navigationum Adminandum ...* 27.5 x 35 cm, Amsterdam 1598/99. (Juha Nurminen)

97. Coronelli, Maria Vincenzo (1650-1718)
'Polo Settentrionale & Boreale et Artico.'
Osa 'Globi del Padre Coronelli gli argonauti, in Venetia'-kartasta. Diameter = 36.5 cm, 1697/1705 (Juha Nurminen)

98. The arctic fauna. Jari Patanen, 2001

102. Phipps, Constantine John (1744-1792)
'Plan of Fair Haven with the Islands adjacent, on the North-West Coast of Spitzbergen, from an actual survey taken 1773.'
Phipps, C.J., *A Voyage toward the North Pole undertaken by his Majesty's Command 1773.* London: printed by W. Boyer and J. Nichols for J.

Nourse 1774. (Matti Lainema)

103. Hondius, Henricus (1597-1651)
'Poli Arctici, et Circumiacentium Terrarum Descriptio Novissima.'
Mercator. Gerard, & Hondius, Henricus, *Atlas sive Cosmographicæ meditationes...*
42 x 43 cm, Amsterdam 1636. (Juha Nurminen)

104. Happel, Eberhard Werner (1647-1690)
'Der auswerffende Moskol-strohm. - Der Verschlingende Moskol-Strohm.'
Happel, E.W., *Relationes Curiosae.* 15.4 x 12.8 cm, Ulm 1675.
(Juha Nurminen)

107. Gerritsz, Hessel (1581-632)
'Carte nautique des bords de Mer du Nort, et Norouest, mis en longitude, latitude, et en leur route, selon les rins de vent.' 112 x 87 cm, c.1628. (Bibliothèque Nationale de France, GE DD 2987, Paris)

114. Champlain, Samuel de (1567-1635), & **Duval, Pierre** (1618-83)
'Le Canada ... Suivant les Memoires de P. Du Val ... Paris 1677.'
Duval, P., *Cartes de geographie les plus nouvelles et les plus fideles.* 54,7 x35 cm, Paris: Pierre Du Val 1679. (The Map House, London)

115. Renard, Louis (fl. 1715-1739)
'Septentrionaliora Americae à Groenlandia, per Freta Davidis et Hudson, ad Terram Novam.' - 'Apud R. & I. Ottens.'
Renard, Louis, *Atlas van Zeevaart en Koophandel door de Geheele Weereldt... naar de laetste Ontdekkingen vernieuwt ... door Reinier & Iosua Ottens.* 48.5 x 56 cm, Amsterdam 1745. (Juha Nurminen)

116. Hudson´s Bay Company trading posts. Jari Patanen, 2001

117. Hearne, Samuel (1745-1792)
'A Plan of the Coppermine River. Surveyed by Samuel Hearne, July 1771.'
Hearne, S., *A Journey from Prince of Wales's Fort in Hudson Bay to the Northern Ocean.* Dublin 1796. (Juha Nurminen)

118. Hearne, Samuel (1745-1792)
'Kaart Aanwyzende de Wegen langs welken de Heer Hearne in de Jaaren 1770, 1771, en 1772 zyne beide Landtogten gedaan heeft ter ontdekkinge van de Kopermijn Rivier onder 't bestuur van de Maatschappy der Hudsons Baai.'
Hearne, S., *Landreis van't Prins van Wallis Fort aan Hudsons Baai, naar den Noorder-ocean.* 35.4 x 48 cm, De Haage 1798. (John Nurminen Säätiö)

124. Murray, John (1745-1793)
'Map Shewing the Discoveries made by British Officers in the Arctic Regions from the Year 1818 to 1826.' Franklin, J., *Narrative of a Second Expedition to the Shores of the Polar Sea in the Years 1825,1826, and 1827.*London 1828. (Juha Nurminen)

127. Hall, James (died 1612)
a) 'The coast of groineland with the latitudes of the havens and harbours as I founde them."
James Hall's manuscript atlas of Greenland. (The British Library, Royal Ms. 17 a.xlviii)

130. Reilly, Franz Johann Joseph von (1766-1820)
'Grönland so weit es bekant ist mit den Inseln Færöer.'
Reilly, F.J.J. von, *Schauplatz der fünf Theile der Welt... Nach und zu Büschings grosser Erdbeschreibung.*Nr 77. 23 x 27.6 cm, Wien 1789–1791.
(Juha Nurminen)

136. Daurkin, Nikolai
Northern Pacific, East-Siberia and West-Alaska. 56 x 71 cm, 1765.
(Russian State Archives of Military History, Fond 846 op. 16 # 23435, Moscow)

137. The charting of Alaska. Jari Patanen, 2001

144. Zatta, Antonio (1742-1797)
'Nuove Scoperte de´Russi al Nord del Mare del Sud si nell´Asia, che nell´America'
Atlante Novissimo. 29 x 40 cm, Venice 1776 (Matti Lainema)

145. Roberts, Henry, & Cook, James (1728-1779)
'Chart of the N.W. Coast of America and the N.E. Coast of Asia

explored in the Years 1778 and 1779. Prepared by ... Henry Roberts, under the immediate Inspection of Capt Cook.' Grav.: William Palmer.
Cook, James, *A Voyage to the Pacific Ocean ... for making discoveries in the northern hemisphere .. Performed under the direction of Captains Cook, Clerke, and Gore ...In the years 1776, 1777, 1778, 1779, and 1780.* London: William Faden (1784), 2. ed. 1794. Dimensions 39.2 x 67.8 cm (John Nurminen Foundation)

147. Sarytšev, Gavril Andrejevitš (1763-1831)
'Tjast' Ledovitogo morja ot ust'ja reki Kolymy k vostoku do mysa nazvannogo kuptsom Sjelaurovym Pesjanoj.' 1787.
Sarytšev, G.A., *Putesjestvie flota kapitana Sarytjeva po severovostotjnoj tjasti Sibiri.* St. Peterburg 1802. (Helsinki University library/Nordenskiöld collection)

149. Jode, Cornelis de (1568-1600)
'Quiviræ Regnu(m) cum alijs versus Borea(m).'
Jode. C. de, *Speculum Orbis terrae.* 34.3 x 22.9 cm, Antwerpen 1593. (The Newberry Library, Chicago, # 135 J9 1593)

150. Kosyrevski, Ivan P. (s. 1680). Map of East-Siberia.
45 x 52 cm, n.1726. (Russian State Navy Archives, Fond 349 op. 45 # 2422, Moscow)

151. Bellin, Jacques Nicolas (1703-1772)
'Carte Réduite des Découvertes des Russes, Entre l'Asie et l'Amérique. Pour servir à l'Histoire générale des Voyages.'
L´Histoire Générale des Voyages. [Publ. av, Abbé Antoine François Prévost.
20,5 x 28,5 cm, Paris 1764. (John Nurminen Foundation)

152. Tširikov, Aleksei I. (1703–1748)
'Karta do Tobol'ska, s Atlasa Rossiiskago, a ot Tobol'ska - s raznych opisanjev i Vojajei Kamtjatskoj ekspeditsii ... Mai 1746.'
A portion of the map. 234 x 85.5 cm.
(Russian State Archives of Military History, Fond 846 op. 16 20227, Moscow)

155. Beaurain, Jean de (1696–1771)
'Carte des deux Regions Polaires Jusqu'au 45° Degré de Latitude.' 22 x 44 cm. Gravé par Aldring. c. 1780. (John Nurminen Foundation)

156. Laurie, Robert (k. 1858), & **Whittle, James**
'North Pole; Extending to the Tropic of Cancer, with the addition of all the New Discoveries.' London: Published by Laurie & Whittle Fleet Street 1st Octr 1801. (John Nurminen Foundation)

159. Ross, John (1777-1856), & **Bushnan, John** (k. 1824)
'A General Chart Showing the Track and Discoveries of H.M. Ships Isabella & Alexander to Davis's Straits & Baffins Bay in an attempt to Discover a Passage into the Pacific Ocean. Commanded by Captn Ross R.N. Drawn under his inspection by J. Bushnan Midn R.N. 1815. J. Walker Sculpt.'
Ross, John, *A Voyage to Baffin's Bay.* London 1819. (Juha Nurminen)

160. Iligliuk & William Edward Parry
Eskimaux Chart no. II. Journal of the Second Voyage for the Discovery of a North-West Passage from the Atlantic to the Pacific. William Edward Parry, R.N.,F.R.S, London 1824. (Juha Nurminen)

161. Vander Maelen, Philippe
Découvertes Boréales. no 9. *Atlas Universel. Quatrième partie. - Amérique septentrionale.* Bruxelles 1827. (John Nurminen Foundation)

162. The expeditions of th e Royal Navy. Jari Patanen, 2001

170. Ross, John (1777-1856), & **Ross, James Clark** (1800-1862)
'To ... William IVth King of Great Britain, Ireland &c. This Chart of the Discoveries made in the Arctic Regions, in 1829, 30, 31, 32 & 33, is Dedicated ...' 44.6 x 61 cm. Published by Capt. Ross R.N. Dec.1834. (John Nurminen Foundation)

173. The north magnetic pole. Jari Patanen, 2001

177. Fullarton, Archibald, & Johnson, J. Hugh
'Arctic Regions. The Arctic Regions, showing the North-West Passage as determined by Cap. R[obert] McClure and other Arctic voyagers. Compiled by J. Hugh Johnson. Engraved by A. Fullarton & Co. - The results of Dr [Elisha

336

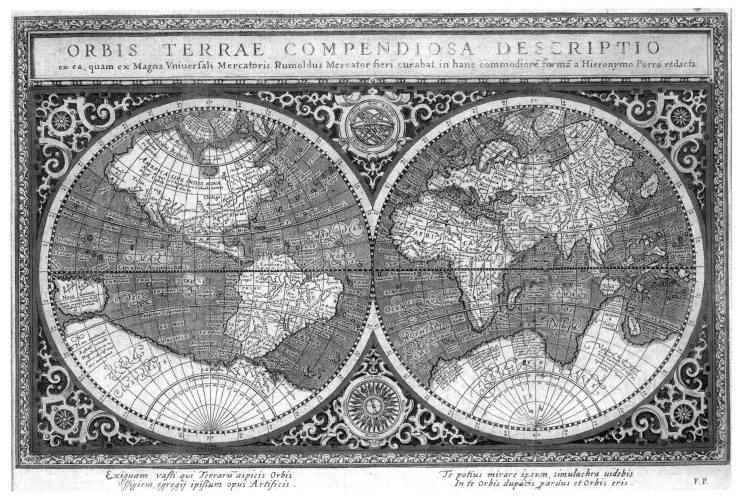

*Exiguam vaſti qui Terrarũ aspicis Orbis
Effigiem, egregij ipißum opus Artificis .*

*Te potius mirare ipſum, simulachra uidebis
In te Orbis dupacis paruus et Orbis eris .*

F. P.

268

Kent] Kane's Expedition 1856. - Wellington Channel, Melville Islands &c.'
Royal Illustrated Atlas. London & Edinburgh: A. Fullarton & Co 1862.
(John Nurminen Foundation)
178. The expeditions of the Royal Navy. Jari Patanen, 2001
180. Philip, George (died 1799)
'Arctic Regions, with all the Discoveries, to 1853.' Vignette 'Capt.
Franklin's Journey from Coppermine River, to the Head of Bathurst
Inlet, & Return by Hood's River.'
Philip, G *General Atlas*. 50.2 x 61 cm, London 1856. (John Nurminen
Foundation)
192. Petermann, August Hermann (1822-1898)
'Karte des Arktischen Archipel's der Parry-Inseln nach den bis zum Jahre
1855 gewonnenen Resultaten, nach Englischen Aufnahmen gezeichnet.'
Petermann's Geographische Mittheilungen. Jahrg. 1855, Tafel 8.
(Juha Nurminen)
198. Renard, Louis (fl. 1715–1739)
'Planisphere Representant Toute l'Etendue du Monde.'
Renard, Louis, *Atlas de Navigation, et du Commerce qui se fait dans toutes les
parties du...* 42 x 26 cm, Amsterdam: Regner & Josua Ottens (1715)
1739. (Juha Nurminen)
204. Petermann, August Hermann (1822-1898)
'Die Amerikanische Nordpolar-Expedition unter Kapitän C.F. Hall
1871/72.'
Gotha: Justus Perthes 1873.
Petermann's Geographische Mittheilungen. Jahrg. 1873, Tafel 16.
(Juha Nurminen)
206. Mercator, Gerhardus (1512-1594), **& Hondius, Henricus**
(1597-1651)
'Septentrionalium Terrarum Descriptio; Juxta mentem Veterum
Geographorum.'
Mercator, G., *Atlas sive Cosmographicæ meditationes*. 10 ed. 18 x 25 cm,

Amsterdam 1630. (Juha Nurminen)
207. Phipps, Constantine John (1744–1792)
'Chart Shewing the different Courses Steered by His Majesty's sloop
Racehorse From July 3d to August 22d. J. Russell sculp.Part of the chart.
Phipps, C.J., *A Voyage toward the North Pole undertaken by his Majesty's
Command 1773*. London: printed by W. Bowyer and J. Nichols for J.
Nourse... 1774. (Juha Nurminen)
208. Jäger Gustav (1815-1875)
'Weltkarte in Nordpolar-Stereprojektion. Nach einer Idee von G. Jäger.'
Gotha: Justus Perthes 1867.
Petermann's Geographische Mittheilungen. Ergänzungsband IV, 1865-67.
Spitzbergen, Tafel 3. (Helsinki University library/Nordenskiöld
collection)
211. The race to the North pole. Jari Patanen, 2001
213. Moss, Edward Lawton
'Sketch Map of Track of Expedition.' 1875-76.
Moss, Edward, *Shores of the Polar Sea. A Narrative of the Arctic Expedition of
1875-6 ... H.M.S. 'Alert'*. London 1878. (Juha Nurminen)
215. Nansen, Fridtjof (1861–1930)
'Vardö 13 augusti 1896.' – 'Det förste Kart Fridtjof Nansen Tegnede paa
norsk Grund i 1896.'
(Nasjonalbiblioteket, Oslo, according to the original)
216. Bergslien, Knud (1827-1908)
'Kart over Dr. Fridtjof Nansen's Polarexpedition 1893-1896. Tegnet af
Knud Bergslien.' Ny revid. Udg. Kristiania: tr. Kristiania Litografisk AB,
Cammermeyer's Boghance 1896. (Nasjonalbiblioteket, Oslo,
Kart NA 2000)
221.Nord-Polar-Karte, Stieler´s Hand-Atlas no 10. 33.2 x 40,5 cm.
Gotha: Justus Perthes 1885 (John Nurminen Foundation)
223. Andrée's flight. Jari Patanen, 2001
225. Peary, Robert E. (1854-1920)

'Sketch Map to illustrate the North Polar explorations of Commander R.E. Peary, USN, Under the auspices of the Peary Arctic Club.'
The Geographical Journal. 1903. - *Meddedelelser om Grønland.* Bd 130, Nr 1 (Lauge Koch), pl. 17 A. (Matti Lainema)
226. **Blumer, Walter** (s. 1888)
'Physiographical Map of Peary-Land (Northernmost Greenland) 1938.' - 'Printed by Kümmerley & Frey, Berne.'
Meddedelelser om Grønland.. Bd 130, Nr 1 (Lauge Koch). pl. 13. (Matti Lainema)
229. **Peary's expeditions.** Jari Patanen, 2001
242. **Mercator, Gerhardus** (1512-1594) & **Hondius, Henricus** (1597-1651)
'Polus Arcticus. - Septentrionalium Terrarum descript.'
Mercator, G., & Hondius, H., *Atlas minor.* 14,5 x 20 cm, Amsterdam 1634. (Juha Nurminen)
243. **Hedenström, Matiass M.** (1783-1845)
'Karta novootkrytym zemlijam na Ledovitom more. 1809.' 79 x 58 cm. (Russian State Archives of Military History, Fond 846 op. 16 # 23419, Moscow)
244. **Nordenskiöld, Adolf Erik** (1832-1901)
'Beeren Eiland.' (Helsinki University library/Nordenskiöld kokoelma)
245. **Petermann, August Hermann** (1822-1898) & **Payer, Julius R. von** (1841-1915)
'Originalkarte zur Übersicht des Standpunktes neuester Polarforschungen bis Ende September 1874. - Provisorische Skizze von Franz Joseph Land ... von Julius Payer.'
Gotha: Justus Perthes 1871.
Petermann's Geographische Mittheilungen. Jahrg. 1871, Tafel 22 (Helsinki University library/Nordenskiöld collection)
247. **A chart of the Hydrological Dept. of Russian Maritime Ministry**
'Karta Severnago Ledovitago Okeana, ot' Enjseiskago Zaliva do ust'ja reki Jany. Sostavlena s russkich' opisej 1734-42 i 1821-23 g.g.'
71 x 106 cm, St. Peterburg 1874 (Helsinki University library/Nordenskiöld collection)
248. **Expeditions of Scandinavians.** Jari Patanen, 2001
251. **Isachsen, Gunnerius** (Gunnar) I. (1868-1939)

'Karta over arbeidsfeltet for den 2. norske polarfærd med 'Fram' kaptein Sverdrup 1898-1902.'
Sverdrup, Otto, *Nyt land.* Kristiania: Aschehoug 1903.
(Frammuseet, Oslo)
252. **Jackson, Frederick** (1860-1938)
'Sketch Map of Franz Josef Land Showing Journeys and Discoveries of Frederick Jackson, F.R.G.S. Leader of the Jackson-Harmsworth Polar Expedition 1894-1896.' - 'Rough Sketch by George Philip & Son, London.'
The Geographical Journal. 1896. (John Nurminen Foundation)
254. **Amundsen, Roald** (1872-1928) & **Hansen, Godfred**
'Map to illustrate the Voyage and Arctic Explorations of Capt. Roald Amundsen. From Surveys by Lieut. G. Hansen, 1903-1906. 'Vignette 'King William Land. Neu-mayer Peninsula.'
The Geographical Journal . 1907. (Juha Nurminen)
258. **Hagen, Høeg,**
Northeast Greenland at the bottom of the Independence fiord 1907.
Ventegodt, O.Den sidste brik. Kobenhavn 1998
259. **Petermann, August Hermann** (1822-1898)
'Karte des nördlichen Theiles von Ost Grönland nach den Aufnahmen von Clavering & Sabine 1823 ... zur Orientirung der Forschungen der Deutschen Expedition 1869/70.'
Petermanns Geographische Mittheilungen. Jahrg. 1871, Tafel 10. (Juha Nurminen)
262. **Ice cover in the Arctic.** Jari Patanen, 2001
267. **Ortelius, Abraham** (1527-1598)
Septentrionales Regiones Septrentrionalium Regionum Descriptio
'Il Theatro del Mondo di Abraamo Ortelius' 7,2 x 10,2 cm, 1598 (Juha Nurminen)
268. **Mercator, Rumold** (1545-1599), **Magini, Giovanni** (1555-1617) & **Porro, Girolamo** (fl. 1567-1599)
Orbis Terrae Compendiosa Descriptio... 'Geographicae Universae tum teris tum novae...', 16.4 x 24.6 cm Venice 1596. (Juha Nurminen)

OTHER PICTURE SOURCES

1. **Scale model**, Cyrenia. Picture: Rauno Träskelin. (John Nurminen Foundation)
6. **The Broighter boat.** (The National Museum of Ireland, Dublin)
7. **Scale model** Hjortspring. Picture: Rauno Träskelin. (John Nurminen Foundation)
8. **Cyrenian merchant vessel.** Kari Jaakkola. (John Nurminen Foundation)
9. **Edge of the pack ice.**(Picture: Derek Fordham)
14. **Kemig.** Ross, John, Appendix to the Narrative of a Second Voyage in Search of a North-West Passage and of a Residence in the Arctic Regiones during the Years 1829, 1830, 1831, 1932, 1833, London 1835. (Juha Nurminen)
15. **Shulanina**, Tulluachiu, Tirikshiu. Ross, John, same as 14. (Juha Nurminen)
16. **G. F. Lyon's drawing** 1562. (Scott Polar Research Institute, Cambridge)
18. **Igluus and Northern Lights.** Murray Smith, D., Arctic Expeditions from British and Foreign Shores from the Earliest Times to the Expedition of 1875-76. Glasgow 1877. (Juha Nurminen)
19. **North Hendon.** (Scott Polar Research Institute, Cambridge)
20. **Bear's head.** (Canadian Museum of Civilization)
21. **Pair of swans.** (Canadian Museum of Civilization)

22. **Wooden map.** (The Greenland National Museum and Archives)
24. **Eskimo in a kayak.** (Kuva: Bryan & Cherry Alexander)
25. **Snow glasses.** (Picture: Bryan & Cherry Alexander)
26. **Igloo.** (Picture: Bryan & Cherry Alexander)
27. **Dog team.** (Picture: Bryan & Cherry Alexander)
29. **Kayak.** W. A. Graah, Undersögelses reise till. ...stkusten af Grönland Köpenhamn 1832 (Juha Nurminen)
30. **Umiak.** W. A. Graah, same as 29. (Juha Nurminen)
31. **Kayaks.** Cook, James, Plates to Cook & King's Voyage. London 1785. (Juha Nurminen)
32. **Carrying a kayak.** Journal of a Second Voyage for the Discovery of a North-West Passage. London 1824. (Juha Nurminen)
33. **Källung weather vane.** Picture: Göran Ström. (Gotlands Fornsal, Visby)
The **Hunning stone**. Picture: Raymond Hejdström. (Gotlands Fornsal, Visby)
34. **Picture stone.** (The National Historical Museum, Stockholm)
38. **The Bayeux Tapestry** . (Centre Guillaume le Conquerant, Bayeux)
39. **Viking ship.** Nordenskiöld, A. E., Vegas färd, Stockholm 1880 (Juha Nurminen)
40. **Ruins of the Kakortok /Hvalsö church** W. A. Graah, same as 29. Köpenhamn 1832. (Juha Nurminen)

of Captain Sir Edward Belcher, C.B., London 1855. (Juha Nurminen)

182. **Reindeer in the tundra.** (Picture: Bryan ja Cherry Alexander)

183. **Musk ox.** (Picture: Bryan & Cherry Alexander)

184. **Seal.** (Picture: Bryan & Cherry Alexander)

185. **Polar bear.** (Kuva: Derek Fordham)

186. **Lieutenant Schwatka's party resting in the Divide Hill area.** The Illustrated London News, 1.1.1881. From a sketch by Mr. H. W. Klutchak, the artist of the expedition. (John Nurminen Foundation)

187. **HMS Assistance in the ice.** Thomas Sewell Robins. (National Maritime Museum, Greenwhich, BHC 4239)

188. **Francis Leopold McClintock.** (National Maritime Museum, Greenwich, BHC 3612)

189. **Charles W. Morgan.** John Stobart. (American Maritime Paintings of John Stobart by John Stobart with Robert Davis, copyright (c) 1991 by M.H.P. Enterprises, Inc. Used by permission of Dutton, a division of Penguin Putnam Inc.)

190. **Whale hunting boat.** De Katholieke Illustratie (John Nurminen Foundation)

191. **Polar explorers' equipment.** The Graphic 24.4.1875 (John Nurminen Foundation)

193. **Sir John Franklin's death.** Thomas Smith. (National Maritime Museum, Greenwich, BHC 1273)

194. **The crew of HMS Alertin on their way to the Pole.** Illustrated London News 4.11.1876 (John Nurminen Foundation)

195. **Vilhjalmur Stefánsson.** (Dartmouth College Library)

196. **Constatine John Phipps.** Ozias Humpry. (National Maritime Museum, Greenwich, BHC 2872)

197. Journal of a *Voyage towards the North Pole* 15. April-24. September by Hon. Constantine John Pipps (and Baron Mulgrave 1775) a record of the expedition of H.M. Sloops Racehorse (Capt. Phipps) and Carcass (Capt. Skaffington Lutwidge with Nelson served as Captains's coxswain) to try for a Northeastern Polar Passage, with historical instroduction and scientific appendix. Printed, with a dedication to George III. 1777, King's 225 (The British Library)

199. **Elisha Kent Kane.** Arctic Explorations: The Second Grinnell Expedition in Search of Sir John Franklin, 1853, 54, 55, Vol. I & Vol. II, Philadelphia 1856. (Juha Nurminen)

200. **An iceberg near Kosoak.** Kane, Elisha Kent, same as 199. (Juha Nurminen)

201. **Crossing the Rotko at Coffee Gorge.** Kane, Elisha Kent, same as 199. (Juha Nurminen)

202. **Charles Francis Hall.** Davis, C. H., Narrative of the North Polar Expedition, captain Charles Francis Hall Commanding U.S. Naval Observatory 1876, Washington 1876. (Juha Nurminen)

203. **U.S.S.Polaris.** Davis, C.H., same as 202. (Juha Nurminen)

205. **A struggle in the ice.** George E. Tyson, Arctic Experiences. New York 1874 (Juha Nurminen)

209. **Payer ja Weyprecht.** Payer, Julius, New Lands within the Arctic Circle. Narrative of the Discoveries of the Austrian Ship *Tegethoff* in the years 1872-1874 Vol. I & Vol. II, London 1876. (Juha Nurminen)

210. **The Tegethoff.** Payer, Julius, same as 209. (Juha Nurminen)

212. **Captain Georg S. Nares.** Murray Smith, D., same as 18. (Juha Nurminen)

214. **HMS Alert at her winter quarters.** Moss, Edward, H.M.S. *Alert* Shores of the Polar Sea a Narrative of the Arctic Expedition of 1875-6. (Juha Nurminen)

217. **Dr. Fridtjof Nansen.** The Graphic 12.9.1896. (John Nurminen Foundation)

218. **The Fram in the ice.** Nansen, Fridtjof, Farthest North, vol. II., London 1897. (Juha Nurminen)

219. & 220. **Scale model the Fram.** 1:48 (2000). Picture: Rauno Träskelin. (John Nurminen Foundation)

222. **Andrée on the ice.** (Andréemuseet, Gränna)

224. **Robert E. Peary.** Peary Robert E., The North Pole, London 1910. (Juha Nurminen)

227. **The Northern Lights.** (Picture: Pekka Parviainen)

228. **The Northern Lights** (Picture: Matti Rikkonen)

230. **Taking soundings.** Peary Robert E., same as 224. (Juha Nurminen)

231. **At the North Pole.** Peary Robert E., same as 224.. (Juha Nurminen)

232. **The Count of Abruzzi.** Luigi Amedeo di Savoia, On the Polar Star, London 1903. (Juha Nurminen)

233. **Peary' calculations.** Peary Robert E., same as 224. (Juha Nurminen)

234. **Five flags at the North Pole.** Peary Robert E., same as 224. (Juha Nurminen)

235. **Sextant.** Picture: Rauno Träskelin. (John Nurminen Foundation)

236. **Peary's calculations.** Peary Robert E., same as 224. (Juha Nurminen)

237. **Artificial horizon.** Picture: Rauno Träskelin. (Juha Nurminen)

238. **Dog team and the polar sun.** (Picture: Derek, Fordham)

239. **Matthew Henson.** (New York Explorers' Club)

240. **Fredrick A. Cook.** (Fredrick A. Cook Society)

241. **Sunset and open water.** (Picture Derek Fordham)

246. **Adolf Erik Nordenskiöld.** Georg von Rosen, oil, 1927. Photo Kaius Hedenström. (Kungliga Vetenskapsakademien, Stockholm)

249. **Nordenskiöld, Palander and the Vega.** (Juha Nurminen)

250. **Otto Sverdrup.** Brögger, W. C. och Rolfsen, Nordahl, Fridtjof Nansen 1861-1893. Stockholm 1896. (Juha Nurminen)

253. **Roald Amundsen.** (Nasjonalbiblioteket, Oslo)

255. **The Gjøa.** Lauritz Haaland. (Norsk Sjöfartsmuseum, Oslo)

256. **Ludvig Mylius-Erichsen.** (Arctic Institute, Copenhagen)

257. **Knud Rasmussen.** (Arctic Institute, Copenhagen)

260. **Vilhjalmur Stefánsson.** (Dartmouth College Library)

261. **New ice.** (Picture: Bryan & Cherry Alexander)

263. **Ice current.** (Kuva: Bryan & Cherry Alexander)

264. **An iceberg washed ashore.** (Picture: Bryan & Cherry Alexander)

265. **Glacier.** John White. (The British Library)

266. **Panorama from Spitsbergen.** Paul Gaimard. (Juha Nurminen)

LITERATURE

Abramson, Howard S., *Hero in Disgrace*. New York 1991

Adams, *Recent Polar Voyages*. London 1880

Ahlgren, Lauri, *Eskimotaidetta*.Taide 3/1964

Ahlgren, Lauri, *Eskimotaide vanhan muotovaailman lähteillä*. Taide 6/1973

Aho, Pekka, *Retkikunta jääkauteen*, Helsinki 1966

Alaska Almanac – more Facts about Alaska. Anchorage 1985

Allen, E. S., *Arctic odyssey; the life of Rear Admiral Donald B. MacMillan*. New York 1963

Allgemeine Historie der Reisen zu Wasser und zu Lande, oder Sammlung aller Reisebeschreibungen. Leipzig 1769

Amdrup, G. C., *Gronland i Tohundreaaret for Hans Egedes Landing*. Kobenhavn 1921

Amundsen, Roald, *Genom luften till 88° Nordlig Bredd*. Stockholm 1925

Amundsen, Roald, *Luoteisväylä Kertomus Gjöan matkasta 1903–1907*. Porvoo 1908

Amundsen, Roald, *Nordvästpassagen af Roald Amundsen*. Stockholm 1908

Amundsen, Roald, *My Life as an Explorer*. New York 1928

Andrée, S. A., *Med örnen mot polen*. Stockholm 1930

Andrews, Kenneth R., *Trade, Plunder and Settlement*. Cambridge 1984

Andrews, William J. H., *The Quest for Longitude*, Massachusetts 1998

Anson, George, *A Voyage Round The World, in the Years MDCCXL, I. II. III. IV*. London 1748

Anspach, Lewis Amadeus, *A History of the Island of Newfoundland*. London 1819

Archer, Christon I., The Spanish Reaction to Cook's Third Voyage, *Captain James Cook and His Times* s. 99–119. 1979

Arima, Eugene Y., *Contributions to Kayak Studies*. Hull, Quebec 1991

Armstrong, Terence, Cook's Reputation in Russia, *Captain James Cook and His Times*. s. 121–128, 1979

Armstrong, Terence, *The Russians in the Arctic*. London 1958

Back, George, *Arctic Land Expedition*. London 1836

Back, George, *Narrative of an Expedition in H.M.S. Terror, undertaken with a View to Geographical Discovery on the Arctic Shores in the Years 1836–37*. London 1838

Back, R.N., *Narrative of the Arctic Land Expedition to the Mouth of the Great Fish River*. London 1836

Bagrow, Leo, *A History of the Cartography of Russia up to 1600*. Ontario 1975

Bagrow, Leo, *A History of Russian Cartography up to 1800*. Ontario 1975

Bagrow, Leo, *History of Cartography*. Chicago 1985

Bagrow, Leo *Meister der Kartographie*. Würzburg 1963

Bagrow, Leo, Sparwenfeld's Map of Siberia, *Imago Mundi* IV s. 65–70. 1947

Bagrow, Leo, The first Russian Maps of Siberia and their Influence on the West-European Cartography of N. E. Asia, *imago Mundi* IX s. 83–93. 1952

Baker, Emerson W. (edit.), *American Beginnings*. Lincoln 1994

Balikci, Asen, *The Netsilik Eskimo*. New York 1970

Bandi, Hans-Georg, *Eskimo Prehistory*. London 1969

Barrington, Daines, *History of the Voyages and Dicoveries made in the North*. London 1786

Barrington, Daines, *Miscellanies*. London 1781

Barrington, Daines, *The Possibility of Approaching the North Pole Asserted*. London 1818

Barrow, John, *A Chronological History of Voyages into the Arctic Regions (1818)*. Devon 1971

Bartlett, R. A., *The log of Bob Bartlett; the true story of forty years of seafaring and exploration*. New York 1931

Batey, Colleen, *Cultural Atlas of the Viking World*. New York 1994

Bartlett, R. A. & Hale R. T., *Northward ho! The Last Voyage of the Karluk*. Boston 1916

Beattie, Owen – Geiger, John, *Frozen in Time – Unlocking the Secrets of the Franklin Expedition*. Saskatoon 1987

Beechey, Frederick W., *Narrative of a Voyage to the Pacific and Beering's Strait in the years 1825, 26, 27, 28*. New Burlington 1831

Beedell, Mike, *The Magnetic North*. Toronto 1983

Belcher, Edward, *The Last of the Arctic Voyages*. London 1855

Bennett, J. A., *The Divided Circle*. Oxford 1987

Bergquist, Lars, *Isvandring med Nordenskiöld*. Stockholm 1981

Bernardi, Jean Frederick, *Recueil de Voiages au Nord*. Amsterdam 1715

Berthon, Simon, *The Shape of the World*. London 1991

Berton, Pierre, *Klondike*. New York 1967

Berton, Pierre ,*The Arctic Grail*. Toronto, Ontario 1988

Bertram, Colin, *Arctic and Antarctic*. Cambridge 1939

Best, George, *The Three Voyages of Martin Frobisher*. Amsterdam 1971

Birket-Smith, Kaj, *Eskimos*. New York 1971

Black, Jeremy, *Maps and History*. New Haven and London 1997

Blake, E. Vale (edit.), *Arctic Experiences*. New York 1874

Blewitt, Mary, *Surveys of the Seas*. London 1957

Boas, Franz, *The Central Eskimo*.Toronto 1974

Bobé, Louis, *Hans Egede, Colonizer and Missionary of Greenland*. Copenhagen 1952

Bobrick, Benson, *East of the Sun The Epic Conquest and Tragic History of Siberia*. New York 1992

Bockstoce, John, *Arctic Passages, A Unique Small-Boat Journey through the Great Northern Waterway*.New York 1992

Bockstoce, John, *The Journal of Rochfort Maguire 1852*. London 1988

Borup, George, *A Tenderfoot with Peary*. New York 1911

Breitfuss, L., Early Maps of North-Eastern Asia and of the Lands around the North Pacific, *Imago Mundi* III s. 87–99. 1939

Bricker, Charles, *Landmarks of Mapmaking*. Oxford 1976

Brody, Hugh, *Maps and Dreams*. New York 1982

Brontman, L., *On the Top of the World*. London 1938

Brooks, Alfred H., *Reconnaissances in the Cape Nome and Norton Bay Regions, Alaska, in 1900*. Washington 1901

Brown, Lloyd A., *The Story of Maps*. New York 1979

Brown, R. N. Rudmose, *The Polar Regions*. London 1927

Bruemmer, Fred, *The Arctic World*. Toronto 1985

Bruton, Eric, *The History of Clocks and Watches*. New York 1989

Bryce, George, *The Siege and Conquest of the North Pole*. London 1910

Bryce, Robert M., *Cook & Peary, The Polar Controversy, Resolved*. Mechanicsburg P.A. 1997

Brögger W. C. och Nordahl, *Fridtjof Nansen 1861–1893*. Stockholm 1896

Bullen, Frank T., *Fighting the Icebergs*. London 1910

Burney, James, *A Chronological History of North-Eastern Voyages of Discovery*. Amsterdam 1969

Burton, Richard F., *Ultima Thule, or, A Summer in Iceland*. London 1875

Byrd, Richard E., *Skyward*. Chicago 1981

Cameron, Ian, *Explorers & Exploration*. Leicester 1991

Campbell, Tony, *The Earliest Printed Maps 1472–1500*. London 1987

Carpenter, Edmund, *Eskimo Relatives*. New York 1973

Carpenter, Kenneth J.,*The History of Scurvy and Vitamin C*. Cambridge 1988

Casson, Lionel, *The Ancient Mariners*. New Jersey 1991

Castrén, M. A., *Nordiska Resor och Forskningar*. Helsingfors ????

Catchpole, Brian, *A Map History of Russia*. Oxford 1990

Chapman, F. Spencer, *Northern Lights*. London 1932

Chevigny, Hector, *Lord of Alaska, Baranov and the Russian Adventure*. New York 1942

Chevigny, Hector, *Russian America The Great Alaskan Venture 1741–1867*. New York 1965

Christy, Miller, *On 'Busse Island', one of the Lost Islands of the Atlantic*. London 1897

Conway, Martin, *The First Crossing of Spitsbergen*. London 1897

Cook, Frederick A., *My Attainment of the Pole*. New York 1911

Cook, Frederick A., *Return from the Pole*. London 1953

Cook, James, *Captain Cook's Third and Last Voyage, to the Pacific Ocean, in the Years 1776, 1777, 1778 1779, and 1780*. London 1785

Cook, John A., *Pursuing the Whale. A Quarter-Century of Whaling in the Arctic*. London 1926

Corner, George W., *Doctor Kane of the Arctic Seas*. Philadelphia 1972

Coxe, William, *Account of the Russian Discoveries Between Asia and America*. London 1804

Crantz , David, *The History of Greenland*. London 1767

Crone, G. R., *Maps and Their Makers*. Kent 1978

Cumming, W. P., *The Discovery of North America*. London 1971

Cumming, W. P., *The Exploration of North America 1630–1776*. London 1974

Cyriax, Richard J., *Sir John Franklin's Last Arctic Expedition*. Plaistow 1997

Danish Arctic Expeditions, 1605 to 1620. Printed for the Hakuyt Society, London 1847

Davis, Thomas D., New Evidence: Peary reached the Pole, *National Geographic*. January 1990

De Long, G. W., *The Voyage of the Jeannette. The ship and ice journals of George W. De Long 1879–1881*. Boston 1884

Dekin, Albert A. Jr., Sealed in Time. Ice Entombed an Eskimo Family for five Centuries, *National Geographic*. July 1987

De Veer, Gerrit, *A True Description of Three Voyages by the North-East towards Cathay and China*. London 1853

Deacon, Margaret, *Scientists at the Sea 1650–1900*. London 1971

Dekker, Elly, *Globes from the Western World*. London 1993

Diebitsch-Peary, Josephine, *My Arctic Journal*. London 1894

Diubaldo, Richard J., *Stefánsson and the Canadian Arctic*. Montreal 1978

Donner, Kai, *Siperian Samojedien keskuudessa*. Helsinki 1915

Dow, George Francis, *Whale Ships and Whaling*. New York 1985

Dudszus, Alfred, *Dictionary of Ship Types*. London 1986

Eames, Hugh, *Winner lose all Dr. Cook and the Theft of the North Pole*. Boston – Toronto 1973

Eggede Mr., *Description et Histoire Naturelle du Groenland*. Copenhague 1763

Ehrensvärd, Ulla, *Pohjoiskalotin historiallisia vaiheita*. Tukholma

Ehrensvärd, Ulla, Sjökortet gav kursen, *Kungliga Biblioteket. Utställningskatalog 79*. Stockholm 1976

Ehrensvärd, Ulla, Cartographical Representation of the Scandinavian Arctic Regions, *Unveiling the Arctic*. Ed.: Louis Rey. Arctic Vol. 37: no.4.Calgary 1984

Ehrensvärd, Ulla, Ryssarnas svenska kartor. *Forum navale*. Skrifter utg. av Sjöhistoriska Samfundet nr. 50, s. 5–12. Stockholm 1994

Elder, William, *Bibliography of Elisha Kent Kane*. Philadelphia 1858

Ellsberg, Edward, *Hell on Ice, The Saga of the 'Jeanette'*. New York 1938

Endige, J. Raymond, Jr., Overland to the Sea Samuel Hearne's Search for the Coppermine River, *Mercator's World* No 1. 2000

Endiger, J. Raymond, Jr., Adrift!, *Mercator's World* No 3. 2000

Fairley, T. C., *Sverdrup's Arctic Adventures*. London 1959

Fejes, Claire, *People of the Noatak*. Volcano 1994

Fisher, David E., *Across the Top of the World*. New York 1992

Fisher, Raymond, *Bering's Voyages, Whither and Why*. London 1977

Fisher, Raymond H., The Early Cartography of the Bering Strait Region, *Arctic* No 4, December 1984

Fisher, Raymond H., *The voyage of Semen Dezhnev in 1648: Bering's precursor with selected documents*. London 1981

Fisher, Robin, *Cook and the Nootka Captain James Cook and His Times* s. 81–97. 1979

Fisher, Robin, *Vancouver's Voyage Charting the Northwest Coast, 1791–1795*. Seattle 1992

Fleming, Fergus, *Barrow's Boys*. London 1998

Ford, Corey, *Where the Sea Breaks Its Back*. London 1967

Forselles-Riska, Cecilia af, *The A. E. Nordenskiöld Collection in the Helsinki University Library*. Helsinki 1995

Francis, Daniel, *Arctic Chase*. United Kingdom 1984

Franklin, John, *Journey to the Shores of the Polar Sea*. London 1824

Franklin, John, *Narrative of a Second Expedition to the Shores of the Polar Sea in the Years 1825,1826, and 1827*. London 1828

Freeman, Andrew A., *The Case for Doctor Cook*. New York 1961

Freuchen, Dagmar, *Peter Freuchen's Book of the Eskimos*. Cleveland 1961

Freuchen, Peter, *I all uppriktighet*. Stockholm 1957

Freuchen, Peter, *I Sailed with Rasmussen*. New York 1958

Freuchen, Peter, *Min Anden Ungdom*. Kobenhavn 1938

Freuchen, Peter, *Seitsemän meren kirja*. Jyväskylä 1958

Freuchen, Peter, *Vagrant Viking, My Life and Adventure*. New York 1957

Freuchen, Peter, *Året runt i Arktis*. Stockholm 1961

Frison-Roche, Roger, *Hunters of the Arctic*. London 1969

Furse, Chris. *Arctic Expedition Handbook*. Smarden 1997

Geiger, John - Beattie, Owen, *Dead Silence*.London 1993

de Gerlache de Gomery, Adrian *Fifteen Months in the Antarctic*. Southampton 1998

Giddings, J. Louis, *Ancient Men of the Arctic*. New York 1967

Gilder, William, *Schwatka's Search*. New York 1881

Glover, R., *A Journey from Prince of Wales s Fort in Hudson Bay to the northern ocean, 1769, 1770, 1771, 1772*. Toronto 1972

Gmelin, Johan George, *Reize Door Siverien Naar Kamtschatka; Van't Jaar 1733 tot 1743*. 1752

Goetzmann, William H., *Looking Far North, The Harriman Expedition*. Princeton N.J. 1963

Goodsell, John W., *On Polar Trails*. Austin, Texas 1983

Gordon, W. J., *Round About the North Pole*. London 1907

Goss, John, *The Mapping of North America*. New Jersey 1990

Gould, Laurence M., *The Polar Regions in their Relation to Human Affairs*. New York 1958

Gould, Rupert T., *The Marine Chronometer*. Woodbridge 1989

Graham-Campbell, James, *The Viking World*. London 1980

Graham-Maxtone, John, *Safe Return Doubtful*. Northhamptonshire 1989

Greely, Adolphus W., *Three Years of Arctic Service*. New York 1886

Greely, Adolphus W., *Handbook of Alaska*. New York 1909

Green, Fitzhugh, *Peary, The Man Who Refused To Fail*. New York 1926

Grierson, John, *Heroes of the Polar Skies*. New York 1967

Grieve, James, *The History of Kamtschatka, and the Kurilski Islands, With the Countries Adjacen*. London 1764

Gruber, Ruth, *I Went to the Soviet Arctic*. New York 1939

Gould, Rupert T., *John Harrison and his Timekeepers*. Greenwich 1987

Hakluyt, Richard, *The Principal Navigation, Voyages Traffiques & Discoveries of the English Nation*. London 1847–1852

Hall, Charles F., *Narrative of the North Pole Expedition*. Washigton 1876

Hall, Charles F., *Narrative of the Second Arctic Expedition made by Charles F. Hall*. Washington 1879

Hall, Charles F., *Life with the Esquimaux*. London 1864

Hansen, Thorkild, *North West to Hudson Bay. The Life and Times of Jens Munk*. London 1970

Harrison, Alfred H., *In search of a Polar Continent 1905–1907*. London 1908

Hartwig, G., *The Polar and Tropical Worlds*. Springfield, Massachusetts 1871

Hayes, Isaac I., *The Land of Desolation*. New York 1872

Hayes, Isaac I., *The Open Polar Sea*. New York 1867

Hayes, J. Gordon, *Robert Edwin Peary. A Record of his Explorations 1886–1909*. London 1929

Hayes, J. Gordon, *The Conquest of the North Pole*. London 1934

Hedin, Sven, *Adolf Erik Nordenskiöld*. Stockholm

Hedin, Sven, *Navalta aavalle*. Helsinki 1913

Hellemans, Alexander, *The Timetables of Science*. New York 1988

Henson, Matthew A., *A Negro Explorer at the North Pole*. New York 1912

Herbert, Wally, *The Noose of Laurels*. New York 1989

Herbert, Wally, *Across the Top of the World The last great journey on earth*. New York 1971

Herrmann, Paul, *Conquest by Man*. New York 1954

Heyerdahl, Tor – Lillieström, Per, *Ingen Grænser*. Oslo 1999

Hintzsche, Wieland, *Die Grosse Nordische Expedition*. Halle 1996

Histoire Générale des Voyages, ou, Nouvelle Collection de Toutes les Relations de Voyages Par Mer et Par Terre. Paris 1759

Hobbs, William H., *Peary*. New York 1936

Holland, Clive, *Arctic Exploration and Development*. New York 1994

Holland, Clive, *Farthest North, A History of North Polar Exploration in Eye-Witness Accounts*. New York 1994

Hornborg, Eirik, *Segelsjöfartens Historia*. Helsingfors 1923

Horwood, Harold, *Bartlett The Great Canadian Explorer*. Toronto 1977

Houston, Stuart C., *To the Arctic by Canoe 1819–1821*. Montreal 1974

Houston, Stuart C., *Arctic Artist*. Montreal 1995

Hovgaard A., *Nordenskiölds rejse omkring Asien og Europa*. Kjøbenhavn 1881

Hoving, Ab J, *Nicolas Witsens Scheeps-Bouw-Konst Open Gestelt*. Franeker 1994

Howse, Derek, *The Sea Chart*. Newton Abbot 1973

Hudson's Bay Company. London 1934

Hunt, Harrison J. and Hunt, Thompson Ruth, *North To The Horizon*. Maine 1980

Hunt, William R., *Arctic Passage*. New York 1975

Hunt, William R., *To Stand at the Pole*. New York 1981

Häkli, Esko, *A. E. Nordenskiöld*. Helsinki 1980

Ingstad, Helge, *Ennen Kolumbusta*. Helsinki 1967

Ingstad, Helge, *Nunamiut*. Stockholm 1954

Ingstad Helge,*Westward to Vinland*. London 1969

In the Polar Regions, Or, Nature and Natural History in the Frozen Zone.

342

London 1882

Jackson, F. G., *The great frozen land*. London 1895

Jackson, Gordon, *The British Whaling Trade*. London 1978

Jacobsen, N. Kingo, *Vitus Bering 1741–1991*. Kobenhavn 1993

James, Alton James, *The First Scientific Exploration of Russian America and the Purchase of Alaska*. Evanston and Chicago 1942

Jefferys, Thomas, *The Great Probability of a North West Passage*. London 1768

Jensen, Jorgen Solarstein, *Danish Maritime Museum Yearbook* s. 14–21, 1997

Johansen, Hjalmar, *With Nansen in the North*. London 1899

Johnson, Donald S., *Phantom Islands of the Atlantic*. New Brunswick 1994

Jones, Gwyn, *A History of the Vikings*. Oxford 1984

Kane, Elisha Kent, *Arctic Explorations, Vol. I–II*. Philadelphia 1857

Kane, Elisha Kent, *The U. S. Grinnell Expedition in Search of Sir John Franklin*. New York 1854

Keay, John (edit.), *History of World Exploration*. London 1991

Keuning, Johannes, Hessel Gerritsz, *Imago Mundi VI* s. 48–66, 1949

Keuning, Johannes, Isaac Massa, 1586–1643, *Imago Mundi X*, s. 65–80, 1953

Keunig, Johannes, Nicolas Witsen as a cartographer, *Imago Mundi. XI*, s. 95–110, 1954

Kirwan, L. P., *The White Road A Survey of Polar Exploration*. London 1959

Kish, George, North-east passage, Adolf Erik Nordenskiöld, his life and times. Amsterdam 1973

Klindt-Jensen, Ole, *Vikingarnas värld*. Stockholm 1967

Klinge, Matti, *Itämeren maailma*. Helsinki 1995

Koldewey, Karl, *The German Arctic Expedition of 1869–70, and Narrative of the wreck of the 'Hansa' in the ice*. London 1874

Kotzebue, Otto von, *A voyage of discovery into the South Sea and Bering Straits in the years 1815-1818*, Vol. I–III. Amsterdam 1967

Kotzebue, Otto von, *The South Sea, Voyage of Discovery*. London 1821

Kretschme, Konrad, *Die Historischen Karten zur Entdeckung Amerikas*, Frankfurt am Main 1991

Laktionov, Aleksandr, *Nordpolen*. Moskva 1960

Lamb, G.F., *Franklin – Happy Voyager*. London 1956

Lamb W. K., *The journal and letters of Sir Alexander Mackenzie*. Cambridge 1970

Leed, Eric, *Shores of Discovery How Expeditionaries Have Constructed the World*. New York 1995

Leslie, John, *Narrative of Discovery and Adventure in the Polar Seas and Regions*. Edinburgh 1831

Lihatsov, Dmitri Sergejevits, *Nestorin kronikka*. Porvoo 1994

Liljequist, Gösta H., *High Latitudes*. Stockholm 1993

Lincoln, W. Bruce, *The Conquest of a Continent*. London 1994

Logan, F. Donald, *The Vikings in History*. London 1992

Lopez, Barry, *Arctic Dreams*. New York 1986

Lubbock B., *The Arctic whalers*. Glasgow 1937

Luigi, Amedeo di Savoia, *On the 'Polar Star' in the Arctic sea*. London 1903

Lundborg, Einar, *När Nobile räddades*. Stockholm 1928

Lyon, G. F., *A Brief Narrative of an Unsuccessful Attempt to Reach Repulse Bay*. London 1825

Lyon, G. F., *The private journal of Captain G. F. Lyon of H.M.S. Hecla during the recent voyage of discovery under Captain Parry 1821–1823*. London 1824

Mackenzie, Alexander, *Voyages from Montreal on the River St. Laurence*. Great Americana 1966

Major, Richard Henry, *The Voyages of the Venetian Brothers, Nicolò & Antonio Zeno, to the Northern Seas, in the XIVth Century*. London 1873

Manby, George William, *Journal of a Voyage to Greenland, in the year 182.* London 1823

Marcus, Geoffrey Jules, *The Conquest of the North Atlantic*. Bury St Edmunds 1998

Markham, Albert Hastings, *A Whaling Cruise to Baffin's Bay and the Gulf of Boothia*. London 1875

Markham, Clements, *The Lands of Silence*. Cambridge 1921

Markham, Clements, *A Life of John Davis, The Navigator, 1550–1605, discoverer of Davis Straits*. London 1889

Markham, Clements, *A Polar Reconnaissance Being the Voyage of the 'Isbjörn'' to Novaya Zemlya in 1879*. London 1881

Markham, Clements, *The Arctic Navy List*. Portsmouth 1892

May, W. E., *A History of Marine Navigation*. Oxfordshire 1973

McClintock, Francis Leopold, *The voyage of the Fox in the Arctic seas. A narrative of the discovery of the fate of Sir John Franklin and his companions*. London 1860

McClure, Robert, *The Discovery of a North-West Passage*. Edinburgh 1865

McClure, Robert, *The North-west passage. Capt. M'Clure's dispatches from Her Majesty's ship, 'Investigator', off Point Warren and Cape Bathurst*. London 1853

McFee, William, *The Life of Sir Martin Frobisher*. New York 1928

McKinlay, William Laird, *Karluk; the great untold story of Arctic exploration*. London 1976

McNaughton, Douglas, Mercator's Secret, *Mercator's World* No 2, 2000

Meri, Lennart, *Hopeanvalkea*. Jyväskylä 1983

Meri, Lennart, *Kamtšatka*. Jyväskylä 1988

Meri, Lennart, *Revontulten porteilla*. Jyväskylä 1974

Michael, Henry N., *Lieutenant Zagoskin's Travels in Russian America, 1842–1844.* Toronto 1967

Miertsching, Johann, *Frozen Ships*. Toronto 1967

Mikkelsen, Ejnar, *Conquering the Arctic ice*. London 1909

Mikkelsen, Ejnar, *Lost in the Arctic; being the story of the 'Alabama' expedition, 1909–1912*. London 1913

Miller, Floyd, *Ahdoolo! (Biography of Matthew A. Henson)*. New York 1963

Mirsky, Jeannette, *To the Arctic!*. Chicago 1970

Mollat du Jourdin, Michel, *Sea Charts of the Early Explorers*. New York 1984

Molett, William E., *Robert Peary & Matthew Henson At the Pole*. Frankfort, Kent 1996

Morison, Samuel Eliot, *The European Discovery of America*. New York 1971

Morison, Samuel Eliot, *The Great Explorers*. New York 1978

Moss, Edward, *Shores of the Polar Sea*. Strand 1878

Mountfield, David, *A History of Polar Exploration*. London 1974

Muir, John, *Travels in Alaska*. Boston and New York 1915

Murphy, Robert, *Vitus Berings Opdagelsesrejser*

Nansen, Fridtjof, *Farthest North Vol. 1–II*. London 1898

Nansen, Fridthof, *In the Arctic*. New York 1925

Nansen, Fridtjof, *In Northern Mists Vol. I–II*. London 1911

Nansen, Fridtjof, *Pohjan pimeillä perillä osat 1–2*. Helsinki 1897

Nansen, Fridtjof, *På skidor genom Grönland*. Stockholm 1890

Nansen, Fridtjof, *The First Crossing of Greenland*. London 1890

Nansen, Fridtjof, *Through Siberia*. London 1914

Nares, Georg, *Narrative of a voyage to the polar sea during 1875–6 in H.M. ships Alert and Discovery… with notes on the the natural history… .* London 1878

Neatby, Leslie H., *In Quest of the North West Passage*. London 1958

Neatby, Leslie H., *Frozen Ships. The Arctic Diary of Johann Miertsching 1850–1854*. Toronto 1967

Nobile, Umberto, *My Polar Flights*. New York 1961

Noice, Harold, *With Stefánsson in the Arctic*. London 1925

Nordenskiöld, Nils Adolf Erik, *Den andra Dicksonska Expeditionen till Grönland dess inre isöken och dess ostkust utförd år 1883 under befäl af A. E. Nordenskiöld*. Stockholm 1885

Nordenskiöld, Nils Adolf Erik, *Explanatory Remarks in Illustration of a Map of Spitzbergen*. Stockholm 1865

Nordenskiöld, Nils Adolf Erik, *Facsimile-Atlas*. New York 1973

Nordenskiöld, Nils Adolf Erik, *Studier och forskningar föranledda af mina resor i höga norden*. Stockholm 1883

Nordenskiöld, Nils Adolf Erik, *Svenska Polar-expeditionen år 1872–1873 under ledning af A. E. Nordenskiöld*. Stockholm 1875

Nordenskiöld, Nils Adolf Erik, *Svenska Expeditionen till Spetsbergen och Jan Mayen, utförda under åren 1864 af A. E. Nordenskiöld*. Stockholm 1867

Nordenskiöld, Nils Adolf Erik, *Vegas Färd Vol. 1–2*. Stockholm 1880

Nourse J. E., *Narrative of the second Arctic expedition made by Charles F. Hall… during the years 1864–69*. Washington 1879

Nurminen, Juha – Ehrensvärd, Ulla – Kokkonen, Pellervo, *Mare Balticum 2000 vuotta Itämeren historiaa*. Keuruu 1995

Nurminen, Juha – Ericsson, Christoffer – Häkli, Esko – Odelberg, Wilhelm –

Okhuizen, Edwin – Pärssinen, Leena, *Koillisväylä viikingeistä Nordenskiöldiin*. Helsinki 1992

Okhuizen, Edwin, Historical and Current Uses of the Northern Sea Route. Part II: The Period 1745-1855. *INSROP Working Paper No 113*, 1998

Osborn, Sherard, *Stray leaves from an Arctic journal; or, eighteen months in the polar regions, in search of Sir John Franklin's expedition, in the years 1850–51*. London 1852

Papers of the Nordenskiöld Seminar on the History of Cartography. Helsinki 1981

Parry, Ann, *Parry of the Arctic – the Life and Story of Admiral Sir Edward Parry*. London 1963

Parry, Edward *Memoirs of Rear-Admiral Sir W. E. Parry*. London 1857

Parry, John Horace, *The Discovery of the Sea*. New York 1974

Parry, William Edward, *Journal of a voyage for the discovery of a North-West Passage from the Atlantic to the Pacific; performed in the years 1819–20*. London 1821

Parry, William Edward, *North-West Passage*. London 1824

Parry, William Edward, *Journal of a Second Voyage for the Discovery of a North-West Passage from the Atlantic to the Pacific; performed in the years 1821–22-23*. London 1824

Parry, William Edward, *Journal of a Third Voyage for the discovery of a North-West Passage from the Atlantic to the Pacific*. London 1826

Parry, William Edward, *Narrative of an Attempt to reach the North Pole*. London 1828

Pasetsky, Vasily, Moscow 1988

Pastoureau, Mireille, *Voies Océanes*. Paris 1992

Payer, Julius, *New Lands Within the Arctic Circle*. London 1876

Payer, Julius, *Die Österreichisch-Ungarische Nordpol-Expedition in den Jahren 1872–1874*. Wien 1876

Payer, Julius, *Upptäcktsresor i Norra Polarhafvet*. Stockholm 1877

Peard, George, *To the Pacific and Arctic with Beechey; the Journal of Lieutenant George Peard of H.M.S. Blossom, 1825–1828*. Cambridge 1973

Pearson, Henry J., 'Beyond Petsora Eastward'. London 1899

Peary Robert Edwin, *Nearest the Pole*. London 1907

Peary, Rober Edwin, *Northward Over the Great Ice* Vol. I-II. London 1898

Peary, Robert Edwin, *The North Pole*. London 1910

Peary, Robert Edwin, *The Secrets if Polar Travel*. New York 1917

Petermann, Augustus Herman, *Papers from Petermann's 'Geographische Mittheilungen'*. Gotha 1869–75

Petersen, Carl, *Den sidste Franklin Expedition*. Kjobenhavn 1860

Phipps, Constantine John (Lord Mulgrave), *A voyage towards the North Pole undertaken by his Majesty's command*. London 1774

Pinkerton Robert E., *Hudson's Bay Company*. New York 1931

Porlákstídir og önnur Skálholtshandrit 1998

Postnikov, Alexei, *Russia in maps: a history of the geographical study and cartography in the country*. Moscow 1996

Postnikov, Alexei *The Mapping of Russian America*. Milwaukee 1995

Pryde, Duncan, *Nunaga, Ten Years of Eskimo Life*. New York 1972

Ptolemy Geographia. Devon 1973

Putman, Robert, *Early Sea Charts*. New York 1983

Pälsi, Sakari, *Arktisia kuvia*. Helsinki 1983

Rae, John, *Narrative of an Expedition to the Shores of the Arctic Sea in 1846 and 1847*. Canada 1970

Ramsay, Henrik, *Nordenskiöld, sjöfararen*. Helsingfors 1950

Randier, Jean, *Marine Navigation Instruments*. London 1980

Rasky, Frank, *The Polar Voyagers*. Toronto 1976

Rasmussen, Knud, *Fra Gronland Til Stillehavet*. Kobenhavn 1925

Rasmussen, Knud, *Greenland by the Polar Sea*. London 1921

Rasmussen, Knud, *Norr om Manniskor*. Stockholm 1919

Rasmussen, Knud, *The People of the Polar North*. London 1908

Rawlins, Dennis, *Peary at the North Pole Fact or Fiction?*. Washington – New York 1973

Rey, Louis. *Unveiling the Arctic*. Calgary 1984

Rich, E. E., *John Rae's Correspondence*. London 1953

Rich, E. E.,*The History of the Hudson's Bay Company 1670–1870*. London 1958

Richards, Robert L., *Dr John Rae*. North Yorkshire 1985

Richardson John, *Arctic Searching Expedition*. London 1851

Richardson, John, *The Polar Regions*. Edinburgh 1861

Rodahl, Kaare, *North, The Nature and Drama of the Polar World*. New York 1953

Roesdahl, Else, *Viikingit*. Helsinki 1993

Roos, Willy de, *North-West Passage*. Camden 1980

Ross, John, *A voyage of discovery, made under the orders of the Admiralty, in His Majesty's ships Isabella and Alexander, for the purpose of exploring Baffin's Bay, and inquiring into the probability of a Northwest Passage*. London 1819

Ross, John, *Narrative of a second voyage in search of a North-west Passage, and of a residence in the Arctic regions during the years 1829, 1830, 1831, 1832, 1833*. London 1835

Ross, W. Gilles, *Arctic Whalers Icy Seas*. Toronto 1985

Russel, Franklin, *The Secret Islands*. New York 1965

Sage, Bryan, *The Arctic & Its Wildlife*. New York 1986

Sargent, Epes – Cunningham, William H., *The Wonders of the Arctic World*. Philadelphia 1873

Sarytschew, Gawrila, *Gawrila Sarytschew's Achtjährige Reise im nordöstlichen Sibirien, auf dem Eismeere und dem nordöstlichen Ozean*. Leipzig 1805–11

Sauer, Martin *An Account of a Geographical and Astronomical Expedition to the Northern Parts of Russia*, London 1802

Saunders, Harold N., *All the Astrolabes*. Oxford 1984

Savours, Ann, *The Search for the West Passage*. London 1999

Scammell, Geoffrey Vaughn, *The World Encompassed*. London 1987

Schley, Winfrid Scott and Soley J. R., *The Rescue of Greely*. New York 1885

Schnall, Uwe, Navigationstechniken, *Europäische Technik im Mittelalter 800 bis 1400 Tradition und Innovation* s. 373–38 ????. Berlin 1966

Schurke, Paul, *Bering Bridge, The Soviet-American Expedition from Siberia to Alaska*. Duluth 1989

Schwatka, Fredrik, *Along Alaska's great river. A popular account of the travels of the Alaska exploring expedition of 1883, along th great Yukon River*. New York 1885

Schwatka, Frederick, *A Summer in Alaska*. St. Louis 1893

Scoresby, William, *An account of the arctic regions with a history and description of the northern whale fishery*. Newton Abbot 1969

Scoresby, William, *Journal of a Voyage to th Northern Whale-fishery*. Edinburgh 1823

Scoresby – Jackson R. E., *The Life of William Scoresby*. Edinburgh 1861

Seaver Kirsten A., *The Frozen Echo*, Stanford 1996

Seaver Kirsten A., The Mystery of the 'Vinland Map', Manuscript Volume, *The Map Collector* No 74, 1996

Seaver, Kirsten A., The 'Vinland Map': who made it, and why? New light on an old controversy, *The Map Collector* No 70, 1995

Service, Robert W., *Ballads of Cheechako*. Toronto 1909

Service, Robert W., *Rhymes of a Rolling Stone*. Toronto 1912

Service, Robert W., *The Spell of the Yukon*. New York 1916

Seton, Ernest Thompson, *The Arctic Prairies*. London 1912

Shackleton, Edward, *Arctic Journeys*. London 1936

Shackleton, Edward, *Nansen*. London 1959

Sherwood, Morgan B., *Exploration of Alaska 1865–1900*. New Haven 1968

Shirley, Rodney W., *The Mapping of the World*. London 1993

Sinkarjov, Leonid, *Siperia* 1980

Simpson, Alexander, *The Life and Travels of Thomas Simpson, the Arctic Discoverer*. London 1845

Skelton Raleigh A., *Explorer's Maps*. London 1970

Skelton Raleigh A., *The Marine Surveys of James Cook in North America 1758–1768 Particularly the Survey of Newfoundland*. London 1967

Skelton Raleigh A., *The Vinland Map and the Tartar Relation*. New Haven 1965

Smith, William D., *Northwest Passage*. New York 1970

Sobel, Dava, *Longitude*. New York 1995

Stamp, Tom, *William Scoresby, Arctic Scientist*. Great Britain 1975

Starbuck, Alexander, *History of the American whale fishery from its earliest inception to the year 1876*. New York 1964

Starokadomskiy, L. M., *Charting the Russian Northern Sea Route*. Montreal 1976

Steelman, Robert, *Call of the Arctic*. New York 1960

Stefánsson, Vilhjalmur. *Discovery*. New York 1964

Stefánsson, Vilhjalmur. *My Life With the Eskimo*. New York 1913

Stefánsson, Vilhjalmur. *The Adventure of Wrangel Island*. New York 1923

Stefánsson, Vilhjalmur, The Arctic as an Air Route of the Future, *National Geographic*, July 1922

Stefánsson, Vilhjalmur, *The Friendly Arctic*. New York 1922

Stefánsson, Vilhjalmur, *The Three Voyages of Martin Frobisher*. Amsterdam 1971

Stefánsson, Vilhjalmur, *Ultima Thule*. London Toronto 1942

Stefánsson, Vilhjalmur, *Unsolved Mysteries of the Arctic*. London Toronto 1939

Steger, Will, North to the Pole, *National Geographic*, September 1986

Stommel, Henry, *Lost Islands*. Vancouver 1984

Struzik, Edward, *Northwest Passage*, London 1991

Sutton, George Miksch, *Eskimo Year*. Norman 1985

Sverdrup, Otto, *Nytt Land 1–2*. Stockholm 1904

Swinton, George, *Sculpture of the Eskimo*. Toronto 1972

Solver, Carl V., *Eskimoisk kartografi*.

Solver, Carl V., *Vestervejen*. København 1954

Tape, Walter, *Atmospheric Halos*. Washington D.C. 1994

Taylor E. G. R., John Dee and the map of North-East Asia, *Imago Mundi*. XII, s. 103–106, 1955

Taylor E. G. R., *The Haven-Finding Art*. London 1958

Thirslund, Søren, Sailing Directions of the North Atlantic Viking Age (from about the year 860 to 1400), *Journal of Navigation* No 1, 1996

Thompkins, Stuart Ramsay, *Alaska Promyshlennik and Sourdough*. Oklahoma 1945

Thordarson, Matthias, *The Vinland Voyages*. New York 1930

Thorén, Ragnar, *Svenska arktiska expeditioner under 1800-talet*. Stockholm 1987

Toennessen, J. N., *The History of Modern Whaling*. London 1982

Tolmachoff, Innokenty P., *Siberian Passage*. New Brunswick 1949

Tooley, Ronald Vere, *Tooley´s Dictionary of Mapmakers*. Hertfordshire 1982

Towards the North. Early Maps from the A. E. Nordenskiöld Collection 15th–19th centuries, Exhibition in Helsinki Fair Centre, Finbland, 7.11.6.1999. Helsinki 1999

Tryde, Ernst Adam, *De döda på Vitön*. Stockholm 1952

Tuck, James A. and Grenier, Robert, 16th-Century Basque Whalers in America, *National Geographic*, July 1985

Turley, Charles, *Roald Amundsen Explorer*. London 1935

Uemura, Naomi, Solo to the North Pole, *The National Geographic*, September 1978

Vaughan, Richard, *The Arctic A History*. Bridgend 1994

Vancouver, Capt. George, *A Voyage of Discovery to the Pacific Ocean*,1801

Vanderlip, Washington, *In Search of a Siberian Klondike*. New York 1903

Vebæk C. L. & Thirslund S., *The Viking Compass Guided Norsemen first to America*. Skjern, 1992

Victor, Paul-Émile, *Man and the Conquest of the Poles*. London 1964

Villarejo, Oscar, M. *Dr. Kane´s Voyage to the Polar Lands*. Philadelphia 1965

Vinner, Max, Rundt Kap Farvel i vikingeskib, *Tidskriftet Grønland* Nr. 3, 1995

Waldman, Carl, *Who Was Who in World Exploration*. New York 1992

Watt, James, Medical Aspects and Consequences of Cook´s Voyages, *Captain James Cook and His Times* s. 129–157, 1979

Waxell, Sven, *The American expedition*. London 1952

Weems, John Edward, *Race for the North Pole*. London 1961

Whitfield, Peter, *The Image of the World*. London 1994

Whitfield, Peter, *The Charting of the Oceans. Ten centuries of Maritime Maps*. London 1996

Whittaker, C.E., *Arctic Eskimo*. London 1937

Williams, Glyndwr, Myth and Reality: James Cook and The Theoretical Geography of Nortwest America, *Captain James Cook and His Times* s. 58–80, 1979

Williamson, James A., *The Cabot Voyages and Bristol Discovery Under Henry VII*. Cambridge 1962

Wilkins, Georg H., *Flying the Arctic*. New York – London 1928

Wilkes, Charles, *The Narrative of the United States Exploring Edition, during the Years 1838,1839, 1840, 1841 and 1842*. Philadelphia 1845

Wilson, Clifford, *Campbell of the Yukon*. Toronto 1970

Wilson, Derek, *The World Encompassed*, London 1977

de Windt, H. *Through the gold-fields of Alaska to Bering Straits*. London 1898

Winter, Heinrich, The changing face of Scandinavia and the Baltic in cartography up to 1532, *Imago Mundi* s. 45–54, 1955

Winter, Heinrich, What is the Present Stage of Research in regard to the Development of the Use of the Compass in Europe?, *Research & Progress* s. 225–233, 1936

Woodman, David C., *Unravelling the Franklin Mystery*. Montreal 1991

Wrangel, Ferdinand P., *Narrative of an expedition to the polar sea, in the years 1820, 1821, 1822 & 1823*. London 1855

Wright, John K, The Open Polar Sea, *The Geographcial Review*. 1953

Zimmermann, Heinrich, *The Third Voyage of Captain Cook*. Fairfield 1988

Zögner, Lothar, Die kartographische Darstellung der Polargebiete bis in das 19. Jahrhundert, *Die Erde* No 109 s. 136–152, 1978

Yermak´s Campaign in Siberia. London 1975

INDEX OF NAMES